To Bruce Mc Donald,
my former student

my Best wishes,

Kathy Berry

# www.wadsworth.com

*wadsworth.com* is the World Wide Web site for Wadsworth and is your direct source to dozens of online resources.

At *wadsworth.com* you can find out about supplements, demonstration software, and student resources. You can also send email to many of our authors and preview new publications and exciting new technologies.

**wadsworth.com**
Changing the way the world learns®

# RELATED TITLES OF INTEREST

## Work Psychology Titles

*Applied Industrial/Organizational Psychology*, 3rd Edition,
by Michael G. Aamodt

*Human Relations in Business: Developing Interpersonal
and Leadership Skills,* by Michael G. Aamodt and Bobbie L. Raynes

*Psychology Applied to Work*, 7th Edition, by Paul M. Muchinsky

*Training in Organizations*, 4th Edition, by Irwin L. Goldstein
and J. Kevin Ford

## Other Related Titles

*Group Dynamics*, 3rd Edition, by Donelson R. Forsyth

*Intergroup Relations*, by Marilyn B. Brewer and Norman Miller

*Psychological Testing*, 5th Edition, by Robert M. Kaplan
and Dennis P. Saccuzzo

*Social Psychology,* by Stephen Worchel, Joel Cooper, Al Goethals,
and James Olson

## Statistics

*Comprehending Behavioral Statistics*, 3rd Edition, by Russell Hurlburt

*Essentials of Statistics for the Behavioral Sciences*, 3rd Edition,
by Frederick J Gravetter and Larry Wallnau

www. infotrac-college. com

P3XX90P51N

# *Employee Selection*

**LILLY M. BERRY**
*San Francisco State University*

Australia • Canada • Mexico • Singapore • Spain
United Kingdom • United States

THOMSON
WADSWORTH

Sponsoring Editor: *Marianne Taflinger*
Editorial Assistant: *Nicole Root*
Technology Project Manager: *Darin Derstine*
Marketing Manager: *Lori Grebe*
Marketing Assistant: *Laurel Anderson*
Advertising Project Manager: *Brian Chaffee*
Project Manager, Editorial Production:
   *Mary Noel*
Print/Media Buyer: *Vena Dyer*

Permissions Editor: *Robert Kauser*
Production Service: *Vicki Moran, Publishing
   Support Services*
Text Designer: *Adrienne Bosworth*
Copy Editor: *Margaret Moore*
Cover Designer: *Roger Knox*
Cover Image: *PhotoDisc*
Compositor: *Scratchgravel Publishing Services*
Printer: *Transcontinental Louiseville*

Printed in Canada
1  2  3  4  5  6  7  06  05  04  03  02

For more information about our products,
contact us at:
**Thomson Learning Academic Resource
Center
1-800-423-0563**

For permission to use material from this text,
contact us by:
**Phone:** 1-800-730-2214
**Fax:** 1-800-730-2215
**Web:** http://www.thomsonrights.com

Library of Congress Control Number:
2002109313

ISBN 0-534-58095-5

**Wadsworth/Thomson Learning**
**10 Davis Drive**
**Belmont, CA 94002-3098**
**USA**

**Asia**
Thomson Learning
5 Shenton Way #01-01
UIC Building
Singapore 068808

**Australia**
Nelson Thomson Learning
102 Dodds Street
South Melbourne, Victoria 3205
Australia

**Canada**
Nelson Thomson Learning
1120 Birchmount Road
Toronto, Ontario M1K 5G4
Canada

**Europe/Middle East/Africa**
Thomson Learning
High Holborn House
50/51 Bedford Row
London WC1R 4LR
United Kingdom

**Latin America**
Thomson Learning
Seneca, 53
Colonia Polanco
11560 Mexico D.F.
Mexico

**Spain**
Paraninfo Thomson Learning
Calle/Magallanes, 25
28015 Madrid, Spain

# Brief Contents

# Contents

# 3 *Job Analysis* 37

## *Part Two*

## ATTRACTING APPLICANTS

# 4 *Compensation and Other Work Rewards* 71

# 5 *Recruitment* *101*

*Part Three*

# LEGAL ISSUES

# 6 *Fair Employment Law* *127*

## *Part Four*

# SELECTION METHODS: PREDICTING JOB SUCCESS

# 7  *The Basics of Selection Measurement*    163

# 11 *Interviews* 288

# 12 *Assessment Centers and Other Simulations* 316

## Part Five

## EVALUATING THE SUCCESS OF SELECTION

## Part Six

## EMPLOYEE DEVELOPMENT

# 16 Employee Training                                             420

# *Preface*

I began thinking of this book some years ago when I contemplated teaching an undergraduate course that had been designed to address personnel issues—specifically the use of employment tests in selection decision making. The course appealed to me for two reasons. At the time, I was teaching the survey course in industrial/organizational (I/O) psychology and, being aware of the tremendous growth in this field, I was finding it difficult to decide what material to ignore in order to fit the course into a one-semester length. It was becoming clear that students needed more than what a single course surveying the field could offer. Since then, I have learned that other instructors have similar thoughts. Some, like myself, offer the survey course and an additional, specialized course. Others have decided to divide the field survey and offer it as two courses, one covering organizational issues and the other covering industrial or personnel issues. The book you have in your hands is for this latter course and for the specialized course on employee selection. It is for those who want a course of study addressing the needs and problems of attracting, selecting, and retaining an effective workforce—by whatever title the course is called, whether personnel psychology, industrial psychology, vocational assessment, human resources, or employee selection.

## *Organization of the Book*

As shown in the table of contents, the book is structured into six parts. These cover the varied aspects of employee selection. At the beginning are six chapters that set the stage, including material on the study and design of work, ways of attracting applicants, and the legal basis of selection. In the center of the book are six chapters addressing the selection methods, instruments, and strategies that are used to predict who will be successful on a job and to make selection decisions. At the end are four chapters evaluating the success of selection through performance appraisal and developing employees through training. A preview of the chapters appears at the end of Chapter 1.

## Narrowing the Practice Gap

The audience I address in this book is mainly students—certainly undergraduates, but also graduate students, particularly those beginning their programs. I believe the book also will be useful to individuals who work in human resources and who need a source of information and ideas about selection. For this reason, I hope this is a book that students keep and use after the course is finished, the degree is earned, and a career is launched. I believe that sending academic knowledge out into the work world with our students is the best way to influence changes toward better practices at work. Personnel psychologists historically have developed technical strategies for collecting and using applicant information and for improving the selection process. These strategies have helped many who applied them at work. Still, the use of faulty selection practices persists in organizations. One reason is an informational gap between what has been learned in research about effective practices and the use of this knowledge in the field setting. In this book, my purpose is to help narrow the gap by presenting technical information in an understandable way, so that students can prepare to use it when they themselves are in a position to make employee selection decisions.

The book has several special features that are meant to serve this purpose, and to enable students to comprehend and use the technical information on selection. First, I have included many discussion summaries and conclusions in the chapters. A "Summing Up" section closes the chapters, which lists some of the high points discussed. Within the chapters readers willl find special "Conclusions" sections. Some of my concluding statements may come across as quite emphatic. I do this because I believe it is often necessary to take a position on important questions toward which research is being directed. I invite the reader to examine my conclusions and agree or disagree with them. I think this can be highly beneficial to student learning, as it leads to discussion and interest and, hopefully, it contributes to use of information from research literature at the workplace. Second, the book is thoroughly referenced. In the reference list at the back, more than 700 sources are cited. The list includes many original theoretical and research articles; reviews and discussions in journals and books; as well as material from trade magazines, government sources, and legal documents. I encourage the reader to make full use of these sources. Although I provide examples of real problems at work and discuss how one might respond to these, the academic literature provides even more ideas about handling problems in the workplace. This is a reason students should read the literature themselves.

## InfoTrac College Edition: A Useful Tool for Papers

Another special feature is the availability of *InfoTrac College Edition*. Those who purchase a new copy of this book receive a complimentary, four-month subscription to *InfoTrac College Edition* with the purchase. *InfoTrac College Edition* is updated daily and contains materials spanning four years. At the end of each chapter, I identify some keywords that can be used to search the *InfoTrac College Edition* database and locate articles that are relevant to the chapter. The database contains full-text articles (not simply abstracts) from research journals and practice-oriented publications. Several research journals that I used in developing this book are available, such as *Personnel Psychology, Journal of Occupational and Organizational Psychology, Human Relations, Administrative Science Quarterly,* and *Journal of Management.* Also, there are many useful trade magazines, such as *HR Focus, HRMagazine, Inc.,* and *Workforce.* The database is found at http://www.infotrac-college.com/wadsworth.

## *Acknowledgments*

Several people have been helpful as I developed this text, and I want to acknowledge their contributions. First, I want to thank the professional staff at Wadsworth and Marianne Taflinger, especially, for her interest and support of this project. I also want to acknowledge the following reviewers; I found their comments and critiques to be extremely useful: Keith Hattrup, San Diego State University; Edward Levine, University of South Florida, Tampa; Roni Reiter-Palmon, University of Nebraska at Omaha; Brian Schrader, Emporia State University; John Tropman, University of Michigan; and Suzanne Tsacoumis, Human Resources Research Organization. Next, I want to express my appreciation to those at San Francisco State University who made it possible for me to have a semester free of teaching and service responsibilities in order to get the book project under way. Also, I want to recognize the students in the I/O psychology master's program at San Francisco State. I tried out many of my ideas on them and they were generous in their responses. Finally, I want to mention my friends and family. I am grateful to those who gently kept after me, especially my sister. Hardly ever did our long distance calls end without her asking, "How's the book coming?"

*Lilly M. Berry*

# Information on the Internet

The Internet is an excellent source of information on employee selection issues. Following is a selection of World Wide Web sites that will appeal to students, researchers, employers, and others who are interested in employment practices.

## Society for Industrial and Organizational Psychology (SIOP) (www.siop.org)

SIOP is the primary professional association for industrial/organizational (I/O) psychologists. Members include I/O professionals who work in varied settings—academic institutions, the corporate world, government organizations, and consulting firms. Students who are planning a career in I/O psychology also may join SIOP. The Web site provides detailed information about the science and practice aspects of the field, and identifies graduate programs that are available. It describes the work that I/O psychologists perform, and reports on a recent survey of their salaries. I/O students and professionals will be interested in the information about SIOP's annual conference and its books, pamphlets, and newsletter. The Web site is also useful to employers. For example, the site contains a "consultant locator" with a list of frequently asked questions. These questions can help a person decide whether an I/O consultant is needed, and if so, how to use the locator to find one. The consultant locater is provided free of charge as a service to the public.

## American Psychological Association (APA) (www.apa.org)

The APA is an important professional association to which a very large number of psychologists belong, including many I/O psychologists and students. The Web site provides information of interest to researchers and students, and to the public. News on psychological issues, including items related to workplace behavior, is available. For those who are considering a career in psychology, the site describes what psychologists do, gives advice on career paths, and reports the results of a salary survey. Also, graduate study programs in many different areas of psychology are identified. APA is an important publisher of books and journals in psychology, including the premier *Journal of Applied Psychology* in which research relevant to human resources and personnel psychology is published. The Web site provides information about this and other journals, as well as special interest books, such as *Ethical Practice of Psychology in Organizations.* In addition, resource books of special interest to students—such as *Mastering APA Style: Student's Workbook and Training Guide*—can be obtained through the Web site.

## International Personnel Management Association (IPMA) (www.ipma-hr.org)

IPMA is a nonprofit membership association for those who work in human resources or personnel departments. The association attracts many who work in the public (governmental) sector, but it is open to those in the private (business) sector, as well. IPMA's specific objectives are to (1) foster fairness and equity in employment, (2) encourage research in HR, and (3) promote the sharing of knowledge among HR professionals. IPMA publishes practitioner-oriented pamphlets, and a journal—*Public Personnel Management.* The Web site describes its products, including employment tests and publications, as well as conferences and practitioner training seminars. In addition, the Web site reports a turnover study being conducted online, and provides links to IPMA's world wide partners in global human resources. Another aspect of the Web site that may be interesting is the online job posting where employers can list and job seekers can search positions available.

## American Society for Training and Development (www.astd.org)

ASTD is probably the largest association focusing specifically on employee training and performance improvement. The association's purpose is to provide information for training practitioners and others who are interested in these and related issues. The association sponsors an annual conference and publishes a trade magazine that is well-known to training practitioners—*Training and Development.* The Web site gives information about the conference and the magazine, as well as ASTD books and audiovisual products. In addition, there is information on careers in training, listings of specialized training resources, such as management development, and an online job bank. ASTD members work in training-related positions in many different countries throughout the world, and its Web site identifies some international links.

## U.S. Department of Labor (DOL) (www.dol.gov)

The U.S. Department of Labor is a governmental agency whose Web site can be helpful to employers, HR researchers, and students interested in workplace issues. The Web site provides details on wages (including the federal minimum wage), worker's compensation, and employee benefits such as health plans. Also, there is information on careers and the current occupational outlook, laws and federal regulations on employment, and a job bank. HR professionals and students probably will be interested to find that the DOL collects data and publishes statistics on employment issues, such as productivity and technology. The Web site offers access to DOL reports and publications, such as those from the Bureau of Labor Statistics, the Women's Bureau, and the Office of Disability Employment Policy. A list of "frequently asked questions," found at www.dol.gov/dol/faqs, can be particularly helpful. For example, this page gives answers to questions about employee safety and health and assistance for dislocated workers.

# INTRODUCTION

To master the "business meal," career advisers say,

Don't talk with your mouth full.
Stay away from messy foods and alcohol.
Silence your cell phone.
Give your full attention to your host.

A business meal is not simply a free lunch. Casperson (2001) pointed out that such meals are conducted for any of several important reasons, such as meeting with a customer or client, closing a business deal, or conducting a job interview. In all of these, it is important to have good table manners. In none, are manners more important than when you are being interviewed for a job. Although the job might have nothing to do with food, how you present yourself in public is often very important. Poor manners and rudeness can hinder any job applicant's chances, but especially if the job involves communicating and interacting with people, such as the jobs for which many psychology and business students are preparing.

A person who has come so far as to be called for a job interview over lunch clearly has taken other appropriate steps to arrive at this point. Let us consider what he or she might have done—and what you might do—to get that interview. First, the person probably began the job search by developing a network of contacts in the relevant field. Marketing professors often advise students about the importance of networking in getting the right job (Felson, 2001; Frey, 2001). If you are a marketing or other business student, or a student in industrial and organizational (I/O) psychology, networking should not be a nerve-racking experience because it is a natural extension of the work for which you are preparing. To develop a network, be sure to include your existing contacts—classmates, teachers, friends, and, if you are currently employed, boss and coworkers. You can expand the network with referrals from these individuals. Second, the job seeker likely had a well-designed résumé.[1]

---

[1]However, it is in poor taste to hand out résumés during networking. If a contact requests your résumé, take the person's address and promise to send one.

To develop an effective résumé, put yourself in the place of the person whom you want to read it. Be direct. Say what you have accomplished and what you can do for an employer. However, you probably will have less than a minute in which to capture the reader's attention. So, keep your résumé short—a page or less—and don't cheat by using small type and narrow margins. Include only relevant information. Use ordinary language, not "bureaucratese." For example, Lovelace (2001) asked which of the following you would call for an interview: the person who "was instrumental in facilitating the architectural parameters for help-desk prioritization algorithms" or the person who "designed the help-desk priority-setting process" (p. 164).

There are two highly interrelated roles in the process of employment— that of the employer and that of the job seeker. Most of the published research and current knowledge on employee selection is oriented toward the employer. However, because each role is essential to the other, a job seeker can draw many important messages from the study of this material. Most of us have been or will be job seekers, and thus we can benefit from learning about employee selection processes. Many of us have been or will be in the position of needing to hire someone; for this role, knowledge of employee selection is a necessity.

## EMPLOYEE SELECTION

Selection is a rationale and a set of procedures by which employers collect information about individuals seeking jobs and use the information to make employment decisions. The purpose of selection is to help an employer identify the most qualified individual for a job. Generally, the term *selection* refers to the initial hiring of employees, although it also can refer to "selection" of current employees for promotion or transfer to other jobs. The responsibility for making selection decisions usually is shared by human resource (HR) or personnel department staff and the manager of the department in which a job opening exists. For example, to hire a new employee for a business firm's marketing department, the HR staff might recruit and identify a small number of applicants who have the appropriate qualifications, and the marketing manager would decide which of these to hire.

Effective employee selection requires more than simply putting an ad in the local newspaper and interviewing those who apply. Although selection does include recruitment and the assessment of applicants' qualifications, it involves much more, as you will learn in this text. For example, selection requires the study of jobs, an understanding of performance, and knowledge of influences such as employment law.

# THE ORGANIZATION IN THE EMPLOYMENT ENVIRONMENT

Employee selection in any organization is open to influences from the outside. As indicated in Figure 1.1, a number of environmental factors can affect an organization's effort to hire and retain a workforce. These include the national and global economy, law and political climate, organized labor, culture and subculture, science and technology, and behavioral and social science. In addition, the available labor supply, customers, and competitors within the community are especially relevant factors. In this section, you will see how such factors can affect organizations and how organizations' responses, in turn, can influence the environment.

Some aspects of the environment, such as the availability of workers, directly alter an organization's ability to hire. Other factors change the organization's environment and cause indirect effects on employee selection. For instance, national economic conditions can change the rate of unemployment, and this, in turn, determines the size of the labor supply. When unemployment is high—as it is periodically—employers need do little more than post a "help

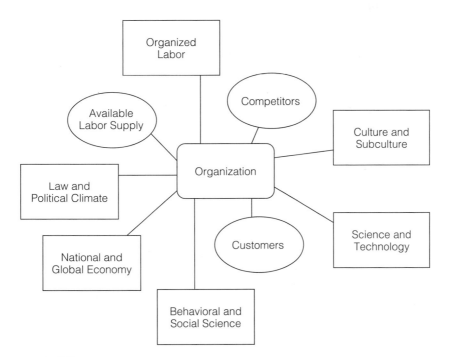

**FIGURE 1.1**

Links between an organization and the surrounding environment. Links between the organization and environmental components are two-way, indicating a reciprocal relationship.

wanted" sign to get a large pool of applicants. When unemployment is low, however, employers have to engage in active recruiting to attract applicants, and they may need recruiters to do specialized searches. Depending on how low the rate of unemployment is, an employer may be unable to hire from outside and may instead have to transfer and train present employees to perform the work needed.

As the marketplace expands and companies move across national boundaries into other countries, other labor supplies become available. However, if a company's workforce is drawn from the host country, cultural difference may become a relevant environmental influence. As I discuss in later chapters, if a business firm establishes operations in a country in which the culture of its workforce is different from the firm's home culture, the difference can pose problems for both selection and management.

Organized labor is another environmental entity that can have indirect effects on employee selection through its influence on the labor supply. In some unionized industries, only union members may be hired. In addition, unionization can have direct effects on selection and related issues. Labor union contracts, resulting from collective bargaining, usually include agreements about pay and job security, and they may stipulate how promotions, transfers, and terminations are decided.

A nation's law and political climate affects organizations' actions in many ways, including the hiring and treatment of employees. In the United States, there are laws on unionization and collective bargaining processes. In addition, fair employment law directly affects selection, whether the organization is unionized or not. As you will see in later chapters, fair employment law developed out of a political climate in which the ideal of equality in employment opportunity was advanced.

If you examine Figure 1.1, you can probably guess that several of the factors listed will interact in affecting an organization's operations. For example, an important interplay occurs that involves customers, competitors, the state of the economy, and advances in technology. When consumer spending levels are high and the economy is strong, manufacturers and businesses have work to be done and jobs to offer. Customers are an important part of the business environment, and organizations must respond to their needs and desires for products and services. Technological advances and business competition can mean that an organization must make changes so as to use improved work equipment and/or develop new product lines to satisfy consumer needs. There are many examples of products that at one time were new and exciting but that later were replaced by something newer and better. For instance, a mid-20th-century company might have been enjoying great success by producing television sets. However, as the years passed, it would have had to make changes in response to business competition and consumer demands for the technologically advanced, big-screen TVs and equipment for home video recording and playback. A company's response to such environmental demands may require redesigning jobs, training some employees, and hiring others who have the skills necessary to use new equipment or to produce a new product line.

The last component of the organizational environment that I include in Figure 1.1 is behavioral and social science. Because the organization is a social entity, its nature can be understood through the behavioral and social sciences. In addition, unlike some other environmental components that constitute constraints to which an organization must respond, behavioral and social science can aid the organization in handling the demands. Industrial and organizational (I/O) psychology, which is the study of work behavior, is the behavioral science most directly relevant to organizational needs. In its beginning, this scientific field was primarily concerned with personnel testing and related employee selection topics. Although these are still important, today the field includes a full range of employment issues. Organizations can draw knowledge from the scientific field to address many needs in addition to selection and retention of productive employees. For example, information is available on how to design jobs, develop work teams, and structure organizations, as well as how to respond to problems in the workplace, such as interpersonal conflict, stress, and dishonesty. I/O psychology is applied in dealing with environmental demands, especially in large organizations, because many people who work for business and government organizations as HR specialists or consultants were educated in I/O psychology and understand its usefulness in their work.

## *Organizational Change and Environmental Effects*

Clearly, environmental changes affect organizations. However, actions taken by organizations in response to such changes can have reciprocal effects on the environment. For example, large-scale environmental factors such as the economy and changes in a nation's population can affect the available labor supply. Currently, in the United States, a large segment of the working population are individuals from the baby-boom generation who are now approaching an age at which retirement ordinarily occurs. It is possible that employers will encourage these employees to retire on schedule, thinking to replace them with younger employees. However, if many employers do this, replacements may be hard to find because growth in the population of younger workers has not kept pace with this group. Quite simply, there may not be enough younger workers to take their places, and the overall effect could be a labor shortage. Other organizational responses, such as retaining some older employees, could prevent the shortage. Global expansion also can have an effect, as when organizations do at least some of their work in other countries, using workforces drawn mostly from the host country.

***The Effects of Downsizing***   Another example of the reciprocal effects of organizational change on the environment is shown in the widespread layoffs and organizational downsizing that took place during the 1980s and '90s, when there were serious changes in the economy and growing competition in the world marketplace. In searching for ways to sustain their companies in this environment, many business leaders paid attention to what others were doing that might help them survive (Mirvis, 1997; Pfeffer, 1995). Some kept a close watch on what was happening among their international competitors. American and Japanese firms, for example, have been following each other's business moves for years (Mroczkowski & Hanaoka, 1997).

Periodic changes in a national economy can be expected to occur, and cutting costs is a common response to an economic downturn. Because the cost of labor is often a firm's greatest expenditure, operating costs can be reduced by cutting the size of the workforce, that is, by "downsizing." Many organizations do exactly this. In a survey of 400 American-based corporations, Mirvis (1997) reported that when asked what had been the firm's response to international competition and a weakening national economy, five of every six firms reported that they had downsized to some extent. Many had shut down plants (64 percent) or sold off part of the business (51 percent). More than one-half had laid off a substantial number of employees. More than one-third had deleted at least some managerial jobs. Many employers believed that productivity would be improved as a result. That is, if only those with jobs essential to the profit-making mission of the firm were retained, then fewer people doing the same amount of profit-yielding work would result in overall increased productivity. This was the idea of the "lean" organization, which conceivably would produce as much as an organization with more employees engaged in unnecessary activity. Maybe this worked, or maybe it was a change in the economy that brought about some improvement. At any rate, within a few years, organizations that had downsized reported that they were rehiring (Jacoby, 1999). Still, the reaction of many organizations to the first sign of economic downturn continues to be hiring freezes and workforce reductions (Conlin, Mandel, Arndt, & Zellner, 2001).

Cutting back on a workforce requires changes in the organization. First, most companies that downsized during the 1980s and '90s had to redesign work roles and reassign—to surviving employees—valuable work functions that had been done by employees who were being laid off. Similar changes resulted from laying off managers. As a group, managers are highly compensated, and a company looking to cut costs certainly would consider reducing their numbers, especially when heavy layoffs in a department made a manager unnecessary. However, whatever a manager had been doing that needed to be continued had to be reassigned. Often, the tasks were given to surviving employees whose jobs had not previously included managerial work. Sometimes, teams were formed and responsibility for managing their own work was given to the team. In any case, training was often needed to prepare survivors for their redesigned jobs and for teamwork. Second, the structure of authority changed in organizations that downsized middle management. Fewer levels of authority between production workers and upper management meant that employees worked on a more equal basis with shared responsibility for all work and decision making. Firms of this type typically had more work done by self-managing teams at all levels of the organization, including production (Jacoby, 1999; Mirvis, 1997). Third, layoffs often included the staff and management of human resource departments, especially when a department was seen as responsible mainly for record-keeping. In such companies, the necessary HR work either was reassigned to surviving managers in other departments or was contracted out to consultants or vendors of human resource services. Some business observers (e.g., Alvares, 1997) think this development was destined and that HR specialists should consider it an opportunity to develop their own HR service companies.

## *Learning From Organizational Change*

Organizations did not always benefit from downsizing, especially if the workforce reduction was primarily to control costs rather than to enhance productivity. Some companies had greater expense due to training and overtime. Others had increased their use of temporary employees and consultants. Morale was low among the surviving employees in many organizations. In some cases, the very employees a firm needed to retain left their jobs and had to be replaced (Mirvis, 1997).

Downsizing is not the only—and often it is not the best—way to respond to changes in the economy. Some business leaders and academicians have argued that the people working in an organization are potentially the main reason the organization can be successful. This argument is based on the experience of innovative employers who disregard conventional thinking on management practices and develop an organization that is fundamentally different from that of firms which view their workforce as a cost to be contained. In fact, during the period when many organizations were laying off workers to control costs, innovative employers were taking action to increase productivity. They made investments in their human resources,[2] introducing new HR practices and adopting a more open stance toward change (Mirvis, 1997). In the innovative organization, a committed and productive workforce is the source of the organization's success. Developing such a workforce depends on the creation of a positive

---

[2] The term *human resources* refers both to the employees who are a firm's "resources" and to the work function performed by HR specialists in the firm.

organizational culture in which employees know they are valued (Cappelli & Crocker-Hefter, 1996; Ferris, Hochwarter, Buckley, Harrell-Cook, & Frink, 1999; Pfeffer, 1995).

An organization that values its employees and considers their treatment to be critical to success, not surprisingly, also responds more positively toward its HR staff. Such employers recognize that the human resource function is essential. A successful organization will have continuing needs for hiring and retaining skilled employees. Those with technical skills will be needed for work in areas of technological advance. Also, those with interpersonal skills will be needed for internal operations and for work with customers and others in the external environment (Pfeffer, 1995). The HR function might be redesigned, however. For example, an HR vendor might provide routine personnel operations or occasional services, such as recruitment for an executive position (Greer, Youngblood, & Gray, 1999). One point in favor of retaining an HR department is that insiders know a lot about the organization, which contributes to a more positive organizational culture. In innovative organizations, the HR manager has a role on the firm's strategic management team, along with the heads of other valued departments. The manager's purpose on the team is to align HR goals with the goals and mission of the organization (Ferris et al., 1999).

# PREVIEW

## *Employee Selection and Related Topics*

All I have said so far underscores the fact that work is a human activity and that all organizations need ways to hire and retain effective employees. As has been true for many decades, today's organization must be able to determine what work is needed, whom to hire, and how to ensure that the work is done well. Both work and the way it is organized have changed in the past and will continue to change. Some work activities and procedures become obsolete in the business environment, and they are changed. Other work activities remain relevant—these are retained. Employee selection is like this. At any one time, there are some brand-new ideas and strategies for addressing employment needs, but many tried-and-true selection methods as well. In the following chapters, you will learn about all of these.

**The Study and Design of Work**    Before meeting with job applicants, it is necessary to understand the work the hiring organization needs. In Chapter 2, you will learn about different kinds of work and jobs. Some of the work mentioned above is discussed, such as teamwork and managerial jobs. Chapter 3 addresses job analysis. Techniques for collecting job information, and using it in job design and employee selection, are described in detail.

**Attracting Applicants**    Certain factors relating to compensation and working conditions are important in attracting applicants. Chapter 4 deals with compensation issues, including the effects of pay levels on employee satisfaction and productivity, and working conditions that applicants will want to know about, such as scheduling. Chapter 5 focuses on recruitment. Labor market changes that affect an employer's ability to recruit are discussed, as are strategies, such as college recruiting.

**Legal Issues**    Chapter 6 addresses employment law. The chapter includes an overview of the history of fair employment law in the United States, which prohibits discrimination on the basis of race, gender, age, and disability. Fair employment programs, such as affirmative action, also are described. Other legal issues are included in other chapters. For example, laws relating to pay setting are discussed in Chapter 4 on compensation, and the right to discharge an employee is discussed in Chapter 15 on performance appraisal.

**Selection Methods and Techniques**    Six chapters are grouped together covering specific selection issues. Chapter 7 presents the principles of measurement that are essential for selection program planning. Employers need to know that their tests, interviews, and other measures yield accurate information. Procedures for evaluating reliability, validity, and related issues, such as how to decide what is a passing score, are covered in Chapter 7. Chapters 8 and 9 focus on testing. Chapter 8 covers ability and knowledge tests, beginning with a discussion of the nature of intelligence. Examples of several ability tests that are used with job applicants are presented. Chapter 9 discusses the use of personality testing for employee selection, as well as testing for employee misconduct, such as drug use. The next two chapters focus on techniques that are used for selection by almost all employers. Chapter 10 presents techniques for gathering information from job applications and résumés, and problems related to obtaining references are discussed. Chapter 11 is about interviews. The traditional job interview is contrasted with a more effective structured interview, and methods for developing questions and scoring are outlined. Chapter 12 focuses on using job simulations to assess applicants' abilities. Work samples can be used to assess performance, as can assessment centers, which simulate managerial work.

**Evaluating the Success of Selection**    Three chapters are concerned with employee performance and show how to evaluate the effectiveness of selection. Chapter 13 presents the rationale for using performance as a measure of selection effectiveness, and it discusses factors that affect the quality of work performance. Chapter 14 examines the methods of performance appraisal, including rating scales and problems such as rater error and personal bias. Chapter 15 describes the usefulness of performance appraisal for validation of selection measures, as well as for performance improvement and employee retention.

**Developing Employee Skill**   Chapter 16 addresses training and shows its relationship to employee selection. Organizations need to provide training for new employees who are not adequately skilled for their jobs and for employees who are promoted or otherwise have responsibilities for which they are not prepared.

## INFOTRAC COLLEGE EDITION

If you purchased a new copy of this book, you received a complimentary subscription to InfoTrac® College Edition. Use it to access full-text articles from research journals and practice-oriented publications. Go to http://www.infotrac-college.com/wadsworth and start your search. There are several ways you can search this online library. For example, you can open the current issues of a journal, such as *Personnel Psychology*. You also can do a keyword search on a topic that interests you. The following keywords can be used to find articles related to the topics discussed in this chapter.

Job search                          Organizational environment
Organizational change

# The Nature of Work

The nature of work can be described from several different perspectives. In this chapter, I discuss some of these perspectives on work and define terms that you will find useful in most discussions of work. First, let me point out that some terms refer to the specifics of work activity and worker capacities. At this elemental level, work is made up of tasks. *Tasks* are cognitive and/or physical operations that are performed actively and with purpose. Worker capacities that are needed for performing tasks are usually described as relevant knowledge, skills, and abilities, or KSAs. Roughly speaking, *KSAs* can be defined as understanding and having information (knowledge); knowing how to do things (skills); and having the basic personal power to learn and develop oneself (abilities). In this and later chapters, you will see examples of these elements of work. Second, on a different scale, some terms refer to organized sets of work activities that people perform at the workplace. An employment *position* is a set of related tasks or activities that are performed by one individual. Each employee in an organization fills a single position. A *job* is a group of positions in which the tasks and work activities are identical or basically the same. Everyone in an organization has a job as well as a position, although the job is likely to be one that others also are performing. In Chapter 3, you will learn about job analysis procedures for studying and understanding the nature of an organization's jobs and the worker capacities that are needed.

Third, some work-related terms summarize jobs and work experiences into more general categories. Jobs that are similar to others in an organization are grouped into a *job family*. The complete work of a business firm can be divided into any number of job families, depending on the complexity of the firm. Two other terms are not closely connected to any single organization. *Occupation* refers to essentially the same job as it exists in multiple organizations. (In some cases, however, the term *job* is used instead of *occupation,* as when one is talking about a job as it exists in general.) A person's occupation does not depend on employment in a specific organization. In fact, someone can be unemployed and still have an occupation. The term *career* has a developmental connotation, and it includes the meaning of occupation. A career refers to changes, in job or organizational level, over the course of an individual's work life. A career, like an occupation, can be developed by employment at one or at multiple organizations.

## THE IMPORTANCE OF WORK

Work is important to us. Notice how much time and effort we expend becoming qualified for work, searching for work, working day after day, working even when we don't have to, thinking about work, . . . and talking about work. You probably have had the experience, in meeting someone for the first time, of being asked, "What do you do?" Perhaps you said that you are a student pursuing a certain major or studying for an occupation. Or, if you have a job or an established line of work that you use to identify yourself, you might have talked about that. Most of us have been asked this question, and we ask it of others. The answers function as "identity labels." Such labels give information about someone's work that helps to determine the relationship between two people and gives clues as to how they should behave toward each other. For example, finding out what work someone does can affect how formally you address the person, whether you show deference—or expect deference, and whether you are likely to have anything further to say to the individual.

The work a person does becomes a critical part of self-identity and affects self-esteem (Albert & Whetten, 1985; Tajfel & Turner, 1986). We learn about the value of certain occupations through the lessons our society and culture give us. Similarly, we come to understand that the value of the occupation gets attached to the person. Thus, we begin to grasp what others think of us as a result of the work we do. All of us want to feel positive about how we are defined, particularly those definitions that are important to self-esteem. Therefore, we develop ways of telling others about the kind of work we do so as to gain positive reactions and preserve our positive self-concept.

### Occupational Prestige

Sociologists have discussed the extent to which society positively values various occupations. Some occupations are considered much more prestigious than others, possibly because of the education and wealth of individuals having these occupations. Also, the level of occupational prestige is something that the average person understands. Subgroups within a country rate occupations about the same, and ratings appear to be stable over time. Although there are national differences, these differences have not been extreme, at least to the extent that countries use the same occupations (Treiman, 1977). Table 2.1 demonstrates the nature of occupational prestige with a list of occupations that

| TABLE 2.1 | OCCUPATIONAL PRESTIGE IN FIVE COUNTRIES | | | | |
|---|---|---|---|---|---|
| | **Country** | | | | |
| **Occupation** | **U. S.** | **Canada** | **Germany** | **Australia** | **Japan** |
| University professor | 78 | 80 | 77 | 81 | 80 |
| Physician | 78 | 83 | 75 | 81 | 73 |
| Civil engineer | 68 | 69 | 68 | 75 | 63 |
| Manufacturing plant owner | 63 | 66 | 68 | 72 | 60 |
| Elementary school teacher | 60 | 57 | 59 | 53 | 56 |
| Journalist or reporter | 52 | 58 | 61 | 50 | 57 |
| Policeman* | 48 | 49 | — | 44 | 46 |
| Construction foreman* | 46 | 49 | 49 | 46 | — |
| Insurance agent | 47 | 45 | 42 | 44 | 30 |
| Truck driver | 32 | 31 | 35 | 26 | 32 |
| Store or shop clerk | 28 | 25 | 28 | 33 | 31 |
| Farm laborer | 21 | 21 | 19 | 28 | 23 |

Table constructed from *Occupational Prestige in Comparative Perspective* (Appendix D, pp. 318–329, 332–337, 348–353, 376–378, 406–409), by D. J. Treiman, 1977, New York: Academic Press.
*Note.* Cell entries are standard occupational prestige scores with a range of 0 to 100. The standard score is a summary measure devised using multiple studies of occupational prestige rating and ranking.
*Data not available for one country.

vary in this respect. Notice, for example, that the occupations of university professor and physician have high prestige. Journalist or reporter has midlevel prestige. Other occupations, such as farm laborer and store clerk, have lower levels of prestige. Also, although the absolute values of prestige scores vary by country, their relative ranks are comparable (Treiman, 1977).

Occupational prestige can contribute to a person's positive self-identity and self-esteem. For example, individuals whose occupations have high prestige are esteemed by others in the society. As a result, they can gain self-esteem from this recognition, which contributes to their positive self-identity. However, it is not only occupational prestige, nor is it the absolute level of prestige, that determines how valuable one's work feels. Some people whose occupations are considered prestigious do not feel that this makes much difference to their self-esteem. Conversely, some whose occupations have little prestige feel that what they do is meaningful and, although others might not value their work, they feel that it contributes greatly to their self-identity.

We gain some understanding of the personal value of work to a person's positive self-identity by considering work that society disparages. Ashforth and Kreiner (1999) discussed the nature and meaningfulness of work to those who perform society's "dirty work." Although such work is recognized as being necessary for society to function, dirty work is considered "tainted." I once overheard my uncle speaking to my teenage cousin about the need to establish an occupation for himself. "I think you should consider going to school to become a mortician," my uncle said. "Yuck! That's disgusting!" my cousin responded. "But, look, it's important work," my uncle argued. "We need people to do it." He did his best to promote the occupation. Nevertheless, my cousin was swayed by the taint, and he never became a mortician.

Ashforth and Kreiner (1999) found that a number of occupations are considered dirty work. In the current research, the concept is broadly defined as involving (1) working directly with physically noxious materials and conditions (e.g., mortician, garbage collector, firefighter); (2) taking a servile role with respect to others (e.g., housemaid); (3) working in contact with others who are stigmatized (e.g., prison guard, psychiatric ward attendant); and (4) engaging in activities of doubtful virtue (e.g., exotic dancer, telemarketer, gambling-casino owner). Some of these categories do not obviously appear to serve a need of society. However, even when they do not, people who do such work can see value in what they do, and they can identify at least indirect benefits that society reaps.

Doing meaningful work is essential in maintaining a positive self-identity and self-esteem, not only for those who do society's dirty work, but for all of us. However, people differ in the strategies they use to establish positive social meaning and status for an occupation. For some, the status associated with a prestigious job can be tapped simply by wearing their "identity labels." Others, who have less prestigious occupations and/or do "dirty work," might need to be careful to avoid negative reactions to their work that could damage self-esteem. Ashforth and Kreiner (1999) point out that occupational and work group cultures provide ways to protect a person's esteem and self-identity. For example, members of the same work group can help each other by identifying valuable aspects of the work that are not apparent to outsiders. The work group also can offer its members a positive and cohesive subculture, and it can be the source of identity as well as social relationships. The work group provides a buffer from outsiders, which allows the person to avoid negative encounters with those who might condemn the work. Importantly, the group provides a more appropriate basis for social interactions. That is, those doing stigmatized work can retain their self-esteem by associating with others performing similar work.

## Conclusions

The question "What do you do?" is loaded with meaning. Clearly, the work someone does can be a critical component of his or her self-identity and self-esteem. Societal, occupational, and work group factors affect the value of work, change individuals' attitudes about work, and influence one's self-respect. It is not unreasonable to expect that organizational factors also might affect the part that work plays in a person's life.

# TYPES OF WORK

Work is described and categorized in various ways, and the labels used to identify jobs and occupations reflect these distinctions. Sometimes, the labels refer to the kinds of tasks or operations performed. For example, the labels "machine operation" and "technical work" reflect specific work operations. Other types of work, such as agricultural or customer service work, are described as being directly involved with the employer's product or service. Some work is more specific to its context or client, such as hospital work, teaching, and law enforcement. In addition, certain work can be described not only by such work content descriptors but, in an important sense, also by its relationship to the organization. "Management" is this type of work, and titles such as "marketing manager" and "director of human resources" are examples. Finally, work can be understood according to how it fits an employer's needs, such as teamwork, shift work, and international work. In the following sections, I discuss these different ways of defining work.

## Occupational Descriptions

Massive amounts of information about jobs and occupations are available to employers, counselors, students, and other users. The best-known source is probably the *Dictionary of Occupational Titles* (DOT). This is a publication in encyclopedic form, containing detailed information on the types of work being done in the workplaces of the United States. Based on this is a second source, the *Occupational Information Network*, which is an electronic database accessed through the Internet.

***Dictionary of Occupational Titles***   The DOT is published by the U.S. Department of Labor (1991), and new editions have come available periodically since the 1930s. Based on summaries of millions of employment positions currently in use by American organizations, the DOT presents full descriptions of the work that defines occupations. Abstracts of jobs included in each occupational category delineate the nature of the occupation, identify the industry in which such jobs are found, and describe the specifics of the work—including work activities and tasks, as well as related job titles. Abstracts are organized into categories of similar occupations. Figure 2.1 provides an example of an abstract.

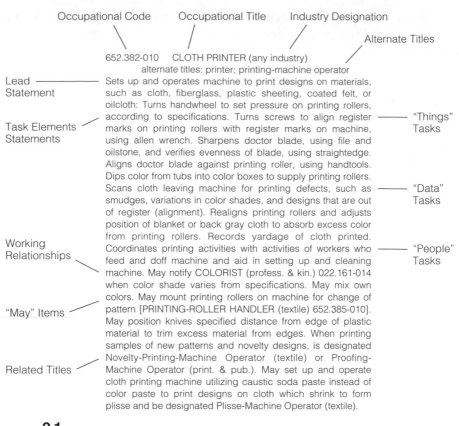

Occupational Code    Occupational Title    Industry Designation

Alternate Titles

652.382-010    CLOTH PRINTER (any industry)
alternate titles: printer; printing-machine operator

Lead Statement —— Sets up and operates machine to print designs on materials, such as cloth, fiberglass, plastic sheeting, coated felt, or oilcloth: Turns handwheel to set pressure on printing rollers, according to specifications. Turns screws to align register —— "Things" Tasks

Task Elements Statements —— marks on printing rollers with register marks on machine, using allen wrench. Sharpens doctor blade, using file and oilstone, and verifies evenness of blade, using straightedge. Aligns doctor blade against printing roller, using handtools. Dips color from tubs into color boxes to supply printing rollers. Scans cloth leaving machine for printing defects, such as —— "Data" Tasks smudges, variations in color shades, and designs that are out of register (alignment). Realigns printing rollers and adjusts position of blanket or back gray cloth to absorb excess color from printing rollers. Records yardage of cloth printed.

Working Relationships —— Coordinates printing activities with activities of workers who —— "People" Tasks feed and doff machine and aid in setting up and cleaning machine. May notify COLORIST (profess. & kin.) 022.161-014 when color shade varies from specifications. May mix own colors. May mount printing rollers on machine for change of

"May" Items —— pattern [PRINTING-ROLLER HANDLER (textile) 652.385-010]. May position knives specified distance from edge of plastic material to trim excess material from edges. When printing samples of new patterns and novelty designs, is designated Novelty-Printing-Machine Operator (textile) or Proofing-

Related Titles —— Machine Operator (print. & pub.). May set up and operate cloth printing machine utilizing caustic soda paste instead of color paste to print designs on cloth which shrink to form plisse and be designated Plisse-Machine Operator (textile).

**FIGURE 2.1**

Example of an occupational abstract. Elements of the definition are identified as they are used in *Dictionary of Occupational Titles* entries.

Adapted from *Dictionary of Occupational Titles*, 4th ed., Rev., by U.S. Department of Labor,1991, Washington, DC: U.S. Government Printing Office.

The foundation and organizing principle of the DOT was drawn from a method of studying and describing jobs, known as *functional job analysis*, which had been developed in 1944 by employment researchers (cf. Fine & Wiley, 1971). In this method of analysis, every job is viewed as containing work tasks and activities that are related to data, people, and things. DOT occupations are defined and scored in these terms, as indicated in Figure 2.1. An occupation is given a score for each of the three categories, with lower scores indicating more complex relationships. For example, "synthesizing" is a highly complex data-relationship (scored 0, on a scale of 0–6). "Serving" is a simple people-relationship (scored 7, on a scale of 0–8). "Operating" is a moderately complex things-relationship (scored 3, on a scale of 0–7). In the figure, the occupational code—specifically, the fourth, fifth, and sixth digits—shows the average data-, people-, and things-related scores for the occupation as a whole.

| TABLE 2.2 | **OCCUPATIONAL GROUPS AND EXAMPLES.** |
|---|---|

| Occupational Division | Example Occupations |
|---|---|
| Professional, technical, and managerial occupations | Architect, engineer, psychologist, physician, writer, attorney, pilot, ship captain, advertising executive, retail sales manager |
| Clerical and sales occupations | Secretary, computer operator, bookkeeper, cashier, receptionist, store clerk, real estate sales agent, advertising sales agent |
| Service occupations | Maid, childcare worker, waitress, bartender, barber, baggage handler, launderer, janitor, security guard, firefighter, police officer |
| Agricultural, fishery, forestry, and related occupations | Farmer, horticulturist, greens-keeper, tree trimmer, farm machine operator, dairy worker, animal care-taker, fisher, forest worker |
| Processing occupations | Tungsten refiner, blast furnace tender, die-casting machine operator, beverage grain miller, cigarette inspector, butcher, egg candler, bakery supervisor |
| Machine trades occupations | Machinist, machine-shop tool maker, grinder operator, drill-press operator, robotic machine operator, automobile mechanic, aircraft mechanic |
| Benchwork occupations | Beadworker, sewing-machine operator, plastic pattern caster, glove turner, glass blower, button maker, packing-line worker, paint-spray inspector |
| Structural work occupations | Welder, riveter, electrician, furnace fabricator, refrigeration mechanic, shipyard painter, bulldozer operator, blaster, carpenter, bricklayer |
| Miscellaneous occupations | Trailer-truck driver, railroad station agent, parking lot attendant, sign painter, miner |

Table constructed from *Dictionary of Occupational Titles*, 4th ed., Rev., by U.S. Department of Labor, 1991, Washington, DC: U.S. Government Printing Office.

You can see that the occupation of cloth printer has moderately complex data-relationships, simple people-relationships, and complex things-relationships.

DOT information is organized into nine occupational divisions. Although the divisions contain seemingly very different types of work, the jobs included do have features in common. The common features provide a rationale for the occupational division. The divisions are identified below, and Table 2.2 gives examples of the occupations in each division.

1. *Professional, technical, and managerial occupations* involve the theoretical or practical aspects of a range of fields including art, science, engineering, education, medicine, law, and business relations, as well as administrative, managerial, and technical work. Most of these occupations require substantial education, at least at the college level.

2. *Clerical and sales occupations* include two related categories. Clerical occupations are concerned with compiling and computing or otherwise systematizing data. Sales occupations are concerned with influencing customers to purchase a product or service.
3. *Service occupations* involve work in and around private households; serving in institutions and commercial establishments; and providing protective service for the benefit of the public.
4. *Agricultural, fishery, forestry, and related occupations* are concerned with growing and harvesting plant and animal life and products. Also included is work concerned with related support services, such as logging, hunting, and caring for public parks and gardens.
5. *Processing occupations* are concerned with refining, mixing, treating, and otherwise preparing materials and substances. Knowledge of processes and formulas is required in some of these occupations. Equipment or machinery, such as vats, ovens, mixers, and grinders, usually are involved.
6. *Machine trades occupations* involve operating machines to cut, abrade, or print a variety of materials such as metal, paper, wood, and stone. Machine assembly, installation, maintenance, and repair are required. The ability to operate machines is of primary importance. Some jobs require blueprint reading and mathematical computations. In less complex jobs, eye–hand coordination may be the most important requirement.
7. *Benchwork occupations* are concerned with using human limbs, hand tools, and bench-based machinery to grind, paint, sew, assemble, or otherwise work with small objects and materials. The work is done at a bench, worktable, or conveyor in a mill, plant, or shop. In more complex jobs, workers read blueprints or follow patterns.
8. *Structural work occupations* involve erecting, paving, and otherwise building structures or structural parts, such as buildings and roads. Stationary machines, hand tools, and portable power tools are used with materials such as wood, metal, concrete, and glass. Knowledge of the nature of materials, such as stress tolerance and durability, is needed.
9. *Miscellaneous occupations* include occupations that are not easily categorized into another division. Included are mining, transportation, packaging and warehousing, utilities, recreation, and graphic arts.

DOT information makes it clear that people perform a great variety of jobs and occupations. The work activities described range from tasks that are simple to tasks that are extremely complex. Because the DOT has focused on providing job-oriented information, this source is useful to employers who may have any of several needs for job-descriptive information. For example, the DOT can be helpful in studying and designing jobs.

***Occupational Information Network* (O\*NET)**   An electronic database, the *Occupational Information Network,* or O\*NET, is being developed by the

U.S. Department of Labor. The O°NET is based on and will replace the DOT when it is complete. The purpose of the O°NET is to provide a national database of occupational information, including extensive data on worker requirements as well as task-oriented information. The database already contains information on more than one thousand occupations. The data have come from two sources: (1) a questionnaire study using a workplace sample, in which job incumbents have described both the work they do and their own job-relevant attributes; and (2) conversions of existing occupational descriptions from the DOT (Peterson, Mumford, Borman, Jeanneret, & Fleishman, 1999).

By the start of the 1990s, it was becoming apparent that public needs for occupational information could no longer be satisfied by the existing DOT. A new informational system would be needed that could describe occupations in a more flexible manner and which could be more easily accessed by a greater number of users. In 1990, the U.S. Department of Labor established an advisory panel of experts to evaluate the DOT and to specify the needs for a new system. In its final report to the government, this panel recognized the value of DOT information but also identified certain issues that needed to be addressed (U.S. Department of Labor, 1993). For example, the DOT traditionally has concentrated on describing tasks. Although the need for task identification would continue, the panel recommended that other information also be provided, particularly details on worker qualifications, such as knowledge and skill requirements.[1] The panel further recommended that changes in users' needs be considered. One such change was an increased need for making cross-occupational comparisons. Comparing multiple occupations is difficult when using the DOT. A new system, in which occupational descriptions use a common framework and more general cross-job terms, would be an improvement. Another potential change in users' needs was for an information system that could be searched quickly and easily. The panel recommended the development of an electronic database with a software interface allowing users to view the data. Such a system would be helpful to employers and also would appeal to individuals who do their own career planning (Dunnette, 1999).

Finally, the advisory panel proposed a content model or framework for structuring the database. The model identifies and defines the contents or categories of information that various users likely will need, such as cross-occupational and job-specific characteristics, as well as worker requirements (Dye & Silver, 1999). The content model is shown in Figure 2.2. Using this model to structure the O°NET database means that the data are organized into the six domains specified in the model. These domains represent electronic "windows" that users can open to reveal information related to a chosen occupation. The first three of the domains discussed below are work-oriented and

---

[1]The DOT does not offer detailed KSA information. Notice that the abstract in Figure 2.1 gives only task information.

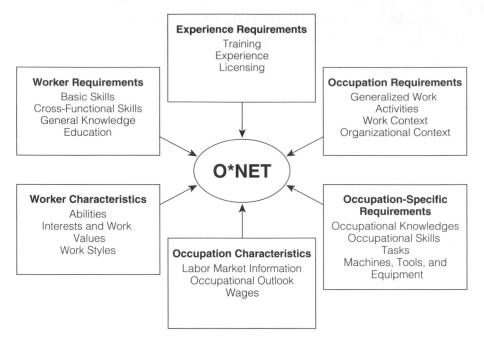

**FIGURE 2.2**

The content model of the *Occupational Information Network* (O*NET) showing the six domains of the database (http://www.onetcenter.org/content.html).

From N. G. Peterson, M. D. Mumford, W. C. Borman, P. R. Jeanneret, & E. A. Fleishman (Eds.). *Development of Prototype Information Network (O*NET) Content Model* (vols. 1 and 2). Copyright 1995 by Utah Department of Employment Security, Salt Lake City, Utah. Reprinted by permission of the American Psychological Association.

address different aspects of an occupation. The other three domains are worker-oriented, referring to personal attributes and experiences that are relevant to an occupation.

Following Figure 2.2, let us consider each of the content model domains in terms of the data that will become available when the database is fully developed.

1. *Occupation requirements* refers to the nature of the work performed. This domain includes general work activities that characterize groups of related occupations; and the physical or social context in which the work is performed, such as whether it is done indoors or outdoors, or involves other people.
2. *Occupation-specific requirements* mainly addresses the specific tasks performed in an occupation. The domain also includes the tools and equipment that are used and job-specific knowledges and skills.
3. *Occupation characteristics* includes broad-scale labor market conditions, occupational outlook, and wage information. This domain comprises links to other databases where such information can be found.

4. *Worker characteristics* are abilities, interests, work values, and styles of behaving. These personal attributes generally influence a person's performance capabilities for a type of work. For example, if you go into a line of work (such as marketing), you might need to have certain abilities (e.g., oral expression), interests (e.g., in enterprising occupations), and values (e.g., for recognition).

5. *Worker requirements* are attributes an individual develops that directly influence work performance. These can be useful in a range of occupations. They include general knowledge and both basic and cross-functional skills, and they are reflected by a person's education. For example, knowledge areas might be sales and marketing, mathematics, and communications media. Examples of skills include information gathering, active listening, and writing.

6. *Experience requirements* also are individual attributes. However, job experience, training, and, for some types of work, having a license are explicitly linked to the type of occupation (Mumford & Peterson, 1999).

The O*NET database, which can be found at http://www.onetcenter.org/, is structured by the content model. Users can access and browse through information on an occupation by entering its title and then selecting domains from the content model to open folders in the database. They can find both narrative and numerical information, describing an occupation at any of several levels of specificity—from the most general overview to the most specific details. That is, the user is able to "drill down" to the level of data needed (Rose, Hesse, Silver, & Dumas, 1999).

To demonstrate the use of the O*NET, I opened the Web site, clicked on the button for O*NET Online, then entered an occupation—real estate agent—for which I was interested in searching. In addition, I requested a "snapshot" (or general overview) of what is required to perform this type of work. My search request brought up the page shown in part (a) of Figure 2.3. You should notice certain features of this page. First, look at the group of buttons on the lower right. One indicates that a list of related occupations can be obtained. Another provides "crosswalk" connections to other information sources, such as the DOT. The Details button allows the user to switch out of the snapshot windows and "drill down" to obtain more specific information about this occupation. Next, notice that the O*NET content domains reproduced on the left depict the extent to which snapshot data are available for this occupation. You can see that some O*NET domains hold complete data, whereas others do not. For example, in the Occupation-Specific Information domain, only tasks are currently available. Because I was interested in occupation-specific information, I clicked on the appropriate button for it (in the group at the top right) and found the snapshot of required tasks. Part (b) of Figure 2.3 shows a brief job description and a sample of the tasks. Notice that the tasks are similar to those listed in the DOT.

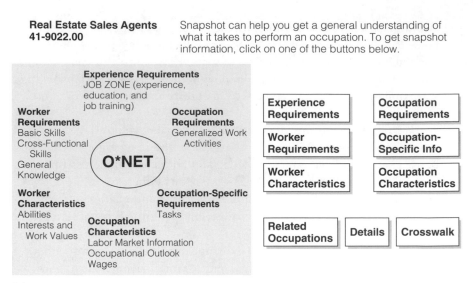

**Real Estate Sales Agents**
**41-9022.00**

Snapshot can help you get a general understanding of what it takes to perform an occupation. To get snapshot information, click on one of the buttons below.

(a)

**Snapshot Occupation-Specific Information for**

**Real Estate Sales Agents**

Description: Rent, buy, or sell property for clients. Perform duties, such as study property listings, interview prospective clients, accompany clients to property site, discuss conditions of sale, and draw up real estate contracts. Includes agents who represent buyer.

Examples of Tasks:
- Displays and explains features of property to client and discusses conditions of sale or terms of lease.
- Answers client's questions regarding work under construction, financing, maintenance, repairs, and appraisals.
- Interviews prospective tenants and records information to ascertain needs and qualifications.
- Solicits and compiles listings of available rental property.

(b)

FIGURE **2.3**

Example of an online search for occupational information on the job of real estate agent. (a) Snapshot window showing O*NET data options. Content domains, shown on the left, indicate the type of data available. On the right are two groups of buttons for accessing the data. (b) Examples of tasks listed in the Occupation-Specific Information domain.

Adapted from http://online.onetcenter.org/.

## Managerial Work Roles

Organizations vary in terms of the product or service they provide, and many jobs reflect such an organization-specific nature. Other occupations are not very different across organizations, however; and comparison information showing their similarities can be helpful to employers. For example, managerial work is needed to some extent by all employers. In fact, some large organizations have a great need for management and hire many individuals for work in this area.

What kind of work do managers do? Occupational descriptions of managerial work can be found in both the DOT and the O°NET. Researchers also have studied the nature of this work. Still, although it can be simply put, this turns out to be a rather difficult question to answer. Even managers often have difficulty saying what it is they do on a daily basis, although they can tell you about their overall responsibilities. Also, like other kinds of work, managers' daily activities change over time, as a result of changes in the business environment. For example, Fogli and Whitney (1998) conducted a study of the roles of retail store managers following a period of organizational downsizing. They found that compared to the 1980s, managers in the 1990s were spending considerably less time on company-specific technical work, such as store operations and expense control, and more time on human resource management and customer service activities. In addition, there is evidence that managers in different countries do somewhat different work. For example, compared to their American counterparts, a sample of Russian factory managers spent more time on routine communications and traditional management activities, such as coordinating and controlling plant operations, and, in general, they spent less time on networking with outside informational sources (Luthans, Welsh, & Rosenkrantz, 1993).

Leadership has long been recognized as an important part of managerial work. Leadership theorists have identified work activities in which a manager might be expected to show leadership, and they have proposed ways a manager can be effective in performing the leadership role (Bass, 1985). Managerial activities that involve leadership include rewarding and motivating subordinates to achieve their goals; directing and coordinating the work of teams; handling interpersonal conflicts; representing the organization; and problem-solving and planning (Yukl, 1989).

Other aspects of managerial and supervisory work have been examined in research. In one early study (Mahoney, Jerdee, & Carroll, 1965), managers working in different departments in several organizations filled out a questionnaire that included two groups of items about managerial work: (1) basic functional dimensions, such as planning and supervision, that any manager might be expected to do; and (2) specialized work activities, such as dealing with employee relations, finance, or sales, which a manager's job might emphasize. The researchers found that most managers spent about one-half of their workday performing five basic managerial functions: planning, informational input and processing, coordinating or exchanging information, evaluating, and supervising. On average, managers spent more of their time supervising than on any other basic function. The rest of the workday was spent on area-specific activities and depended on the focus of the managerial job.

Mintzberg (1980) developed a theoretical typology of the work roles[2] a manager performs that includes but goes beyond leadership. He based the typology on empirical research suggesting there is great similarity among managers in the roles they perform. In his view, most differences between managers can be described as resulting from the emphasis of certain roles over other roles in their jobs.

Mintzberg's (1980) typology is composed of ten work roles that describe what managers do in the course of fulfilling their responsibilities. Any single managerial job is thought to involve some level of each role. The ten roles are divided into three categories: interpersonal, informational, and decisional. *Interpersonal roles* are primarily concerned with interactions and relationships to people. This category includes three sets of related activities. In one, a manager has a symbolic role as representative or figurehead of an organization or a unit. In another set of work activities, a manager has a leadership role with respect to subordinates. In this, the manager hires, trains, motivates, and otherwise interacts with subordinates. In other activities, a manager has a liaison role, in which he or she networks with outside contacts to get information relevant to the organization's environment. Performance of a manager's interpersonal roles is essential to obtaining information and to performance of the second group of roles. *Informational roles* concern the transfer of information. In one set of informational activities, a manager acts as a monitor, receiving and collecting information and developing expert knowledge of the organization's issues. In the disseminator role, a manager yields this information to the organization. In the role of spokesperson, a manager speaks for and transmits information from the organization. Because information access and handling are necessary for making decisions, a manager's performance of informational roles contributes to the next category—the decisional roles. *Decisional roles* include four sets of work activities in which a manager decides for the organization. In the role of disturbance-handler, a manager must deal with threats to the organization. In the entrepreneurial role, a manager must initiate changes that will allow the organization to take advantage of opportunities in the environment. The negotiator role means that a manager makes decisions for the organization in major negotiations, such as with unions. As resource allocator, a manager decides how the organization will expend its resources.

Clearly, managerial work that includes many of these roles is highly complex and can involve a heavy workload of information processing, decision making, and strategy development. In such cases, the manager has a central role in the flow of information and in handling threats and disturbances. In Figure 2.4, you see an occupational description from the DOT. In the task statements, this shows how one managerial job can include such work roles.

---

[2]A work role is a set of task-related behaviors that are expected to be shown by the person doing the job.

166.167-034 MANAGER, LABOR RELATIONS (profess. & kin.)
alternate titles: labor relations representative

Manages labor relations program of organization: Analyzes collective
bargaining agreement to develop interpretation of intent, spirit, and
terms of contract. Advises management and union officials in
development, application, and interpretation of labor relations
policies and practices, according to policy formulated by DIRECTOR,
INDUSTRIAL RELATIONS (profess. & kin.) 166.117-010. Arranges
and schedules meetings between grieving workers, supervisory and
managerial personnel, and BUSINESS REPRESENTATIVE, LABOR
UNION (profess. & kin.) 187.167-018, to investigate and resolve
grievances. Prepares statistical reports, using records of actions
taken concerning grievances, arbitration and mediation cases, and
related labor relations activities, to identify problem areas. Monitors
implementation of policies concerning wages, hours, and working
conditions, to ensure compliance with terms of labor contract.
Furnishes information, such as reference documents and statistical —— Refers to external
data concerning labor legislation, labor market conditions, prevailing    information-collecting
union and management practices, wage and salary surveys, and              activities
employee benefits programs, for use in review of current contract
provisions and proposed changes. May represent management in
labor contract negotiations. May supervise employees and be known
as Labor Relations Supervisor (profess. & kin.). May be employed by —— Variants of the
firm offering labor relations advisory services to either management      occupation in which
or labor and be known as Labor Relations Consultant (profess. &           people-related activities
kin.). May be employed by governmental agency to study, interpret,        are more complex
and report on relations between management and labor and be
known as Industrial Relations Representative (government ser.).

> Complex data-related
> or informational tasks

**FIGURE 2.4**

Managerial work relationships in a managerial occupation. This example shows task statements describing data-related, or informational, tasks and people-relationships.

Occupational description adapted from *Dictionary of Occupational Titles,* 4th ed., Rev., by U.S. Department of Labor, 1991,
Washington, DC: U.S. Government Printing Office.

Notice that the primary role in this occupation is informational; the occupation
includes a high level of complex data-related tasks and associated decision
making. Variants of the occupation put more emphasis on complex interpersonal relationships.

Managerial work is extremely important to the functioning and success of
an organization, particularly because management forms the connective tissue
between the various units that make up an organization's structure. Managerial
work is involved in every move an organization makes. Therefore, understanding the nature of managerial work is essential, and in the following sections, we
will return to the question of what managers do.

## Conclusions

In its detailed descriptions of tasks and work relationships defining jobs
and occupations, the DOT demonstrates that there are many different
types of work. Some of these, such as managerial work, show organization-

specific attributes as well as cross-occupational similarities. The new approach of the O*NET yields task information, indicates worker requirements, and makes cross-occupational comparisons easier to perform. The comprehensive information provided by the DOT and the O*NET is particularly useful to employers, for example, in the analysis of existing jobs, design of new jobs, and planning for future employment needs. In addition, one of the original purposes of the DOT was to satisfy vocational counseling needs for person–job matching. In this respect, vocational and career counselors can obtain information about a client's personal work history, interests, and abilities, and then compare the information with occupational descriptions to advise the individual about the kinds of work that might be suitable. The O*NET makes this matching process even easier (Dunnette, 1999).

## The Organization of Work

Jobs are embedded in an organization, and they are affected by their organizational context. In addition, features of the social environment of business can influence work done in an organization. Broad contextual factors, such as culture and society, are potentially important in determining the nature of work, and researchers are interested in learning how such effects occur. For example, some research has focused on the extent to which people of a particular culture assign value to individual and collective work activities. In North America and in northern and western Europe, cultures are mainly individualistic in their values. That is, there is more concern about the needs, goals, and activities of individuals than of groups. In other cultures, such as those in some Latin American, Asian, and African countries, values are collectivistic. The focus is on the needs, goals, and activities of groups rather than individuals (Hofstede, 1980; Triandis, 1989).

Such differences might be relevant to the design of jobs and to the definition of working relationships. Obviously, it is good to know about cultural differences if an organization's workforce is multicultural or if an organization expands or relocates to another country. In this section, I discuss how several features of an organization's structure and its social environmental context can influence how jobs are designed and performed.

### Job Design

A question to be answered by anyone thinking of establishing a business is "What work needs to be done?" Answering the question generally means identifying or defining the tasks that need to be performed to produce a certain consumer product or service. Doing this will show what kind of work is needed; how much is needed; and how the work might be structured and work relationships defined. If the work is substantial and the business owner plans to hire employees, he or she will need to design jobs and establish positions.

Job design results in a more or less deliberately conceived division of labor and an organizational structure that defines job relationships and decision-making authority. The particular organizational structure that emerges depends on the simplicity or complexity of the jobs designed. This, in turn, is affected by labor market conditions and the business owner's values and orientation to work.

When labor market conditions are such that few workers are available who can perform complex and difficult work, job design tends to result in simplified jobs. Such jobs include only a few, easy-to-perform tasks. A worker repeats the same tasks over and over throughout the workday. For example, in some of the benchwork occupations described by the DOT, simple work is performed on an assembly line, in which an employee performs one or two operations and then passes the materials on to other employees for the remaining work.

Simplified jobs require less in terms of knowledge, skills, and abilities, and they can be performed—with some on-the-job training—by workers who have low levels of education or experience. In a tight labor market, such workers are more likely to be available and at a lower wage rate. Many employers facing these labor market conditions or other constraints of the business environment decide to design jobs in this way. Most basic production or service work can be broken down into its elements and simple jobs designed from the elements. This job design, based on Frederick Taylor's (1916) classical studies of production work design, allows a business to employ relatively unskilled workers and make the best use of the available labor supply.

This simplified job design produces a certain organizational structure. Let me demonstrate. Once an employer has reduced basic production work to its elements and designed simplified jobs, a need for other jobs appears that had not been apparent before. Supervisory and managerial jobs are needed to oversee and supervise the performance of these simplified jobs. Supervisory and managerial work includes the complexities of basic production work, such as planning a production procedure. It also includes work that directly resulted from simplifying production, such as coordinating work activities and overseeing the production process. The resulting organizational structure becomes more "vertical" or hierarchical with the addition of supervisory and managerial jobs because the simplified job design requires removing decision-making authority from the production line and adding authority to the managerial jobs. Employees doing production work are at the lower levels of the hierarchy in that they have little authority in their jobs. Rather, they are supposed to follow job design specifications that are given to them. Some decision-making authority is available to their immediate supervisors. However, when the nature of production work is such that many different kinds of jobs are developed, the authority available to individual supervisors is limited, and more authority for overall management and steering of the organization's operations is reserved for those higher up in the management ranks.

Although apparently economical in that an employer can use generally low-cost production workers, use of the simplified job design strategy has certain costs. For one thing, managerial positions cost more to fill. Managerial jobs are varied, complex, and difficult, and they can involve high levels of decision making and accountability. Complex jobs generally require greater knowledge, skill, and ability, and they often require specialized education and experience. Individuals already well qualified for such work are less numerous in the labor supply than individuals who are less qualified, so they can demand higher wages. Therefore, an employer might do well to ask whether the cost savings of hiring a less expensive production crew is used up by hiring more expensive managerial employees. Furthermore, in using the simplified job design approach, some employers have found that they have created repetitive, monotonous, and deadening production jobs. Productivity of employees on these jobs declines and other costly problems appear, such as absenteeism. In fact, early organizational theorists pronounced this kind of work as demeaning to the worker. They proposed that people need to have at least some complexity in their work, such as having a say in how it is done, in order to stay interested and motivated (cf. Argyris, 1957; Likert, 1967).

Instead of simplifying jobs, an employer might choose to design jobs so that they are more complex. It is possible to organize work into only a few categories and to hire people for each category to do everything that needs to be done. This design strategy results in a complex and varied job in which a worker performs a complete process of work on a single product or service. Such "whole" jobs include routine and simple tasks as well as work involving greater responsibility and decision making. For example, a new bookstore might open with a few employees all of whom attend book fairs, make purchasing decisions, advise customers, ring up purchases, stock shelves, and sweep up after closing.

Of course, there is a downside to this strategy, as well. An employer using such a job design approach would hire individuals according to their ability to perform the complex activities of these jobs, as he or she could assume they also would be able to perform the simple tasks. Therefore, an employer might have to pay more for performance of the simple tasks than if someone had been hired specifically to do them. However, the richness of "whole" jobs, in terms of employee decision making and responsibility, means that less supervision is required and that a business can operate with fewer managers. This translates into cost savings. It also means that the organizational structure is "horizontal" or "flat"—there is little differentiation of employees in terms of authority, as more individuals hold equal ranks. Many decisions are made by employees, with relatively less authority reserved for managers. However, as you might imagine, giving up decision-making authority can make a business owner nervous, as the quality of decisions made by employees might not be good, and many employers are disinclined to share their authority (Manz, 1992). As a result, they undermine the flat organizational design.

**Job Enrichment**     As a result of the experience with job simplification, and of concerns about the quality of employee decision making, organizational researchers have developed compromise strategies for redesigning jobs. Sometimes, jobs that had been simplified are redesigned to be enriched in some manner. Job *enlargement* is a way of improving a job by increasing the variety of its tasks. Tasks are added, at roughly the same level of complexity as the original job. Generally, the enlargement simply means that an employee has different things to do. Job *enrichment* involves expanding the job to include more complex tasks and increasing the scope of responsibilities. An enriched job can include responsibilities for planning and making job-related decisions. The purpose of both forms of job redesign is to increase the worker's interest and motivation. However, job redesign probably should not merely enlarge the job. Rather, to gain real motivational improvements, redesign should increase the level of complexity in the tasks and allow at least some decisional responsibilities (Lawler, 1969).

## *Teamwork*

In an effort to increase employees' control over their jobs and to allow their participation in organizational decision making, many employers have added elements of teamwork to existing job designs. An early example of such enrichments is the quality circle, in which production employees meet and discuss ways to improve product quality. Members of a quality circle devise innovations for the organization to use, which may or may not be implemented. Quality circles continue to be used by organizations, and they are the precursor of the popular "total quality" approach for improving product and service quality (Guzzo & Dickson, 1996).

In recent years, employer interest in teams has increased (Devine, Clayton, Philips, Dunford, & Melner, 1999). Researchers are interested too, and published research on teamwork has mushroomed. For example, in the 1990s, several summaries and discussions of large bodies of research literature on work team interactions and performance have been published (cf. Guzzo & Dickson, 1996; Guzzo & Shea, 1992). Also, if you look through current issues of any of several research journals (e.g., *Journal of Applied Psychology*, *Group & Organization Management*, *Academy of Management Journal*, or *Human Relations*), you will be convinced of the high level of research interest. Varied issues are being studied, many of which are relevant to understanding the kinds of work activities that teams perform.

**The Work of Teams**  Work teams are defined and structured in several ways, depending on the group's purpose and staffing needs. Teams often are identified by their membership. Top management teams are identified this way, as are various cross-functional teams that draw their members from different organizational units. Teams also can be differentiated in terms of whether there is a temporary or an ongoing need for them. Ad hoc committees, task forces, and special project teams have a temporary nature. They are established to meet, do a one-time work project, and then disband. Standing committees and production crews have an ongoing or recurrent purpose.

Teams can be distinguished by the primary focus of the work they are supposed to do. Some teamwork is oriented primarily toward production outcomes, and the collective power of the team is meant to serve production performance. Manufacturing production teams and other work crews are like this. A road construction crew, made up of workers and their supervisor, is an example. Self-managing teams and self-regulating work groups also focus on production tasks, although they differ from the traditional production team in an important respect. These teams are structured with interdependent work roles, and they are meant to operate autonomously. In such teams, all participants learn to perform all tasks, including team leadership. These are versatile teams because the group controls all aspects of the work, and participants' roles are interchangeable. This means a team can function even if a member is absent.

Other teamwork is primarily process-oriented. Unlike production teams, in which the group's interaction is largely incidental to its product-oriented purpose, group interaction processes are foremost in the purpose of other teams. In the process-oriented team, the group's purpose is to develop and use its unique interactive capacities to reach goals that individuals working separately could not accomplish. Process-oriented teams are established specifically for information exchange and discussion, problem solving, decision making, and planning. Typically, the goal is to develop ideas and plans that can benefit the organization. For example, the discussion that goes on in quality circles is meant to yield ideas for product improvement. Research and development (R & D) project teams and cross-functional teams are primarily process-oriented. The purpose of these and similar groups includes creative problem solving, decision making, and strategy development.

In both production- and process-oriented teams, the essential group process of interaction can be influenced by the design and context of the team. The nature of the work goals and tasks constitutes one factor that can change interactions and determine how well a team performs. For example, a group with poorly defined goals does not perform as well as a group with clear and specific goals (Weldon & Weingart, 1993). When a team is assigned an uncertain task—that is, a task in which no one is sure whether work procedures will be effective—the team does not perform as well as when task procedures are certain. Sometimes, when a task is uncertain, the group does not perform well because members lose faith in their team's ability to succeed and they begin working independently. When there is greater task certainty, however, members are more likely to believe that the group can succeed, and this affects their performance (Gibson, 1999).

You might already have observed that certain kinds of jobs are more likely than others to include teamwork assignments. Managerial work includes roles and activities that are oriented toward interactional processes and teamwork. For example, motivating and inspiring employees to reach their goals are managerial work activities that feature interactive processes. In addition, high-level managers often must work in teams of their peers. Informational exchange and innovation are managerial work activities that are especially important in organizations that operate in a rapidly changing environment. One purpose of top management teams is to brainstorm innovative ideas for changes an organization can make to more effectively adapt to such a business environment (cf. West & Anderson, 1996). Clearly, the team context is appropriate for this kind of creative work.

**Teams in Industry**   I hear a lot of talk these days about the widespread use of teams in American business firms. Teamwork, it seems, is something that all working people should expect to do at some time. I am ready to believe it. However, I would like to know exactly how prevalent organizational team use is and also what kinds of work teams are doing.

Evidence from a randomly selected sample of organizations shows that teams indeed are enjoying widespread use (Devine et al., 1999). This study indicated that nearly half (48 percent) of all U.S. organizations were using some kind of team in their operations. Most of those using teams were large establishments with multiple departments. Team use was found across all industries; unexpectedly, however, there was relatively greater team use in nonprofit, public service organizations than in either blue-collar or white-collar business firms.

Although production teams were in use, the most common type of work group was the process-oriented team. These teams were set up to gather and exchange information to solve quality problems, formulate organizational strategy, and develop or research new product lines and markets (Devine et al., 1999). Another study, describing the work of teams in industry, was a longitudinal analysis of senior management teams in hospitals. The teams in this study were multidisciplinary and process-oriented. Their purpose was to develop innovative ideas and strategies for making changes that would help a hospital adapt in a changing health-care environment. The study examined several teamwork factors, including the group's resources and interaction processes, as well as individual member characteristics. The researchers reported the overall best predictor of team innovation to be the group's process of interaction. Interaction processes that were especially effective included goal-oriented discussion, high levels of member participation, and showing support for innovativeness (West & Anderson, 1996).

## *Conclusions*

Because so many teams are process-oriented, I recommend that employers give more attention to staffing teams and preparing employees for teamwork. As a method of working, teamwork differs from individual work, and it requires special understanding and skill. Most employees are hired and trained to perform individually, and although they might perform well on an "individual" job, they might not have the necessary capabilities for teamwork. For example, some otherwise satisfactory employees lack knowledge of effective communication, have not learned strategies for making effective group decisions, and do not understand the impact of conflict on group interactions. An issue that needs research concerns effective selection procedures that employers can use to identify "teamworkers," either in an organization's current staff or in an applicant pool.

## ARRANGEMENT OF WORK

Real-world organizations operate on a time schedule and have a physical location in the business community. In some important ways, these temporal and physical features, like other contextual factors, influence the nature of work people do. In the final pages of this chapter, I discuss two of these factors: (1) work scheduling and (2) international expansion of business firms.

### *Work Shifts*

Although many organizations operate only during the daytime, other organizations conduct two or three work shifts for a 24-hour operation. For example, public service providers, such as hospitals, utility companies, and fire and police departments, operate on shifts. Some manufacturing and transportation organizations also run around the clock, with shifts scheduled to cover the 24-hour period. In a three-shift schedule, for example, the day shift can run from 7 a.m. until 3 p.m., with the evening shift following from 3 until 11 and the night shift from 11 p.m. until 7 a.m.

**Night Work**    The night shift is different from other shifts in two ways. One, workers have trouble performing the very tasks on which they excel in the daytime. Two, the nature of the work is more or less different from that performed in the daytime. For example, security guards' jobs in some companies are strictly nighttime jobs. Other nighttime work, such as that of hotel desk clerks and police officers, involves tasks that vary somewhat from day work tasks. Additionally, for some night jobs, the work context changes in terms of the presence of others, such as coworkers and customers.

Workers have personal difficulty adjusting to night work, and their work performance usually suffers. Not surprisingly, sleep disturbance is one of the most common personal problems. Even those on permanent night work, such as security guards, have more trouble sleeping than workers on other shifts (Alfredsson, Akerstedt, Mattsson, & Wilborg, 1991). Sleep loss, and the resulting fatigue and drowsiness during the shift, affects both shift performance and the workers' days off, because recovery takes longer and leisure time is upset (Bohle & Tilley, 1998; Totterdell, Spelten, Smith, Barton, & Folkard, 1995). In general, night workers are less productive, and they have more accidents, particularly in the last hours of the night shift (Craig & Condon, 1984; Levin, Oler, & Whiteside, 1985).

Worker assignment to night work can be arranged basically in two ways—in fixed or in rotating shifts. In a fixed-shift system, certain employees are assigned permanently to the night shift. You might think this seems unfair because always working at night and sleeping in the day can disturb one's lifestyle. However, the alternative also has disadvantages. In a rotating shift system, all employees take turns working on all shifts, which means that the night work is temporary for everyone rather than permanent for some. How the schedule is rotated is another variable. In forward rotation, workers rotate their assignments with the clock—from an evening shift to a night shift and then to a day shift. In backward rotation, they go *against* the clock, as from an evening shift to a day shift and then to a night shift. Rotating shifts also vary in terms of how fast the rotation is. It is possible for workers to change shifts as quickly as every few days or as slowly as every few weeks.

Night workers on rotating shifts generally have the same kinds of performance problems and personal difficulties that night workers on fixed shifts do. However, the effects are more severe. Research indicates that rotating shift workers find it more difficult to adapt to the changing sleep/wake cycles and they experience more stress, especially on shifts that rotate quickly and against the clock (Jamal & Baba, 1992; Paley & Tepas, 1994; Wilkinson, 1992). Attitudes are affected also. In one study, nurses evaluated rotating night shifts more negatively than rotating day or evening shifts (Bohle & Tilley, 1998).

You might be thinking that some people probably like night work. If so, you are correct. Individuals do vary in their attitudes toward night work. There are good reasons for working at night. Some have to do with the nature of the work and working conditions, such as a quieter workplace. Other reasons are more personal. For example, nurses sometimes choose permanent night work in order to share child-care responsibilities with a day-working spouse. Research has shown that those who specifically choose permanent night work have fewer of the health problems that interfere with work performance (Barton, 1994; Barton & Folkard, 1991).

In general, for an organization that must operate at night, the recommendation about night work is this: It is better to arrange fixed shifts and allow workers to choose their assignments. If not enough people choose a permanent night shift, the next best arrangement is a forward-rotating shift that rotates slowly.

## Working in Other Countries

Some large companies, in an effort to reduce costs and increase performance, expand their operations by establishing branches in other countries. A labor force has to be provided for the foreign branch, and one seemingly effective way for companies to do this is to send some of their own domestic employees and to hire additional workers from the host country. Although American organizations have sent technical employees, they are especially likely to relocate managerial personnel to the branch to oversee the developing operation. Host-country nationals usually are hired for the production work. Employees who are sent on foreign work assignments typically are selected on the basis of their having been effective in the domestic assignment. The reasoning is that if they are good at their jobs at home, then they will be good abroad. The unstated assumption is that the job is the same.

Experience has shown that there is a problem with this manner of staffing the foreign branch because a large number of employees working abroad do not finish their work assignments. Dissatisfied, they return home early. Across branch locations and industries, it has been estimated that anywhere from 16 to 50 percent of overseas employees return before completing their work assignments (Black, 1988; Tung, 1988). In addition, some researchers point out that the failure rates would be even higher if they included those expatriate workers who psychologically withdraw from their work responsibilities, even though they do not actually return early (Black, Gregersen, & Mendenhall, 1992).

Of course, early returnees have been questioned about the cause of the problem. Because of their responses, some researchers conclude that retention failure is due at least partly to the inability of an employee and his or her family to adjust to life in another country. Some think that better selection procedures would help by identifying employees who personally would be better able to adjust. Also, cross-cultural training programs often are suggested as being a good way to prepare employees and to prevent some of the common misunderstandings that occur between people of different cultures (Black & Stephens, 1989; Tung, 1981).

Researchers also have been giving some thought to the validity of the assumption that managerial work is the same the world over. It is reasonable to suppose that changing the cultural context of a manager's job might change the work itself. One of the most obvious differences in the work situation of an expatriate manager is that the people he or she supervises often are host country citizens with a cultural background that differs from that of the manager's previous domestic subordinates. As I noted earlier in the discussion of individualism and collectivism, culture can affect the way people perform interactive work. Therefore, it is reasonable to expect that the cultural context can modify the work relationships between a supervisor and his or her production employees. The results of a study done in the early 1990s suggest how supervision might vary as a function of culture. The study focused on how production employees in different countries deal with things that happen during the course of working. In Japan, supervisors reported that their best performers handle unusual events by checking policy manuals or consulting their supervisor. However, British and American supervisors said that their best performers rely on their own experience to know how to handle such things (Smith, Peterson, & Misumi, 1994). Think how such supervisory work might change for a manager who moves from one of these cultures to the other. In some cases, undoubtedly, an expatriate manager is unable to determine whether such contextual factors have changed the work needed or, if so, how the work has changed. It is thought not to be unusual for an expatriate manager to experience ambiguity and conflict in his or her work roles (Black, Mendenhall, & Oddou, 1991).

Another sign of change in the expatriate manager's job is when the managerial behaviors that were effective in the domestic location are not effective in the foreign location. Managers do not always make adjustments in their behavior when they relocate to another country to work with people from a different culture (Tse, Francis, & Walls, 1994). For some, however, the transported management style is not fully successful. One study reported that American expatriate managers working in Hong Kong behaved very much like American managers working in the United States. However, while such behavior was effective for the domestic managers, it was not related to effective job performance for the expatriates (Black & Porter, 1991). This may mean that many expatriate managers do not have adequate cross-cultural knowledge or a repertoire of effective alternative behaviors. Or it may mean that they tend to be unaware that some aspects of their work have changed and that different behavior is required.

In these examples, the implication is that a manager's work is not the same in a foreign location as in the domestic location. Managers who are relocating to a foreign branch need to understand that their jobs might change and that new tasks and responsibilities, as well as new ways of working, might be required. As to how an employer might prepare managers, I recommend identifying potential cultural differences; studying the domestic manager's existing job and comparing it to the job designed for the foreign branch; and incorporating the results of these studies into a training program for relocating managers.

## SUMMING UP

The purpose of this chapter is to show the breadth of human work activity and to identify factors that influence how work is structured and jobs are designed. The discussion also is meant to suggest issues that employers need to take into account in staffing or other human resource functions. Summing up, we can draw the following conclusions:

- Work is personally important; it contributes to our identities.
- Society and culture strongly influence the nature and value of work.
- The DOT and the O*NET are important sources of occupational information.
- Currently, there are many different occupational types and millions of jobs.
- Labor market conditions affect how jobs are designed in organizations.
- Complex jobs involve a whole process of work, including decision making.
- Teamwork allows workers to participate in decision making.
- Process-oriented teams are good for innovations and problem solving.
- Work varies according to the time of day a job is performed.
- Managerial work includes people relationships and process-oriented tasks.
- The job of an expatriate manager differs from domestic management.

## INFOTRAC COLLEGE EDITION

Would you like to learn more about the issues reviewed in this chapter? If you purchased a new copy of this book, you received a complimentary subscription to InfoTrac College Edition. Use it to access full-text articles from research journals and practice-oriented publications. Go to http://www.infotrac-college.com/ wadsworth to start your search. You might open current issues of a journal that you know is likely to have relevant articles, such as *Personnel Psychology*. You probably will want to do a keyword search. The following keywords can be used to find articles related to the topics of this chapter.

| | |
|---|---|
| Vocational planning | Managerial work |
| Job enrichment | Cross-functional teams |
| Production teams | |

# JOB ANALYSIS

Here's an assignment for you. Develop a description of all the tasks and activities you perform in the course of doing your job. (Refer back to the definitions at the opening of Chapter 2, if you need to.) Start by recalling all the things you did on a typical workday, such as maybe last Wednesday. Write these down, and then estimate how much time you spent doing each of them. While doing this, you probably will remember that there are some important elements of your job that you do not do every day and, in fact, did not do last Wednesday. Put these on another list and estimate how much time you spend on them per week on average. In this activity, you are using one of the basic techniques for collecting job information: the work diary. It is sometimes used to collect information from job incumbents, as a first step in a job analysis.

Job analysis is the systematic study of a job or job family. Specifically, it is the collection of information about tasks and observable work behaviors that are performed on a job and that can be verified either directly (e.g., physical actions) or indirectly by inference (e.g., decision making, by its product or outcome) (Harvey, 1991). Job analysis also includes information about the context in which work is performed, such as work equipment, materials, and relationships with others. For example, turn back to Figures 2.1, 2.3, and 2.4 and examine the occupational descriptions shown. Notice that task statements are listed and contextual features of the work are identified. The goal of job analysis is to describe what the worker does in performing a job. Therefore, the information collected should be at least indirectly observable to others. Harvey (1991) pointed out that any aspect of work that does not have an observable component cannot be described in a job analysis. Also, job analysis focuses on work behavior that is independent of the person. That is, it is the work and the work process that are important, rather than the personal attributes of a job incumbent. You will see later that we can infer personal attributes from tasks and work activities and, although they might be helpful in performing a job, they are not part of the job per se. Finally, because job analysis is a study of observable and verifiable behavior, it can be checked for accuracy. Job analysis results can be replicated—like other psychological research—by others studying the same jobs (Harvey, 1991).

Why do we do job analysis? There are several organizational needs for job information that can be satisfied only by the systematic study of jobs. As I discussed in Chapter 2 concerning the development and structuring of an organization, the question "What work needs to be done?" must be answered in order to accomplish the purpose and goals of the organization. Job analysis provides the basis of job design, and it allows an organization to establish that its purpose and goals actually are expressed in terms of the work being done.

In Chapter 2, you learned about the general nature of work, including some useful terminology. In the present chapter, the focus is on job analysis. Here, you will learn about the organizational needs for job analysis. You will see that the various human resource functions in all organizations must be based on accurate and complete information about jobs. In this respect, job analysis is the foundation for employee recruitment, compensation, selection, performance appraisal, and training. In this chapter, I discuss how to conduct a job analysis in order to obtain the job information for these purposes.

# PREPARING TO CONDUCT JOB ANALYSIS

## Uses of Job Information

The methods of job analysis vary as to the types of information they yield. Therefore, before conducting a job analysis, questions such as "What is the nature of the need?" and "How will job information be used?" must be posed and answered. This gives direction to the project. It is an essential step in deciding how and by whom a job analysis will be done.

Organizations need job information for many purposes, as indicated in Table 3.1. For example, an organization that does not have written job descriptions might need to develop them. A systematic job analysis can be helpful for writing these descriptions. Job descriptions themselves are useful for other human resource purposes, such as planning for future workforce needs and employee recruitment. Also, a company might need to design new jobs or redesign existing ones. Organizational changes, such as downsizing, can bring about a need for redesign. Job analysis information on existing and anticipated job tasks is essential in job redesign. Similarly, job analysis is needed in developing employee training. Another use of job information is for classifying jobs into job families. Job classification is needed for compensation systems, and also for moving employees from one job to another. The same job analysis may or may not be appropriate for these different uses, however. Clifford (1996) found that a job analysis done for compensation classification purposes was not appropriate for organizing jobs into job families for training and employee transition.

TABLE

3.1

**TABLE**

**3.1**    **POTENTIAL USES FOR JOB ANALYSIS INFORMATION**

| Organizational Need | Job Information Needed |
|---|---|
| Developing job descriptions | Tasks and work context information; worker requirements |
| Job design and redesign | Task and work context information; anticipated job changes |
| Classification of jobs | Job information on multiple jobs |
| Compensation and job evaluation | Job information on multiple jobs |
| Recruitment | Job descriptions |
| Employee selection | Worker requirements for performance |
| Employee training | Task and work context information |
| Performance appraisal | Information on critical tasks |

The most important use of job analysis information is for developing and preparing measures to be used in employee selection and performance appraisal. Employee selection has a complex relationship to job analysis. First, employee selection is the centerpiece of important fair employment law and litigation. In this legal arena, tests and other measures used for selecting employees are required to be based on information from a job analysis. In some cases, the selection device is literally drawn from the details of a job analysis. In addition, employee selection decisions can be based on performance appraisal information, such as when an employee is "selected" for promotion or advancement to a higher ranking position. For such uses, performance appraisal also needs to be based on job analysis information.

An organization can experience a special need for job analysis when it faces problems of employee discrimination or other fairness issues. For example, if a firm's selection procedures result in unfair discrimination in hiring new employees or in making promotional decisions, a new job analysis might be required. Similarly, if existing job designs do not consider the possibility of hiring persons with disabilities, a job analysis might be conducted for the purpose of developing accommodations to such individuals.

**Conducting a Job Analysis Project**    Deciding to conduct a job analysis to provide for one or more of these needs means that an organization must consider how to manage the project and, specifically, who can do the job analysis. Large organizations that have HR people who have the necessary skills for doing job analysis often choose to conduct the project in-house. A well-trained job analyst is a good source of information about the needs for job analysis and about job analysis techniques that can be used to obtain job information. A trained job analyst can work with other HR personnel to make effective use of job analysis results. Organizations that do not already have such capability might decide to hire skilled job analysts in order to do an in-house job study, particularly if there will be an ongoing need for job analysis. On the other hand, an organization can hire a consultant to perform a job analysis. This can be reasonable, especially if the need is not great or is only short-term.

The specific purpose of a needed job analysis determines whether it should be done by an organization's staff or by an external consultant. For some uses, such as when stringent scientific or legal requirements are involved, job analysis must be conducted by means of a sophisticated methodology, which requires expert job analysts. For example, job analysis for the purpose of developing and validating[1] selection tests requires such expertise. If the company already has HR personnel with this capability, the job analysis can be done internally. Otherwise, the company probably should look for a qualified consultant (Van De Voort & Stalder, 1988).

## Sources of Job Information

Where do we get information about jobs? For any particular job being studied, one or more of several information sources will be available. Some information can be obtained from printed or electronic resources. Other information comes from seeing a job performed or from talking with those who know the job.

**Documents and Published Research**   The study of company documents and published research on job analysis is usually the place to start in conducting a job analysis. Written information about the company often is available. The organization also might have documents that describe the work being performed, such as announcements of positions available, training manuals, equipment operation instructions, records of customer complaints, and performance records identifying tasks that incumbents perform. Records of job analyses previously conducted by the company also may be available. Even if these studies are outdated or not on the specific jobs being studied, they can be informative.

Various published materials can be consulted for job-relevant information. As discussed in Chapter 2, you can find specific information about many different kinds of work by looking in the *Dictionary of Occupational Titles* (DOT, 1991) and by accessing the *Occupational Information Network* (O*NET) at http://www.onetcenter.org/. The occupational abstracts published in the DOT were developed by job analysts who reviewed and consolidated job information received from many different employers who had made use of a particular job. Similarly, the O*NET is being developed from a large sample of data

---

[1]"Validation" refers to the process of establishing that a test or other instrument actually measures what it is meant to measure.

obtained from employees at many different organizations. The O\*NET includes a broader range of information than the DOT, including worker requirements, which makes it an especially valuable source of information. For example, Figure 3.1 (a and b) shows samples of the types of knowledges and skills that are found in the O\*NET database.

Published research on a range of issues important to job analysis methodology can be accessed from public and university libraries. For example, two publications that can help someone planning a job analysis are *The Job Analysis Handbook for Business, Industry, and Government* (1988) and a chapter on job analysis in the *Handbook of Industrial and Organizational Psychology* (Harvey, 1991). Together these sources represent the most extensive knowledge of job analysis available. Procedures for conducting a job analysis are described and discussed thoroughly, and strengths and weaknesses of the methods are identified. This is publicly available information that can help an employer decide how to conduct a job analysis project.

**Job Incumbents and Supervisors**    Some sources of job information are people. Those who perform the job in question or who supervise its performance are the most frequently contacted sources. There are some advantages in this. First, job incumbents have an up-close familiarity with the work activities of the job under study. The immediate supervisor has an understanding of the job, although it is different from an incumbent's because a supervisor is involved in overseeing performance of the job. Second, it can be "politically" wise to feature job incumbents and supervisors in a job analysis. Doing so can increase the apparent or "face" validity of job analysis results, which can be essential for certain uses of job analysis. That is, the work described by the job analysis needs to look like what job incumbents actually do. To omit these job information sources might require some explaining. Generally, if anyone knows what a job involves, it probably is the person who does it or the one who supervises it.

Although you might need to include incumbents and supervisors in a job analysis, you should be aware that there are potential problems in doing so. One is that job incumbents simply might not want to be bothered with what amounts to extra work. I found myself in such a position on a job I had years ago. My work group was asked by job analysts in our HR department to accumulate work diary information about our daily activities. The HR staff carefully explained the need for the job analysis. They promised that the data collection would take only a short time, and they agreed that we would record our data only once a day. Still, we found participation tedious and felt that it added to our workload. We joked that part of our jobs now was to do job analysis paperwork.

Another reason that incumbents sometimes do not want to participate in a job analysis is that they feel nervous about what the results are going to mean

**Details of Knowledge for**

**Marketing Managers**

Knowledges are organized sets of principles and facts that apply to a wide range of situations. All knowledge areas important to this occupation are shown in this window.

( ◎ ) Importance          (  ) Level Required          (Submit)  You can view detailed areas based on their importance or the level of expertise required.

Use this key to get an idea of how important each area is to this occupation.

**Importance Key**

100 ☐ Extremely important

☐ Very important

☐ Important

☐ Somewhat important

0 ☐ Not important

| Importance | Knowledge | Description |
|---|---|---|
| 100 | Sales and Marketing | Knowledge of principles and methods involved in showing, promoting, and selling products or services: including marketing strategies and tactics, product demonstration and sales techniques, and sales control systems. |
| 92 | Administration and Management | Knowledge of principles and processes of business and organizational planning, coordination, and execution; including strategic planning, resource allocation, manpower modeling, leadership, and production methods. |
| 83 | Mathematics | Knowledge of numbers, their operations, interrelationships, and applications; including arithmetic, algebra, geometry, calculus, and statistics. |

FIGURE **3.1 (a)**

Example of online search for the job of marketing manager. Samples of important knowledges.

From http://online.onetcenter.org/

---

for them in terms of changes. Part of the role of those conducting a job analysis is to get commitment from participants. Usually, a good strategy is to explain the need for the study and allay fears about adverse job changes. Of course, this is not always possible. Even if incumbents are assured that the purpose is to study jobs and not individual performance records, and even if resulting job changes are minor, people sometimes react as if they have been

### Details of Skills for
### Marketing Managers

Skills are developed capacities that facilitate learning and performance of activities that occur across jobs. All skills important to this occupation are shown in this window.

 Importance        ◯ Level Required        （Submit） You can view detailed areas based on their importance or the level of expertise required.

Use this key to get an idea of how important each area is to this occupation.

**Importance Key**

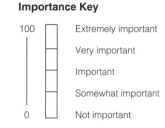

| Importance | Skill | Description |
|---|---|---|
| 96 | Speaking | Talking to others to effectively convey information. |
| 88 | Active Listening | Listening to what others are saying and asking questions as appropriate. |
| 88 | Idea Generation | Generating a number of different approaches to solving problems. |
| 83 | Reading Comprehension | Understanding written sentences and paragraphs in work-related documents. |

FIGURE **3.1 (b)**

Samples of important skills.

From http://online.onetcenter.org/

---

personally assaulted. I once was responsible for getting a group of job incumbents to participate in a job analysis. I explained the project honestly, including the possibility of job redesign. The incumbents agreed to participate, and during the data collection, they even seemed to enjoy being involved. However, the simple job changes that were highlighted by the job analysis were resisted actively. If I hadn't known it before, this experience certainly made clear how very personal a job is to the one who performs it daily.

People's motivations affect their actions, of course. Therefore, we can expect that the quality of job information provided by incumbents can be influenced by such psychological factors as motivation, and we should not be surprised to find that there are errors in the information job incumbents provide.

Morgeson and Campion (1997) reviewed the published literature in an attempt to identify the psychological sources of inaccurate job information. They found 16 possible sources of inaccuracy. For example, they found that an informational work overload could lead to incomplete reporting of job information. Other sources of inaccuracy were carelessness and psychological processes such as withholding effort, resisting participation, and impression management. When a job informant focuses on impression management, the information given is more likely to reflect what he or she *wants* the job to be. In general, the reviewers found that the particular inaccuracy in job information depended on the measure being used. In this respect, I have more to say about inaccuracies in a later section of this chapter.

## Conclusions

Complete and accurate job information, which only carefully conducted and documented job analyses can provide, is needed for most organizational uses of job information. In deciding how to conduct a job analysis, organizations must consider the primary need for the job study. If an organization does not have the necessary personnel—with skill in using job analysis methodology—to provide for this primary need, it should not attempt an in-house project. The better investment would involve hiring a consultant with the necessary expertise to conduct the project.

A well-done job analysis requires preparation. Preliminary information should be compiled concerning the need for job analysis, the job to be studied, and the appropriate job analysis methodology. This basic information forms the rationale and general strategy of the project. Plans should be outlined for collecting information from job incumbents and supervisors because they have personal knowledge of the job. The plans should recognize potential difficulties in obtaining the participation of these subject-matter experts, and some thought should be given to possible inaccuracies in the job information. Skilled job analysts can be a real asset in dealing with such difficulties. Also, the quality of job analysis data is sometimes improved by using a larger number of job informants.

## RESEARCH METHODS USED IN JOB ANALYSIS

At this point, I will describe some general research methods that are routinely used in conducting job analysis. In some job studies, these methods are the sole means of getting information. In other studies, they are used in concert with one or more specialized job analysis techniques. The general research methods include observations and various survey techniques incorporating interviews and questionnaires.

## *Observation*

Observation can be a straightforward way of getting job information to answer two important questions: "What work is being done on the job?" and "How is the work being done?" Observational methods are particularly appropriate for initial study when little information about a job exists. The method calls for recording observable work behavior. It yields detailed information about tasks performed; materials and equipment used; work processes and procedures followed; and interactions with coworkers, subordinates, and supervisors. Observation can be done in any of several ways. Frequently, a job analyst directly observes someone performing the job during a sampling of the performer's work period. Most often, the performer is the job incumbent, although this does not have to be the case. For new jobs being developed, the job analyst can observe a simulated performance. In addition, self-observation is possible, in which the job analyst role-plays the performer and records his or her own activities in doing the job.

Direct observation by a job analyst has certain advantages. For one, the data have face validity. That is, the information looks right when it is reviewed by job incumbents. They recognize it as being what they do on the job. More importantly, observational data provide a basis for dealing with inconsistencies in job information obtained by more subjective methods (Martinko, 1988). For example, if job incumbents and supervisors report discrepant information, then observation of the job can be used to clarify the discrepancy. Another advantage of direct observation is its effectiveness for studying a variety of work activities, including the process of group interaction in working teams. In teamwork, as in individual work, an observer records how the work is being done and what work relationships are involved.

There are also disadvantages in using direct observation to collect job information. One is that job performers sometimes are uncomfortable when someone watches them work, and they may change their behavior because of this. Another disadvantage is that it takes longer to compile and analyze observational data—compared to questionnaire data, for example. Observation also can be expensive, depending on how long the observations continue. If a limited time sample of performance is observed, it is less costly (Martinko, 1988; Pape, 1988).

## *Interviews*

Most job analyses involve interviewing throughout the job analysis process. Interviews are good for initial gathering of task information. Sometimes, instead of directly observing a work process, job analysts interview individual job incumbents and ask questions about what they do on the job, and they interview supervisors to get their views of the work activities of the job. Interviews also can be used to finish the data collection process. More frequently, however, interviewing takes place in an interim stage and contributes to the development of a list of tasks and/or KSAs (Knowledges, Skills, Abilities). This list is used further to develop a questionnaire for the final data collection.

Individual interviewing needs to be conducted carefully, and the data that are gathered must be recorded immediately so as to obtain and preserve as much accuracy as possible. The job analyst should come to the interview well prepared with preliminary information about the job and be ready to speak with the job informant using appropriate work terminology. Such interviews should take place at or near the location of the work because this makes it easy for a respondent to include information about equipment and other contextual features of the work. A good strategy to improve the quality of interview information is to structure the interview process with a line of questioning, developed from previous document study, that alludes to possible tasks. In the interview, the job analyst should plan to ask probing questions and allow the individual to thoroughly describe the work. The interview should not be rushed. Enough time should be allowed for the informant to describe the job and for the job analyst to record information. The point of the interview, which should be explained to incumbents, is to get as much information as possible about the job (Gael, 1988).

**SME-Groups**   A job analysis interview can be conducted in a group setting. Because job incumbents and supervisors are widely recognized as having extensive, firsthand job knowledge—and are called subject-matter experts, or SMEs—they often are interviewed as a group. For all group members to have a chance to fully participate, an SME-group should be fairly small, say 5 to 10 people. SME-groups can be assembled for gathering information at various stages of job analysis. The group interview is conducted for some of the same reasons as individual interviews. For example, SME-groups are used to develop a list of tasks or to get information about the work context. In addition, and even more likely, SME-groups evaluate and refine task statements and lists that have been developed by other means, such as by observation or individual interviews. Sometimes, they also identify KSAs that are implied by task statements or that appear to be required on the job (Gael, 1988).

Depending on the purpose of an SME-group, the job analyst who conducts the group interview can have a more or less active role to play. Generally, however, the interview should be structured with questions or objectives for the group to accomplish. For example, if a group is supposed to evaluate a list of tasks, the job analyst will need to lead the group through an item-by-item assessment of the tasks and encourage members to offer suggestions for revising, deleting, and adding tasks.

**Work Diaries**   The work diary that I asked you to complete at the opening of this chapter is a technique that lies at the boundary between interviewing and self-observation. In a work diary, a job incumbent self-observes by following instructions from a job analyst. The incumbent records what he or she did during a period of observation, often a workday, though it can be longer. Recording after short intervals, such as a half hour, sometimes is recommended in order to ensure that complete data are recorded. Because it is done by incumbents with no need for costly materials or interventions, the work diary is an inexpensive method to use. However, it also is an inexact method. There is little control over how specific the recorded tasks are. Also, job incumbents may not stay within the requested time intervals or accurately record their work activities (Freda & Senkewicz, 1988).

## Questionnaires

Observation and interview techniques can be the primary methodology of a job analysis. However, in many cases, these techniques are secondary to the objective of developing a job analysis questionnaire. Many job analyses start with observations of work being performed or individual interviews with incumbents. Statements describing tasks, and sometimes KSAs, often are developed by job analysts using observational and interview data, and these statements are given to an SME-group for evaluation and revision. Finally, job

**Task**
**Performance**
Do you perform this
task on your job?
0 No
1 Yes

**Relative Time Spent**
How much time do you spend on this task
compared to other tasks?
1 Very little time
2 Less than average amount of time
3 Average amount or same as other tasks
4 Moderate amount of time
5 Very much time

**Frequency of**
**Performance**
How often do you
perform this task?
1 Very rarely
2 Not often
3 Fairly often
4 Frequently
5 Very frequently

**Importance**
How important is this task in performing
your work?
1 Not important
2 Slightly important
3 Moderately important
4 Important
5 Very important

**Criticality**
How critical is it that you perform this task effectively? What would happen if you
performed it ineffectively?
1 Not critical.
2 Slightly critical. If performed ineffectively, slight difficulties would result.
3 Moderately critical. If performed ineffectively, corrections would be needed.
4 Critical. If performed ineffectively, hard-to-correct difficulties would result.
5 Very critical. Difficulties would be impossible to correct.

FIGURE **3.2**

Rating scales used on job analysis questionnaires.

---

analysts set up the statements as items in a questionnaire and devise rating scales for job informants to use in responding to the items. Typically, a questionnaire asks respondents to evaluate each work activity that they do on the job and to assess how important or critical a task is to overall success on the job. Also, questionnaires often ask about the amount of time spent doing a task and how frequently it is performed. Figure 3.2 shows how such rating scales might look.

Because they are in written form and can be mailed, job analysis questionnaires are a convenient way to collect information from large numbers of job incumbents and supervisors. They can be used to include incumbents in related jobs or in the same job at branch locations. Although sometimes only a sample of job incumbents is surveyed, it often is desirable to invite all incumbents to participate, and questionnaires make it easy to do this.

**Job Rating Errors**    When job incumbents do not have the necessary verbal skills for filling out complex questionnaires to accurately portray the job, supervisors can be the better source of questionnaire information. However, substituting supervisors for incumbents might not be the best strategy because of another problem that can appear. Researchers have found that incumbents and supervisors do not always agree in what they say about a job. In addition, job incumbents themselves do not necessarily agree in how they describe their work (cf. Mullins & Kimbrough, 1988).

Concerning incumbent–supervisor disagreement, reviewers of research report that incumbents say they perform tasks that their supervisors say they do not, and supervisors identify tasks that incumbents say they do not perform (Cornelius, 1988; Harvey, 1991). How can this be? I saw it happen once in a job analysis. Some incumbents reported that their responsibilities included work—such as caring for the office plants—that the supervisor never mentioned, nor was it in any existing job description. Also, the office supervisor believed that certain other tasks were the responsibility of the staff, yet these were not mentioned by anyone.

Generally, such discrepancies are taken to mean that there is error in the *reporting* of job information. In other words, such differences are not considered to be real differences in the work performed but, rather, inaccurate assessments of a job as reported on a questionnaire. The accuracy of job information gathered by a questionnaire is assessed, in most job studies, by the extent to which there is interrater agreement among the questionnaire respondents. Interrater disagreements can be due to an imperfect instrument. For example, a questionnaire may contain language that is unfamiliar to some respondents, making it difficult for them to report on the job and resulting in answers that are inconsistent with those of others.

I have no doubt that problematic questionnaires can account for some of the differences observed. In addition, I think that some of the inaccuracy has its source in the kinds of social psychological influences described by Morgeson and Campion (1997). As I mentioned earlier, such factors as impression management can affect how a person describes a job. Another possibility is that observed discrepancies between job informants are not solely a problem of reporting. Rather, it might be that real work differences are being described by different SMEs. Currently, a line of research is developing that explores the nature of the differences in information reported on job analysis questionnaires. Some researchers propose that the way to understand how two people doing the same job can describe it so differently is to examine the nature of their personal relationship with the job. For example, a person might perceive a job differently after working at it for a long time than when he or she started doing the job. To study the effects of long-term job experience, Richman and Quiñones (1996) referred to the research on memory, which indicates that people have a harder time remembering how often something is done if it is part of the everyday routine. In their laboratory study, they found evidence that job incumbents with more experience actually give less accurate estimates of how frequently they perform a task than incumbents with less experience. The researchers explained that for newcomers each performance stands out in memory, but for experienced workers performances blend together over time.

It is possible also that the quality of an incumbent's performance influences how the job is described. For instance, two employees on the same job might differ in terms of the amount of time they spend on different tasks, and if so, they could be expected to describe their jobs differently, which would reflect this time difference. If their most time-consuming tasks vary in how important they are to success on the job, then the one who spends more time on important tasks would perform better and be evaluated higher than the one who spends more time on tasks that are not very important. Some researchers have not been able to show that high- and low-performing incumbents describe their jobs differently (Conley & Sackett, 1987). Others, however, who used a complex means of differentiating high and low performers, did find the expected effect. High performers described their tasks quite differently than low performers and they concentrated their efforts on more important job tasks (Mullins & Kimbrough,1988).

In addition to the variables of experience and quality of performance, a third possible reason for differences in incumbents' reports is that characteristics of the job and its organizational context might have an influence. For example, some job incumbents might have more autonomy than others on the same job and, as a result, more freedom in deciding how to perform the work. In jobs that lack autonomy, performance could be expected to vary little, and the job information supplied by the incumbents should generally be in agreement. In jobs with autonomy, however, employees can decide how to perform their work. Therefore, performance could be expected to vary among them, and their assessments of the job likely would vary also. Some research suggests that it is because of such job factors that information reported by incumbents sometimes looks as if different jobs are being performed (Borman, Dorsey, & Ackerman, 1992; Lindell, Clause, Brandt, & Landis, 1998). For example, the employees included in Mullins and Kimbrough's (1988) study performed a job (university police patrol officer) in which there was worker autonomy. The results showed that high- and low-performing incumbents described their work activities in such different ways that it looked as if they were actually on different jobs. Such distinctions in job information should not automatically be treated as error.

The message from these studies is this: Choose job informants carefully. Do not assume that all SMEs will provide the same information. Be aware that an informant's relationship with the job affects the information he or she is able to provide. Length of experience and quality of performance, and possibly other personal characteristics, can influence how a job is assessed. Job characteristics and work context features can have effects also. In choosing informants, notice whether the job appears to have differentiating features such as autonomy.

# Conclusions

Behavioral research methods are the basics of job analysis. In fact, a job analysis is a kind of field study involving observation, individual and group interviews, and survey questionnaires. Job analysts use these methods in different phases of the data collection process. Initially, they use observational strategies and interviews to get information about what tasks a job might include. Then an SME-group often will use this information to develop a questionnaire. With a questionnaire, data collection is more complete, as large numbers of job informants can be included in the job analysis. However, a job analyst must be cautious in questionnaire data collection and interpretation, as inaccuracies are not uncommon. Both personal and job context factors appear to influence the quality of job information. Although we might want objective job information, job incumbents have only their subjective experience to report. At best, they tell us about the job as they understand and perform it.

## SPECIALIZED JOB ANALYSIS TECHNIQUES

In this section, you can see the basic research methods playing roles in some specialized job analysis techniques. Observation is used to start a job analysis in certain of these techniques and SME-group interviews are involved in many of them. Specially developed questionnaires play a central role in many of the newer techniques. A large number of specialized job analysis techniques and instruments have been developed and are being used. For example, the Fleishman Job Analysis Survey (F-JAS) is a job analysis questionnaire focusing on worker abilities (Fleishman, 1992). This instrument has been used to collect information on required abilities for the U.S. Department of Labor's *Occupational Information Network* (O*NET; Peterson, Mumford, Borman, Jeanneret, & Fleishman, 1999).

In the following pages, I discuss task inventory analysis, the Position Analysis Questionnaire, the job element approach, and the critical incidents technique. Although several other specialized techniques and instruments are available, I discuss these four because they represent a range of methods that are useful for different purposes.

### Task Inventory Analysis

Task inventory analysis (also called task analysis) aims primarily to identify the essential tasks of a job. By specifying tasks, the method grounds the job

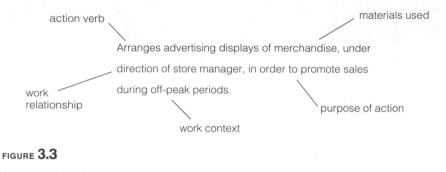

**FIGURE 3.3**

Anatomy of a task statement.

analysis in the realm of observable work behavior. In so doing, the technique makes it possible for a job study to be replicated and the results verified, which is an important feature. In this sense, the method is advantageous over other techniques that are not task-oriented and do not yield directly observable behavior, as you will see later in this section.

The task inventory analysis technique was originally developed by the U.S. Department of Labor (1972) for studying a single job or job family. Usually, the job study is conducted in-house by an organization's staff alone or with the aid of a consulting team. In the task analysis process, a complete inventory of all tasks performed on the job is developed.

Depending on the complexity of the job, a task inventory can contain 200 or more items. The inventory is developed using direct observation of job performers, individual interviews with incumbents and supervisors, and SME-group interviews. Using the information gained through these methods, job analysts develop task statements to describe the job. Although these can be simple statements describing physical actions, task statements often are multi-faceted, not only indicating what action a job performer takes, but also specifying what purpose, what materials or equipment, and with whom or in what work context. Figure 3.3 gives an example showing the components of a task statement.

**Developing Task Statements**    Task statements begin with an active verb, which expresses the action taken. In this way, a statement conveys the observable nature of a task. For example, some action verbs, such as "align" and "build," clearly are physical in connotation. Others are not obviously physical, such as "study" and "determine." Are these used in a task analysis? When the task analysis technique was first developed, researchers believed that task statements should describe physical activities only, because these are the most directly observable actions taken. Obviously, however, a job cannot be fully described unless the data include some mental or cognitive activities. In many jobs, cognitive tasks are the most important, although they might be the least

| TABLE 3.2 ACTION VERBS WITH CONNOTATIONS FROM THE PHYSICAL TO THE COGNITIVE | | |
|---|---|---|
| **Physical Verbs** | **Midrange Verbs** | **Cognitive Verbs** |
| Align | Balance | Compose |
| Arrange | Calculate | Conduct |
| Count | Classify | Coordinate |
| Decorate | Compare | Counsel |
| Inspect | Compile | Create |
| List | Contact | Design |
| Order | Discuss | Develop |
| Polish | Estimate | Diagnose |
| Pour | Examine | Evaluate |
| Record | Implement | Formulate |
| Replace | Inform | Interpret |
| Score | Prepare | Persuade |
| Sort | Observe | Plan |
| Sweep | Recommend | Predict |
| Type | Review | Reconcile |
| Wrap | Search | Resolve |

observable to an outsider. As a result, the technique of task analysis evolved so as to allow cognitive task statements and to provide a way to verify them as job behavior. Many commonly used action verbs such as "promote" and "assess," refer to cognitive tasks and such verbs make the task somewhat more observable in that they hint at physical or social activity. Using these verbs along with terms suggesting an observable outcome of the cognitive activity can make the task verifiable. For example, one's task might be to "promote a project proposal in order to gain a contract." (See Table 3.2 for a list of action verbs that vary from the physical to the cognitive.)

Generally, job analysts like to select terms that convey, as much as possible, what a job performer actually does. The more abstract verbs do not do this very well. A discussion among members of a job analyst team with whom I once worked illustrates the point. We were writing task statements for a complex administrative job—and struggling to come up with the best term for one particular task. At one point, someone asked the critical question "What exactly does someone do to marshal support for a project?" The verb "marshal," although it had been used in our SME-group discussions, seemed not to convey enough meaning to describe the action involved. We needed to find a potentially more observable term. (Can you think of one?)

---

**TABLE**

**3.3**    EXAMPLE OF DUTY AND TASK STATEMENTS

---

**Duty**

- Initiate, design, and implement programs and procedures for maintaining health and safety of clients, staff, and visitors.

**Task**

- Evaluate health and safety programs in order to establish legality.
- Design updated program elements to meet legal guidelines, with assistance of administrative analyst.
- Inform staff and clients of proper procedures in case of accidents or other emergencies.
- Develop an on-site emergency plan to be used in case of earthquake, fire, or other natural disaster.
- Investigate injury accidents, with assistance of staff, in order to prepare appropriate reports to health and safety officials.

---

As you might imagine, in developing a task inventory, job analysts spend a lot of time writing task statements. In addition, they organize the task statements into related groups and write a "duty" statement that describes each group of tasks. A duty is something that is accomplished through performing the associated tasks. On a questionnaire, a duty statement helps respondents comprehend the nature of the job being described. See Table 3.3 for some examples of duties and tasks.

**Questionnaire Development**    A task inventory provides the items for a task analysis questionnaire. Rating scales are constructed according to the kind of information needed. Most task inventory questionnaires at least include ways for a respondent to report that a task is or is not required on the job and to rate how important or critical a required task is. For task inventories that contain many task statements—most of which are part of the job—and call for many ratings, the process of completing such a questionnaire can be extremely time consuming. This is a good reason to limit the number of different ratings to the minimum necessary. Sometimes, task inventory questionnaires have asked for four ratings of each task: both importance and criticality, and time spent and frequency ratings. It seems to me that all of these ratings have to do with task importance. Doing something frequently or spending a lot of time on it can indicate to a job incumbent that the task is important. Some tasks are not only important but even critical because failing to effectively perform them has a serious negative impact on the job as a whole. For a task analysis that will be used for multiple and varied purposes, such as developing employee selection instruments and training, job analysts might think it is necessary to know about various aspects of task importance. However, research indicates that these rating scales are redundant to a great extent. Job informants especially find it difficult to distinguish between the concepts of importance and criticality, as these are almost completely redundant (Sanchez & Fraser, 1992). Time spent and task importance also appear to be redundant to some extent (Friedman, 1990). Therefore, it seems that there is little advantage in having respondents complete all of these ratings. Not only are they time consuming to do, but multiple ratings may increase inaccuracies. The best overall strategy probably is to ask respondents if they perform a task and, if so, how important the task is.

**Extracting KSA Information**    Responses to questionnaires can be summarized with some simple descriptive statistics to show how job incumbents as a group describe the job. These include the percentage of incumbents saying they perform the task versus those who say they do not. Also, ratings can be analyzed by calculating the mean and standard deviation of the ratings given each task by all informants. For a task that all incumbents say they perform, we might want to know how important it seems to the incumbents on average. The mean score of the importance ratings would show this, and the standard deviation would show the extent to which the job informants agreed in rating the task's importance.

A task inventory questionnaire does not ask job incumbents to identify the knowledge, skill, and ability needed on the job. Rather, task information yielded by the questionnaire provides the basis for inferring necessary KSAs. To accomplish this, job analysts first assess the questionnaire data to identify the important tasks. Next, they make judgments as to what KSAs might be needed in order to perform each of these tasks. Then, they organize the inferred KSAs into separate groups showing the different areas of knowledge and the skills and abilities that are needed to perform the job. It is crucial that the judgments be made carefully and that the links between the inferred KSAs and the observable tasks are specified in documenting the task inventory analysis. Users must be able to see how the inferred KSAs are needed on the job.

KSA information extracted from the analysis of tasks is useful if the task analysis is meant for employee selection purposes. Such information can be especially useful if selection measures are being developed and/or evaluated. The advantage of the task inventory analysis for this purpose is its job relatedness. A performance test, for example, might be developed and evaluated for its capacity to assess an important job skill identified in the task inventory analysis. There will be more about this use of task analysis in a later chapter.

In conclusion, task inventory analysis is appropriate for any organizational purpose that requires detailed task information collected on a relative or within-job basis. When a task inventory questionnaire asks for ratings that are specific to a job, such as the importance of task A relative to task B, the resulting data are more valuable for job-specific uses, such as developing a selection test or a technical training program for the job studied. However, these kinds of data are less helpful when the purpose is to make some sort of cross-job comparison, such as classifying jobs into job families, or assessing the use of a selection measure that has been developed and used by another organization for a similar job. For such purposes, task inventory analysis is not appropriate, because the task ratings are too specific to the details of the job. The broader characteristics are camouflaged. To see the broad outlines, it is better to use a different job analysis method, one that can determine whether a certain job is similar enough to another that they might be considered the same (Harvey, 1991).

## Position Analysis Questionnaire (PAQ)

The Position Analysis Questionnaire, or PAQ, is a standardized questionnaire for conducting job analyses (McCormick, 1976; McCormick, Jeanneret, & Meacham, 1972). The instrument resulted from research in which many different jobs were analyzed. From these studies, certain work behaviors were identified that appeared to be common to all jobs. This meant that work could be understood as composed of a limited number of behavioral dimensions—or ways to work. Because of its focus on work behavior, the PAQ is considered a worker-oriented instrument. The worker-oriented elements of the PAQ are not tasks, nor are they personal attributes. Rather, they are aspects of the job performance process. That is, they are worker behaviors that make up the fundamental parts of what is being done. They include certain adjustments that are made to the work context (McCormick, 1976). For example, as shown in Figure 3.4, worker-oriented job elements can include various information processing operations, such as combining information or data. The PAQ includes 194 items referring to different elements of work behavior. These elements are organized into six groups as follows:

- Informational input, concerning how and from what sources a worker gets job-related information
- Mental processes, such as reasoning, using knowledge, and making decisions
- Work output, referring to physical activities and use of equipment in the work process
- Relationships with others, as in communication and supervision
- Job context, referring to the physical and social context of work performance
- Other job characteristics, such as shift work or special job demands

Six rating scales are used for evaluating the elements. These ratings include "extent of use on the job," "relative amount of time spent," and "importance to the job" (McCormick, 1979). Notice that the PAQ sample shown in Figure 3.4 calls for importance ratings.

2 MENTAL PROCESSES
2.2 Information Processing Activities

In this section are various human operations involving the "processing" of information or data. Rate each of the following items in terms of how *important* the activity is to the completion of the job.

| Code | Importance to This Job (I) |
|------|----------------------------|
| N | Does not apply |
| 1 | Very minor |
| 2 | Low |
| 3 | Average |
| 4 | High |
| 5 | Extreme |

39 |_|_Combining information (combining, synthesizing, or integrating information or data from two or more sources to establish new facts, hypotheses, theories, or a more complete body of related information, for example, an economist using information from various sources to predict future economic conditions, a pilot flying aircraft, a judge trying a case, etc.)

40 |_|_Analyzing information or data (for the purpose of identifying *underlying* principles or facts by *breaking down* information into component parts, for example, interpreting financial reports, diagnosing mechanical disorders or medical symptoms, etc.)

41 |_|_Compiling (gathering, grouping, classifying, or in some other way arranging information or data in some meaningful order or form, for example, preparing reports of various kinds, filing correspondence on the basis of content, selecting particular data to be gathered, etc.)

42 |_|_Coding/decoding (coding information or converting coded information back to its original form, for example, "reading" Morse code, translating foreign languages, or using other coding systems such as shorthand, mathematical symbols, computer languages, drafting symbols, replacement part numbers, etc.)

43 |_|_Transcribing (copying or posting data or information for later use, for example, copying meter readings in a record book, entering transactions in a ledger, etc.)

44 |_|_Other information processing activities (specify) _____

FIGURE **3.4**

Items from the Position Analysis Questionnaire. These items are in the category of mental processes, describing information processing activities.

From "Position Analysis Questionnaire," E. J. McCormick, P. R. Jeanneret, and R. C. Meacham, copyright 1992 by Purdue Research Foundation, Purdue University, West Lafayette, Indiana 47907. Reprinted by permission.

The PAQ is filled out by job incumbents, or sometimes by others, such as supervisors and job analysts. In completing the questionnaire, the job informant first assesses each element as to whether or not it is a part of the work performed. Each rating scale includes the alternative "does not apply" for respondents to use if the job does not include the element. The data obtained from a PAQ analysis include statistical summaries of the ratings that show the extent to which various elements are part of the work required. In addition, more complex analyses can be obtained that profile the job and compare it with PAQ databases on other jobs. Because the PAQ is a copyrighted instrument, permission to use it will need to be arranged. Data analysis services can be purchased from PAQ Services, in Logan, Utah.

**Strengths and Weaknesses**    The PAQ has been the subject of much research, and there is evidence that it is a reliable and valid measure of worker behavior (McCormick, 1976, 1979). One of its strengths is its versatility. Because of the general nature of its worker-oriented elements, it can be used to analyze a wide variety of jobs. However, the high reading level required to use the instrument is a serious difficulty in many jobs. Job informants need to be able to read at the level of a college student. Obviously, not all jobs require such reading skill. Therefore, many job incumbents will not be able to use the instrument. Supervisors who have the necessary reading ability can complete the PAQ in place of incumbents. Job analysts—because they need to have high verbal abilities for their own jobs—also might be able to complete the PAQ for an incumbent, but probably only if the job analyst is familiar with the work (Harvey & Lozada-Larsen, 1988).

Worker-oriented instruments such as the PAQ can highlight similarities in jobs that have few tasks in common. Whether this is an advantage or a disadvantage depends on the main purpose of the job analysis. For instance, sometimes, two jobs that are scored similarly on the PAQ as involving many of the same worker activities actually involve tasks that are quite different. The jobs of police officers and homemakers, for example, have been found to be similar in that they both do trouble-shooting and handle emergencies (Arvey & Begalla, 1975). If a job analysis is needed that can identify and evaluate the tasks of these jobs, then the PAQ is not appropriate to use because it cannot yield such information. The PAQ is not the best procedure to use when the job analysis is for writing job descriptions or developing new selection procedures or training programs. A task inventory analysis or similar task-oriented procedure is better for these purposes.

Because it is not uncommon that many different tasks involve the same worker behaviors, the PAQ is good for matching up jobs that are similar in their work elements. Therefore, the PAQ is a good method for any organizational need—such as classification—that involves showing different jobs to include the same worker activities. For example, if a selection instrument has been developed and found to be valid in predicting success on one job, then showing that another job includes the same worker activities might mean that the instrument could be used to hire employees for both jobs. However, in order to establish that the instrument can be used equally well for both jobs, the job analysis must show that the two jobs, in essence, are the same. The PAQ is capable of making such cross-job comparisons.

## Job Element Approach

The job element approach to job analysis (Primoff, 1975) was developed at the U.S. Civil Service Commission to be used by employers in government and private industry to identify the most important worker requirements of a job.

Originally, it was meant for use with industrial and clerical jobs. Sets of job elements were developed for supervisors and incumbents to use in analyzing these jobs. Later, it became obvious that the method could be used to isolate and identify elements in any job. Today, employers can draw elements from prepared lists. In addition, they can define and write other elements that they know are required by a job (Primoff & Eyde, 1988; Primoff & Fine, 1988).

Like the PAQ, the job element method is worker-oriented. However, the worker-oriented job elements are KSAs and related attributes that are required on a job. For example, job elements can include relevant job *knowledge*, such as knowledge of the principles of accounting; *skills*, such as skill in operating office machines; *abilities*, such as those needed in managing a team; and *other* personal attributes, such as dependability. More examples are listed in Table 3.4.

In comparison with task inventory analysis, the role of job analyst is minor in both the job element and PAQ job analyses. Mainly, the job analyst supports and manages the job study project and analyzes the data collected. A job element analysis begins with an SME-group. Because the objective is to identify the critical KSAs for a job, SME-groups must include job incumbents who perform at a superior level and their supervisors. These individuals can be expected to thoroughly understand the job in question. The SME-group must develop a complete list of all the job elements involved and identify everything

| TABLE 3.4 | JOB ELEMENTS AND SUBELEMENTS FOR ASSISTANT MANAGER'S JOB |
|---|---|
| **Elements** | **Subelements** |
| Ability to manage a program | Ability to coordinate a program |
| | Ability to distinguish priorities |
| | Ability to operate under pressure |
| | Ability and willingness to delegate |
| Ability to analyze and solve problems | Ability to identify problems |
| | Ability to handle multiple problems at the same time |
| | Ability to make objective and unbiased decisions |
| | Ability to reason |
| Leadership | Ability to get things done through people |
| | Self-motivation |
| | Ability to handle controversial matters |
| | Honesty and integrity |

Adapted from "Job Element Analysis," by E. S. Primoff and L. D. Eyde, 1988, in S. Gael (Ed.), *The Job Analysis Handbook for Business, Industry, and Government,* Vol. 2, p. 815. Copyright 1988 by John Wiley & Sons, Inc., New York, NY 10276. Adapted by permission.

that might be needed for superior performance on the job. In the next phase, the SMEs work independently to rate the accumulated job elements in order to answer four questions about each one. These ratings are as follows:

- To what extent does a *barely acceptable* worker have this element?

    _____ all have, _____ some have, _____ almost none have

- How important is this element in identifying *superior* workers?

    _____ very important, _____ valuable, _____ does not differentiate

- How much *trouble* is likely to result if this element is ignored?

    _____ much trouble, _____ some trouble, _____ safe to ignore

- Practically speaking, how many openings can we fill if we demand this element?

    _____ all openings, _____ some openings, _____ almost no openings

Job analysts collect and score the ratings. They use a formula for combining ratings that indicates the importance and practicality of each element. Combined over all the SMEs, a total value for each job element is derived. Elements that have high values are those that represent the critical aspects of the job (Primoff, 1975).

The technique is meant to provide a rational basis for finding and organizing a battery of selection instruments and, in the process, to show that the battery can be used validly (Primoff, 1975; Primoff & Eyde, 1988). The critical job elements are used to identify suitable existing measures for employee selection purposes. Job elements with high values are compared with the KSAs that are assessed by existing, well-developed tests. If the KSAs rated as being critical to performance on the job in question are the same as those evaluated by a valid test, then it would be appropriate to use the test to select employees for the job.

**Strengths and Weaknesses**  A criticism of this method is that it skips the task identification phase, which means that it cannot provide direct connections between a job's tasks and the contents of tests or other measures that might need to be developed. In other words, it is not an appropriate technique when the main use of the job analysis is to develop and validate selection instruments. The critics are right, of course. Tasks are not identified. SMEs are not asked to specify how they know the KSAs are needed on the job. Like other worker-oriented approaches, the job element method is not appropriate for any purpose that requires direct task information, such as developing job-specific selection tests.

However, *because* it does not focus on tasks but, rather, addresses broad worker characteristics, job element analysis has an advantage: It can be used effectively to assess and compare elements of jobs in different settings or across organizations. That is, the technique accommodates the idea that the validity of an instrument used effectively in one setting can generalize to use of the instrument in an essentially identical setting. This describes the concept of validity generalization, discussed further in Chapter 7.

Job element analysis is economical in three ways: One, SMEs play a major role in conducting the project. Two, no time is spent identifying specific job tasks and duties. Three, there is no job analysis instrument to develop or purchase. Such economical features could provide real advantages. If we are entering an era, as it sometimes seems, in which elaborate and highly detailed job analyses are no longer necessary for employee selection purposes, then organizational needs might be satisfied by job studies that do little more than classify a job into the appropriate job family. Then, if the "same" job family is found elsewhere, and selection procedures already have been established for filling positions in that setting, all we might need to do—in order to use those procedures—is to show that the two job families are essentially the same (Schmidt, Hunter, & Pearlman, 1981; Zedeck & Cascio, 1984). This capitalizes on the idea of validity generalization, and it could make job analysis an inexpensive process. The job element approach already represents a move in that direction.

## Critical Incidents Technique

The critical incidents technique (Flanagan, 1954) was originally developed in order to establish job requirements and evaluate job performance in military units. However, the technique soon was extended to a range of jobs in civilian organizations. The critical incidents technique differs from the job analysis methods discussed so far. One, it is primarily a qualitative, rather than a quantitative, method. Unlike the others, the technique does not call for ratings of items. Two, it collects neither tasks nor KSAs. The elements of a critical incidents analysis are worker actions that vary in their quality. Three, although it can be used to do job analyses for other purposes, the technique is mainly used to provide a foundation for developing performance appraisal instruments. In Chapter 14, you will learn about several appraisal instruments based on this type of job analysis.

To use the critical incidents technique, the job analyst collects detailed information about observed performance behavior, usually in interviews with supervisors or job incumbents. The technique is used to identify and describe the critically important incidents that occur in the course of performing a job. These incidents show the kind of behavior that makes the difference between succeeding or failing on a job. An example is shown in Figure 3.5.

The interview in a critical incident analysis is structured so as to promote full descriptions of observed worker behaviors. The informant may describe

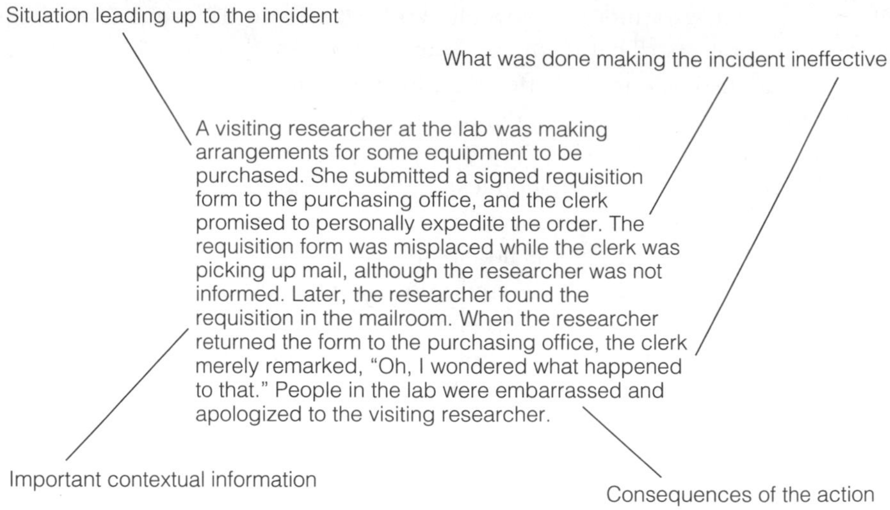

Situation leading up to the incident

What was done making the incident ineffective

A visiting researcher at the lab was making arrangements for some equipment to be purchased. She submitted a signed requisition form to the purchasing office, and the clerk promised to personally expedite the order. The requisition form was misplaced while the clerk was picking up mail, although the researcher was not informed. Later, the researcher found the requisition in the mailroom. When the researcher returned the form to the purchasing office, the clerk merely remarked, "Oh, I wondered what happened to that." People in the lab were embarrassed and apologized to the visiting researcher.

Important contextual information

Consequences of the action

**FIGURE 3.5**

Components of a critical incident describing ineffective work behavior of a purchasing office clerk.

either highly effective or highly ineffective actions that have been observed. The job analyst encourages the informant to provide

- the situation leading up to the incident.
- exactly what was done that made the action effective (or ineffective).
- important contextual information, such as when and where the action took place.
- the consequences of the action.

After the critical incidents are collected, they need to be organized into categories. McCormick (1979) described a comparatively simple procedure for this that was suggested by Bouchard (1972). Using this procedure, job analysts first sort the mass of material according to what aspect of the job each incident addresses. This results in a limited number of categories or job dimensions. Next, they examine and order critical incidents in each category and write brief dimension descriptions.

**Strengths and Weaknesses**   One of the drawbacks of the critical incidents technique is that it is so labor intensive. Hundreds—maybe thousands—of critical incidents might need to be collected. It is extremely time consuming for job analysts to do this through individual interviews. It is less time consuming if it is done by SME-groups. For some jobs, it is possible to assemble a group that can brainstorm, and develop and write critical incidents. However, SMEs must have reasonably good verbal skills for this to be effective. For incumbents, and even supervisors in many jobs, this skill level cannot be assumed (Brownas & Bernardin, 1988).

The critical incidents technique is not the best approach for organizational uses that require complete information on the work performed because the data can be deficient. Critical incidents may not have been collected for all the important behaviors in a job. Also, because of their nature in describing workers' actions, critical incidents data can be contaminated by containing personal characteristics of some performers. It is better to reserve this technique for performance appraisal uses and to select another method for other organizational needs. If a critical incidents analysis is particularly desired, then for general purposes it is better to begin the job analysis with a task-oriented procedure and use the critical incidents analysis to develop incidents for each task (Harvey, 1991).

## Choosing the Best Method

The decision about which job analysis method to use depends on a number of things. The first consideration is how job information will be used. If an organization plans to do nothing more than develop a few job descriptions, then a simple procedure involving interviews of job incumbents and their supervisor about work performed should suffice. However, most job analyses are meant to satisfy more than one need. An organization might plan a job analysis for a number of purposes, ranging from job classification and compensation to the development of employee selection and performance appraisal procedures. (Refer back to Table 3.1 to review the variety of ways job analysis is used.) These purposes require different kinds of job information, and for each the information is used in somewhat different ways. Some functions need primarily to have details about tasks. Others need both KSAs and task information. Some functions are better served by general and abstract information on worker-oriented elements, such as when there is a need to relate jobs in an organization to jobs elsewhere.

For a job analysis that is going to be used for more than one purpose, task inventory analysis is a good single technique. In addition, it is possible to select more than one technique and combine them in a multimethod job analysis. This strategy has much to recommend it because methods can be selected specifically for what they do best. Each of the four techniques reviewed here has strengths. Let me briefly summarize these: (1) Task inventory analysis yields detailed job-specific task information and it ties KSAs to tasks, which is useful for training and selection needs. (2) PAQ analysis provides information on the human processes involved in work, and this is useful in profiling, comparing, and classifying jobs. (3) The job element technique yields information on essential KSAs, which can be used in job classification and selection. (4) The critical incidents technique identifies effective and ineffective work incidents, which are useful in performance appraisal.

These techniques overlap in what they do well. If more than one can provide equally for an organization's need, then other considerations should be made in deciding the kind of job analysis to conduct. First, an important issue to consider is how participants respond. Job informants often complain about the amount of time they spend participating in job analysis. In particular, they dislike having to fill out long, difficult questionnaires. Task inventories can be long, not only because of the number of tasks listed but also because tasks often have to be rated two or three times. The PAQ is another long instrument. However, the PAQ can be difficult because of the abstract nature of the elements and the high reading level required. Second, job analysts have opinions about the techniques they use. In one study, job analysts reported that they used task analysis and job element methods more frequently and that they liked these methods better than the PAQ and critical incidents techniques (Levine, Bennett, & Ash, 1979). Another study similarly found that job analysts evaluated the PAQ less positively than other methods used for employee selection purposes. The researchers thought it was probably because PAQ information is abstract and difficult to use in devising selection plans (Levine, Ash, & Bennett, 1980).

Finally, another consideration in deciding how to conduct a job analysis is cost. The costs of job analysis include both direct and indirect expenses. If a consultant is involved, obviously his or her fee has to be considered. If the organization decides to conduct the job analysis in-house, HR staff time will be used, and there might be secondary costs if training is required on the use of job analysis methodology. In addition, whether a job study is done in-house or by a consultant, there are costs in taking incumbents and other SMEs away from their jobs to participate in a job analysis. Costs also are incurred in either developing a questionnaire or obtaining the use of an existing one. All of these costs will need to be considered. However, the final assessment of the value of a method will depend on what is gained from a job analysis. To satisfy important needs for job information, it might be worth making a greater investment in a job analysis.

## SPECIAL NEEDS FOR JOB ANALYSIS

Job analysis is a workplace methodology oriented mainly toward serving certain organizational needs that have become fairly routine. However, there are some special uses of job analysis that are somewhat out of the ordinary. Two of these special uses are (1) the study of managerial work and (2) the study of future jobs.

## Managerial Jobs

All the job analysis methods I describe in this chapter are general-purpose methods in that—hypothetically at least—they can be used to analyze any job. However, when it comes to managerial jobs, you might wonder whether the work is too complex to be analyzed by ordinary job analysis methods. Sometimes, it seems that a manager's workday is filled with a wide range of work activities, carried out by following various procedures, involving many different people both in and out of the organization, and for purposes that are not always clear. Also, these activities seem to vary by the manager's title and the function of the organizational unit.

How can jobs of this sort be studied in a job analysis? They can, of course, and have been. Managerial jobs, like other complex occupations, such as professional and scientific jobs, have been the focus of job analyses conducted for organizational purposes. A few questionnaires have been developed specifically for managerial job analysis. The Position Description Questionnaire (Page & Gomez, 1979), for example, is a worker-oriented questionnaire meant for comparing different managerial jobs. Items refer to managerial function dimensions, such as supervising, long-range planning, controlling, and customer relations. However, development of specialized managerial instruments for job analysis has proceeded slowly, and the job elements included in managerial questionnaires are similar to those on worker-oriented, general-purpose questionnaires. Usually, in fact, managerial job analyses use the same methods as other job analyses use. Harvey (1991) summarized four categories of work dimensions that general-purpose and managerial questionnaires have in common. These include interpersonal work, such as supervision of employees; information processing, such as that involved in policy and procedures development; mechanical or technical activities, such as operating office equipment; and aspects of the work context, such as work schedule.

Interestingly, managerial job analyses have been conducted for extra-organizational or research purposes. For example, an early research report described a cross-organizational study using a job analysis questionnaire made up of items referring to basic managerial functions and job-specific work activities (Mahoney, Jerdee, & Carroll, 1965). Results showed that the time spent on basic managerial roles varied across different managerial specialties, with some managers concentrating much of their effort on a single managerial function. Some were mainly planners, for example, as most of their work focused on determining goals, policies, and courses of action. Also, work activities differed depending on the manager's organizational rank, as shown in Figure 3.6. A more recent study was conducted that also used basic job analysis techniques (Kitzman & Stanard, 1999). Individual interviews were conducted, from which a questionnaire was developed. The questionnaire included both task statements and KSA statements, and rating scales called for time-spent and criticality ratings. The questionnaire was used to survey police chiefs with the purpose

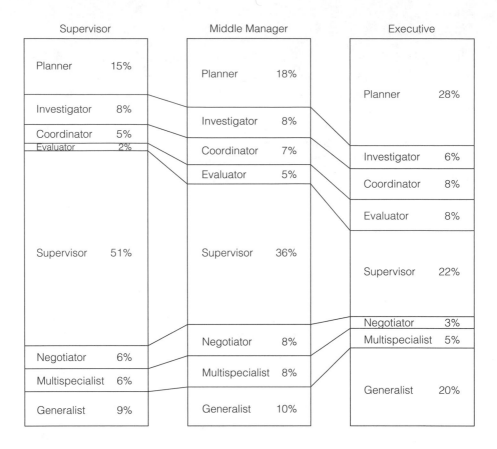

Notes:
   Total percentages do not add up to 100% due to rounding.
   Investigator roles involve informational input and processing.
   Coordinator roles include informational exchange.
   In multispecialist and generalist positions, managers divide their time more equally among roles.

FIGURE **3.6**

Work roles performed by managers at three levels of organizational rank. The study considered the proportion of work roles in managers' jobs at three organizational levels, including first-line supervisors, middle managers, and high-ranking executives.

Adapted from "The Jobs of Management," by T. A. Mahoney, T. H. Jerdee, and S. J. Carroll, 1965, *Industrial Relations, 4*(2), p. 109. Copyright 1965 by Blackwell Publishers, Inc., Cambridge, MA 02142. Adapted by permission.

of identifying essential functions in running a large police department. The researchers concluded from the results that the police chief's job is that of a "government business manager." The work of all chiefs included leadership, communication, public relations, and interactions with other agencies. However, there were some differences due to the relative size of the organization. Chiefs in larger departments spent more time than those in smaller departments on activities such as budgeting and negotiating.

Managerial work clearly can be quite specialized, although there always seems to be a core of common functions. The question is, Does the common core in these jobs justify their being classified together? Or is it reasonable to suppose that differences, such as organizational rank and department size and function, make managerial jobs different enough that they belong in different job families? Worker-oriented techniques, such as the job element and PAQ methods, that can be used in cross-job comparisons would appear to have a particular advantage for answering such questions.

## Future Jobs

Over time, the business environment undergoes change, and this influences work done in business firms. One result is that some jobs become obsolete while others appear for the first time. It is fairly easy to recognize this process in retrospect, especially to see the impact of technological advances. If you look at history, you can discover jobs that went out of existence because they provided products and services that were no longer needed. For example, long ago there were many jobs involving the use of horses for transportation. Craftsmen constructed equipment, such as harnesses and carriages, and service providers operated stables and handled the driving. This industry collapsed and a new one grew, as the gas-powered engine increasingly was used in transportation. Old jobs dropped out of existence. New jobs were created. Entirely different products—cars and trucks—were produced, and new services were offered, such as engine repair.

Often, the greatest effect of new technology is to define a new way of performing the jobs we have. Rather than suddenly making our jobs obsolete, it gradually changes them. For example, much of what we have been doing in business for many years involves communication, such as with customers and suppliers. We used to do this work by going across town to speak with someone, writing a letter, or later and more conveniently, ringing up someone on the telephone. Now, we have telecommunications equipment and services that have revolutionized business communications. We send "letters" electronically; make a single conference call and simultaneously talk with people in different parts of the world; and send a facsimile of a signed document in the time it takes to make a telephone call. You can see how just one branch of technology has changed many jobs in many industries. I am sure you can think of other technologies that have similarly affected jobs.

Sometimes, it is not technology that changes the way jobs are performed. Rather, a social organizational factor is involved. Today's move toward teamwork is an example. Teamwork is a social process that influences the way work is done. Many jobs, as I discussed previously, have been modified so as to include teamwork. Whereas work procedures that are changed by technology involve working with new equipment, jobs that are modified by team processes involve working through interpersonal interactions.

When jobs become obsolete, when existing jobs undergo major change, and when entirely new jobs need to be done, organizations must respond. In the midst of such change, employee terminations can be required. Employees might have to be retrained for different work activities. New jobs might have to be designed. Recruitment must begin and new employees hired. In all of these situations, there is a need for job analysis.

But how does one do a job analysis when the full impact of the expected change has not yet occurred? General-purpose job analysis methodology is used to guide the project, although typically some provision must be made to get an accurate forecast of what is likely to happen. In a study of the impact of new technology introduced in the U.S. Postal Service, researchers combined the PAQ with a task analysis to examine the effects of new equipment on cognitive tasks (Koubek, Salvendy, & Noland, 1994). Often, SME-groups are assembled to generate data on expected job changes. The identity of SMEs will vary to some extent. If an existing job is expected to undergo major revisions, superior performers on the existing job and their supervisors should be included in the job analysis. For example, in a task analysis of teamwork jobs, an SME-group of incumbents from newly established work teams was assembled. The SMEs identified tasks and KSAs that they had found to be relevant in their team assignments (Neuman & Wright, 1999).

For a job that does not exist, there are no incumbents or supervisors, of course. At best, there are incumbents and supervisors of similar jobs. A job analysis can include these individuals in an SME-group, depending on their awareness of the conditions that are bringing about the future job. More importantly, people who are familiar with the organization's strategic plans for the future, and those who know about technological advances, must be included as job information sources.

Special techniques have been proposed for conducting analysis of future jobs, such as Schneider and Konz's (1989) strategic job analysis. This technique uses general-purpose job analysis methods and adds a segment in the data collection phase that specifically addresses the anticipated job change. SME-groups are assembled to create a list of issues relevant to the future job. This information provides a basis for developing task statements and KSA statements, which are then rated by the SMEs as to their importance in the future job. Defining both tasks and KSAs is a necessary emphasis because the job analysis will be needed for multiple purposes, such as designing the future job and developing employee training for it.

Some say the world of work is changing at an increasingly fast rate of speed. I'm not sure that changes are coming any faster now than they have been for a long time. Possibly, this is part of the psychological process of personally experiencing change in our own lives. However, I am confident that we can expect more of the kinds of changes that we already have seen to affect jobs. There probably will be other changes, the likes of which we have never dreamed. Job analysis methodology has to be able to operate at the edge of this future. So far, job analysts have modified existing analysis techniques in order to use available sources of information about future jobs. Thus, the basic general-purpose job analysis is the best technique we have. In the future, we may need some entirely new ways of analyzing jobs. I think we will accept the challenge.

## SUMMING UP

The purpose of this chapter is to discuss job analysis. Organizational needs and uses and the sources of job information are discussed. The main feature of the chapter is the job analysis methodology. Summing up, we can make the following conclusions:

- One of the most important reasons for a job analysis is to improve employee selection procedures.
- A job analysis is a practical field research study involving observation, interviewing, and survey questionnaires.
- Most job analysis projects involve an SME-group that identifies tasks and/or KSAs.
- Inconsistencies in questionnaire data may be due to either inaccuracies or real differences in the experience of job informants.
- Examples of specialized job analysis techniques are task inventory analysis, the PAQ, job element approach, and critical incidents.
- In task inventory analysis, task information is collected from which KSAs are inferred.
- The PAQ and the job element approach differ in their data collection strategies, although both can make cross-job comparisons.
- Critical incidents are most useful for performance appraisal purposes.
- To choose the best method for a job analysis, consider the need for job information, the requirements of the techniques, and organizational costs.
- Two special issues are the study of managerial work and job analysis of future jobs.

## INFOTRAC COLLEGE EDITION

To learn more about the issues discussed here and about related topics in research and practice, use your subscription to InfoTrac College Edition to

access articles from research journals and other publications. Go to http://
www.infotrac-college.com/wadsworth to start your search of this online library. You can enter search terms of your own choosing, or you can use the
following keywords to find articles relevant to this chapter.

Job descriptions                     Task analysis
Job analysis questionnaires

# COMPENSATION AND OTHER WORK REWARDS

Many undergraduate students come to talk with me about psychology-related careers. Often, they have questions about what kinds of work are done by people with psychology degrees, where they are employed, and how much education they need. Sooner or later, in one fashion or another, they ask, "How much money could I expect to make?" Of course, this is not merely idle curiosity. For some, it is probably the main reason they come to see me.

Compensation is a complex concept because there are multiple ways of compensating someone for his or her work. Wages are what people think of, first. Wage levels are what my students are most interested in, when they ask the money question. However, compensation also includes benefits and other payments, such as bonuses. Related rewards include opportunities for advancement and career growth. In addition, there are nonmonetary features of jobs that are rewarding. These include the nature of the work involved, work relationships, and the work environment.

Monetary compensation is a highly valued outcome of working that is considered by anyone conducting a job search, accepting a job offer, or deciding to quit a job. Although indirect and nonmonetary rewards are important, they cannot fully substitute for pay. Generally, they are taken into account secondarily, after direct pay has been considered. Research has confirmed that job applicants usually have an amount of pay in mind, which is based on their knowledge of what competing organizations are paying. The applicant will not consider a job, regardless of how attractive it is in other ways, if the pay offer is not this high (Rynes, Schwab, & Heneman, 1983).

## IMPORTANCE OF COMPENSATION IN EMPLOYMENT

The employee selection process is affected by pay and benefits levels and by programs for administering pay increases. Applicants are attracted by the compensation for a job. Employees are more or less satisfied with various aspects of their pay. Pay satisfaction, in turn, is implicated in how hard people work at their job, how productive they are, and how they respond to pay increases. Pay satisfaction also helps to determine how likely a productive employee is to quit his or her job.

## Attracting Applicants

By advertising the amount of compensation in open-position announcements, employers use money to attract applicants. Considerable evidence shows that this is an effective strategy. Money and the promise of money are enticements to many people. A high level of pay offered in position announcements can make a job more attractive to job seekers (Cable & Judge, 1994; Gerhart & Milkovich, 1992; Rynes, 1987). Offering high pay levels results in greater numbers of applicants and more applicants with high qualifications (Holzer, 1990; Krueger, 1988). Mitchell and Mickel (1999) believe that people's satisfaction with their lives is connected to the money they have or potentially might have.

The pay being offered for a job provides other important information about the job and organization. From the level of pay, applicants can infer the type of work and how high the job is in the organizational hierarchy. To knowledgeable job seekers, getting information about an organization's pay programs, which show how pay is distributed within the organization, is even more helpful. This information suggests the organization's orientation and values, and it can attract applicants who will fit the organization. For example, pay-program information that identifies whether incentive pay is offered for individual efforts, or variable bonuses are available for team outcomes, can be of interest to job seekers (Cable & Judge, 1994; Gerhart & Milkovich, 1992; Spence, 1973; Welbourne & Cable, 1995).

Job seekers are sometimes attracted by the benefits an organization offers, although this depends a great deal on the individual. I do not believe that my students were referring to benefits when they came in to ask about what they could expect to earn in a psychology-related job. Certainly, none corrected me when I began to talk about wages. Gerhart and Milkovich (1992) reviewed studies suggesting that graduating students do not place much value on benefits in deciding whether to accept a job offer. Perhaps this is because many students are unaware of the range of benefits organizations offer, and because benefits that most quickly come to mind, such as retirement, are not personally very relevant. However, some benefits, such as flexible work schedules, probably are attractive to younger job seekers, especially workers with small children and college students who have class schedules to accommodate.

## Effects of Pay on Employee Work Behavior

Once an applicant is hired for a job, does compensation have any effect on work behavior or employee loyalty? There is evidence that it does. When the level of pay is satisfactory, an employee's productivity and retention on the job are affected.

**Pay Satisfaction**    Research and theory on job satisfaction indicates that there are several ways in which people may be satisfied with their jobs. For example, any of the following may be satisfying: the nature of the work, working conditions, work relationships, promotional opportunities, and pay (cf. Locke, 1976). Pay satisfaction is considered in many research studies. Standardized job satisfaction instruments typically include one or more questions about pay (e.g., Smith, Kendall, & Hulin, 1969). However, on most job satisfaction instruments, pay-related items usually refer to pay level only. Heneman and Schwab (1985) developed and validated a questionnaire to correct this. As indicated in Table 4.1, their Pay Satisfaction Questionnaire (PSQ) addresses four aspects of satisfaction with compensation—pay level, raises, benefits, and pay administration.

Potentially, pay satisfaction can be affected by any aspect of compensation. People who earn high wages are more likely to be satisfied with their pay than those who earn lower wages, especially when the pay level meets or exceeds their expectations (Berkowitz, Fraser, Treasure, & Cochran, 1987; Gomez-Mejia & Balkin, 1984). Pay satisfaction also can be affected by pay raises and by the policy used to grant a raise. For example, in one study, employees who received information showing that the pay raise they received was higher than the usual amount recommended by policy were more satisfied than employees who received the recommended amount (Scott, Markham, & Vest, 1996).

**Employee Productivity and Turnover**    It is reasonable to ask whether satisfied employees are more productive and more likely to stay on the job than those who are not satisfied. Many studies have focused on productivity and overall job satisfaction. There is a relationship here, but it does not appear to be very strong (Iaffaldano & Muchinsky, 1985). The relationship probably is more complex than many studies have considered. Productivity may be more closely connected to some aspects of job satisfaction than to others. In addition, the relationship may not be straightforward and may be influenced by policies for administering pay raises. For example, Gerhart and Milkovich (1992) discussed a study (Gerhart, 1990) in which the relationship between performance and pay level was nonlinear. Average performers earned more than poor performers; however, there was not much difference between the average and the best performers in the amount of pay received. Satisfaction of the high performers might be depressed by a policy that appears so unresponsive to their productivity.

Researchers are interested in the relationship between levels of job satisfaction and turnover, mainly because turnover can be dysfunctional. An organization always has a price to pay when employees leave—in terms of recruiting, selecting, and training replacements. Sometimes, the price is worth it if

TABLE

4.1    PAY SATISFACTION QUESTIONNAIRE (PSQ) ITEMS

The statements below describe various aspects of your pay. For each statement, decide how satisfied or dissatisfied you feel about your pay, and put the number in the corresponding blank that best indicates your feeling. To do this, use the following scale:

| 1 | 2 | 3 | 4 | 5 |
|---|---|---|---|---|
| Very Dissatisfied | Dissatisfied | Neither Satisfied nor Dissatisfied | Satisfied | Very Satisfied |

|  | Code* |
|---|---|
| 1. My take-home pay. | L |
| 2. My benefit package. | B |
| 3. My most recent raise. | R |
| 4. Influence my supervisor has on my pay. | R |
| 5. My current salary. | L |
| 6. Amount the company pays toward my benefits. | B |
| 7. The raises I have typically received in the past. | R |
| 8. The company's pay structure. | S/A |
| 9. Information the company gives about pay issues of concern to me. | S/A |
| 10. My overall level of pay. | L |
| 11. The value of my benefits. | B |
| 12. Pay of other jobs in the company. | S/A |
| 13. Consistency of the company's pay choices. | S/A |
| 14. Size of my current salary. | L |
| 15. The number of benefits I receive. | B |
| 16. How my raises are determined. | R |
| 17. Differences in pay among jobs in the company. | S/A |
| 18. How the company administers pay. | S/A |

From "Pay Satisfaction: Its Multidimensional Nature and Measurement," by H. G. Heneman III and D. P. Schwab, 1985, *International Journal of Psychology, 20*, pp. 129–141. Copyright 1985 by International Union of Psychological Science. Reprinted by permission of Psychology Press, Ltd., East Sussex, UK.

*L = level, B = benefits, R = raise, S/A = structure/administration.

the employee has not been satisfactory. However, if a productive employee leaves, the cost is great. Productive employees, of course, need to be retained.

Studies of why employees quit their jobs have considered the effects of an employee's level of performance, likelihood of finding another job, and level of satisfaction. Less productive employees actually are more likely to quit than more productive employees (McEvoy & Cascio, 1987), especially those who are dissatisfied with their jobs generally (Spencer & Steers, 1981). In addition, the rate of unemployment, which can determine whether a better job is available, affects employees' decisions to quit. McEvoy and Cascio (1987) reviewed studies showing that productive employees who quit did so during periods of low unemployment. Of course, this is an effective strategy for a person looking for a new job because more jobs are available. However, for the employer, it is a difficult time to try to replace a productive employee.

Satisfaction with pay can predict turnover. Employees who are dissatisfied with their pay are more likely to quit (Motowidlo, 1983; Weiner, 1980). Sometimes, an employee is less satisfied with an organization's pay policies than with the actual level of pay received. Gerhart and Milkovich (1992) reviewed theory and research suggesting that productive employees might be better served by working for a company that offers piece rates, commissions, or other performance-contingent pay in which high performance levels are rewarded. If a company's pay program does not reward individual productivity, this fact will become apparent. If potentially productive applicants recognize that productivity is not rewarded, they are unlikely to accept a job offer. However, if hired, such an employee might show a decline in performance, or eventually leave the organization (Brown, 1990; Spence, 1973).

## Effects of Benefits on Employee Work Behavior

As you will see later in this chapter, organizations offer a variety of employee benefits. Some of these are useful in attracting applicants, as I say above. Other benefits, such as retirement pensions and life insurance, are more oriented toward the long-term retention of employees. Because retirement income is based on years of service and earnings as well as age, someone who has worked for a company for most of his or her working life and experienced salary growth in the process is increasingly disinclined to quit the job as time goes by. Retirement benefits often are not specifically portable from one organization to another. Even if they are, the person may have to accept a position and/or a pay cut if his or her years of experience are not relevant at another company.

Some experts are concerned that offering such benefits may not be constructive for an organization. Voluntary turnover in fact is reduced by service-oriented benefits, especially among men who have years of contributions in a pension program (Mitchell, 1983; Schiller & Weiss, 1979). At first thought, it seems that this might have been expected. Through benefits and, not insignificantly, through pay level, the organization has been providing costly enticements to retain someone who supposedly is a productive and valued employee. There are at least two underlying difficulties in the situation, however. One is that no distinction is being made here between functional and dysfunctional turnover. Some senior employees likely are worth retaining. Other long-term employees undoubtedly are not productive and may not be satisfied with their jobs. However, the power of high pay and service-oriented benefits probably is enough to keep the employee from voluntarily leaving the job. Another difficulty is pay policies that add permanent pay increases to an employee's base pay. Over a long period, this results in a pay level that would be hard for almost anyone to actually "earn." It seems to me that it is not solely the effect of service-oriented benefits but also a matter of compensation policy that has caused this costly problem.

Other benefits and employer-provided rewards are more innovative, less costly, and less likely to create such difficulties. In addition, they may be more attractive to junior employees. For example, in the future, employees may be offered flexibility in both work hours and work location. Currently, some employees are being offered the option of "telecommuting," in which they do their work at home at least one day a week while maintaining telephone contact with the workplace. Variations on this strategy are expanding to include more than occasional work at home. One study (Hill, Miller, Weiner, & Colihan, 1998) evaluated the benefits of "teleworking" in which office workers at an organizational branch gave up their space at the branch location and moved into a "virtual office" for their entire work time. The "virtual office" included workspaces in the employees' homes and at customer locations. The employer provided the employees with mobile electronic equipment so that they could perform the full range of work tasks at multiple locations. In general, the employees were very positive about the arrangement. They felt they were more productive because of reduced commuting time, fewer distractions during work periods, and the ease of working on a flexible time schedule. Flexibility was a particular benefit. Teleworking allows a person to work whenever and wherever it feels right, such as at the person's peak periods. In addition, working at home allows an individual to more easily take care of family responsibilities, such as caring for sick children or an elderly parent, which can be difficult in traditional work arrangements.

## Conclusions

Organizations need to consider compensation and benefits in order to conduct employee selection procedures. Pay levels and pay policies can influence the extent to which qualified applicants are attracted to open positions. Pay levels and policies also can determine whether the productivity potential of a new employee is realized. Satisfaction with compensation and benefits enters into the picture, in predicting employee performance. Pay satisfaction also affects whether an employee quits. Turnover can be costly, particularly if a productive employee leaves. High performers who quit tend to do so at a time when more jobs are available, but this is the time when it is difficult for a company to find an equally qualified person.

Costs are involved in all steps of the recruitment, selection, and employment process. First, it is necessary to get high-quality applicants interested. Then, the employer must hire them, help them to become fully productive, and, if they are high performers, must have ways to encourage them to stay. Many benefits are designed to encourage employee retention and to control turnover. Some benefits appeal to senior organizational members, and these can have powerful effects on their continued retention. Other benefits and rewarding work conditions are appealing to junior employees, and employers can advertise these in the effort to attract high-quality job applicants.

# SETTING PAY LEVELS

How does an organization go about deciding how high to set wage levels? There are a number of considerations to be made in deciding this. These include legislated wage requirements, collective bargaining agreements, and wages paid by competitors.

## Legislation Affecting Pay Levels

The Fair Labor Standards Act (FLSA) of 1938 and its amendments constrain the wage-setting practices of American businesses because the act defines the minimum wage level. Also, the FLSA defines and specifies rates for overtime pay and identifies job categories (e.g., managerial and professional) that are considered "exempt" from overtime pay. In addition, the FLSA contains safeguards for fair compensation. The Equal Pay Act (EPA), which is a 1963 amendment to the FLSA, requires that employees doing equal work be paid equally (more about this law in a later section). Two other laws should be mentioned, as they pertain to employee benefits. The Employee Retirement Income Security Act (ERISA) was passed in 1974 to control the administration of employer-provided retirement systems. The Consolidated Omnibus Budget Reconciliation Act (COBRA) was passed in 1985, in the midst of organizational downsizing, in order that employees who lose their jobs can continue their health insurance.

## Union Influences on Pay Levels

Pay levels and pay policies typically are important union issues. Research indicates that when employees have not been satisfied with their pay, they are more interested in having a union represent them in wage-setting contract negotiations (Hamner & Smith, 1978; Schriesheim, 1978). If an organization's employees are represented by a union, then a formal labor contract will be negotiated. This contract will define wage levels as well as other aspects of compensation and benefits. In the collective bargaining sessions conducted to negotiate a contract, the two parties—representatives of management and of the union—present their proposals on the issues and attempt to reach agreement. Both parties usually must move from their original positions to a compromise position.

Indirectly, collective bargaining also affects the wage levels adopted in nonunionized firms. This happens in various ways. Most importantly, it occurs because an employer must establish wage levels that are competitive with those of other firms in the same industry, which can include unionized firms. That is, wages paid in unionized firms change the size of the "prevailing wage" and in this manner affect what a nonunionized company must pay in order to attract applicants. This effect is pronounced during times when the national economy begins a decline and, yet, multiyear labor contracts established before the decline are still in effect. In addition, some nonunionized companies are highly sensitive to the possibility of a union coming in, and they will voluntarily increase compensation in an effort to keep that from happening (Milkovich & Newman, 1987).

## Labor Market Effects on Pay Setting

The wages paid by a company's competitors in the same industry or in the broader labor market will influence the company's pay levels. As stated earlier, a lower limit on wage levels is established by law; that is, at least the minimum wage must be paid. Beyond that, what other companies are paying will provide both lower and upper limits. In order to control the costs of its consumer product or service, a business will need to go no higher than the upper limit. If a company pays more than this, its labor costs may be higher and such costs will be translated into higher consumer prices, which in turn will make the company less successful. If a company pays very much less than competitors and does not offer other appealing features to make up for a low base pay, it will have a harder time attracting applicants. Therefore, companies need to set pay within the prevailing wage range in order to control labor costs and, at the same time, make themselves attractive to high-quality applicants.

## Paying Above or Below Competitors

With all of these contingencies—the legislation, collective bargaining, and competitors' pay levels—you might think that employers have very little leeway in setting pay levels. Compared to what might be without these constraints, employers apparently do not have a great deal of discretion in pay setting. It might seem to be the best strategy simply to aim for the average of pay levels currently being offered in the marketplace. Some employers do exactly this. They pay the average rate (Leonard, 1988).

Organizations can survive while paying either higher or lower than average wages, however. One way companies pay lower than the industry average is to offer a compensation package that includes a lower base pay rate in combination with benefits and other rewards that have high applicant appeal but low employer cost. For example, a company might set base pay at a lower rate but emphasize the potential for wage increases of a performance-contingent pay program. In addition, a lower-paid job with valuable benefits, such as on-site child care, might offset the impact of a smaller paycheck for some applicants. An employer also can offer a higher-than-average base wage and expect to control the cost of this through increased productivity of those hired. Employees who are hired at a higher rate of pay might feel obligated to work harder and to be more productive. Whether they actually do, of course, is not certain. According to equity theory (Adams, 1965), however, this is a reasonable expectation. Some employees report that they do work harder in higher-paid jobs (Levine, 1993) and in jobs that have improved work conditions (Hill et al., 1998). Other ways to control the cost of offering higher wages include making modifications in jobs that result in reduced numbers of employees. For example, jobs might be consolidated to include more variety in tasks and more responsibility for decision making, such as in self-managing work teams. The employer then would need to make a great effort to recruit and hire employees who are able to perform such jobs. Gerhart and Milkovich (1992) describe the experience of Japanese automakers operating in the United States in which careful screening of job applicants is conducted in order to hire highly capable employees for self-managing teams.

Some employers are able to hire high-quality employees because of the kind of work they offer. Work in such an organization can offer the opportunity to learn and to perform interesting work or work that is socially valuable. Such work sometimes is literally its own reward. Most of us would like to work at something we enjoy or find interesting. Some people feel this is important enough to counteract the effects of lower pay. Many nonprofit organizations, in fact, depend on this appeal and may even get a certain amount of their work done by volunteers.

## Conclusions

In deciding how high to set wage levels, an organization must consider certain factors that affect pay levels. Laws, such as the Fair Labor Standards Act, constrain wage-setting practices. Collective bargaining affects wage rates for both unionized and nonunionized companies. Also, wage rates paid by business competitors have to be taken into account, as these can determine both upper and lower pay limits. A company has to be careful about paying more than industry competitors because labor costs can drive up the costs of consumer products. However, if a company pays much lower compensation than competitors, it will have a harder time hiring employees who will perform effectively. Employers are not locked into paying the average rate, however. There are ways for an employer to pay higher or lower wages than the market. Offering an attractive package of compensation, benefits, and other rewards can appeal to applicants. Wage costs can be offset by productivity management and job modifications to increase intrinsically motivating job activities.

## TECHNIQUES FOR GATHERING WAGE INFORMATION

Information about appropriate pay levels for jobs may be obtained by conducting wage surveys of other employers. A wage survey yields a range of rates that competitors pay. This information provides a basis for documenting the *external equity* or fairness, of the compensation plan in that it confirms that the adopted pay rate is comparable to what others in the business community are paying.

To conduct a wage survey, an employer needs to decide which companies within an industry or labor market are relevant. An effort should be made to survey those firms that use the same types of jobs and that draw from the same labor sources as the employer does. In addition, the employer needs to decide how many companies to contact, how to combine the information gathered from different companies, and how often to update the survey. Surveying more than one competitor is necessary to give a reliable measure, although, of course, those surveyed must have relevant information about the jobs being evaluated. Information also needs to be recorded describing the number of positions within the job that the contacted organization has, and what the range and median pay levels are (Henderson, 1988).

### *Job Evaluation*

Companies usually conduct wage surveys to get information on the current rates being offered in the business community. In addition, some companies conduct a job evaluation study to establish the *internal equity* of their pay systems. The differences in the rates of pay for different jobs within an organization need to be viewed as being appropriate and equitable in order for individuals to feel they receive relatively fair pay.

Job evaluation studies determine the value of a job to an organization and define appropriate pay levels for job families. Job analysis information (as discussed in Chapter 3) is used in job evaluation studies, especially those involv-

| TABLE 4.2 | JOB FACTORS USED IN JOB EVALUATION |
|---|---|

| Factor Label | Description |
|---|---|
| 1: Knowledge required by the position | Nature of knowledge and skills needed; how knowledge and skills are used in work. |
| 2: Supervisory controls | How work is assigned; employee's responsibility for carrying out work; how work is reviewed. |
| 3: Guidelines | Nature of guidelines for performing work; judgment needed to apply or develop new guidelines. |
| 4: Complexity | Nature of assignments; difficulty in identifying what needs to be done; difficulty and originality involved in performing work. |
| 5: Scope and effect | Purpose of work; impact of work product or service. |
| 6: Personal contacts | People and conditions under which contacts are made (except supervisor). |
| 7: Purpose of contacts | Reasons for contacts; skill needed to accomplish work through person-to-person activities. |
| 8: Physical demands | Nature, frequency, and intensity of physical activity. |
| 9: Work environment | Risks and discomforts imposed by physical surroundings; safety precautions necessary. |

Adapted from *How to Write Position Descriptions Under the Factor Evaluation System* (pp. 29–30), by U.S. Office of Personnel Management, Staffing Services Group, Washington, DC: U.S. Government Printing Office, 1979; 1989 printing.

ing the assignment of monetary value to knowledge, skills, working conditions, and other requirements of jobs. These job requirements, you recall, can be determined by job analysis.

**Job Evaluation Techniques**    A variety of job evaluation techniques are available. One is a simple procedure for whole-job ranking. With this technique, all jobs in an organization are ranked in terms of their relative worth to the organization. For whole-job ranking to be a reliable technique, multiple job evaluators are required, and evaluators must be familiar with all the jobs in the organization. Therefore, only small organizations are likely to be able to use this technique effectively.

Other job evaluation techniques involve the use of compensable job factors. These are qualities and requirements of jobs that have monetary value to an organization. Any job requirement or characteristic that has monetary value could be considered a compensable factor. Usually, broad categories of factors are identified that are compensable for all jobs to one degree or another. Typically, these include elements, such as skill, effort, responsibility, and working conditions, that are compensable for all jobs to some degree. Table 4.2 describes some of these factors.

The point-factor technique is the method of choice for many organizations. It is useful in large and complex companies in which many different jobs need to be evaluated. It is not specific to any job. Rather, it consists of broadly defined compensable factors and levels within these factors. It is a procedure for assigning value-points, and it results in a single number of points for each job. They represent the total worth of the job to the organization. The points are used to place the job at the appropriate pay level in the compensation structure.

A point-factor evaluation study begins with defining the importance and weight of the compensable factors as they exist in the job being studied. Jobs vary in terms of how important individual factors are. Some factors can be very important and carry a great deal of weight, whereas others are of minor importance. For example, a job might require considerable specialized knowledge that counts for as much as 40 percent of the total point value of the job, whereas physical demands might be insignificant and contribute no more than 2 percent of the total points. The points earned for all factors that are relevant in a job determine the total point value for the job (Henderson, 1988). For example, in Table 4.3, you see that the levels of the complexity factor describe work differing in terms of clarity and alternatives and that the levels earn more points as the work becomes more complex. Suppose we compare two jobs. Job A might be at level 2 on this factor, which means that the job involves work with related steps and processes and that decisions are a matter of choice among a few alternatives. Job B might be evaluated at level 4, in which there are varied duties involving unrelated processes such as those involved in professional work, and difficult decisions must be made. Notice that these two levels have quite different point values: Level 2 is worth 75 points and level 4 is worth 225 points. The points earned for complexity in jobs A and B would be added to points earned on other factors for these jobs, to obtain a total point value for each job. Differences between the jobs would be shown, not only in their total scores but also in the pattern of different factor levels. Although job B shows higher complexity, job A might have a higher level on the work environment factor, if job A involves working with dangerous machinery and job B does not.

Job evaluation plans have been developed for wide use. A point-factor job evaluation system was designed by the U.S. Government's Office of Personnel Management, which provides detailed information about factor levels, such as those shown in Tables 4.2 and 4.3. This system is used for evaluating many different jobs in the federal government, and it shows considerable strength in making accurate and valid assessments. Another job evaluation system, called the Hay Plan, was developed and is offered by the Hay Associates consulting group. This system combines a point-factor structure with factor comparisons on key or benchmark jobs. The Hay Plan is used by many organizations for evaluating managerial and professional jobs. Major job factors are *know-how*, including technical and human relations knowledge and skill, *problem-solving*, and *accountability* (Henderson, 1988).

| TABLE 4.3 | LEVELS OF THE COMPLEXITY JOB FACTOR |
| --- | --- |

| Level | Points | Description |
| --- | --- | --- |
| 1 | 25 | Tasks are clear-cut and directly related. Little or no choice in deciding what needs to be done. Actions to be taken are readily discernible. Work is quickly measured. |
| 2 | 75 | Duties involve related steps, processes, or methods. Decisions involve choices among a few easily recognizable alternatives. Actions to be taken differ in the source of information, the kind of transactions or entries, or other factual differences. |
| 3 | 150 | Duties involve unrelated processes and methods. Decisions depend on analysis of subject, phase, or issues in each assignment, and course of action is selected from many alternatives. Work involves conditions and elements to be identified and analyzed. |
| 4 | 225 | Duties require many unrelated processes and methods, as in administrative and professional fields. Decisions include assessment of unusual circumstances, variation in approach, and incomplete or conflicting data. Work requires decisions on interpreting data, planning work, or refining methods and techniques. |
| 5 | 325 | Duties require many unrelated processes and methods applied in a range of activities or substantial depth of analysis, as in administrative and professional fields. Decisions include major areas of uncertainty in approach, methodology, or interpretation and evaluation processes resulting from changes in program, technological developments, unknown phenomena, or conflicting requirements. |
| 6 | 450 | Work consists of broad functions and processes of an administrative or professional field. Assignments have breadth, require effort, and involve phases pursued concurrently or sequentially with support from others within or outside the organization. Decisions regard undefined issues and require extensive probing and analysis to determine the nature and scope of a problem. Work requires effort to establish concepts, theories, or programs or to solve problems. |

Adapted from *Instructions for the Factor Evaluation System*, by U.S. Civil Service Commission, 1977, Washington, DC: U.S. Government Printing Office.

## Pay Equity

The Equal Pay Act (EPA) was passed in 1963 and made it unlawful to pay unequal wages to men and women working on equal jobs. Historically, women had earned less than men regardless of their jobs, and the EPA seemed destined to change this. Some things did change. No longer do employers explicitly advertise for a man or a woman when a position opens up. Prior to the mid-1960s, want-ad columns that listed "help wanted male" and "help wanted female" were commonplace. However, for the most part, the EPA made little improvement at a national level in the overall earnings of women. U.S. Census

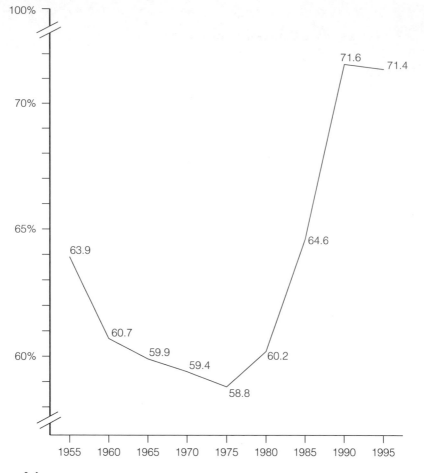

FIGURE **4.1**

Women's earnings compared to men's. Data on annual earnings over 5-year periods from 1955 to 1995. Data points are percentages of women's earnings to men's earnings across all jobs nationally.

Adapted from *Median Annual Earnings for Year-Round, Full-Time Workers, by Sex, in Current and Real Dollars, 1951–98,* by U.S. Department of Labor, Women's Bureau,2000. http://www.dol.gov/dol/wb/. Prepared with original data from U.S. Bureau of the Census, *Current Population Reports.*

Bureau statistics indicated that for many years, women's earnings hovered around 60 percent of men's (see Figure 4.1). In 1965, two years after the EPA was passed, the average was 60 percent, and in 1995, it was 71 percent (U.S. Department of Labor, 1978, 1994, 2000a). That is, approximately 30 years after the EPA, the women's wage gap had been reduced by about 11 percentage points. In 1999, U.S. Census Bureau data showed a rate of 73 percent, which is an improvement consistent with previous years. The gap appears to be closing by about 6 percentage points every 10 years. If this persists, women should be earning the same wages as men in about 2035.

There is ongoing discussion about why a wage gap still exists. Although explanations have been offered to account for the difference, a portion of the gap between men's and women's wages is unexplained, and it might be due to past or present discrimination (Treiman & Hartmann, 1981). Some experts have observed that women have not moved as rapidly as men into high-level and highly paid executive positions. Table 4.4 shows evidence of this. Only 29.8 percent of those holding management jobs in 1998 were women. Also, relative to the percent of men in the labor force, the percent of women is increasing rapidly, and these increased numbers continue to fill the lowest-paid jobs (Henderson, 1988). Historically, women have had access to fewer occupations than men, and their occupations are paid at lower rates. This is one of the most likely reasons that passage of the EPA has not removed the wage gap. The occupations that have been most accessible to women are in clerical, nursing, teaching, and service areas. Table 4.4 shows 20 occupations in which nearly half of some 60 million women were employed in 1998. Notice that some jobs are held almost exclusively by women. At least 90 percent of those holding jobs as secretaries, receptionists, bookkeepers, nurses, and hairdressers are women. The occupational difference between women and men is important to understand because it suggests a reason for the wage gap. Women and men do not do the same jobs. They have different job titles and they are in different job classifications, which results in different market rates of pay.

**Comparable Worth**    The EPA defines equal work as referring to work that requires equal skill, effort, and responsibility and is performed under similar working conditions. (Notice that these are terms used in job evaluation as compensable factors.) The EPA says also that the compared jobs are not required to be *identical* but, rather, to be substantially equal. These two aspects of the law are important because they suggest how to determine whether women's pay differences are due to differences in the value of their jobs. The idea that (1) equal work might be determined by compensable job factors rather than by job titles and descriptions and that (2) jobs can be equal without being identical gave rise to the highly debated issue of comparable worth. The comparable worth argument is that jobs should be paid the same wages if they have the same value to an employer, as this would constitute being "substantially equal." Jobs that have similar contents—that is, similar tasks, duties, and classifications—would have the same value and deserve the same wages. Further, jobs that do not have similar contents but are similar in their requirements for skill, effort, and responsibility, would be paid the same because of their comparable value to the employer. In summary, in the reasoning of comparable worth, if job evaluation outcomes show that two jobs have comparable value to an organization, then they should be paid the same wages.

| TABLE 4.4 | EMPLOYMENT OF WOMEN IN THE UNITED STATES: THE LEADING OCCUPATIONS IN 1998 | | |

| Occupation | Number Employed | Percent of Total Women Employed | Percent of Women Compared to Men |
|---|---|---|---|
| Clerical and sales, total | 10,656,000 | 17.5 | |
|    Secretaries | 2,868,000 | | 98.4 |
|    Cashiers | 2,367,000 | | 78.2 |
|    Sales supervisors, proprietors | 1,890,000 | | 40.0 |
|    Bookkeepers, accounting clerks | 1,604,000 | | 93.0 |
|    Sales workers, other | 967,000 | | 68.3 |
|    Receptionists | 960,000 | | 95.5 |
| Professional, technical, and managerial, total | 8,236,000 | 13.6 | |
|    Managers, administrators | 2,287,000 | | 29.8 |
|    Registered nurses | 1,879,000 | | 92.5 |
|    Elementary school teachers | 1,639,000 | | 84.0 |
|    Accountants and auditors | 941,000 | | 58.2 |
|    Secondary school teachers | 697,000 | | 56.9 |
|    Investigators, adjusters (not insurance) | 793,000 | | 75.6 |
| Service, total | 5,125,000 | 8.4 | |
|    Nursing aides, orderlies | 1,703,000 | | 89.0 |
|    Waiters, waitresses | 1,079,000 | | 78.3 |
|    Cooks | 873,000 | | 40.9 |
|    Janitors, cleaners | 777,000 | | 34.8 |
|    Hairdressers, cosmetologists | 693,000 | | 90.8 |
| Machine operation and benchwork, total | 2,296,000 | 3.8 | |
|    Machine operators | 915,000 | | 32.2 |
|    Fabricators, assemblers | 693,000 | | 33.1 |
|    Textile machine operators | 688,000 | | 72.1 |
| Total all employed women | 60,771,000 | | |

Adapted from *20 Leading Occupations of Employed Women: 1998 Annual Averages,* by U.S. Department of Labor, Women's Bureau, 1999. http://www.dol.gov/dol/wb/

You may be wondering whether other countries have problems of pay equity. Current international reports indicate that they do. Many of the same issues are being discussed, such as why women's wages are low, and what, if anything, can be done about it. Many countries also have equal-pay laws that prohibit gender pay discrimination. For example, Canada's Human Rights Act, drafted in the 1970s, requires equal pay for work of equal value.

Some of the shrinkage in the women's wage gap in the United States and in other countries probably has occurred because of both voluntary and court-ordered pay-equity adjustments. For example, the Canadian government currently is adjusting pay schedules and is preparing to pay back wages to 230,000 previously underpaid public service workers in various job classifications, including clerical, educational, and hospital service workers (*Canada NewsWire*, 2000). In the United States, both private and public sector organizations have made adjustments. Some large U.S. corporations, such as Kodak and Eli Lilly, have voluntarily conducted pay-equity studies and made pay adjustments for their employees (Erbe & Shiner, 1999). In the public sector, eight states— Minnesota, Washington, Connecticut, Iowa, Montana, New York, Oregon, and Wisconsin—have implemented pay-equity laws that cover state employees (Gardner & Daniel, 1998). Some of this state action has been voluntary, although it likely was triggered by the U.S. Supreme Court case of *Gunther v. County of Washington* (1981). Wage discrimination was found in this case, as the defendant's job evaluation showed that the job of female prison matron, although not identical to the job of male prison guard, was substantially the same and worth 95 percent of it. Yet, the matron's job paid only 70 percent of the male guard's.

Repeatedly, both here and in other countries, concern is voiced about the economic burden that comparable worth adjustments might cause. Henderson (1988) points out that many such concerns are based on fear rather than reasoning. For example, the concern that costs of upgrading all jobs would bankrupt an organization is ill-founded because the pay for only some jobs would be increased. The pay for other jobs would remain the same, and for some it might even be downgraded.

Market rates might be modified by comparable worth adjustments. As I mentioned earlier, some jobs are female-dominated and, historically, have been paid at lower rates. Whatever the reason for beginning this practice, the result has been that working women have had fewer occupational choices than men, as you can infer from Table 4.4. As more and more women have entered the labor force—squeezing into the same relatively few occupations— market rates have remained low. An employer can always get someone out of the increasingly large labor supply to take a job at the low rate of pay. As you know, two variables that determine the going rate for a job are (1) the number of job seekers and (2) the amount that competitors are paying. If some employers begin to pay better rates, others soon will need to improve their rates in order to attract quality applicants. Therefore, employers need to pay attention to what market competitors are doing with respect to comparable worth adjustments.

## Conclusions

Two types of compensation information are needed in order to show that pay structures are appropriate and equitable. External equity is established by means of wage surveys. Internal equity, which shows that pay rates within an organization are equitable, is established with job evaluation studies. Job evaluation techniques range from whole-job rankings to complex procedures in which compensable factors are identified and each job is scored as to its monetary value. Compensable factors usually include skill, effort, responsibility, and the conditions under which work is done.

The methods used to determine and document pay equity become especially important when the issue of gender wage inequity is considered. The Equal Pay Act was meant to prohibit wage discrimination. However, women's earnings did not show great improvement as a result. Even as women have gained more education and work experience and have worked for longer uninterrupted periods, they still earn substantially less than men. For most of the past 50 years, women have averaged no more than 60 to 70 percent of men's wages. Conditions that contribute to this wage gap include the fact that a relatively large number of women currently are entering the labor force in low-paid jobs. Most female-dominated occupations historically have been paid at lower rates, and organizations using market rates to set pay levels continue this practice. In addition, most women perform jobs that are at least superficially different from those performed by men.

The EPA defines equal work but leaves open to interpretation how to establish equality of jobs. A comparable worth interpretation of the concept advocates use of job evaluation techniques and posits that jobs which have the same value to an employer should be paid the same wages. Recently, court-ordered and voluntary comparable worth adjustments have been made in public- and private-sector organizations. Market rates may change as a result of such adjustments. Still, in the past, progress has been slow and uneven, and it may continue to be so.

## COMPENSATION POLICIES AND PLANS

A compensation plan includes a pay structure that shows base pay levels for all jobs used in an organization. Pay policies also describe how employees receive pay raises and bonuses. This section considers how some compensation plans are designed.

Effective compensation systems have two main objectives. They must reward high-quality and productive work behavior, and they must encourage the retention of effective employees. Compensation comprises direct and indirect monetary and nonmonetary elements. Certain benefits and indirect compensation, such as health insurance, appeal to applicants and employees. Typically, these are simply a part of being employed by the company and, while they may act to retain employees, usually they are not incentives. Some intangible rewards, such as good work conditions or interesting work, may have both retentive and incentive power. Direct monetary compensation has great potential to motivate performance, and a pay plan should be designed with this in mind. Compensation should reward employee behavior that an organization requires in order to succeed in the marketplace.

## Merit- and Performance-Pay Plans

Conventional merit- and performance-pay plans are meant to link pay to performance on the job. The typical merit pay structure lists several levels in the pay grade for each job. For an employer to use such a structure to motivate productivity, behavioral standards are needed, although these may or may not have been developed. Behavioral standards define the level of performance that an employee must reach in order to advance to the next level of pay. Each pay raise an employee receives in a merit system is supposed to be based on a performance appraisal showing that he or she has demonstrated behavior at or beyond the behavioral standard.

In many ways, merit pay plans can be and are corrupted. For one thing, employees quickly learn that performance is not the real link to pay. Pay raises often are given for flimsy reasons—for "acceptable" performance or for showing up regularly for work. Also, supervisors who complete a performance appraisal and approve a raise may be unaware of the existence of any behavioral standards, or they may be concerned about what happens if an employee does not get a raise. These are all reasons that merit pay plans often do not function as performance incentives. However, notice that the problem is not entirely due to the structure itself. A plan to reward good performance and not reward poor performance is inherently reasonable and potentially motivating. Rather, the greater reason for the plan's ineffectiveness is the manner in which it is used to reward staying on the job and putting in average performance. Heneman (1990) reviewed research indicating that this undermines a merit system. The studies showed that there was not a strong relationship between performance ratings and merit pay raises, which means that many raises were given for reasons other than performance.

Another problem with conventional merit pay programs concerns what happens when an employee reaches the highest level in the pay grade. Most conventional pay systems have caps on pay grades. Administrators have ways to get around these caps, which can create problems. For example, to control the costs of having many employees at the highest pay level, employees who are approaching the top level of a pay grade sometimes are given raises that are relatively smaller than those given to employees at lower levels (Lawler, 1989). If the merit plan has been used frivolously to give raises to employees who have not earned them, this is probably just as well. At least, it might slow down the ineffective use of the merit plan. However, if these employees are worthy of raises, they might be led to feel that they are not as valuable as newer employees. Another method of dealing with a capped pay grade is promotion. Many organizations are structured explicitly with lines of progression from one job to another. Presumably, these primarily are for career growth, such as when an employee has developed new skills on the current job and now is qualified for a more difficult job. However, sometimes promotions are not used for the purpose of advancing an employee with potential but, rather, for the purpose of salary growth. Some employees are promoted as a way of getting around a pay grade cap.

Merit plan designers need to be clear about exactly what they intend to reward. Most compensation plans cannot simultaneously reward high performance and retention. It is better to design different features to accomplish these two objectives. To reward seniority and encourage employees to stay with the organization, an employer can make pay adjustments based on the passage of time. One way to do this is to periodically adjust base pay rates for cost-of-living expense and to match the market rate. Cost-of-living increases do not function as incentives, of course. Like the pay raises granted in conventional merit plans, cost-of-living increases are added to base pay. This makes the increase permanent. However, because performance levels fluctuate over time, monetary rewards for performance also must fluctuate over time. To effectively reward high-quality performance, temporary pay adjustments should be made in the form of bonuses to the most productive employees. Bonuses of significant size should be granted, depending on an individual's performance. A range of values needs to be offered. Some employers report that they award anywhere from 0 to 30 percent of an employee's pay as a bonus (cf. Cascio, 1991). In order for pay to actually operate as a performance motivator, large bonuses must be given only for high-quality productivity. Small amounts given to all employees regardless of performance are discouraging to high performers and will undermine the system.

**Skill-Based Pay**    Almost all pay plans are job-based, which means that pay is based on the value of the job. However, in skill-based plans, the idea is to pay on the basis of employee skills, knowledge, or competencies, not on the basis of the job performed. Those who have higher levels of skill receive higher pay. Pay increases are awarded when an employee develops new skills of value to the organization. Before you conclude that such plans reward *potential* instead of performance, let me add that skill-based pay plans usually do not stand alone. Rather, they are combined with conventional merit or performance pay plans.

In actual practice, companies using skill-based pay are faced with the problem of how reasonably to measure competence, if not by the extent to which it is expressed in performance. Thus, in actuality, this approach becomes one in which "competence" is more about using skills than having them, and this leads back to a performance-based compensation plan (Armstrong & Brown, 1998).

So, what does an employer accomplish by adopting a skill-based plan? It is thought to be useful for certain types of organizations, such as research and development (R & D) organizations of which professional level employees are a key component. Perhaps the main advantage for these organizations is that highly skilled employees can be encouraged to work outside job boundaries, and in the process some jobs can be eliminated. There are disadvantages, however. Because employees are being rewarded for attaining new skills, the organization's training costs will increase. In addition, there is a risk that employees will leave the organization, taking the new skills with them (Armstrong & Brown, 1998; Shareef, 1998).

As you learned earlier, market surveys and job evaluation studies identify appropriate pay levels and establish the equity of pay systems. Skill-based pay, obviously, is a new idea. Few organizations have used such plans. As a result, there is very little market information available to identify skill-based market rates and to establish external equity of the pay plan. Armstrong and Brown (1998) reported that in the United Kingdom only 17 to 20 percent of companies had or were even planning a skill-based pay system. In the United States, only 14 percent had such pay plans. Therefore, with little direction from the market, a company must depend on internal studies to assess equity. Given that job evaluation has emerged for use with job-based pay systems, you may rightly wonder whether it can function for skill-based systems. The basic methodology of job evaluation might be used to guide an employee competency evaluation study, although it is not an easy fit. Job evaluation techniques do include knowledge and skill components among the factors considered. However, these factors are job-based requirements. To adapt the methodology, a company would have to make adjustments so that it wouldn't drift away from a skills orientation.

Skill-based pay systems are attractive to some employers because they seem to provide a way to break away from the sense of entitlement for scheduled pay raises that merit plan employees often develop. Skill-based pay seems to promise an easier way for managers to make the difficult decision of appropriately granting pay raises. As an employee, I like the idea of paying employees for the skills they have. Others, who are paid by such systems, say they do too (Shareef, 1998). As an employer, however, I doubt that the evaluation process will be any easier, or any less prone to error, than the conventional job-based plan. Whether or not skill-based pay is better is something we will probably learn from those companies that are now experimenting with it.

## *Teamwork Incentives*

Most compensation policies and plans are designed to reward individual efforts. This is appropriate for at least two reasons. First, most jobs are performed individually and performance should be rewarded accordingly. Second, when jobs include team activities, individual performance may need to be taken into account. Team members vary in their contributions, and individuals who contribute most to a team may receive relatively less from team-based rewards than members who contribute little. As a result, the better performer may leave the organization. Gerhart and Milkovich (1992) provide a good example of how this can occur. They point out that in professional sports teams, star performers are paid more than other team members. If a star did not receive the individually based bonus, some competing team likely would offer it and entice the player away.

In many cases, there is a need for cooperative teamwork and teamwork incentives are appropriate. The incentives may or may not take individual differences into account. Skill-based pay sometimes is cited as a way to compensate when self-managing groups are a key element of an organization's work structure. Recall from previous discussion that in self-managing groups, all members learn and perform all the work done by the group, including management of the team. In a skill-based pay system, individual employees can earn rewards based on the skill development made possible by their membership in the self-managing group. If skill-based pay is part of a merit pay plan, this increase would be added to base pay.

Some group-oriented incentives are not added to base pay but rather are types of bonuses. Profit sharing is an organization-wide strategy in which employees' base pay is frozen or reduced in exchange for a chance to receive shares in the annual profits the company makes. Because the payoffs are determined by many other people in the company, it is doubtful that this strategy motivates either individual or team performance. In addition, there is a downside that will be apparent to some employees. If the company is not very profitable, the return to employees may not even replace the reduction in base pay (Gerhart & Milkovich, 1992).

**Gainsharing.**    Gainsharing is an explicit team-oriented method of paying for performance. It is a plan for awarding bonuses to team members on the basis of outcomes of the team's productivity. The link between pay and performance in gainsharing is clearer and more relevant to employees working in teams than it is to employees in profit-sharing plans. There is evidence that gainsharing can improve team performance and productivity (Hatcher & Ross, 1991; Wagner, Rubin, & Callahan, 1988). However, employees do need to be involved in the development of the plan. They must understand how it operates, and they must approve of it. Even then, high-performing team members may not feel that they personally are equitably rewarded by the team-based bonuses.

Gainsharing is largely a private-sector innovation, as the focus is on profit making. In the public sector, bonuses would be considered a waste of tax money. However, some public organizations have redefined "gains" in terms of goals attained at a budget savings. Goalsharing plans for providing teams of public employees with productivity incentives drawn from budget savings have been tried in a few cases. These have been found to have some potential. However, as is true in the private sector, public employees also must have a role in developing the goalsharing plan (Patton & Daley, 1998).

## *Benefits*

Few employee benefits are required by law. In the case of most benefits, employers choose whether or not to offer them and, if so, in what form. Health care insurance, for example, comes in various forms, from a fee-for-service plan to a prepaid health maintenance, or HMO, plan. Some benefits are quite appealing to applicants and employees. They can motivate an applicant to seek employment with a company that offers them. They can encourage employees to stay with a company in order to retain them. Health insurance is one such benefit. For many, a compensation package must include adequate coverage in this area.

Other benefits are likely to appeal to some employees, but not necessarily to all. For example, life insurance might be provided. Company dining rooms might be subsidized so that employees can get low-cost meals. Parking spaces often are provided free of charge. Many family-related benefits might be available, including help with caring for an elderly parent. Because benefits are not equally desirable to employees, many employers offer them "cafeteria-style," which allows employees to choose what is most individually valuable. This also helps to control employer costs as there will be no need to pay for benefits that no one wants.

**Family-Friendly Benefits**    Organizational policies have been developed over the past decade or so that are meant specifically to assist employees with family responsibilities. See Table 4.5 for the kinds of family benefits that are available. Why would employers want to provide family benefits? Osterman (1995) proposed that there might be several reasons. One reason is that these programs are meant to prevent or solve work problems that develop when employees have to handle family difficulties. Problems at home can result in productivity loss, absenteeism, and turnover. Another reason is that family-friendly programs are part of the strategy of employers who are attempting to develop innovative organizations that yield high productivity and high organizational commitment.

TABLE

4.5    FAMILY-FRIENDLY BENEFITS

| Category | Examples |
| --- | --- |
| Family-care resources | Child-care resources and referral services<br>On-site and near-site child care<br>Elder-care resources and referral services |
| Job scheduling variations | Part-time employment<br>Job sharing<br>Telecommuting<br>Flextime<br>Compressed workweek<br>Shift |
| Leaves | Sick leave for family care<br>Leave for adoption<br>Leave sharing |
| Counseling and other resources | Employee assistance programs<br>Fare subsidies<br>Homework assistance |

Adapted from *A Review of Federal Family-Friendly Workplace Arrangements: A Report to Congress by the U.S. Office of Personnel Management,* by U.S. Office of Personnel Management, Office of Workforce Relations, 1998, Washington, DC: Author.

The increase in family-oriented benefits sometimes is said to have resulted from societal changes, including the increased number of working women and the number of dual-earner and single-parent families. The programs do benefit those working women who are responsible for family caregiving. The programs also can be beneficial for other employees. Some working men make use of family benefits. In addition, some benefits, such as flexible work schedules, are appealing to those who do not have family responsibilities. A survey of U.S. governmental agencies found that more than one-third of the federal workforce makes use of alternate work schedules (U.S. Office of Personnel Management, 1998).

Some employees are thought likely to respond negatively toward employer-provided family benefits, mainly as a result of what they believe is fair. Organizational justice theory (Leventhal, 1976) predicts that when an organization's goal is perceived to be increased productivity, employees will consider it equitable to reward individual performance (with benefits, as well as pay). When an employer appears to be aiming to enhance team performance, the theory predicts that employees will expect team members to be rewarded equally. Therefore, employees might consider family benefits as violating one or both of these principles. Reports in business newsmagazines (e.g., Jenner, 1994) suggest that benefits are not considered fair if they are available to only some employees and that a backlash against family-friendly programs might be developing. The suggestion refers especially to child care. Childless employees and employees with children who are unable to get child-care benefits are predicted to be unhappy. Kossek and Nichol (1992) did find that those on a waiting list for on-site child care felt frustrated. However, a more recent study found little evidence of generalized negativity or an impending backlash (Rothausen, Gonzalez, Clarke, & O'Dell, (1998). Although employees who did not use the company's child-care center responded less positively toward the center than users did, they were not less positive in their general work attitudes and behavior.

**Work Schedule Alternatives**    Flextime is a flexible work schedule in which starting and quitting times are flexible around a core period when all employees are present. Flextime is an attractive benefit to many employees, as it allows them to adjust their work schedules in order to take care of family and personal needs and to avoid inappropriately using sick leave. In a survey of managers from different organizations, the reaction to flextime was generally positive. Women managers and managers with family responsibilities who had access to flexible work hours felt more satisfied with their jobs and more committed to the organization (Scandura & Lankau, 1997). Research has shown that the effects of flextime are widespread and positive. Productivity, job satisfaction, and satisfaction with the schedule are increased, and absenteeism is reduced (Baltes, Briggs, Huff, Wright, & Newman, 1999).

Other work schedules, though not appealing to all employees, may be considered desirable by some. These include night shifts and compressed workweeks. On a compressed workweek, an employee gets an extra day off by working four 10-hour days. The compressed workweek has fewer positive effects than flextime. Baltes et al. (1999) found that although employees were satisfied with the schedule and with their jobs as a whole, absenteeism was not reduced and productivity did not increase. It might be that increasing the length of the workday simply increases the amount of time employees are not working at peak levels, which might account for the lack of productivity improvement in the compressed workweek. Whether the night shift is considered a benefit depends on individual preferences and how the shift is structured. Barton (1994) found that some employees personally prefer to work at night, sometimes for family reasons but not always, and that those who do want night work prefer a fixed shift over a rotating shift.

## Conclusions

A pay plan identifies pay levels for all jobs and specifies pay adjustments. The purpose of merit- and performance-pay plans is to reward employees for high-quality performance. Some might accomplish this, if behavioral standards are available and supervisors use them carefully to document a pay adjustment. However, most of these plans fall very short of this goal. They are better at rewarding employee retention than employee productivity. Compensation plans can accomplish these two objectives, but only through different means, such as cost-of-living increases and bonuses awarded to high performers.

Other varied ways to reward productivity are being explored. First, skill-based pay is meant to reward employees for gaining competencies. Although there are difficulties with this strategy, it might be effective in organizations with many professional employees. Second, team incentive plans are being developed to reward team productivity. One of the most promising of these plans is gainsharing, which is a method for awarding bonuses for team results. Third, employers offer a variety of benefits, including some that may encourage productivity.

Family-related benefits are attracting attention in the business community. In most organizations, these benefits are seen as a way to prevent work problems, to avoid losing good employees, and to gain high organizational commitment from employees. Alternative work schedules, especially flextime, may be used to accomplish these aims. Flextime has widespread and positive effects, such as increased productivity and decreased absenteeism. This is something for employers to consider instituting if they do not already have it.

# NONMONETARY REWARDS

Some people get a great deal more out of their work than simply a paycheck. Nonmonetary aspects of work can be rewarding. Employers have learned that they can use features of the work itself and of the work environment to attract and employ high-quality employees. The very earliest studies in which workers were questioned about what they found satisfying about their jobs revealed that a variety of nonmonetary rewards were appealing to at least some employees (Hersey, 1936).

## *Intrinsic Rewards*

Theories generally have viewed work motivation as being outcome-oriented. That is, a performance outcome is satisfying and the opportunity to obtain such outcomes is motivating. The rewarding aspects of performance can be either intrinsic or extrinsic. Intrinsic outcomes are satisfying in and of themselves. For example, accomplishing something that one finds challenging is intrinsically satisfying. Extrinsic outcomes are desirable, not because they themselves are satisfying, but because they are useful for attaining other satisfiers. Pay and benefits are extrinsic rewards.

Early motivation theorists, such as Maslow (1943) and Herzberg (1966), attempted to show how employees could be motivated to perform well if they were given opportunities to engage in intrinsically satisfying work. Although individual differences generally were considered important in determining exactly what work activities would be intrinsically satisfying, certain aspects of work likely would satisfy most employees. Theorists thought that jobs should be redesigned to include some of these intrinsically satisfying features. For example, redesigned and enriched jobs might include complex, challenging, and important work as well as an opportunity to participate in decision making.

The rationale for enriching jobs is that people will find intrinsic value in doing work that is challenging, important, and responsible and that motivation toward high-quality performance will be improved. The work team is a way to put this strategy into operation. Self-managing work teams are particularly effective as a way to enrich jobs, because the team is responsible for completing a work "whole," including the most complex tasks. All team members learn and do all assignments, and the team is responsible for making decisions about work planning, scheduling, and quality control (Cannon-Bowers, Oser, & Flanagan, 1992). Are such work activities intrinsically valuable to employees? Are they actually motivating? It appears that they are. Productivity and work quality are high in these teams, as are job satisfaction and organizational commitment (Cohen & Ledford, 1994; Cordery, Mueller, & Smith, 1991). However, as motivation theorists expected, individual differences count, and self-managing teams are not appealing to everyone. Culture seems to be one of the reasons why. International firms have found that some employees resist self-managing teamwork. Kirkman and Shapiro (1997) suggest that the resistance may be due to cultural differences in achievement orientation, attitudes toward decision making, and interest in working alone or with others.

Early thinking on how intrinsic motivators might affect employee behavior was that they would add to the total rewards received from the job. That is, one could be paid well and have satisfying work to do at the same time. This seems reasonable. However, some research has indicated that the effects are not always additive and that extrinsic rewards can depress intrinsic satisfactions (Deci, 1972). In other words, paying someone to do something they like doing might make them like it less. Later research found conditions under which extrinsic rewards did not have this effect. One study suggested that extrinsic rewards do not depress intrinsic satisfaction among those who are strongly attracted to the intrinsic aspects of their work (Phillips & Freedman, 1985). There has been much study and discussion of this issue with no clear conclusion. For the purpose of employer strategy, maybe it doesn't much matter. It isn't as if companies aren't going to pay people for their intrinsically valuable work. Also, if the intrinsic value of one work experience is depressed by extrinsic rewards, perhaps another will not be.

## Work Conditions

In addition to making work more intrinsically satisfying, work conditions might be modified so that simply being at work would be better. For example, many employees might find it rewarding to have a clean and safe workplace, or to have better supervision and good coworker relationships. Job satisfaction surveys often ask about relationships at work and show that positive interactions with supervisors and coworkers are satisfying. Good interpersonal relationships at work might reasonably be expected by any employee. Therefore, although the presence of good relationships might not improve work behavior, poor relationships are likely to be detractors.

**Harassment and Violence**    Andersson and Pearson (1999) noted that the "business world was thought by many to be one of the last bastions of civility" and that coworker relationships were "characterized by formality yet friendliness, distance yet politeness" (p. 453). Still, their review of research indicated that aggressive behavior does occur in the American workplace, and not infrequently. For example, more than 20 percent of the companies surveyed in one study had experienced violent acts, and in an additional 33 percent, violence had been threatened (Romano, 1994). A national survey conducted in 1993 showed that during the previous year, one out of every four full-time workers was harassed or attacked while at work. Whereas attacks came more often from customers and clients, most of the harassment involved interpersonal conflict and was perpetrated by coworkers and bosses (Northwestern National Life Insurance Company, 1993). In a union survey of construction and building maintenance workers, more than a third of the respondents reported having witnessed or been a victim of harassment or violence on the job. Most of the harassment was verbal (52 percent of incidents reported), although in 39 percent of the reports, both verbal and physical attacks were involved (McCann, 1996). Andersson and Pearson's (1999) theoretical model of how such harassment and violent behavior develop proposes that small things such as rudeness, snide comments, and other incivilities at work can increase in importance and spiral out of control to a point at which the small things escalate into violence.

Such work conditions undoubtedly are serious for some employees. The Northwestern National Life (1993) study reported that victims of harassment and violence were angry, fearful, and generally distressed. In addition, they said their productivity had been affected and that they had thought about quitting. Is there a general concern that interpersonal relationships might go sour? Perhaps not. In the union survey reported by McCann (1996), most respondents (84 percent) said they felt their workplace was safe, even though a notable number of them had witnessed harassing or violent acts. Some researchers point out that the chance of armed violence at work is actually relatively small. Even so, employers may need to resolve problems of aggressive behavior (VandenBos & Bulatao, 1996). Interpersonal conflict that leads to intimidation and harassment must be controlled in order to create a workplace in which employees can perform effectively.

## Conclusions

Nonmonetary work outcomes can be intrinsically satisfying, and they can motivate productivity and employee loyalty. Certain aspects of work are thought likely to satisfy most employees, and jobs can be enriched to include these. Job enrichment is a way to make work more important, complex, and challenging and to allow employee participation in decision making. Self-managing work teams are designed in this way. The work done by these teams apparently is rewarding, because productivity, job satisfaction, and organizational commitment generally run high in self-managing teams.

While looking for nonmonetary conditions that might function as performance reinforcers, we sometimes uncover a poor situation that needs correction. Employers often need to restore or improve work conditions so that employees' performance is not hindered. Employees value good relationships with supervisors and coworkers. When poor relationships exist, these are likely to detract from productivity. Although not all harassment and violence is generated as a result of conflict between coworkers and supervisors, much of it is. Victims are personally harmed, and their productivity and retention are adversely affected. Employers should pay attention to signs of aggressiveness and develop ways of responding. Most employers rely on preemployment screening as a way to avoid hiring individuals who might behave violently. Most also have procedures for hearing complaints and for aiding terminated employees. The U.S. Postal Service has a highly responsive employee assistance program that includes both violence prevention and threat management (Kurutz, Johnson, & Sugden, 1996). The program focuses on employee selection in an effort to hire appropriately. Program policy emphasizes that employees have a right to a safe work environment, and it takes a strong stance against aggressive behavior. Procedures are outlined for making employee termination safe and effective.

## SUMMING UP

The purpose of this chapter is to discuss how compensation and other rewards received for work can influence employee selection, management, and retention processes. Summing up, we can make the following conclusions:

- Pay levels and pay policies can attract applicants.
- Employee satisfaction with pay affects productivity and turnover.
- Wage levels are influenced by laws, union activity, and competitors.
- A company can offer more or less than the average wage, depending on what else is in the compensation package and what is expected in return.
- Wage surveys and job evaluation studies provide evidence of the extent to which a pay structure is externally and internally equitable.
- Most job evaluation techniques involve identifying and weighting compensable job factors.
- Earnings of working women continue to lag behind those of men.
- Conventional merit- and performance-pay plans usually are effective for employee retention, but ineffective in rewarding productivity.
- Bonus plans that are carefully administered have potential for motivating high performance, including that of teams.
- Employers offer a variety of benefits, including family-oriented programs.
- The intrinsic value of satisfying work and good work conditions can operate as effective nonmonetary rewards.
- To have effective work conditions, employers may need to correct an existing situation, such as employee harassment.

## INFOTRAC COLLEGE EDITION

If you purchased a new copy of this book, you received a complimentary subscription to InfoTrac College Edition with your purchase. Use it to access full-text articles from research journals and practice-oriented publications. Go to http://www.infotrac-college.com/wadsworth and start your search. There are several ways you can search this online library. For example, you can open the current issues of a journal, such as *Personnel Psychology*. You also can do a keyword search on a topic that interests you. The following keywords can be used to find articles related to the topics discussed in this chapter.

| | |
|---|---|
| Pay satisfaction | Teleworking |
| Pay equity | Wage surveys |
| Incentive pay | Employee assistance programs |

# RECRUITMENT

Help wanted really badly.
Wanted: Experienced anybody.
Help wanted: An adult.
You'll do. Sign here.

These are titles of business magazine articles[1] that reflect humorously how exasperated—even desperate—some employers have felt as a result of trying to hire new employees at a time when the economy is strong and unemployment is at a very low rate. Clearly, one cannot fill a job opening unless someone wants it and applies for it. In a tight labor market, job ads sometimes draw few applicants and, of those, the best may turn down a company's offer. At such times, it can seem to an employer as if there is no one out there who wants a job.

As I stated in Chapter 1, the state of the national economy and the associated level of unemployment affect an employer's ability to hire. When unemployment is low, active recruitment is absolutely necessary. In the past, employers and most researchers emphasized selection procedures and ignored recruitment. This orientation usually was not problematic because many people were looking for jobs and applicants made themselves available without any special encouragement. People would send unsolicited résumés or walk in off the street and ask if there were any openings. During such times, employers felt little need to develop innovative recruitment methods. Mainly, they needed effective ways to reduce a large applicant pool to a small number of job seekers from whom to hire. However, the employment situation can and does change periodically. The available labor supply can increase or decrease, as can organizational demand for new hires. In the late 1980s, economists predicted that a serious decline in the level of unemployment would occur by the year 2000 that would initiate a long-term labor shortage (cf. Bernstein, 1987; Johnston, 1987). At that time, the prediction seemed hard to believe. When

---

[1]John Fried, *New York Times Magazine*, 3/5/00; Bronwyn Fryer, *Computerworld*, 11/15/99; David H. Freedman, *Inc*, 11/99; Michael Stern, *Canadian Business*, 10/8/99.

the day came—at the end of the 20th century—that job openings began to go unfilled, it was an unpleasant surprise to employers. In response, some employers set aside their standards and were willing to hire almost anyone. Others took a more active, but perhaps not more effective, approach. They began "raiding" other companies, trying to draw away people who already had good jobs. Competitors' employees were being offered even higher compensation and better benefits than they already had, plus thousands of dollars as a "signing" bonus for accepting an offer. In the popular press, writers referred to the raids as recruiting wars, and much off-the-cuff advice was offered on how to get the better of one's competitors. We have to wonder about the efficacy of these tactics, however. How likely is the recruit to stay with the new employer? Is it worth the cost to hire someone who may be recaptured soon by yet another competitor?

## THE NATURE AND CONTEXT OF RECRUITMENT

Recruitment is defined as those organizational practices and decisions that determine the number and identity of individuals who are interested enough to apply for a job (Rynes, 1991). It is an organization's way of actively reaching out and inviting applicants. Many organizational theories describe an organization as a structure that has permeable boundaries, through which it interacts with the outside environment. As Figure 5.1 illustrates, recruitment is a process involving such cross-boundary interactions with the environment. Because recruitment operates on an organization's boundaries, it is affected by both environmental and organizational forces, as I discuss next.

### Labor Market Changes Affecting Recruitment

Changes in the labor market can have powerful effects on a company's behavior and success. Certainly, the overall rate of unemployment affects organizations. So do a number of other characteristics of the labor supply, such as the availability of skilled versus unskilled workers, especially trained specialists; the proportion of young, midcareer, and older workers; and the geographic locations and lifestyles of workers. At the beginning of the 21st century, the U.S. national unemployment rate was lower than it had been in 30 years. The rate had been gradually declining for some time. At the end of 1998, the U.S. Bureau of Labor Statistics reported the rate of unemployment to be at 4.4 percent of the civilian labor force. In spring 1999, the rate had dropped to 4.3 percent. By spring 2000, the rate was at 4.1 percent.[2] However, even when

---

[2]The U.S. Bureau of Labor Statistics provides a monthly updated report on the national unemployment rate. Check the Web site at http://www.bls.gov/home.htm. The rate for February 2002 was 5.5 percent.

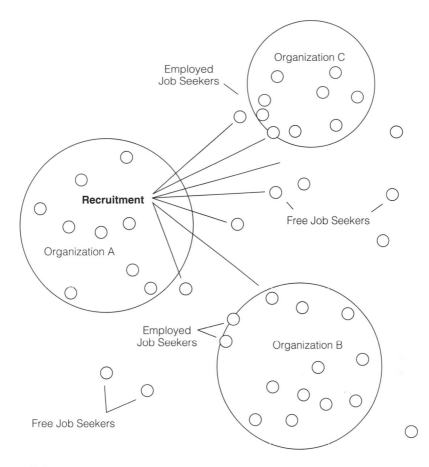

FIGURE **5.1**

Recruitment of unemployed and employed  job seekers. Organizational boundaries are permeable, allowing recruitment to attract applicants from other organizations as well as from among the unemployed.

unemployment is high and many are seeking jobs, the population does not grow at an even rate and it may be difficult to find young workers, for example. Shortages also can occur in some types of occupations or in certain geographical areas, independent of the national rate of unemployment. (See Table 5.1 for variations in geographic areas.) In spring 2000, the lowest regional rate of unemployment in the United States was in the Midwest, at 3.3 percent. (By comparison, the Western region showed a rate of 4.5 percent.) During that time, the more westerly section of the Midwestern region recorded a rate of 2.7 percent. This particular geographic section continuously records the lowest rate and has done so since 1989 (U.S. Department of Labor, 2000b).

There have been previous periods in which there was a strong economy and low unemployment, of course, such as during the 1950s and 1970s. During

<table>
<tr><td>TABLE<br>5.1</td><td colspan="4">CIVILIAN LABOR FORCE UNEMPLOYED BY GEOGRAPHIC REGIONS AND STATES, MARCH 2000</td></tr>
</table>

| Geographic Region and States* | Civilian Labor Force ( in thousands) | Unemployed ( in thousands) | Percent of Labor Force |
|---|---|---|---|
| Northeast | 26,364.9 | 980.9 | 3.7 |
| New England states | 7,200.1 | 183.1 | 2.5 |
| Middle Atlantic states | 19,164.9 | 797.8 | 4.2 |
| South | 49,295.6 | 1,916.1 | 3.9 |
| South Atlantic states | 25,605.8 | 883.2 | 3.4 |
| East South Central states | 8,328.5 | 339.7 | 4.1 |
| West South Central states | 15,361.3 | 693.1 | 4.5 |
| Midwest | 33,881.2 | 1,123.7 | 3.3 |
| East North Central states | 23,475.2 | 843.0 | 3.6 |
| West North Central states | 10,406.0 | 280.7 | 2.7 |
| West | 31,673.7 | 1,422.9 | 4.5 |
| Mountain states | 9,034.1 | 330.0 | 3.7 |
| Pacific states | 22,639.5 | 1,092.9 | 4.8 |

*New England = Connecticut, Maine, Massachusetts, New Hampshire, Rhode Island, and Vermont. Middle Atlantic = New Jersey, New York, and Pennsylvania. South Atlantic = Delaware, District of Columbia, Florida, Georgia, Maryland, North Carolina, South Carolina, Virginia, and West Virginia. East South Central = Alabama, Kentucky, Mississippi, and Tennessee. West South Central = Arkansas, Louisiana, Oklahoma, and Texas. East North Central = Illinois, Indiana, Michigan, Ohio, and Wisconsin. West North Central = Iowa, Kansas, Minnesota, Missouri, Nebraska, North Dakota, and South Dakota. Mountain = Arizona, Colorado, Idaho, Montana, Nevada, New Mexico, Utah, and Wyoming. Pacific = Alaska, California, Hawaii, Oregon, and Washington.

Adapted from *Local Area Unemployment Statistics*, U.S. Department of Labor, Bureau of Labor Statistics, 2000b. http://stats.bls.gov:80/news.release/laus.t01.htm.

these earlier periods, employers behaved much the same way as they behaved in the more recent years. Rynes (1991) cited articles from business magazines published during the earlier periods, indicating that employers had reduced their standards; attempted to entice applicants with bigger salaries; varied their recruiting activities, adding more expensive methods; and searched over wide geographic areas. Employers did the same in the late 1990s. For example, businesses in Wisconsin tried to attract out-of-state job seekers. Former residents of the state were notified of the existence of a Web site that posts available jobs and promotes Wisconsin as a good place to come to work (Johnson, 2000). Such a strategy might be effective because it seems to recognize that unemployment is higher in some other regions and that people who used to live in Wisconsin might be interested in coming home. Other employers, in facing the reality of the labor market, quit looking for the elusive "top level" recruit and began using other approaches to the problem. Some stopped recruiting. For example, some businesses reduced the number of hours they were open. Others recruited, but from the inside. They began redesigning jobs, adding teams, and reassigning current employees. Some continued to recruit from outside, but from among the classically hard-to-hire. That is, they looked at welfare recipients, ex-convicts, and the hard-core unemployed. They recognized that at the low rate of unemployment, these individuals were about all that were left without jobs. These groups require different recruitment and employment strategies and different post-hire attention (Flynn, 1999b).

**Recruitment for Selection or Placement**    When I was a student, "employee selection and placement" was a commonly used phrase in industrial/organizational psychology courses. However, almost everything discussed in my textbooks and classes focused on selection. Placement was ignored. Being shy, I hesitated to ask what was meant by the term "placement." Instead, I thumbed through old textbooks and finally found a definition. It seemed that placement was a rather old-fashioned concept, in contrast to selection. In selection, the employer finds the right person for a particular job opening. (This is the approach that organizations usually take.) In placement, however, the employer finds or makes the right job for a particular person. This approach seemed old-fashioned to me because at the time there were many more applicants than there were jobs. That is, the unemployment rate was high at the time. It had been a while since a serious drop in the unemployment rate had occurred, and textbooks and class discussions covered the more topical issue of selection.

The placement approach makes sense at any time when the unemployment rate is low and jobs—but not applicants—are plentiful. Placement can be implicit in an employer's actions. When employers focus on finding individuals with potential and then make adjustments to accommodate and develop them, they are using a placement approach in recruitment rather than a selection approach. Redesigning jobs, adjusting lines of career progression, and training or otherwise developing the employee are signs of this approach. Wernimont (1988) identifies several employer actions that indicate placement, including creating new jobs or restructuring existing ones, allowing employees to share jobs, and providing vocational-interest testing and skills training to prepare recruits for jobs.

Employers may search for "top performers" and, using a placement orientation, find or create work for them to do or provide opportunities for their further development. In addition, an employer may choose to take this approach with individuals who are less interesting to other employers. Those who are willing to consider hiring welfare recipients, for example, might look for trainability rather than skills and plan to develop the employee according to his or her potential. Flynn (1999b) observes that training is absolutely necessary, even in basic "come to work" skills, as this person may never have had a job and is unlikely to be qualified for work. Still, such employees can be good low-cost hires. There are tax breaks for employers who hire people who are on welfare. In addition, although there is high turnover, for some of these employees, a job is a real step up, and they stay and become good performers.

## Legal Issues Affecting Recruitment

Indirectly, some legislative action addresses recruitment although there is little in the way of specific requirement. Title VII of the Civil Rights Act of 1964 made it unlawful to make employee selection decisions on the basis of someone's race or sex. However, Title VII focuses almost entirely on hiring procedures rather than recruiting. Early court decisions and federal agency reports, which interpreted the law for purposes of implementation, also primarily addressed selection decisions and gave little attention to recruitment. It was not until the Equal Employment Opportunity Act of 1972, which amended Title VII, that anything specific to recruitment procedures was required. Targeting federal employers, this measure required that they devise programs by which to recruit minorities for certain federal jobs in which there was underrepresentation (Lee, 1999).

An interpretation of Title VII appeared in a 1978 document published by the federal government titled *Uniform Guidelines on Employee Selection Procedures*. This document, as I discuss in Chapter 6, informed employers as to how they could conduct fair employee selection. The *Uniform Guidelines* also identified some aspects of recruitment that could contribute to compliance with the law on fair employment. Basically, in mentioning recruitment, the *Uniform Guidelines* addressed an employer's posture toward soliciting minority and female applications. An employer could adopt one of two postures, each of which would influence the pool of recruits, and the employer's posture would be considered in cases where the selection procedures appeared to be discriminatory. Over time, by having adopted one posture, an employer's "reputation may have discouraged or 'chilled' applicants of particular groups from applying because they believed application would be futile" (*Uniform Guidelines*, 1978, p. 38291). In such a case, recruitment would be negatively affected. The employer would appear disinterested and unlikely to hire a minority or female applicant, and so these job seekers would not bother to apply. Methods of determining employment discrimination depend on who applies as well as who is hired. Therefore, this employer might not appear to be discriminating because if few apply few can be hired. In fact, however, such a "chilling" reputation has the discriminatory effect of denying equal opportunity at the recruitment level.

On the other hand, an employer's posture toward minority and female applicants might be positive and encouraging. Some employers are willing to go beyond simply refraining from unfair discrimination and take more proactive, affirmative steps to correct past inequities. Although not specifically requiring affirmative action, the Civil Rights Act does recognize its value, and the *Uni-*

*form Guidelines* mirrors this encouragement. As understood at the time this document was published, affirmative action referred to recruitment. Voluntary affirmative action was meant to recruit minorities and women for openings in jobs in which these groups were underrepresented. Affirmative action recruiting was supposed to be a way of seeking out and making it clear to minority and female job seekers that their applications were welcome and encouraged. In practice, however, affirmative action programs have changed over the years since the *Uniform Guidelines* interpreted the Civil Rights Act. Because these programs appear now to have much more to do with employee selection than with recruiting, I hold further discussion of the issue until Chapter 6.

## Effects of Organizational Characteristics

In the discussion above, you can infer ways in which an organization's behavior can determine the processes and outcomes of recruitment. For example, an employer's posture with respect to minorities and women, and an employer's willingness to hire anyone other than "top performers," are two characteristics that affect recruitment. In fact, several organizational variables affect recruitment strategies and recruitment success. Rynes (1991) outlines these as including (1) an employer's ability to modify job vacancy characteristics to make an opening more attractive; (2) the selectivity or stance an employer takes toward recruiting from among "less desirable" job seekers; (3) an employer's position on timing a recruitment effort prior to need; and (4) the existence of norms for how recruitment is done in an organization. Concerning the fourth variable, for example, norms exist about how to recruit executives and professionals as compared to production and service workers.

An organization might use any of several methods to make itself attractive or to appear an "employer of choice" to job seekers. As I mentioned in Chapter 4, companies make adjustments in base pay and offer bonuses for accepting a job offer. This is especially likely for employers seeking capable people in new or developing occupations, such as those in the field of information technology (IT). Much of the recruiting competition I described earlier is focused on such occupations, in which there are relatively few experienced or trained job seekers. Benefits also are useful in making a vacancy appealing. The practice-oriented literature abounds in advice on how to use these and other rewards to make vacancies in either private- or public-sector organizations more attractive to those who might be considering a new job. For example, in a survey of government agency managers, one of the "best practices" for recruiting IT professionals was to market the organization as offering a contrast to the high pressure and travel requirements of the private sector (International Personnel Management Association [IPMA], 1999a). Any number of such existing and inexpensive perquisites can be used to distinguish an employer from others and to make the organization more attractive.

In tight labor markets, many employers are advised to cut the time it takes to recruit and hire. Consultants often are quick to point out that "top performers" are desired and pursued by many other employers and that any delay in an organization's process will cause a hiring opportunity to be missed because such employees are snapped up quickly. There is little evidence indicating that employers improve their hiring success by rushing recruitment, although long delays are likely to cause some high-quality applicants to be lost to a faster-acting competitor (Rynes, 1991). However, effective timing of recruitment—even recruiting before there is an opening—might make an employer appear more attractive to a job seeker.

Advertising certain characteristics of the organization and its environment can make an employer's vacancies more interesting to job seekers. Some organizations market their location (IPMA, 1999a), especially when they are situated in or near a fabulous city and want to recruit out-of-the-area applicants. Other firms make known whatever employee-related programs they have in place, such as work-family and employee assistance programs. Diversity programs are thought to be appealing to many job seekers. Other benefits and opportunities can be helpful, even those that appeal to only a few employees. Offering college-level internships and scholarships for summer employment of high school students, for example, might make an employer more generally attractive (Anderson & Pulich, 2000). Employers who adopt an employee placement approach, as described earlier, in which an effort is made to find a place for a good applicant, may be viewed by job seekers as both innovative and attractive. For example, a former student of mine teamed up with a long-time acquaintance, and the two of them marketed themselves as a high-level "job share" in human resources. They found that only some companies were willing to talk with them about such an arrangement. Primarily, those companies were known as risk-takers in their business strategies and were interested in innovations.

Job seekers do seem to respond to organizational attractiveness. A sample of college recruits who visited a company's workplace were questioned after the site visit about their reactions. The researchers found that overall evaluations of the company and of its location, as well as ratings of how likable the host was, predicted how likely recruits were to accept job offers (Turban, Campion, & Eyring, 1995). Still, employers must be careful not to mislead job seekers into believing a position offers more than it actually does. One reason is that employees who realize they have been deceived by a sharp-witted recruiter do not remain on the job. In a survey of graduate management alumni, 55 percent of the sample said that psychological contracts or obligations which had been developed at the time of recruitment were broken by the employer (Robinson & Rousseau, 1994). These violations resulted in either actual turnover or plans to leave. Some years ago, I was interviewed by an employer who gave me some very positive information about a job vacancy that persuaded me to accept the job offer, but which turned out not to be entirely true. Within a month or so, I realized I had been misled by the recruiter's flimflam. Like subjects in Robinson and Rousseau's (1994) study, I looked for another job and left soon. Another reason that employers should be careful about excessive promises is that it might spoil their chances of benefiting from a traditionally good source of recruitment—that is, referrals from current or previous employees. Those who have been treated poorly in any way are unlikely to refer their friends to the employer. They might even engage in some negative marketing, as customers sometimes do when they are dissatisfied with a company's product or service.

## Whom to Recruit

Employers usually want to attract a pool of the best applicants so that the most effective employees can be hired. However, there are two difficulties with this approach. First, it is not always possible for a company to attract and hire the very best. Second, it is not unusual for employers to overlook sources of good applicants. Rynes (1991) describes a theory (Thurow, 1975) in which both jobs and job seekers are viewed as being arrayed in hierarchies. In this view, employers who have the best jobs are those at the top of the job hierarchy, and they attract the best applicants—those at the top of the people hierarchy. Employers who are further down on the job hierarchy can get only those applicants that are less marketable. Whenever there are labor shortages, either overall or in certain occupational niches, all employers have to move down a notch or two in order to fill any vacancies they have. If the recruits at the lower levels of the people hierarchy have deficiencies, these will have to be corrected by the employer through training.

There is some evidence that employers actually do become less selective and more willing to consider alternative job seekers when there is a tight labor market. As I mentioned at the start of this chapter, during such times, some employers lower their standards. Others train their present employees and promote them into vacancies that are hard to fill (IPMA, 1999a). Still other employers, like those in earlier times of shortage, consider sources of applicants that usually are ignored. The experience of American manufacturers during World War II is a good example of this latter response. At that time, a labor shortage occurred because of the military need for a large proportion of young adult males—men who had been working in industrial jobs. When they left, it looked as if there would be no one to run the factories. However, women were available. Previously, they had limited job opportunities. Of necessity, employers tapped this source of labor and filled their industrial job vacancies. This turned out to be a very effective strategy, as women workers performed jobs previously thought possible for men only. Currently, welfare recipients—another underemployed group—are being recruited partly as a result of the 1996 welfare reform law. A report by the U.S. Department of Labor (2000b) indicates that companies participating in the government's "welfare-to-work" program had hired over 410,000 welfare recipients by April 1999. However, most of these individuals have few job skills. To make it easier to employ welfare recipients, Flynn (1999b) recommends working with a local agency that specializes in placing the hard-to-hire and providing thorough training. Another group that is underemployed but could be recruited is people with disabilities. Although individuals with moderate disabilities are almost as likely to be employed as individuals without disabilities, the employment opportunities of those who are severely disabled are bleak. Although education can improve a disabled person's chance of employment, only 52 percent of those with severe disabilities who are college educated were employed in 1998, compared to 90 percent of nondisabled workers (U.S. Department of Labor, 2000d).

## Conclusions

At certain times, and for certain job vacancies, little is required of an employer in the way of recruitment because job seekers appear without any special encouragement. However, at other times, an organization must take action. Recruiting is a process that crosses the boundary between an organization and its environment, and some environmental conditions require a vigorous response. The state of the labor market is an external influence of major importance to recruitment. A low rate of unemployment in general, or in certain occupations, can mean that employers have to struggle to find applicants. During such times, though, we see the most creative solutions. While some employers simply push for better results from the same recruitment practices, such as offering higher monetary enticements, others begin to consider more innovative ways to attract recruits. If an organization is unable to offer bonuses or higher compensation, there is little choice but to consider other strategies. It is also during such times of labor shortage that social progress can occur, such as when employers begin to recruit job seekers they previously turned away.

Although an organization may have no direct control over changes in the labor force, it does have control over the way it responds to the changes. In their responses, organizations themselves are changed, not only in superficial ways such as increasing the amount of money going into recruiting efforts, but also in deeper and more comprehensive ways. For example, in realizing that certain recruits are difficult to attract, an organization may adopt a placement approach to recruitment and look for high-potential job seekers before a vacancy exists for them. In contrast, a company might turn its recruiting effort inward and develop its current employees to fill vacancies by redesigning jobs and tightening up operations to accomplish the same work with fewer employees. Any of these and other changes can result in improved recruitment practices. While it is difficult for organizations to hire during times of low unemployment, this

| TABLE 5.2 | RECRUITMENT SOURCES |
| --- | --- |

| Category | Examples |
| --- | --- |
| Job posting locations | Major and community newspapers |
| | Academic and professional newsletters |
| | Business magazines |
| | Professional and trade journals |
| | Internet job sites |
| Agencies | Local unemployment office |
| | Employment agencies |
| | Executive search firms |
| College recruiting | College placement office |
| | Job and career fairs |
| Internal resources | Employee referrals |
| | Career transitions |
| | Job rotation |
| | Realistic job preview programs |

situation seems to have some long-range positive effects, as the recruitment practices being elicited are anything but passive.

# RECRUITING SOURCES

Employers recruit applicants through a number of different sources. Mainly, recruitment sources are (1) locations in which to post a job vacancy announcement and (2) people whom to inform that an opening exists. For example, newspaper ads, Internet job sites, employment agencies, and current employees are some recruitment sources. Table 5.2 lists these and other sources. Recruitment varies in terms of how actively the employer is seeking applicants. A passive approach can amount to no more than informing current employees that the company is hiring, or advertising in public sites, such as newspapers. Sending out recruiters from the HR department to arrange and conduct interviews, or engaging a search firm to do this, indicates a more active stance.

## Posting Job Ads

Putting a "Help Wanted" sign in a store window is the most basic way to post a job ad. It is an inexpensive source of recruits and is flexible in that it can be used for various job openings. This method can be useful in times of high unemployment when many people are out on the streets looking for work. However, a "Help Wanted" sign is always a limited source of recruits because it reaches relatively few job seekers and conveys little information that will allow a job seeker to decide whether to apply.

Paying for and placing an advertisement in a newspaper is an improvement over the "Help Wanted" sign because newspapers and the like reach more people who are looking for jobs. Also, depending on how much an employer can pay, many details can be included, describing job requirements, compensation, and benefits, in addition to information about the organization, such as its location and reputation in the marketplace. Any local newspaper is likely to have job ads, and those with a special Sunday edition will have pages and pages of them. Trade and business journals and professional newsletters also publish job announcements. For example, the American Psychological Association's newsletter, the *APA Monitor*, lists ads recruiting psychologists with various specialties for academic, community, and business positions.

**Internet Recruiting**    The latest twist in locations for job ads is the Internet. Some employers are quite enthusiastic about the potential of this source. It has the capacity to make posting and updating ads easy and can reach job seekers quickly. If job posting is teamed up with online procedures for job seekers to apply for open positions, the recruitment process is expedited. Ad space for job postings can be purchased from several commercial Web sites. In addition to recruiting through such commercially available sites, some organizations use their corporate Web sites and develop their own recruitment source at such independent locations.

A difficulty for most employers using Internet recruiting is deciding where to place an ad. About 18,000 Web sites exist where employers can announce job openings (Day, 2000). Some of these sites will be relevant to the kind of job opening an employer is seeking to fill, but others will not be. Commercial sites often promise a lot of résumés from job seekers. However, the key is not quantity but, rather, relevance and quality. Sifting through a mass of responses from job seekers who are inappropriate for the job can be tedious, time consuming, and costly for an employer's recruiting staff. Similarly, employers have had difficulty with Internet postings because the right job seekers often do not seem to be visiting the sites. One employer who was looking for employees who could handle the now old-fashioned COBOL computer language concluded that unless one is looking for people with skills in the latest technology, the Internet may not be the best source (Caggiano, 1999).

Not surprisingly, management services for outplacing Internet recruiting are now being marketed to employers. Such services provide employers with software and consulting and can help in several ways, such as by finding the right sites and placing job ads simultaneously at multiple job sites (Day, 2000). Even employers who have had success with Internet recruiting recognize that using this recruitment source takes special skill. In addition, Internet recruiting should not be expected to replace other recruitment sources. It should be part of a larger recruitment process (Caggiano, 1999). Owners of some commercial job sites agree. In spring 2000, a job fair was conducted at the World Trade Center in New York, which attracted 83 recruiting companies and 5,000 potential recruits. The job fair was sponsored by an online recruiting business. This company makes most of its money through online operations. Yet, company management recognized that real-world interactions are needed in recruitment, even for those who have computer-based jobs to fill (Maroney, 2000). Because a job fair brings job seekers and recruiting employers together, in person, they get a sense of each other that might not be possible in strictly online interactions.

## Posting With Agencies

Employers often post their job vacancies with employment service agencies, including the U.S. Employment Service and numerous fee agencies. Look in the telephone directory's Yellow Pages in any large city under "employment agencies" and you will see pages of listings and ads for agencies proposing to match employers with job seekers. Many of these agencies offer a full spectrum of recruiting services and will locate recruits for a broad range of jobs. Others are specialists, offering to find recruits for technical, sales, or managerial positions. Some employers contract with an employment agency to supply all of its recruitment needs. Others use an agency for certain searches only, with the remaining recruiting done by HR staff.

Like company recruiters, employment agencies try to attract recruits by posting ads in various printed sources, such as newspapers and telephone directories. In addition, these agencies use the Internet to search for appropriately qualified applicants. Many job posting sites also let job seekers post their résumés where potential employers or recruiting agencies can view them. Although agencies in general may use Internet sources less than company HR staffs do, about one-third of agencies do use the Internet as part of their recruitment activities (Kay, 2000).

Executive search firms are specialty recruiting agencies that locate recruits for high-level managerial and executive positions. (These are listed under "executive search firms" in the Yellow Pages.) These specialized recruiters often are hired when a company must find a new president or another member of its top management team. Although the use of an executive search firm often is costly, there can be advantages to an employer. For example, an outside recruiter sometimes is needed to provide an element of objectivity in a search process that has become internally politicized. Also, a search firm may be needed simply because the company's own recruiters have been unable to locate acceptable executive recruits.

## College Recruiting

Traditionally, colleges have been a source of professional, technical, and managerial recruits, and considerable recruiting is done on campuses. Colleges and universities have career and job placement offices for their students, in which employers are invited to post information about job openings. A placement office sometimes is a simple operation with bulletin boards available for posting jobs that students can peruse. Increasingly, placement offices are making posted information available by touch-tone telephone and/or the Internet. In addition, colleges regularly sponsor job or career fairs in which company representatives come to campus and conduct recruiting interviews with students who are nearing graduation.

Because campus recruiting occurs regularly and makes research samples readily available, many studies have been conducted using campus interviews. Therefore, the context of college recruiting is one of the few areas in recruitment that has received real attention from researchers. These studies have not always shown that college recruiting is an effectively used source of recruits. Although students—especially those getting degrees in business and professional fields—are of interest to college recruiters, many managerial and professional jobs in fact are filled by individuals recruited through other sources. Employers often are interested in job seekers who are experienced and who might be drawn away from their existing jobs with other companies (Bretz, Boudreau, & Judge, 1994). Upcoming changes in organizational demands, such as a greater need for quick response in a competitive market, might mean that employers increasingly will try to recruit experienced employees who can be available immediately and can perform with little training or development. In their survey, Rynes, Orlitzky, and Bretz (1997) found that more than half of the externally advertised jobs requiring a college degree were taken by experienced applicants rather than new graduates. As predicted, experienced recruitment was judged superior to college recruitment in terms of the time it took to bring new employees up to full productivity. Even so, the employers evaluated their college recruiting programs as a successful part of their recruiting process. They viewed college recruiting as having certain advantages for identifying qualified applicants while containing recruitment costs.

The question of how college recruiting is helpful to an organization was addressed in a study by Powell and Goulet (1996), who asked whether assessments made by recruiters of the applicants they interviewed were considered in later organizational decisions about these applicants. They found that college recruiters' impressions of applicants did affect the organization's decision to grant a follow-up interview; however, they had no effect on whether an applicant received a job offer. On the other hand, campus recruiters can influence applicants' impressions of a vacancy and the recruiting organization, and in this way recruiters indirectly influence applicants' attraction to the organization and like-lihood of accepting a offer (Turban, Forret, & Hendrickson, 1998).

Interest in new college graduates is not likely to cool down. In fact, in the near future, organizations may become more interested because of the ex-pected decline in experienced workers due to increased retirements within the next few years. College recruiting already is being promoted as a good way to replace these worker losses. Skill requirements of jobs appear to be increasing. However, educational attainment also is increasing. Of adults age 25 and older, 24 percent have college degrees, compared to 10 percent some 30 years ago. Also, more of today's high school graduates are going to college than in the past. As you can see in Figure 5.2, 66 percent of the nation's high school gradu-ates in spring 1998 entered college in the fall. This is an increase over the 63 percent that entered in 1993 (U.S. Department of Labor, 2000c). We can ex-pect that HR professionals will continue coming onto campuses for job and career fairs.

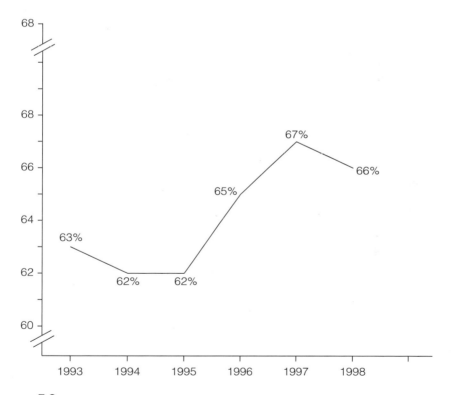

FIGURE **5.2**

New high school graduates enrolling in college. In the 1990s, more high school graduates were going to college than in previous years.

From *Futurework: Trends and Challenges for Work in the 21st Century: 1—The Workforce* (chart 1.2, p. 3), by U.S. Department of Labor. http://www.dol.gov/dol/asp/public/futurework/report/chapter1/main.htm;downloaded April 21, 2000.

## *Referrals*

Another traditionally used recruitment source is employee referrals. An employer simply informs current employees that openings are available and accepts their leads for possible applicants. Although it is not clear that new employees hired through referrals are better performers, a consistent message from research is that turnover is lower (Rynes, 1991). There has been much discussion about why this might be. One intriguing idea is the realistic information hypothesis, which proposes that some recruitment sources, such as referrals, provide more realistic information about the job and organization that better prepares the recruit. For example, a study compared employees recruited through informal sources, such as employee referrals, with those recruited through formal sources. Those informally recruited said they felt they had received accurate job information and were better able to cope as a result (Saks, 1994).

The idea that referrals result in more accurate and complete information makes a lot of sense to me. I can imagine that when someone recommends a friend or an acquaintance to his or her employer that the person would be careful to give an honest and complete assessment of what it is like to work there, including the organization's negative as well as positive features. However, what would be the outcome if an employer began to give rewards to employees for referring applicants who were subsequently hired? This is happening in some organizations. Employers have discovered that employee referrals are an inexpensive way to get loyal employees, and they are encouraging referrals with bonuses. One company was reported to be giving $1,000 to any employee who referred an applicant that was hired, or $2,000 if the new hire was a technology worker. In a further push for referrals, the company held a drawing for employees who had referred successful recruits in which it gave away two big prizes—a new car and an all-expense-paid vacation (Joyce, 1999). One might wonder whether such tactics will affect the quality of job information that employees give to those they refer to the company. As I discuss in a later section, one concern that recruiters have is how much information to give a recruit. If one tells a recruit too much, he or she might decline a job offer. Assuming that employees who make referrals have thought of this, the effectiveness of referrals might be damaged in an employee's eagerness to recruit someone.

## *Recruiting Internally*

Most companies have some kind of internal recruiting system through which current employees can be identified and considered for other jobs in the organization. A variety of career transitions—promotions, lateral transfers to jobs at the same hierarchical level, and transfers to other locations—are possible as a result of an internal recruiting system. This system usually includes qualifications information, information on career paths, and listings of eligible employees. Generally, an employer will consider the internal recruitment source before advertising the opening externally.

Although there was intense downsizing of American organizations over the past two decades, employers have learned that it is possible to cut too deeply and new employees may need to be hired. In addition, staffing needs can vary across different functional areas in an organization and a company might find itself in the untenable position of laying off employees in one section and recruiting new ones for another section. In a tight labor market, it becomes especially clear to companies that they need ways to retain employees. Companies have developed a number of creative ways to solve this problem by emphasizing internal recruitment for job vacancies. These solutions include (1) long-term preventive measures, such as the cross-training that takes place in job rotations, in which employees learn by doing a series of different work assignments; and (2) measures that address more immediate needs, such as a "bank" of available jobs and employees that can easily be accessed by managers with vacancies and by employees looking for a placement (Martinez, 1998).

**Job Rotation**     Some firms rotate employees from job to job in a planned series of lateral moves through the organization. These transfers can be made within the same organizational function (e.g., within the finance department) or across functions (e.g., from finance to the human resources department), and they can involve relocations to other company worksites. Job rotation has been used for developing employees in all types of jobs and at all hierarchical levels. For example, in Chapter 2 I discussed the self-managing work team, in which all members are rotated through all work assignments of the team. More often, job rotation has been used in the development of managers, and there is evidence that business and administrative knowledge and skills are gained this way. However, technical and specialty learning also can be accomplished through job rotation (Campion, Cheraskin, & Stevens, 1994).

Job rotation can be understood as a method of both employee development and internal recruitment. By giving current employees opportunities to learn new job skills and knowledge and to gain highly relevant experience, a company invests in its current staff. This can result in high payoffs when there are job vacancies to be filled. In such cases, a recruitable person is available who is experienced and knowledgeable about both the job and the organization. Potentially, job rotation allows recruitment of skilled employees who have experience in the very positions that are vacated. They are likely to have more company knowledge than outside recruits. In addition, they have had a very realistic trial on the job. This combination of features can make an internal recruit a highly attractive applicant. Campion, Cheraskin, et al. (1994) found that employees involved in job rotation were more likely to be perceived as having greater administrative and business knowledge and skill. In addition, more involvement in job rotation was associated with career progress. Job experience that results in new learning can identify current employees who are appropriate for higher level positions.

You might guess that knowing about vocational interests; that is, the kind of work someone is interested in doing, would be helpful in determining whether an otherwise attractive applicant would be appropriate for a specific vacancy. In fact, recruiters routinely do try to appeal to what they assume are job seekers' interests in order to get applicants. They are not always right about their interests, of course. This is one of the difficulties in searching for individuals who have skills in new fields, such as information technology. A recruiter might overestimate the value of high compensation, for example, relative to a recruit's interests in working in the forefront of technology development. Although the vocational interests of external recruits might be difficult to assess, information on interests might easily be gathered and used in internal recruitment. In-house career guidance programs usually involve consideration of a person's interests and may include vocational-interest testing.

Concerning the concept of person–job fit, it is hypothesized that people make career transitions and, over the course of their careers, they gravitate to jobs that provide a better personal fit for themselves (cf. Gottfredson & Daiger, 1977). As you might suppose, a person's abilities are an important part of what determines this gravitational force toward a better fitting job (Wilk, Desmarais, & Sackett, 1995). However, vocational interests add something unique in understanding occupational and job changes. Dawis (1991) reviewed studies showing that interests predict employee retention. To some extent, they are associated with job satisfaction, and, although secondary in importance to ability, they reflect differences in job performance ratings.

Finding the right fit might mean that a person moves from job to job across different organizations. However, the movement can occur within an organization. Job rotation can allow an employee a chance to try out various jobs to see which, if any, provide a good fit. Companies that offer job rotation, especially rotations within and across organizational functions, likely are providing opportunities for individuals to find work that fits their abilities and interests, as well as a vehicle for self-recruitment.

## Conclusions

Several sources of recruitment are available to employers. Some yield better results than others. Whether a company does its own recruiting or hires an employment agency to do this work, careful decisions must be made about how to advertise the vacancy. Ads need to be placed in locations where they will be seen by the targeted job seekers. A variety of printed sources can be used, and some have high potential for reaching the appropriate job seekers. The Internet is a similar source of recruits. Whether it is better than print sources is not clear. It might be better for some jobs or for some needs, such as recruiting applicants in distant locations. A poll of graduating college students recently reported that most students use both the Internet and printed resources for job searches. Those with technical degrees, such as engineering, were as likely as others to use both sources (International Personnel Management Association [IPMA], 1999b). Generally, a good approach for employers is a recruitment program that includes varied sources.

A college campus is a good place to announce a job vacancy. College recruiting traditionally has been able to attract talented recruits for technical, professional, and managerial jobs, and it remains an important part of many organizations' recruitment process. Some recruiters come looking for graduates with technical or business degrees. Others are interested in graduates who have a well-rounded education (Hickins, 1999). Employers often seek new graduates specifically because of their fresh ideas, open-mindedness, creativity, and willingness to learn.

One of the best ways to announce a job opening is to let current employees know about it. Employee referrals have long been recognized as a good source of retainable employees, probably because recruits get an honest description of what it is like to work for the recruiting company, so there are no surprises. In past years, these referrals have been cost-free to the employer. The major rewards to a referring employee probably were the satisfaction of being a good citizen or having a friend as a coworker. However, if an employer pays for referrals, the recruiting strategy may not be effective because the employee may become more interested in the monetary reward than in sharing complete and honest information with the recruit.

Internal recruiting is something that most organizations do to some extent. For some companies, it is a major part of the recruitment program and is the first step taken in filling a vacancy. Only if there are no internal applicants for a vacancy is the position then advertised externally. After years of downsizing, many companies are making efforts to retain and develop the employees that remain with them. Some do this through job rotation. Often, this opportunity is opened to managerial employees and used as a means of career development. In job rotation, employees gain experience and skill in new areas of work, and they have a chance to assess how interesting the work is and whether such a job would be a good personal fit. In essence a job preview, job rotation can be an effective way to recruit from among a company's own employees.

## RECRUITMENT INFORMATION

An important question in recruitment concerns the type, amount, and timing of information to be given to job seekers. Generally, companies need to provide enough of the right kinds of information to accomplish their purposes, and the information must be timed appropriately so that it is useful to job seekers as well as employers. Recruitment information must draw the attention of high-quality job seekers and retain their interest long enough for the company to initiate employee selection procedures and consider making a job offer. That is, job seekers must be attracted and their attrition from the applicant pool must be controlled. From the standpoint of the job seeker, recruitment information must be complete enough that he or she can assess whether the job might be a good fit and can make an informed decision about whether to pursue a job offer.

Different kinds and amounts of information may be necessary to satisfy these different needs of the two parties. To market themselves and to attract the attention of job seekers, companies communicate the positive features of the job and organization in advertisements and recruiter-provided materials. In these, work assignments and reporting relationships can be outlined, and KSAs and other job requirements can be defined. Compensation and benefits and promotional opportunities usually are indicated. If compensation information is not given, job seekers might not consider the vacancy (Ÿuce & Highhouse, 1998). Information on organizational profitability, and on the firm's values and culture, can be mentioned. According to research, job seekers can be attracted by information that a company has affirmative action policies or work-family programs (Bretz & Judge, 1994; Highhouse, Stierwalt, Bachiochi, Elder, & Fisher, 1999). Job seekers also draw their own conclusions, based on recruitment material, about what opportunities a job might provide, such as the chance to do challenging work. They also have opinions on how important such opportunities are, which determines whether they are likely to pursue a job offer. Powell and Goulet (1996) asked college recruiting interviewees to evaluate a list of job attributes in response to a job opportunity they were considering. The researchers did a factor analysis of the participants' evaluations of these attributes and found that they fell into two categories—attributes referring to the job itself, and attributes referring to compensation and environment. These are listed in Table 5.3. The mean scores are ratings of how important the attribute is. Notice, by the bold values, that the first eight attributes plus the overall evaluation of the job opportunity define factor 1 (the job itself). The remaining four items refer to factor 2 (compensation and environment). The researchers found these attributes to be important to the recruits, as they affected their decisions on whether to accept a follow-up interview or job offer.

What kind of information should an employer try to convey to get the best effect? At the beginning of recruitment, when the main task is to get job seekers' attention, positive and general information about the job and organization are appropriate. General information is more useful to the job seeker than specific information at this early stage (Barber, Daly, Giannantonio, & Phillips, 1994). Although later in their searches, job seekers will be interested in details,

## 5.3  JOB OPPORTUNITY ATTRIBUTES FOLLOWING A RECRUITMENT INTERVIEW

| Attribute | Mean[a] | SD | Factor[b] 1 | 2 |
|---|---|---|---|---|
| Opportunity to learn | 5.66 | 1.08 | **.79** | .19 |
| Opportunity to use my abilities | 5.46 | 1.28 | **.76** | .24 |
| Variety of activities | 5.12 | 1.28 | **.76** | .09 |
| Opportunity for rapid advancement | 4.69 | 1.37 | **.74** | .20 |
| Challenging and interesting work | 5.24 | 1.35 | **.83** | .27 |
| Competent and sociable coworkers | 5.24 | 1.16 | **.72** | .22 |
| Opportunity to show effective performance | 5.59 | 1.09 | **.63** | .42 |
| Job security | 4.89 | 1.40 | **.57** | .27 |
| Location | 5.11 | 1.53 | −.06 | **.79** |
| Salary | 4.78 | 1.33 | .49 | **.60** |
| Reputation of company | 5.40 | 1.35 | .38 | **.73** |
| Training programs | 5.37 | 1.34 | .46 | **.60** |
| Overall evaluation of job opportunity | 4.96 | 1.70 | **.59** | .47 |
| Eigenvalue | | | 6.67 | 1.16 |
| Percentage of variance accounted for | | | 51 | 9 |

[a]Mean importance ratings on a scale of 1 (very weak) to 7 (very strong).
[b]Bold entries represent the highest factor loading a variable had on either factor. Factor 1 refers to "the job itself"; factor 2 refers to "compensation and environment."

From "Recruiters' and Applicants' Reactions to Campus Interviews and Employment Decisions," by G. N. Powell and L. R. Goulet, 1996, *Academy of Management Journal, 39*(6), p.1625. Copyright 1996 by Academy of Management, Pace University, Briarcliff Manor, NY 10510-8020. Reprinted by permission.

at this first contact, general information is sufficient to determine whether further contact with the recruiting organization is desired.

In general, job seekers start with incomplete information about a job vacancy and about how a recruiting organization would react to their application. Recruiters can provide information concerning both. Some information conveyed by recruiters is direct and consciously selected in order to cause the job seeker to form a positive impression. Recruiters also indirectly convey information about the vacancy or their interest in the job seeker. Subtle, covert messages are sent through recruiter behavior. These messages allow a job seeker to infer the nature of the job and the organization beyond what is verbalized (Rynes, 1991). Research shows that recruiters can influence job seekers' attraction to a company in this way because they can change the person's perception of the job and the organization (Turban, Forret, & Hendrickson, 1998). Recruiter behavior also can reflect the company's likely interest in the job seeker and imply whether a follow-up interview could be expected. As I discussed earlier, a job seeker's decision about an offer can be predicted from how he or she reacts to an interview in which a job opportunity was described (Powell & Goulet, 1996).

The structure of the recruiting interview can influence whether and how easily a job seeker can get needed information. Some recruiting interviews are dual-purpose in that they combine recruitment with preliminary employee selection. Other interviews are for recruitment only. These different interview designs modify what a recruiter does and vary the kind of information that is conveyed. Recruiters in dual-purpose interviews, of necessity, must split their time between giving information about the job and organization, and getting information from the job seeker. Most job seekers in dual-purpose interviews are unable to get as much information as those in recruitment-only interviews. This is because the selection aspect of the dual-purpose interview creates a need for the applicant to perform and make a good impression. The person's attention is divided between focusing on job information messages from the recruiter and monitoring his or her own behavior. Thus some information that the recruiter gives is not received because of the distraction and stress of self-presentation (Barber, Hollenbeck, Tower, & Phillips, 1994). It can be an advantage for both company and job seeker if the company splits the two functions and focuses on recruitment only during the first interview. Although some high-ability, low-anxiety job seekers actually can attain the necessary information in a dual-purpose interview, many others cannot. A company recruiting in a tight labor market probably would not want to discourage these other job seekers by conducting an unnecessarily difficult recruitment interview.

**Realistic Job Information**   There are reasons that employers would want to help job seekers get information. Certainly, a company would want to provide whatever information is needed to attract good applicants. Also, an employer might want to provide the kind of information that allows an applicant to determine whether the vacant job is a good fit, given his or her interests, personality, and abilities. Think what might happen if a recruit accepted a job offer without having received this information. Because the success of employee referrals appears to be due to the realistic information that is provided for a recruit, perhaps other recruitment sources should convey equally realistic and balanced information. Realistic information includes negative as well as positive information. Generally, recruiters are cautious about communicating negative information because it might cause an applicant to drop out of recruitment. This is a reasonable concern. However, the outcome may have less to do with the negativity than with the timing of the information.

Realistic job previews (RJPs) are structured programs that are meant to provide realistic job information to applicants who are seriously being considered for employment. These programs vary in terms of how and in what form information is conveyed and in what phase of the recruitment process it is given. RJP information may be as simple as printed materials or an interview with a person who knows the job and the company. Or it can be as complex as a sample of work or a trial period on the job. RJPs often are given in the late pre-hire stage, after a job offer is made but before the offer is accepted. This late pre-hire RJP appears to have the best results in terms of employee retention (Phillips, 1998).

In considering the value of providing realistic job information, we should look at (1) the degree to which the information is actually perceived as being negative and (2) the time during recruitment at which it is conveyed. When recruiting information is being developed, some thought should be given to how job seekers will respond to its different elements. Although recruiters usually want to be as positive as possible in order to cast a wide net for recruits, it is probably not possible to avoid giving some negative information. We can expect that some kinds of information, for example, time pressures and night shifts, are going to be perceived negatively by most people. (See Table 5.4 for some ways that researchers have defined negative versions of job information elements.) Even so, there are likely to be individual differences. For example, team-based work mentioned in job ads was evaluated more positively than individual work by one group of subjects, but not by another group in the same study (Highhouse et al., 1999). Travel requirements in a job might be viewed positively by some job applicants. However, certain employers hope that a job ad that includes the phrase "no travel required" will be evaluated positively (IPMA, 1999a).

As mentioned above, negative information appears to have better results if it is timed for the pre-hire period. If given very early, as in job ads, it is likely

TABLE

**5.4** POSITIVE AND NEGATIVE EXAMPLES OF FOUR JOB ATTRIBUTES

| Job Attribute | Positive Example | Negative Example |
|---|---|---|
| Time pressures | There is ample time to complete tasks before they are due. | Many tasks you will be asked to perform have time deadlines that are difficult but necessary to meet. |
| Closeness of supervision | Your supervisor stays out of your way and lets you do your job. | Your supervisor frequently looks over your shoulder to make sure you are on top of things. |
| Supportiveness of the culture | Expectations are high but will be recognized when these expectations are met. | Expectations are high and you can expect to be criticized for poor performance but seldom praised for good performance. |
| Interactions with others | The job requires frequent interaction with friendly and courteous people. | The job requires frequent interaction with employees and customers who have not had their earlier concerns handled to their satisfaction. |

From "Realistic Job Previews: A Test of the Adverse Self-Selection Hypothesis," by R. D. Bretz, Jr., and T. A. Judge, 1998, *Journal of Applied Psychology, 83*(2), p. 332. Copyright 1998 by American Psychological Association, Washington, DC 20002-4242. Reprinted by permission.

to discourage job seekers and they may self-select out of the applicant pool. Bretz and Judge (1998) found that subjects who received negative information in written job descriptive material responded negatively. The researchers found also that applicants do not always consider a job further when they have received early negative information, especially when they have other opportunities. Of course, even when realistic information is given late in the pre-hire period, dropouts still might occur. Phillips (1998) reasoned that a person who receives realistic job information and perceives that the job will be a poor fit will be unlikely to continue in the application process. However, in contrast to this hypothesis, Phillips's (1998) meta-analysis showed that when a person received the realistic job information late in the pre-hire period, attrition was actually reduced.

RJPs have been shown by many studies to reduce subsequent employee turnover (McEvoy & Cascio, 1985; Phillips, 1998; Premack & Wanous, 1985; Reilly, Brown, Blood, & Malatesta, 1981). Researchers have attempted to understand why. Although the answer is not clear, we might speculate that those who do not drop out when they are given realistic and negative information (1) have found a job that fits, (2) have found that a job meets their expectations, (3) have become committed to taking the job despite any failings it may have, or (4) have ideas on how they can cope with difficulties of the job. Any or all of these possibilities might explain why late pre-hire RJPs are effective in employee retention.

## Conclusions

The two parties involved in recruitment activities have different but complementary needs for information. Job seekers need to get enough good information to decide for themselves whether they will pursue a job offer. Job seekers usually want specifics about the kind of work involved and some details about compensation and the organization. Recruiters need to provide enough good information to attract job seekers and to keep them interested long enough to decide whether the job will be offered to any of them.

Early in the recruitment process, it is best for companies to provide general and positive information about the job and organization because job seekers can make use of this to evaluate and flag the vacancy as a possibility to pursue. In this way, objectives of both job seekers and recruiters are being met. Insufficient or negative information at this point, however, can cause the job seeker to drop the vacancy from further consideration. Some methods of providing information can be detrimental to job seekers' needs and ultimately may not be satisfactory to recruiting organizations. Interviews with a recruiter in which the functions of recruitment and selection are combined provide an example. Recruiter behavior often carries subtle messages through which a job seeker learns about a vacancy and what might be expected from the organization. The process of receiving these subtle messages can be disrupted in a dual-purpose interview, however. In such an interview, the job seeker must try to get information and at the same time perform well enough to keep the recruiter interested. In the process of performing, the job seeker is likely to miss potentially useful messages from the recruiter.

Because organizations have post-hire objectives for finding recruits who can be retained, there is good reason to consider providing a realistic preview of the job and company, including negative information. Studies have shown that realistic job previews can reduce employee turnover, although attrition also can occur as a result. The key is timing. Realistic information that is given late in the pre-hire process has the best effects. Dropouts are less likely and, later, employee turnover is reduced.

## SUMMING UP

An employer can select a new employee for a job opening only if someone applies. In this chapter, the purpose is to discuss how applicants are recruited. Summing up, we can make the following conclusions:

- The labor market is highly important. It affects all employers' hiring efforts.
- In a labor shortage, recruitment innovations are required. Employers cannot rely on techniques designed when labor was plentiful.
- Employers may take a placement approach—hiring any high-quality applicant and then finding a place for him or her.
- Market conditions and societal values can bring employers to consider underemployed groups, including the long-term unemployed.
- Printed and electronic job advertisements and interviews with recruiters are common ways to appeal to job seekers.
- College recruiting is a traditionally used method of getting fresh talent, although experienced recruits often are favored by employers.
- Employee referrals yield retainable employees.
- Internal recruiting from an organization's own staff can be effective.
- Realistic job previews given late in the pre-hire period have good results in terms of job offer acceptances and employee retention.

## INFOTRAC COLLEGE EDITION

Would you like to learn more about the issues reviewed in this chapter? If you purchased a new copy of this book, you received a complimentary subscription to InfoTrac College Edition with your purchase. Use it to access full-text articles from research journals and practice-oriented publications. Go to http://www.infotrac-college.com/wadsworth to start your search. You might open current issues of a journal that you know is likely to have relevant articles, such as *Personnel Psychology*. You probably will want to do a keyword search. The following keywords can be used to find articles related to the topics of this chapter.

| | |
|---|---|
| Labor shortage | Recruiters |
| Job fairs | Internet job sites and recruiting |
| Executive search firms | |

# FAIR EMPLOYMENT LAW

From sections in Chapter 4 on wage setting and pay equity, you may have had the impression that employment in the United States is controlled by law. By the end of this chapter, you will be convinced of this. You will see that the law extends far into the employment process. In every way that selection can be defined—from selection for initial hire to "selection" for termination—laws govern what an employer may do. Although working people have had some degree of legal protection for more than a century, it was only 40 years ago that employers began to be seriously constrained in the kinds of employment practices they were allowed. Fair employment and freedom from discrimination became the rights of workers. This chapter provides an in-depth discussion of the laws, court decisions, and federal agency guidelines that govern employee selection.

## STRUCTURE OF THE LEGAL SYSTEM

Let us begin by taking a quick look at how the legal system of the United States is structured and identify those who play a role. The U.S. Constitution is the supreme or highest law, and it provides certain protections for working people. In the Constitution, certain powers and limitations are assigned to the federal government, whereas other powers are handed down to the states. Individual states have their own state constitutions. These must be consistent with the U.S. Constitution. For example, if a proposal to amend a state constitution is found to be in conflict, it cannot stand because the U.S. Constitution is the higher law. This is what it means for something to be "unconstitutional."

The federal government regulates certain activities of the nation, such as those involving relationships between states. Other activities, such as those relating to employment, may be shared with the state governments. Federal law governs employment issues, including the minimum wage, employee tax withholding, and unfair employment discrimination. State and local governments sometimes regulate slightly different employment questions, such as whether to allow benefits for domestic partners comparable to those for spouses. State laws also may address the same issues as federal law. The question of which law takes precedent depends on what the state law requires. If state laws provide less protection than the federal, then federal law prevails. However, state laws sometimes provide broader protection than federal law. In this case, an employer first must meet the more stringent state requirement. In so doing, the employer also meets the relatively less demanding federal requirement.

The U.S. Congress frames and passes laws. Similarly, at the state and local levels, laws and ordinances are enacted by state legislatures and local governing bodies. In all of these, some source of enforcement for the new law must be identified. Regulatory agencies are established for this purpose. In addition, the courts provide for enforcement. Decisions of the courts and guidance provided by regulatory agencies function as directives on how people must comply with the law. In actuality, neither court decisions nor agency guidelines are law per se. However, they function to interpret, explain, and uphold existing laws. Court decisions and agency guidelines are especially helpful on points at which the law is unclear or silent. In fact, in some areas where no formal law has been enacted, federal and state court decisions function in place of the law. This is known as "common law."

## The Judicial System

Within the judicial system of government, there is a hierarchy comparable to that of the lawmaking system. Figure 6.1 depicts this hierarchy and shows the routes that employees may take to have their complaints heard. The judicial system includes the U.S. Supreme Court and a number of lower courts. The Supreme Court is superior to all other courts. This includes U.S. courts of appeal and district courts. It also includes courts at the state level—a state's supreme court, state appellate or appeals courts, and district courts. U.S. district courts hear cases on issues that are under federal jurisdiction; that is, those relating to the Constitution or to federal law. Appeals of district court decisions are directed to one of the U.S. courts of appeal. These courts are established by region and are commonly referred to as "circuit" courts. For example, the Ninth Circuit covers the West Coast region. State courts reflect a similar structure and process. Cases are heard at the lowest level in state district courts. Appeals of state district court decisions go to the state appellate courts, and these may be reviewed by the state's supreme court.

Although it does not always do so, the U.S. Supreme Court may review decisions of either the U.S. circuit courts or the state supreme courts. In this chapter, you will learn about many cases that the Supreme Court chose to review. For example, in *Cleveland Board of Education v. LaFleur* (1974), the Supreme Court reviewed court of appeal decisions in two different circuits

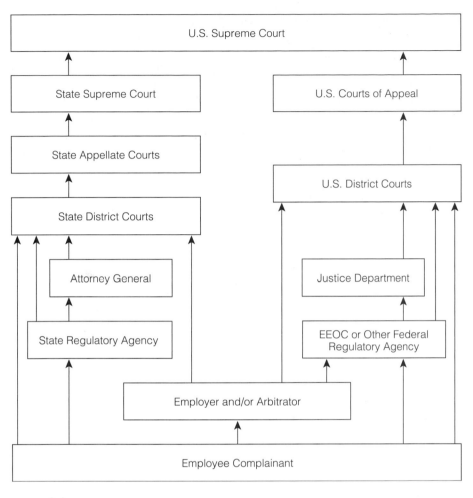

**FIGURE 6.1**

Multiple possible routes of a complaint made by an employee through the legal system hierarchy.

Adapted from *Legal Aspects of Personnel Selection in the Public Service,* by L. W. Seberhagen, M. D. McCollum, and C. D. Churchill, 1972, Chicago: International Personnel Management Association.

concerning the constitutionality of mandatory pregnancy-leave policies. These policies had been established by local school boards in Ohio and Virginia. In both school districts, pregnant teachers were required to take unpaid leave some months prior to giving birth. The circuit court decisions concerning these mandatory leave requirements were contradictory. The Fourth Circuit found the Virginia requirements to be acceptable, whereas the Sixth Circuit judged the Ohio requirements as unconstitutional. The Supreme Court concluded that the leave requirements, in fact, were in violation of the teachers' constitutional rights.

## Constitutional Amendments Related to Employment

Certain amendments to the U.S. Constitution, although not specific to employment, nonetheless protect individuals' employment rights. The Fifth Amendment is directed toward agencies of the federal government. It provides that a person shall not be deprived of life, liberty, or property unless there is "due process of law." The Fifth Amendment has wide applicability, and the concept of "due process" expresses an ideal of fairness. Cases not covered by other laws may be brought to court based on a charge that due process has been violated. For example, in *Frontiero v. Richardson* (1993), the U.S. Supreme Court reviewed a case involving a married female Air Force officer who alleged that the application of certain military service regulations had violated her Fifth Amendment rights to due process of law. The officer had sought to increase benefits for her spouse as a "dependent," but she was unable to meet the requirement that he be dependent on her for more than half of his support. Under the same regulations, male service members' spouses were considered as dependents regardless of whether they were dependent on their husbands for any part of their support. The Supreme Court ruled that the military regulations, which used classifications based on sex, did violate the Fifth Amendment and were unconstitutional.

**Fourteenth Amendment**    The Fourteenth Amendment to the U.S. Constitution is addressed to state governments. It includes the "due process" clause and also states that citizens shall be accorded "equal protection under the law." The amendment was passed soon after the Civil War and was meant to protect the rights of newly freed slaves. However, it yields protection to all citizens. In addition, the concept of "liberty," which appears in both the Fourteenth and Fifth Amendments, has been interpreted to encompass a range of employment-related freedoms. For example, the case of *Cleveland Board of Education v. LaFleur* (1974), described above, was filed under the Fourteenth Amendment. In its decision, the Supreme Court noted that the freedom of personal choice, including the right to bear children, is one of the liberties protected by this amendment.

**Early Civil Rights Acts**    The Fourteenth Amendment—and, similarly, the Thirteenth Amendment, which abolished slavery—granted power to Congress to enact legislation to uphold these constitutional rights. The Civil Rights Acts of 1866 and 1871 were designed to do that. The 1866 Civil Rights Act granted to all citizens the rights held by White citizens, such as in making contracts and bringing lawsuits. The Civil Rights Act of 1871 allowed lawsuits to be filed against state and local governments. The U.S. Supreme Court has applied the 1866 act in cases of employment discrimination, because employment can be understood as a way of making and enforcing contracts. As you already know from Chapter 5, a later Civil Rights Act was passed in 1964. This newer Civil Rights Act did not repeal the earlier Act of 1866. Rather, the two are considered parallel prohibitions of racial discrimination (Seberhagen, McCollum, & Churchill, 1972).

## FAIR EMPLOYMENT LAWS

All branches of the U.S. government have participated in the movement toward fair employment. The legislative branch writes and enacts laws. The judicial branch plays a role in interpreting and enforcing the laws. The executive branch participates in the process through presidential executive orders. In fact, much of our current employment law has roots in the mid-20th century, during which time more than one president issued executive orders denouncing discrimination (Kellough, Selden, & Legge, 1997). In 1941, President Franklin D. Roosevelt issued an executive order establishing a government program to combat employment discrimination. In 1961, President John F. Kennedy issued an executive order calling for employers to take "affirmative action," or proactive steps, toward fair employment. In 1965, President Lyndon B. Johnson prohibited discrimination by federal agencies and businesses holding federal contracts, with the issuance of Executive Order 11246. Although many presidents since have signed executive orders addressing discrimination, Executive Order 11246 remains important, as you will see later in this chapter.

### Equal Pay Act

The Equal Pay Act was passed in 1963. It was the first of several fair employment laws passed within a few years. Because I discussed the EPA in Chapter 4, I simply list it here. Recall that the law requires equal pay when equal work is being performed by men and women. Thus, sex discrimination in compensation and benefits is prohibited.

### Civil Rights Act of 1964

The Civil Rights Act of 1964 provides protection against discrimination in several different areas of life, including voting rights, housing, public education, and employment. The framing of the law began when Kennedy was president, during a time of civil unrest. At first, the legislative measure was written primarily as a means of prohibiting racial discrimination. There was considerable disagreement in Congress, however, and in an attempt to defeat the measure, its opponents added language that would prohibit sex discrimination as well as racial discrimination. The reasoning was that while many legislators might support protection against racial discrimination, they would be unlikely to want to extend protection to women. However, the effort to defeat the bill was not successful. The bill passed.

Title VII is the section of the Civil Rights Act that applies to employment. The Equal Employment Opportunity Commission (EEOC) was created by the act to function as the regulatory agency charged with ensuring that employers complied. In 1972, Title VII was amended to add state and local government employers to the list of those already covered—which included businesses, educational institutions, labor organizations, and employment agencies.

Title VII provides broad coverage of employment practices and specifies that it shall be unlawful for an employer

> (1) to fail or refuse to hire or to discharge any individual, or otherwise to discrimi-
> nate against any individual with respect to his compensation, terms, conditions, or
> privileges of employment, because of such individual's race, color, religion, sex, or
> national origin; or (2) to limit, segregate, or classify his employees or applicants for
> employment in any way which would deprive or tend to deprive any individual of
> employment opportunities or otherwise adversely affect his status as an employee,
> because of such individual's race, color, religion, sex, or national origin. (section
> 703a)

Certain exceptions were written into Title VII, section 703. These generally fall into three categories: (1) granting of preferences or preferential treatment, (2) permissible differentiation or discrimination, and (3) acceptability of employee selection strategies. First, Title VII does not prohibit employers from granting preferences to veterans, and under certain conditions, employers also may give preferential treatment to American Indians. However, employers are not required to give preferential treatment to individuals or groups because of numerical differences between an employer's workforce and the surrounding population. Second, discrimination may be permissible when there is a need to protect national security. Discrimination also may be permissible in a few situations in which religion, sex, or national origin is a bona fide occupational qualification, such as when being Jewish is required to perform as a rabbi. Third, preemployment inquiries, seniority systems, and professionally developed ability tests may be used, provided there is no intent to discriminate. If a particular employment practice results in a discriminatory effect, Title VII specifies that the practice will not be considered unlawful if the user demonstrates that it is job-related for the position and consistent with business necessity.

***Griggs v. Duke Power Company* (1971)**   In the late 1960s and early 1970s, there was a flurry of court cases in which widely used employment practices were evaluated against the requirements of the new law. One case in particular is important. The U.S. Supreme Court decision in *Griggs v. Duke Power Company* (1971) set the standards for fair employment in at least two ways. The first concerned the importance of discriminatory intent. The second concerned evidence of "reasonable business necessity" for employment procedures that discriminate. Before Title VII was passed, the defendant in this case had openly discriminated on the basis of race in employee assignments. Black employees were assigned to jobs in which the pay for the highest position was lower than the lowest position in jobs held by White employees. Later, after Title VII was passed, the company allowed Black employees to transfer to other jobs but required the employees to have a high school diploma in order to transfer. At the same time, the employer instituted a requirement that new and transferring employees pass two aptitude tests—one measuring general intelligence and the other measuring mechanical comprehension.

The Supreme Court's review and ruling on this case defined points of law that would later become part of Title VII. First, the Court pointed out that, although the law does not require preferences to minorities, it does require that tests or other hiring practices not discriminate. The Court also ruled that it is not necessary to prove discriminatory intent. Rather, the *consequence* of an employment practice is the key to a Title VII violation. Further, if a plaintiff proves that an employment practice does have a discriminatory effect, then the practice is disallowed unless the employer can prove that it is reasonably necessary to the operation of the business. The Court decided that the use of tests and other measures can be proven to be a business necessity only if they can be shown to be a reasonable measure of job performance, such as through scientific evidence of validity. In this case, the Court concluded that the company could not use either the high school diploma or the general intelligence test because the evidence had not shown that these predicted successful job performance (U.S. Office of Personnel Management, 1979).

**Civil Rights Act of 1991**    Two decades later, the Civil Rights Act of 1991 was passed, which made a number of changes in the federal law. For example, the 1991 act extended protection to American workers employed in foreign branches of American companies (Geidt, 1991–92).

Most importantly, the new federal law was intended to modify certain decisions made by the U.S. Supreme Court in a 1989 case.[1] *Wards Cove Packing Company v. Atonio* (1989) involved minority workers who filed a complaint against their employer, a salmon-canning company, charging racial discrimination on the basis of an imbalance in the company's workforce. Most of the low-level, unskilled canning jobs were performed by minority employees, whereas the higher-level, noncanning jobs were filled by Whites. In Congress, three different aspects of the decision in *Wards Cove* were debated. The first issue was whether someone bringing a charge of discrimination

---

[1]This shows the balance of power that exists between the legislative and judicial branches of government.

would have to identify the specific practice that caused the discrimination. Or could a person simply cite evidence of a bottom-line racial imbalance? In this case, the Supreme Court had ruled that the specific practice had to be identified. In framing the Civil Rights Act of 1991, Congress agreed that the practice *should* be identified. However, when specific practices could not be separated out for analysis, Congress decided that a bottom-line assessment would be acceptable. On a second issue, Congress disagreed with the Supreme Court. The question concerned the burden of proof. That is, once a plaintiff provides persuasive evidence that discrimination has occurred, does the burden for showing whether the discriminatory practice is permissible remain with the plaintiff or shift to the defendant? In the *Griggs* case, discussed earlier, the burden shifted to the defendant, who then had the opportunity to show that the practice was job-related and demanded by business necessity. In *Wards Cove*, the Supreme Court ruled that the burden did not shift but, instead, remained with the plaintiff to demonstrate how the practice was discriminatory. The Civil Rights Act of 1991 overturned *Wards Cove* on this point. The act specified that if a legally sufficient case of discrimination is established, the burden shifts to the employer to provide evidence on business necessity.

The third point of debate in framing the 1991 act concerned the evidence used to defend a discriminatory employment practice. In *Wards Cove*, the Supreme Court held that the employment practice did not need to be essential or indispensable, but only that it serve a legitimate business goal. The Court had been concerned about requiring employers to meet standards that were too high. There was considerable controversy in Congress, also, over this point. Some legislators who supported the Supreme Court's reasoning argued that making the standards too high would simply result in employers using racial quotas for hiring in order to avoid challenges. Others argued that employers must be required to show evidence of a significant relationship between the employment practice and success on the job. The outcome was that the 1991 act was passed without resolving this issue. No specific language was included to define "business necessity." Therefore, as it was before *Wards Cove*, the definition of this term remains a matter for the courts to decide (Varca & Pattison, 1993).

## Age Discrimination in Employment Act of 1967

In 1964, the Civil Rights Act called for the U.S. Department of Labor to conduct a study on age discrimination. This study led to the Age Discrimination in Employment Act (ADEA), which was passed in 1967. The act prohibited employment discrimination against individuals because of their age and specified ages 40 to 65 as the protected class. This age range represented the period of life in which it was most likely that workers would experience age discrimination. The upper limit of 65 was chosen because it was the age when most people retired. However, studies conducted by the government over the next few years showed that many employees were subject to mandatory retirement at age 65. This finding resulted in a 1978 amendment to the ADEA that restricted mandatory retirement. The amendment removed the upper age limit entirely for employees of the federal government, and it extended the limit of protection to age 70 for employees of all other employers (Stone, 1980). In 1986, the ADEA was again amended to remove the upper age limit for all. Now, the ADEA prohibits employment discrimination on the basis of age for individuals over age 40.

**Court Rulings on Terminated Older Employees**   Several cases have been brought to court recently concerning an employer's right to engage in organizational cost-savings and terminate high-paid employees who are over 40. Does this violate the ADEA? The answer is not clear, but it seems to hinge on whether the cost-cutting measure is actually a pretext for age discrimination. For example, in a case tried in the California state courts, high-salaried older employees were laid off following a company buyout. The state appellate court decided that the employer's actions did not constitute discrimination. The court's opinion was that employers must be allowed to make economic decisions and may engage in personnel cost-cutting if they actually make the decision on the basis of costs (*Marks v. Loral Corporation*, 1997). However, the California state legislature passed a law in 1999 that effectively overturned the court's decision. The new state law says that differentiating between employees on the basis of salary in deciding who will be terminated may be discriminatory if older workers as a group are affected. This provision is at variance with certain federal circuit court decisions, and it is not clear how this will play out. Many employers will want to stay abreast of what is happening on this issue (Flynn, 1999a).

Similar employer actions have been examined in the federal courts. In one case, an organization had eliminated an entire job classification and laid off full-time employees after finding that the work could be done more cheaply by part-time employees. The Eighth Circuit Court concluded that the action was not a pretext for age discrimination even though the affected employees had been over 40 years old (*Tuttle v. Missouri Department of Agriculture*, 1999). The point is that terminations can be made for legitimate business reasons, but they must not be an excuse for age discrimination. Another case demonstrates this. In *Wichman v. Board of Trustees of Southern Illinois University* (1999), the Seventh Circuit Court decided that the employer had discriminated against an employee by terminating him because of his age. The employer had argued that the termination was part of a restructuring plan to reduce costs. Other evidence, however, indicated that this was a pretext. At a meeting in which the restructuring was discussed, a supervisor was reported to have commented that it was necessary to "cut down the old, big trees so that the little trees underneath" could grow. The little trees, of course, referred to younger employees who benefited from the restructuring.

**Older Workers Benefit Protection Act**    As I mentioned in Chapter 4, a law related to the ADEA addresses employee benefits. The Older Workers Benefit Protection Act (1991) forbids age discrimination in benefits among employees who are age 40 or older. In addition, it establishes minimum standards for waiving claims against the employer in connection with early retirement, layoff, or other termination. In this act, Congress legislated very specific requirements for what the waiver of rights must include. These are summarized in Table 6.1. Notice, in particular, that there are strict requirements for the time that is allowed for an employee to consider signing a waiver and reconsidering once it has been signed. The detail included in this law is notable. The U.S. Supreme Court decision in *Oubre v. Entergy Operations, Inc.* (1998) shows how important these specifications are. A severance agreement signed by the plaintiff in this case was found to be unlawful because it had multiple flaws. It gave the employee only 14 days to consider signing the severance agreement. It did not allow her the 7 required days to change her mind and did not mention the ADEA. The Supreme Court noted that it could not overrule requirements that Congress had so precisely defined. Employers are well advised to stick to the letter of the law.

## Immigration Reform and Control Act

Passed in 1986, the Immigration Reform and Control Act pertains to the employment of aliens. For our purposes, there are two important aspects to this law. First, employers are prohibited from discriminating against legal aliens, that is, those who are not citizens but who have been admitted to the United States for temporary or permanent residence. It is not unlawful, however, to show a preference for a U.S. citizen over a legal alien when the two are equally qualified. Second, employers are forbidden to hire or continue to employ illegal aliens. To establish that an alien is legally authorized to work, the law requires that an employer must determine that the person has the proper work authorization documentation and must file paperwork attesting to this.

## Disability Employment Law

Two laws contribute to the protection of persons with disabilities. The Rehabilitation Act of 1973 was the first of these. This law prohibits discrimination against disabled individuals in employment with the federal government and with federal contractors (i.e., companies that contract for federal projects). The second law passed was the Americans with Disabilities Act (ADA) of 1990.

**TABLE 6.1** — **MINIMUM STANDARDS FOR CLAIMS WAIVERS UNDER THE OLDER WORKERS BENEFIT PROTECTION ACT**

| Waiver Directed to | Waiver Requirements |
| --- | --- |
| Any employee or group | Are written in terms and language that the employee understands. |
| | State that rights under the ADEA are being waived. |
| | Cover no rights or claims that arise after the person signs. |
| | Offer a payment in exchange for waiving the rights that is greater than what the person is already owed. |
| | Advise the person to get legal advice before signing. |
| Single employee | Allow at least 21 days to decide whether to sign. |
| | Allow 7 days after signing in which to revoke the waiver. |
| Group of employees | Allow each employee at least 45 days to decide whether to sign. |
| | Allow 7 days after signing in which to revoke the waiver. |
| | Include information about those eligible for the action: |
| |     Employee class or group eligible |
| |     Factors determining eligibility |
| |     Job titles of those eligible |
| |     Ages of those eligible |
| | Include information about ages of those not eligible for the action. |

The ADA extends the prohibition against disability discrimination to all other employers who have 15 or more employees.

A disability is defined by the ADA as a physical or mental impairment that substantially limits a person's major life activities. The types of major activities to which the law refers are defined by the Rehabilitation Act. These activities include "caring for one's self, performing manual tasks, walking, seeing, hearing, speaking, breathing, learning, and working." The ADA states that an employer shall not discriminate against a qualified disabled person because of the disability, in job applications, hiring, promotion, compensation, or termination. A qualified disabled employee is someone who can perform the job, either with or without reasonable accommodation. An employer is required to make reasonable accommodation to the person's limitations in order to enable him or her to perform the job, unless this would cause the employer undue hardship. Reasonable accommodation might mean making the physical workplace facilities accessible and usable, or it might mean making other changes such as modifying equipment or revising work schedules. Employment selection procedures also must not adversely affect a disabled applicant, unless the selection method can be shown to be job related for the position and consistent with business necessity. In general, the ADA rules out preemployment medical examinations and inquiries about disabilities. However, under certain conditions, examinations may be required after a conditional offer of employment has been made.

**Court Rulings on Disability Employment**    Two cases have been reviewed by the Supreme Court, addressing an important question about disability. The question concerns whether mitigating or corrective measures should be considered in determining whether an ADA-protected disability exists. *Sutton v. United Airlines* (1999) is the key decision on this issue. The case involved sisters whose uncorrected vision was 20/200 but with corrective lenses was 20/20 or better. After being denied jobs as pilots, the sisters sued the employer claiming disability discrimination on the basis of their *uncorrected* vision. The lower courts rejected their claim that they had a substantially limiting disability. In the Supreme Court's review of the case, the primary issue was whether a correctable impairment constitutes a disability. Because the employees wore eyeglasses that corrected their vision, the Supreme Court rejected their claim of an ADA-protected disability. The Court noted that the law speaks concretely in the present tense. Although a person might become disabled if correction was not available, the ADA describes a disability as something that *presently* limits the person. With their vision corrected, the employees could not be considered as having a substantially limiting disability. The second case concerning corrective measures is *Murphy v. United Parcel Service* (1999). In this case, an employee claimed that his uncorrected high blood pressure was the basis for his employer's decision to deny him work as a driver. As in *Sutton*, the Supreme Court ruled that when controlled by medication, the employee's high blood pressure did not qualify as a substantially limiting disability.

These decisions on mitigating measures attracted a certain amount of media attention. Public reports and interpretations of the *Sutton* and *Murphy* decisions apparently led many advocates of the disabled to believe that the ADA would no longer protect against employment discrimination. However, analysis of these decisions suggests that by narrowing the interpretation of "disability," the focus of protection is more clearly directed to some 43 million disabled Americans whose impairments are not correctable and on whose behalf Congress framed the ADA. Further, the Supreme Court pointed out that the use of corrective measures does not automatically mean that a person's condition is excluded from ADA protection. Rather, such determinations must be made on an individual basis. For example, a correction may not be fully effective. Also, in certain circumstances, a corrective action itself might be disabling, as when medications have severe, negative side effects. This point is important. The Court held that considering measures taken to correct a condition is the only way that "disabling corrections" can be evaluated in determining the existence of an ADA-protected disability. "Disabling corrections" might include medical treatment that causes side effects such as severe drowsiness or nausea, and surgeries that correct one disabling condition but result in another, such as colostomies (McGarity, 2000).

## Conclusions

Protection against unfair practices is extended from the Fifth and Fourteenth Amendments to the Constitution. However, fair employment law in the United States was developed mainly during the mid- to late-1900s. Several federal laws were passed during that time that provided specific protection from employer actions that discriminate against individuals on the basis of their race, sex, age, disability, and other personal attributes. These laws were directed toward a range of employee selection practices, including hiring, compensation, and termination. Title VII of the Civil Rights Act was particularly important, not only because of the extent of its coverage but also because of the activity surrounding its enforcement. Here, the dynamic nature of the law becomes apparent. The federal courts are essential in interpreting and extending fair employment law, and Supreme Court decisions, such as in *Griggs v. Duke Power Company*, have resulted in Title VII amendments. Actions of the Supreme Court also have triggered legislative debate and the making of new law.

## IMPLEMENTATION OF FAIR EMPLOYMENT LAW

By now, it may seem as if an employer would need to hire at least one attorney simply to make sure that the company's human resource procedures are not discriminatory. Many large companies do employ attorneys and human resource professionals who know about employment law for this reason. However, small and middle-sized businesses may not be able to afford the expense of a legally trained staff. Instead, they rely on their own understanding of the law. They also may use government-provided resources for everyday needs, and call a lawyer only when additional help is needed. This may be the case where you work.

In Figure 6.1, at the start of this chapter, the paths for resolving complaints are identified. Notice that the employer represents an important basic step in resolving employment discrimination complaints. Developing a process for investigating and dealing with employees' concerns can be one of the most effective actions an employer can take. Complaints often can be worked out informally and inexpensively. In recent years, complaints filed with the EEOC have increased, and a great number of lawsuits have been filed. As a result, employer involvement in handling complaints has been welcomed. The Civil Rights Act of 1991 encouraged employers to develop complaint procedures, including negotiating settlements through arbitration. Under certain conditions, arbitration can produce a binding decision that can stand up in court. However, the process must be voluntary. Employees must not be deprived of their right to take a complaint to court.

## Court Rulings on Arbitrating Discrimination Charges

Arbitration itself has been an issue in several court cases. The government has long supported arbitration in disputes involving collective bargaining agreements between union and employer. However, is it legal to arbitrate antidiscrimination law? If so, can employers make arbitration mandatory? Two Supreme Court decisions demonstrate the differences in legal thinking about arbitration. The first was in an early case, decided in 1974. In *Alexander v. Gardner-Denver Company,* a union member filed a grievance contending that he had been wrongfully discharged from his job because of his race. The grievance was heard and decided in arbitration. The arbitrator found the termination to be proper and based on job performance. As a result, the charge of racial discrimination was not discussed. The employee then filed a complaint in federal court under Title VII charging racial discrimination. The complaint was not given a formal trial by the lower courts as it appeared there was no genuine issue remaining after arbitration. However, the Supreme Court reviewed the case and ruled that an individual could not be barred from filing a Title VII suit, regardless of the outcome of a union grievance (Fitz, 1999). In discussing the decision, the Court stated that an arbitrator's role is to interpret collective bargaining agreements, not to decide in matters of public law. Further, the Court interpreted the rights conferred by Title VII as being individual in nature, and as such, these rights could not be determined by collective bargaining agreements. By definition, such agreements are group oriented (Kim, 1998). Therefore, in this decision, arbitration was not an acceptable way to handle a discrimination complaint.

The next important case on this issue is *Gilmer v. Interstate/Johnson Lane Corporation*, decided 17 years later, in 1991. Here, the Supreme Court endorsed the lower court's decision to accept mandatory arbitration of discrimination complaints. In the *Gilmer* case, the employer had required the employee to sign an agreement stating that disputes would be settled through arbitration. When the employee was fired, at age 62, he sued the employer charging age discrimination. In court, the employer proposed that the dispute be sent back for arbitration in compliance with the signed agreement. The district court denied this, ruling that a discrimination complaint was not appropriate for arbitration. The circuit court reversed this decision and ruled that, in this situation, the complaint could be arbitrated. The Supreme Court reviewed the case and affirmed the circuit court's decision that the discrimination complaint was arbitrable. Unlike the union member in the *Alexander* case, the employee in the *Gilmer* case effectively had waived his own individual right to sue by signing the arbitration agreement. Thus arbitration was acceptable for resolving discrimination complaints when an employee had agreed to arbitration.

The case of *Duffield v. Robertson Stephens & Company* (1998) is a final example of the distinctions being made on arbitration of discrimination claims. In this case, as a condition of employment, the employer had been required to sign an agreement to use arbitration to resolve disputes and to waive her right to pursue discrimination claims in court. The employee later sued, charging sex discrimination, and further asked that the employer be prohibited from making arbitration mandatory. The employer responded by referring to the *Gilmer* decision, in which arbitration of discrimination complaints had been appropriate. The district court agreed and decided in favor of the employer. However, the circuit court reversed, observing that the Civil Rights Act of 1991 had effectively overruled the *Gilmer* decision in instances of mandatory arbitration. The court noted that although the 1991 act encourages arbitration of discrimination complaints, this does not mean that employers can force employees to resolve complaints in this way, even if they have signed an arbitration agreement. The Supreme Court has not chosen to review this case but has allowed the circuit court's decision to stand (Fitz, 1998).

So, what can we conclude? First, with respect to employment discrimination disputes, employers should not attempt to make arbitration mandatory. Employees have a right to have their complaints heard by a regulatory agency such as the EEOC and by the courts. Employment policies requiring arbitration of civil rights claims that an employer already has in place should be revised. Second, the employer is not prevented from offering voluntary arbitration. Undoubtedly, some employees will see an advantage in voluntary arbitration because it is generally quicker, cheaper, and less stressful than filing a lawsuit (Geidt & Cobey, 1999).

## Regulatory Agencies

As you can see, the judicial system represents a major source of interpretation and enforcement of the law on employment discrimination. Information on court decisions can be helpful to employers. Another source of interpretation and enforcement is the state and federal regulatory agencies. When a federal or state law is passed, some provision is made for monitoring, overseeing, and enforcing the law, and a government body is identified as having overall responsibility for this. At the state level, typically a "commission" or an "authority" is established and may be called a Fair Employment Practices Agency (FEPA). At the federal level, more than one regulatory agency may be identified. When the Civil Rights Act was first passed in 1964, many different federal agencies were involved and had overlapping responsibility for the regulation of fair employment practice. The number of those involved has been reduced, as has the scope of their responsibilities. At present, some responsibility for regulation remains with the U.S. Department of Justice and the U.S. Department of Labor—specifically, the Office of Federal Contract Compliance (OFCC). However, most of the authority has been assigned to the Equal Employment Opportunity Commission (EEOC).

The EEOC began operation in 1965 and currently has authority for enforcing Title VII of the Civil Rights Act, the Equal Pay Act, the Age Discrimination in Employment Act, Section 501 of the Rehabilitation Act, and Title I of the Americans with Disabilities Act. The EEOC is constituted by five commissioners and a general counsel. All positions are appointed by the president of the United States and confirmed by the U.S. Senate. Commissioners are appointed for 5-year staggered terms, and the general counsel for a 4-year term. In addition to its headquarters, the EEOC operates 50 field offices.

The main work of the Equal Employment Opportunity Commission is to investigate and resolve charges or complaints filed by individuals who believe they have suffered employment discrimination. Each year, between 75,000 and 80,000 new charges of discrimination are filed with the EEOC. In addition, complaints are referred by state regulatory agencies. The commission regularly carries a backlog of cases that are at some stage of progress. The all-time high number of such cases was 111,345 in 1995. However, special initiatives to encourage voluntary settlements improved the handling of complaints and resulted in a sharp reduction of the backlog in 1998. The number of pending cases dropped by more than one-half to 52,011. The initial handling of EEOC complaints involves identifying those that have potential merit. These are investigated to determine whether there is a "reasonable cause" suggesting discrimination. If so, the EEOC initiates conciliation to help the employee and the employer voluntarily resolve the issue. If conciliation is not successful, the EEOC may file a lawsuit or may issue a "right to sue" letter to the employee. On average, conciliation appears fairly successful. Between 1992 and 1999, 28 percent of the cases showing reasonable cause were resolved through conciliation (U.S. Equal Employment Opportunity Commission, 2000a).

In court, the EEOC files "friend of the court" (i.e., *amicus curiae*) briefs to present the commission's own position on relevant issues. It also files lawsuits on behalf of discrimination victims. In 1998, nearly $90 million in benefits was recovered through such litigation. For example, the EEOC filed a suit in a U.S. district court in 1998 against a large construction company charging racial and sexual harassment. The lawsuit arose from employee complaints reported to the EEOC concerning harassment that included racist and sexist graffiti in the public toilets provided for employees at the construction worksite. In early 2000, the case was resolved with a settlement of $1.3 million awarded to some

100 African American and/or female former employees. In addition, the company was required to implement a policy prohibiting harassment. In discussing the case, the EEOC trial attorney concluded that racial and sexual harassment was "no more acceptable at construction sites" than it was at other workplaces (U.S. Equal Employment Opportunity Commission, 2000b).

In addition to its primary work of investigating charges of discrimination, the EEOC has other responsibilities. The commission supports and provides funds for state and local fair employment practices agencies. It is responsible for providing public access resource materials, such as seminars and an Internet site (found at http://www.eeoc.gov/), and provides outreach and technical assistance to employers. It also develops and publishes guidelines that interpret the laws it enforces. A number of these documents can be found at the EEOC's Internet home page or by contacting a field office.

## Uniform Guidelines *of 1978*

Soon after the passage of Title VII, in 1966, the EEOC developed guidelines for employers describing what the law required and outlining how to determine whether an employment practice was discriminatory. At about the same time, the Office of Federal Contract Compliance (OFCC) also issued guidelines for federal contractors who were subject to Executive Order 11246. (Recall that this was issued by President Johnson in 1965 and that it prohibited discrimination by businesses doing contract work with the federal government.)

The two sets of guidelines were not in complete agreement on several points. Federal contractors were particularly disadvantaged. They needed to conform with the OFCC guidelines because they had federal projects under way. They also needed to conform to the EEOC's guidelines on Title VII because they were businesses in the private sector. Because of the conflicting messages between the coexisting guidelines, these employers often were at a loss as to what to do. As a result of this difficulty, the regulatory agencies made a new and concerted effort to establish a *uniform* federal position on discrimination. This led to the 1978 *Uniform Guidelines on Employee Selection Procedures*. These guidelines superseded the previous EEOC and OFCC guidelines, and applied to all who were subject to Executive Order 11246 and/or Title VII.[2] All four federal agencies that were involved endorsed the document, and each agency affirmed that it would apply the *Uniform Guidelines* in carrying out its own responsibilities.

The stated purpose of the *Uniform Guidelines* is (1) to provide a single set of principles that can assist employers and other users in complying with federal law that prohibits practices that discriminate on the basis of race, color,

---

[2]The *Uniform Guidelines* do not address an employer's responsibility under the ADEA or the ADA. Other guidance documents address those responsibilities.

religion, sex, and national origin; (2) to provide a framework by which to assess the proper use of selection procedures; and (3) to encourage all users to establish that their selection procedures are valid (section 1607.1b).

The *Uniform Guidelines* define and discuss the requirements in language that closely mirrors that of Title VII. First, users are identified as being any employer, labor organization, employment agency, or licensing or certification board that is covered by EEO law. Generally, the guidelines are addressed to employers of a certain size—those with at least 15 employees working as much as 20 weeks per year. Second, the affected employment procedures and decisions are described. The procedures are those used as a basis for making selection decisions, such as tests, job application evaluations, and interview ratings. The law applies to any procedure or practice that is used to make any employment decision. Employment decisions include hiring, promoting, transferring, demoting, and terminating employees, as well as selecting employees for training or other employment opportunity.

An important purpose of the *Uniform Guidelines* is to help employers determine whether their employee selection practices are discriminatory. Section 1607.3 defines a discriminatory practice as one that has an "adverse impact" on the employment opportunities of persons of any race or ethnic group or either sex, unless the procedure has been validated or otherwise is justified by business necessity. Defining discriminatory selection practices in this manner has important implications. Adverse impact is a practical or operational definition referring to the use of selection procedures that result in discriminatory effects. If an employer's assessment shows that a selection procedure has an adverse impact, it is discriminatory unless it is justified. However, if the procedure is shown not to have an adverse impact, for the purposes of the *Uniform Guidelines*, it is not discriminatory. I say more about conducting adverse impact assessments in a later section.

One can argue that an employer's attitude toward the employability of members of a sex, race, or ethnic group might be discriminatory and yet the methods of adverse impact would not reveal this discrimination. The concept addressed here is that of unequal or disparate treatment. Members of a sex, race, or ethnic group have been treated unequally when they are denied employment opportunities that are available to others, because of practices used in the past that are now known to have been discriminatory. For example, in the past, managerial jobs were reserved for male applicants by means of employment practices designed to disqualify female applicants. This past practice currently may affect the employment opportunities of women. The *Uniform Guidelines* comment on disparate treatment and recommend that members of the group discriminated against by a prior practice should now be allowed to qualify under less stringent selection procedures. Beyond this, there is little to instruct employers on resolving disparate treatment (section 1607.11).

TABLE

6.2    SELECTED EEOC REGULATIONS AND GUIDELINES

| Title 29 CFR[a] Part Number | Description |
|---|---|
| 1602 | Record-keeping and reporting requirements under Title VII and the ADA |
| 1604 | Guidelines on discrimination because of sex |
| 1605 | Guidelines on discrimination because of religion |
| 1606 | Guidelines on discrimination because of national origin |
| 1607 | Uniform guidelines on employee selection procedures (1978) |
| 1608 | Affirmative action appropriate under Title VII, as amended |
| 1611 | Privacy Act regulations |
| 1614 | Federal sector equal employment opportunity |
| 1620–21 | Equal Pay Act, and procedures |
| 1625–26 | Age Discrimination in Employment Act, and procedures |
| 1630 | Regulations to implement the equal employment provisions of the Americans with Disabilities Act |
| 1640 | Procedures for coordinating the investigation of complaints or charges of employment discrimination based on disability subject to the ADA and section 504 of the Rehabilitation Act of 1973 |

[a]Regulations and guidelines are published annually by the U.S. Equal Employment Opportunity Commission in Title 29 of the *Code of Federal Regulations* (CFR), parts 1600 through 1699. The CFR can be found in libraries, or it can be accessed online through the U.S. Government Printing Office.

## Other EEOC Guidelines

The EEOC has published several other documents explaining the laws it regulates.[3] Table 6.2 lists a selection of these documents. These documents can be instructive for employers. They represent the commission's interpretation of the law and also often include summaries of Supreme Court decisions. For example, current information is available defining what constitutes a disability under the Americans with Disabilities Act. The definition has been updated to include the Supreme Court rulings on the use of corrective measures, which

---

[3]As EEOC regulations are developed, they are published first in the *Federal Register* and later are entered into the *Code of Federal Regulations* (CFR), which is published annually. EEOC regulations appear in CFR Title 29, Parts 1600–1699. Many libraries carry the CFR. It also can be accessed online: http://www.access.gpo.gov/nara/about-cfr.html#page1

came from the *Sutton v. United Airlines* (1999) and *Murphy v. United Parcel Service* (1999) cases discussed earlier (U.S. Equal Employment Opportunity Commission, 2000c).

***Guidelines on Discrimination Because of Sex***    This document was first published in 1972 and was amended at later dates to further define sex discrimination under Title VII. The document identifies and discusses employer actions that can adversely affect someone because of the person's sex. In some sections, these guidelines clearly address the rights of both sexes. For example, it is noted that the meaning of bona fide occupational qualification (BFOQ) is limited in application. An employer's desire for an employee of one sex or the other because of the supposed preferences of clients and customers, does not constitute a BFOQ (section 1604.2). Much of the discussion, however, centers on the inequitable treatment of, or denial of opportunities to, women. The *Uniform Guidelines* indicate that some states may have laws limiting the employment of females, such as in jobs that involve lifting or working at night. However, these laws are discriminatory, and they are superseded by Title VII (section 1604.2). Employer policies that restrict the employment opportunities of married women are denounced as discriminatory and unlawful (section 1604.4). Employer policies that limit the availability of fringe benefits to women also are discriminatory. An example is when benefits are made available to the wives and families of male employees, but are not equally available to the husbands and families of female employees (section 1604.9). Also, a fringe benefit program must not treat pregnant employees differently than it treats other employees with regard to health insurance or leaves of absence. An amendment to Title VII—the Pregnancy Discrimination Act of 1978— made it unlawful to discriminate against women because of pregnancy and childbirth. The guidelines on sex discrimination note that employers must treat any pregnancy-related disability the same as disabilities caused by other medical conditions.

**Sexual Harassment**    In amending the sex discrimination guidelines, the EEOC has interpreted sexual harassment as an action constituting sex discrimination. Therefore, it is a violation of Title VII. Sexual harassment is defined as unwelcome sexual advances, requests for sexual favors, and other sexual conduct when this activity (1) is made a condition of a person's employment; (2) is the basis for decisions affecting a person's employment; and/or (3) interferes with a person's work performance or creates a hostile work environment (section 1604.11). This section of the *Uniform Guidelines* is written in sex-neutral terms, which means that either males or females can be sexually harassed, by either males or females. Sexual harassment can be opposite-sex or same-sex behavior, and it can be perpetrated by either coworkers or bosses (U.S. Equal Employment Opportunity Commission, 1990).

## Conclusions

Employers are participants in the implementation of fair employment law. They monitor their own employment practices, find remedies for unfair procedures, and may provide arbitration for settling disputes. Employers are instructed on meeting the requirements of the law by the EEOC and other regulatory agencies through their guidelines, legal interpretations, and commentary. The *Uniform Guidelines* are particularly helpful in informing employers about what constitutes a discriminatory selection practice. Nondiscrimination law is enforced through mechanisms involving both the regulatory agencies and the courts. Although the government generally keeps watch over employment practices, enforcement of these laws is based primarily on the resolution of complaints. Control comes especially through EEOC investigation of discrimination charges, conciliation efforts, and/or court proceedings.

## CONSIDERATION OF LAW IN EMPLOYEE SELECTION

Have these laws made any difference? Recent studies indicate that there have been gains in public sector employment. A study evaluating the diversification of state and local government workforces nationwide showed some improvement in minority employment (McCabe & Stream, 2000). The researchers examined data from 1980 to 1995, with respect to gender and Black/White racial composition of the workforce. Over the 15-year period, there was a pattern of gradually increasing employment of women, especially of African American women, compared to White men. In 1980, nationwide, these workforces were 48.8 percent White men and 6.6 percent African American women. In 1995, the percentage of White men had declined to 43.5 percent, and the percentage of African American women had increased to 8.5 percent. The percentages of other minority groups and White women also increased during this period, but not by as large a margin.

Friedman (1997) proposed that because of the federal government's role in enforcing Title VII, we might view the government as having a special responsibility for treating its own employees fairly. He described a 1996 study of the practices of federal agency employers, which was conducted by the U.S. Merit Systems Protection Board. The study looked at career advancement of minorities and nonminorities. There were three important findings: (1) The employment status of minority employees has improved in important ways since 1978. Minority employment in the federal government now exceeds that of the civilian labor force. Also, minority and nonminority employees in administrative and high-level professional jobs are being promoted at generally equivalent rates. (2) Despite these improvements, the career experience of minority employees is different from that of nonminority employees. Minority employees have not advanced as far as White male employees. The difference in advancement is not fully explained by differences in education and experience, and it may be due partly to subtle biases. (3) Different racial and ethnic groups vary in their perceptions of how minorities are treated in government employment. Many minority employees believe they have not received equal treatment, whereas nonminority employees generally believe that discrimination against minority employees is minimal. Thus, according to these studies, minority employment has improved as a result of fair employment law. Still, progress has been slow and equity has not been reached.

## Adverse Impact Assessment

For the purposes of evaluating whether an employer's practices are discriminatory, the *Uniform Guidelines* define employment discrimination as "adverse impact." Further, the *Guidelines* give detailed instructions on how to determine whether an adverse impact has occurred. The first requirement in assessing selection procedures for adverse impact is careful record-keeping. Employers must gather and record data on applicants and employees, including the sex and race or ethnicity of each individual (section 1607.4b). The race and ethnic classifications considered in gathering the data are those specified by the EEOC: White (non-Hispanic), Black (non-Hispanic), Hispanic, Asian or Pacific Islander, and American Indian or Alaskan Native. Employers must generate and keep records for all such groups that make up more than 2 percent of the labor force in the relevant geographic area. They must collect the data for each job in which selection decisions have been made. For smaller businesses (i.e., with less than 100 employees), the data-gathering process has been simplified somewhat. Still, an employer must keep annual records for each job showing (a) the number of applicants considered for hire or promotion by sex and race or ethnicity; (b) the number of persons hired, promoted, and terminated by sex and race or ethnicity; and (c) the selection procedures used in making these decisions.

Using this information, the employer determines whether an overall or *bottom-line* adverse impact has occurred in the selection process. Two assessments are conducted. One assessment uses a race/ethnicity breakdown of the data, and the other uses a breakdown by sex. (An example using race/ethnicity data is worked out in Table 6.3.) The basic procedure of adverse impact assessment is straightforward. It requires the use of two simple measurement concepts: (1) the *selection ratio*, which is the proportion of applicants who are considered acceptable in the selection process; and (2) the *four-fifths rule of thumb*, which is a decision strategy for determining adverse impact by comparing the selection ratios of different groups.

<table>
<tr><td>TABLE</td></tr>
<tr><td>6.3</td><td>EXAMPLE OF BOTTOM-LINE ADVERSE IMPACT ASSESSMENT</td></tr>
</table>

**Bottom-Line: 114 applicants, 21 hired**

| Race/Ethnicity | Number Applied | Number Hired | Selection Ratio[a] | Comparison Ratio[b] |
|---|---|---|---|---|
| White | 70 | 14 | .20 | — |
| Black | 20 | 3 | .15 | .75[c] |
| Hispanic | 24 | 4 | .17 | .85 |
| Total | 114 | 21 | | |

[a]Number hired divided by number of applicants.
[b]Smaller selection ratio divided by largest selection ratio.
[c]Adverse impact.

In a bottom-line assessment, the selection ratio is the number hired relative to the number applying. Thus, as you see in Table 6.3, the selection ratio for each of the groups is determined by dividing the number hired by the number of applicants. The next step in a bottom-line assessment is to highlight the group that has the highest selection ratio. This group's ratio is used as the standard against which the others are compared. Comparison ratios are calculated by dividing the selection ratios of the other groups by the selection ratio of the standard. These comparison ratios indicate whether each group was selected at a rate that is at least four-fifths, or 80 percent, of the most frequently selected group. If the ratios of the groups meet this criterion, then the employer may accept this as bottom-line evidence that there was no adverse impact. In this case, no further analysis or other action is required. However, if any of the groups were selected at a rate less than 80 percent of the standard, then the criterion is not met and the employer should conclude that adverse impact has occurred.

When a bottom-line assessment shows that an adverse impact has occurred, the employer must conduct an additional and slightly different adverse impact assessment. It uses the same basic procedures but is conducted on each component of the selection process. The purpose of this component assessment is to isolate the source of the effect that was shown by the bottom-line assessment. Often, a selection process contains multiple components, and sometimes these operate as "hurdles," in that an applicant must "pass" on one selection component in order to be considered in the next. To do an adverse impact assessment on the selection components, an analyst breaks down the data per measure and does an assessment for each. An example is shown in Table 6.4. This example uses the data from the bottom-line assessment in Table 6.3 and includes two measures—a test and an interview. In the analysis

| TABLE 6.4 | EXAMPLE OF ADVERSE IMPACT ASSESSMENT OF SELECTION COMPONENTS: TWO MEASURES |

**1. Test: 115 applicants tested, 49 passed test**

| Race/Ethnicity | Number Tested | Number Passed Test | Selection Ratio[a] | Comparison Ratio[b] |
|---|---|---|---|---|
| White | 70 | 32 | .46 | — |
| Black | 20 | 7 | .35 | .76[d] |
| Hispanic | 24 | 10 | .42 | .91 |
| Total | 114 | 49 | | |

**2. Interview: 49 interviewed, 21 passed interview and hired**

| Race/Ethnicity | Number Interviewed | Number Passed Interview | Selection Ratio[c] | Comparison Ratio[b] |
|---|---|---|---|---|
| White | 32 | 14 | .44 | — |
| Black | 7 | 3 | .43 | .98 |
| Hispanic | 10 | 4 | .40 | .91 |
| Total | 49 | 21 | | |

[a]Number who passed test divided by number tested.
[b]Smaller selection ratio divided by largest selection ratio.
[c]Number who passed interview divided by number interviewed.
[d]Adverse impact.

of the first selection component, we enter the number of unscreened applicants and compare this to the numbers who passed on this first measure. In each analysis of the selection components, the data to be compared are the numbers who were considered by the measure compared to the numbers who passed on the measure. In the assessment of the final component, the number who passed the previous hurdle is compared to the number who were hired. As the example shows, each of these component analyses involves (1) calculating selection ratios, (2) identifying the group that most frequently passed on each measure, and (3) determining whether the four-fifths criterion is met. Through this process, the source of the adverse effect that was indicated in the bottom-line assessment is exposed.

In making their investigations, the EEOC ordinarily uses the four-fifths rule to determine whether discrimination exists in employee selection. Most employers should use this rule also. The rationale for using the four-fifths rule is that, in most situations, it is appropriate and practical and can easily be administered by most employers. However, it is sometimes necessary to calculate the statistical significance of differences in selection rates. When large numbers of new employees are hired, for example, employers are cautioned that differences in the selection ratios of groups may appear small but still may constitute adverse impact. If a great many were hired and the bottom-line assessment shows that a "near effect" has occurred—that is, the selection ratio of one group is barely 80 percent of the standard—then a statistical test of the difference is needed. On the other hand, there are occasions in which the sample is so small that reason alone suggests that a difference exposed by the four-fifths rule is actually due to chance. For example, sometimes the difference between the selection ratio of a group, when compared to the group used as the standard, is so unstable that selecting one more person in the comparison group and one fewer person in the standard completely shifts the "adverse impact" from one group to the other. Here, the four-fifths rule does not perform as an indicator of adverse impact, and the EEOC does not expect an employer to take action in such a case (U.S. Equal Employment Opportunity Commission, 1979).

**Employer Alternatives**    If an employer discovers that adverse impact exists in one or more components of a selection procedure, then action must be taken. The *Uniform Guidelines* identify a number of alternatives that are available to employers. One alternative is to demonstrate, through a rigorous validation study, that the measure showing adverse impact is a valid predictor of job performance. The *Uniform Guidelines* addresses the issue of validation by presenting detailed procedures on how to prepare for and conduct validation studies (section 1607.5).[4] A second alternative action is suggested when the selection measure showing adverse impact cannot be validated. For example, an employer may have been using an informal or unscored procedure, such as an unstructured interview. Here, the employer has the option of eliminating the procedure or modifying it into a measure that is formal, scorable, and possible to validate. A third alternative is for an employer to exchange the troublesome measure for another procedure that is job related and will minimize or eliminate the adverse impact. Generally, employers are advised that when two or more procedures are available that have substantially equal validity, they should use the procedure that has less adverse impact. In discussing this option, the *Uniform Guidelines* indicate that it is permissible and may be helpful to combine measures into a composite (section 1607.3b).

**Research on Alternative Measures**    In the third alternative action, the *Uniform Guidelines* suggest that employers can choose measures that have equal validity, but less adverse impact. It appears, however, that in 1978 when the *Guidelines* were published this was less a reality than a reasonable-sounding hypothesis. Early on, when employers looked for selection tests that

---

[4]I discuss validation studies in Chapter 7.

had high validity and low adverse impact, usually they found one or the other, but not the two in combination. Cognitive ability tests, for example, have been found to have high validity for predicting job performance in most and perhaps all jobs. However, these tests also show adverse impact on racial minorities. For example, some studies have found that differences in the group mean scores of White and Black test takers are equal to about one standard deviation (Gottfredson, 1988; Hunter, 1986; Hunter & Hunter, 1984). An average score difference of this size is extremely influential in adverse impact assessments. According to one analysis, a cognitive ability test showing a difference of one standard deviation between groups will have an adverse impact in all cases except when an employer makes very little use of the test and lowers the passing score to a point that 95 percent of all those who take the test pass it (Sackett & Ellingson, 1997). Of course, this is hardly an effective use of cognitive ability tests. In fact, if employers plan to hire 95 percent of those who take a test, they may as well not use the test at all. Because well-developed cognitive ability tests are highly capable of predicting job performance, employers typically are interested in using them in a moderately selective fashion, at least, such as in accepting no more than 25 to 50 percent of those who apply.

Researchers presently are exploring the possibility of combining measures that show low adverse impact with high-validity cognitive ability tests to create a composite that hopefully will perform as suggested by the *Uniform Guidelines*. Researchers have proposed that carefully structured interviews, as well as measures of personality and biographical data, might have potential for reducing adverse impact when combined with a cognitive ability test. One study found that such a composite did show lower adverse impact than the cognitive ability test alone, but not by much. Only when the composite was used in a very unselective manner—that is, in which 90 percent of those assessed were accepted as passing, was there no adverse impact. Also, including measures that individually show low adverse impact did not always reduce the composite's level of adverse impact. Sometimes, in fact, adverse impact was higher in the composite than when the cognitive ability test was used alone (Schmitt, Rogers, Chan, Sheppard, & Jennings, 1997).

Other research has explored the use of personality tests in a composite with a cognitive ability test. Certain aspects of personality—specifically, work orientation and conscientiousness—have been used to predict performance on many jobs (Barrick & Mount, 1991). These measures do not show the same high validity for predicting job performance that cognitive ability tests do. However, adverse impact is lower (Ones, Viswesvaran, & Schmidt, 1993). Some researchers suggest that cognitive ability and personality may predict different dimensions of job performance (Hattrup, Rock, & Scalia, 1997). Most studies would not have revealed this because job performance usually is treated as a single dimension, and varied test scores are compared to the same overall measure of job performance. Hattrup et al. (1997) proposed that cognitive ability tests may be better able to predict task performance, whereas tests assessing the work orientation aspect of personality may better predict contextual work performance. (Contextual work behavior is more related to the organization's climate and culture than it is to the technical aspects of work.) Organizations likely have different needs for emphasizing either task performance or contextual performance, and so it would be helpful in using test scores if they knew how to give more weight to one dimension of performance relative to the other. In their research, Hattrup et al. (1997) found that work orientation in personality correlated more strongly with contextual performance than with task performance, while the reverse was true for cognitive ability. They also found that adverse impact could be reduced by emphasizing the prediction of the work context dimension of performance. However, contextual performance had to be weighted very heavily, for example, counting as much as five times that of task performance. Even then, adverse impact was not removed unless the composite was used rather unselectively to pass 80 percent of those taking the combined test. These findings suggest that only for an organization that values contextual performance much more than task performance is such a composite likely to be of value. In that case, the personality test alone might be more helpful than the composite.

A field study further showed the limited effectiveness of using a personality and cognitive ability test composite (Ryan, Ployhart, & Friedel, 1998). These researchers gathered data from two groups of applicants for firefighter and police officer jobs. They conducted analyses showing the effect on adverse impact of (1) using a cognitive ability test alone, (2) using a personality test alone, and (3) combining the tests in a composite. In the police officer sample, the analyses showed that adding a personality test did not compensate for the adverse impact of the cognitive ability test. At moderate to low selectivity—where 50 percent or less pass on the measure—there was adverse impact against African Americans regardless of whether or not the personality test was used. In the firefighter sample, similar effects were found. At moderate to low selectivity, the cognitive ability test, used alone or in combination, showed adverse impact against African Americans. When one scale on the personality test was analyzed separately, it showed no adverse impact on the traditionally protected groups (African Americans, Hispanics, and women). In contrast, however, it showed adverse impact on male and White applicants. Thus, the composite did not yield the hoped-for effects in the field setting.

In conclusion, the research has not supported the proposal offered in the *Uniform Guidelines* that valid selection procedures that show no adverse impact are readily available. Personality tests have characteristics suggesting that they might be good alternatives for certain procedures that show adverse impact. That is, they are formal and scorable, and they are less open to bias than informal, unscorable procedures. They also show less adverse impact than cognitive ability tests. However, they do not show the same high validity for predicting job performance that cognitive ability tests do. Further, the studies have not been able to support the hypothesis that a composite with high validity and low adverse impact results from combining these measures. Although yet hopeful that such a composite can be developed, the researchers have not found that combining personality and cognitive ability tests is effective in this regard. They warn employers to proceed cautiously when thinking of adding personality tests, especially if their main purpose is to reduce adverse impact shown by cognitive ability testing. A composite using a personality test is not likely to have the desired effect.

## Affirmative Action

Affirmative action was one of the most controversial and hotly contested issues of the latter part of the 20th century. Throughout Title VII's 35-year existence, the regulatory agencies, the courts, and employers alike have been challenged by affirmative action. Some observers question whether the practice can endure (Kellough et al., 1997). How have we come to this point? What will be the ultimate outcome for affirmative action?

In order to evaluate the impact of political activity surrounding this issue, we need to be clear on our terms. In some popular press reports, "affirmative action" is used to express the entire arena of fair employment law and litigation. However, this is a misuse of the term, and it does not help our understanding of events. The first purpose of this section is to define "affirmative action" and relate it to other concepts of equal employment opportunity. Then, we can address the question of what may come from the controversy.

### Affirmative Action as Related to Adverse Impact and Recruitment

The assessment and remediation of adverse impact is a routine practice through which employers must make a sincere effort to avoid discriminatory action. As such, this routine practice is sometimes considered to be "passive" nondiscrimination. Early in the history of EEO law, it was reasoned that if employers refrained from discrimination in employee selection, eventually there would be equal employment opportunity among men and women of different races. However, it also was recognized that this would take a very long time. In 1965, President Johnson spoke about the need to take a more active step in helping people overcome the years of past discrimination. Something more than passive nondiscrimination would be needed. An "affirmative" action would have to be taken in order to move the nation more quickly toward equality. At that time, it was generally recognized and accepted that one such effort would be the active recruitment of job applicants. Employers would have to reach out to minority members and women and urge them to apply for job openings. The idea was that if these individuals were in the applicant pool, then by using nondiscriminatory selection procedures, employers could hire minority members in greater numbers.

Recruitment of minority and female applicants was an obvious extension of nondiscriminatory law. It was considered a proactive step that the EEOC would take into account in their investigations. The introductory section of the 1978 *Uniform Guidelines* as published in the *Federal Register* noted that in certain situations the routine procedure for assessing adverse impact would not automatically be applied: "An employer who has conducted an extensive recruiting campaign may have a larger than normal pool of applicants" (p. 38291). Therefore, the application of the four-fifths rule might make the employer appear to have engaged in discriminatory action when in fact it was just the opposite. This meant that the EEOC would consider active recruitment to be a valuable affirmative action and would take this into account in evaluating adverse impact.

**Affirmative Action as Related to Employee Selection**    At the time the civil rights bill was being debated in Congress, employers were concerned about what such a law would require with respect to their selection procedures. As a result, certain assurances were written into Title VII for the benefit of employers. For one, Congress authorized the use of tests for selection purposes. It was not considered unlawful for an employer to administer and use the results of any professionally developed ability test if the test was not used to discriminate (section 703h).

A second assurance directed to employers in Title VII was that they would not be *required* "to grant preferential treatment to any individual or to any group because of the race, color, religion, sex, or national origin of such individual or group on account of an imbalance which may exist" in the numbers employed relative to the labor supply (section 703j). However, in 1965, President Johnson's Executive Order 11246 conveyed a somewhat different message concerning preferences than Title VII had. Recall that the order focused on prohibiting employment discrimination in the federal government and called for special efforts to increase the number of minorities in federal jobs. In 1969, the OFCC took the first aggressive step toward affirmative action that went beyond recruitment and influenced the selection process. In what was known as the "Philadelphia Plan," the OFCC established employment targets for the construction trades in the Philadelphia area. Contractors who submitted bids for federal projects in the area were required to include details about their plans for affirmative action before their bids would be considered. An affirmative action plan had to specify the contractor's goals for hiring Black employees and include timetables for reaching those goals (Lee, 1999). The purpose of making affirmative action obligatory and focusing on their hiring practices was to get federal contractors to address the underutilization of minority employees. Still, employers were told they were not required to hire anyone who did not have the needed qualifications. What was expected was a "good faith" effort to reach the stated goals (Jones, 1985; Kellough et al., 1997).

This extension of affirmative action into the selection process was controversial from the start. Kellough et al. (1997) noted that requiring goals and timetables formulated on the basis of race, ethnicity, or sex was a change which implied that preferences would be extended to qualified minorities and women in federal contract work. The selection process would not be neutral but, rather, would take account of an applicant's personal status.

In the 1978 *Uniform Guidelines*, the EEOC encouraged voluntary affirmative action, although it emphasized the point that affirmative action is not required of private employers. This statement is in keeping with the Title VII section cited above, in which employers were assured that preferential treatment would not be required in order to remedy an existing racial or gender imbalance in their workforces. However, the message is ambiguous. Part of the difficulty has to do with the fact that, throughout, the Civil Rights Act does not identify a protected class as being a particular race, color, religion, sex, or national origin, which suggests that the law protects *all* of us against employment discrimination. However, assuring employers that they will not be required to give preferences muddles the clarity of this point. It appears that the language in this section has shifted so that a protected class—specifically, minorities and women—is implicitly defined. Similarly, the EEOC's interpretation conveys a mixed message. Employers are assured in the *Uniform Guidelines* that there is no intention "to impose any new obligations" regarding affirmative action (section 13b). At the same time, however, the EEOC presents an affirmative action policy statement that had been developed to help public employers design affirmative action plans. The policy statement is attached to the *Guidelines* as an appendix, and it is recommended to all private employers. It instructs users in the steps to take, including (1) analyzing whether the percentages of sex, race, or ethnic groups in the workforce are comparable to those in the relevant labor supply; (2) setting goals and timetables; (3) recruiting qualified members of underutilized groups; (4) revamping selection procedures; and (5) initiating measures to assure that qualified members of underutilized groups are included within the pool from which a selection is made (section 1607.17). Although the language of the policy statement is quite directive and pointedly includes the selection process, users again are assured that affirmative action is voluntary. It seems to me that the language of the appendix, like other sections on affirmative action in the 1978 *Uniform Guidelines*, reflects a very careful interpretation of Title VII, in light of Executive Order 11246, so as to neither require nor disallow preferences. However, as you will see, later EEOC guidelines are more strongly worded.

**Responses to Affirmative Action**    Supreme Court decisions over the past two decades show that it is not affirmative action *recruiting* that is questionable. Rather, it is selection-related activities, such as reserving opportunities for minorities and women (Riccucci, 1997). The stance of the Supreme Court has changed over time. At first, the Court was relatively supportive of programs that took account of race, ethnicity, and sex in selecting employees. Later, the Court began to apply strict standards in evaluating these programs.

The first Supreme Court decision addressing affirmative action was the *Bakke* decision (*Regents of the University of California v. Bakke*) in 1978. Although this case referred to academic admissions, it is relevant to employment because it involved considering an applicant's race in making selection decisions. The University of California had instituted a policy in which the medical school reserved admission slots for students of color. The Supreme Court ruled that this program of reserved admissions violated both Title VII and the Fourteenth Amendment's equal protection clause. However, the Court did not completely disallow the use of race in admissions decisions. Legality would depend on whether student diversity could be shown to contribute to education (Riccucci, 1997).

In other cases, the Supreme Court compared the affirmative action plan to what Title VII *permits* for voluntary affirmative action. In the case of *United Steelworkers of America v. Weber* (1979), a federal contracting firm had attempted to increase its minority workforce in certain skilled trades and had reserved half the slots in its training program for Black workers. The Supreme Court ruled that this practice was in keeping with Title VII because the plan reflected the purposes of the law. First, it extended opportunities to minority employees in order to compensate for past discrimination. Second, it did not unnecessarily trammel the interests of others. Third, it was a temporary plan, to end when racial balance was achieved (Gullett, 2000). The standard developed in this case later was used by the Supreme Court in deciding *Johnson v. Transportation Agency, Santa Clara County* (1987). Here, an applicant's sex was considered in a hiring decision. To fill a job opening for a dispatcher, the employer had selected a female applicant ahead of a male applicant with higher qualifications. The male applicant challenged the plan as causing reverse discrimination. The outcome of the case was about the same as in the *Weber* case. The Supreme Court found the affirmative action plan acceptable, viewing it as having been designed to eliminate a pattern of workforce imbalance. No woman had ever held the dispatcher's job (Gullett, 2000).

In 1989, there began a series of judgments that redirected legal thinking on affirmative action. Several court decisions addressed "set-aside" programs, in which public project funds were set aside or earmarked for contracts with companies owned by minorities or women. The cases were tried under the Fourteenth Amendment of the Constitution, and the decisions demonstrate the difference between the comparative permissiveness of Title VII and the strict standards of the Constitution. *City of Richmond v. Croson* (1989) was a precedent-setting case involving a municipal set-aside program. In deciding whether the program was constitutional under the Fourteenth Amendment, the Supreme Court applied what is known as the "strict scrutiny" test, under which a program must meet two criteria: (1) There must be a compelling government interest, such as when a program compensates for past discrimination. (2) The program must be sufficiently narrow in tailoring to meet its goals, such as when there is no effective alternative. The Supreme Court ruled that the City of Richmond's affirmative action plan did not meet these criteria; thus it was unconstitutional. The outcome was that both state and local affirmative action programs, which included set-asides, would be subjected to stringent criteria in judgments of their constitutionality (Riccucci, 1997).

At the time, the courts treated federal set-aside programs more positively than those of states and municipalities, presumably because federal programs had the support of the U.S. Congress. In 1995, however, this changed. In its ruling on *Adarand Constructors v. Peña, U.S. Secretary of Transportation,* the Supreme Court reversed its previous decisions on federal set-asides. Notably, the Court decided that the strict scrutiny test applied in the *Croson* case also would apply in cases involving federal affirmative action set-aside programs. Federal programs, like state and local programs, would be considered unconstitutional unless they met the strict scrutiny standards (Riccucci, 1997).

During the 1990s, affirmative action was debated throughout the nation. Several state initiatives were filed. Some state measures promoted affirmative action, but several others condemned it. In California, Governor Pete Wilson spoke against affirmative action in campaigning for his second term. The University of California decided to revoke its policy of considering race, ethnicity, and sex in student admissions. And California voters passed Proposition 209, an initiative designed to amend the state constitution so as to prohibit the consideration of race, sex, color, ethnicity, and national origin in actions that either discriminated against or granted preferences to persons in California's public education system, employment in the state's public agencies, or employment by contractors on state-funded public projects. Soon after the proposition was passed, it was challenged in federal court as being unconstitutional under the Fourteenth Amendment. The reasoning was that prohibiting affirmative action, which would have benefited minorities and women, amounted to an obstacle to members of these groups in receiving equal protection under the law. The district court agreed and ruled the measure to be unconstitutional. However, the circuit court reversed the decision. By prohibiting preferential treatment, the Court concluded that the measure actually had advanced the cause of equal protection (Kellough et al., 1997). The Supreme Court has not reviewed the case, allowing the circuit court's decision to stand.

The EEOC also has responded to the affirmation action controversy by strongly endorsing voluntary affirmative action. The commission issued special guidelines instructing employers on how to develop affirmative action plans under Title VII and assuring those who adopt such plans that they will be supported in this effort (U.S. Equal Employment Opportunity Commission,

1999). One purpose of the new guidelines is to recognize that many employers already "have changed their employment practices and systems to improve opportunities for minorities and women" and to affirm that this must continue (section 1608.1a). Further, in a remarkably explicit statement, the EEOC interpreted the protected class and purpose of Title VII by noting that "Congress enacted Title VII in order to improve the economic and social conditions of minorities and women by providing equality of opportunity in the workplace" (section 1608.1b). Continuing, the commission stated that it is difficult to believe that Congress intended to expose employers who support this ideal to charges that they have violated the very law they were upholding in their voluntary affirmative action plans. Thus, the EEOC stands firm on the subject of affirmative action. The guidelines assure employers that EEOC investigations of discrimination charges will take account of any affirmative action plan an employer has in place.

## Diversity Management

Diversity management programs go beyond the categories specified by the EEOC for equal employment opportunity and aim to produce a heterogeneous mix of people in work organizations. The purpose of these programs generally is to recruit, select, and retain a workforce that is diverse in varied ways. In broadly defined diversity management programs, the stated aim is to recognize the organizational value of developing a workforce of men and women with a full spectrum of racial, ethnic, cultural, linguistic, and individual characteristics (Slack, 1997).

Some observers view the affirmative action movement and its backlash as having been the source of workforce diversity programs. The impetus for diversity programs can be found within the civil rights movement. In the early 1960s, the primary issue under discussion, which led to the Civil Rights Act, was discrimination against Black citizens. However, this focus shifted as other groups also were recognized clearly as having experienced employment discrimination, such as American Indians. Gradually, the EEOC added other racial and ethnic minority groups and refined the list of those who needed to be considered in employers' reports to the commission. As the years passed, EEOC's definition of minority status came to recognize many different racial and ethnic groups.

There are problems with such listings. One problem has to do with who is left off of a list that is based on historic employment disadvantage. An argument could be made for including some regional groups, such as the Acadians in Louisiana, or other groups of European ancestry who have suffered employment discrimination in the United States, such as Irish Americans. In addition, although Title VII includes religion as a category for nondiscrimination, the EEOC has not yet identified groups who may have been victims of both ethnic and religious discrimination, such as Jewish groups. The listing could go on, and a case might be made for yet others who have been victims of discrimination because of personal characteristics such as sexual orientation.

Another problem emerges from the attempt to be all-inclusive in identifying disadvantaged groups. In the EEOC's listing of protected groups, we have drifted rather far afield of the original point of the early legislative debates. The civil rights movement of the 1960s was centered on the rights of Black Americans. Title VII and Executive Order 11246 implicitly were meant to improve the employment opportunities of Black workers. However, by identifying the specific members of a protected class, especially a class that includes many groups, the emphasis on African Americans has been diluted. Some observers are similarly critical of diversity management programs because this same broad-spectrum approach is being taken. The attempt of diversity programs to be fully inclusive has reduced the relative emphasis on prohibiting racial discrimination. As a result, diversity management, like affirmative action, diverges from the nation's original aim of improving employment opportunities for African Americans (Grossman, 2000).

It is probably too early to say what diversity programs will accomplish. So far, little evaluation research has been done. Ivancevich and Gilbert (2000) point out that most of what is published on these programs could be described as simply "hype and rhetoric." Case studies, which could be helpful in advancing our understanding of diversity programs, mostly have been promotionals or advertisements for a diversity-management consulting package. They present a single view of a program, use no discernible evaluation methodology, and are slanted in the direction of supporting the program. There is very little research that evaluates the organizational outcomes of diversity management, especially studies that use organizational effectiveness criteria to assess the innovation.

Researchers clearly are interested in studying diversity at the workplace. Ivancevich and Gilbert (2000) proposed a paradigm for research that calls for moving beyond hiring statistics to address the dynamics of interaction in diverse workforces. Similarly, Barry and Bateman (1996) theorize that diversity objectives and organizational constraints may be pitted against one another, resulting in "social traps" for decision makers. Using social psychology and conflict management reasoning, the theorists propose solutions that may improve the dynamics of these interactions.

## Conclusions

By its very nature in prohibiting discriminatory practices, EEO law has influenced employee selection in important ways. Through the *Uniform Guidelines*, employers learn how to evaluate their selection procedures for adverse impact and what to do if they find a discriminatory procedure. On the positive side, this routine practice of adverse impact assessment has resulted in more careful attention to the effectiveness of procedures used in selection. EEO law encourages the development and use of selection measures that are valid predictors of job performance. In no instance does the law require an employer to hire someone who is unqualified for the job. Employers also are encouraged to improve their selection practices, and researchers are looking for valid alternatives that do not show adverse impact. On the negative side, employers sometimes have simply discarded valid selection tests in favor of other procedures that do not show adverse impact, in order to avoid challenges and EEOC investigations.

Affirmative action has affected employee selection in other ways. Although it is not required of most employers, the EEOC encourages the voluntary development of affirmative action in order to improve employment opportunities for minorities and women beyond what is required by law. One form of affirmative action focuses on recruitment. Active recruitment of minority members and women indirectly influences the selection process by changing the composition of the applicant pool. Another form of affirmative action is more aggressive and directly affects selection. Goals and timetables for hiring underutilized groups are set in these affirmative action programs. Often, reserved slots or set-asides have been included, in which selection depends on the applicant's race, ethnicity, or sex. There has been a public reaction to these selection-oriented affirmative action programs, and court rulings during the 1990s were not supportive. The outcomes of the controversy over affirmative action are likely to influence the selection process. The initiation of diversity management programs suggests the direction the next change may take.

## Summing Up

The purpose of this chapter is to discuss fair employment law and to show how employment practices for employee selection have been affected by enforcement of the laws. Summing up, we can make the following conclusions:

- Employment law is developed and enforced by a balanced system of state and federal legislatures, courts, and regulatory agencies.
- Since the 1960s, fair employment law has provided protection against discrimination by race or ethnicity, sex, religion, age, and disability.
- Title VII of the Civil Rights Act is critically important.
- Supreme Court decisions have brought about amendments and revisions of the law on discrimination.
- Charges of discrimination may be resolved in arbitration.

- The EEOC is the designated regulatory agency for fair employment law and is responsible for investigating charges of discrimination.
- The *Uniform Guidelines* discuss ways to comply with Title VII.
- Employers must routinely conduct adverse impact assessments.
- If a selection procedure shows adverse impact, its use may be justified if it validly predicts job performance.
- Personality and cognitive ability test composites are being evaluated for their potential as valid, nondiscriminatory selection alternatives.
- Although encouraged by the EEOC, Title VII does not require affirmative action.
- Active recruitment of minority and female applicants is an extension of Title VII and indirectly affects employee selection.
- Aggressive affirmative action that directly influences employee selection has been the focus of federal lawsuits, public controversy, and political action.
- Diversity management is projected as the next evolutionary step in equal employment opportunity.

## InfoTrac College Edition

Want to learn more about the issues discussed here? Use your subscription to InfoTrac College Edition to access an online library of research journals and other periodicals. Go to http://www.infotrac-college.com/wadsworth and enter a search term. Any of the following terms can be used in a keyword search to find articles about some topics reviewed in this chapter.

| | |
|---|---|
| Civil rights act | Age discrimination |
| Immigration reform | Disability employment law |
| Religious discrimination | Minority employee recruitment |

# THE BASICS OF SELECTION MEASUREMENT

Suppose you own a business and you need to employ some people to work for you. Whom should you hire? What work would you expect them to do? How likely is it that they could successfully perform the work? How would you know that an applicant has high potential? How could you be sure not to hire an incompetent or unscrupulous person? Underlying these questions is the suggestion that there are important differences between people that one should consider in making selection decisions.

An individual differences perspective is the basis for psychological measurement. According to this perspective, people vary in their abilities and other attributes from one extreme to the other. The purpose of psychological measurement is to provide ways to identify how and to what extent people are different. For example, individuals differ in the level and nature of their intelligence. Large differences in intelligence are discernible to the average observer. However, an employer is likely to attract job applicants that are not very different in intelligence, and these small differences are not easily identified by the average observer. Therefore, if an attribute that is difficult to distinguish has to be evaluated for a hiring decision, an employer will need a sensitive measuring device.

In this chapter, I discuss the basic elements of psychological measurement in the employment setting and show how measurement contributes to sound selection decision making. Understanding the basics of measurement is essential in learning how to use a variety of tools and techniques for the purposes of employee selection or performance evaluation. The study of measurement is essential for those who design and develop precise selection instruments. It is necessary for HR people who use selection instruments in the business setting and for those who interact with consultants or contractors on selection projects.

# Psychological Measurement in Employee Selection

The use of psychological measurement permits us to assign numerical values (or scores) to observable indicators of a psychological attribute. A test of cognitive or mental ability, for example, is often used in employment. From the scores obtained on such a test, the user can infer the level of a person's cognitive ability in areas such as verbal facility or mathematical reasoning. Notice that the measurement is indirect. The instrument reflects the outward indication of an internal attribute. That is, the level of cognition is inferred from the person's test performance. Using a finely graded numerical scale, we can assign precise values to slight variations in attributes. Thus, individuals can be distinguished from one another more precisely with a high-quality test than by an average observer.

## *Measurement Precision*

The concept of precision is inherent in measurement. Precision refers to (1) the degree to which a measure can recognize subtle distinctions in the attribute being studied and (2) the extent to which the resulting measurement is exact. Procedures and instruments for assessing differences among individuals vary in terms of precision. Using some procedures, we simply classify individuals into a few broad categories. These are relatively crude measures. Other measures make refined distinctions on an attribute and allow a user to infer the magnitude of differences among individuals. Thus, as you will see, the level of precision in a measure determines the statistical procedures that can be used to analyze measurement data. The different levels of measurement precision are indicated by the term *scales of measurement*. Four scales of measurement have been defined, including the nominal, ordinal, interval, and ratio scales. You might find any of these scales used in employee selection. Examples of their uses and strengths are shown in Table 7.1.

**Nominal Scale**   The lowest level of precision is the nominal scale of measurement. At this level, individuals are classified into different categories. The categories are qualitatively different and mutually exclusive. That is, they differ in kind, and a person may belong to only one category, such as either male or female. In Chapter 6, you learned about adverse impact assessment in which individuals were classified by their sex, by race or ethnicity, and by whether they were hired or not. Notice that these classifications are nominal scale measurement data. Such categories are naturally occurring groupings. It is also possible, for convenience, to create categories in which to classify people. For example, an organization might survey employees about their reactions to work scheduling by having them check the schedule they liked best from the following categories:

1_____ day shift; 2_____ evening shift; 3_____ night shift.

| TABLE 7.1 | SCALES OF MEASUREMENT | | | | |
|---|---|---|---|---|---|
| | **Measurement Characteristics** | | | | |
| | Assigned Category | Rank Ordering | Equal Intervals | True Zero | Example |
| **Scale** | | | | | |
| Nominal | x | | | | Race/ethnicity classification |
| Ordinal | x | x | | | Ranks of employee performance |
| Interval | x | x | x | | Cognitive ability test |
| Ratio | x | x | x | x | Count of items produced |

Numbers can be assigned to the categories in nominal scale measurement to make data more easily recorded. For example, I have numbered the work shifts above. However, such numbers function only as category labels. They have no numerical meaning and should not be used in mathematical operations, such as in calculating a mean score. (Doing so would produce nonsensical results.) At this level of measurement, only limited data analysis is possible. Frequencies and percentages of individuals in each category can be calculated. A few statistical procedures using nominal data are available, such as the chi-square test, which shows whether the category frequencies are significantly different from chance occurrence.

**Ordinal Scale**    At the ordinal level of measurement, the same categorical information is available as at the nominal level. In addition, the numbers assigned to categories yield information about how the categories are related. Ordinal scale measurement is a hierarchical ordering or ranking of individuals from low to high on some attribute. This systematic ordering allows the inference that an individual at one rank has a higher level of the attribute than those in lower-ranked categories. Ordinal measurement is used frequently in work-related research and practice. For example, as discussed in Chapter 2, studies of occupational prestige ask participants to rank a list of occupations from the least to the most prestigious. Also, as you will learn in Chapter 14, performance appraisal sometimes requires a supervisor to rank-order subordinates in terms of how well they perform on the job.

The precision of the ordinal scale is greater than that of the nominal scale. Still, ordinal measurement is limited because the magnitude of the difference between ranks is not known. That is, we do not know how much higher one rank is, compared to the ranks above and below it. For example, an employee who is ranked highest by a supervisor is considered the best performer, but he or she may not be much better than the person ranked second. The person ranked second, however, may be a much better performer than the one ranked third. From ordinal data, we cannot tell how far apart the ranks are. We know only that there is a hierarchical relationship between the categories.

The numbers used to reflect the ranks have some numerical meaning. The median, or midmost, rank can be identified. However, we cannot calculate a sensible mean score because we do not know the size of the difference between ranks. Some statistical tests can make use of ordinal data. In addition, percentiles can be calculated and are a commonly used method of interpreting such data. As I discuss later in this chapter, the percentile in which an ordinal scale score falls indicates the percentage of other scores earned that were lower than this.

**Interval Scale**   Measurement at the interval level is even more powerful. Categorical information shows differences between individuals and there is a hierarchical distribution of scores, as there is at the ordinal level. In addition, precision is greater than in the lower scales because the scale units or intervals are known to be equal in size. That is, the difference between one point and another is the same across the scale. The advantage is that the numbers assigned to the categories take on added meaning. They express the magnitude of difference between the scores.

There is disagreement about whether much behavioral research actually reaches an interval level, mainly because the size of the interval does not always appear to be equal across the scale. However, work-related research and selection practices often are *accepted* as having interval-level precision. For example, ratings are used in a variety of work-related research, such as opinion surveys, and they are a common means of evaluating employee performance. For these uses, interval-level rating scales must be designed so that respondents will interpret the intervals between response categories as being of equal size. Here is the weak point in the argument that ratings yield interval-level data—the difference between rating scale points may not be equal in the minds of respondents. Another instrument, in which interval size equality might be more easily argued, is a written test. For example, a job knowledge test might be constructed with each of 100 questions worth 1 point. Correct answers on a test can be summed and individuals' scores can be compared. The value of the interval does not change in summed scores. Thus, the difference between test scores of 55 and 60 can be presumed to be exactly the size of the difference between test scores of 70 and 75, that is, 5 points or interval units.

The advantage of the interval scale of measurement is that it allows the use of many mathematical operations. With interval data, a mean score and standard deviation can be calculated to precisely describe the distribution of scores. Interval measurement also meets the requirements of many powerful statistical tests for testing hypotheses about the attribute being studied. Therefore, researchers often proceed as if they were confident that a measure had actually reached interval scale precision, in order to take advantage of the statistical tests that can be used with data at this level of measurement (Kiess, 1989; Shavelson, 1996).

Interval measurement has one limitation, as indicated in Table 7.1. There is no absolute zero point on an interval scale (as there also is not at the two lower levels). Certainly, a zero may be assigned to an interval scale point, but this is arbitrary, because there is no way to know what defines a zero amount of a psychological attribute. For example, on a job knowledge test, if a person answers none of the questions correctly, we cannot conclude that the person knows *nothing*. That is, we cannot assume that a zero test score equals zero knowledge. This is because we are not measuring knowledge directly, and we are asking only a sample of what could be asked on the test. Similarly, because there is no true zero, we cannot draw conclusions about how much of the underlying attribute an individual has, relative to others. In other words, we could not infer that a person who answers 50 percent of the questions correctly knows twice as much as someone who answers 25 percent. Only if we have a true zero point do we know that the unit on the test is equal to the unit of the underlying attribute.

**Ratio Scale**     The highest level of measurement is the ratio scale. This scale has all the advantages of the other scales. Also, a true zero point is known, which defines the absence of the attribute being measured. Ratio scale measurement is clearest in physical measures, such as height, weight, or arm length. These measures sometimes are needed in work-related research, such as in designing equipment that disabled employees can use. Ratio level precision also can be reached in some cases in which the object of interest can be counted (Bordens & Abbott, 1996; Shavelson, 1996). Examples are the number of errors made by employees on a quality-control task; the number of items produced by employees in factory jobs; the number of sick-leave days taken; and the amount of employee earnings. Some performance appraisal instruments reach ratio scale precision. In these measures, employee productivity is assessed objectively with a measure of production in which the units produced by an employee are counted.

The advantage of the ratio scale is that the attribute is *directly* measured. The zero point on the test is the same as zero on the attribute. This allows conclusions about the proportion or ratio of the attribute among individuals. For example, by knowing the zero point, not only can we conclude that one employee produces a specific amount more than a second employee, but we also can know that the person produces twice as much as the other. Knowledge of the zero point allows exact measurement of such ratios.

In selection measurement, the ratio level of precision is not often reached. For many human attributes of interest in the workplace, there is no absolute zero point. This seems to be no great problem, however, because measurement at the interval level is sensitive, and powerful statistical procedures have been devised for use with interval scale measurement.

## Criterion and Predictor Measures

Psychological measurement is used for two purposes in employee selection. First, an employer needs to know what work must be done and what constitutes successful work performance. The selection variable addressed here is the *criterion*. It is the behavior that the selection process is meant to predict. Second, an employer must get information about a behavioral attribute that might be associated with successful work performance. This is the *predictor* variable. This variable relates to the criterion and is used to predict it. The two variables are inherently connected. They are two parts of the same process. The term "selection measures" refers both to instruments used as criterion measures and to instruments used as predictor measures. The *use* of an instrument identifies it as either a predictor or a criterion measure. Some instruments, such as rating scales, can serve as either predictor or criterion measures, depending on how they are used.

How does an employer determine what are relevant criteria and predictors? The major source of information is a job analysis. Recall from Chapter 3 that a job analysis yields detailed information about the work that needs to be done and about employee attributes—such as knowledge and skills—that are required to successfully perform the work. This information is used to locate or develop measures of the necessary worker attributes, for use as predictor measures. By defining successful work performance, job analysis information also is useful for identifying appropriate performance criteria and developing an effective performance appraisal instrument.

## Developing a Selection Measurement Plan

Good selection decision making pays off. Although some employers consider the costs of employee selection generally to be excessive, other employers recognize the long-term value of making the right selection decisions. Research has found that when an employer can be very selective and hire only the best applicants, company performance improves, as does the company's image as a high performer (Becker & Huselid, 1992; Delaney & Huselid, 1996). High-precision measures give an employer the ability to be highly selective in hiring because these measures can identify applicants who will be productive and successful (Schmidt, Hunter, McKenzie, & Muldrow, 1979).

Employers can develop selection measures in-house or obtain them from outside sources. For many organizations, it is reasonable to do both. Instruments for certain uses will be available from commercial suppliers. However, measures that assess attributes unique to a job will have to be developed by the employer. Information about how to obtain and use existing measures and how to create new ones is available to employers through research journals and other academic sources. When a company's HR staff makes use of these information sources, the company benefits (Terpstra & Rozell, 1997). To determine exactly what measures are needed, a coherent selection plan must be developed. Russell and Peterson (1997) describe a procedure for planning through which an organization can realize its major goal for selection—that is, to become highly selective in hiring. The plan helps the organization stay focused on selection procedures that are valid, result in minimal adverse impact, and are not excessively expensive.

To do selection planning, we start with a job analysis. From this, required worker capacities and other attributes are determined. Next, the academic literature on tests and other selection methods is reviewed to identify possible measures that might assess these capacities and attributes. Study of the literature should yield a description of each existing measure or procedure that might be used. Details about these measures are recorded, including what attribute is measured, how accurate the measure is, how it is scored, and how much it will cost to use it. Using the information gained from the job analysis and the selection literature, we then evaluate the chosen measures as to their potential validity for assessing one or more of the required worker attributes for this job. At this time also, the efficiency and costs of the measures, and their likelihood of adverse impact, must be evaluated. The central feature of a well-conceived selection plan is a matrix showing a summary of information about necessary worker attributes and potentially useful predictor measures. An example of a selection plan matrix is shown in Figure 7.1.

In the process of constructing the matrix, the HR specialist discovers where existing measures can be used and where new measures will have to be created. Notice, in Figure 7.1, that enough information is given about the possible measures that an informed decision can be made about which to include in the final selection plan. For some worker attributes, more than one valid measure is identified. These alternatives can be weighed in terms of how much they contribute to the overall effectiveness of the final selection plan and according to their efficiency, costs, and potential adverse impact. In this particular example, the use of three existing measures (the math and verbal tests and the biographical inventory) can be arranged at a low cost. The other three measures would need to be developed specifically for this job and probably would be more expensive than the existing measures partly because of their developmental costs (Russell & Peterson, 1997).

**Information Sources on Selection Measures**    As mentioned earlier, employers can obtain measurement information from academic research journals. Two journals that frequently publish articles on selection are *Journal of*

Measurement Methods

| | Aptitude or Achievement Tests | | Interview | Self-Report | Simulation | |
|---|---|---|---|---|---|---|
| | Basic Math Test | Test of Verbal Comprehension | Skilled Trades Selection Interview | Environmental Reactions Biographical Inventory | Situational Judgment Test | Work Sample |
| **Worker Characteristics** | | | | | | |
| Ability to add, subtract, multiply, and divide and use formulas | X | | | | | |
| Ability to understand verbal instructions and warnings | | X | X | X | | X |
| Ability to communicate orally with others | | X | X | X | | |
| Ability to develop alternative solutions to a problem and choose the best alternative | | | X | X | X | X |
| Ability to work in a noisy environment | | | | X | | |
| Ability to work at heights | | | | X | | |
| **Other Factors** | | | | | | |
| Anticipated adverse impact | High | High | Low | Low | Moderate | Moderate |
| Anticipated develpment cost | None | None | Moderate | None | Moderate | Moderate |
| Anticipated operational cost | Low | Low | High | Low | Low | HIgh |

**FIGURE 7.1**

Example of a selection plan matrix showing measurement options.

From "The Test Plan," by T. L. Russell and N. G. Peterson, 1997, in D. L. Whetzel and G. R. Wheaton (Eds.), *Applied Measurement Methods in Industrial Psychology*, p. 133. Copyright 1997 by Consulting Psychologists Press. Reprinted with permission.

*Applied Psychology* and *Personnel Psychology*. These research journals are carried by college libraries as well as some public libraries and can be accessed in databases available on the Internet. Other sources of information found in libraries are the *Mental Measurements Yearbook* and *Tests in Print*, both of which are updated and reissued every few years. These reference sources contain descriptions of a large number and variety of tests, including tests that can be used for selection purposes (Conoley & Impara, 1995). Critical reviews and evaluations are written by testing experts. The *Mental Measurements Yearbook* also includes a list of test publishers who can be contacted directly for information about their tests and other measures. Be aware that reputable test publishers will provide potential users with detailed information about the development of a test and will be able to show evidence that the test is valid for measuring an attribute. If a test supplier is unable to provide such evidence, do not accept the measure. Many "tests" that are promoted in the marketplace have been quickly thrown together and are worthless.

## Conclusions

The purpose of selection planning is to find or develop measures that will allow an employer to be selective and hire only the best applicants. To accomplish this, HR providers must have access to thorough job analyses and to information on available selection measures. Because it is likely that not all selection needs can be provided by off-the-shelf instruments, the organization must be prepared to develop some measures. For this, knowledge of psychological measurement is required, and the developer must be able to access and use high-quality research on measurement issues.

Most human capacities that are of interest in the workplace are measured indirectly with instruments that assess indicators of an underlying attribute. Such measures vary in how precise they are. Although ratio scale instruments provide the most sensitive and precise measurement, few selection measures reach the ratio level. Most selection instruments are not ratio scale because the attribute of interest is psychological and there is no known zero point from which to start the measure. Interval scale measures are quite sensitive and provide more information than measures of lower scale. For some attributes, it may not always seem likely that a predictor measure can be found that yields interval scale scores. Rethinking the design of an ordinal scale instrument so as to use ratings sometimes can increase the instrument's precision to the interval level. This requires careful development in order to establish equal rating intervals. It is often worthwhile to make such an effort, however, because powerful statistical methods are available for interval scale data.

## REQUIREMENTS OF EFFECTIVE SELECTION MEASURES

The basic goal of selection measurement is to detect and gauge the extent of real differences among individuals. To reach this goal, the measures we use for criterion purposes must reflect true differences in individuals' job performance. Similarly, for predictive purposes, we must be sure that the instruments used can precisely measure levels of attributes required by the job. In actual practice, interval scale measures, such as tests and well-developed rating instruments, are usually the best we have for reaching these selection goals. Most of what I have to say in this section refers to interval scale measures, especially tests. However, keep in mind that the same standards of quality should be applied to any predictor or criterion measure.

## Standardization

The standardization of selection measures refers to control. In order for a measure to accurately assess an attribute, it will have to be controlled so that bias does not enter and spoil the results of the measure. Three aspects of selection measurement must be controlled: administration, scoring, and interpretation of scores. Most of what is known about standardization is discussed in terms of testing. However, the principles of test standardization are useful in standardizing any measure.

**Administration**   The administration of a selection measure is standardized by making sure that conditions remain exactly the same each time it is administered. These conditions include materials, such as instructions, test questions, answer sheets, and allowable aids or resources. Also, the time allowed for the test and the equipment, furniture, and other testing-room conditions must be standardized. In order to accomplish such standardization, test administrators often arrange for applicants to be tested in groups, and they put everything in writing. Questions and answer sheets are printed (either in hard copy or on a computer screen). Instructions are written down and given to a single test taker or are read by the test administrator to a group of test takers. In addition, the test is timed, and the testing room is maintained with well-functioning equipment and comfortable seating. The reason for this scrupulous control is that variation in test-taking conditions can hamper a test's ability to accurately measure levels of the attribute being tested (Cronbach, 1970).

   There are certain exceptions that can be made. Test takers who are disabled must be given special accommodations if the disability would not prevent them from performing the job but might prevent them from performing the test. For example, tests that require abilities that the job does not require can disadvantage a disabled applicant. A job that does not require vision might be performed by an applicant who lacks eyesight. If so, the test administrator must accommodate the person's disability, such as by providing a reader or a taped transcript of a written test.

**Scoring**   The possibility for bias in testing is especially great if rules for scoring are not specified and if those who score the tests are allowed to use their own discretion in deciding whether or not answers are correct. If a test scorer is allowed personally to decide the accuracy of a response, then the scorer's understanding of the question will influence the score, resulting in a contaminated measure. To prevent such bias from entering the scores, the test scoring must be standardized. Correct answers, or conditions under which answers may be considered correct, must be defined beforehand and a scoring key or guide developed so that the impact of the person who scores the test is minimized. In some selection measures, in which applicants report information in their own words, an evaluator or scorer uses a scoring guide as a template to determine whether the person's response could be considered accurate. In objective tests, scoring has previously been determined and the scorer need not interpret answers. Answers are either correct or incorrect. Such tests can easily be made machine-scorable to fully control scorer bias.

**Score Interpretation**    What does a score on a test mean? In some instances, a raw score can be taken literally. The raw score on a ratio-scale measure exactly reflects the true score. If your new bathroom scale says you weigh 152 pounds, this "score" needs no interpretation. (You might have various reactions to it, but you do know what it means.) However, as I discussed earlier, most selection instruments are not ratio scale measures. At best, an interval scale can be assumed, and often the measure is no better than ordinal. At these levels, a person's scores must be interpreted according to how well others scored. Otherwise, these scores have no meaning.

To standardize scores, a test is administered to a large sample of individuals who are similar to those who later will be taking the test for selection purposes. This group is the *standardization sample*. It is also called the *normative sample* because the distribution of the group's scores provides test norms that are used to interpret scores of later test takers. The *percentile* is a statistic that is frequently used to describe a score distribution of the standardization sample and to establish test norms. Raw scores earned by the sample are converted into percentile scores. A percentile score indicates the percentage of those in the standardization sample who scored below the raw score. Percentiles result in an ordered ranking of scores from lowest to highest. The median score of the distribution corresponds to the 50th percentile, which indicates the average performance of the group. The 25th and 75th percentiles identify the lowest one-quarter and highest one-quarter of all scores. When the test is used, new scores are interpreted against the normative sample. The percentile within which a new raw score falls indicates how well a test taker did compared to the normative group. A raw score that falls at the 75th percentile is relatively good, since 75 percent of the normative sample scored lower.

Percentiles are a useful way to interpret scores partly because they are easily understood by most people.[1] However, percentiles do not give a lot of information. They show the rank of a test taker's score relative to the standardization sample and indicate that there are differences among the people taking

---

[1]Scores on the Graduate Record Examination (GRE), a test required for entry into many graduate programs, are reported in terms of percentiles.

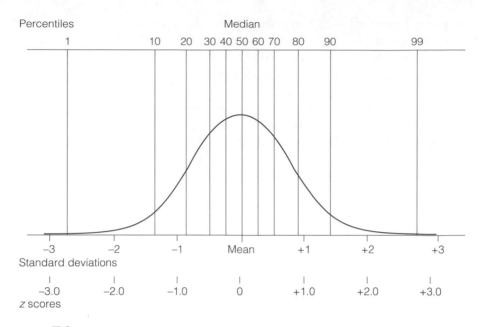

**FIGURE 7.2**

Percentiles and z-scores in a normal distribution. A percentile score represents the cumulative percentage of scorers at lower levels. Because most test takers earn scores near the median, the difference between midrange raw scores is exaggerated in percentile equivalents, whereas the difference between scores at the ends of the distribution is minimized in percentiles. This effect is apparent in the difference between percentiles of 40 and 50 compared to the difference between percentiles of 10 and 20.

the test. They do not show the actual size of the differences in raw scores. Percentile transformations of raw scores exaggerate the difference between scores that fall near the median and diminish the difference between scores that fall near the ends of the distribution. You can detect this in Figure 7.2. Notice that scores falling between the 50th and 70th percentiles, although 20 percentile points apart, would be less than one standard deviation apart. A score at the 99th percentile, however, would be more than one standard deviation from a score only 9 percentile points away at the 90th percentile.

If interval-level scaling of a test or rating can be assumed, such that the difference between scores is equal, then a more powerful statistic can be used to summarize the score distribution. Standard scores, such as $z$ scores, are more informative than percentiles because they show the distance between scores in a distribution. Transformation of raw scores to standard scores retains the exact relationship that exists between the scores. Therefore, if the intervals between scores are equal, this equality is retained in the standard score. To convert raw scores to $z$ scores, the mean and standard deviation of the raw scores are needed. Subtract the mean score from each raw score, and divide the difference by the standard deviation. The resulting $z$ score describes the distance of the score from the mean in terms of standard deviations. Hypothetically, $z$ scores can range from −4.00 to +4.00, although most scores will fall within three standard deviations from the mean, as you can see in Figure 7.2. When a $z$ score is 0, it is equal to the mean of the normative group. Standard scores are informative, although they can sound strange. To learn that a score of 0 is average may be puzzling to many people. If this is a problem practically, the scores can be modified to make them all positive (Anastasi, 1982).

## Reliability

The reliability of an instrument shows the extent to which it measures accurately and consistently. In reliable measurement, differences in a distribution of scores accurately reflect individuals' levels of an attribute. In other words, the reliability of a measure expresses the extent that the measure is free of error. Standardization of a measure improves its reliability because standardization controls error sources. Reliability also shows whether an instrument measures consistently. Inconsistent measures suggest that extraneous variables are affecting scores. For example, suppose a person correctly answers 45 questions out of 50 on one form of a test, but on a supposedly equivalent form given later, he or she answers only 20 questions correctly. Neither of the two scores can be trusted to indicate a reliable measure because human attributes are more consistent than this.

Empirical evaluation of a test's reliability makes it possible to estimate how much of a sample's score differences are due to error rather than to the true attribute. Generally, we think of an error source as being anything that is irrelevant to the attribute we want to measure. By standardizing test administration and scoring, we can control the operation of certain irrelevant variables that we suspect might influence test scores. For example, machines used in a test setting might vary as to how well they operate, which could account for some of the differences among test takers' scores. Also, the testing room might be quiet when one group is tested but noisy when another group is tested, which could make a difference in test scores. Obviously, known sources of error can be controlled. However, some sources are not apparent, and it may be unclear how they affect a measure's scores. For this reason, an estimate of reliability can help determine how much undefined error remains in scores.

In employee selection, evidence of reliability is needed for both predictor and criterion measures. The purpose is to determine that each instrument is accurate and consistent enough that it can predict its own scores. That is, a reliable measure yields scores that are associated strongly enough that knowing one score earned by a person will allow us to predict a second score earned by the same person. If an instrument cannot do this, then we cannot accept it as reliable. Reliability is a necessary condition of validity. That is, an instrument that is unable to predict itself cannot be expected to accurately predict a score on any other measure. In employee selection, this is exactly what we ask selection measures to do. We depend on reliable and valid predictors to accurately measure job-related attributes so that we can use the scores to predict how well an applicant would later perform on a criterion measure that also is reliable and valid. This is why reliability is essential.

Research on reliability usually focuses on tests or ratings. The methods for estimating test reliability are relevant for other test-like instruments, whereas procedures for assessing rater reliability are relevant for measures that require judgments and the use of ratings. In general, reliability is assessed by obtaining two sets of scores from a test or rating scale and examining the degree of association between the scores through a correlational analysis. The degree of reliability is summarized in the correlation coefficient. Various techniques exist for computing correlation coefficients, although a commonly used one is the Pearson product-moment correlation. The particular technique required for estimating reliability will depend on how the scores or ratings have been obtained. Reliability is estimated for tests and test-like measures through procedures for test–retest, alternate or parallel forms, split-halves, and interitem reliability. The reliability of ratings is estimated by interrater and intraclass correlational procedures.

**Test–Retest**    In a test–retest study, the two sets of scores to be correlated are obtained by administering the same test to the same individuals at two different times. Individuals' test scores are correlated with their retest scores. The resulting correlation coefficient, which is used as the reliability estimate, indicates the degree of association or consistency between the test and retest scores. Because the same test is administered at both times, the reliability coefficient shows the test's *stability,* or the extent to which scores can be generalized without concern that they are affected by random changes that occur over time.

The test–retest method has some constraints relative to the length of the time interval. If the interval is very short, such as a few hours, memory or practice effects can influence the retest scores and artificially increase the size of the correlation coefficient, which overestimates the test's reliability. For example, test takers may remember how they responded to items on the test and respond exactly the same way on the retest. On the other hand, if the interval is very long, say more than 6 months, a more serious problem arises because real changes can occur in the individual, such as new learning. These changes can result in substantially different test scores, which will artificially reduce the estimate of reliability (Anastasi, 1982). To minimize both of these problems, it is better to choose an interval of moderate length, such as a few weeks. A shorter interval could be used if the test being evaluated has many and/or complex items that test takers are unlikely to specifically remember.

**Alternate or Parallel Forms**   The alternate or parallel forms method can be used to assess reliability when there are concerns about memory effects. With this method, there are two test administrations. However, two different forms of the test are used. The scores on the two forms are correlated, and the resulting reliability coefficient shows the extent to which the two forms are not different, but are actually comparable versions of the same test. Thus, the reliability coefficient provides an estimate of *equivalence*. If the tests are administered on two different occasions, the reliability estimate also indicates stability over time, but not if the tests are administered one after the other in the same sitting.

The alternate forms method is difficult and time-consuming. Two versions of the same test must be constructed covering the same subject matter. Questions should be at about the same level of difficulty and expressed in similar terms. This is not easy to do. Often, test developers construct alternate forms by randomly drawing a sample of items from a bank of items that have been devised to have content similar to that of the original test. This method does not always produce equivalent forms, however. Recently, a procedure was reported which is especially effective for developing parallel forms of tests that have multidimensional content. Using a procedure called "item cloning," the researchers reconstructed each item on the original test to produce an alternate test made up entirely of parallel forms of the original items (Clause, Mullins, Nee, Pulakos, & Schmitt, 1998).

**Split-Halves**   The split-halves method of estimating reliability involves one test and one administration. After the test is given, it is split in half. One difficulty with this method is deciding the best way to split the test. In the past, most users divided the test by the odd- and even-numbered items. In this way, if there was a difference in the difficulty of items from start to finish, which would cause test takers to perform less well at the end, this effect would not be reflected in the reliability coefficient. Similarly, if a test is long and individuals get tired toward the end and do not perform as well, the reliability estimate would not show this. The odd–even method does require that items be independent of each other, however. That is, if a test contains groups of related items, they cannot be split this way. It is better to move the groups intact to one or the other half.

Once a test is split, the two halves are scored as if they were individual tests, and participants' scores on each half are correlated. The resulting reliability coefficient is generally understood as providing a measure of the *internal consistency* of the whole test. That is, the reliability estimate shows the extent to which the test is internally consistent in measuring the same content. In a related sense, because the test is effectively divided into two small tests, the reliability coefficient also can be understood as showing the extent to which the two tests are equivalent in content.

| TABLE 7.2 | SUMMARY OF METHODS FOR ESTIMATING RELIABILITY | | |

| Method | Procedure | Measure | Limitations |
| --- | --- | --- | --- |
| **Tests and Test-Like Measures** | | | |
| Test–retest | One instrument, administered in two sessions to one sample | Stability or consistency over time | Memory and/or practice effects may result in overestimation of reliability |
| Alternate or parallel forms | Two versions of one instrument administered in two sessions to one sample | Equivalence of forms and stability over time | Difficulty and costs of developing equivalent forms; possible practice effects |
| Split-halves | One instrument, split in half; halves treated as two tests | Internal consistency and equivalence of halves | Content must be homogeneous; split may not be optimal; adjust for short length |
| Interitem | One instrument administered; items compared | Internal consistency | Content must be homogeneous; dichotomous and continuous scoring use different statistics |
| **Ratings and Other Judgment Measures** | | | |
| Interrater and intraclass | One instrument used by two or more evaluators rating two or more individuals | Consistency between raters and rating score distributions | Judgment bias; lack of knowledge of rated attributes; weak rating instrument |

Although this method is appealing as a quick and economical way to assess reliability, it has a disadvantage. Cutting the test into halves can underestimate the test's reliability unless some adjustment is made. This is because the measure of reliability depends on the number of items (Cureton, 1965). All things being equal, the longer the test, the greater its reliability. By splitting the instrument into two small tests, the resulting measure of reliability is not as strong as it would be if the tests were full length, as is the case with parallel forms reliability. The Spearman-Brown formula provides a solution to this problem, as it estimates the reliability of the whole test from data on the two halves. The formula is widely reported in split-halves reliability studies (Anastasi, 1982). (See Table 7.2 for a summary of the reliability methods.)

**Interitem Reliability**   With this method also, reliability is estimated from one test, administered once. The interitem method solves the problem of the split-halves method on how best to split the test. Although the test is not actually split when assessing interitem reliability, the rationale is something of this sort. That is, instead of settling on one way to split a test, we would consider all possible splittings; calculate a correlation coefficient for each; and then average these to get the reliability coefficient for the test. The reliability coefficient reflects the consistency among items throughout the test. There are two statistical procedures for estimating interitem reliability of a test without actually splitting the test. The Kuder-Richardson formula KR20 is the most commonly used for this purpose. It is appropriate for tests composed of items that are scored as correct or incorrect. A different formula is required for tests using items that are scored otherwise, such as personality tests in which more than one answer can be correct and earn score points. Cronbach's (1970) formula for *coefficient alpha* is commonly used with such instruments.

Internal consistency reliability, whether assessed by the interitem or split-halves method, is constrained by the extent to which the test's content is homogeneous. Internal consistency is an appropriate measure of reliability only for tests that measure one content area. If a test is multidimensional, in that it addresses very different subjects, such as vocabulary and mathematical reasoning, there may be little or no relationship in test takers' responses to the different types of items. As a result, an internal consistency measure will underestimate reliability. For multidimensional tests, the better strategy would be to obtain a different measure of reliability, such as stability through test–retest or equivalence through the alternate forms method.

**Reliability of Ratings**   So far, I have discussed techniques for assessing the reliability of objectively scored tests and similar instruments. However, some measures, such as interviewers' ratings of applicants and supervisors' ratings of employees, are not objectively scored. They rely on judgments or subjective assessments. Potentially, some part of individuals' scores on these measures is not due to real differences between the individuals but, rather, to human error on the part of examiners. In any measure that involves subjective judgments, the scores include some amount of uncontrolled judgment error.

The reliability of judgment measures indicates the extent to which rater error is present. Often, little effort is made to assess the reliability of raters in the business setting, although sometimes *interrater agreement* is assessed. The procedure for this is weak, however, and it does not yield a reliability coefficient. It is simply a matter of recording the percentage of times that raters agree in their assessments. Because percentages of agreement are nominal scale categories, little can be done with them. With categorical data, remember, the mathematical operations required to calculate a reliability coefficient are not possible.

There are empirical techniques for assessing rater consistency, if the raters use a well-designed rating instrument with interval scale precision. When there are two raters, interrater reliability can be estimated through correlational procedures, such as the Pearson product-moment correlation. Intraclass correlations can be estimated when there are three or more raters evaluating the same individuals. These techniques yield reliability coefficients that show the consistency of raters in terms of the rating score distributions generated. Certain steps can be taken to improve the reliability of raters, as I discuss in later chapters on predictor and criterion measures that involve ratings (e.g., interviews, assessment centers, and performance appraisal). For example, in their meta-analysis, Conway, Jako, and Goodman (1995) found that when interviewers work in panels there is higher reliability than when they work separately. Also, providing interviewers with a structured line of questioning improves the reliability of their ratings. Such standardizing efforts can increase the likelihood that all the raters are judging the same attribute.

## Validity

In a general sense, the validity of a measure is the extent to which the instrument actually measures what it is supposed to measure. More specifically, validity refers to what the scores mean and to the consequences of interpreting them as having a certain meaning. One way to understand validity as score interpretation is to consider *invalidity*. With an invalid measure, a low score might occur because the instrument is missing something relevant or because it contains something irrelevant that interferes with a person's demonstration of the attribute being measured (Messick, 1995). Therefore, a valid math test, for example, would need to measure mathematical ability and not a different attribute that might interfere with showing this ability, such as reading comprehension in understanding mathematical "word" problems. In a related sense, validity also refers to how scores on a measure are used. A person's score on a math test might be used validly to infer the person's facility for performing mathematical work on a job. However, the score might not be valid if it is used to predict overall job performance if other attributes, such as oral and written verbal ability, are not measured by the test but are important requirements for the job. In making selection decisions, we need instruments that yield valid information about attributes required for performance on the particular job.

## Conclusions

The single, most important conclusion we can draw at this point concerns the absolute necessity for reliability in measurement. Employee selection requires that both predictor and criterion measures be able to function reliably and validly. Only then is it possible to accurately assess potential in applicants and make effective selection decisions. Reliability of a measure is the first requirement of a valid measure. When an instrument is unreliable, it is not a valid measure of anything. If an instrument has high reliability, this means it consistently measures something. Whether or not that "something" is actually the attribute we intended to measure is a question of validity. Reliability of measurement is diminished by various error sources including the limitations of the instrument and/or the examiner. Standardization provides ways to control these extraneous variables and to reduce the amount of error in score distributions. Thus, standardization can improve the reliability of a measuring device and contribute to its validity.

# VALIDATION OF SELECTION MEASURES

Some selection instruments appear to have validity. On the surface, they look as if they measure some job attribute. This is what is known as *face validity*. The face validity of a selection measure can be important. Applicants may react differently depending on whether the instrument or procedure appears to be job relevant. For example, low face validity might cause an applicant to feel less motivated to perform well on a test or to become less interested in pursuing a job offer. As a result, decreased motivation might cause the individual to actually perform less well than he or she otherwise could (Chan, Schmitt, DeShon, Clause, & Delbridge, 1997; Smither, Reilly, Millsap, Pearlman, & Stoffey, 1993). Employers need to know about such effects because adjustments might be possible to increase the face validity of an otherwise quality instrument. However, test users should not depend only on face validity. What an instrument appears to measure may not be what it actually measures, and assessing the instrument's technical validity requires going beyond its appearance. Rather, validity is shown by studies, through which evidence is gained, evaluating the measure against an indicator of the attribute. In this section, you will see how this is done. (Table 7.3 contains a preview of validation methods.)

## *Criterion-Related Validation*

The purpose of criterion-related validation is to determine the empirical relationship between a selection instrument and a criterion measure. This will show how useful the instrument is as a predictor of performance on the job. Two commonly used methods for demonstrating criterion-related validity are the predictive validity technique and the concurrent validity technique. These techniques can be used for measures that reach the interval level of precision, such as tests. Both techniques involve the correlation of scores on the predictor measure with scores on the criterion measure. The correlation coefficient, which—in validity studies—is called the validity coefficient, estimates the extent to which test scores can predict criterion scores.

TABLE 7.3    METHODS FOR ASSESSING VALIDITY OF SELECTION MEASURES

| Method | Measure of Validity | Requirements and Constraints |
|---|---|---|
| Criterion-related | Empirical evidence of instrument's ability to predict a criterion measure | Predictive or concurrent strategy can be used; needs reliable measures and large validation sample; range restriction |
| Content | Rational evidence of relevance; representative sample of job | Thorough job analysis; must assess reliability of measure; judgment error possible |
| Construct | Rational evidence of construct's relevance to job; empirical evidence of convergence on construct and divergence from unrelated construct | Job analysis adequate to show construct relevance; adequate existing tests; effective choice of unrelated tests; large validation samples |

**Predictive Validity**    Two identifying features of the predictive validity technique are (1) use of job applicants as participants in the study and (2) a time interval between testing and collecting criterion data. In a predictive validity study, the validation sample is a group of unscreened applicants. The test is administered to these applicants, and then their responses are filed away, unscored, until a later time. Ideally, we would hire the whole group of applicants in order to evaluate how well each of them performs on the job. Realistically, however, we will not be able to do this. Instead, selection activities for these applicants will go on as usual. Whatever selection procedures are used ordinarily in the organization, such as applications and interviews, will be used and hiring decisions made. (Remember, the test is not scored or used at this time. It has been filed away. The validation strategy would be seriously compromised if the test were used to make hiring decisions during its validation.) After the applicants, who were hired by routine procedures, have been on the job for a while, their job performance is evaluated. Usually, the supervisor completes a performance rating, and this serves as the criterion measure. At that time, the tests are brought out of storage and scored, which yields the validation sample's test score distribution. The test scores of those who were hired are correlated with their performance rating scores, and the resulting validity coefficient is the estimate of the test's predictive validity.

In predictive validity studies, it is always better if we can obtain criterion scores for all members of the validation sample. This makes it possible for us to see whether high scores on the test are associated with high scores on the performance measure and whether low test scores are associated with low performance scores. This is the kind of relationship we look for in a validity study, of course. It tells us that the test can effectively differentiate applicants who will be successful job performers from those who will not be. However, in the usual case, we will not have complete information on the validation sample. Some applicants will have been screened out by the routine selection procedures described above. If the organization's routine procedures are any good at all, most of those who were hired from the validation sample will have become reasonably good performers by the time we take the criterion measure. If so, these individuals will not vary much in terms of their job performance. (This is what is meant by the term "restricted range of abilities.") Also, as a result of the employer's screening, we will lack criterion data on those who were not hired, who possibly were the ones who would have been poor performers. This lack may prevent us from fully assessing the test's ability to predict poor performance. Why do we need to know this? Here's one reason: If those scoring low on a test can perform as well as those scoring high, then the test does not validly predict job performance. However, unless we have criterion information that shows how low test scorers fare on the job, we cannot know how well they can perform, and our validity evidence is weakened.

Sometimes, however, an organization's routine selection procedures are low quality and they result in hiring decisions that are little better than random choices. This actually can be an advantage for our validity study. Organizational procedures that result in what is effectively random selection means that those who were hired and thus remain in the validation sample will include both high and low test scorers. This will allow us to assess whether the test can validly predict performance across a full range of scores. Therefore, if it is not possible to hire an entire validation sample, then we might hope that "selection as usual" results in a representative sample of test scores.

**Concurrent Validity**   In a concurrent validity study, there is no time interval between the predictor and the criterion measures. The two measures are taken at the same time. This can be an advantage because complete data for the validity estimate are immediately available, and there is no danger that test scores will be prematurely used. In concurrent validation, the sample is made up of an organization's current employees who are already on the job for which the test is being prepared. They are given the test and their work performance is evaluated concurrently. Then, the scores are correlated. The correlation coefficient expresses the concurrent validity of the test to predict the performance measure.

This technique has some of the same drawbacks as the predictive technique, although the problems are not necessarily worse (Barrett, Phillips, & Alexander, 1981). First, the distribution of performance ratings on employees in the sample is likely to show a restricted range. As with the predictive technique, the organization's selection decisions may have produced a group that was similar in their abilities from the time they came on the job. In addition, changes likely will have occurred during the terms of their employment so that neither highly successful nor unsuccessful performers are available for the validation sample. Those who were not performing well probably were transferred or terminated, or they may have quit. Those who were highly successful on the job may have been promoted, or they may have quit to take better jobs. A second limitation of the concurrent technique has to do with potentially important differences between the validation sample and later job applicants who will take the test as part of an actual selection process. Individuals in these two groups are likely to differ in their motivation to perform well on the test. The stakes will be higher for real job applicants than for current employees who are simply participating in a study. In addition, the current employees may differ from the job applicants because learning has occurred on the job. Such differences can be important because a test's validity for use with applicants depends on the similarity of the validation sample to later test takers.

**Handling Constraints**    The quality of a criterion-related validation study, whether conducted with the predictive or concurrent technique, depends on a good criterion measure of job performance. For certain jobs, such as in production, ratio scale productivity measures may be available. For most jobs, however, the criterion measure will be a supervisor's rating of job performance that includes productivity as well as other employee behaviors. At best, these ratings will have come from a well-developed interval-scale performance measure that has been shown to be reliable and valid. If this is the case, then we can be assured that the criterion measure does not constrain the test validation study. However, the rating scale often is an instrument of lower quality. In addition, performance appraisal ratings, like interviewers' ratings, can contain errors due to the rater that will limit the reliability of the measure. Of course, ratings are unreliable, we cannot depend on them to provide a valid assessment of job performance, and this weakens the validity study. The best solution for a test validation study is first to establish that the criterion measure is reliable and can accurately identify different levels of performance. Ratings that do not provide this information—such as when all employees are evaluated as performing at the same level—are useless for a validation study. The test will appear to be invalid even if it is not. Therefore, unless it is possible to determine that an existing criterion measure is reliable and relevant, or that such a measure can be developed for the study, a criterion-related validity study will not be feasible (Society for Industrial and Organizational Psychology, 1987).

Another factor that can affect the feasibility of a criterion-related validity study is the size of the sample. A validation study requires a large sample in order to be statistically powerful enough to detect a true effect and to show that a test is valid when it actually is. We cannot be confident of our study's result if we have no more than 15 to 20 people in the sample. The required sample size is too large for many small organizations. Hollenbeck and Whitener (1988) devised a way for relatively small businesses to validate a selection testing system using a sample of minimal size. The procedure can be used to conduct a concurrent validity study in a company that has as few as 84 employees on staff in various jobs, or to conduct a predictive validity study in a company that hires as many as 84 people a year for various jobs. The procedure begins with a job analysis to identify important elements of jobs throughout the organization. Next, a battery or set of tests is collected in which individual tests measure these job elements. In a concurrent validation study, each job element test is given to every employee whose job includes the element. Individuals' job element scores are then correlated with evaluations of their performance on these same elements. The overall correlation coefficient expresses the validity of the test battery for predicting organization-wide performance. Thus, the procedure allows a small organization to construct and validate a test battery that can function effectively in selecting for jobs throughout the organization (Hollenbeck & Whitener, 1988).

## Content Validity

The objective of a content validation study is to establish that a logical or rational relationship exists between the contents of an instrument and the contents of a job. The rationale of the strategy is that if a test is made up of a representative sample of a job's content, then an applicant who can perform the test also will be able to perform the job. In general, this is sound reasoning. In any specific instance, the truth of it hinges on the extent to which the test's sampling of job content is truly representative of the job. The aim of content validation, then, is to develop a convincing argument that the test constitutes a representative sample of the job.

You can probably guess that the foundation for content validation is a thorough job analysis. The job analysis is used in two general approaches to content validation. The first and more common approach is to develop the contents of a new test directly from the job analysis, thereby establishing content validity during the test development process. In the second approach, used with existing tests, panels of judges evaluate the test items to determine whether they sample the tasks and requirements of the job, as identified in the job analysis.

Test content can comprise a job sample in different ways. One, the tasks or work activities identified by a job analysis can be used as test content. Work sample tests are examples, such as operating a machine to produce some item. With work sample tests, the relationship between the test and the job is often apparent. A typing test can be content-valid for secretarial and similar jobs that require heavy keyboard use, if it samples an important part of the work. Two, a test can sample important areas of knowledge required on the job. Here, the relationship between test and job content is less apparent because job knowledge tests are written tests rather than performance tests.

To make a convincing argument for the content validity of such tests, the job analysis must demonstrate that certain areas of knowledge are needed to perform certain work activities. The test items must refer to this knowledge somewhat clearly. For example, a written test used to hire safety inspectors in a manufacturing plant might include questions about certain toxic substances and effective safeguards for using them.

## Construct Validity

Construct validation includes the reasoning of both the criterion-related and content validity techniques. First, a rational relationship exists between the content of the test and the underlying attribute or construct.[2] Second, an empirical relationship exists when test scores correlate with scores on a previously validated test of the construct. Commercial test developers use the construct validation method to validate tests that employers can purchase. Large organizations also sometimes use the technique to develop and validate tests. An organization can have unique needs for applicant testing that require developing and validating its own instrument. For example, suppose a job analysis was done which revealed certain required KSAs that appeared to refer to a common underlying construct. The company might decide to develop its own test, perhaps because no existing test exactly or conveniently measures the attribute. Some tests might not measure it completely, whereas others might be too long.

To construct-validate a test, first, job analysis is used to guide the development of test items. Second, empirically validating the test against a criterion requires two existing measures: a previously validated test of the construct, and a valid test of a different and unrelated construct. For example, if a new test is being developed to measure social intelligence, an existing test of this construct is needed as well as an unrelated measure, such as a math test. Third, all three tests are administered to a validation sample. Then using a criterion-related strategy, an analyst correlates scores on the new test with scores on each of the existing tests. (The existing tests function as the criterion measures.) Two aspects of empirical validity are needed in order to demonstrate construct validity. To show *convergent* validity, scores on the new test must correlate strongly with the existing test of the construct. (That is, the new test converges on the existing test of the same construct.) To show *discriminant* or *divergent* validity, the new test must *not* correlate strongly with the test of the unrelated construct. (The new test diverges from an unrelated test.) If evidence of both convergent and discriminant validity is shown, then the test can be accepted as construct-valid (Campbell, 1960).

---

[2]A construct is a trait or an attribute that is hypothesized to be the basis for exhibited behavior.

As I pointed out at the start of this discussion, employers need to know what a test actually measures, as well as whether it can be used to predict job performance. Construct validation is a powerful strategy that can provide for both of these needs. First, using a job analysis, the construct is identified as a basis for KSAs that are clearly required on the job. This establishes the relevance of the construct and its usefulness in predicting job performance. Second, the evidence of convergent and discriminant validity more or less identifies the construct. Messick (1995) points out that a construct-valid measure theoretically is one of a number of ways to "represent" a construct, and any of these will vary in terms of how valid the representation is. A measure may underrepresent a construct, such as when a test does not fully assess all of its important aspects. Also, a measure may overrepresent the construct because it taps into unrelated constructs that are not actually examined in the validation study. (This is a reason for carefully choosing the unrelated test in a validation study.) For adequate construct validity, we must know that the construct identified from job analysis is the basis for the required KSAs and that it is the same construct the instrument is measuring. If we can be sure of this, then we can assume that our test is construct-valid for our use.

## Validity Generalization

In early discussions of validation, test validities were considered to be situation-specific. That is, the validity of an instrument was believed to be dependent upon the particular situation in which it was used. Any change in the use of a test was thought to require a new validation study. For example, if a test validated for use in hiring for one job was going to be used for a different job, it had to be revalidated. If a test validated in one organization was borrowed by another organization for use on the same type of job, it also had to be revalidated. The reason was that situational differences were considered to be such strong sources of error, a test's validity coefficient could not be trusted to reflect its validity in a new situation. That is, the validity of the test for its previous use was not generalizable to the new use.

The main reason test validities were thought to be limited in this way is that validity coefficients of the same instrument did vary from one situation to another. The validity of aptitude tests for predicting performance on similar industrial jobs was found to vary widely from one validation study to another (Ghiselli, 1966). Most researchers recognized that some part of the variability in criterion-related validity coefficients probably was due to errors in the research. However, it became widely accepted that the effect of differences in the situation were real and accounted for much of the variability in validity coefficients.

Over the past two decades, considerable research has focused on the concept of validity generalization, with the aim of discovering the extent to which test validity coefficients are stable enough to generalize from one use to another. This new research has been done by means of a statistical method known as *meta-analysis*. This procedure involves locating a large number of previously conducted validation studies and using the evidence from each study as the unit of analysis in the meta-analysis. In other words, a meta-analysis is a study of other studies.

In the initial studies, researchers using meta-analysis to examine selection test validities discovered that the previously suspected measurement error in validation research had been underestimated. The error was much worse than we thought. An extensive program of meta-analytic research demonstrated that variations in validity coefficients from one situation to another were due to weaknesses in validation studies. Small samples, unreliable criterion measures, and restricted range in scores on predictor and criterion measures were common problems (Hunter, Schmidt, & Jackson, 1982; Schmidt & Hunter, 1981a). The small size of the typical validation sample was a particularly serious source of error. Reporting on validation done in industry, researchers estimated that roughly half of the samples used were no larger than 40 or 50 individuals (Schmidt, Hunter, & Urry, 1976). In one study, Schmidt and Hunter (1981b) found that about 72 percent of the variance in validity coefficients was due to measurement weakness (such as unreliability); however, most of the error resulted from using a validation sample that was too small. When the sample in a criterion-related study is too small, the study will not reflect the test's true validity. Small sample size remains a problem in criterion-related validation. Although published meta-analyses are showing that sample sizes in organizational studies have increased somewhat, the average validation sample still is too small to adequately assess a test's validity (Salgado, 1998).

The meta-analytic research conducted over the years has resulted in better techniques for estimating the generalizability of validity coefficients (e.g., Hunter & Schmidt, 1990). The research also has demonstrated that situational specificity is something of a myth (Lubinski & Dawis, 1992). Meta-analytic studies have shown that many test validities can be transported across jobs and organizations. It is no longer considered necessary for an employer to struggle through a criterion-related validity study in an attempt to revalidate an instrument in order to use it for similar jobs. Cognitive ability tests, in particular, have been shown to be valid in a wide range of jobs and settings (Schmidt & Hunter, 1981b). This does not mean that all cognitive tests are equally valid for all jobs. Validity generalization does not eliminate the need for good judgment on the part of the researcher (Guion, 1991). Employers who are putting together previously validated tests for use in selecting employees for a different job will still need to analyze the job and demonstrate that the tests are relevant to the required KSAs. What has changed as a result of the validity generalization research is the general requirement of revalidating a test for every new use.

## Conclusions

I cannot overemphasize the importance of establishing the validity of selection measures before they are used. Actions are taken, based on the assumption of validity, that affect people's lives and the success of organizations. How to establish validity is a decision that depends on the need and anticipated use of a measure, as well as an organization's available resources for conducting a validity study. The method of content validation is beneficial because it can show the relevance of a measure to job requirements. In the past, criterion-related validation was thought to yield the best and most defensible validity evidence. However, as discussed earlier, criterion-related validity studies are not always feasible. Frequently, this is because of the lack of an adequately large validation sample. If an employer presses forward with a criterion-related study despite a limited sample size, the effort to validate the measure will be disappointing. Still, meta-analytic studies of past research show that many such ill-designed validation studies were done, possibly because of the view of validity as being situation-specific. In such settings where a large sample cannot be obtained, it might be better to conduct a content validity study and use professionally developed instruments that have validity across settings.

The potential of instruments showing high levels of construct validity seems particularly promising for generalizability. In summary, construct validation includes rational evidence of the relevance of an instrument's content to an underlying construct. It also provides empirical evidence of the instrument's ability to predict other representations of the construct. In so doing, validation identifies the construct. The extent to which a test accurately and fully represents a construct determines how generalizable the scores are (Messick, 1995). In a broad sense, "work performance" might be considered a single construct. Organizational settings and job titles might be other constructs that are unrelated to the construct of work performance. If so, it would be of great value to know this. A construct-validated test with the ability to predict work performance in one sample could be accepted as being valid for other samples because the test would be predicting exactly the same criterion.

## USING MEASUREMENT IN SELECTION DECISION MAKING

Reliable and valid predictor measures are not always used to their full capacity. Although it would seem rather pointless to develop high-quality predictor measures and then not use the information they provide, this does happen. Sometimes, applicant information is not considered in a selection decision because a manager already has someone in mind to hire. On other occasions, a manager may simply look over test scores and other information on applicants and then make a hiring decision based on his or her own judgment. There are a variety of reasons why this manager's selection decision is likely to be flawed. One is that the quality of the manager's judgments probably is not as good as he or she believes. Such judgments tend to introduce new error into the process. Also, the way the manager combines the data from the predictor measures (i.e., by "looking over" test scores) is another judgmental process of which the person probably is not aware. There are better ways to combine and make use of predictor information.

At this point, you and I need to change our focus. So far, I have discussed the preparation of measures for a selection program. Now, we need to turn our attention to the actual use of individual applicants' scores to predict their performance on the job. Three final measurement issues need to be discussed: (1) combining and using applicant information in selection decision making, (2) setting passing or cutoff scores, and (3) establishing the overall utility of selection.

## *Predicting an Applicant's Job Performance*

Any of several procedures might be effective in helping a manager use predictor data in making selection decisions. I will describe three that are commonly used: multiple regression, multiple cutoffs, and multiple hurdles. Each method provides ways to combine and order individual scores on objective and/or judgmental measures.

**Multiple Regression**   With multiple regression, we can combine scores on different predictor measures and obtain a single score for each applicant that can be used to decide whom to hire. Multiple regression is an extended version of the basic procedure for using a single test score to obtain a predicted performance criterion score. Therefore, let us begin with simple regression.

Regression shows the relationship between scores on a predictor and a criterion measure, and it is the statistical method upon which correlation is based. If an employer has conducted a criterion-related validation study on the predictor measure, the necessary information for a regression analysis of the validation sample's scores will already be available. A correlation coefficient shows the relationship between predictor and criterion for the validation sample as a *group*. Regression analysis allows us to examine this relationship at the *individual* level. That is, with regression analysis, we can predict someone's job performance, based on the person's test score. In order to do this, we start by examining the predictor and criterion scores of the sample. The relationship between the two variables can be described graphically by a scatterplot of observed scores through which a regression line has been drawn, as shown in Figure 7.3. The regression line is calculated from the scores and represents the "best fit," or most likely criterion score for each predictor score. That is, the

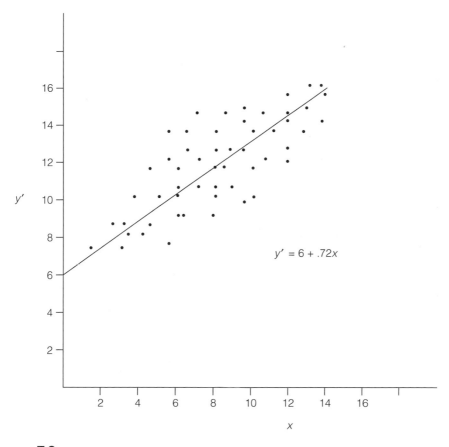

$$y' = 6 + .72x$$

**FIGURE 7.3**

Scatterplot of test ($x$) scores and predicted criterion ($y'$) scores, showing regression line and regression equation. The intercept is at 6 on the $y$-axis and the slope of the regression line is .72.

regression line is a running mean of criterion scores at each predictor score point. If an employer planned to use only the one measure to make hiring decisions, the regression line could be used directly to estimate the future performance of an applicant. He or she would locate the applicant's test score on the $x$-axis of the graph, then moving up to the regression line, would simply read off the corresponding score on the $y$-axis. Usually, however, an employer uses more than one predictor measure and needs a way to combine predictor scores. Therefore, a regression equation is needed for predicting applicants' criterion scores from one or more predictor scores.

The regression equation for one predictor takes the form $y' = a + bx$, in which

$y'$ = the predicted criterion score
$a$ = the intercept, or point where the regression line intercepts the $y$-axis

$b$ = the slope of the regression line
$x$ = the predictor score

The actual values of $a$ and $b$ are determined by data from the validation sample. These values describe two characteristics of the regression line, as generated by the data. The correlation coefficient between predictor and criterion, which was found in the validation sample, is used in determining the value of $b$. Once established, $a$ and $b$ function as constants in the regression equation used. In the example shown in Figure 7.3, the regression equation was determined to be $y' = 6 + .72x$. The intercept ($a$) is at 6 on the $y$-axis. This is the predicted level of performance for someone scoring zero on the test, and it represents a starting point for predicting the criterion. For any score on the test, we add 6 to the weighted value of $x$ to get the value of $y'$. The slope ($b$) of the regression line is the amount of increase in performance for every increase on the test. Thus, the value of $b$ is a weight that is applied to the applicant's test score. In the example, each test score is weighted at .72 of its point value in predicting the criterion score. For example, if an applicant scores 11 on the test, we would predict a performance score of $y' = 6 + .72(11)$, or $y' = 14$.

The major advantage of regression analysis is that it provides an objective way to combine applicants' scores on multiple predictor measures so as to make full use of the scores in selection decision making. Just as we need to know how to use a single test score to predict performance, so also do we need to know how to get and use a composite score. The mathematical operations of multiple regression are similar to those for regression with one predictor, specifically because multiple regression is an extension of simple regression. The regression equation for one predictor is $y' = a + bx$. For two predictors, the equation is $y' = a + bx_1 + bx_2$. For three predictors, it is $y' = a + bx_1 + bx_2 + bx_3$. More predictors could be added in the same way. However, this is not realistic for the employment setting, mainly because it is difficult to find many different measures that can predict a job performance criterion. Sometimes, two predictors are identified that are independent of one another and measure different aspects of a criterion. Usually, though, predictor measures overlap in their prediction of a criterion. That is, to some extent they predict the same thing. As more predictors are added, the overlap is likely to increase and the extent of their unique predictive ability declines. Thus, an important difference between simple and multiple regression is the addition of statistical procedures for taking account of the overlap between predictors.

In multiple regression, as in simple regression, data from a sample of test takers are needed. Similarly, the relationship between multiple predictors and a criterion measure is examined through a multiple correlational study. The multiple correlation statistic $R$ shows the combined relationship that exists between the predictors and the criterion measure, and $R^2$ expresses the amount of variance in the criterion scores explained by the predictors. Importantly, $R^2$ includes an adjustment for correlations between the predictors. That is, the procedure accounts for overlap. In the multiple regression equation, values of $b$ for the multiple predictors will include the adjustment for overlap.

Suppose we want to use two tests to predict the score on a performance criterion measure. One is a vocabulary test $(x_1)$ and the other is a job knowledge test $(x_2)$. The multiple correlational study has been done, and the values of $a$, $b_1$, and $b_2$ have been determined, yielding the following regression equation: $y' = 2 + .31(x_1) + .55 (x_2)$. Now, suppose an applicant scores 42 on the vocabulary test $(x_1)$ and 60 on the job knowledge test $(x_2)$. Substituting the scores into the formula, the predicted performance score would be $y' = 2 + 13 + 33$, or $y' = 48$. In use, both tests would be given to all applicants and $y'$ scores would be calculated for all applicants. If the employer has established a minimum satisfactory performance score (let's say 42, for this example), then each $y'$ score can be evaluated against the minimum to determine whether an applicant is acceptable for hire. If the employer needs only a few new employees, then the predicted criterion scores for the group can be ranked and, using top-down selection, those with the highest composite scores can be hired.

Multiple regression provides an objective and systematic means for obtaining composite scores on multiple measures. In addition, a variety of predictor measures can be accommodated with the method. There are some constraints, however. First, because the procedure is complex, some HR staff may be reluctant to use it. However, computer software is available that can make the data analysis painless. Second, multiple regression requires that all applicants take all tests and other measures. This can be a problem if an organization plans to use its more expensive measures only to evaluate a smaller, screened group of applicants. Third, the multiple regression model makes certain assumptions that may or may not be appropriate with certain data. The relationship of the predictors to the criterion variable is assumed to be linear, in that performance increases at a constant rate as test scores increase. In addition, the model assumes that scores on the different predictors are additive and can compensate for one another. A high score on one measure is assumed to compensate for a low score on another. Using the example above, suppose another person earned 95 on the vocabulary test and 30 on the job knowledge test. The predicted criterion score for both this person and the earlier applicant is 48. That is, the two individuals are predicted to show the same overall performance. Is this a good prediction? A user of multiple regression needs to consider whether the assumptions are appropriate given the nature of the job requirements. For many measures used in employment selection, they are appropriate. However, if not, then a different strategy for combining predictor information is needed.

**Multiple Cutoffs**    When the multiple regression model is not feasible to use because the linearity and compensatory assumptions are not appropriate, the multiple cutoff method may be better because it can more easily handle curvilinear relationships between predictor and criterion, and scores that are not compensatory. Sometimes, a certain level of an attribute is optimal for job performance. Lower levels are not enough for good performance, and higher levels might make no difference or possibly be detrimental to performance. That is, the relationship between predictor and criterion is not linear. It is conceivable that various attributes might relate to performance in this manner. The relationship is easy to understand when physical or perceptual abilities are involved. For example, commercial drivers need to have a minimum level of vision to perform their work and another ability cannot compensate for this. Once an applicant meets the minimum visual requirement, greater visual ability will make little or no difference in performance.

If performance on a job has such prerequisite conditions, it is necessary that predictor measures not be misapplied. Scores on critical measures may not be combined with those on other measures. For example, if an employer uses a perceptual test along with a general aptitude test and then combines the scores in a composite, the essential score on the perceptual test can easily be overlooked. Cronbach (1970, p. 437) shows how this can happen. In his example, individuals were being selected for training in submarine detection. The equipment that would be used required the ability to hear and judge sound qualities. Selection was based on a composite score of mechanical comprehension tests and tonal judgment tests. The applicants whose overall scores were high were sent to sonar training. Many who were predicted to do well in training, in fact, failed. The reason? Their ability to hear and judge differences in tones was poor. However, the composite score—by allowing a high mechanical comprehension score to compensate for a low tonal judgment score—had not revealed the perceptual weakness.

The multiple cutoff procedure requires that users establish minimum cutoff or passing scores for all predictors. Each applicant is given all tests or other measures, and all applicants are considered at one time. If an applicant scores lower than the cutoff score on any of the measures, he or she is disqualified. In the above example, those who scored low on the tonal judgment tests would not have been sent to sonar training. Applicants whose tonal judgment scores were high enough but who scored low on the mechanical comprehension test also would have been disqualified, leaving only those who scored at least the minimum on both tests.

The advantage of the multiple cutoff method is that it is simple, intuitively reasonable, and acceptable to employers. A serious weakness is that it provides no guidance on how to select from the applicants who pass the multiple cutoff points because scores are not combined. One way to overcome this is to use multiple regression at this point to calculate composite scores for those who passed the multiple cutoffs. If not all predictor measures have a strictly curvilinear relationship with the criterion, multiple regression can be used to combine scores and rank the acceptable applicants. That is, if score increases above the minimum on some measures are associated with increased job performance, and if, at high score levels, scores can compensate for one another, then multiple regression can provide an objective way to make top-down selection decisions from the group of acceptable applicants.

**Multiple Hurdles**   Whereas multiple regression and multiple cutoffs involve single-stage selection decisions, the multiple hurdles approach is a sequential method of selection decision making. The method involves arranging predictor measures in an administrative sequence with each measure constituting a hurdle, as depicted in Figure 7.4. At each hurdle, applicants' scores are compared to the measure's cutoff score. Applicants whose scores do not reach the cutoff on any measure in the sequence are disqualified at that time and are not further examined. Therefore, screening decisions are made at every step in the process. Because not all applicants are examined on all measures, the multiple hurdles process is economical, especially with large numbers of applicants. At the final stage, only those who passed all hurdles remain. The final decision may be to hire all of them. Having passed all hurdles means that everyone in this group is qualified on all measures. Decisions to hire fewer than this could be made by randomly choosing from the remaining group. Instead, the accumulated scores on the predictor measures could be combined into a composite score for each applicant and used in top-down selection. Some employers use the score on the final measure to make the selection decision.

Predictor measures can be organized into multiple hurdles in various ways. Figure 7.4 shows one way. The particular design depends on the purpose of using the strategy. In an early study, Cronbach and Gleser (1965) evaluated various testing sequences to find those that had high economic utility. They found one procedure that was both economical and effective in predicting performance. In this sequence, all applicants were screened on the first predictor. Three selection decisions were made at this point: (1) Those who did not reach the passing score were disqualified. (2) Those who clearly surpassed the cutoff score were hired. (3) Those who were close to the borderline were tested further with the next measure in the sequence. The procedure was economical because the first screen sharply reduced the applicant sample and relatively few required a second or third screening before a decision could be made.

Multiple hurdles may be effective for different purposes depending on how the measures are ordered and what use is made of the accumulated scores. In a study evaluating different versions of this method, Sackett and Roth (1996) used two tests to make up four sequence options. The options were identical in that those who did not pass a screening test were disqualified. Those who passed were given a second test. Selection decisions are made either by using only the score on the second test or by using a composite of the two test scores. The four options differed according to which measure was used as the screening test and how much weight the screen was given in the final selection decision. In their simulation study, the researchers evaluated the

Reduction of Applicant Pool          Measure at each Hurdle

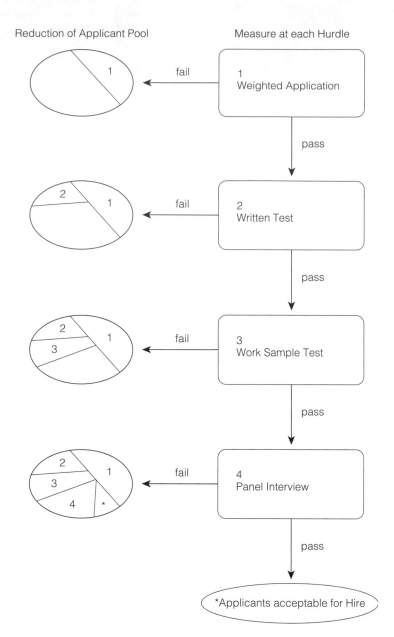

**FIGURE 7.4**

A multiple hurdles selection process. At each hurdle, any applicants who pass go to the next hurdle. Any who fail are disqualified. At each hurdle the applicant pool is reduced so that at the final stage only a small number remain as acceptable applicants.

effects of these differences. They found that a composite of the two test scores provided a better prediction of job performance. Using only the second score in making selection decisions was a waste of information. Discarding the screening test score in the final decision was equivalent to assigning the same score to all those who passed the test.

In a multiple hurdles procedure, the order in which measures are given is thought likely to make a difference in selection decisions. For example, sometimes it might be a good idea to place the most valid measure at the first hurdle, because the first disqualifications would be based on a valid predictor of job performance. Later hurdles could be used to disqualify applicants for other reasons. Such reasoning highlights the possibility that an employer may have more than one objective for the selection program. Sackett and Roth (1996) recognized that modern employers often need to meet objectives for minority hiring as well as performance prediction and that measures valid for one purpose are not necessarily valid for the other. In their study, they found that reversing the order of the two tests had an important effect because of the nature of the tests. One test was known to show adverse impact whereas the other did not. Options that increased the influence of the latter test in the selection decision were more effective for minority hiring. One option, in which this test was used as the screen and selection was based on a composite score, produced the highest level of minority hires. This same option also was one of the best two for predicting job performance. These advantages would make it a good choice for an employer needing to balance performance hiring with minority representation.

The multiple hurdles approach has good potential for helping an employer make effective selection decisions. It can be an economical procedure for high-performance hiring. With careful planning, it also can provide a means for increasing workforce diversity. The extent to which an employer can actually realize these objectives depends on how well the hurdle structure is organized and how the measures are combined for the final selection decision.

## Setting Cutoff Scores

A cutoff score on a criterion measure may be needed in any selection decision making system. In systems using multiple cutoffs or multiple hurdles, passing scores on predictor measures are absolutely necessary. So, where do we get cutoff scores?

Setting cutoff scores always involves human judgment. Procedures are available for making the process somewhat more objective. However, an element of subjectivity always remains. If we have criterion-related validity evidence for a predictor measure, we can find the point in the distribution of scores that is associated with the lowest acceptable performance level on a criterion measure, and then label this point as the cutoff score. Of course, the criterion measure is likely to be a performance rating, which means that the cutoff score is based on the judgment of supervisors. Recognizing that judgment is always involved, we might try to make the judgment process as systematic and error-free as possible. Some methods for setting cutoff scores aim to do exactly that.

Two commonly used methods are those devised by Angoff (1971) and Ebel (1972). Using Angoff's method, judges examine each item on a test and rate how likely a minimally qualified employee would be to answer the item correctly. The judges' ratings are averaged for each item, and the item averages are summed to get the cutoff score for the test. In a slightly different version of Angoff's original method, judges are asked to envision a group of minimally qualified employees and then estimate the proportion of them who would answer each item correctly. Proportions are averaged across judges for each item and summed over items to get the cutoff score. Angoff's method is less complex and time consuming than Ebel's. Using Ebel's method, judges are asked first to rate the relative importance of the items to the job, and then to evaluate the likelihood that a minimally qualified person would answer each item correctly. The cutoff score for the test is determined by averaging the two ratings per item across raters and summing over items.

Some professionals doubt the value of either method because judges' ratings obtained in studies using these methods have not been shown to be highly reliable (Cascio, Alexander, & Barrett, 1988). Steps might be taken to improve the reliability of judges and rating instruments. A starting point would be to ask who can perform well as a judge using Angoff's procedure. Who would have a conception of the "minimally qualified employee" and know whether the person could answer a test question? Certainly, he or she would have to be someone close to the job and familiar with different levels of performance quality. Those most likely to have this knowledge are experienced supervisors on the job. To the extent that judges are not so knowledgeable, we can expect variability in a group's ratings. Therefore, to improve the accuracy and consistency of ratings, we should first establish that the judges have the necessary knowledge for the task. Next, we might try to improve the rating process. The Angoff method has been interpreted and used in a variety of ways, and the variations might be important. Hudson and Campion (1994) noted that studies varied as to whether or not judges were given correct answers to the items they evaluated. In their own study, the researchers found that having the answers was a helpful aid in judging item difficulty. Judges who were given answers made more accurate and reliable judgments than those who were not given answers, at least on the easiest and hardest items. This research suggests that simple improvements in the rating task might have important effects on cutoff score-setting.

Another possible response to the problem of setting cutoff scores is simply to not use them. This avoids the problem altogether. For any measure that has a linear relationship to the performance criterion, as many selection measures do, we might simply use top-down selection with no minimum score to decide whom to hire (Cascio et al., 1988). This would not be possible, of course, for measures that are used to screen applicants on the basis of an essential physical or perceptual capacity, nor would it be possible in multiple hurdle decision making except at the final stage. Otherwise, it is a reasonable approach. In most cases, there is little to show that a person who is one point below a cutoff score is much less likely to be a good performer than a person who is one point above. The "cutoff" on most selection measures is better envisioned as a section of a distribution rather than a single point. We can usually assume that there is not much real difference between scores that are closely situated along a distribution. Small differences between scores are likely due to measurement error.

A variation of top-down selection that is based on this reasoning is a procedure called *banding* (Cascio, Outtz, Zedeck, & Goldstein, 1995). The basic idea of banding is that a test score distribution can be divided into sections or "bands" such that the scores within a band can be assumed to be roughly equal. Any numerical difference is considered to be due to error. In one way of dividing the distribution, the sections are conceptualized as *fixed bands*. In another procedure, they are *sliding bands* because the distribution is redivided after an applicant is selected, which allows the band to "slide" from one area of the distribution to another. In either banding procedure, the width of the score bands depends on the test's reliability. The bands are narrow when reliability is high and wide when reliability is low. (Remember, reliability refers to the accuracy of the measure or, conversely, the amount of error the scores likely contain.)

Because scores within a band are not considered to be different, they can be treated as tied scores. Therefore, establishing bands of scores allows an employer to use the top-down strategy with a certain freedom (Murphy, 1994). The decision about which to select from a group of tied scorers can be made randomly or on the basis of some other variable, such as the applicant's race or ethnicity. Parenthetically, one of the most common uses of banding has been to counteract adverse impact (Murphy, Osten, & Myors, 1995). In practice, when fixed bands are used, the top scorer is selected first and then others can be selected from the band, as if their scores were tied. If everyone in the first band is hired and still more employees are needed, then a second band is identified and used in the same way. When sliding bands are used, the procedure is slightly different. After the top scorer of a band is selected, the band is recalculated *without* the top scorer. Thus, it slides down the distribution to include individuals at the next lower score. By considering these scorers as being tied with those remaining from the first band, the next selections can be made as before. After the top scorer is selected, any other scorer in the band can be chosen, either randomly or on the basis of another variable.

The purpose of banding was to provide an alternative to a previously used procedure for increasing workforce diversity. Known as *race norming*, the procedure involved the use of within-group percentiles. This required calculating a percentile score for each applicant based on the performance of a normative sample of the same race or ethnicity. Therefore, individuals' scores were compared only to the scores earned by others of the same group, and it resulted in a percentile score distribution for each racial or ethnic group of applicants (Hartigan & Wigdor, 1989). To use this procedure, an employer combined the percentile scores of test takers of one ethnic group with those of other ethnic groups to create a consolidated list of percentile scores. Then, selection proceeded top-down from the list. This was meant to allow an employer to hire the top scorers of each ethnic group, thereby increasing diversity. However, because within-group percentiles represents a system for granting preferences, the 1991 Civil Rights Act made it illegal.

Test score banding itself is controversial. The most severe criticism is that when there are large numbers of applicants, banding leads to the conclusion that the only defensible form of selection is random selection ( F. L. Schmidt, 1991; Schmidt & Hunter, 1995). This, of course, strikes at the heart of selection measurement. Also, the method may have a legal problem similar to that of race norming. Selecting from the bands by considering an applicant's minority status might conflict with the 1991 Civil Rights Act. A study by Truxillo and Bauer (1999) found that whether an applicant considered test score banding to be fair depended on the person's belief that it was associated with affirmative action. Employers should carefully consider how they explain their use of banding to applicants, in order to reduce any negative reactions.

## Utility of Selection Programs

For many years, personnel psychologists have considered it only reasonable that employers should get information on how effective their selection procedures are. In 1939, Taylor and Russell discussed the practical efficiency of selection tests and devised expectancy tables to help personnel specialists evaluate the ability of selection to meet an organization's needs. In the early assessments, the standard procedure for evaluating the utility of a selection test was to calculate (1) the percentage of satisfactory employees before the test was used, (2) the validity of the test, and (3) the selection ratio, or percentage of test takers who passed the test. Entering these data into the Taylor-Russell tables, the user was able to determine the percentage of successful employees that could be expected from using the test.

The next major step in the development of utility assessment centered on the kind of information that business managers might like to have. It was assumed, in some discussions, that managers were more interested in dollar estimates than percentages and that they would be receptive to utility evidence based on cost accounting (e.g., Brogden & Taylor, 1950). Soon, this assumption was widely accepted. As a result, utility analysis became a way to demonstrate the dollar value of selection. The index of utility was defined as $SD_y$, which is the standard deviation of the performance score distribution in dollars. Various techniques for estimating $SD_y$ were suggested. The earliest of these was developed by Schmidt, Hunter, McKenzie, and Muldrow (1979) to use in a utility study in which supervisors estimated the dollar values of products and services provided annually by employees. The procedure is fairly simple and is appropriate to use if levels of job performance in an organization can be assumed to be normally distributed. Supervisors are asked to estimate the dollar value of job performance of two employees: (1) the average employee on the job (whose performance would be at the 50th percentile, or the mean of the distribution of performance ratings) and (2) the superior employee (whose performance would fall at the 85th percentile, or one standard deviation above the mean). After these estimates are collected, they are averaged across supervisors. The difference in average ratings between the two performance levels corresponds to the size of the standard deviation and is used as the utility estimate, $SD_y$.

Other procedures consider the average salary of individuals performing the job. Reasoning that the value of any HR intervention can be viewed as a proportion of employee salaries, Hunter and Schmidt (1982) recommended a simple procedure with the value of selection being set at 40 percent of salary costs. To estimate $SD_y$ in an organization, simply multiply the average annual salary of those working on a job by 40 percent. A more complex procedure that uses salaries was proposed by Cascio and Ramos (1986), in which the dimensions of the job first are identified and rated in terms of importance. This determines the weight of each dimension in the total job. The average annual salary for the job is then apportioned to each dimension according to its weight. Next, performance ratings on the dimensions are collected for each employee. Then, the overall organizational worth of each employee's performance is calculated by multiplying the dollar value of each dimension by the employee's rating on that dimension and then totaling these values. $SD_y$ is the standard deviation of the distribution of the values across employees.

Researchers have been making an effort to provide ways for HR practitioners to convince managers that high-quality selection is worthwhile. They have designed utility assessment methods to provide monetary information because they assumed that was what managers wanted. Perhaps this was not a good assumption in all situations. Reviewers have observed that managers often do not use the utility information they have available (cf. Boudreau, 1991). Some researchers have found that managers are more supportive of selection programs when only validity information is presented (Latham & Whyte, 1994). Whyte and Latham (1997) found that experienced managers were less persuaded by the presentation of an elaborate utility analysis than by a simple discussion of validity.

Several researchers have attempted to discover why managers are not more receptive to utility evidence. One possibility is that utility analysis procedures are too complicated. Some psychologists and HR practitioners have reported that they themselves find utility analyses hard to understand and explain (Macan & Highhouse, 1994). Managers may react similarly. In one study, managers were given reports on utility analyses that differed in the complexity of the method used and were asked to rate how useful the information would be. The managers responded that the most useful utility analysis was the one conducted by the simplest procedure—the "40% of average salary" method (Hazer & Highhouse, 1997).

How a utility analysis is presented—and for what apparent purpose—is likely to affect managers' reactions to the information. In Whyte & Latham's (1997) study, the manner of presenting the utility analysis seemed unnecessarily heavy handed. It included detailed written and videotaped explanations and a videotaped endorsement by an expert. Cronshaw (1997) thought the managers in that study felt they were being coerced into supporting the selection program and reacted accordingly. If managers are provided with utility analyses for informational purposes, rather than for marketing a selection program, then perhaps a more even-handed approach would be better, regardless of whether utility is couched in terms of dollars or percentages.

## Conclusions

A major goal of the modern organization is to find and hire the best available employees. Organizations perform better if they can reach this goal. The quality of an organization's selection program is critical in determining whether the goal is reached. How well the program functions in this way can be estimated by examining its overall utility. Utility assesses the improvement in performance quality that will result from using the selection program.

To be effective, a selection program must be fully implemented. To ensure this, a strong program will contain guidance on how the employer can implement the selection program's provisions. Guidance is needed in several areas. First, because most selection involves multiple measures, the program needs to include information on how to interpret and use scores from different instruments. The second need for guidance is for a strategy that the employer can use to choose one or more high performers from among finalists. The most pleasant and yet often the most difficult task in selection decision making is having to choose one person to hire from among several highly qualified applicants. The effective selection program will provide a strategy to help the employer make this decision.

## SUMMING UP

The purpose of this chapter is to discuss the role of psychological measurement in the development and use of employee selection measures. Summing up, we can make the following conclusions:

- Psychological measurement is used in selection to distinguish real differences among applicants.
- The precision of a selection measure depends on its scale of measurement.
- A selection plan can help determine when existing predictor measures can be used and when others must be developed.
- A measure's reliability in providing consistent information is assessed with test–retest, alternate forms, split-halves, or interitem techniques.
- Standardization controls error in measurement and improves reliability.
- The reliability of ratings indicates the consistency of judgments.
- Predictor measures can be validated with criterion-related, content, and construct validity techniques.
- Construct validity combines elements of content validation to show relevance and criterion-related validation to show the relation to known measures of the construct.
- If a test's validity generalizes across situations and uses, the test may be used in a new setting without revalidating the instrument.
- With multiple regression, scores from multiple measures are combined into single scores for use in selection decision making.
- Cutoff scores are often needed, such as for multistage decision making using the multiple hurdles strategy.
- Test score banding is an alternative to strict top-down selection.
- The overall value of a selection program can be described by its utility.

## InfoTrac College Edition

To learn more about the issues discussed here and about related topics in research and practice, use your subscription to InfoTrac College Edition to access articles from research journals and other publications. Go to http://www.infotrac-college.com/wadsworth to start your search of this online library. You can enter search terms of your own choosing, or you can use the following keywords to find articles relevant to this chapter.

Employee selection planning        Interrater reliability
Predictive validity                         Meta-analysis

# TESTS OF ABILITY AND KNOWLEDGE

Not so many years ago, textbooks and college instructors routinely defined intelligence as "what IQ tests measure." At the time, many psychologists did not consider it scientifically defensible to offer a definition of general intelligence that went beyond a researcher's ability to test or measure the construct. However, more recently, with the development of cognitive approaches, psychologists are discussing definitions that are richer in meaning.

How would you define intelligence? Sternberg and Kaufman (1998) observed that how this question is answered often depends on *who* answers. Members of different cultures generally consider intelligence to be the cognitive, social, and behavioral attributes that are valued and that are necessary for living in the culture. Many theorists and researchers have considered the capacity to learn and adapt to the environment, and to understand and control oneself to be part of what defines the construct. Although the definitions may be expressed in varying terms, the research suggests that a common core of cognitive abilities is present in most definitions of intelligence. The construct appears to be highly complex and to involve various abilities and knowledge. One model of intelligence was based on a factor analysis of data collected over a period of 60 years (Carroll, 1993). In this model, intelligence is described as a three-layer, hierarchical structure. The lowest layer includes many specific and narrowly defined abilities, such as spelling. The highest layer is a broad general intelligence factor. The middle layer is interesting because of the kinds of abilities included. First, it includes flexible and creative thinking, or "fluid intelligence." It also includes accumulated knowledge, or "crystallized intelligence." Second, it includes processes, such as perceiving, learning, remembering, and forming ideas.

The purpose of this chapter is to examine the nature and use of ability tests in employee selection. I begin with a discussion of the content of ability tests, focusing particularly on intelligence or mental abilities. Next, I discuss the mechanics of ability testing and consider some developments that have far-reaching effects on how selection testing is done. Then, I describe some standardized tests varying in content that are commonly used in employee selection.

# THE CONTENT OF SELECTION TESTS

Selection tests can be distinguished according to *what* they measure and *how* they measure. At this point, let us consider what is being measured—that is, the content of an ability test, particularly the cognitive or mental ability test. Later, I will discuss how ability tests are structured and what tasks are involved.

## Background of Intelligence Testing in the Workplace

Groundbreaking in employment testing took place in the early 1900s with an "intelligence" test that was developed especially for use in classifying men who were inducted into the army during World War I. This test, known as the Army Alpha, was unique in two ways: It was a written, group-administered test, and it was designed to be used for work-related purposes. The test consisted of items on reasoning ability, arithmetic, ability to follow directions, and knowledge of general information. Because many recruits were unable to read English, a second test was designed, called the Army Beta, which was a nonlanguage test. As a result of the successful use of these tests for military selection—which was widely reported to the public—the idea of testing caught on. The use of tests spread like wildfire. They were used for educational purposes and for employee selection in business, industry, and government.

Soon, however, it became apparent that there were problems with intelligence testing in the workplace. First, early intelligence tests were meant to provide a global measure of intelligence. However, an examination of the tests being used made it clear that they were made up of items addressing only certain abilities. Mainly, they were measures of verbal comprehension, such as are involved in academic tasks. Mechanical and other practical or vocational abilities, though recognized widely in the academic community as being part of intelligence, generally were not included. Following the lead of psychologists who designed the Army Alpha, most employment test writers had included a selection of items referring to learned skills, abilities, and academic knowledge in their tests. However, some tests simply measured numerical and verbal ability, with a few items on abstract reasoning. The problem was that if intelligence tests were to be used effectively in employee selection, users needed to know what they were measuring, and different tests probably would be needed.

A second issue that needed clearing up concerned whether intelligence tests were measuring raw talent or learned abilities, or both. For a time, test developers distinguished their tests in terms of aptitude and achievement. Aptitude tests were meant to measure a relatively homogeneous content area relating to a specific ability, such as mechanical or artistic aptitude, that might have an inborn aspect but that could have developed from a variety of learning experiences. Intelligence tests had more heterogeneous content than aptitude tests, including items that address multiple aspects of ability, and provided a more global assessment of intelligence. Achievement tests were narrow in scope and provided a measure of the effects of specific learning, such as a test for a college course. However, even these distinctions soon began to break down. It was difficult to construct aptitude tests that did not include the effects of learning or achievement. Also, employers came to realize that any of these test types might be used to evaluate applicants as to their abilities on the job, and they began to develop their own. Anastasi (1982) noted that as more personnel specialists were trained in psychological measurement, the more the achievement tests they constructed began to look like intelligence tests. This was especially true as the achievement tests began to place less emphasis on recalling specific facts and focused more on broad areas of knowledge that may have been attained through schooling or work experience.

Today, most of these tests are called ability tests. Little is made of the source of the abilities that are tested in various so-called aptitude and achievement tests. Ability tests usually measure both natural talent and the crystallized knowledge that results from learning. The job knowledge test is something of an exception. It is focused on factual information learned on the job itself, on similar jobs, or through similar educational experiences. Thus, the job knowledge test is more clearly an achievement test that is specific to the job. Selection tests today include cognitive or general mental ability tests that contain heterogeneous content and resemble intelligence tests. Other tests focus on specific abilities, and they are used singly or combined in test batteries. Table 8.1 shows the kinds of abilities that are measured in selection testing.

## The Psychometric Approach to Intelligence

The psychometric approach to the study of intelligence reveals the nature of intelligence by measuring signs of it in behavior. This is one of the oldest approaches to the study of intelligence, and it is the basis for employee selection testing. Its history extends back to the late 1800s, when methods for measuring mental capacity were being developed. Spearman (1904) postulated a general intelligence factor as existing in all aspects of intelligent functioning and as determining an individual's level of capacity. His thinking influenced the development of the first test of intelligence. The test was the 1905 Binet-Simon Scale, which had been prepared for the purpose of assessing the general mental capacity of retarded schoolchildren (Binet & Simon, 1916). Ultimately, this work led to modern intelligence tests, such as the Stanford-Binet Intelligence Scale and other IQ tests used for testing in educational settings.

**Factor Theories of Intelligence**    In employment testing, intelligence has been conceptualized in two ways, (1) as having a single and unitary basis, with multiple specific manifestations, and (2) as involving multiple basic factors,

| TABLE 8.1 | TYPES OF ABILITIES MEASURED IN ABILITY TESTS | |

| Ability | Item Types | Examples |
| --- | --- | --- |
| Verbal | Vocabulary, language use, analogies | Acorn is to oak, as egg is to (a) bacon (b) tree (c) seed (d) hen |
| Numerical | Computation, number series, problem solving | Which number completes the series? 1, 2, 4, 8, 16, _____ ? (a) 4  (b) 32  (c) 48  (d) 96 |
| Abstract thinking | Syllogisms, categorical and figural relationships | Which figure completes the series? |
| Mechanical | Mechanical information, physical forces, tool use | Which of the cartwheels carries more weight? |
| Spatial | Object components, relationships, rotations | Which picture is a duplicate of the first? |
| Perceptual speed | Number and word comparisons | Check the pairs that are the same. 0196374_____ 0169374  4796310_____ 4796310  Olivia Anderson_____ Olivia Andersen  Alison Nichols_____ Allison Nichols |

each of which has specific manifestations. The first view reflects Spearman's (1904, 1927) early theory of intelligence. He proposed a two-factor model, positing a general factor of intelligence as the underlying basis for all intelligent activity. He called this the $g$ factor, a term that still is used in research discussions. In addition, Spearman proposed that multiple specifics, or $s$ factors, are present which reflect intelligence in specific activities. Any relationship that exists between tests of specific factors is understood to be due to the influence of the $g$ factor. That is, if the contents of two tests are highly correlated, then the tests are "saturated" with the $g$ factor and, therefore, they are measuring aspects of $g$. In contrast, when tests are measuring different $s$ factors, their intercorrelation is reduced, as is the influence of $g$. It is reasonable to conclude, from this psychometric view of intelligence, that if the $g$ factor runs through all abilities, then an assessment of intelligence might be used to predict performance in any situation. Furthermore, a single test, such as abstract reasoning, that is shown to be highly saturated with $g$, could be used as a measure of intelligence. It would not be necessary to use multiple specific tests to measure such a unitary construct. For the same reason, it would not be necessary for an intelligence test to have heterogeneous content, because $g$ is itself conceptualized as reflecting all aspects of intelligence.

The second perspective on intelligence is that a number of distinctly different basic factors exist, from which specific abilities emerge. In this view, the combination of the multiple basic factors makes up intelligence, and nothing more general than these need be postulated. In this view, the combined individual strengths of the basic factors determine the level of overall intelligence and, conceivably, one basic factor can substitute for another (Hull, 1928). In the multiple-factor theory, the best test of intelligence would be a battery of individual tests measuring the multiple basic factors.

A leading proponent of multiple-factor theory, whose thinking was highly influential in test development, was Thurstone (1938). He proposed several basic factors, or primary mental abilities, such as abilities with words, numbers, and space. In tests, these primary factors might be represented with varying strengths, depending on what activities a test involves. For example, a test might be mainly an arithmetic test and so would be most heavily weighted by the *number* factor. However, it also may have a slight weight from the *word* factor because the instructions and items are expressed linguistically.

**Content of Intelligence Tests**   What do intelligence tests measure? Spearman (1904, 1927) introduced a method for analyzing and identifying the contents or factors that are measured in tests. (This methodology is reflected in his psychometric theory, i.e., in the definition of $g$ and $s$ factors.) Later theorists (e.g., Thurstone, 1947) further advanced the methodology toward what we know as factor analysis. Briefly, in a factor analysis to determine what a test measures, a researcher begins with a complete matrix of intercorrelations between the parts of the test (i.e., items or subtests). At the end of the factor analysis, a factor matrix results which shows a limited number of relationships, or *factors,* that are more or less present in each part of the test. When a test can be explained by one factor, it means that all parts or items of the test are "loaded" heavily or saturated with one factor and related very little to any other factor. When the test is explained by two factors, some parts of the test are heavily loaded on one factor and not on the other, whereas other parts show the reverse pattern. Labeling the factors is a judgment process. The researcher needs to examine the parts of the test and the strengths shown by the loadings on the different factors.

## Conclusions

Although some early developers of mental ability tests were influenced by Spearman's g factor concept, most were finally persuaded that intelligence was a multiple-factor construct, such as Thurstone described, and the result was a number of multiple aptitude test batteries that contained tests of various primary mental abilities. Recently, however, there has been renewed interest in the g factor. The reasons for this have to do with the results of several studies that have evaluated what mental ability tests and test batteries measure. First, the tests in multiple aptitude batteries often show high intercorrelations, which indicates that a general factor, or psychometric g, is being measured by the tests in the battery (Olea & Ree, 1994; Ree & Earles, 1991; Ree, Earles, & Teachout, 1994). Many studies have shown that general mental ability, whether measured by a single test or a battery, is predictive of job performance (Hunter, 1986; Jensen, 1984). Also, as discussed previously, validity generalization studies have shown that cognitive or mental ability tests have broad application for various jobs and organizational settings (Schmidt & Hunter, 1981b). Although we are not ready to discard the idea of multiple basic abilities, we are increasingly willing to consider that a single general factor of intelligence might also be operating in employment testing.

## THE MECHANICS OF TESTING

A variety of ability tests are used in testing job applicants. They differ somewhat in their content. They also differ in how they are administered, scored, and interpreted, as I discussed, in general terms, in the section on test standardization in Chapter 7. At this point, let us look at some of these differences from the standpoint of using ability tests.

### Administration of Ability Tests

Our first question in administering a test is whether it is a group test or an individual test. Few ability tests are administered individually to job applicants. Those that are given this way typically are *performance tests* that involve a sensory or physical activity and use some type of special equipment. For example, a hearing test using an audiometer is an individually administered test of hearing sensitivity in which a test taker judges the quality and loudness of variously pitched tones. Another commonly used individual test is a typing test in which an applicant's speed and accuracy on a typewriter, computer, or other keyboard is assessed.

Most ability tests are administered to groups of test takers. As you learned in Chapter 7, group testing can make the standardization of a test easy to maintain. Testing a group requires fewer administrations, and this means testing conditions are less likely to cause error in the test. Although there are costs in group testing, mainly because a group has to be scheduled and test conditions arranged, the costs generally are not great. However, for individually administered tests that require the time of a test administrator giving personal attention to each applicant, the costs can be considerable.

Group testing is made possible by the use of *written tests*, which are also called *pencil-and-paper tests*. Both written tests and performance tests have timing requirements, and timing is a distinguishing feature of tests. *Speed tests* sharply limit the amount of time a test taker has for completing the test. A speed test can involve a performance task, such as placing small pins in holes on a board. A speed test also can be a written test, such as comparing names or numbers and indicating whether they are the same or different. Speed tests are simple. Most people could do them with complete accuracy—if they had enough time. What is being assessed, however, is a person's ability to work quickly without making a lot of mistakes. Such tests are appropriate for jobs, such as in production and clerical work, that have an important requirement for quick thinking and action. Other tests are referred to as *power tests*. They are meant to assess an applicant's depth of ability, or power. Many written tests of mental ability or job knowledge are power tests. The items are difficult and most people could not answer all of them correctly—even if they had a lot of time. Strictly speaking, a power test is not a timed test because accuracy, rather than speed, is being evaluated. However, because of the needs for standardization, even these tests have a time limit, albeit a generous one.

**Computer-Assisted Testing**    Increasingly, written tests are being administered by computer. Conventional written tests are computerized by means of software that is used to store the test and to instruct the computer in presenting items, accepting a test taker's responses, and scoring the test. Once the initial work is done to computerize a test, administration and scoring costs are low. Standardization of testing conditions can be maintained, and reliability appears to be as good as for the conventional test (Greaud & Green, 1986).

One potentially important difference between pencil-and-paper and computerized versions of tests has been observed. The difference is attributable to features of the computer administration process, especially of speed tests, and it shows up in test scores. A meta-analysis of test results from computerized and conventional tests first showed the difference. Scores on computerized versions of power tests correlated at .97 with conventional power tests, but computerized speed tests correlated at .72 with conventional speed tests (Mead & Drasgow, 1993). The researchers suggested that the reduced correlation might have been due to differences between test takers in the motor skills that are required for responding to test items via computer. Another study, using scores on the computerized and conventional versions of the General Aptitude Test Battery (GATB),[1] also found a difference on speed tests (Van de Vijver & Harsveld, 1994). Individuals taking the test by computer were significantly faster. They completed more items in the same time period than those using the pencil-and-paper version. However, they also were significantly less accurate. The researchers suggested that their inaccuracy may have resulted from a shift in the individual's test-taking strategy that was caused by using the computer. That is, a person may feel greater pressure to work fast when using a "fast" computer than when using a pencil-and-paper test. Also, presenting items one at a time on a computer screen may discourage item-skipping. (Item-skipping, when a person does not know the answer, is a good strategy on speed tests.)

## Scores on Ability Tests

To be effective for employee selection purposes, predictor measures must be free from bias, and passing scores must be carefully defined and used fairly. These requirements are particularly relevant in a discussion of ability testing. First, most of the research on the reliability, validity, and fairness of predictor measures has been conducted using written ability tests. Second, certain federal requirements for fairness in selection are couched in terms of objectively scorable measures, such as written ability tests. Further, much of the discussion of test fairness refers to the meaning and use of ability test scores to make employment decisions.

**Selection Test Fairness**   The term "test fairness" has been used to refer to various ways in which unfair discrimination in testing may occur. One possibility, which was suggested in the early studies of intelligence testing, was that test items reflect only the white, middle-class experience. Researchers thought that this cultural difference might cause minority applicants to score lower on selection tests than white, middle-class applicants. Considerable discussion of such possible unfairness took place during the 1960s. Soon, research was being done to evaluate the extent to which standardized ability tests might have systematically biased effects. In the midst of this activity, the *Uniform Guidelines* (1978) identified fairness as a concept relevant to the standards for criterion-related validity studies. The term "unfairness" was defined as follows:

---

[1]The GATB is a speed test of general mental ability developed by the U.S. Department of Labor, for use by state employment offices in testing and placing job seekers.

When members of one race, sex, or ethnic group characteristically obtain lower scores on a selection procedure than members of another group, and the differences in scores are not reflected in differences in a measure of job performance, use of the selection procedure may unfairly deny opportunities to members of the group that obtains the lower scores. [section 1607.14b(8a)]

The *Uniform Guidelines* went on to identify conditions under which employers might need to evaluate their tests for statistical evidence of test unfairness with criterion-related validity studies. Actually, it was noted that in the practical business situation, statistical evaluation probably would not be technically feasible because the methodology for these validity studies required such large samples. Most employers simply would not have enough employees in a job class to perform the studies appropriately. Therefore, the standard was being addressed mainly to large employers and commercial test developers.

Researchers looking for evidence of bias already had identified ways that tests might be unfair. One possibility was that, whereas a test might be valid for the majority group, it might not be valid for a minority group. The test scores of the minority group might have no relationship to how these individuals perform on the job. This is called *single-group validity*. Another possibility, known as *differential validity*, was that a test might be valid for both groups, but differentially predictive. In this case, the test is valid because increasing test scores are associated with increasing levels of performance for both groups. However, the relationship between a test score and a person's job performance is proposed to differ depending on the identity of the individual. That is, the test scores of one group do not mean the same, in terms of work performance, as the scores of the other group. In either type of bias, researchers should examine tests for constant error.

Academic researchers had found that regression analysis could be used to examine the statistical relationship between test scores and performance criterion scores and to show whether or not there was constant error in a test.[2] Recall that there are two features of the regression line that, once generated from test data, function as constants in predicting the criterion—the slope and the intercept. In part (a) of Figure 8.1, you see a scatterplot of scores (represented by the ellipse form) and a regression line indicating a valid predictor of a single undifferentiated sample. The scores of the groups within the sample completely overlap. The relationship of their test scores to criterion scores is exactly the same. Part (b) of Figure 8.1 shows a similarly valid predictor of two groups with scatterplots showing identical regression lines, but there is a difference in the mean scores of the groups. Does this indicate test unfairness? No, as the term is defined by the *Uniform Guidelines*, it does not. Also, in the statistical sense of the word, it does not, because the slope and the intercept of the regression line are the same for both groups. This is the kind of pattern

[2]The procedure is known as the "Cleary model" because of Cleary's (1968) studies of educational test score distributions.

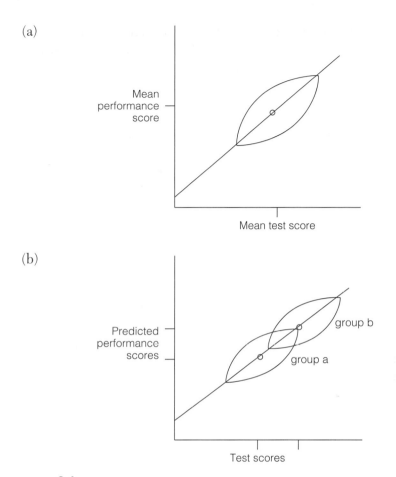

**FIGURE 8.1**

(a) Scatterplot and regression line used to predict performance from a single undifferentiated group's test scores.
(b) Scatterplots and regression lines showing a valid test for two groups with different mean scores.

that might be observed when one group does better on a test and on a performance measure because the group is made up of people with more training and work experience. Such a test is not unfair for use in selecting high performers for the job. If the groups can be distinguished by their ethnicity, then this pattern shows adverse impact on the lower scoring group. However, the finding of adverse impact, in itself, is not a showing of statistical unfairness. Rather, as expressed in the *Uniform Guidelines*, a finding of adverse impact is a signal that a study of test unfairness might legally be required.

If a test is valid for one group but not for the other, as in the proposed single-group validity, different regression lines would be shown in the scatterplots of scores for two groups, as demonstrated in part (a) of Figure 8.2. In this, the regression line for group a shows that the test is not valid because an increase in test scores is not associated with an increase in performance scores. That is, the slope of the regression line for group a is zero, and the regression line is flat. However, the test is valid for group b, as shown by the slope of its regression line, which has a positive, greater-than-zero value. On the other hand, if a test is proposed to have differential validity, the slopes of the regression lines of both groups are predicted to have positive, nonzero values, which indicate that increases in test scores are associated with increases in criterion scores and that the test is valid for both groups. However, if there is differential validity, a difference in the values of the slopes is predicted, as shown in part (b) of Figure 8.2. The slope value difference tells us that the test scores of one group predict different performance scores than are predicted by the same test scores of the other group.

Another way that bias might be shown is when the regression lines of the two groups have different intercepts, although the slopes are identical. Notice in part (c) of Figure 8.2 that the regression line of group a intercepts the $y$-axis at a higher point than the regression line of group b. This means that the predicted performance of a test score from group a is greater than the predicted performance of the same score from group b. If group a is a minority group and b is the majority group, then the same performance can be expected from a minority applicant scoring lower on the test as from a majority applicant scoring higher on the test. This is the kind of test unfairness that psychologists were most concerned about, and it is what is being referred to in the *Uniform Guidelines'* definition of the concept. If an employer uses the regression line for the majority group in deciding to accept or reject job applicants—as it usually is because in small samples there usually are not enough minorities to calculate separate regression lines—then it is unfair to minority applicants because this regression line underpredicts their performance.

I have described three ways that test-criterion score relationships might be biased. So, what is the evidence that these various forms of bias actually affect a test's ability to predict performance? Although many studies were done, and careful reviews of these were published, there is very little evidence that such biases are present in standardized ability tests. Reviews of studies on well-designed single-group validity and differential validity indicated that these patterns of test-criterion score relationships occurred no more frequently than chance (Boehm, 1977; Hunter, Schmidt, & Hunter, 1979). Whereas there is some evidence indicating the operation of intercept bias, the evidence is not strong, and the bias effect may be as likely to be to the benefit of the minority group as to its detriment (Bartlett, Bobko, Mosier, & Hannan, 1978). For example, about 8 percent of the intercept differences were significant in a review of studies involving Hispanic test takers. Intercept bias tended to be in the direction of performance overprediction for the minority group, however, rather than underprediction as would be expected (Schmidt, Pearlman, & Hunter, 1980).

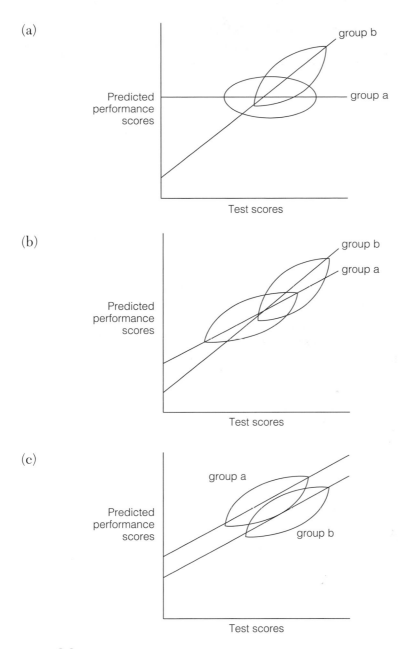

**FIGURE 8.2**

(a) Scatterplots and regression lines showing single-group validity. Group b's regression line slope is positive, indicating validity. Group a's regression line slope equals zero, indicating the test is not valid for this group.

(b) Regression lines showing differential validity. The slopes of the regression lines are both positive, indicating validity for each group. The value of the slopes differ, indicating differential performance prediction for the two groups.

(c) Intercept bias. The slopes of the regression lines are the same for each group. The values of the intercepts differ, indicating test unfairness.

In conclusion, the research indicates that if they are valid, ability tests do not underpredict the performance of minority applicants. However, there has been some concern that these findings may be cloaking a real difference resulting from use of criterion measures that are biased in the same way as a test could be (cf. Sackett & Wilk, 1994). The typical performance criterion measure is a supervisor's rating and most supervisors are nonminorities; therefore, the performance measure could be culturally biased against minorities. This possibility was investigated recently using a very large set of concurrent validation data on the General Aptitude Test Battery. With this data set, it was possible to study the extent to which performance prediction was affected by the rater. Rotundo and Sackett (1999) examined the differences between Black and White employees' ratings when all were rated by a White supervisor and when each was rated by a supervisor of the same race. They reasoned that if there is culture bias in performance ratings, it would be expressed in ratings provided by a different-race rater, but not in ratings provided by a same-race rater. However, in neither analysis was there evidence of predictive bias. Rater race did not affect the relationship between mental ability test scores and performance ratings. This study provides unique support to the regression literature on test unfairness, and it contributes to the conclusion that a well-developed and valid mental ability test, such as the GATB, does not cause biased predictions, even when it is used to predict a judgment measure of performance.

## Computer Adaptive Testing

As described earlier, the computerization of pencil-and-paper ability tests assists in the administration and scoring of tests. Computer adaptive testing (CAT), however, is a potentially more powerful alternative to conventional testing, because it more effectively uses the computer's capacity (Weiss & Vale, 1987). By means of software designed for adaptive testing, the computer "interacts" with the test taker. In the process, the computer both develops and administers a customized or tailored test. Items are selected for the test taker from a stored bank of items that have been validated to represent different levels of difficulty on the test. The computer uses the person's responses to earlier test items to select later test items.

Unlike conventional testing, which is based on classical test theory, CAT is based on item response theory (IRT) (Lord & Novick, 1968). In fact, classical test theory is not useful for guiding computer adaptive testing because it assumes that the items in a test are fixed and that individual test takers are given the same test (Drasgow & Hulin, 1990). These are not appropriate assumptions in CAT, because items are not fixed and individuals are given different "tests" that have been customized especially for each person. IRT is a better basis for CAT because it makes no such assumptions about tests but, rather, focuses on item characteristics. Item response theory is a group of mathematical models that can be used to describe test items in terms of how difficult they are and how well they distinguish among individuals who have different levels of ability. A test developer can use the models to infer a person's underlying ability level based on his or her responses to a set of items that have known levels of difficulty and discriminability. Generally, if we know how easy or difficult the test items are, then we can infer an individual's ability level from the difficulty of the questions answered correctly.

CAT has several features that might appeal to employers. First, because individual tests are tailored to the person, test security is greater than in conventional testing. Second, test length can be shortened by using only questions at the appropriate levels. Thus, test takers do not spend time answering questions that provide no information about their ability levels (i.e., questions that are so easy that anyone could answer them, or so hard that the person is guessing). Third, the CAT can be designed to yield the most precise measurement or to make use of a cutoff score.

In general, a CAT yields a more precise measure of any test taker's ability because more items at the appropriate level are included in the customized test. In the typical pencil-and-paper test, the overall difficulty is at the level of the average test taker, and the most precise measure the test provides is for the person of average ability. Individuals who have either high or low ability are measured less precisely by the conventional test because the test contains fewer items at their level. For example, unless there are some questions that are too difficult for a test taker to answer, the test cannot show the person's upper limit and cannot distinguish him or her from other high-ability individuals. To make a conventional test assess low- and high-ability individuals more precisely, additional easy and difficult items would have to be added, and this could make the test too long. This problem does not occur with computer adaptive testing. To test a person, more items at the appropriate level of difficulty are selected from the bank of items. Relatively few items are selected that are too easy or too hard. This means that the CAT can be shorter for each person and yet provide a precise measure at all ability levels.

Item response theory answers a number of technical questions in the design of a CAT concerning (1) how to start the test, (2) how to select the best items, (3) how to get a test score or estimate of a person's real ability level, and (4) how to end the test (Weiss & Vale, 1987). First, the CAT starts with an item that estimates the test taker's ability level. Unless some biographical information is available on the test taker that would indicate otherwise, such as educational level, a good assumption is that the test taker is an average person. Each item in the CAT item bank has been developed and calibrated specifically to measure different levels of difficulty. Therefore, the computer randomly chooses an item from those that are calibrated at average difficulty and presents it as the first question. Second, if the test taker answers the first question correctly, the computer selects the next question from a set of items that represent a slightly higher level of difficulty. If the individual answers the first question incorrectly, the second item is selected from those at a slightly lower level of difficulty. The same process continues until the difficulty level is found beyond which the person cannot answer correctly.

Third, a score on a CAT can be conceptualized as an estimate of a person's performance on a very complete test with items at many levels of difficulty. This "very complete test" exists in the computer's item bank, of course, and the computer's adaptive procedure allows the score on the full test to be estimated from a well-chosen sample of the items. Each time an item is administered and the person responds, the computer updates its estimate of the person's level of ability. Notice that we start with an estimate of average ability. After the first response, we have one bit of information with which to revise the estimate to either slightly above or slightly below average, depending on whether the answer was correct. Each new ability estimate is based on information available to the computer which shows the probabilities that an item would be answered correctly by individuals who have various levels of ability. The distribution of probabilities for an item, which is called the *item response curve*, shows how likely a person with a known level of ability would be to answer correctly. By comparing the test taker's answer to the probability distribution for the item, the computer generates a new ability estimate and also a standard error of measurement, which indicates how likely it is that the ability estimate is wrong. The testing process continues with new items administered and new ability estimates and standard errors generated after each response. As the standard error of the estimates becomes smaller, the estimated score approaches the person's actual ability level, as shown in Figure 8.3.

Fourth, depending on how precisely we want to measure the test takers, we can direct the computer to end the test when the standard error of an ability estimate is less than a certain cutoff level. If we want to be very sure that an ability estimate is accurate, we can set the standard error cutoff near zero. There are other ways to end a CAT. Drasgow and Hulin (1990) point out that while the computer can be directed to give all test takers the same number of items, this will result in variations of measurement precision among the test takers. That is, fewer items will be needed for some test takers than for others, to reach the same accuracy of measurement. Instead, a cutoff test score can be used to end a CAT. Employers are not usually interested in obtaining the most precise measure of an applicant's ability. For selection purposes, they often want to identify only those applicants who pass a cutoff score. To accomplish this with a CAT, a cutoff score on the test must be established that represents the necessary ability level for someone who can satisfactorily perform the job. The computer uses this score and the standard error of an individual's ability estimate to determine when the test taker is clearly above or below the cutoff point.

So far, the use of CAT technology to develop tests appears to have been limited mainly to test developers and organizations that use tests on a large

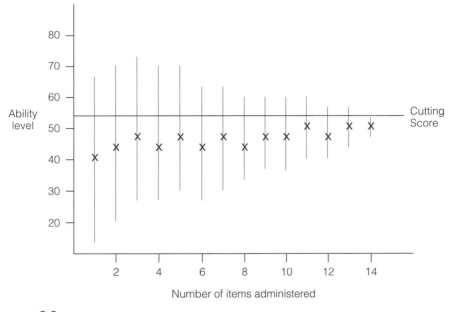

FIGURE **8.3**

CAT ability estimates compared to a cutting score. The lines bracketing the x scores represent the standard error of measurement. When the ability estimate plus the standard error clears the cutting score, the test is ended. This test taker did not pass.

From "Adaptive Testing," by D. J. Weiss and C. D. Vale, *Applied Psychology: An International Review, 36*(3/4), p. 255. Copyright 1987 by Blackwell Publishers Limited. Oxford, UK. Reprinted by permission.

scale. For example, an equivalent CAT version of the Armed Services Vocational Aptitude Battery, which is used for selection and classification by the military services, was developed (Cudek, 1985). Other standardized mental ability tests that are used for employment purposes have been offered commercially as a CAT. For example, the developers of the Differential Aptitude Tests (DAT), which is a widely used mental ability test battery, offered a CAT version. In the late 1980s, it was evaluated positively as showing equivalence with the pencil-and-paper version (Henly, Klebe, McBride, & Cudeck, 1989). Also, a study conducted during 1994 using the CAT versions of three of the DAT tests found them to be useful in predicting the performance of trainees for oil refinery jobs (Alkhadher, Clarke, & Anderson, 1998). However, since its 1987 publication, the CAT version appears to have been neglected and is now technologically out of date (Wise, 1995).

As yet, there has been little use of CAT methodology in private industry to develop CATs in-house. However, this may change if employers begin to make use of CAT-equivalents of the standardized tests they purchase. The difficulty, as in any test development and evaluation, is that large samples are essential, which will limit the development of CATs to large employers. Overton, Harms,

Taylor, and Zickar (1997) reported on an in-house CAT developed by a large private industry employer. The primary motivation for constructing the CAT was concern about test security and the unavailability of an alternate form of an existing pencil-and-paper test. The developers realized their intention to improve test security. However, the resulting CAT was not fully satisfactory. The test had been designed to use a fixed number of items that were found to be extremely difficult and more time consuming than the conventional test. Still, the researchers were optimistic about the potential of adaptive testing and believed that adjustments in the item bank and use of a different cutoff scoring strategy could improve their CAT.

## Conclusions

Ability testing has had a tremendous impact on employment selection. The impact is so pronounced that in many discussions, the term "test" is used to signify any selection predictor measure. Ability tests are widely recognized as providing the most useful information for selection purposes. Historically, ability test theory and methodology have been used to guide the development and evaluation of various predictor measures. New developments in the construction, administration, and scoring of selection techniques have evolved from beginnings in ability testing, particularly in mental ability or intelligence testing. The importance of ability tests can be seen in the literature on employment discrimination. Although it is recognized that any predictor measure may be unfair, in fact, the methodology for statistically assessing measurement bias is test methodology, and the usual test evaluated for discrimination is an ability test. The importance of ability tests in the evolution of selection measurement, perhaps, can be seen most clearly when computers are used. At first, computers were used simply as filing cabinets for selection test data. They were places to store test items and individuals' scores. Then, they were used as "page-turners" to assist in the administration of written ability tests. Now, we have the capacity to use the computer as an individual "examiner" in adaptive testing. Drasgow and Hulin (1990) indicated some of the possibilities for using CAT methodology for a variety of selection measures including work sample performance tests, assessment center activities such as business games, and various dynamic visual and spatial tasks.

## STANDARDIZED ABILITY TESTS

Much of selection testing is done by means of standardized ability tests that can be purchased from test developers. Tests are available for many different abilities that may be needed on the job. In this section, we will look at some examples of commercially available tests.

## Tests of General Mental Ability

Some general mental ability tests are single measures that provide a global estimate of intelligence. Others are organized into a battery of tests that were designed to assess multiple abilities, but also measure general mental ability. Here, we will look at a single test and a battery that are used in industry. Both are classics in employee selection testing.

**Wonderlic Personnel Test**    The Wonderlic Personnel Test is a single measure of general mental ability. It was developed in 1938 from an earlier test—the Otis Self-Administering Test of Mental Ability—and it has been used in business, industry, and government since that time. The test is offered in 16 comparable or similar forms, and it is available in French, Spanish, and American Spanish and English. It has been reviewed many times in the *Mental Measurements Yearbook*, and is well-known as a brief measure of general intelligence, or psychometric *g*.

There are a total of 50 items in the Wonderlic, with a time limit of 12 minutes. Tests are scored by counting the total number of items out of 50 that were answered correctly. Item content includes vocabulary, logical reasoning, arithmetic problem solving, and geometric figure analysis. The items range from very easy to fairly difficult. The Wonderlic uses a spiral omnibus format, in which the easiest items of the various types included in the test are presented first, with the next easiest items following these, and so on, until the most difficult ones are presented at the end. A spiral omnibus arrangement of items makes a single time limit reasonable and easy to administer. It also solves the test developer's problem of having to decide which content group of items to present first (Anastasi, 1982).

The Wonderlic's publisher reports good reliability, documented with test–retest reliability coefficients between .82 and .94, and alternate forms reliability coefficients between .73 and .95. A variety of validity evidence has been provided, including 22 published studies in which the Wonderlic was used. Meta-analytic reviews of cognitive test validities are discussed, indicating that such tests are more predictive of job performance than other selection measures. A reviewer agreed that the Wonderlic, like other general mental ability tests, is likely to be valid to some degree for most jobs (Schmidt, 1985). The widespread use of the Wonderlic has resulted in an extensive database of many thousands of test scores, from which group norms have been derived. These are made available to users for interpreting their applicants' scores. Tables are provided showing the distribution of scores by demographic characteristics, such as educational level, gender, age, and ethnicity, and by occupation or job.

| TABLE 8.2 | MEAN SCORES ON THE WONDERLIC PERSONNEL TEST FOR A SAMPLE OF JOBS | | |
| --- | --- | --- | --- |

| Job | *n* | *M* | *SD* |
| --- | --- | --- | --- |
| Engineer | 584 | 28.6 | 6.7 |
| Department head | 614 | 28.0 | 6.7 |
| Purchasing agent | 292 | 26.9 | 7.7 |
| Lab technician | 505 | 26.4 | 7.7 |
| Computer operator | 2,122 | 25.1 | 7.6 |
| Bookkeeper | 1,092 | 23.8 | 7.1 |
| Circulation manager | 619 | 23.3 | 7.8 |
| General office worker | 5,949 | 22.8 | 7.0 |
| Reservations agent | 5,515 | 22.2 | 9.9 |
| Shop apprentice | 760 | 21.8 | 7.6 |
| Meter reader | 530 | 20.0 | 7.8 |
| Mail clerk | 1,193 | 19.8 | 7.5 |
| Food service worker | 1,256 | 19.4 | 8.4 |
| Material handler | 804 | 18.2 | 8.2 |
| General factory worker | 11,537 | 17.5 | 8.1 |
| Custodian | 812 | 16.7 | 8.6 |

From "Job-Specific Applicant Pools and National Norms for Cognitive Ability Tests: Implications for Range Restriction Corrections in Validation Research," by P. R. Sackett and D. J. Ostgaard, 1994, *Journal of Applied Psychology, 70*(5), p. 682. Copyright 1994 by American Psychological Association, Washington, DC 20002-4242. Reprinted by permission.

The mean scores, standard deviations, and number of applicants tested for 80 different jobs have been collected and are listed in the test manual (Sackett & Ostgaard, 1994). A sample of these data is shown in Table 8.2 for 16 of the 80 jobs.

**Differential Aptitude Tests (DAT)**    The DAT is a battery of eight tests. It was originally designed in 1947, following the multiple-factor theory of intelligence testing. The multiple tests have been evaluated for their ability to independently predict the different ability areas, and the evidence is strong that they can do so. In addition, there is evidence of high intercorrelations among the tests, which suggests that there is a general mental ability factor running through performance on all of them. Five of the tests (verbal reasoning, numerical reasoning, abstract reasoning, spelling, and language usage) contain 40 items each. Mechanical reasoning has 60 items, and space relations has 50. A speed test of perceptual speed and accuracy has 100 items. Scores are generated for each of the eight content areas and for total ability.

There is evidence that the eight tests are reliable. Internal consistency reliability ranges from .80 to .95 among the tests, and alternate forms reliability ranges from .73 to .90. The battery is appropriate for testing the scholastic ability of high school students and adults, and validity information consists mainly of correlations with educational aptitude and achievement tests. A serious criticism of the DAT is that little effort has been made to analyze and report on its validity for predicting work-related criteria. Meta-analysis techniques could be used to analyze data from years of work-related use, since the DAT has been used for selection purposes throughout its existence (Anastasi, 1982; Hattrup, 1995).

A partial DAT battery, including two tests—the verbal and numerical reasoning tests—is available and appears to be as good as the complete DAT in terms of validity for predicting school achievement. A composite calculated by summing the raw scores on the two tests can be used as a valid index of scholastic ability. The test publisher recently reported correlations of the composite with the College Board's Scholastic Aptitude Test, at .68 on the verbal SAT and .77 on the math SAT. In addition, the composite correlated at .76 with the academic ability score on the Armed Services Vocational Aptitude Battery[3] (ASVAB) (Hattrup, 1995). Given the strength of the partial battery, an effective strategy for employers might be to use it, instead of the full battery, as a less time-consuming measure of general mental ability. If applicant information is needed on specific abilities, single tests of these might be obtained.

## Tests of Special Abilities

For some kinds of work, a general mental ability test or test battery may be more than is needed. Instead, a test that measures a specific type of ability is preferred. An employer also might want to use one or more special ability tests in addition to a general mental ability test depending on the complexity and difficulty of the work. Many specialized ability tests are available. In the next pages, we will consider some examples.

**Mechanical Abilities**  Some jobs, such as in engineering, construction, and manufacturing, require at least some understanding of mechanical concepts. A test that has a long history of use for such jobs is the Bennett Mechanical Comprehension Test. First published in 1940, it was among the special ability tests developed in response to the finding that most of the general intelligence tests being used were tests of academic ability that did not adequately measure practical or vocational abilities. The test is designed for use in selection of industrial employees and trainees for jobs that require mechanical abilities. It has been widely used by industrial and military employers and is currently

[3]The ASVAB is used for selection and placement of individuals in military service jobs.

available in two forms. It is a pencil-and-paper test, using questions with pictorial illustrations that demonstrate physical relationships. There are 68 items and a 30-minute time limit. Routinely, it is group administered. A tape-recorded reading of test questions is available for use with applicants whose reading ability is limited. Spanish and American English versions of the written and tape-recorded tests are available. The Bennett's internal consistency reliability is in the .80s on each form. Criterion-related validity studies indicate that the test is valid for predicting job performance in the mechanical trades and engineering (Ghiselli, 1966).

The Revised Minnesota Paper Form Board is a related test involving spatial relationships. It is meant to test a person's ability to think in terms of objects in space. Introduced in 1930, the test has a long history of use for both educational and employee selection purposes. Although it is a pencil-and-paper test, language is not required. The items consist of drawings of geometric figures, such as squares, that have been cut into pieces. Each item presents a drawing of the disordered pieces, and the test taker selects one of several alternatives that depicts the reassembled figure. This is a speed test; there are 64 items and a 20-minute time limit. Norms from industrial samples are available to employers showing scores of both job applicants and employees. Test–retest and alternate forms reliability coefficients range from .71 to .85. The test correlates with other tests of spatial relations and mechanical abilities. It is widely recognized as a valid test of spatial ability (Thayer, 1985).

**Perceptual Abilities**    Many jobs, especially those requiring mechanical skill, require at least minimum levels of sensory abilities, such as hearing and seeing, and employers may need ways to establish that the requirements are met. The most commonly used vision test is the Snellen letter chart, which gives a measure of distance vision. (This is the familiar poster hanging in optometrists' offices, with the big "E" at the top.) The test is used by having a test taker identify the smallest line of letters he or she can read from a distance of 20 feet, and comparing that to what the average person can see. Visual acuity of 20/30 means that the test taker must be as close as 20 feet away from what others can see from 30 feet away.

Most jobs need more than basic sensory abilities, of course, and performance on a job may require the ability to mentally process sensory information. Many different types of clerical and related work, such as proofreading, typing, filing, data entry, and bookkeeping, have special requirements for perceptual speed and accuracy. The Minnesota Clerical Test is an appropriate measure for assessing this ability. The test was first developed in 1931 and, like the other standardized tests described here, is a classic in personnel selection. It is also used in educational institutions for counseling students who are interested in clerical work. The test contains two subtests, involving comparisons of numbers and of names. The items are pairs of either identical or dissimilar names or numbers. The test taker responds by checking off the identical pairs. There are 200 items on each subtest and a time limit of 15 minutes for the whole test. Scores are calculated for each subtest by subtracting the number of incorrect from the number of correct answers. The Minnesota Clerical has good test–retest reliability, with coefficients at .86 and .87 for the names subtest and at .81 and .83 for the numbers test. There are studies showing criterion-related validity, using both production measures and supervisors' ratings. Also, the test correlates well with other tests of clerical aptitude, verbal and numerical ability, and typing speed. Norms are provided, showing the scores of clerical applicants, trainees, and employees. However, the most recent reviewer of the test found that the norms needed updating (Thomas, 1985).

**Physical Abilities**    Many jobs, such as in the building trades and manufacturing, involve considerable physical labor. Other jobs, such as police work and firefighting, also have important physical ability requirements. Some organizations rely on job analysis to define the physical requirements, and they develop content-validated work sample measures for the specific job. The physical requirements of jobs need to be evaluated carefully. One reason is that there is potential for discrimination here, particularly against disabled applicants. Any physical standard that is used in selecting new employees needs to be established as being a real requirement for the job. In addition, physical abilities are not highly interrelated, and they are not necessarily predictable from a general measure. J. C. Hogan (1991) identified the types of physical abilities that may be involved in work. These include whole-body physical abilities, such as (1) muscular strength, such as for lifting; (2) endurance, such as in loading materials and climbing; and (3) balance, such as in using a ladder or scaffold. For certain jobs, whole-body physical activities are less important than coordinated perceptual-motor skills, in which muscular responses depend on sensory information and feedback.

Two standardized perceptual-motor skill tests are commercially available. These are the Crawford Small Parts Dexterity Test and the Purdue Pegboard. Both have long been used in industry for testing finely coordinated perceptual-motor skills or manual dexterity. Both are performance tests involving a testing apparatus that consists of a board and small materials to be manipulated. The Crawford test has two parts, yielding two scores. In one part, test takers use tweezers to pick up and position a pin in a small hole on the board and then to place a collar on each pin. In the second part, they place small screws in threaded holes in the board and use a screwdriver to fasten them down. There are 36 holes for each part of the test. Scoring can be done in either of two ways. One, the time required for a test taker to complete all 36 items in each part can be measured and used as the two scores. This means that the test must be individually administered. Two, the test can be speeded by applying a time limit of 3 minutes for part I and 5 minutes for part II. The score would then be the number of items completed in each part. This allows the test to be group administered. The Purdue Pegboard test uses a similar apparatus and similar tasks, but does not use tools. It also contains two parts. In the first, test takers insert pegs into small holes with the right hand, left hand, and then both hands in successive trials. The second part is an assembly task in which they assemble pegs, washers, and collars in each hole. The Purdue is a speed test with scores reflecting the amount of work done in the allotted time. Both the Purdue and the Crawford were developed during the 1940s and have been used extensively for industrial employee selection.

## Conclusions

Employers have many ability testing options for meeting their selection needs. Purchasing the use of a standardized test can be an effective and economical strategy. As I discussed earlier, validity generalization research has shown that reliable and valid ability tests can be used effectively for jobs that are similar to those included in the tests' validity studies. In addition, valid tests of general mental ability can predict performance in most jobs. Routinely, test publishers provide norms for employers to use in scoring tests. They provide data on the validity and reliability of the tests and identify the samples used in these studies. Conservatively, an employer needs to establish that the jobs for which a test is being used are similar to those used in a test's validation study. Conducting a job analysis to identify ability requirements and to provide content validity for the use of the test is the best way to establish that a standardized test meets an employer's needs.

## DEVELOPING A JOB KNOWLEDGE TEST

In Chapter 7, I discussed the development and use of a selection plan, through which an employer could determine the nature and extent of the needs for predictor measures. Recall that a selection plan is based on a thorough job analysis, involves a study of selection resources and literature, and results in a matrix specifying commercially available measures. The matrix also highlights job requirements for which there is no available instrument and for which one will need to be developed. A frequent need for in-house development is for a means of assessing job knowledge. New employees often need to have at least a minimum level of specialized knowledge at the time they are hired. An employer who has conducted a task inventory job analysis may use it to both develop and content-validate a written test that provides a representative sample of the knowledge required on a job.

The U.S. Civil Service Commission issued a guidebook for developing written tests that follows the content validation model (Gavin, 1977). The first step is to define the objectives by specifying what job content will be measured and how the test will be used in selection (i.e., to screen out or rank applicants). Second, the entire test development project is planned, including the test's format, timing, length, and specific content. The culmination of the planning is a written test content outline that documents the reasoning and procedures of the test development. The test content outline demonstrates how and to what extent the test can be considered to adequately sample the knowledge required on the job. That is, it provides the evidence of content validity. (Table 8.3 shows an example of a test content outline.) Third, the job knowledge test is constructed. Items are written, evaluated, revised, and then assembled for a pilot study or pretesting of the test. Careful attention must be given in testing items to confirm that they are (a) meaningful and relevant to the knowledge required on the job, (b) clearly and accurately stated, (c) written at the appropriate level of difficulty, (d) able to distinguish between the most- and least-knowledgeable of applicants, and (e) free from grammatical and proofreading errors. Fourth, before the test is used, the administration and scoring of the test must be standardized, and its reliability assessed. The test must be administered at least once to a sample of individuals who are similar to potential applicants for the job, in order to obtain a measure of reliability. The sample's tests also can be used to conduct an item analysis. By examining the responses of high-scoring versus low-scoring test takers, the difficulty and discriminability of the items can be determined, and adjustments in the test can be made if needed (Gavin, 1977).

The best format for the test is one that uses multiple-choice or true–false items, because they can be scored objectively and, thus, are less prone to score bias. Because a job knowledge test is a power test, enough time should be allowed for all except very slow test takers to consider and answer all questions. A rule of thumb is to allow 1 minute for ordinary multiple-choice items and 2 or 3 minutes for items that are especially complex or require extra reading or calculations. However, the final decision about time allowance should be determined in the pilot study of the test. The length of a job knowledge test will depend on the number of critical job knowledge areas and how important they are in the job's tasks. Often, such tests have about 100 items. Generally, a test developer should plan to write enough items to adequately measure each knowledge according to its importance. One way to determine the importance of a knowledge is to use the task inventory analysis to find out the number of duties that are associated with the knowledge. More items should be written for important knowledges and fewer items for less important knowledges.

Special care should be taken to produce items for the test that clearly relate to the job. This is essential for showing the content validity of the test. In addition, it is helpful if applicants can recognize that the test is job related.

| TABLE 8.3 | EXAMPLE OF A JOB KNOWLEDGE TEST CONTENT OUTLINE |
|---|---|

**Type of Test**

Job Knowledge

**Job**

Accountant I

**Test Objective**

To measure knowledge of accounting terms and procedures. Knowledge at the level needed for successful performance of a diversity of routine accounting tasks in municipal government. Scores will be used to rank applicants in the last phase of a multiple hurdle selection program.

**Item Format**

Multiple-choice (4 alternatives)

**Test Length**

100 items

**Time Allowed**

2 hours

| Knowledges Sampled | | Number of Items |
|---|---|---|
| Area I | Balance Sheet | **8** |
| | Classification of balance sheet items | 4 |
| | Relation of balance sheet to income statement | 2 |
| | Debit and credit balance | 2 |
| Area II | Cost Accounting | **8** |
| | Cost analysis | 3 |
| | Billing and collection procedures | 3 |
| | Inventory pricing procedures | 1 |
| | Depreciation allowance | 1 |
| Area III | Assets | **7** |
| | Fixed assets: Accounting treatment of purchase and disposition | 4 |
| | Intangible assets: Accounting treatment of goodwill, leasehold improvements, patents, and trademarks | 3 |
| | | . . . |
| | | . . . |
| | | . . . |
| Area VII | Ratios | **3** |
| | Types: Working capital ratio, acid test ratio | 1 |
| | Capital turnover and inventory turnover | 2 |

Adapted from *Guide to the Development of Written Tests for Selection and Promotion: The Content Validity Model*, by A. T. Gavin, 1977, Washington, DC: United States Civil Service Commission, Personnel Research and Development Center, Technical memorandum 77-6, p. 37.

Studies have shown that applicants react more positively to selection testing and to the organization when the job relevance of a test is apparent to them (Bauer, Maertz, Dolen, & Campion, 1998; Smither, Reilly, Millsap, Pearlman, & Stoffey, 1993). Establishing a test's relevance is particularly important for a content-validated test because its validity depends on rational rather than empirical evidence.

## SUMMING UP

The purpose of this chapter is to examine the nature and use of ability tests for employee selection. Summing up, we can make the following conclusions:

- Ability tests usually include items addressing both natural talent and accumulated knowledge.
- General mental ability is conceptualized in testing as psychometric *g*.
- Tests are distinguished by whether they are speed tests or power tests.
- Selection test fairness holds particular importance for ability testing.
- Computer adaptive testing can be used to develop a short but precise ability test that is customized for each individual.
- The Wonderlic Personnel Test is a brief test of general mental ability.
- Standardized tests offer employers options for testing applicants' special abilities.
- Job knowledge tests can be developed and content-validated in-house.

## INFOTRAC COLLEGE EDITION

Want to learn more about the issues discussed here? Use your subscription to InfoTrac College Edition to access an online library of research journals and other periodicals. Go to http://www.infotrac-college.com/wadsworth and enter a search term. You can use any of the following terms in a keyword search to find articles about some topics reviewed in this chapter.

| | |
|---|---|
| Aptitude tests | Computerized testing |
| Test fairness | Cognitive tests |

# TESTS OF PERSONALITY AND CHARACTER

# CHAPTER 9

Do you believe that some jobs require people who have not only the abilities to do the work, but also a certain personality or disposition? For example, does it seem obvious to you that sales, or counseling, or legal work, might require specific and different personalities? If so, you are not alone. Many people, both now and in the past, have considered this to be reasonable. It has not been easy to prove, however.

Personality tests are used, typically in a battery of other tests and selection measures, to evaluate aspects of an applicant's personal nature and values and to predict the kind of personal conduct that can be expected. Some aspects of personality and character have been found to predict the quality of work performance. Other aspects predict the extent to which a person can be expected to conduct him- or herself well and to be a good organizational citizen. In this chapter, we will consider these relationships between personality, character, and work behavior, and examine some tests that are used in making selection decisions on this basis. First, I will discuss personality testing. Later in the chapter, I will discuss testing designed to detect employee counterproductivity and misconduct.

## PERSONALITY TESTING FOR SELECTION

Early in the 20th century, at the encouragement of industrial psychologists, many employers began to include various kinds of tests in their selection procedures, including personality tests. At first, the use of tests for employment purposes was very carefully considered and documented. Guion (1976) reviewed the work of Freyd (1923) and others, during the early part of the century, whose work defined the principles of effective selection testing. Their standards were very much in keeping with those of today. For example, to determine what attributes a job required, personnel researchers conducted a job analysis. Tests were then found or developed to assess the attributes required on the job, and the tests were validated against a criterion measure of job performance. Sound familiar? The purpose, then as now, was to predict performance, and measures needed to be standardized and validated. Users of tests were advised that they must periodically evaluate the tests to make sure they were still performing as expected, and be prepared to make adjustments if things changed.

By midcentury, however, it was clear that employers were not keeping to the standards of effective testing. This was partly because fewer industrial/organizational (I/O) psychologists were involved in personnel selection than had been involved earlier. (They were busily researching other issues.) Employers had given the task of selection testing to personnel managers or secretaries who knew little or nothing of the standards of good testing practice. Unfortunately, this coincided with a time when tests were extremely popular. Everyone was in love with testing. Employers were eager to have tests for selection. Tests were obtained and used without a job analysis having been done, without any validation effort, and without ever checking to see if the device predicted job performance. Often, in fact, tests were simply borrowed from other employers. This was bad news for employee testing in general and especially for personality testing. As you know, by the mid-1960s, racial discrimination in selection was a national issue, and many employers had to demonstrate that their tests were valid—or else stop using them. Most employers had not routinely collected test validity information. Whereas some ability tests had a certain amount of face validity that could be used to justify their use, it was often difficult to show that personality tests were valid for predicting job performance. Under the best circumstances, personality tests do not predict job performance as strongly as cognitive or mental ability tests do, and when they are used indiscriminately without the foundation of a job analysis, it is difficult to justify their use for most jobs.

Evaluations of personality tests used for selection had been reviewed and reported in the professional literature in the 1940s and '50s. The reports were not entirely encouraging. For example, Ghiselli and Barthol (1953) located 113 criterion-related studies that had been published between 1919 and 1953 which showed correlations between personality test scores and measures of work proficiency. Most correlation coefficients were positive, although few were very high, and there was considerable variability between the coefficients, even within the same occupational group. The average correlation for sales personnel was .36. However, for supervisory jobs, the correlations averaged only .14. The reviewers expected that supervisory jobs would be better predicted than that. Because of the many low values and the fact that some correlation coefficients were negative, they recommended that employers be cautious in using personality tests. A later review of the validity of personality tests for selection by Guion and Gottier (1965)[1] conveyed a similar message. Their evaluation of empirical validation studies and of the statistical significance of validity coefficients led them to conclude that personality measures were not a good basis for making employment decisions. However, they observed that the designs of the studies they reviewed often were poorly conceived and carried out. Further, they noted that there was little theoretical underpinning in the typical study, to suggest why anyone would expect personality traits to correlate with job proficiency. Others also found reason to be doubtful about the way personality measures had been used, and yet to be hopeful about the future of theory in the realm of personality testing. For example, in college textbooks, personality tests were considered not to be appropriate for direct use in selection, although they possibly had an indirect role in the selection process (Cronbach, 1970).

Actually, the early reviewers now appear not to have been unduly censorious (Hogan, Carpenter, Briggs, & Hansson, 1985). Instead, they seem to have provided a wake-up call, alerting academic researchers that some attention needed to be given to the use of personality tests in selection. Admittedly, it was not a very loud alarm because nearly 20 years passed before any new academic interest in personality testing was shown. This did *not* mean that personality tests were not being used. They were, for both managerial and nonmanagerial applicants (Tett, Jackson, & Rothstein, 1991). However, not until the mid-1980s did I/O psychology researchers pay much attention to personality testing for selection. At that time, it was new theoretical work that sparked the interest.

## Personality Theory

Personality theory provides a framework for understanding certain aspects of human nature. It is used to describe and explain human motives and behavior from several different psychological perspectives. For example, clinical psychologists use personality theory to understand and treat disordered behavior. In other areas of psychology, personality theory is used to learn about normal behavior. In I/O psychology, personality theories are applied in various explanations of work motivation, job satisfaction, leadership, and other aspects of organizational behavior.

The term "personality" has two meanings. First, personality is an individual's reputation within the social groups to which he or she belongs—family, friends, or work associates, for example. This is personality from an external point of view. It is public, relatively objective, and usually described in terms

---

[1]This review often is cited as being responsible for discouraging the use of personality testing in employee selection and causing the topic to be abandoned by selection researchers.

of traits, such as dominance, cautiousness, and maturity. Second, personality refers to the internal or psychic structures and processes that are used to describe how or explain why a person behaves in a distinctive way. Different theories of personality offer specific terms that can describe the inner workings of a person's nature. Most traditional personality theories, such as Freudian or psychoanalytic theory, address inner structures and processes. We could argue that "personality" refers to both the public reputation and the inner causes of behavior, although the two aspects of personality are scientifically quite different. For example, in explaining a person's social reputation, we might use concepts referring to internal processes (Hogan, 1991).

**The Five-Factor Model of Personality**   In the 1930s, some psychologists collected a very large database of personality trait terms that ordinary people use in describing one another (Allport & Odbert, 1933). Their rationale for this was that the language we use has evolved from and reflects our social reality; therefore, we should be able to describe personality by finding out how people talk about themselves and others. Some years later, Cattell (1947) used 140 of these terms to conduct a study in which peers rated each other. A factor analysis showed that 16 factors were needed to account for the intercorrelations of the peer ratings. Fiske (1949) attempted to replicate this result but, instead, he found that as few as five factors could describe the data. In a few years, Fiske's findings were corroborated, as others reported that the same five factors could be used to characterize personality (cf. Borgatta, 1964; Norman, 1963). Since that time, many studies have shown that the five-factor model, also known as the Big Five model, has a great deal of value for guiding research on personality. It was this theoretical model that, in the 1980s, drew the interest of researchers to personality testing in industry.

Possibly, the greatest disagreement among researchers is how to label the five factors. (Recall from Chapter 8 that labeling factors is not empirical but, rather, is a judgmental process. Based on Norman's (1963) labeling, the five factors are as follows: (1) extraversion, or sociability; (2) emotional stability, which is also called emotionality or neuroticism; (3) agreeableness; (4) conscientiousness; and (5) openness to experience, which is also sometimes called culture (Barrick & Mount, 1991; R. T. Hogan, 1991). These factors and some of the terms used to describe them are shown in Table 9.1.

Beginning with the early studies on personality traits, many researchers have come to the same conclusion: Personality can be described by five primary constructs that are represented in the five-factor model. The factors are broader and at a higher level of abstraction than the many specific personality traits that have been identified. Therefore, the five-factor model often is viewed as a useful taxonomy or theoretical framework within which other traits can be placed and by which other personality structures can be interpreted (Digman, 1990).

| TABLE 9.1 | THE BIG FIVE PERSONALITY FACTORS: LABELS AND DESCRIPTIONS | |
|---|---|---|

| Main Label[a] | Alternate Label | Factor Descriptions |
|---|---|---|
| Extraversion | Sociability | Talkative, gregarious, ambitious, enthusiastic, energetic |
| Emotional stability[a] | Neuroticism[a], emotionality | Anxious, fearful, insecure, depressed, bad-tempered |
| Agreeableness | Likability | Warm, good-natured, tactful, compliant, flexible |
| Conscientiousness | Dependability, conformity | Thorough, orderly, responsible, achievement-oriented, hard-working |
| Openness to experience | Culture | Imaginative, interested, cultured, broad-minded, enlightened |

[a]All factors are known as having both a positive and a negative pole. Only Emotional Stability or Neuroticism is typically described by its negative side.

## The Relationship of Personality to Work Behavior

In their meta-analysis, Barrick and Mount (1991) found the five-factor model to be a useful structure for formulating and testing hypotheses about the ability of personality tests to predict job performance criteria. They reviewed 117 criterion-related validation studies, conducted between 1952 and 1988, that had used measures interpretable by the five-factor model. As a group, these studies had examined the validity of personality tests for predicting performance and other employee behavior in five different occupational groups—professional, police, managerial, sales, and skilled/semiskilled work. The researchers hypothesized that two of the five personality factors—conscientiousness and emotional stability—would emerge from the data as valid predictors across all jobs. Their reasoning was that conscientiousness includes specific traits such as persistence, planfulness, carefulness, responsibility, and hard work, and that these characteristics are important in accomplishing all kinds of work tasks. They reasoned that neuroticism or the negative side of emotional stability, which includes traits such as worry, nervousness, moodiness, and self-pity, would inhibit successful work behavior on any job. The researchers also expected that extraversion and agreeableness would predict performance for sales and managerial employees, because facility in interpersonal interaction is likely to be important in performing this work. Finally, they thought openness to experience should be positively correlated with training performance, in general. Results of the meta-analysis supported two of their hypotheses. First, there was clear evidence that conscientiousness was a valid predictor for all jobs. Second, extraversion was found to be valid for sales and managerial jobs. The other three hypotheses were not supported.

A few months later, Tett, Jackson, and Rothstein (1991) reported on a related meta-analytic study. They, too, had evaluated the relationship between personality and performance. Specifically, they set out to determine the importance of using a theoretical approach to personality trait selection in validation studies. That is, they asked, Would it be more productive to use a theory, like the five-factor model, to frame hypotheses about which personality traits would predict job performance and which would not? They thought this would be preferable to simply exploring, using a broad spectrum approach, to see whether anything would turn up. In their meta-analysis, they classified the studies as being theory-driven and confirmatory in nature, if the author gave a rationale for evaluating specific traits relative to job performance. They classified studies as exploratory when no rationale was given to suggest that some traits could be expected to correlate with performance. Because job analysis is a means for identifying job-related personality characteristics, Tett and his colleagues also considered whether researchers conducting theory-driven studies had used job analysis to select traits.

As hypothesized, Tett et al. (1991) found that the validity coefficients established by confirmatory or theory-driven studies were significantly greater than those derived from exploratory studies. Also, validities were higher in studies that used job analysis to link personality traits to job requirements. Both findings emphasize the value of theory in guiding validation research. The researchers examined the theory-driven studies further, in search of evidence pertaining to the Big Five personality factors. They found, in these studies, that a broad spectrum of personality traits were related to job performance, including the traits categorized as Big Five factors. The results of this analysis were generally supportive of the previous meta-analysis done by Barrick and Mount (1991). In addition, Tett et al. (1991) found significant evidence for some personality traits that the previous researchers had hypothesized but had not been able to show. In this later study, both agreeableness and openness to experience showed strong positive relationships to the performance criteria. High scores on these personality constructs predicted higher job performance. Also, the correlations showed that the neuroticism factor negatively affected job performance. Again, the results of these studies demonstrate the value of using a theory in selecting traits that might be reasonably expected to predict performance, and of designing the research to confirm that the traits are related to performance.

## Conclusions

The five-factor model recently has excited the interest of many researchers studying employee selection testing, and relationships between measures of the factors and work performance are being reported almost daily.

Still, we should be careful not to go overboard. It is not a good idea to rely too much on a single theoretical model. Tett et al. (1991) expressed the need for caution with respect to embracing the five-factor model. Whereas such a macroscopic approach to the study of personality unquestionably is valuable in guiding validity research, it should not distract us from the need for studies investigating measures of personality traits that are narrower and more specific than the Big Five factors. To be useful in employee selection, personality tests need to allow the user to link specific traits to performance on the job. Schneider (1996) sounded a critical note concerning overreliance on the five-factor model. He observed that using this model as the answer to all our questions about the relationship of personality to work performance is likely to cause the model to become just another fad. Fads, by their very nature, are replaced. He thought we would do better to focus on behavior as the key to understanding how personality is related to performance outcomes. According to Schneider, as far as work is concerned, it is not so much what people *are* that counts but, rather, what they *do*. He predicted that unless research on personality in the workplace is broadened beyond validity studies using the five-factor model, the study of work-related personality issues will fade, as it did 30 years ago.

## PERSONALITY TESTS

Personality tests historically have been classified into one of two broad categories—projective or objective—which differ in terms of rationale and format. In projective tests, a test taker is presented with test stimuli that have ambiguous meanings. The idea is that the individual will *project* his or her unconscious personality structures onto the ambiguous test stimuli and will respond in a uniquely personal way. The well-known Rorschach, or inkblot, test and the Thematic Apperception Test (TAT) are examples of projective personality measures. In contrast, objective personality tests are made up of unambiguous items with clear response alternatives that can be scored objectively. Such tests are designed in the form of self-report inventories or questionnaires. The rationale of these tests is that a person has enough self-knowledge to provide an accurate personality report. An example is the Minnesota Multiphasic Personality Inventory (MMPI).

### Examples of Personality Tests Used in Selection

Many personality tests, including the MMPI and most projective measures, have been developed primarily for clinical use, and they often are individually administered by a clinical psychologist. Their use for selection purposes has been limited mainly to high-level managerial and executive positions or to high-security jobs.

One projective test that departs from this description is the Miner Sentence Completion Scale, developed in 1961 to provide a measure of a person's motivation to manage. In developing the test, Miner (1985) believed that a projective technique would be more effective than an objective test because he was interested in accessing unconscious motivation for management. However, he used verbal (sentence fragments) rather than pictorial stimuli, as other projective tests do, in order to avoid certain problems that occur in projective testing and particularly to eliminate the need for a professional psychologist to interpret test responses. The test's 40 items consist of incomplete sentences that the test taker finishes. It requires 20 to 30 minutes and can be group-administered. The test yields six to nine scores depending on which form is used. Originally, the test was designed to identify scientists in research and development (R & D) who would be good managers for departments in hierarchically structured organizations. Two additional forms of the test later were designed for selecting managers and professionals working in other types of organizations. The test responses have to be individually evaluated by a scorer, and a scoring guide is included in materials provided for users. However, scorer reliability depends on how experienced the test scorer is. Generally, scorers require special training. Using reliability data reported in various published studies, Miner (1985) estimated that the average reliability coefficient for experienced scorers was .91 and for less experienced, .76. A reviewer of the test pointed out that although some studies have questioned the reliability and validity of the instrument, the weight of the evidence supports Miner's assessment that the test can be used reliably and validly (Leong, 1992). However, because reliability in testing is essential, and because inexperienced test scorers tend to be unreliable, I would say that training is absolutely necessary.

**Standardized Self-Report Inventories**  Most selection programs that incorporate personality tests use self-report inventories rather than projective tests. Relatively speaking, objective personality tests offer a number of advantages for employment use. They can be group-administered and machine-scored, or they can be hand-scored by someone without special expertise. Thus, they are less time consuming and less expensive to administer. The procedures for test administration can be standardized and scoring norms are more easily established.

There are a number of self-report inventories that purport to measure some aspect of the normal personality. Several are well-developed and have solid backgrounds of research and practical use for employment purposes. I have selected three well-known instruments as good examples of personality inventories, which I will describe in the following paragraphs. The best

| TABLE 9.2 | TEST SCALES IN SELECTED PERSONALITY INVENTORIES |
|---|---|

| Personality Inventory | Scale Labels |
|---|---|
| California Psychological Inventory, Revised Edition (CPI) | Dominance, Capacity for Status, Sociability, Social Presence, Self-Acceptance, Independence, Empathy, Responsibility, Socialization, Self-Control, Good Impression, Communality, Well-Being, Tolerance, Achievement via Conformance, Achievement via Independence, Intellectual Efficiency, Psychological-Mindedness, Flexibility, Femininity-Masculinity |
| Gordon Personal Profile—Inventory (GPP-I) | Ascendancy, Responsibility, Emotional Stability, Sociability, Self-Esteem (total), Cautiousness, Original Thinking, Personal Relations, Vigor |
| Revised NEO Personality Inventory (NEO-PI-R) | Neuroticism (Anxiety, Angry Hostility, Depression, Self-Consciousness, Impulsiveness, Vulnerability, total); Extraversion (Warmth, Gregariousness, Assertiveness, Activity, Excitement-Seeking, Positive Emotions, total); Openness (Fantasy, Aesthetics, Feelings, Actions, Ideas, Values, total); Agreeableness (Trust, Straightforwardness, Altruism, Compliance, Modesty, Tender-Mindedness, total); Conscientiousness (Competence, Order, Dutifulness, Achievement-Striving, Self-Discipline, Deliberation, total) |

Information from *Tests in Print*. Lincoln, Neb: Buros Institute of Mental Measurements, University of Nebraska Press, 1999.

approach for an employer in using these or any other personality measure is the same as for using commercially available instruments of any sort. Begin with a job analysis, to establish the personality requirements for the job. Next, locate instruments that assess the needed traits. Finally, evaluate the evidence that shows the extent to which the traits are assessed reliably and accurately. (Recall from Chapter 7 that *Tests in Print* and *Mental Measurements Yearbook* are good sources of this information.)

The California Psychological Inventory (Revised) (CPI) was first published in 1956 and was revised and updated in 1987 (Gough, 1987). The CPI is a long self-report inventory, containing more than 400 items and taking as much as an hour to complete. The test provides scores on 20 specific personality scales, such as dominance, flexibility, and self-control. The scales describe personality in terms of interpersonal behavior. (See Table 9.2 for a listing.) In addition to the 20 scale scores, other scores can be obtained for special purposes. For example, the level of "managerial potential" can be calculated from test takers' responses. You might be wondering about the relationship of these personality scales to the five-factor model discussed earlier. One reviewer (Bolton, 1992) pointed out that several factor analyses have shown that the CPI does include the Big Five factors. However, the CPI was developed empirically rather than by a theory, and it is not scored on the five factor dimensions, although the reviewer wished that it would be.

Normative data are available for CPI users. The original CPI was noted for the very large samples (6,000+ for males and 7,000+ for females) on which norms were based. The revised CPI offers norms that are based on a smaller set of data selected from the original normative samples. It is not clear whether there are plans for collecting new normative data. A variety of reliability evidence is provided, including internal consistency, test–retest, and parallel forms (comparing English and French forms). After examining the range and quality of this evidence, Bolton (1992) concluded that the CPI probably is more reliable than the user's manual suggests. He estimated that the actual reliability coefficients range from .70 to .90 across the scales. Considerable validity evidence has been gathered over the years, beginning with the CPI's empirical development through criterion-related validity studies using nontest criteria. For example, the CPI has been validated against both academic and job performance criteria. Several studies have found significant relationships between CPI scores and job performance in law enforcement jobs (cf. Hogan, 1971; Mills & Bohannon, 1980). The CPI is a classical personality instrument. Despite any weaknesses, it is one of the best measures of normal personality.

The Gordon Personal Profile-Inventory (GPP-I) is another classic. First published in 1951 as two separate tests—the "Profile" and the "Inventory"—the current instrument combines the two. The GPP-I measures ten personality constructs, as indicated in Table 9.2. These constructs were identified from factor analysis of responses to the test items. In the test, unrelated items that appear to be equally acceptable are grouped in sets of four (or tetrads). There are 38 tetrads, taking 20 to 25 minutes to answer. A forced-choice response strategy is used in order to control the operation of response tendencies such as social desirability. That is, the test taker must answer by choosing two alternatives in each tetrad—the most and the least descriptive of his or her personality.

Extensive group norms are available. Most are based on college and high school student samples, which reflects the fact that the GPP-I has been used extensively for academic guidance and counseling. Although norms for employee groups are somewhat limited, a sample of nearly 2,500 employed individuals provides normative data on adult workers. Interitem reliabilities are in the .80s. Both long-term (4 years) and short-term (2 months) test–retest reliabilities are provided, which range from .68 to .88. Overall, the GPP-I is quite stable and the constructs are measured reliably. The test has been validated against other tests. In addition, many criterion-related validity studies have been conducted in employment, educational, and military settings. These studies have shown correlations in the .20s and .30s with educational and work performance criteria, indicating that the scores can predict reasonably well. This test, like the CPI, was developed long before the five-factor model appeared, although it is recognized as anticipating the five-factor model and you can see in Table 9.2 that some of the constructs are similar to the Big Five factors. However, it has not been adjusted for scoring along these lines. Gordon reportedly is disinclined to reduce the test to five constructs because doing so may obscure some important distinctions that are present in the existing test. The evidence indicates that the GPP-I is useful for employment purposes, as it stands (Guion, 1998a).

The Revised NEO Personality Inventory (NEO-PI-R) is another multidimensional self-report inventory that is designed to assess the normal personality. The NEO-PI-R has been structured using 30 specific traits or facets of personality that are ordered and scored according to the five-factor model. The test was first published in 1978 and originally was based on analysis of traits drawn from natural language. In 1985, it was published with subscales measuring three of the Big Five factors (Juni, 1995). The current NEO has facet scales for all five factors and is the most explicit measure of the five-factor model. (See Table 9.2 for a listing of the scales.) Compared to many personality inventories, the NEO-PI-R is a fairly short test, requiring only 30 to 40 minutes for test takers to complete 240 items. An even briefer version, the NEO-FFI, has 60 items focusing on the Big Five and takes 10 to 15 minutes to complete. The full test is available in other languages, including Spanish and German, and a modified version is available for use in the United Kingdom.

Norms are provided for users, based on a 1,000-person sample, which was selected so as to be representative of the 1995 U.S. population in age, gender, and race (Botwin, 1995). The user's manual presents data showing internal consistency reliability that is strong for the five factors (.86 to .95) and acceptable (.58 to .87) for the facet subscales. The test has been validated, typically by comparing it to similar normal personality instruments, such as the CPI. In addition, factor analysis has shown that the test validly represents the five-factor model (Costa & McCrea,1992). The NEO has been widely used for counseling and clinical purposes. However, Costa (1996) has argued that, because the test is a valid representation of the five-factor model, it also can be used successfully for employee selection purposes. He discussed research evidence showing significant relationships between the five-factor scales and supervisor ratings of job performance. The strongest of these relationships was for conscientiousness. This finding, as we have seen, corresponds to those from other studies of conscientiousness and work performance (e.g., Barrick & Mount, 1991).

**Response Distortion in Self-Report Inventories**   Not infrequently, students ask me whether it is not true that job applicants can fake their responses to personality tests. This question is asked also by test developers and researchers. It is a serious question because if tests are faked, then their validity may be compromised.

The research indicates that "faking" is a complex issue, and it may be helpful to define some terms at this point. Generally, response distortion occurs when test items are transparent enough that the social desirability of their meanings can be assessed by test takers. Theoretically, the social desirability of test items can influence responses either because the person is self-deceptive or because he or she is deliberately trying to make a good impression. Faking, or intentional distortion, refers to the latter type of behavior; that is, to impression management (Paulhus, 1986). Hogan (1991) discussed research on impression management, which indicates that this is a personal tendency or trait. Individuals who score high on impression management are aware of what is socially desirable in the given context, and they deliberately try to fit in. Special scales have been designed to detect signs of impression management. Standardized personality instruments sometimes contain these. If there are concerns that this type of response distortion is affecting employee selection decisions, then scales to detect it might be used to adjust scores and control the effects. Self-deceptive response distortion appears to result from different mechanisms than impression management. Here, the individual genuinely believes that the very positive self-descriptions are true. The person is not faking, although the responses are considered to be distorted in the direction of social desirability. R. T. Hogan (1991) discussed evidence that individuals who think of themselves in such favorable ways actually are well-adjusted. This type of response distortion might better be left unadjusted or uncontrolled, because when controls are applied, they might reduce the predictive power of a test that includes well-being, adjustment, or emotional stability constructs.

Considerable research has addressed the question of whether job applicants deliberately raise their scores on standardized personality tests. Most of the studies show that when subjects are told to "fake good" (i.e., answer so as to make the best impression), they can make their scores more positive[2] (cf. Hough, Eaton, Dunnette, Kamp, & McCloy, 1990; Orpen, 1971). Whether many applicants actually do this is another issue, because people do not always do what is actually possible for them. For example, in one study, a sample of soldiers were tested twice, being told at one time to answer honestly and at another time to fake the test. Their responses were later compared to those of a group of army applicants who had been routinely tested in the course of volunteering (Hough et al., 1990). The comparison confirmed that the soldiers could fake their tests. In addition, when they were told to answer honestly, their responses were similar to those of the army applicants. This suggested that deliberate faking might not be much of a general problem in applicant testing.

Other studies, however, have shown that some job applicants do distort their test responses. Then, the question is whether these response distortions damage the predictive ability of the personality tests. Some studies suggest that they do not (e.g., Barrick & Mount, 1991). Ones, Viswesvaran, and Reiss (1996) conducted a meta-analysis to examine the effects of social desirability on measures of the Big Five factors, as well as on several other measures including job performance and counterproductive behavior. The results of the

---

[2]They also can "fake bad" and make their scores more negative, which someone might do if he or she wished not to be selected for something on the basis of test scores.

analysis led them to conclude that the personality measures were not unduly susceptible to socially desirable responding. Actually, they reported that social desirability was associated with real differences between test takers in emotional stability and conscientiousness, which is consistent with previous observations about the adjustment of self-deceivers. The researchers discussed the theoretical distinctions between self-deception and impression management, and noted that evidence indicates that both types of response bias are associated with emotional stability and conscientiousness. This would suggest that although test-item social desirability does affect test takers' responses, it is not a serious problem as far as test validity is concerned. However, the question of whether response distortion damages the validity of the test is not yet resolved. Researchers continue to study the issue. For example, one study found that (1) a group of job applicants had more positive personality profiles than a group of job incumbents and that (2) the applicants whose scores on conscientiousness were extremely high (three or more standard deviations above the mean) were very likely to be hired (Rosse, Stecher, Miller, & Levin, 1998). We cannot be absolutely sure that any one person with an extremely high conscientiousness score is *not* telling the truth. However, statistically, a score that is three standard deviations away from the mean is quite rare, and a good guess would be that the test item responses are distorted. Until we establish the meaning of response-distorted scores, the question of whether test validity is affected is a difficult one to answer.

## Conclusions

Employers have many alternatives from which to choose when planning to include a personality test in an employee selection program. Self-report inventories often are an attractive choice because they have been developed and validated to measure personality constructs that are related to effective job performance. Self-report inventories are comparatively inexpensive and convenient to use in group testing, have the advantages of offering standardized administration and scoring norms, and do not require psychological expertise for interpreting the responses. A possible disadvantage is that these tests may be susceptible to response distortion. Test takers can deliberately influence their scores, and some actually do. However, the research shows that the validity of standardized personality tests is generally durable enough to withstand the effects of response distortions, although concerns about the problem remain. There are ways to control response distortions, such as scales scored for this purpose. In addition, when planning how to use personality test scores to make hiring decisions, an employer might consider defining a "window" of acceptable scores, rather than simply using a top-down strategy.

# TESTING FOR EMPLOYEE MISCONDUCT

When the misconduct of an employee seriously affects other employees, a company may need to answer to legal charges of "negligent hiring." For example, following a serious incident in which one employee harms others, an employer may be sued as being negligent in hiring a person who would place others in danger. In the past, employers relied on reference checks to obtain information about the trustworthiness and integrity of job applicants. However, this was not always satisfactory. For various reasons, as I will discuss in a later chapter, references often do not provide adequate information. Many employers looked to testing for the solution to the problem. Today, several tests are available for use in evaluating the honesty and integrity of job applicants. Some of these tests actually are personality inventories that have been designed to assess certain features of a person's nature. Other tests are questionnaires about dishonesty and illicit behavior. Physiological tests are used for some purposes, also. Generally, the tests that predict employee misconduct fall into two categories—honesty or integrity tests, and drug tests.

Employee counterproductivity and misconduct can reduce worklife quality for all employees and skyrocket employer costs. Some misconduct at work seriously affects human life. For example, aggressiveness and violence have been the source of workplace injuries and fatalities. In addition, workplace accidents often involve drug and alcohol use as a causal factor. These events also can result in injuries and death, as well as property destruction. Employee misconduct and counterproductive behavior often are directed toward the organization itself and can be quite expensive. This includes employee theft, embezzlement, sabotage, and vandalism. It includes interpersonal misconduct, such as sexual harassment, as well as malingering, misuse of paid time and equipment for personal needs, and abuse of sick leave. Robinson and Bennett (1995) developed a typology of deviant workplace behavior, in which they distinguished between how serious the act is and whether such acts are directed toward the organization or individuals. Figure 9.1 shows four types of deviant work behavior that vary in these ways, including production, property, political, and personal deviance.

The exact costs of such behavior often are difficult to estimate, especially when considering the loss of capital assets and indirect costs, such as legal proceedings and medical care for injured individuals. Another difficulty in estimating these costs is the fact that some forms of inappropriate behavior, such as theft and the misuse of work time, go undetected and/or unattributed to any individual. As a result, the range of cost estimates typically is broad. One estimate was $40 billion to $50 billion (Lipman & McGraw, 1988), and another was between $6 billion and $200 billion annually. At any rate, whatever the actual amount, the message is clear: Employee misconduct is expensive, and employers want to control these costs.

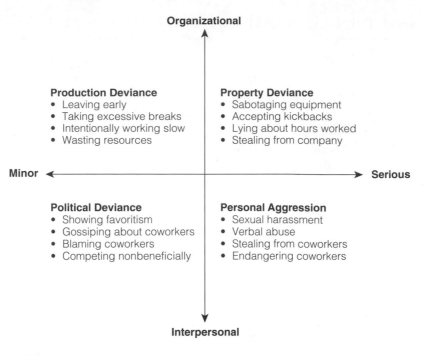

FIGURE **9.1**

Typology of deviant work behavior. Deviant behavior at the workplace can be categorized by how serious it is and by whether it is directed toward the organization or individuals. Behaviors listed are examples of the category, not a full listing.

From "A Typology of Deviant Workplace Behaviors: A Multidimensional Scaling Study," by S. L. Robinson and R. J. Bennett, 1995, *Academy of Management Journal, 38*(2), p. 565. Copyright 1995 by Academy of Management. Reprinted by permission.

## *Honesty and Integrity Tests*

Increasingly, employers are using tests to screen job applicants for potential misconduct and counterproductive behavior. Polygraph, or lie detector, testing of applicants was the approach taken by many employers in the 1970s and early 1980s, although some pencil-and-paper tests were available at the time. However, in the mid-1980s, a movement began that was aimed at prohibiting employers from using the polygraph to screen job applicants. Several state laws were passed, limiting or barring the use of the preemployment polygraph test. Also, the American Psychological Association (APA) reported that scientific evidence did not show the polygraph to be valid for employee screening. Finally, in 1988, the federal Employee Polygraph Protection Act was passed. This prohibited most employers from using polygraph testing for applicant screening (Sackett, Burris, & Callahan, 1989).

When employers were unable to use polygraphy, they turned to the pencil-and-paper tests that increasingly were being developed for this purpose (Sackett et al., 1989). The Polygraph Act did not make written honesty tests illegal, although in the preliminary studies leading up to the act, this was considered, and Congress made plans to later evaluate the use of written tests. This evaluation of written honesty tests took place over the next 3 years. In 1990, the Office of Technology Assessment (OTA) reported to Congress that the available evidence was insufficient to either prove or disprove the validity of the written tests for applicant screening. Regulation of the tests was not recommended; however, Congress was asked to continue monitoring, mainly because the OTA thought misclassifying individuals as being dishonest would have serious consequences for individuals. The American Psychological Association also reported to Congress on this issue (Goldberg, Grenier, Guion, Sechrest, & Wing, 1991). The APA report criticized the use of cutoff scores because they might lead to the simplistic view that test takers are either honest or dishonest, based on one score-point. However, the APA report found that the criterion-related validation evidence was positive and certainly strong enough to indicate a degree of validity. On a practical note, the APA report also pointed out that companies must have some way to deal with the problems of employee theft and that integrity tests offer a solution which is superior to that of the very limited alternatives—mainly, the analysis of handwriting or nonverbal cues in interviews.

**Types of Integrity Tests**    Sackett et al. (1989) identified two basic types of honesty or integrity tests. The first type, which they called *overt* integrity tests, are made up of two kinds of items. Some are about attitudes toward theft and other dishonest behaviors, such as whether you think minor theft should be punished. Other items are about a person's actual dishonest behaviors in the past, such as how much money you stole or whether you used drugs in the past year. Most of the earlier honesty and integrity tests were of the overt type. A well-known example is the Reid Report.

The Reid Report was first published in 1969, and it has had considerable use since that time. The test is made up of four parts, including scales measuring integrity attitudes, antisocial history, recent drug use, and work history. The score on each part yields an evaluation of the test taker as recommended, recommended with reservations (borderline), or not recommended. In addition, an overall evaluation is provided based on the least favorable of the part evaluations. The test has relatively high reliability, in both internal consistency and test–retest assessments. Some validity evidence is provided, including correlations with personality inventories. However, a reviewer noted that because the construct the Reid is supposed to measure is not fully described, the value of this evidence is not clear. A more severe criticism concerned the use of a cutoff score (Murphy, 1995). Dichotomous scoring (honest or dishonest) is exactly the concern regarding integrity testing that the APA presented to the U.S. Congress (discussed above).

The second type of integrity test is *personality-based*. These tests contain personality test items, such as questions about whether you like to take chances, are a hard worker, and respect the views of authorities. User instructions show how to score the tests and draw inferences about a person's tendencies to engage in counterproductive behavior. They are distinguished from overt tests by the fact that they do not obviously draw attention to their actual purpose in assessing integrity. Also, they appear to be more broadly oriented and to assess various forms of employee deviance, whereas overt integrity tests usually focus more specifically on theft and other similarly dishonest behaviors. How different are they, actually? In fact, little is known about the links between overt and personality-based measures. Hogan and Brinkmeyer (1997) addressed this question. They analyzed the intercorrelations between responses to the Reid Report and to the Employee Reliability Index, which is an integrity test drawn from the more general Hogan Personality Inventory. The Reliability Index contains four subscales on impulse control, attachment, avoiding trouble, and hostility. The researchers found greater similarity between the two integrity tests than they had expected. They found that the two tests were measuring similar underlying constructs and showed similar correlations on personality dimensions. The conscientiousness factor also was found in both instruments. These results led the researchers to conclude that the Reid Report measures more than simply "honest" behavior.

Several other tests are classified as personality-based integrity tests. The Personnel Reaction Blank (Gough, 1971) is described as an aid for hiring dependable and conscientious employees. The test is based on the CPI and yields a single overall score from items on internal values, self-restraint, dependability, and acceptance of convention, among others. The user's manual indicates that the test is appropriate for nonmanagerial jobs, and it provides norms for several different groups. Reliability varies between samples, from .65 to .97, with the highest values obtained from samples of "delinquents." The manual presents some evidence of criterion-related validity, using supervisor ratings of work performance. However, a reviewer evaluated both the reliability and validity evidence as being weak (Sundre, 1998).

Another integrity test is largely personality based, although it includes some overt scales. This is the Employee Reliability Inventory[3], which was first published in 1986. It is offered as a test of employee reliability and productive work behavior. Requiring only 12 to 15 minutes, the test yields scores on several different scales, including emotional maturity, conscientiousness, trustworthiness, job commitment, alcohol and substance use, safe performance, and

---

[3]Note that this is not the same test as the similarly named Employee Reliability Index mentioned earlier.

courtesy. Normative data are provided on a large number of job applicants. Both internal consistency and test–retest reliability are at acceptable levels. The main weakness is the validity evidence. A reviewer noted that although the test is usable, the validity evidence is not strong (Guion, 1995).

**Validity of Integrity Tests**   As you can see from these examples, integrity tests are not problem-free. For most, the difficulty is in showing that the test is valid for predicting employee honesty and integrity. Reviewers of the tests described here identified what they thought was a problem in the validity evidence and offered recommendations for ways to improve it. Despite these difficulties, however, the reviewers recognized that these tests have some degree of usefulness, especially in view of the few alternatives that are available to employers.

An important question in the validation of integrity tests concerns what criterion to use. In the early evaluations of honesty tests, validity studies often used polygraph examinations as the criterion measure. Perhaps, at the time, test developers were interested in demonstrating that a written test could do what the polygraph had been doing to help an employer control employee theft. Apparently they were right. Sackett and Harris (1984) found a mean validity coefficient of .49 from nine studies, indicating that honesty tests could predict polygraph results. However, as the use of the polygraph for employee screening began to be questioned, many test developers stopped this as the criterion measure in their validity studies. Instead, they began to use organizational criteria, such as detected theft, turnover, and supervisors' ratings of performance. Although detected theft may seem to be the most appropriate criterion for an honesty test validation, there is a problem with using this as a criterion measure. Because very little theft is detected and attributed to the guilty party, this criterion measure is likely to be inadequate to assess the actual validity of a test (Sackett et al., 1989). This is a restriction of range problem. Recall from Chapter 7 that when a criterion measure shows little difference between employees, such as when all are evaluated as satisfactory performers with few evaluated as very good or very poor, then it will not be clear whether the test validly predicts different performance levels. Similarly, when a criterion measure is unable to identify more than a few thieves, we cannot determine whether the integrity test is valid. As a result of this kind of problem, validation studies often use job performance as the criterion and supervisors' ratings as the criterion measure, reasoning that employee misconduct will demonstrate itself in various aspects of job performance and that this will be apparent to the supervisor. Ones, Viswesvaran, and Schmidt (1993) conducted a meta-analysis of 180 separate validation studies yielding 665 validity coefficients. They found that overall the validity studies showed that the use of organizational criteria is a good strategy. From this sample, the researchers identified and analyzed a number of predictive validity studies in

Source: United Feature Syndicate, Inc., August 15, 2001. (*San Francisco Chronicle*). Reprinted by permission of UFS, Inc.

which job applicants' integrity test scores were correlated with their later job performance as measured by their supervisors' ratings. The average validity coefficient in these studies was .41, which is strong evidence that integrity tests are valid in predicting overall job performance.

Response distortion, possibly, is another problem for integrity tests. Originally, some researchers thought that overt honesty tests were most likely to be affected because the content is transparent as to what is being measured. However, because it is possible to fake personality tests, we must ask whether response distortion is a problem for both personality-based and overt integrity tests. Given that employers are likely to want honest employees, would it not be reasonable to expect applicants to present themselves as honest? Is there anything in these tests that can get an honest report from individuals who are prone to be dishonest? Actually, there might be. One suggestion is that in taking such tests we all project ourselves. People who do dishonest things think they are not the only ones—they believe others are dishonest, too, and they report this on honesty tests. In a similar sense, basically honest people see others as being honest also, and their responses reflect this (Cunningham & Ash, 1988). Still, not all researchers accept this view, and some consider that there is a potential for faking which might damage the validity of these tests. Cunningham, Wong, and Barbee (1994) reported three experiments in which they examined the extent to which the Reid Report could be faked. In two experiments, subjects were encouraged to try to score high on the test, were given information about the nature of the items, and were offered money for high scores. Under these conditions, subjects were able to score high. However, their scores were no higher than those of a group of job applicants taking the test. From this, we can conclude that responses can and may actually be distorted. In a third experiment, however, subjects were asked to respond to the Reid Report as if they wanted a job, and then, at the end of the test, the subjects were overpaid. The researchers found that the subjects' scores actually predicted whether or not they would return the overpayment. This finding indicates that the Reid Report is still able to validly predict honest behavior despite the response distortions that may occur.

# Drug Testing

Because drug and alcohol use is associated with low-quality job performance and workplace accidents, substance use is a serious problem in business and industry. An estimated 40 percent of work accidents resulting in serious injuries or fatalities involve the use of drugs or alcohol (Cowan, 1987). Drug use also is significantly related to absenteeism. In one study, those who tested positive for drugs showed an absence rate that was 59.3 percent higher than those who tested negative. In addition, those who tested positive for drugs were 47 percent more likely than others to be fired (Normand, Salyards, & Mahoney, 1990).

Over the past 30 years or so, national concerns about the serious effects of drug use in the United States have increased. The Drug-Free Workplace Act, which applies to federal employers and contractors, was passed in 1988. Although the act specifies that employers need to offer rehabilitation, it also allows for sanctions, including termination of those who are caught using drugs at work. The Americans with Disabilities Act (ADA) recognizes drug addiction and alcoholism as medical conditions and requires employers to make reasonable accommodation to those who are *recovering* addicts or alcoholics. However, the ADA also clearly states that current drug or alcohol users are not protected. Further, it does not prohibit employment testing to identify users.

**Types of Drug Tests**   Drug testing usually is conducted by urinalysis.[4] A sample of a test taker's urine is chemically analyzed to determine whether specified drugs are presently being used. These tests are not fully satisfactory for a number of reasons. For one thing, urinalysis is costly. The specimens are collected by a trained test administrator and sent to an outside laboratory for analysis. Typically, the analysis is conducted in two stages. First, a screening test is run. Second, those specimens in which the screen showed signs of drugs are subjected to a confirmation test in which the presence of a specific drug is established. In addition, if the drug test is used with job incumbents, the costs will be multiplied by the frequency of testing.

A more troubling problem with urinalysis is its ability to identify current use of drugs. For example, a false-positive test may result because a person is taking certain over-the-counter or prescribed drugs that mimic the presence of an illicit drug. In contrast, unless the test is carefully monitored, false-negative results can be obtained because an individual provides a false or altered specimen. Another problem of accuracy is that the presence of some substances appears to be overestimated depending on how the drug is metabolized. For example, cocaine can be detected 25 hours after it was used, and marijuana can be detected for as long as 120 hours after it was used (Rosen, 1987). This may not be

---

[4]Hair samples can similarly be analyzed for traces of drugs. However, a different measure is obtained because hair analysis indicates whether drugs have been used over a longer period of time, sometimes as much as 3 months.

a problem if the employer is looking for a pattern of drug use rather than present drug intoxication. However, the question then needs to be considered as to whether such results are valid for assessing job behavior and performance.

Urinalysis is not an accurate test for alcohol consumption. It does not show whether an individual has used alcohol while at work or whether there is alcohol presently in a person's blood (Normand, Lempert, & O'Brien, 1994). Breathalyzers and blood tests are more accurate measures of alcohol use. Employers historically have not used tests of any type to detect alcohol use at work. Rather, they have relied upon supervisors to identify and deal with alcohol users. However, many managers currently believe that testing is the preferred method. Hartwell, Steele, and Rodman (1998) studied workplace alcohol testing programs and found them to have several features that distinguish them from ordinary drug testing programs. First, organizations that test for alcohol use are more likely to test job incumbents than applicants. Second, drug testing is more prevalent than alcohol testing. The researchers found that 36 percent of organizations with more than 50 employees tested for alcohol use, whereas 54 percent tested for drugs. However, alcohol testing programs increasingly are being implemented at worksites, especially in larger organizations. Third, urinalysis is used by most (72 percent) alcohol testing programs. Blood tests or Breathalyzers were used by about one-quarter of those that tested for alcohol. The researchers speculated on why urinalysis is preferred over the more effective Breathalyzer. They thought perhaps it was simply more convenient to add alcohol to an order for urinalysis that had already been arranged for drug testing.

Drug testing is distinguished from other types of employee selection testing in several ways. One, drug testing is conducted both as a pre-hire assessment and as a post-employment method of detecting drug use by job incumbents. As a post-employment test, *selection* is involved in that individuals are "selected" for some special treatment, which may be rehabilitation, discipline, or termination. Two, the test itself is different from most employee selection tests. Urinalysis is a physiological procedure that might be considered a medical assessment. Although medical examinations are sometimes required for jobs, such as when vision or hearing requirements exist, these examinations are of a different order than drug tests. Three, drug tests are not always tied to specific job requirements, although in some cases they might be. For example, in certain jobs, such as pilot or truck driver, safety requirements are clear that an employee must not be drug- or alcohol-intoxicated while working. Finally, because drug tests are used primarily to disqualify or screen out drug users, there is no intrinsic benefit in passing a drug test (Arthur & Doverspike, 1997). This may be especially important to incumbents who are tested. Whereas an applicant may consider passing the drug test as simply getting over the final hurdle before being hired, there is little for a continuing employee to feel good about in passing a routine drug test. Such psychological processes may explain employees' negative feelings about drug testing.

**Reactions to Drug Testing**   Employers see the value of drug testing in terms of safety and economy. Drug tests can help an employer avoid hiring applicants who are drug users, and they can help identify employees who are using drugs at work. Do employees also see value in drug testing? Although some employees do, at least in certain circumstances, other employees react negatively. The negative reaction is not about testing *applicants*, however. It is about the periodic testing of incumbent employees.

You might guess that drug users react negatively to drug testing, and some research suggests that negative responses do come more often from frequent drug users than from infrequent users (Murphy, Thornton, & Reynolds, 1990). However, many employees are favorable toward drug testing when there is a need to protect the quality of work and to enhance workplace safety (Murphy et al., 1990; Tepper, 1994). The acceptability of drug policies—specifically, policies that involve punitive actions following drug use detection—actually depends on who is asked. Tepper (1994) reported that laboratory subjects considered termination to be appropriate for employees using drugs while working on safety-sensitive or dangerous jobs, whereas they preferred rehabilitation or counseling for drug users on other jobs. Employees who actually worked on safety-sensitive jobs, however, thought termination policies were generally less fair than policies involving rehabilitation. Also, the opinions of employees who had been tested differed from those who had not been tested. Both tested and untested employees were concerned about policy fairness. However, untested employees thought invasion of privacy was an important issue, whereas tested employees were more concerned about the practice of singling out those who would be tested.

Organizations should not ignore employees' reactions to drug testing. Just as adjustments can be made in ordinary selection tests to make them more clearly job-related, so also can adjustments be made in how drug testing programs are conducted. When safety issues are present in certain jobs, or when high costs result from low-quality work performance, all employees should be made aware of this. Improvements might be made in the procedures for testing, also. Testing all employees generally is more acceptable than random selection or singling out only certain employees to be tested. The punitiveness of the consequence of positive test results also affects employees' reactions. Programs in which individuals have an opportunity to be rehabilitated are generally preferred.

## Conclusions

Most selection tests are meant to accomplish two purposes: (1) to screen in, or to identify, highly suitable applicants who could be hired, and (2) to screen out, or to disqualify, applicants who are unsuitable for hire. Tests that are used to assess the potential for employee misconduct are mainly focused on screening out individuals, and this has contributed to their being controversial. The public's negative response to honesty and integrity tests probably was because of their association with the polygraph, which was viewed as unnecessarily invasive for ordinary employment use. As more than a decade has elapsed since the polygraph law was passed, the controversy surrounding integrity tests appears largely to have subsided, especially when their use is restricted to applicant testing. Even the concerns that a company's image might be damaged by offensive integrity test items appear no longer to be a problem. Most applicants do not object to integrity test content. Sackett and Wanek (1996) concluded that applicants do not perceive integrity tests as negatively as critics have suggested they would.

A determinant of the reactions to drug testing is whether the tests are given to incumbent employees. When they are, employee reactions tend to be negative. It is quite a different experience, for example, to be given a drug test or an integrity test as an employee than to be given one as an applicant. If an applicant fails such a test, he or she is not usually given feedback about the test failure. Usually, the denial letter sent to an applicant is the same polite sort that is sent to a person who is not being hired because of inadequate experience or anything else. No specific reason is given. However, if an employee is given such a test, feedback certainly is given. Whatever the outcome of the test, the person will learn the result. If an employee fails, he or she may be disciplined, sent to rehabilitation, and/or terminated. When tests are given to incumbents, the fairness of the procedures and the apparent purpose of testing are likely to become relevant in ways that are not relevant to applicants. For example, if workplace safety is recognized as a compelling reason for testing and the procedures for testing seem to be fair, then employees can be expected to react favorably.

## SUMMING UP

The purpose of this chapter is to explore the nature of tests of personality and character as they are used for employee selection. Summing up, we can make the following conclusions:

- The five-factor model is a useful taxonomy for describing the normal personality.
- Conscientiousness is a valid personality predictor of job performance.
- Self-report inventories have advantages over projective personality tests for use in employee selection.
- The Revised NEO Personality Inventory is designed to test the Big Five personality factors.

- Faking can be a problem in self-report inventories, and procedures have been devised to detect response distortion.
- Employee counterproductivity and misconduct are serious problems in today's workplace.
- Written honesty and integrity tests, some of which are personality-based, can be used to predict employee misconduct.
- Drug tests are used in testing both applicants and incumbents.
- Employees often react negatively to incumbent drug testing policies and procedures.

## InfoTrac College Edition

Would you like to learn more about the issues reviewed in this chapter? If you purchased a new copy of this book, you received a complimentary subscription to InfoTrac College Edition with your purchase. Use it to access full-text articles from research journals and practice-oriented publications. Go to http://www.infotrac-college.com/wadsworth to start your search. You might open current issues of a journal that you know is likely to have relevant articles, such as *Personnel Psychology*. You probably will want to do a keyword search. The following keywords can be used to find articles related to the topics of this chapter.

Five-factor model or          Employee theft
    Big Five personality          Executive personality
Conscientiousness          Employee drug testing

# APPLICATIONS AND OTHER PERSONAL HISTORY ASSESSMENTS

What do people put on their résumés? A list of achievements? A list of leisure-time activities? An employment objective or a reason for leaving one's last job? In a recent business magazine article, an employer commented on résumés reviewed in the course of finding a new employee. He was most interested in some of the optional items that applicants listed on their résumés. He gave some "interpretations" of the reasons cited for leaving a previous job. For example, when someone wishes to "pursue other interests," it is simply another way of saying they were no good at what they'd been doing. Saying that one "needs a new challenge" means they were bored stiff. And "organizational restructuring" actually means they got fired. However, he observed, none had said what was probably true of most—that they "want more money and more time off." The commentator thought that what applicants said about their leisure activities would interest other employers, because many employees do these things at work as well as during leisure time. The applicants listed a wide variety of leisure interests on their résumés. However, he found that nobody owned up to any of the real things people spend their leisure time doing—drinking, using drugs, gambling, watching TV, and shopping (Cleary, 1999).

All joking aside, the article highlighted some of the difficulties with using self-reports of personal history information for screening job applicants. With both résumés and employer-designed application forms, response distortion can be a problem. This is important because the job application is a frequently used method of evaluating applicants (Levine & Flory, 1975). Most employers include some kind of personal history assessment in their employee selection procedures. Generally, it is a job application form that is filled out by the applicant, although many employers either request or will accept individuals' résumés.

In this chapter, I discuss the various types of job applications, including standard and weighted application forms, as well as some test-like application instruments. In addition, I will discuss the use of applications for assessing education and experience, and the need for collecting references.

# APPLICATION METHODS

The main purpose of the job application is to gather information about aspects of an applicant's personal history that are job-relevant, such as education and previous work experience. This information is used to predict performance on future jobs and to hire new employees.

The underlying rationale of application procedures is based on the principle of consistency of behavior. This is a common theme in the study of individual behavior. Looking back at the discussion of testing, you can see that the consistency principle is basic to aspects of test reliability. It refers to the stability of behavior, specifically the stability of knowledge, skills, and abilities (KSAs), but also to motivation and interests. The consistency principle also identifies how the educational and work experience features of personal history can be important in predicting future performance. That is, an applicant can be expected to engage in certain needed work behaviors if there is evidence that he or she has shown these behaviors in the past. The assumption is that the individual has not lost the capacity or the motivation to perform since the time of the past experience. Previous work experiences that are the same as or similar to those of the job opening as well as certain educational experiences can provide evidence of past behavior. The key question is whether or not these past experiences are accurately sampled by application procedures.

## Standard Application Forms

The typical job application is used routinely to gather two kinds of information. Some information is needed for HR record-keeping on employees, such as name, address, phone number, social security number, and the name of a person to contact in case of emergency. Other information, such as education and work experience, is used to screen applicants against job requirements and, often, to inform interviewers about applicants. Both of these selection uses potentially are risky because application forms sometimes contain discriminatory items. You will recall from Chapter 6 that Title VII allows the use of any employee selection device, including an application, provided it does not unfairly discriminate against applicants. The EEOC's *Uniform Guidelines* (1978) requires most employers to evaluate their selection procedures in an adverse impact assessment. Job applications are used in selection decision making to screen out applicants. Generally, they provide a means for making the first cut in the applicant pool. Therefore, employers must include them in adverse impact assessments.

Application forms also need to be examined before they are used in order to establish that they do not contain items suggesting that the employer intends to discriminate. It would be difficult to prove that an employer's motive is *not* discriminatory if data are being gathered that, in fact, provide the basis for a discriminatory decision. When an employer is examining an application form, certain types of items should be flagged and revised or removed. First, direct questions about an applicant's race, ethnicity, national origin, sex, religion, age, and disability must not appear on application forms. Of course, some of this information will have to be gathered in order to conduct adverse impact assessments. However, because applications are used to make or influence selection decisions, they must not be used also to gather EEO data. Separation of EEO documentation from selection decision making is not difficult to accomplish. Employers usually gather the needed personal information by sending a special "affirmative action" form to all applicants so as to collect these data separately and in a confidential manner. Second, some questions that are found on application forms *indirectly* yield information that might discriminate. For example, an application with an item calling for the preferred form of address—Mr., Mrs., Miss, or Ms.—provides information about the sex of the applicant, and for women it also can provide information about their marital status. Such information might be the source of a discriminatory selection decision. Other application inquiries are similarly inappropriate because they access information about historical and discriminatory differences among individuals or because they invade an applicant's privacy. For example, asking whether a person has ever been arrested is inappropriate because being arrested for a crime is not the same as being convicted. Further, African American men historically have had a higher arrest record than their numbers in the population would predict, and many of these arrests have not led to convictions. Table 10.1 contains examples of questions that are inappropriate for application forms.

At this point, you might be thinking that by now employers surely would be sensitized to the necessity for nondiscriminatory selection procedures and that it would be unusual for a job application to include such items. I believe that a great many employers are sensitive to this need. Certainly, there have been improvements in the design of application forms since the time, 35 years ago, when application forms routinely included explicitly discriminatory items such as those identified in Table 10.1. However, some researchers have reported that not all application forms are free of problematic questions. In the early 1980s, Burrington (1982) examined the application forms used in state agencies throughout the United States. She found that all of the forms contained at least one item that was inappropriate in some way, either because it was explicit in calling for information about protected group status or because it invaded an applicant's right to privacy. The average application form contained eight inappropriate items. Some of the explicit questions were constructed so as to include an "EEO" disclaimer; that is, to make the response optional. For example, 32 percent of the forms included an item asking for the applicant's date of birth, with a disclaimer making the response optional. However, 46 percent of the sample asked for the applicant's birthdate without the disclaimer. Ten years

**TABLE 10.1** EXAMPLES OF APPLICATION ITEMS YIELDING POTENTIALLY INAPPROPRIATE INFORMATION

| Explicit Items | Indirect Items (implying) |
|---|---|
| What is your sex? | Please circle preferred title: Mr. Mrs. Miss Ms. (sex; marital status of women) |
| What is your marital status? | How many children do you have? What are their ages? (sex) |
| What is your date of birth? | In what year did you finish high school? (age) |
| What is your race? | Please attach a recent photograph of yourself. (sex, race, ethnicity, age) |
| Where were you born? | What language is spoken in your home? (national origin) |
| Do you have any handicaps or disabilities? | What is the general state of your health? (disability) |
| What is your religion? | Are you able to work on weekends? (religion) |

after this study, Vodanovich and Lowe (1992) reported that organizations still were using forms with inappropriate items. All the application forms the researchers examined contained at least two items that were questionable in some way, and the average form included seven such items. Further, forms used by private companies contained significantly more inappropriate items than those used by government or public employers. The researchers reported that the most frequent inappropriate question was one about past earnings or minimum acceptable salary. What is wrong with this question? Because of the historical difference in the earnings of men and women, such a question is thought to have a harsher effect on the employment opportunities of women than of men, specifically in terms of fair compensation.

Perhaps there will be more improvement soon. Regulations have been developed at the state level concerning the questions that must not be included on application forms. Fair employment practice agencies in several states have published their own lists of impermissible questions, including those that ask about an applicant's age, sex, religion, health, and economic status (Ash, 1991). These lists are available to business organizations. Hopefully, employers will obtain and use them in evaluating their application forms.

**Résumés**   Often, résumés[1] are used in selection, especially in hiring individuals for managerial, professional, and technical positions. In filling such

---

[1] Résumés are also referred to as curriculum vitae, or CVs.

positions, employers solicit résumés instead of an application, whereas in other jobs, they often accept a résumé along with an application form.

Résumés function in the same way that an application form does. The main difference is in terms of the items of personal history that are provided. In a sense, a résumé is an application form in which the *applicant* decides what questions to answer. Although the format of résumés may differ from application forms, in content they resemble applications. Frequently using the same or similar questions, résumés appear to be modeled after the traditional standard application form. Because of this, they may suffer from the same problems. For example, résumés sometimes include personal information that could cause a discriminatory effect if an employer used the information to make a selection decision. Although the information is voluntarily provided, it is inappropriate in the same way that an application item with an EEO disclaimer is inappropriate, and an employer must not base the selection decision on the discriminatory information.

Beyond the routine information showing how to contact the applicant, résumés have some common features. First, and most importantly, résumé writers describe their educational programs and degrees and give a history of work experiences. Typically, résumés convey about the same brief amount of detail on work accomplishments and educational course work that standard application forms do. The brevity might be because it is commonly believed that employers are unwilling to read more than a two-page résumé. Second, many résumés begin with an employment objective that identifies career plans or the type of work being sought. Often, this objective is couched in terms exactly fitting the employer's open position. This is meant to express interest in the position. Depending on how difficult it is to get a job, some individuals will have more than one version of their résumé. In these versions, the applicant organizes and describes personal history material somewhat differently under slightly different employment objective statements. Third, résumé writers sometimes include optional items of personal information, such as volunteer work activities that may be relevant to the open position, memberships in professional or other work-oriented associations, accomplishments that are not cited elsewhere, and even hobbies or leisure-time activities.

**Response Distortion**    As I discussed in Chapter 9, personality test scores are distorted when applicants fake a test and try to present themselves more positively in order to make a good impression. For the same reason, applications and résumés are likely to contain response distortion. Falsification of the amount and quality of education and work experience is thought to be a fairly common problem in job applications and résumés. The education and experience qualifications desired by employers are generally well known to applicants because they are listed in job advertisements. Therefore, it may be especially easy to distort a work history to match known or presumed job requirements.

Do applicants actually give false information on applications and résumés? Currently, there is very little published research on these questions. However, it is widely believed, by I/O psychologists and HR consultants, that applicants do give inaccurate and/or incomplete information. For example, in a recent HR magazine article, a consultant was interviewed who stated that many job seekers give false information, and increasingly so. She reported a poll showing that the percentage of résumés containing distorted information had risen from 18 percent in 1979 to 36 percent in 1997 ("Avoiding 'Truth or Dare,'" 2000). It might be that fluctuations in the labor market make applicants more or less likely to give accurate information. In recent years, you remember, organizations laid off employees and went through a period of rather severe downsizing, making jobs hard to get. The consultant mentioned other polls in which many college students said they were willing to falsify their résumés to get a job, if they had to, and some said they already had done so. An earlier published study described the types of information that applicants falsify. Goldstein (1974) found that the most commonly distorted information was in response to application items asking how long a person had worked on a specific job and the amount of earnings. On questions about length of time on a job, 57 percent of applicants gave information that did not agree with previous employers' records. Also, 72 percent misrepresented their earnings. Distortion this frequent, especially about the amount of experience, should alert employers to be careful about relying heavily on standard applications and résumés for applicant screening purposes. The potential for response distortion is also a good reason to check applicants' references, as I discuss later.

## *Evaluating Education and Experience*

Employers use standard application forms and résumés to screen applicants based on their education and work experience. In a selection hurdle process, those who pass the initial screening undergo further evaluation with selection methods such as testing and interviewing. Often, however, use of application material does not end with the preliminary screening but extends further into the selection process. For example, applications that are initially screened-in often are further reviewed by a manager, prior to conducting an interview. The manager may rate each applicant's level of training and experience and, on this basis, decide whom to interview. In addition, the application sometimes is used to guide the interview. Whether the job application is valid for any of these multiple uses is a question employers need to consider seriously.

The initial screening of applications frequently is done by an HR assistant who checks to see that the applicant has the desired number of years and type of education and experience. These educational and experience requirements should have been determined by a job analysis although, unfortunately, they often are not. Sometimes, instead of having an HR assistant go through paper copies of applications and résumés, an employer conducts the initial screening by computer. Computer software is able to sort through a database of application materials using keywords and will screen out applications that do not contain the keywords. An organization that does a lot of online recruiting and has equipment for scanning paper copies of applications into the database may find this especially appealing. The quality of both methods of screening, however, depends on two requirements: using a job analysis to determine needs for education and experience, and identifying effective keywords. Whether a person or a computer conducts the screening, if the requirements are not directly job-relevant, and if the keywords are inadequate, then the screening will not be valid.

**Accuracy of Measurement**    Job applications can be evaluated in terms of how well they are conceptualized as measures of past behavior. Typically, the traditional standard application has three weaknesses in this respect. First, most applications ask only about formal education and previous paid jobs. A person's history of learning and experience includes much more than this, of course. People develop work-related knowledge and skills in a variety of settings, not simply at school or on paid jobs. For example, people often are self-taught, and many volunteer their time in community service organizations performing work for which they are not paid. Usually, however, these kinds of experiences are not considered on job application forms, although sometimes they are clearly relevant.

Second, an assumption underlying the traditional job application is that the nature and level of education and experience are good signs or indicators of an individual's knowledge, skill, and ability. There are problems with this assumption—and with the manner in which applications yield information on education and experience. Application blanks usually ask applicants to provide brief summary statements describing their past work experience. These descriptions are used as signs of an applicant's ability to perform a specified job. Samples of actual work behavior are not provided. The distinction between signs and samples is important for certain selection methods, such as job applications, that depend on evidence of content validity. As discussed in Chapter 7, to have content validity, a selection measure must clearly be representative of the job and must sample job knowledge or work-related behavior in some way. For example, performance tests provide samples of a person's ability to perform tasks that are part of or representative of the job. Similarly, a job knowledge test provides a sample of the person's knowledge. However, the traditional standard application does not yield samples of past experience. Often, it produces only superficial information about an applicant's previous work, such as company name, job title, and the length of time the person held the position. To make use of such information, the employer must infer that the work experience included opportunities for the person to develop job-related KSAs. The user also must infer that the KSAs actually were developed and exhibited

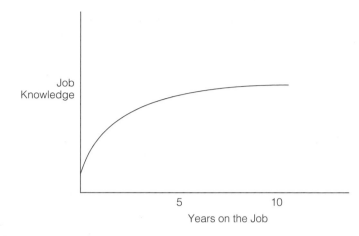

FIGURE **10.1**

Relationship between time on a job and level of job knowledge. The hypothetical curve shows increasing knowledge up to about 5 years on the job and a plateau soon afterward.

Based on information from *Performance in four Army jobs by men at different aptitude (AFQT) levels: 3. The relationship of AFQT and job experience to job performance* by R. Vineberg and E. N. Taylor, 1972. Alexandria, VA: Human Resources Research Organization (HUMRRO).

on the previous job (Schmidt, Caplan, Bemis, Decuir, Dunn, & Antone, 1979; Wernimont & Campbell, 1968). The accuracy of these inferences is questionable. One reason is that the quality of opportunities for individuals to develop KSAs varies between and within employment settings. For example, training and opportunities to learn new skills on the job may be available for some employees and not for others. Another reason is that individuals differ in their inherent ability and motivation to take advantage of the opportunities that are available to them. As you are aware, some students perform extremely well—earning high grades and honors—whereas others earn such poor grades that they barely graduate. Similarly, some employees can and do take advantage of opportunities at work. They learn and perform at high levels, and they accomplish a great deal. Others, on the same job, learn and do very little, and they accomplish only enough to avoid getting fired.

Third, the relationship between the level of a person's knowledge and ability and the length of time that he or she has held a job or been with a company is not completely linear. Schmidt, Hunter, and Outerbridge (1986) discussed evidence showing that only for about the first 5 years on a job is there a linear relationship between knowledge and time. That is, with relatively new employees, there is an increase in job-related knowledge associated with increasing time on the job. Beyond 5 years, however, there is a plateau. The plateau indicates that employees have learned almost all they are going to learn about the work. Graphs of the relationship show essentially no further increase in job knowledge after this point. (See Figure 10.1 for a demonstration of such a graph.)

**Validity of Work Experience for Predicting Job Performance**    In comparison to the vast numbers of studies on the validity of tests, relatively little published research has addressed the validity of job applications. Until recently, the research was limited mainly to exploratory studies that simply looked for any relationship that might exist between experience and performance. In a frequently cited meta-analytic review of such research, Hunter and Hunter (1984) examined validity coefficients from 425 mostly unpublished studies. In these studies, years of experience on the present job was correlated with ratings from the employees' supervisors. The average correlation between experience and performance was .18. This value is comparable to correlation coefficients found in other exploratory studies of the experience–performance relationship. For example, in another meta-analysis, McDaniel and Schmidt (1985) reported an average correlation of .15 between experience on similar jobs and current job performance in 89 studies. These two values indicate that experience is a positive but weak predictor of job performance. However, the individual studies in the meta-analyses used varied measures, allowing only a broad exploration of the issue. Perhaps stronger relationships between past experience and future performance might be shown by research using a more focused approach.

Since the 1980s, researchers have given more attention to the question of using experience to predict job performance. Theoretical development, in particular, has made a valuable contribution by identifying important individual and work context variables that may be used to precisely focus research and expose the nature of the experience–performance relationship. Schmidt and Hunter developed an empirically based theoretical model that traced the mechanisms through which experience influences job performance (Schmidt, Hunter, & Outerbridge, 1986). They based this on Hunter's (1983) earlier work showing that job performance was influenced indirectly by the effect of an individual's general mental ability on the level of job knowledge. In their theoretical model, job experience was added as a variable and proposed to affect performance in the same way as general mental ability. That is, experience was proposed to have a direct effect on the acquisition of job knowledge, but only indirectly would it affect job performance. Further, the indirect effect on performance was proposed to occur primarily through the effect of experience on job knowledge. The complete model is depicted in Figure 10.2.

In order to test the model, Schmidt and his associates (1986) conducted a path analysis of four existing studies of military personnel. The path analysis confirmed the model, showing that the greatest value of higher levels of work experience was increased job knowledge. Measures of experience were directly and strongly related to job knowledge test scores (.57), as had been predicted. Job knowledge, in turn, was shown to be the best predictor of performance. The level of job knowledge predicted both work sample performance (.66) and supervisors' ratings of performance on the job (.34). (These values

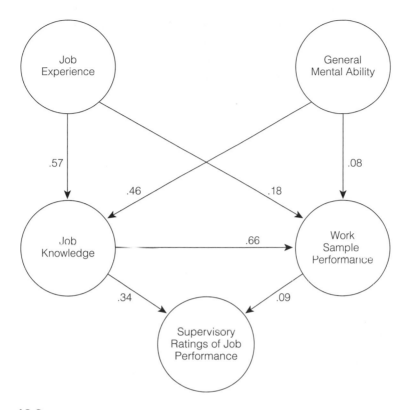

FIGURE **10.2**

The Schmidt-Hunter theoretical model showing the indirect effects of work experience and general mental ability on job performance, through the direct effects that each variable has on job knowledge and work sample performance. Correlation coefficients from path analysis of data are grouped according to experience categories.

Adapted from "Impact of Job Experience and Ability on Job Knowledge, Work Sample Performance, and Supervisory Ratings of Job Performance," by F. L. Schmidt, J. E. Hunter, and A. N. Outerbridge, 1986, *Journal of Applied Psychology, 71*(3), figure 3, p. 437. Copyright 1986 by American Psychological Association, Washington, DC. Adapted by permission.

are shown in Figure 10.2.) The results of this analysis should be understood in view of the samples that were included in the four studies. Specifically, the participants had relatively low levels of job experience—2 or 3 years, on average, and they were performing jobs that were moderately complex. This brings up certain questions: Is the impact of work experience as pronounced among those with more years of experience? Is there a difference due to the complexity of the job?

In related research, McDaniel, Schmidt, and Hunter (1988) investigated questions similar to these. They examined the effects of varying lengths of experience and levels of complexity on job performance, using existing data from 947 samples. Overall, the researchers found that as years of experience increased, performance improved. However, the specific amount of job experience had a strong moderating effect on this relationship. Lower levels of experience showed a higher correlation with job performance than did higher levels of experience. The strongest association with job performance, in which the correlation coefficient was .49, was among employees who had less than 3 years of experience. In comparison, among employees who had 12 or more years of experience, the correlation coefficient was .15, which indicates that years of experience is not as useful for predicting the performance of more senior applicants. The cognitive complexity of the job also moderated the relationship between experience and performance. The researchers found that work experience was a somewhat better predictor of performance when the job was not highly complex. In samples of employees with less than 3 years of experience on low-complexity jobs, the correlation between experience and performance was .54. In comparison, among those on high-complexity jobs, the correlation was .42. McDaniel et al. (1988) interpreted this result in terms of the effects of experience on job *knowledge*. They suggested that work experience has a greater impact on performance in low-complexity jobs because there are few ways, other than on-the-job experience, in which one can gain the knowledge required for this work (i.e., in semiskilled and unskilled occupations). On the other hand, for high-complexity jobs, such as in the professions and skilled trades, a person can obtain the needed knowledge from both work experience and formal education, because of the relatively large number of educational programs available. Therefore, in these jobs, work experience is not as important in predicting performance.

**Effective Measures of Work Experience**    Most studies of the relationship between work experience and job performance, like those discussed above, have used time on the job as the predictive measure. Most job applications in use also ask about time on previous jobs. However, experience can be measured in other ways, and how a variable is measured in a study can affect the study's outcomes. Therefore, it is helpful to know what to expect from measuring work experience and job performance in various ways. Quiñones, Ford, and Teachout (1995) developed a conceptual framework describing the different aspects of work experience and listing the possible ways to measure them. The framework reflects two general dimensions—level of specificity and measurement mode—that are inherent in the kinds of measures used in research. Level of specificity refers to the breadth of focus in a measure, and it includes task-, job-, and organization-level measures. There are three measurement modes. *Time* measures are the ones used in most studies. They are quantitative measures such as years on a job. *Amount* measures, which also are quantitative, are defined as counts of work experience, such as number of tasks performed. *Type* measures describe different qualitative aspects of work experience, such as the complexity of a job. Figure 10.3 shows the nine ways to combine specificity and mode. As you can see, these measures describe quite different ways of assessing work experience, and they might reveal different views of how

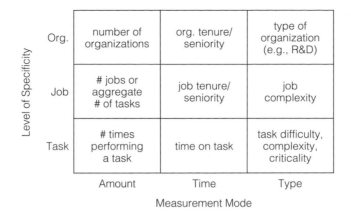

FIGURE **10.3**

Conceptual framework showing work experience measures in three levels of specificity and three modes of measurement.

From "The Relationship Between Work Experience and Job Performance: A Conceptual and Meta-analytic Review," by M. A. Quiñones, J. K. Ford, and M. S. Teachout, 1995, *Personnel Psychology, 48*(4), figure 1, p. 892. Copyright 1995 by Personnel Psychology, Inc., Bowling Green, Ohio. Reprinted by permission.

experience relates to job performance. Quiñones et al. (1995) predicted that task-level measures of the amount of experience (i.e., the number of times a task was performed) would be the strongest predictor of later job performance because these measures provide a sample of what a person was actually doing in the previous experience.

In their meta-analysis, Quiñones and his associates (1995) found the average correlation across all studies to be .27. This established that there was a positive relationship between work experience and job performance. It also demonstrated that a variety of measures could be used to predict job performance. Consistent with industry practice and traditional job applications, most of the studies they reviewed had used time and job-level measures, such as years on a specified job. Still, they identified enough studies to test all specificity-mode combinations identified in the model. The meta-analysis confirmed that some measures of experience were much more effective than others in predicting job performance. First, measures of the amount of work experience were particularly strong, correlating at .43 with job performance. This value was significantly greater than the correlations of time measures (.27) and type measures (.21). Second, task-level measures also were strong, showing a correlation coefficient of .41. This was significantly greater than the correlations of job-level measures (.27) and organization-level measures (.16). Although not part of their theoretical framework, the researchers further reported that the type of criterion measure used to assess job performance had a notable impact on the experience–performance correlation. Productivity measures or other objective assessments, such as work samples, were significantly stronger than supervisors' ratings or other subjective measures of performance (with a correlation of .39 compared to .24).

This study demonstrated that the most valuable work experience information for predicting job performance is information at the most specific level (i.e., tasks performed) and information that shows the amount of experience (e.g., number of tasks performed). To the extent that a measure is more general and assesses time or type of work, the information it yields is less predictive of future performance. Therefore, employers should obtain information about the amount of experience on specific job-related tasks so that they can be more confident of the validity of previous experience for evaluating job applications.

## Conclusions

Standard application forms and résumés have three important limitations for employee selection purposes. First, they can yield personal history information that is inappropriate for an employer to collect. Some application forms call for information that could lead an employer to make discriminatory selection decisions, and some résumé writers voluntarily include such information. Employers need to remove discriminatory items from their application forms, and they must guard against using such information in deciding whom to hire, even if applicants volunteer it. Second, standard application forms and résumés are likely to be distorted and may contain outright falsifications. The only recourse for an employer who wants to use these methods for hiring is to follow up with background checks. Third, information on education and work experience, as collected by traditional applications and résumés, has limited value because of weaknesses in the design of these measures. Research has shown that experience is a better predictor for low-complexity jobs and for relatively inexperienced applicants. For other jobs and for more experienced applicants, the usual application listing of job titles and years with a company without details on what was actually done is not useful for making effective hiring decisions. Also, experience appears to be indirectly related to job performance, and it is affected by differences in individuals' general abilities and motivation. Thus, for most jobs, it is better for an employer to develop and validate a new application instrument that can provide quantifiable information on the level of job knowledge or on the previous performance of specific tasks.

## SCORED APPLICATION INSTRUMENTS

Standard application forms, typically, are not scored. Sometimes an evaluator assigns points for the amount of education and experience an applicant reports. Often, however, an HR assistant or a manager simply examines the infor-

FIGURE **10.4**

Theoretical relationship between background data, KSAs required for the job, and success on the job.

mation to see whether it is comparable to what is on the job announcement. When used in this way to screen applicants or to inform managers prior to an interview, an application can lead to a biased selection decision. A numerically scorable application form can be constructed, however, which provides several advantages. Such an application can standardize the use of application information in screening. Scoring also makes it possible to determine whether the application information is valid for predicting performance on the job.

Information on individuals' personal backgrounds—commonly labeled as biographical data or biodata—has been shown by research to predict job performance and other employee behaviors. Employers can use this information to construct scorable application blanks and related instruments. The rationale for measures using biodata is that past experiences influence the development of various areas of knowledge, skills, abilities, and other personal attributes that contribute to an individual's capacity for work. Information about a person's experiences and accomplishments, therefore, can indicate the extent to which the person may be qualified for a certain job. This relationship between past experience and job-related KSAs is depicted in Figure 10.4.

The use of biographical data in employee selection has a long history. The initial idea came from professional men in the insurance business more than a century ago. In 1894, Colonel Thomas L. Peters reported that he and his colleagues in the Georgia Association of Life Insurers had been using a list of biographical or personal history items to select new life insurance salesmen. The questions included items such as number of residences during the previous 10 years, place and date of birth, amount of real estate owned, occupation during the previous 10 years, and experience in insurance sales (Owens, 1976). A few years later, several published reports described how personal history information could be analyzed empirically and how item responses could be weighted for scoring. For example, Goldsmith (1922) described the procedures for developing a test-like application blank, which would make use of personal history items in the selection of salesmen. Viteles (1932) reported an effective procedure for objectively scoring items on an application form that was used to select taxi drivers. By the 1940s, several instruments had been developed using biographical data. Some had been designed with multiple-choice response categories and resembled attitude questionnaires or personality inventories. Owens (1976) found several reports on the use of scored application instruments in the armed forces of World War II. In one report, Guilford and Lacey (1947) showed that a scored biodata application form, on average, correlated with Air Force pilot training success at levels of .35 to .40. Clearly, as these early studies demonstrated, valid scorable application instruments can be constructed to collect personal history information.

In this section, I discuss three types of application instruments that can be used effectively to collect background data: behavioral consistency instruments, weighted application blanks, and biographical inventories. These instruments have important characteristics in common: (1) All three are designed to collect information on an applicant's background of personal experiences. (2) Relevant experiences and accomplishments are identified from job analysis. (3) Quantitative evidence of validity is obtained for each measure. (4) Applicants' responses are scored and can be used systematically in selection decision making.

In some ways, these application instruments are quite different. Only the weighted application looks like an application blank. Behavioral consistency instruments use an open-ended response format, asking applicants to compose answers in their own words about their education and work experience. As a result, this application looks like a personal narrative or an essay. The biographical inventory uses a closed response format, such as ratings and multiple-choice items, to collect a full range of personal information. Because of the formatting, the biographical inventory resembles a self-report personality test.

## Behavioral Consistency Application

The behavioral consistency application is an open-ended questionnaire used for collecting samples of job-related personal experience data. It can function in place of a standard job application blank or as a supplement to an application. The procedure was developed in the late 1970s by the U.S. Office of Personnel Management (OPM) (Schmidt, Caplan, et al., 1979). The OPM researchers based the procedure on the following four points: (1) Past experience can be used to predict future job performance. (2) Knowledge and ability gained from experience in any setting can be used in assessing work experience. (3) Samples of actual work performed provide stronger predictions of future job performance than mere signs that developmental opportunities were available. (4) Samples of past performance can be obtained from applicants' own personal history reports. The behavioral consistency application thus enables the employer to obtain information about what an applicant actually accomplished in previous work experiences in educational settings, on paid jobs, or in any other work arrangement.

TABLE
10.2 **EXAMPLE ITEM ON BEHAVIORAL CONSISTENCY APPLICATION**

| Component | Item Content |
|---|---|
| Job dimension | Ability to analyze complex and technical data, using quantitative reasoning |
| Question | What have you done in the past that shows that you have analytical and quantitative abilities? |
| Answers to include | a. The problem or objective |
|  | b. What you actually did and when |
|  | c. The outcome or result |
|  | d. The percentage of credit for the result you claim |
|  | e. Name of someone who can verify the information |

Adapted from *The Behavioral Consistency Method of Unassembled Examining* (Technical Memorandum 79-21), by F. L. Schmidt, J. R. Caplan, S. E. Bemis, R. Decuir, L. Dunn, and L. Antone, 1979, Washington, DC: U.S. Office of Personnel Management.

**Developing the Instrument**    Developing a behavioral consistency application begins with a job analysis through which critical dimensions of the job are identified. Developed from the job itself, the instrument thus attains content validity. Schmidt, Caplan, et al. (1979) used Primoff's (1975) job element method of job analysis in creating the procedure. As you will recall from Chapter 3, an advantage of the job element approach is that it yields required KSAs *directly*, through an SME-panel. (By comparison, in task analysis, the job analyst must identify KSAs indirectly by examining tasks.)

The instrument consists of a small number of work dimensions that have been judged by the SME-panel as being critical to success on the job. These are listed as items, along with a standard set of questions. An applicant responds by writing detailed answers to the questions for each dimension. For example, Schmidt, Caplan, et al. (1979) identified five KSA dimensions that were critical to the job of budget analyst. The dimensions were analytical and quantitative reasoning ability, interpersonal interaction skill, ability to organize work, writing ability, and oral communication skill. The questions—which are the same for all dimensions—call for specific information relating to an achievement on each dimension. This information includes the objective or problem solved by the achievement, what was actually done, the outcome, the amount of credit claimed, and the identification of someone able to verify the information. An example item is shown in Table 10.2.

Before a behavioral consistency application can be used, response descriptions must be developed showing the kinds of achievements that applicants might be expected to report. These descriptions are evaluated and scaled as

| TABLE 10.3 | EXAMPLE RESPONSE USED AS A MIDSCALE (3.5) BENCHMARK ON ANALYTICAL AND REASONING ABILITY DIMENSION |

| Component of Answer | Essay Response |
| --- | --- |
| a. Objective | While working as a compensation analyst, I was asked to develop a report on the prevailing wages and fringe benefits of various classifications of trash collection employees in the San Francisco area. These wages are required by the McNamara-O'Hara Service Contract Act to be paid on federal government service contracts. |
| b. What was done | During the month of September 1971, I analyzed various types of data on wages and fringe benefits obtained from sources such as an internal survey, Bureau of Labor Statistics surveys, union agreements, and discussions with company officials in the area. |
| c. Outcome | Using my best judgment of the wages and fringe benefits, I issued an official wage determination and justification which was used on government service contracts in the area. |
| d. Credit | About 75 percent of the wage determination effort was my own, the remainder being supervisory. |

*Note.* Response was evaluated at 3.6 on a scale of 1 to 5 and was one of three responses demonstrating the 3.5 benchmark.

Adapted from *The Behavioral Consistency Method of Unassembled Examining* (Technical Memorandum 79–21), by F. L. Schmidt, J. R. Caplan, S. E. Bemis, R. Ducuir, L. Dunn, and L. Antone, 1979, Washington, DC: U.S. Office of Personnel Management.

rating scale benchmarks, for scoring applicants' responses. To develop the scaled benchmarks, responses to the items are collected from a sample of employees who have the same job for which the instrument is being developed. The sample's responses are read and rated by members of an SME-panel. The ratings are averaged, and those responses that receive an average rating at or near a specific rating score are used as the benchmark for that score. (An example of a benchmark representing 3.5 on a 1 to 5 rating scale is shown in Table 10.3.) Later, when the instrument is being used for employee selection, a rater studies the benchmark descriptions, then reads and evaluates applicants' responses and assigns an appropriate rating scale score to each. Summing the dimension scores provides a total score for each applicant that an employer can use in selection decision making.

The advantages of this procedure include the fact that it is developed through a content validation procedure, and that it yields detailed information about real work accomplishments that the employer can verify. In addition, it provides a standardized method of scoring that allows the user to compare and distinguish between applicants in terms of their potential for the job. A possible drawback of constructing an entire application with the method is that it may represent a daunting task to an applicant. For example, when I once asked to apply for a job that was being advertised, I was sent a behavioral consistency application containing several work dimensions. I found responding to the form difficult and extremely time consuming. Finally, I decided it was simply too much and abandoned it. Apparently, I was not alone in my reaction. Ash and Levine (1985) found that only 56 percent of their research sample completed the behavioral consistency form they were sent, whereas at least 78 percent of those sent other application forms completed and returned them.

## Weighted Applications

The weighted application blank initially was developed primarily to provide for standardized scoring of personal history information, particularly in the areas of education and work experience. Like the behavioral consistency measure, the weighted application needs to be developed individually for a job or job family, mainly because educational and experience requirements vary across jobs. This means an employer is likely to require more than one version of the application. Weighted applications are constructed empirically, which can allow them to include some items from a previously used standard application form. Responses to items are collected using a closed response format. In the developmental process, any of several closed response categories might be considered, such as selecting one alternative from two or more discrete alternatives, or selecting an alternative from a continuum (e.g., as in a rating scale). I discuss response categories further, in the section on biographical inventories.

**Developmental Process**   To develop a weighted application blank, the developer first identifies a large set of personal history items that have potential value for predicting desirable employee behaviors. This set of items can be drawn from existing applications and from other sources, such as the research literature on employee background data. Some items will appear to be related to the job, whereas others will not. For example, items may concern past training or work experiences, interests, leisure activities, length of time at one's present address, or other personal experiences. Next in the developmental process, the items are scrutinized as to the extent to which they might have a discriminatory effect on members of one or more legally protected classes. The items also need to be examined as to whether they may constitute an invasion of privacy. Any that seem to be problematic in these ways should be removed.

Finally, the instrument is evaluated in a criterion-related validity study, typically using current employees. The developer should give careful thought as to what criterion needs to be predicted. Any of several aspects of successful employee behavior might be considered, such as performance, absenteeism, or turnover. The criterion selected depends on why the employer needs the application. Often, it is desirable to adopt performance criteria, such as performance on the job or in training. The developer also must determine what measure of the chosen criterion can be obtained. A commonly used criterion measure of job performance is the supervisor's rating.

A convenient procedure for conducting the validity study, which also yields the basic data for weighting the items for scoring, includes the following steps:

(1) Using the criterion measure, the developer divides the sample of current employees into two criterion groups—one that scores high on the criterion measure and the other that scores low on the measure. Assuming a performance measure is used, high and low performers are identified by their scores on the criterion measure. (2) The criterion groups are divided further into two groups, each with high and low performers. One group is used immediately as the validation sample. The other group will be used in a later cross-validation study to confirm the validity of the developed instrument. (3) The personal history items being considered for the weighted application are administered to the validation sample. (4) The responses of each criterion group are evaluated to identify those items on which the high and low criterion groups differ significantly. Only those items that clearly distinguish between the criterion groups should be included in the weighted application. These items will be the most valid for predicting the criterion measure. (5) The values of the differences between the groups on these items are used to establish weights for scoring applicants' responses. (6) The weighted application then is administered to the cross-validation sample, and their responses are evaluated to establish that the criterion group differences reflect those of the validation sample.

Developing the scoring weights for a weighted application blank involves systematically relating item responses to performance criterion levels. There are several statistical procedures for doing this, including correlational and regression methods. However, the vertical percent method is relatively simple, as it is based on the above developmental procedure. Referring to England's (1971) work, Weiss (1976) provided guidance on using this method of developing scoring weights. The basic information needed is that already obtained from the validation sample. Mainly, we need to know how many from each criterion group responded to an item by selecting each response alternative. An example of the responses to one application item is shown in Table 10.4. As you see, each alternative was used by some individuals in the sample. As a first step, the developer calculates the percentage differences between the criterion groups for each response category on the item. For example, in Table 10.4, for the "less than high school" response alternative, the difference is 5% minus 30%, or –25%. For the "some college" response, the percentage difference is 45% minus 10%, or 35%. The percentage differences then are converted into values that can be used as weights. Weiss (1976) noted that various schemes exist for converting such values to weights, although he found little difference in their effectiveness. Essentially, all that is needed is to define weights that are roughly proportional to the percentage differences. The conversions shown in Table 10.4 are one way to weight items. For example, a weight of –2.5 is given to the percentage difference of –25% and a weight of 3.5 to the difference of 35%. As you can see, item response categories that show a large difference will contribute a heavy weight, or high value to the score of applicants who respond this way. Response alternatives that show a small percentage difference will contribute less weight to a scored application.

| TABLE 10.4 | PROCEDURE FOR DEVELOPING SCORING WEIGHTS FOR WEIGHTED APPLICATION BLANKS | | | |
|---|---|---|---|---|
| Application Item: Education | Criterion Group Performance | | Criterion Group Percent Differences | Differences Converted to Weights |
| | High | Low | | |
| Less than high school | 5% | 30% | −25% | −2.5 |
| High school diploma or equivalent | 15% | 25% | −10% | −1.0 |
| Some college | 45% | 10% | 35% | 3.5 |
| College degree | 30% | 10% | 20% | 2.0 |
| Postgraduate study | 5% | 25% | −20% | −2.0 |
| | 100% | 100% | | |

When the weighted application blank is put into service, the user calculates total scores for all applicants by algebraically summing the weights of the item responses selected. Total scores are used in selection decision making, such as for screening in a multiple hurdle process or for combining with scores on other measures in a multiple regression. (Refer to Chapter 7 for a discussion of selection decision making.)

## Biographical Inventories

Construction of a biographical inventory, like the behavioral consistency and weighted application instruments, begins with careful consideration of the criteria to be predicted. Most biographical inventories are designed to predict job performance criteria, although criterion measures may vary. Objective measures of productivity and accomplishments on the job sometimes are available. Supervisors' ratings also can be used as a criterion measure. Decisions about criteria will depend on the particular job or job family for which the biographical inventory is being constructed. For example, a study involving multiple samples of managerial and professional staff employees used progression or rate of promotion within the organization as the criterion (Carlson, Scullen, Schmidt, Rothstein, & Erwin, 1999). The researchers measured progression in terms of salary increase and job level achieved.

**Biodata Item Development**    A biographical inventory is composed of multiple-choice items that allow an applicant to describe him- or herself in terms of demographic, experiential, and/or attitudinal variables. Questions might concern personality traits and personal adjustment, as well as social, educational, and occupational experiences. Often, biodata items are factual and verifiable, but items about feelings, values, and opinions also may be included.

How does the developer of a biographical inventory find appropriate material for the instrument? Behavioral theory might be used to identify potentially valid experiences and personal attributes. However, it is more likely that this information will come from a job analysis. As discussed previously in this chapter, background experiences are conceptualized as influencing the development of job-related KSAs. The experiences affect learning and memory and, in this way, they cause changes in an individual's capacities for work. Therefore, a job analysis can be used to identify relevant aspects of background experience through which KSAs and other job-related attributes might have been developed and expressed in behavior. These experiences can provide the basis for item construction.

A helpful illustration appeared in a report on developing items for an inventory used to select apprentice electricians (Mumford, Costanza, Connelly, & Johnson, 1996). The job analysis for this job showed that mechanical ability was one of the important KSAs required to perform the work. It was known that applicants typically were young adults with a high school education and some work experience in general construction, but with no training or experience in electrical work. Therefore, the researchers decided, experiences that occurred in high school, leisure activities, or previous construction work would be used in assessing the extent to which applicants had developed the necessary mechanical ability. For example, items such as the following were written: "In high school, how well did you do in shop courses?" and "How often have you been able to make repairs on your car?" In the first example, the item taps into the construct of mechanical ability and addresses performance outcomes. In the second, the same ability construct is being assessed, but in a different past experience. Items should be constructed so as to sample an individual's actual learning and performances, rather than simply asking about exposures to situations in which a learning experience could have occurred (although might not have). That is, instead of asking whether an applicant took shop classes in high school, it is better to ask how well he or she performed in shop classes.

In summary, the procedure for writing biodata items is as follows: First, identify the setting or situation. It should be one that most applicants for the job would have encountered. In the above items used for selecting electricians, the first item's opening—"in high school"—identifies the setting, a common one to which most applicants had had exposure. Second, focus on experiences occurring in the setting that either might lead to the development of required KSAs or indicate that they had previously been developed. In the first item above, the question "How well did you do in shop courses?" addresses an experience that might lead to the development of mechanical ability. The second item, about repairing a car, addresses behavior indicating that the ability had already been developed. Third, identify experiences in which people's accomplishments vary. Both of the above example items are likely to yield variations in the responses of different individuals. For example, some people will have

| TABLE 10.5 | RESPONSE CATEGORIES AND EXAMPLES OF BIODATA ITEMS |
|---|---|

| Category | Example |
|---|---|
| Dichotomous | Did you enjoy high school?    a. yes    b. no |
| Continuum;<br>one response only | How interesting were your college math classes?<br>a. Very interesting      c. Slightly interesting<br>b. Moderately interesting   d. Not at all interesting |
| Continuum,<br>plus escape option;<br>one response only | How old were you when you got your first job?<br>a. under 12         c. 19 or older<br>b. 13–18          d. have never had a job |
| Discrete or<br>noncontinuum;<br>one response only | Which of the following types of books are you most likely to<br>read during your leisure time?<br>a. mystery novels     c. self-improvement books<br>b. classic literature    d. biographies of famous people |
| Discrete or<br>noncontinuum, plus<br>escape option;<br>one response only | When you were a teenager, which of the following did you<br>most enjoy?<br>a. playing ball       c. hiking<br>b. hunting or fishing  d. playing tennis<br>                e. I did not enjoy any of these |
| Discrete or<br>noncontinuum;<br>multiple responses<br>as appropriate | Check all of the following activities that you currently do on a<br>regular basis.<br>a. going out with a group of friends<br>b. attending parties<br>c. attending family gatherings<br>d. spending quiet evenings at home |
| Continuum,<br>multiple item<br>question with<br>common stem;<br>respond to all | Using the rating scale at the lower right, rate each of the<br>following as to its value or importance to you.<br>a. being able to work outdoors  (1) very important<br>b. having a secure job for life   (2) moderately important<br>c. having interesting work to do (3) slightly important<br>d. being in a supervisory position (4) not important<br>e. having time for family activities |

Based on information from "Background Data," by W. A. Owens, 1976, 1983, in M. D. Dunnette (Ed.), *Handbook of Industrial and Organizational Psychology,* p. 613.

done well in shop classes, whereas others will have done poorly. Such differences are necessary in weighting and scoring item responses (Mumford & Stokes, 1992).

Designing response categories for biodata items depends on the nature of the experience or behavior, as well as the structure of the question. Owens (1976) identified seven categories of item response used in formatting a biodata instrument. Table 10.5 describes these response categories and shows an example for each. Owens believed that items using a response continuum are preferable to items using a list of discrete response choices, as they are more effective for statistically validating a biographical inventory. Also, he suggested that items requiring single-choice responses are better than items that allow an applicant to choose more than one of the responses. With the latter, he thought individuals tend to "spread themselves thinly" and that their multiple endorsements yield less information in data analysis.

## Using Biodata Instruments

**Scoring**    To develop a usable biographical inventory, scoring weights and procedures for combining item scores must be determined. There are a number of methods for developing scores, depending on how the instrument was constructed. The rational method involves scoring on the basis of established content- or construct-valid scales. The more frequently used methods involve an empirical procedure. Correlational and regression techniques can be used to empirically key a biodata instrument for scoring. Also, as I discussed in the section on weighted application blanks, the vertical percent method can be used. Briefly, to use this method to develop scores, item responses first are analyzed to determine the extent to which they are related to criterion levels in the validation sample. The value of this relationship for each response then is converted into a weight that is assigned to the response alternative. The weight is used as an item score for applicants who select the alternative. To obtain a total score for an applicant, the item scores are algebraically summed.

**Reliability**    Studies of biographical inventories have reported generally strong reliability estimates. However, the technique used to assess reliability must be appropriate for the instrument. For example, Mumford et al. (1996) conducted internal consistency reliability studies for biodata instruments that had been developed using a construct validation procedure. Reliabilities ranged from .67 to .70, and these values did not notably shrink when the scales were administered to new samples. Because the scales of the inventory had been designed specifically to measure a small number of constructs, the internal consistency technique was an appropriate method for assessing reliability as it shows the extent to which item content is similar across the instrument. However, this technique is less useful for measuring the reliability of many empirically developed instruments that are made up of heterogeneous content and in which there would be little reason to expect strong correlations *within* the instrument.

For most empirically developed instruments, the better assessments of reliability come from the test–retest and alternate forms methods. Test–retest reliability studies have indicated stability in biodata instruments, depending on the length of the retest interval. For example, one study reported a test–retest reliability coefficient of .85 after a 19-month interval (Chaney & Owens, 1964). In another study, Owens's instrument, the Biographical Questionnaire, was readministered after a 5-year interval and reliability coefficients of .56 and .58 were found (Shaffer, Saunders, & Owens, 1986). This study also showed that objective background information was more reliable and less likely than subjective information to change during this lengthy time interval. The alternate forms reliability technique may not be a realistic strategy for those in the workplace who want to develop and use a biodata measure, mainly because there often is no alternate form. Further, because empirically developed instruments usually are made up of varying content without a clear structure of constructs, an alternate form would be difficult to develop using the recommended procedure. In studies assessing the reliability of tests, for example, the usual strategy is to create a pool of items representing the constructs being tested, and then randomly sample from the pool to create the parallel form. However, this procedure is inappropriate for most empirically developed biodata instruments because of their heterogeneous content. A different technique has been reported that was created specifically for constructing an alternate biodata form (Clause, Mullins, Nee, Pulakos, & Schmitt, 1998). The technique involved an "item-cloning" procedure, in which items from the original instrument were rewritten on an item-by-item basis. The researchers found that this was an effective strategy as most of the items they developed for the new version of the instrument were assessed as being parallel to the originals.

**Validity**   With respect to validity, several research reviews have found biodata instruments to be effective predictors of various criteria, and in some cases the validity is as high as that of cognitive ability tests. For example, in their meta-analysis, Hunter and Hunter (1984) found that biodata was valid for predicting job tenure or longevity measures (.25), promotion (.26), training success (.30), and supervisors' ratings of performance (.37). Mumford and Stokes (1992) discussed later reviews showing validity coefficients comparable to these. They concluded that empirically developed biographical inventories are among the best for predicting training and job performance. In addition, recent research has explored the effectiveness of using biodata measures along with tests of general mental ability and personality. Mount, Witt, and Barrick (2000) wanted to know whether biodata measures so overlap personality and cognitive ability tests that nothing is gained by using a biodata instrument along with the other two measures. In fact, they found that the biodata instrument did not completely overlap the other two measures. They concluded that empirically keyed and validated biodata measures can make a unique contribution to the prediction of criterion scores over and above that contributed by cognitive ability and personality tests. The researchers reported strong criterion-related validity for the battery of three measures, with a multiple correlation of approximately .40.

**Problems**   Three types of problems or constraints have been observed in instruments using biographical data. First, the validities of scoring keys tend to decline over time. This decline of validity has been observed in many studies, including the meta-analysis reported by Hunter and Hunter (1984). Mumford and Stokes (1992) speculated on why this might occur. One possibility is that confidentiality of an instrument's scoring key might be breached over the period of time in which the instrument is used. Also, a restricted range of responses may result from long-term use of the key in hiring new employees. In a practical sense, what the decline of validity means is that employers must periodically reevaluate their biographical inventories and weighted application blanks, and they may need to modify scoring keys to retain an adequate level of validity. However, in their study, Reiter-Palmon and Connelly (2000) found that the decline of validity over time was at least partly due to the atheoretical manner in which most biodata item pools are developed. They discovered that if a rational and theory-based approach was used to develop items that were relevant to performance on the job, then loss of validity over time was minimal.

Second, several studies have found subgroup differences in the biodata response patterns that might be problematic. For example, Mumford and Stokes (1992) discussed experience differences between individuals of different age, gender, and ethnicity that differentially predict future work performance. In particular, studies have shown that the predictive ability of background information varies for men and women. For example, items that ask about participation in certain high school team sports, such as football and baseball, may not be predictive for female job applicants because many women did not have the opportunity to participate in these sports. Revisions in biographical inventory items, response alternatives, and item weights may be needed whenever there is reason to believe that gender or other group differences in experience might affect the validity of items.

Finally, like other self-report selection methods, biodata instruments are susceptible to various response distortions. These include outright faking, as well as inaccuracies due to more subtle causes, such as carelessness, lack of self-insight, memory errors, and impression management or responding in socially desirable ways. How prevalent is response distortion in actuality? Some studies have addressed this question. For example, Becker and Colquitt (1992) found that research subjects could fake a biodata instrument when they were told to do so. In the workplace, however, there were fewer faked responses than were actually possible, indicating that many applicants do answer honestly. Also, the researchers found that only certain items were faked. Compared to items that were answered honestly, faked items were *less* objective, historical, and verifiable, and they were *more* job related. In another study, Stokes, Hogan, and Snell (1993) studied the extent of social desirability in the responses of job incumbents and applicants. They found that the applicant sample responded in more socially desirable ways than did the incumbent sample. However, the difference depended on the type of item. On items referring to previous work experience and training, there was little response distortion; however, on items asking about work preferences and style, and in self-evaluations of previous job success, applicants gave socially desirable responses. Together, these studies indicate that response distortion does occur. It seems to occur especially when the information is obviously job-relevant and not readily verifiable.

We might ask whether socially desirable responses are particularly damaging to the validity of a biodata instrument. In other words, does this type of response distortion really matter? In their study, Stokes et al. (1993) could not show that it does. In fact, they found that there were more valid items in the categories to which applicants had given socially desirable responses. Others also have observed such a relationship between the social desirability rating of items and the items' validity (cf. Mumford & Stokes, 1992). Researchers have suggested ways to explain the effect, including the possibility that these items are valid, *not* because of the response distortion, but because they are the most clearly job related. Kluger and Colella (1993) reasoned that while applicants may generally be susceptible to the social desirability of item response alternatives, they are likely to react to an item's desirability for the specific job they are seeking. These researchers investigated the effects of warning research subjects against response distortion. The warning did have an effect. For some, it triggered a more honest response. For others, it probably caused a different, *faked* response. In either case, the effect depended on the "transparency" of individual items in terms of their seeming desirability for the job. When the job desirability of an item was transparent, the warned subjects were less extreme on average and yet more variable in their responses than the unwarned subjects. This result meant that the warning changed the responses of those who were inclined to fake, but it did not necessarily make them any more honest.

## Conclusions

Scored application instruments represent a major improvement over the use of traditional standard application blanks and résumés. The necessarily thorough process of developing and validating a scored application instrument addresses several limitations of the standard application. Although the developmental process is extensive, the results are worth the effort. The research evidence on biographical inventories shows that these measures can validly predict job performance. They can make an important contribution to the selection process, whether they are used alone or in combination with other valid instruments such as cognitive ability and personality tests.

Large organizations often have the capacity to develop their own application instruments. Those that can develop scored applications in-house should do so, because these instruments generally need to be custom designed for a job or job family. A practical reason for developing an instrument in-house is that very few validated biodata instruments are available commercially. Small organizations may not have the necessary HR expertise or the numbers of employees needed for developing and empirically validating a scored instrument, especially a biographical inventory. For some small organizations, a weighted application may be possible, as it requires a smaller validation sample. Another possibility is to use the behavioral consistency method to identify relevant work dimensions for an application supplement, and to develop rating scale benchmarks that evaluators can use to score applicants' responses to the supplement.

# REFERENCE REPORTS

Reports from references traditionally have been used in employee selection. In 1979, Muchinsky reported that most employers (82 to 99 percent) were contacting references before making hiring decisions. Obviously, many employers view the reference report as an effective selection method. But is it, really? Is it an effective way to verify information received from applicants and to obtain additional background data? In this section, I discuss the problems that cast doubt on the value of reference checks and the demands that currently are making reference checks necessary.

## *Obtaining and Using Reference Reports*

The methods of obtaining reference reports and the type of information sought vary among employers. Some invite written reference materials to be sent through the mail, whereas others interview references by telephone. Some employers want specific information from references and may have developed a long list of questions to be answered. For example, a reference might be asked to (1) verify a range of factual information given by an applicant, such as years on the job and number of promotions; (2) evaluate and comment on an applicant's personality, character, and behavioral style; (3) evaluate and comment on an applicant's performance on the former job; and (4) indicate willingness to rehire the individual. Other employers adopt a very casual stance in seeking reference reports. They may ask only for very general impressions. In fact, some leave it to the reference to decide what to report about an applicant.

For most purposes, it is better to develop a structured report form or questionnaire that can be mailed to a reference or used as the interview protocol in a telephone interview. In developing a questionnaire, a good general approach is to start by determining the purpose of the reference information in the selection process and identifying the kind of information that would be most helpful. A job analysis should be used to accomplish this and to establish that the needed reference information is related to performance on the job and/or to employee behavior at the place of work. The developer also should guard against requesting any discriminatory information that is disallowed on any other selection instrument. Because reference reports increasingly are difficult to obtain, the developer might approach the task by identifying information that cannot be obtained by any other means and that would be acceptable to provide about a former employee of one's own organization. For example, tests might be used to assess an applicant's personality and integrity, and validated application procedures might be used to collect background information from the applicant. The reference questionnaire then could be devoted to verifying application details and obtaining other information about an individual's behavior as a good organizational citizen at the previous workplace. To encourage a response from the reference, an appropriately designed questionnaire also should include a statement signed by the applicant giving permission for the former employer to give the requested information.

Many employers prefer to conduct a telephone interview to collect reference information. Realistically, this procedure has two advantages. Reference reports can be obtained more quickly, and answers to the interviewer's questions can be clarified. However, the telephone interview has costs as well as benefits. First, the interviewer must be trained. Second, detailed information obtained during the interview must be recorded in writing. Employers may expect to get information from a telephone conversation that a reference would be unwilling to write down and sign. However, this is risky, for both the prospective employer and the former employer. In order to protect itself from potential lawsuits, the prospective employer must maintain a written record of the telephone interview. The former employer may be open to legal proceedings if the information provided in the interview is inaccurate and/or cannot be documented as being true.

**Reliability and Validity**    The typical reference report is not effective as a predictor of successful job performance. Muchinsky (1979) reported that relatively little research on the method had been published, but what had been indicated that the method suffers from measurement weaknesses. Specifically, reliability and validity are low. A commonly cited problem accounting for the low validity is restriction in the range of reference assessments (Muchinsky, 1979). That is, few differences between applicants are identified regardless of any differences there might have been in individuals' actual behavior. Also, reference reports are highly positive. Very little unfavorable information is ever given. Such reports collected on a group of applicants will not distinguish one person from another, and little of value will be added to the selection process.

Problems have been uncovered that can account for the low levels of reliability, and these give insight into reasons for the low validity of reference reports. One problem is that references reporting on a single individual are inconsistent. That is, there is low interrater reliability. If references cannot agree on a single individual, we cannot expect their information to validly predict job performance. (The essential difficulty is that we do not know which report to accept as correct.) Reference letters written for students applying for graduate school have similar problems (Baxter, Brock, Hill, & Rozelle, 1981). They tend to be highly favorable and show few distinctions among students. Also, multiple assessments of a single student vary among references.

No doubt, part of the unreliability of reference reports is due to personal biases and errors committed by references. First, it is not unreasonable to suspect that some reference reports contain deliberate distortions. For example, a supervisor might be pleased to discover that a poorly performing employee is seeking another job and might assist in this by giving prospective employers a reference report that emphasizes the person's best qualities and ignores weaknesses. Second, reference reports are likely to contain inadvertent errors. These occur for various reasons. Sometimes, the individuals whom applicants identify as their references actually are inappropriate for the purpose. References need to have had certain exposures and abilities before they can adequately provide useful information. A reference should not attempt to answer questions about a former employee without having had an opportunity to closely observe the individual's performance. Also, a reference may not be a capable judge of an applicant's job qualifications. As researchers have learned from studying performance appraisals, people differ considerably in their abilities to evaluate others' job performance. For example, some supervisors use a low standard of comparison that results in lenient evaluations of their subordinates. Others use high standards and their evaluations are more severe. Such characteristics are reflected in the reference reports they provide.

Reference letters might say more about the letter writer than they do about the person being evaluated (Baxter et al., 1981). Intrigued by this possibility, Judge and Higgins (1998) examined the effect of a reference person's disposition on the letters produced. They studied two samples of reference letter writers. One was a group of students who first watched a videotape showing an employee's performance and then wrote reference letters. The other was a sample of faculty members who wrote letters for graduate school applicants. As predicted, individuals in both samples whose dispositions were positive wrote more favorable letters. The researchers also found that the length of the letter was related to its favorability, with longer letters being generally more favorable.

Some research has been conducted to determine whether reference information can be made more useful by quantifying its content. If so, an employer would have a way to score reference reports. Peres and Garcia (1962) developed such a procedure. They found that the personal traits mentioned in letters could be extracted and grouped into a few categories, such as dependability, cooperativeness, and mental agility. These trait categories then could be compared to the needs of the job, and a score obtained by counting the number of traits mentioned for each important trait category. Later, other researchers examined the method in a validity study (Aamodt, Bryan, & Whitcomb, 1993). The resulting validity coefficients were higher than usual for studies of reference reports, which indicates that the procedure has some potential.

## Legal Problems With Reference Reports

A major difficulty in using reference reports is that former employers may be unmotivated to provide reference reports or even fearful of doing so. An employer who has negative information on a former employee may feel that it is risky to share that information because the former employee might sue, charging defamation. As a result, many employers have developed organizational policy stating that they will provide only minimal information in response to reference requests. Often, the information is nothing more than a confirmation of dates of employment and positions held. The reason this is a problem for prospective employers is that they, also, must protect themselves against being sued. Prospective employers face the possibility of being charged with legal negligence if they hire someone who creates a dangerous condition in the workplace. The most direct way to avoid hiring such an employee is to get information from former employers.

Burns (1997) discussed a law review article by Adler and Peirce (1996) that analyzed the risks to which employers are exposed with respect to employment references. The authors observed that although the courts and state legislatures have attempted to encourage the exchange of information between employers, they have not provided enough legal protection for employers to allow this. Instead, employers find themselves in a sticky situation. From the standpoint of any employer, it will be in their best interests to give as little information as possible about a former employee and to get as much information as possible about a prospective employee.

**Defamation Lawsuits**    Apparently, what employers fear is not losing a defamation lawsuit but, rather, having to face one. Relatively few defamation suits are filed and, of those that are, employers usually can defend themselves (Burns, 1997). Defending oneself in a lawsuit is expensive and time consuming, however. It is understandable that an employer would prefer to adopt a "no comment" policy, rather than respond to requests for reference reports and risk a defamation lawsuit.

To legally demonstrate defamation, the plaintiff—that is, the former employee—must show that the employer made a false statement to another party, such as a prospective employer, that both disparaged the individual's employment qualifications and harmed his or her opportunities for getting a job. The defamatory statement can have been made in either written or oral form, which means that talking with a prospective employer may be just as risky as writing something down and signing it. In the past, defamation generally referred to statements presented as fact; however, more recently, the distinction between fact and opinion has become somewhat blurred. A statement of "opinion" now might be considered defamatory if it implied falsely that it was based on fact (Adler & Peirce, 1996; Green & Reibstein, 1988).

Certain defenses are possible for an organization to use in a defamation lawsuit. First, "truth" can be an especially strong defense. However, it is sometimes difficult to prove that an allegedly false statement was actually true. Usually, a reference can show that he or she honestly believed that an evaluation of a former employee was true. If documented evidence is not available, however, it can be difficult to convince a jury of a statement's actual truth. Second, a signed form consenting to the evaluation sometimes is effective in countering charges of defamation. As mentioned above, a good strategy for a prospective employer is to ask applicants to sign a statement on the reference report form giving permission for a former employer to provide the information. Third, the most effective defense possibly is "qualified privilege," which means that two parties who have a legitimate interest may communicate freely. To claim qualified privilege, an employer needs to show that a reference report was provided only in response to a direct request from a legitimate party—i.e., a prospective employer—and that this privilege was not abused, such as by giving a false report (Adler & Peirce, 1996).

**Misrepresentation and Negligent Hiring**   A former employer also can be sued if the reference misrepresents the former employee's qualifications and harm results from the prospective employer's use of this information in hiring the individual. This can occur in two ways: "intentional misrepresentation" and "negligent misrepresentation." In the first case, the former employer is considered to have deliberately misled the prospective employer. In the second, the former employer gave a report without making any effort to establish that the information provided was accurate. In either case, if the prospective employer uses the misleading information to hire the applicant and the person causes some injury at the new workplace that could have been avoided had accurate information been received, then the former employer can be sued by the injured party. For example, Adler and Peirce (1996) described a case in which a former employer provided a positive reference report on a former employee— a school administrator—without looking into the individual's record. Had this been done, it would have revealed that the employee had engaged in sexual misconduct while at work. Another school hired the individual, based on the positive reference report. Later, following an incident in which he was alleged to have molested a child at the new school, a suit was filed against the former employer, charging negligent misrepresentation.

As I mentioned earlier, under certain conditions, the present employer of an employee who causes harm at work may be charged with "negligent hiring." This liability addresses an organization's duty to provide a safe work environment for employees. If an employer hires someone who causes a harmful situation injuring others, and if this could have been anticipated by checking the applicant's references but the employer failed to do so, then there is a risk that the employer will be sued by those injured. For example, if an employee engages in violence at work and kills a coworker, the victim's family might sue the company charging negligent hiring. Being unaware of the potential harm the employee might cause is not an adequate defense if there was no background check. The employer should have discovered the potential for problems and, by not contacting references, was derelict in its duty.

## Conclusions

As a selection instrument, the reference report is weak. References typically provide unreliable reports, and rarely is there evidence that the information can validly predict employee behavior. It would seem that reference reports are not worth the trouble it takes to get them. However, employers are caught in a legal snarl on this point. No matter what they do or fail to do about references, there is risk of legal action. To avoid defamation lawsuits, an employer must be careful about communicating negative information to other employers. Yet, declining to cooperate with prospective employers is not a good option. All organizations need to do some form of background checking. Often, they must find former employers who are willing to share information on whether an applicant is likely to cause harm if hired.

To remedy the situation employers face, some state legislatures have passed laws meant to protect former employers who provide reference reports. However, these laws vary as to whether they protect references who communicate anything other than job performance information. Signs that an employee is unfit are not always demonstrated by job performance. In negligent hiring case decisions, the definition of "job-related requirements" often is considerably broader than requirements shown by a job analysis. For example, "nonrapist" would be unlikely to show up in the list of required KSAs for an outside repairman's job. However, in negligent hiring lawsuits, this is the kind of information that is crucial for an employer to have discovered (Ryan & Lasek, 1991). Adler and Peirce (1996) suggested legal reforms that would improve the communication of such information. One improvement is to strengthen the qualified-privilege defense, making it apply whenever former employers respond to prospective employers' requests for reference information. Another is to protect the former employer's honest opinions about a former employee.

Improvements also can be made in the procedure for conducting background checks and collecting reference reports. First, background checking does not depend entirely on former employers. Public records can be searched and used to verify applicants' self-reports. Criminal records should be checked in hiring for certain sensitive jobs, such as those involving outside repair or service workers and health or child care personnel. For jobs involving operation of a motor vehicle, state license and driving records should be checked. In addition, colleges and universities usually are willing to verify dates of attendance and degrees or credentials earned. Ryan and Lasek (1991) pointed out that some lawsuits are related to hiring individuals who lack required KSAs, such as when a health care worker's lack of educational qualifications result in harm to an organization's clients. Paying close attention to the job analysis and required KSAs can help define appropriate sources of the information needed. Second, the best use of reference checks is to obtain information about a former employee's behavior that is not accessible through other selection methods. When a prospective employer contacts a reference, the legitimacy of the request should be made clear. Signed permission should be obtained from the applicant and sent with the request. It also may be worthwhile to offer a former employer the option of writing a reference letter in lieu of the questionnaire. Although a mix of questionnaires and free-form letters might not contribute to the reliability of reference reports, it is a way to encourage reluctant references to respond.

## SUMMING UP

The purpose of this chapter is to examine the nature and value of applications and related personal history instruments for use in employee selection. Summing up, we can make the following conclusions:

- A psychological principle referring to the consistency of behavior is the foundation of personal history measures.
- Traditional applications and résumés have little validity in selection.
- Applications, like other selection methods, must not be used to obtain discriminatory information.
- Depending on how its validity is measured, past work experience can be a valid predictor of job knowledge and future performance.
- Scorable instruments for collecting personal history information represent a major improvement in job application design.
- Behavioral consistency applications focus on sampling applicants' job-related accomplishments and call for narratives written by the applicant.
- The scores on weighted applications are empirically derived from the responses of current employees.
- Biographical inventories contain multiple-choice items on various aspects of personal history, not simply education and experience.
- Research shows that empirically developed and scored biodata instruments are among the best predictors of job performance.

- Employers should custom-develop and validate their own scored applications.
- Reference reports, although traditionally used in selection, typically are neither reliable nor valid.
- Lawsuits relating to reference checks sometimes are filed against former or present employers.

## InfoTrac College Edition

To learn more about the issues discussed here and about related topics in research and practice, use your subscription to InfoTrac College Edition to access articles from research journals and other publications. Go to http://www.infotrac-college.com/wadsworth to start your search of this online library. You can enter search terms of your own choosing, or you can use the following keywords to find articles relevant to this chapter.

Job applications               Biodata
Reference checking          Negligent hiring

# INTERVIEWS

# chapter 11

People sometimes do funny things in job interviews. One applicant reportedly got his interview off to a really "crummy" start by eating a bag of cheese snack crackers while waiting in the lobby. Then, he extended a hand covered with orange dust when the interviewer came out to greet him ("Adventures in Interviewing," 1998). Much of today's practical advice on interviewing concerns what applicants should and should not do, and most of it is based on common knowledge of culturally correct interpersonal behavior. Examples: Ask questions about the job and the organization. Be assertive. Dress appropriately. Leave pets and children at home. Have your lunch before or after but not during the interview.

Does it matter whether or not an applicant is aware of the latest interviewing etiquette in order to get a job, especially if the job does not require such interpersonal skill? A study by Ramsay, Gallois, & Callan (1997) provides insight on this question. These researchers asked if there are identifiable social rules that apply to the job interview and, if so, what are the effects of social rule-breaking on interviewers' evaluations of applicants' qualifications? They surveyed experienced interviewers on the kinds of behavior that should or should not be shown in a job interview, and factor-analyzed interviewers' responses. They found that identifiable social rules do exist. Two basic types of behavior were described in these rules. The most important was a group of specific "interview presentation skills." This factor included behaviors such as using positive terms to describe one's skills and experience, relating the job to future career goals, and showing evidence of having prepared for the interview. The second factor referred to general "interpersonal competence" and included interpersonal skill, self-confidence, and taking an active role in the interview. So, what happens if the applicant breaks the rules? Does the interviewer keep in mind that job interviews are anxiety-provoking and excuse the person's odd behavior? Or is social rule-breaking considered to reflect a lack of competence and result in a negative evaluation? Ramsay et al. (1997) found some evidence of both. Violation of certain rules was attributed to the applicant's nature. For example, when interviewees seemed not to have prepared for the interview, interviewers tended to evaluate this behavior unfavorably, as showing lack of effort. However, other forms of social rule-breaking were attributed more to the anxiety-provoking situation. Breaking general interpersonal competence rules (e.g., failing to show self-confidence) were viewed as being understandably due to anxiety. Also, interviewers' overall ratings of suitability for hire were closely related to an applicant's social rule-following, particularly if the person showed strong interpersonal competence.

If applicants' interpersonal skills affect interview outcomes, does this imply that we should advise job seekers to get training to improve their social skills and impress interviewers? Not necessarily. Certainly, poor social skills can prevent an interviewer from recognizing the existence of other talents, and this might lead to a faulty selection decision. However, some training is meant to teach impression management skills and help trainees learn how to create diversions and manipulate the interview. Polished impression management skill can result in an applicant being evaluated more positively than his or her job skills would warrant, and this, too, might lead to a faulty selection decision. Perhaps our best approach is to focus on enhancing interviewers' skills in managing the interview so that they obtain more accurate information on which to base the selection decision.

In this chapter, the focus is on the interview as a selection method. I begin by discussing the nature and uses of the traditional job interview, as well as some of its failings. Next, I describe the structured interview, which is a solution to many of the problems associated with the traditional job interview. Finally, I concentrate on the interviewer, who plays the central role in this selection procedure. My focus is on how the interviewer behaves in interacting with applicants and evaluating them, and on what affects this behavior.

## THE TRADITIONAL JOB INTERVIEW

Job interviews can be designed and conducted in several different ways, with varying results. The usual interview conducted in the workplace on a daily basis is the weakest of the designs. This interview tends to be an unstructured, meandering conversation with an applicant. It is not standardized. The interviewer has not previously decided on the questions that he or she will ask and, in fact, different applicants probably will be asked different questions. Often, the questions are vague, as in "Tell me something about yourself." Many interviewers take no written notes on what the person says. When an interview is finished, the interviewer evaluates the applicant's behavior and makes a judgment as to his or her suitability for employment. Often, however, this is a superficial, verbal evaluation with no rating or other numerical grading of the applicant's interview performance.

An employment interview is used for two basic purposes. It is used to promote the organization and recruit applicants. It also is used to obtain oral information from applicants in order to assess their suitability for a job with the organization. In many cases, these two uses of the interview are combined in a single meeting. However, there are good reasons for conducting separate interviews for the two purposes. One reason is that the interviewer's role varies between the two interviews. When conducting an interview to get information for a selection decision, the interviewer must get the applicant to talk most of the time—as by asking open-ended questions—and the interviewer must listen. However, when the purpose is recruitment, the interviewer's role is to promote the organization and capture the applicant's interest. Therefore, in this interview, the interviewer needs to do most of the talking. When the two purposes are combined in a single meeting, the tendency is for an interviewer to neglect the selection purpose and talk excessively.

## Evolution of the Job Interview

Widespread use of the job interview was documented early in the 20th century and has remained popular. Surveys of business firms in the United States have shown heavy reliance on the interview for selection decision making: 93 percent of firms in 1930, 94 percent in 1957, and 99 percent in 1965 used interviews in selection (Spriegel & James, 1958; Ulrich & Trumbo, 1965). The job interview currently is the second most frequently used method of employee selection, surpassing all except job application and résumé screenings in the extent of use. Almost never is a person hired without at least a brief interview, and sometimes more than one interview is required. In some instances, an interview provides the only information used in a selection decision.

**Studies of Interview Validity**   Reports on the use of the job interview as a selection device began appearing early in the 20th century, although little quantitative evidence was available by which to evaluate the interview's validity. Most articles offered advice on how to conduct an interview, or described an employer's experience with the method and reported that managers and personnel people believed it was effective. Then, as now, users liked the method and believed that interviewers could predict future job performance. However, there was little evidence of this. On the contrary, some early studies demonstrated that even experienced interviewers' judgments were not reliable, and this brought validity into question (Guion, 1976). Despite the interview's popularity and widespread use, concerns soon were voiced in the professional literature about both validity and economic utility. Interviews are time consuming and expensive. Any selection procedure that requires the time and effort of HR specialists and/or managers to give individual attention to applicants is expensive because of these labor costs. Therefore, if an organization plans to make the necessary investment in such a costly method, it should have documented evidence that the method is valid for selection purposes. Otherwise, there is no basis for assuming effectiveness.

One of the most important reviews of early research on the interview was conducted by Wagner in 1949. He found 106 articles purportedly addressing the question of interview effectiveness. However, only 25 of the total reported any quantitative data that could be used to assess validity or reliability, and many of these studies were seriously inadequate in terms of their research methodology. A large number of personal attributes had been advocated in the reviewed articles as being suitable for evaluation by interviewers, including physical appearance, voice quality, manner, and intelligence. However, the quantitative studies indicated that only the evaluations of intelligence showed acceptable levels of interrater reliability. Also, only the ratings of intelligence were highly correlated with a criterion measure, which was usually a test of general mental ability, not a job performance measure. Based on the reviewed studies, Wagner (1949) made several important points. One, he emphasized that many factors which had been included in interview evaluations could be measured more effectively by other means. For example, it would be better to use a general mental ability test, instead of asking interviewers to evaluate applicants' intelligence. He recommended that use of the interview be reserved for evaluating attributes which could not be measured better in any other way. Two, he stressed that interview evaluations, like all selection methods, needed to be job related. Regardless of how validly or reliably a personal attribute could be rated, considering it in interview evaluations would be justified only if the attribute was related to success on the job. Wagner's points were on target 50 years ago and they remain so today.

Wagner observed that, although the interview's validity was doubtful, it was a popular method and it probably would continue to be. There seemed to be no substitute for meeting applicants face-to-face. Given this, and the probability that interview validity depended on the particular situation and interviewer, he recommended that interviewers develop skills in observing relevant behavior and in ignoring irrelevant behavior. He also recommended that the interview be standardized. This was meant to keep the interview centered on its objectives and to prevent the aimless rambling and lengthy digressions that often occurred. Finally, Wagner proposed that the interview would best be reserved for three situations: (1) when nothing more than rough screening was needed; (2) when the number of applicants was so small that more valid procedures would not be worth the effort; and (3) when certain attributes were needed that could be uniquely well evaluated in an interview.

Fifteen years passed before the next review of interview research was published. During that time, many researchers and commentators roundly criticized the efficacy of the job interview. For example, in their 1955 *Annual Review of Psychology* report, Wallace and Weitz stated that the use of interviews in business was ubiquitous, although there was little, if anything, positive that could be said about interviewing. Similarly, Dunnette (1962) noted that nearly all employers were using "this costly, inefficient, and usually nonvalid selection procedure" (p. 291) without performing or reporting research to evaluate the method. Many other researchers agreed with these assessments and complained bitterly that employers were paying no attention to the reports that interviews were not valid. As Wagner (1949) had predicted, employers were showing no signs of abandoning the method.

In the mid-1960s, Mayfield (1964) and Ulrich and Trumbo (1965) published the next reviews. Both articles concluded that interrater reliability of the traditional job interview remained at unacceptably low levels, especially when interviewers worked separately. Although interviewers might have used the same approach in conducting their separate interviews, they differed in their interpretations of the information they obtained. In most interviews, it also looked as if applicant assessments were affected by interviewers' personal biases and by their tendency to make snap judgments. As could be expected, interview unreliability was a major difficulty in showing validity. Neither of the research reviews found much evidence of interview validity. In fact, validities were low even in studies that reported fairly high reliabilities. This meant that even if interviewers agreed in their evaluations, the attributes they evaluated were not strongly related to criterion measures. The most encouraging note concerned a few interviews that had been standardized in some fashion. Both Mayfield (1964) and Ulrich and Trumbo (1965) found that standardization had positive effects. Higher interrater reliabilities were reported when interviewers were trained, or given questions and a rating scale to use in evaluating applicants. The higher reliabilities probably were due to interviewers obtaining the same type of information from applicants and weighting it similarly. There was some indication that the more standardized interview had greater validity than the traditional unstructured interview.

Researchers of this period were still concerned about the economic utility of the job interview, and they emphasized that the interview must contribute something unique to selection. For this reason, the reviewers recommended that interviews be validated apart from any ancillary or supplementary data available for interviewers to review. If the method was to be worth its cost, it had to be shown to yield information beyond what was already available through less expensive methods. For example, although intelligence was being

TABLE

**TABLE**

**11.1**    POTENTIAL LEGAL DIFFICULTIES OF UNSTANDARDIZED INTERVIEWS

| Party Affected | Difficulty | Source of Difficulty |
|---|---|---|
| Applicant | Difficult to examine or challenge interview decision | Basis for evaluation and decision is ambiguous |
| | | Evaluation process cannot be reviewed |
| Employer | Heavy burden of proof, if challenged | No preventive measures or controls for discrimination |
| | | Reliability evidence not available |
| | | No written record of questions |
| | | Decision criteria not defined |
| | | Validity evidence not available |

estimated by interviewers, in fact, when test scores were known, interviewer assessments of intelligence were not incrementally valid beyond the test. The reviewers surmised that interviewers might be able to assess work motivation and interpersonal competence, which could be observed in interviews and might be valid predictors of performance. However, they recommended that employers use interviews in a very limited manner, such as in the final phase of a multiple-hurdle selection procedure.

## Discrimination in the Traditional Interview

Undoubtedly, you noticed in the above description that prior to the passage of EEO law, interviewers routinely evaluated personal attributes that today might be considered discriminatory, or at least inappropriate. For example, interviewers evaluated job candidates' physical appearance. As you know, it was not until the mid-1960s that legal constraints were placed on job applicant assessments. The EEOC's *Uniform Guidelines* (1978) identified the job interview as a selection procedure that must not unfairly discriminate. The document indicated that if an employer plans to legally justify the use of a job interview that adversely affects applicants' employment opportunities, then it, like other selection procedures, must be validated.

Employers are not legally prohibited from using subjective or unvalidated interviews. However, such interviews can be difficult to justify when there are challenging discrimination claims. Table 11.1 identifies some of the reasons subjective interviews can be problematic. Because subjective interview decisions are inherently ambiguous, candidates find it difficult to challenge them. If there is a legal challenge, the burden on the employer to substantiate the interview is heavy. Researchers often have pointed out that the potential for legal challenge is a good reason to structure and standardize the job interview. For example, differences in interviewer assessments due to applicant race are lower in structured than in unstructured interviews (Huffcutt & Roth, 1998). Structured interviews also are more easily defended in court than are subjective or unstructured interviews. Verdicts are more likely to favor the employer when interview assessments are job-related and objective, and when the interview process clearly is standardized and consistent (Williamson, Campion, Malos, Roehling, & Campion, 1997). Researchers have found it gratifying that, in making their decisions, judges consider the same factors that I/O psychologists have been recommending for years.

## Conclusions

Over the next two decades following the reviews published during the 1960s, research on job interviews changed. Researchers became more interested in learning about the interview process. Studies focused on identifying factors that influenced interviewers' judgmental and decision-making processes. Variables that might bias the interview were studied. In addition, as the earlier reviews had foreshadowed, a body of research literature on methods of standardizing and structuring the interview began to accumulate. Researchers spent less time deploring the fact that employers were still using this costly and inaccurate method. Instead, they focused on the conditions under which interviews were valid and on how to design interviews that could contribute to a valid selection program. Time had demonstrated that employers wanted the interview and that they would continue to use it. Researchers decided to help them design an effective one.

Currently, the research evidence implies that selection interviews are more valid than was previously believed. However, we must be careful in drawing such a conclusion. It is true that highly structured and standardized interviews show high validity. In fact, even otherwise unstructured interviews that use quantitative evaluation procedures can be shown to have some validity. However, the typical interview conducted in the workplace is likely to be substantially less structured and less standardized than even the most "unstructured" interview examined in research (McDaniel, Whetzel, Schmidt, & Maurer, 1994). The reason is this: In order to assess interview validity in a validation study, interviewers must have used a rating instrument that produced quantitative assessments of job applicants. This is the critical point. Only quantitative data can be correlated with a criterion measure in such a validation study. The ordinary interview conducted in the workplace probably would not qualify to be included in a research evaluation of validity—even as an "unstructured" interview—because quantitative ratings data simply are not collected. This means that the research has not fully evaluated the job interview currently in use, and the validity estimates reported may be overestimates of the actual validity of many job interviews conducted in business today. Only for those businesses that presently use structured or standardized interviews can we conclude that the job interview is now more effective than it previously was.

## STRUCTURED INTERVIEWS

So far, every question about the reliability and validity of the job interview appears to be answered by some reference to the need for standardizing or structuring the interview. What exactly is meant by this? Several terms have been used to refer to structured interviews, including "standardized," "systematic," "patterned," and "guided," and although they do not mean the same, these terms often are used interchangeably. Campion, Palmer, and Campion (1997) defined structuring as including any enhancement of the interview that is meant to improve its measurement properties, particularly its reliability and validity. Campion, Pursell, and Brown (1988) demonstrated how this could be done, by outlining a six-step procedure for structuring job interviews. The procedure included instructions for making an interview job-relevant. It required that interviewers use the same questions for all interviewees and that applicants' answers be quantitatively scored. Also, interviewers would need instruction on conducting the interview. Campion et al. (1997) reviewed the research on structured interviews and summarized the many ways that job interviews had been structured. Table 11.2 lists several of the components or requirements of structured interviews. Notice that some requirements focus on what is covered in the interview, whereas others refer to the process of interviewing or evaluation.

## *Getting Ready to Interview*

Determining and standardizing the questions to ask in an interview are two of the most important aspects of interview structuring. However, requiring use of predetermined questions may be difficult for interviewers to accept, especially when they have been accustomed to completely free-form interviewing. As you will see later, it may help to give interviewers some amount of freedom in questioning, such as allowing them to choose from a list of comparable questions.

Training can prepare interviewers and improve their effectiveness. Training is indispensable for those who have little or no experience. Interviewers need training on various points. They need to become fully familiar with the job for which candidates are applying. They need to understand the questions

| TABLE 11.2 | CONSIDERATIONS IN STRUCTURING THE JOB INTERVIEW |
|---|---|
| **Structural Feature** | **Actions to Achieve Structure** |
| Interviewer preparation | Control use of ancillary information |
| | Train interviewers on all aspects of interview |
| Question preparation | Use job analysis |
| | Develop past-oriented or situational questions |
| | Increase length of interview or number of questions |
| | Develop performance-anchored rating scales |
| Interview process | Ask all candidates the same questions |
| | Limit prompting or elaborating on questions |
| | Allow candidate questions only after interview |
| | Take detailed notes |
| Evaluation | Rate answers to all questions |
| | Use multiple interviewers: panel or serial |
| | Use same interviewers for all candidates |
| | Combine ratings statistically |

Based on information from "A Review of Structure in the Selection Interview," by M. A. Campion, D. K. Palmer, and J. E. Campion, 1997, *Personnel Psychology, 50,* 655–702.

that have been developed and learn how to interpret answers. They need some instruction on how to use rating scales that are anchored with performance descriptions[1] and on how to avoid making common rating errors. If interviewers are allowed some discretion in the choice of questions they can ask, they need to be coached on the appropriate use of a set of comparable questions. Interpersonal skills training may be needed also, because being able to put candidates at ease is beneficial in gaining more complete and comprehensive information from them.

**Problem: Use of Ancillary Information**   In preparing to conduct an interview, it appears that many—if not most—interviewers begin by looking over applicants' materials, including job applications, résumés, reference reports, and/or test scores. Campion et al. (1997) pointed out that use of such ancillary information is a problem for both the reliability and the validity of the interview.

---

[1]Rating scales with performance description anchors were discussed previously, in Chapter 10, in the section on behavioral consistency applications. They will be discussed further in Chapter 14 on performance appraisal.

If pre-interview information is not equally available on all candidates, reliability suffers. If interviewers review applicants' materials, we cannot be sure that the estimated interview validity is actually due to the interview. Rather, it may be because the reviewed materials are valid. As I mentioned above, if interviewers are effective in assessing attributes, such as intelligence, it may not be because they are particularly good at this, but because they have looked at other, more valid assessments of the attribute (e.g., intelligence test scores). Interviewer use of ancillary material can disrupt interview structure in another way. In most unstructured interviews, interviewers use ancillary material to frame the questions they will ask. This practice generally results in different questions for different candidates, a loss of standardization and structure, and damage to the reliability and validity of the interview. Thus, it is not a good idea for an interviewer to review ancillary materials preparatory to an interview.

## Preparing Interview Questions

**Job-Relevant Questions**    A key difference between structured and unstructured interviews is the use of a job analysis to develop questions. A job analysis provides the basis for writing questions that are job relevant and that can be asked equally well of all candidates for a job. Any of the job analysis methods can be used in developing questions. The most frequently used is the critical incidents technique.[2] As you will see in the discussion of performance appraisal in Chapter 14, a critical incidents job analysis is particularly helpful in identifying important behavioral dimensions of a job and describing different levels of employee performance quality on these dimensions. The descriptions of the dimensions easily can be turned into interview questions, and the levels of performance can be used as rating scale anchors. This makes the rating of applicants' responses to questions an easier task for interviewers to accomplish.

Research on interviews has long stressed the importance of job analysis in improving interview validity. Certainly, job analysis can be expected to contribute to validity by increasing the job relatedness of questions. With better questions, interviewers can obtain relatively more job-relevant information and relatively less extraneous information from candidates. Studies have documented that using a job analysis can produce a structured interview with high validity. For example, from their meta-analysis, McDaniel et al. (1994) reported average validity coefficients of .50 for highly structured, situational interviews that had been designed using a job analysis. By comparison, validity coefficients for interviews that were not based on job analysis averaged .29.

A lingering question, for which the answer is not entirely clear, brings up the possibility that job analysis might prime the interview to perform like a test. That is, given that job analysis places stronger emphasis on cognitively

---

[2]For a quick review of critical incidents job analysis, see Chapters 3 and 14.

related KSAs than on other attributes, perhaps it produces an oral examination of cognitive ability. If so, this might explain why structured interviews, based on a job analysis, are so much more valid for predicting job performance. Campion et al. (1997) were unable to clearly determine whether this might be happening. Some studies they reviewed showed little relationship between structured interviews and ability tests (e.g., Pulakos & Schmitt, 1995), whereas other studies showed that they were highly correlated (e.g., Campion, Campion, & Hudson, 1994). So, again, we are face-to-face with the question of whether interviews—even structured interviews—are valid for assessing anything beyond what the less expensive tests do. Some studies have not been able to show that they are (e.g., Campion et al., 1988). Others, however, have reported incremental validity of structured interviews beyond cognitive ability tests (Campion, Campion, et al., 1994; Pulakos & Schmitt, 1995). Probably, we will see more study of this question in the future.

**Experience-Based and Situational Questions**   Much of what determines whether an interview is considered structured or unstructured is the type of questions used. In the traditional job interview, the questions often are general in nature and have little to do with the job. An interviewer may ask an applicant to identify his or her strengths and weaknesses, or simply to "tell me something about yourself." These questions give the *candidate* license to determine the interview content. In contrast, questions for a structured interview focus on candidates' preparation for the job. In their review, Campion et al. (1997) found four types of structured interview questions: background, past behavior, job knowledge, and situational questions. These questions contribute varying levels of interview structure. Of the four types, background questions contribute the lowest level. They focus on a candidate's past work experiences in particular job-related areas. For example, if a job involves close interaction with coworkers, a candidate might be asked, "What experience have you had in working on team projects?" Structure is low in such a question because it does not address specific teamwork issues and probably will yield a variety of answers from candidates that will be difficult to compare. Also, such questions probably will use a general rating scale, which itself does not contribute much structure to an interview.

The other three types of questions produce more highly structured interviews. Each type calls for a specific sample of job-related behavior from candidates. A question may focus on past work activity, present job-related knowledge, or hypothetical work situations. (See Table 11.3 for some example questions.) First, past-oriented questions ask candidates to describe what they did in previous work or other experience that shows how they actually handled a situation similar to what they might face on the job in question. For example, a candidate might be asked, "Think about a time when you had to make sure that a group of workers met strict deadlines. What did you do that was most

### 11.3 EXAMPLES OF EXPERIENCE-BASED AND SITUATIONAL QUESTIONS

| Type of Question | Examples |
| --- | --- |
| Past-oriented work experience | Think about a time when you had to evaluate an employee who was not performing well on the job. How did you handle that situation? |
| | Think about a time in your previous work experience when equipment that you maintained apparently was being misused, causing it to require extra maintenance and repair. What did you do to deal with this? |
| | Can you give an example from your previous experience in which you had to make sure that a group of workers met strict production deadlines? What did you do that was most effective in getting the group to do its work on time? |
| Job knowledge | What kinds of documentation do you think would be needed if a company wanted to discharge a poorly performing employee? |
| | What kinds of information should an office equipment installer provide for users of the new machinery? |
| | What actions do you think would be best for a team leader to take when the team members are engaging in conflict among themselves? |
| Situational | Suppose one of the employees you supervise and evaluate is not performing as well as the company expects. His next performance review is due in a week and you have scheduled a meeting with him to talk about this. How would you handle the meeting? |
| | Imagine you work on a job that requires you to set up and maintain machines for office workers to use. In the course of doing your job, suppose you find that some of the users are particularly hard on the machinery, which results in extra repair and maintenance. What would you do in such a situation? |
| | Imagine that you are the leader of a work team and you find out that one of the team members is not doing his share of the work but, instead, is relying on the others to pick up the slack. How would you handle this situation? |

effective in getting the group to do its work on time?" Second, with a related type of question, a candidate's job knowledge can be sampled. For example, "What actions do you think would be helpful for a team leader to take when team members are engaging in conflict among themselves?" Finally, in a situational interview, the questions ask for reactions to hypothetical or future work situations. The interviewer describes a hypothetical incident and asks the candidate what he or she would do if this happened (Latham, Saari, Pursell, & Campion, 1980). For example, a candidate might be asked, "Imagine that you are the leader of a work team and you discover that one of the team members is not doing his full share of the work, but instead is relying on the others to do the work. How would you handle this situation?" As you can see, these three types of questions call for answers that are highly specific to the job which applicants are seeking. The questions are meant to elicit samples of behavior, and as a result they lend a great deal of structure to the interview.

It is reasonable to expect that questions which contribute higher versus lower levels of structure also will increase interview validity. There is some indirect evidence of this. Biodata studies have shown that questions calling for samples of past work behavior can raise validity levels of biodata instruments (cf. Mumford & Stokes, 1992). However, because interview research often does not distinguish effects due to question type from effects due to job analysis or other sources of structure, it is difficult to decipher the impact of the questions used. A few studies have attempted to determine whether work experience–based or situational questions are better. However, when considered together, the studies do not present a clear distinction. In some, questions about past work behavior are associated with higher validity (e.g., Campion, Campion, et al., 1994; Pulakos & Schmitt, 1995). In other studies, situational questions yield the more valid interviews (e.g., McDaniel et al., 1994). Actually, we could expect that situational and past experience–based questions contribute differently to interviews because they are inherently different. For one thing, questions about past experience are more verifiable. Also, situational questions may be tapping into different constructs, such as motivation. Situational questions appear to require a certain amount of self-insight and awareness of intentions. In practice, it is probably a good idea to include a variety of job-related questions because each type contributes validity, albeit for different reasons. The best interview probably includes some job knowledge questions, some past-behavior questions, and some situational questions.

**Anchored Rating Scales**   An essential part of a structured interview question is a rating scale that uses descriptions of work behavior to anchor scale points. Anchored rating scales are designed using the same job analysis information, typically from a critical incidents study. Because the rating scale points are anchored with performance descriptions that are specific to each question, anchored rating scales allow interviewers to more easily score candidates' answers. By quantifying interviewers' evaluations, use of the rating scales also makes it easier to determine interview validity.

The development of anchored rating scales for interview purposes can benefit from the research on performance appraisal. As I discuss in Chapter 14, rating scales used to evaluate dimensions of employee performance on the job vary as to how scale points are anchored.[3] Some provide minimal information. For example, performance rating scale points sometimes are anchored simply by placing numbers at the ends and at the midpoint of the scale, such as "1 . . . 3 . . . 5," or by adding evaluative terms, such as "unsatisfactory . . .

---

[3]See Figures 14.3, 14.4, and 14.5 in Chapter 14 for examples of rating scale anchors.

average . . . superior." However, more effective scales used for performance appraisal have been developed using critical incidents job analysis. These scales are anchored with detailed behavioral descriptions of performance. Behaviorally anchored rating scales are meant explicitly to assess job-relevant dimensions, and they are used in performance appraisal to control mistakes that supervisors make in rating employee performance.

The same procedure can be followed in developing questions and anchored rating scales for interview purposes. In a critical incidents job analysis, supervisors or other subject-matter experts are consulted regarding employee behavior that varies in its effectiveness on the job. For example, Table 11.4 shows four questions using performance descriptions to anchor a 1–5 point rating scale with a good answer at scale point 5, a marginal answer at 3, and a poor answer at 1. Interviewers need to be given as much information as possible about the meaning of the scale points. Certainly, for a highly structured interview, an example answer at each scale point and some indication as to whether it is a good or a poor answer will be helpful to interviewers.

Behaviorally anchored rating scales can improve the accuracy and validity of an interview because the performance anchors provide objective information against which to compare candidates' answers. This is particularly so if the anchors are examples of what a candidate might say. Then, the interviewer's task is simply to determine the anchor point description that is most similar to a candidate's answer and assign the score of that description. Effectively anchored rating scales increase the likelihood that interview ratings will be based on job-relevant information from candidates. They also can help to focus an interviewer's attention on job requirements and prevent the distraction of irrelevant information.

## Structuring the Interview Process

Certain processes will be valuable in conducting any interview, regardless of whether it incorporates other features of a structured interview. Notetaking during an interview is one such process. As you undoubtedly have noticed, students vary as to whether they are personally inclined to take notes in class. Some simply do not. Others take more or less detailed notes and use them to study in the same way that they study their textbooks. Taking notes in class and then reviewing them helps students remember the material covered. This can improve their ability to use the material to answer questions on exams and to apply the knowledge they gain for other personal and work uses. Similarly, interviewers vary in terms of their propensity to take notes. Some interviewers, like some students, simply do not take notes. Others take detailed and extensive notes, summarize each of a candidate's answers, and write down initial reactions or evaluations of the candidate's performance. Notetaking in job interviews contributes to an interviewer's ability to recall a candidate's

**TABLE 11.4　ANCHORED RATING SCALES FOR STRUCTURED INTERVIEW QUESTIONS**

| Question | Rating Score and Anchors | | |
|---|---|---|---|
| 1. After repairing a piece of machinery, why would it be necessary to clean all the parts before putting it back together? | 5 | Good | Dust and dirt can result in wear and tear on moving parts. Also, to inspect for wear and damage, parts need to be clean. |
| | 3 | Marginal | Parts will go back together easier, and the machine will run more smoothly. |
| | 1 | Poor | So it gets a cleaning, I guess. |
| 2. Can you provide an example from your previous work experience showing that you can analyze complex technical data? | 5 | Good | Reviewed and analyzed financial records of a business my employer was considering for purchase, reported on the value of the business, and wrote a proposal that served as the basis of my employer's offer. |
| | 3 | Marginal | Analyzed bills being considered in Congress as to their potential impact on the operation of the agency where I worked, and reported my assessments to my supervisor. |
| | 1 | Poor | Collected operating budget estimates from department supervisors, and relayed them to the general manager. |
| 3. On some jobs, it is necessary to climb a ladder to the height of a four- or five-story building and do the work. How would you feel about doing that? | 5 | Good | Working at heights doesn't both me. I have done similar work before [gives example]. |
| | 3 | Marginal | I don't think it would bother me to work at heights. I know that this is part of the job. |
| | 1 | Poor | Heights make me nervous. I would do it only if necessary. |
| 4. If you had an idea on how to improve the procedures your work group was using but you knew some of the group would not want to make the change, what would you do? | 5 | Good | I would explain the idea in an open meeting and try to show the benefits. |
| | 3 | Marginal | I would ask them why they are against the change, and I would try to persuade them to give it a try. |
| | 1 | Poor | I would tell the supervisor. |

Adapted from "Structured Interviewing: Raising the Psychometric Properties of the Employment Interview," by M. A. Campion, E. D. Pursell, and B. K. Brown, 1988, *Personnel Psychology, 41*, pp. 30–31. Copyright 1988 by Personnel Psychology, Inc. Bowling Green, Ohio (questions 1 and 3) Adapted by permission; "Structured Interviewing: A Note on Incremental Validity and Alternative Question Types," by M. A. Campion, J. E. Campion, and J. P. Hudson, Jr., 1994, *Journal of Applied Psychology, 79*, table 1, p. 999. Copyright 1994 by American Psychological Association, Washington, DC (question 4) Adapted by permission; and *The Behavioral Consistency Method of Unassembled Examining* (Technical memorandum 79-21), by F. L. Schmidt, J. R. Caplan, S. E. Bemis, R. Decuir, L. Dunn, and L. Antone, 1979, pp. 47–50, Washington, DC: U.S. Office of Personnel Management (question 2).

answers to questions. It improves his or her ability to evaluate the person's interview performance. In addition, taking and using notes helps interviewers make decisions about the relative suitability of applicants for hire. Notetaking during or immediately after a job interview contributes strongly to structuring the interview process, and it improves the interrater reliability of candidate assessments.

**Controlling Questioning**   Although highly structured questions and anchored rating scales may have been prepared for an interview, if interviewers fail to use them, or if they use them improperly, the structure contributed by the questions and rating scale anchors is compromised. What results is a relatively unstructured interview with reduced validity. Thus, candidate questioning remains the single most important aspect of a structured interview. Reviewers have identified three aspects of interview question control that contribute to structure (Campion et al., 1997). First, each question must be asked of each candidate in exactly the same order and in exactly the same manner. Meeting this requirement increases the likelihood that comparable information will be obtained from each candidate. Interview structure and standardization will be lowered if interviewers change the questions or the order in which they are asked. However, a certain amount of flexibility might be allowed and still maintain standardization. For example, if equivalent questions can be constructed for each dimension, then interviewers may select slightly different questions for different candidates. Remember, however, that maintaining a standardized line of questioning is an essential aspect of a structured interview. Therefore, the alternate questions must truly be equivalent. To the extent that they are not, the interview is less highly structured (Conway, Jako, & Goodman, 1995).

A second way to control questioning is to limit prompting and follow-up questions. Although some interviewers might believe that this type of interactive behavior with an interviewee is the "art" of the interview, these behaviors actually constitute sources of error. Still, because interviewers may react negatively to being told they cannot ask probe or follow-up questions, some employers allow interviewers to use planned prompts or probe questions, and a standard follow-up for all candidates, such as "Is there anything else you want to add?" (Robertson, Gratton, & Rout, 1990). Follow-up and probe questions are meant to clarify what a candidate has said and to gain full information. To the extent that such questions accomplish this, they might contribute to an interview's validity. Huffcutt and Arthur (1994) found that structured interviews could include a certain amount of follow-up without damage to validity. However, an employer needs to limit the use of probe and follow-up questions. Mainly, an employer must try to guard against extending these interviewer privileges to such an extent that candidates are coached into giving the right answers.

A third way to control questioning is to disallow questions from candidates until after the structured interview has been completed. Many job applicants are interested in getting information about the job and organization. However, allowing a job candidate to use time in the structured interview to ask his or her own questions disrupts the conduct of the interview, degrades its standardization, and effectively turns the meeting into an unstructured or recruitment interview. This can mean that the interviewer obtains little or no job-relevant information from the candidate. Further, some job applicants are aware that "taking over" the interview with their own questions can both distract the interviewer from gathering information and distort the interview outcome in the candidate's favor.

**Multiple Interviewers**   Job interviews sometimes involve two or more interviewers. There are two ways to arrange this. In serial interviewing, individual interviewers meet separately with each applicant. The serial interview can be conducted the same as an ordinary, single interview with each interviewer asking the same questions. Or the separate interviews might be specifically planned so as to divide the questions among interviewers. In panel interviewing, a group of two to five interviewers meet with each candidate. Procedures for how a panel will operate also vary. One member might be responsible for asking all questions, or the responsibility for asking questions might be shared among members. If probes are allowed, one panel member might ask the main questions, with different members asking the follow-up questions. At the end of questioning, all members independently rate a candidate's responses.

Using multiple interviewers can increase the accuracy of candidate assessments. One reason is that the personal biases of a single interviewer carry less weight when they are consolidated with the evaluations of multiple interviewers. Another possibility is that a broader range of relevant information is gathered by multiple interviewers than by a single interviewer. For example, when serial interviewers ask different planned questions, validity might be increased because a broader range of information is obtained (Campion et al., 1997). There is evidence that reliability is higher when multiple interviewers examine candidates. In a meta-analysis of interrater reliabilities, Conway and his associates (1995) found that the overall average correlation between raters was .70. When this value was considered according to the type of interview, the researchers found that the average reliability coefficient for panel interviews was .77, whereas the average for interviews conducted separately was .53. There could be two related reasons for the difference in these values. Panel interviewers hear the same candidate responses, and it could be expected that their ratings of the responses would be similar. However, serial interviewers are likely to hear somewhat different information, either because a candidate gives different answers to the same question or because the interviewers ask different questions. Conway et al. (1995) found that standardizing the questions affected the reliability of both types of interviews, but it had a stronger effect on serial interviews. This suggests that the reliability of serial interviews is lower because different questions are asked and samples of applicant information are not comparable.

The use of multiple interviewers in either a panel or a serial interview is commonly used with other means of structuring, especially standardized questions. Multiple interviewing also can be used to good advantage in an otherwise unstructured interview because it has potential for providing a more consistent sample of applicant information.

## *Evaluations in the Structured Interview*

There are two main issues relating to evaluation and decision making in interviews. The first is the method with which to combine ratings on individual questions or dimensions in order to form a total score for each job candidate. This sometimes is done subjectively. However, it can be done in a more objective manner by defining weights that give higher values to the more important questions or dimensions, as is done for items on weighted application blanks. The second issue concerns how to combine or consolidate ratings across interviewers, such as when a panel is being used. Sometimes this is done by consensus. It also can be done using some actuarial procedure, such as summing or averaging the interviewers' ratings. In structured interviews, objective procedures should be used for both purposes because errors can be introduced when ratings are subjectively combined and when interviewers discuss candidates in trying to reach consensus.

**Overall Ratings and Total Scores**   To maintain the high structure of an interview that uses detailed job-related questions and anchored rating scales, interviewers must rate a candidate's answers on all questions. Ratings of multiple aspects of a candidate's performance are preferable to a single, overall rating because each question has been designed to elicit a relevant sample of behavior that has been weighted in terms of importance. This makes it easy for an interviewer to evaluate each sample with minimal subjectivity in the process. However, some interviewers prefer to give a single, overall rating to a candidate's performance. The disadvantage of this is that the interviewer will use a subjective process to decide the overall assessment. The subjective process likely will involve the interviewer's own sense of the relative importance of the different questions answered, as well as the formation of a general impression of the candidate. Whenever rating requirements are less question-specific and more general in nature, subjectivity is introduced. For example, when interviewers are required to rate broad dimensions that might be implied from multiple questions, instead of rating answers to single questions, the rater has less clarity on how the individual answers are relevant and the amount of weight in the rating they should carry. Thus, dimension ratings—like the single, overall rating—may contain error because the rater has subjectively weighted and combined a candidate's answers (Conway et al., 1995).

When an interviewer rates a candidate's answers to multiple questions, the ratings can be objectively consolidated into an overall evaluation or total score. Questions that are based on a job analysis already have their own predetermined weights, relative to their importance on the job. Interviewers do not have to subjectively weight the ratings to obtain a total score. This can be done statistically, which avoids the potential bias of subjectivity. Sometimes, however, interviewers are asked to do more than rate candidates' answers to single questions. An interviewer might be asked also to provide an additional overall rating of a candidate or to combine ratings on single questions into a composite. Asking interviewers to do this, however, invites subjectivity because they probably will use a subjective process to weight and combine the different ratings. Such an introduction of subjectivity into an otherwise structured interview is likely to damage validity. When questions have been developed using a job analysis, it also should be used as the basis for statistically weighting and combining ratings.

One reason we sometimes invite interviewers to apply their own sense of what is important in job candidates' interview responses is . . . we think they have some special knowledge of this. Some actually might be able to make good predictions, but not all. There is evidence that interviewers show individual differences in their abilities to make valid interview assessments. Dougherty, Ebert, and Callender (1986) found a marked difference in the effectiveness of the three corporate interviewers they studied over a period of several months. One interviewer gave ratings that were highly valid in predicting applicants' later performance. The judgments of the other two interviewers were simply not valid. Interviewer validity probably is affected by what an interviewer attends to in a candidate's behavior and by how much weight is given to certain answers (Zedeck, Tziner, & Middlestadt, 1983). In making decisions about candidates, Graves and Karren (1992) found that effective interviewers tended to consider and weight the same two behaviors—oral communication and interpersonal skill. Interviewer differences in effectiveness actually may be a function of how well-prepared interviewers are and the kind of interview they conduct. When interviewers are trained and use a structured and standardized procedure in interviewing, there is little indication of individual differences in their assessments (Pulakos, Schmitt, Whitney, & Smith, 1996).

**Statistical Consolidation Versus Consensus**    Just as it is preferable to statistically weight and combine a single interviewer's ratings of a candidate on different questions, so also is it better to sum or average ratings across multiple interviewers. Several studies have shown the value of statistical procedures over consensus-taking in structured interviews (cf. Campion et al., 1997). However, when multiple interviewers are used in a panel, the interviewers tend to discuss candidates' answers during the rating process. The problem is that if discussion is allowed, it can bias individual interviewers' evaluations of a candidate. For this reason, the preferred strategy is to disallow discussion, permit interviewers to draw their own conclusions and independently evaluate candidates' answers, and statistically consolidate the ratings across interviewers.

It may seem that discussion could lead to greater agreement among raters. This may be so; however, interrater agreement does not necessarily increase interview validity. Some individuals can strongly influence the decisions of others. If such an individual is a more effective interviewer than others on a panel, then his or her influence could be expected to improve the panel's ratings. However, if the individual is not a more effective rater, then he or she could have a negative effect on the panel. Still, interviewers often are interested in discussing candidates, and some employers want to permit this in order to accommodate them.

Some research suggests that interviewer discussion is not always damaging and that limited consensus decision making might be allowed in a structured interview. Pulakos et al. (1996) thought the problems found in earlier studies actually were due to the use of unstructured interviews. They proposed that structuring would protect interviews from the inaccuracies and problems that have occurred in consensus decision making. To determine this, the researchers conducted a validity study of a structured interview and compared the validity of statistical consolidation to that of consolidation by consensus. The interview was highly structured and conducted by trained interview panels. Following each interview, interviewers independently rated the candidate's answers to each question. During this rating period, no discussion was allowed. When the independent ratings were completed, interviewers were permitted to discuss their ratings. If their ratings were similar, nothing further was required. However, if the ratings differed by more than one rating scale point, the panel members engaged in a consensus-discussion at the end of which they agreed to adjust their ratings. In the analysis, Pulakos et al. (1996) found that a statistical consolidation of individuals' ratings per candidate correlated at .32 with a performance criterion measure. The consensus ratings correlated with the criterion measure at a level of .35. The difference between these validity coefficients was significant although, in a practical sense, the difference is not large. It indicates that allowing a consensus discussion does not damage validity, given that the interview is highly structured and that interviewers are trained extensively. Consensus decision making may not be worth the extra time it takes, if improved validity is being sought. However, if it makes a structured interviewer more acceptable to interviewers, it might be worth the effort.

## Conclusions

Structuring has been a good solution to the previously well-documented weaknesses of the traditional job interview. In the past, reviewers concluded that interviews were neither reliable nor valid probably because they were not standardized (Arvey & Campion, 1982; Harris, 1989; Schmitt, 1976). Research evaluating the validity of job interviews has been more positive in recent years, and the change appears largely to have resulted from increased study of structured interviews. Clearly, interviews can be reliable and valid, but this depends on the extent to which they use standardized procedures and incorporate high levels of structure (Campion, Campion, et al., 1994; McDaniel et al., 1994).

Interviews can be structured in many different ways. In this section, I discussed several that appear to be necessary for reliability and validity. Probably, any of these elements of structure could help to improve an employer's interview. Some, undoubtedly, would contribute more structure than others. Certain features of structuring are essential. Job analysis is required to develop job-related interview questions and performance-anchored rating scales. Interviewers must control the conduct of the interview by asking the same questions of each candidate and rating each answer. The employer must provide in-depth training for interviewers. Certain other features of the structured interview appear to be less critical, such as disallowing probe questions and prohibiting panel interview discussion of candidates. Some of these features might be made flexible, if the interview is otherwise highly structured, in order to make it seem less mechanical and more acceptable to interviewers.

## INTERVIEWER ATTRIBUTES AND BEHAVIOR

Although I ended the above discussion by observing that researchers now are more positive about the effectiveness of interviewing than they were in the past, I would not like to give the impression that the problem of unreliable and invalid interviews has gone away. The improvement of the job interview clearly depends on the extent to which measures are taken for standardizing and structuring. Job interviews are conducted daily that have no such improvements. In these interviews especially, the accuracy of applicant evaluations depends on the individual abilities and behavior of interviewers. In this final section of the chapter, I discuss some of the variables that might contribute to differences in interviewers and the accuracy of their evaluations.

### Preparing for Interviewing

Interviewers differ as to whether they prepare for conducting job interviews. Some give very little attention to preparation. This usually results in an erratic line of questioning or takeover of questioning by the job candidate. Other interviewers prepare by reviewing candidates' job applications, résumés, and other ancillary materials. As I mentioned earlier, this can result in an interview which has little validity beyond that of the pre-interview application materials.

Errors will result because different information likely is obtained from ancillary materials on different applicants. For example, pre-interview application review will contribute to a general impression of the job applicant, which will remain with the interviewer and affect not only how the interview is conducted but also the evaluation of the person.

Better preparation for interviewing would be to review job analyses, job descriptions, or other job-related materials describing the required KSAs and other attributes. It would be helpful to an interviewer if the job dimensions to be evaluated had already been identified and if questions had been framed. However, if this has not been done, then the interviewer personally should define the dimensions and develop questions. Even better preparation would be to provide formal training for the interviewer that includes instruction and practice on conducting an interview and on how to avoid making common errors in rating. As I discussed previously, the research on structured interviews has demonstrated that interviewers can conduct a valid interview and provide ratings that are predictive of future job performance. However, this is not an intuitive process. Interviewers must *learn* how to do it.

## Interviewing Behavior

How an interviewer behaves depends on his or her own attributes and goals, as well as the interpersonal dynamics that develop within an interview. For example, a study of campus interviewing showed that an interviewer's priorities—to recruit or to screen applicants—influenced the campus interviewer's behavior (Stevens, 1998). Those who were focused primarily on promoting their company and recruiting applicants tended to monopolize the interview. They talked 50 percent more than interviewers who were concerned also with screening. They offered twice as much information, and they asked only half as many questions as their more selection-oriented counterparts. As a result, of course, the recruiting interviewers collected relatively little information from interviewees that could be used to evaluate their suitability for a job with the company. I suspect that many workplace interviews with job applicants are conducted in the same way with the same result, especially when an interviewer has not prepared. Such behavior, when the purpose is selection, indicates that the interviewer has lost control of the interview.

To obtain enough information to make an evaluation, an interviewer must allow and encourage the candidate to do most of the talking. When this does not occur, the interviewer will base evaluations on a general impression of the candidate or on information gained from pre-interview examination of ancillary materials. Interviewers also should be aware that some candidates might attempt to distract the interviewer by asking questions of their own, in order to avoid being asked interview questions that might be difficult. If a candidate knows he or she looks good "on paper," but does not wish to answer job-related questions, the individual might maintain the paper image by consuming interview time in this way. An interviewer who is not adequately prepared to control the interview is susceptible to this type of manipulation.

In addition to asking the questions and then listening, interviewers should take notes on what a candidate says and use them to decide on the individual's suitability for hire. Notetaking is beneficial because it increases the listener's attention to and understanding of the candidate's information. Notes also help in recalling what a candidate said. Some research demonstrates that notetaking can contribute to more accurate assessments of interviewees (Burnett, Fan, Motowidlo, & Degroot, 1998; Macan & Dipboye, 1994). Both the act of writing notes and the content of notes make a difference. Interviewers who voluntarily take notes have been found to make more valid evaluations than those who do not take notes. Behavioral notes are particularly useful. Interviewers who write down behavioral information about a candidate, such as what activities the person performed on a job, make more valid evaluations than interviewers who take other types of notes, such as notes on mannerisms (e.g., "good eye contact") (Burnett et al., 1998).

**Impression Confirming**   An interviewer should not review a candidate's application materials in preparing for an interview, because doing so can lead to bias. The problem occurs because the interviewer forms a pre-interview impression of an applicant from the ancillary materials and then conducts the interview in a manner so as to confirm the impression. Impression-confirming behavior also can be initiated when a general impression is formed at the start of an interview, such as might be based on an applicant's personal appearance.

Impression-confirming behavior can include cognitive distortion, such as when an interviewer pays attention to certain information provided by the candidate and ignores or discounts other information. Impression-confirming is commonly seen in an interviewer's overt behavior, such as in the kinds of questions asked. Interviewers who develop their own questions for individual applicants—and thus conduct a largely unstructured interview—may design questions that confirm their assessments of application materials. Research shows that this is especially likely when the application review suggests that the applicant is relatively unsuitable for the job. For such candidates, the questions are more likely to be framed so as to elicit negative information (Binning, Goldstein, Garcia, & Scattaregia, 1988). Interviewers also tend to ask these candidates more difficult questions and fewer positive questions than they ask candidates whose applications show moderate or high qualifications (Macan & Dipboye, 1988). An interviewer's interpersonal interaction with a candidate also differs depending on whether a negative or a positive impression has been formed. Further, candidates react accordingly, so a job candidate can become a contributor to a self-fulfilling prophesy by responding in a way that is consistent with an interviewer's behavior, whether that behavior is positive or negative. Dougherty, Turban, and Callender (1994) found that interviewers who had a positive pre-interview impression of a candidate exhibited greater positive regard and personal warmth in their interactions. In response, the candidate behaved positively and attempted to establish rapport with the interviewer.

As you might conclude, impression-confirming is a bias that seriously affects the interview. It reduces its value as a selection device, not only because of the curtailed use of the interview as an information-gathering tool, but also because this kind of behavior places an additional burden on the need for validity in the pre-interview application materials. If application materials are not valid, impression-confirming behavior carries the invalidity forward into the interview. If they are valid, such an interview is probably a waste of time.

**Personal Biases**   Demographic variables, such as sex, age, and race or ethnicity, potentially are at the source of some impression-confirming or other assessment biases. In the past, as you know, such applicant characteristics were overtly considered in selection decisions. Fair employment laws, of course, have prohibited selection discrimination. As a result, job interviewers may have become sensitized to the unfairness of taking demographic variables into account, and they may now be more careful to avoid making discriminatory decisions. Another possibility is that the bias remains, but is now more covert and enters only indirectly into interview evaluations through some other variable.

Most of the research investigating race and ethnicity effects has compared the differences in interview scores between Black and White applicants. Reviews of the earlier studies found the results to be largely inconsistent (Harris, 1989). In some studies, Black candidates received lower interview evaluations than White candidates (e.g., Parsons & Liden, 1984). In other studies, they received higher evaluations (e.g., Campion et al., 1988). Although there still is inconsistency in research results, it now appears that racial group differences in interview assessments are relatively minor. In 1998, Huffcutt and Roth meta-analyzed the results of 31 published and unpublished studies that had been conducted between 1970 and 1996. These studies included comparisons of interview scores of Black and White interviewees, as well as a few studies that included Hispanic applicants. Overall, the studies showed that there was still variability in the direction and extent of group differences. On average, however, White interviewees received ratings that were less than one standard deviation (.25) higher than those of Black or Hispanic interviewees. Further examination of the data showed that certain moderator variables were operating. One moderator was the complexity of the job. When a job was highly complex (e.g., technical management or nursing), Black and Hispanic candidates received higher overall evaluations than White candidates. The reviewers surmised that because experience and educational requirements for such jobs are high, minority candidates may represent a select group that is sought in industry. A second moderator was interview design. Group differences were lower when an interview was highly structured than when it was relatively unstructured. That is, candidate race had less impact on ratings in structured interviews. Huffcutt and Roth (1998) thought structuring might be suppressing the use of stereotypes in interview decision making. This is yet another reason to recommend structured interviews.

Only a few studies have assessed the effect of applicant age and, according to Harris's (1989) review, the results of these are inconsistent. Age appears to interact with other variables, and some studies consider both age and gender of job applicants.

Harris found that gender studies conducted in the early 1980s more often reported that females received lower interview ratings than males, whereas studies conducted later in the decade showed little difference in these ratings. Perhaps, as in all forms of illegal discrimination, interviewers were becoming more aware and were trying to avoid sex discrimination. Raza and Carpenter (1987) suggested another possibility—that demographic variables, such as applicant sex and age, do not directly affect interview evaluations and hiring decisions. Rather, they suggested, the effect on interview outcomes is indirect, occurring mainly through intervening variables, especially attractiveness. They expected that the greatest direct impact of sex and age would be on an interviewer's evaluation of an applicant's physical attractiveness and that attractiveness would indirectly affect interview decisions. Raza and Carpenter (1987) conducted a field study that generally supported the hypothesized relationships, at least as far as applicant sex was concerned. The strongest direct impact of sex was on assessments of attractiveness, with relatively minor effects on hiring decisions. In the case of applicant age, however, the predictions were not upheld. Interviewers evaluated older applicants negatively on multiple measures. Female interviewers considered them less attractive. Both male and female interviewers rated them less intelligent. Male raters also rated them as less hirable.

More recent studies have focused on attractiveness bias, particularly as it might affect female job candidates. For example, in one study, researchers wanted to know whether overweight applicants—especially females—are disadvantaged in employment interviews (Pingitore, Dugoni, Tindale, & Spring, 1994). They developed videotapes of simulated job interviews using professional actors as job applicants. The male and female actors appeared as their normal weight in half of the videotaped interviews, and in the other half, they were made up with prostheses to appear 30 pounds heavier than normal. Student raters viewed the videotapes and rated applicants' suitability for hire. The results of the study showed hiring bias against both overweight applicants and female applicants in general, and particularly against overweight females.

Being physically unattractive can be a disadvantage in job interviews. However, some researchers have suggested that physical appearance might be somewhat double-edged in its effect, as far as women are concerned. That is, although attractiveness is an advantage to some applicants in some situations, it might be a disadvantage in other cases. Heilman and Saruwatari (1979) found that physical attractiveness had different effects for men and women depending on the type of job they sought. For male applicants, attractiveness was an advantage regardless of whether they applied for managerial or nonmanagerial jobs. For women, however, attractiveness was an advantage only when they were seeking nonmanagerial jobs. Heilman (1983) hypothesized that such a bias occurs because interviewers evaluate personal attributes as to whether they fit the perceived job requirements. Managerial jobs have long been occupied by men, and these jobs have become male gender-typed. In such jobs, a female applicant might be seen as a "poor fit" because she is viewed as having fewer of the attributes of a successful manager, for example, assertiveness and competitiveness. If she is attractive, the interviewer might view her as even more unlikely to have these attributes.

Reactions to women applying for managerial jobs might have changed, of course. Because of the increased numbers of women actually working as managers, the use of biasing stereotypes in interviews might have declined. In a study in 1996, Marlowe, Schneider, and Nelson considered this possibility. They thought that managers who have more experience in hiring and promoting candidates for managerial positions would show less gender- and attractiveness-bias because of their longer exposure to female managers. In their field experiment, managers with high or low experience reviewed simulated résumé materials that included a photograph of the "candidate." The managers rated the candidates in terms of their suitability for initial hire and promotability to an executive vice presidency. Results of the study showed significant effects for both the physical attractiveness and gender of applicants, indicating that the evaluations were biased. As a group, the managers rated attractive candidates as more suitable for hire and more likely to be promoted. Similarly, they rated men as more hirable and promotable than women. Although the effects were generally smaller for the more experienced managers, less attractive females were disadvantaged regardless of the level of rater experience. Managers with low levels of experience considered them to be less hirable, whereas the more experienced managers considered them less promotable. The results of this study are consistent with other studies showing that a job candidate's physical attractiveness is a compelling variable in interviewers' judgments. Unattractiveness is a disadvantage for female candidates in managerial as in other jobs.

## Conclusions

What can we conclude about interviewer biases in job candidate ratings, especially considering that the research seems so inconsistent? Several explanations for the inconsistencies have been offered. For example, fair employment laws might have caused a change in interviewer behavior in recent years. Interviewers might now be more sensitive to the issues of fair employment, and maybe they try to avoid making discriminatory decisions. Interviewers in industry may have become more sensitive to the potential for EEO complaints and lawsuits, and they may try to avoid any decision that might result in one. (I think employment interviewers do tend to be alert to this.) Also, perhaps there are more women and minority members who, having personally experienced discrimination, are now in a position to change things. That is, perhaps there are more who will evaluate positively and hire "one of their own." This might not be entirely off base because some race-similarity research on employee performance appraisal has shown that supervisors rate subordinates of the same race higher than they rate subordinates of a different race (e.g., Kraiger & Ford, 1985). The effect also has been observed in interviewing studies in which interviewers give higher ratings to applicants who are of the same race as they (Lin, Dobbins, & Farh, 1992).

Another explanation of the inconsistency in studies of interviewer biases is that it is due to research methodology that clouds the issue. One point in the methodology explanation is that lab research done in university settings using students as raters has serious shortcomings in that it is not a good simulation of the workplace. Student raters may have little experience and motivation and expect no consequences for a poor performance as a research subject. Critics ask us to compare this to what takes place in industry when interviewers are experienced and motivated and must take responsibility for the decisions they make. If I could be sure that real interviewers greatly contrast with students in this respect, I would agree that lab research does not tell us much about the workplace. However, I am not entirely convinced.

There is one aspect of the research methodology explanation that should get more attention. This has to do with the overinterpretation of failed research results. What does it mean when an expected effect is not shown in a study? We do not know. We can only guess. If a researcher expected to observe race, sex, or age effects in interview ratings, but the study failed to show these effects, there are any number of explanations of why the expected result was not shown. One that might especially appeal to a researcher is that interviewers no longer consider these demographic characteristics. Of course, it is possible that it is the best explanation. However, the researcher cannot know whether it is the best, unless the study design included a special feature capable of supporting such an interpretation. I think researchers sometimes need to remind themselves to be especially cautious in interpreting the meaning of "no effect" in their research analyses. Failing to find interview differences may not mean that there weren't any.

## SUMMING UP

In this chapter, the purpose has been to examine and evaluate job interviews and explore the possibilities for improving this popular selection method. We can sum up as follows:

- The job interview is one of the most frequently used selection methods.
- Early studies of interviewing reported low reliability and low validity, and researchers recommended against using the method.
- A key difference between structured and unstructured interviews is the use of a job analysis to prepare questions.
- Questions for structured interviews may address behavior in past work experiences or reactions to hypothetical situations.
- Rating scales need to be anchored with performance descriptors.
- All candidates for the same job must be asked the same questions in the same order, and there is little room for probing.
- A carefully structured interview can be a valid selection method.
- Interviewers often make errors, such as when they use the interview to confirm previous impressions and allow their personal biases to influence their decisions.

## InfoTrac College Edition

If you purchased a new copy of this book, you received a complimentary subscription to InfoTrac College Edition with your purchase. Use it to access full-text articles from research journals and practice-oriented publications. Go to http://www.infotrac-college.com/wadsworth and start your search. There are several ways you can search this online library. For example, you can open the current issues of a journal, such as *Personnel Psychology*. You also can do a keyword search on a topic that interests you. The following keywords can be used to find articles related to the topics discussed in this chapter.

| | |
|---|---|
| Job interviews | Structured interview |
| Employment interviewers | Employee communication ability |

# ASSESSMENT CENTERS AND OTHER SIMULATIONS

CHAPTER

*12*

The most direct way to find out if someone can do a job is to let them try it. A "job tryout" is the most realistic and concrete of all selection methods. The job itself comprises the contents of this technique, and job performance is the behavior ultimately evaluated. In job tryouts, applicants are hired temporarily (with little in the way of screening) and are placed on the job for a predetermined period of time.[1] During the tryout period, job performance is monitored and evaluated. If the temporary employee is able to successfully perform the job, he or she is retained as a regular employee. Otherwise, the person is terminated.

The basic idea of hiring for a job tryout is reasonable. If an applicant can perform a time sample of the whole job, then he or she probably can do the job thereafter on a daily basis. The job tryout often is used by employers who have little else in the way of selection measures. However, they can use it to meet various needs, as follows: (1) when other selection methods are in place, but no one is available to administer them; (2) when a new hire is needed immediately; and/or (3) when there are too few job applicants to make other selection measures worth the effort. If the person hired is an acceptable performer, then the job tryout is an economical method. If not, there can be serious problems. If the temporary employee does not have full capacity to perform the job, time and materials are likely to be wasted, and equipment can be damaged by inept operation. Substandard products or services and customer dissatisfaction are possible results, as well. Of course, such problems reduce the employer's successful operation, and they increase monetary costs. If the tryout period shows that the individual is not acceptable, the employer will need to terminate him or her and start the recruitment and hiring process over again. Thus, the job tryout is a chancy and potentially expensive procedure to use—especially if the tryout period is long or if the job involves expensive equipment or otherwise has a sensitive nature.

---

[1]Methods similar to the job tryout are probationary hiring and job rotation. Job rotation is a form of internal recruiting and can be used to try out an employee for promotion or transfer to another job.

316

Job simulations, which are the focus of this chapter, are nearest to the job tryout in terms of realism. Although they show less fidelity to the job than the job tryout, simulations mimic the work contents, and the responses evaluated are similar to those required on the job. Simply put, a job simulation uses tasks like those in the job as the contents of the selection measure, and it calls for test performance that is more or less comparable to job performance. The rationale is that if a representative sample of the job is obtained, it can be considered to be a miniature version of the job, and any applicant who can successfully perform it can be assumed capable of performing the whole job. Because the job simulation can be evaluated as to its measurement quality, the user can be assured of its outcomes. In addition, because the simulation method is conducted prior to placing an applicant on the job, it carries less risk and expense for the employer than the job tryout.

In this chapter, I discuss job simulation methods that are used in employee selection. These include situational judgment tests, work sample performance tests, and assessment centers.

# JOB SIMULATION TESTS

Job simulations are distinguished in terms of the fidelity of the measure to the job. High-fidelity measures simulate the job most realistically. A work sample test, in which applicants perform a sample of the job, is an example of a high-fidelity measure.

Low-fidelity simulations, although clearly job-relevant in content, often use hypothetical material and are less directly reflective of the actual job. In low-fidelity simulations, a work situation is presented to an applicant—either orally or in writing—and the applicant responds as to how he or she *might* deal with it (Motowidlo, Dunnette, & Carter, 1990). For example, the situational interview is considered a low-fidelity job simulation. The interviewer describes a work situation or problem that might be encountered on the job, and the interviewee says how he or she would deal with it. (Refer back to Table 11.3 for some examples of such questions.) Like other low-fidelity job simulations, both the situation described in the situational interview and the applicant's response are hypothetical rather than factual.

## Written and Video-Based Situational Tests

Situational judgment tests are low-fidelity simulations. To construct such a test, realistic descriptions of work situations are drawn from a job analysis and used as items on the test. Either a written or a video-based format can be used in a situational judgment test to present work situations and to collect applicant responses. After each situation is presented, the applicant responds either by

Imagine that part of your job involves setting up and maintaining machines for office workers to use. In the course of doing your job, you have discovered that some of the office staff mishandle the machinery, causing it to require more maintenance and repair. What would you do about this?

Most likely, I would _____        It is least likely that I would _____

a. Tell my boss the reason for the increased maintenance and repair costs.

b. Alert the office manager that maintenance and repair costs are due to some staff misusing the machinery.

c. Post signs alerting users as to the need for careful use of the machinery.

d. Suggest to the office manager that no one be allowed to operate the equipment unless they have received training.

e. Warn the office staff that after a point you will be unable to repair the equipment and there may be no money for replacements.

**FIGURE 12.1**

Example of a written situational judgment test item and response alternatives. Applicants would select one response to represent the most likely action taken and another to represent the least likely action taken.

---

writing out a statement of what he or she would do in the situation or, more typically, by choosing one of several multiple-choice responses. For an example, see Figure 12.1. Sometimes, applicants are asked to choose both their most- and least-likely response from an array of response alternatives. In situational judgment tests, as in situational interviews, hypothetical rather than real job behavior is elicited, even though very realistic job situations might be depicted. For this reason, situational judgment tests show lower fidelity than simulations calling for actual performance of real job tasks, such as work sample performance tests, which I discuss later.

Over the past two decades, as convenient video equipment has become available, several video-based situational judgment tests have been developed. For example, video-based tests have been devised for selecting metropolitan transit operators (Smiderle, Perry, & Cronshaw, 1994); insurance agents (Dalessio, 1994); employees in the hotel and hospitality industry (Jones & DeCotiis, 1986); hourly retail store employees; and nursing home caregivers (Weekley & Jones, 1997). Typically, in these tests, the video depicts the process of a problem arising in a work situation. At the point when the problem becomes apparent, the scene freezes and the applicant is instructed to select an on-screen response alternative that best describes how he or she would handle the problem.

The video format can have certain advantages over a written test. More detailed and realistic work situations that have richer meaning can be presented by using the video format (Weekley & Jones, 1997). Because of this, applicants may react more positively to a video-based situational judgment test. For many job applicants who are more accustomed to watching TV than to reading, responding to a video-based test may seem to be a more natural activity and more acceptable than taking a written test. A video-based test may be especially appealing if the video includes voice-over narration and a reading of response alternatives. For jobs that do not involve reading, the video might be a more valid presentation mode. A comparison of situational judgment tests showed that test takers' scores on a written test were correlated positively with measures of the individuals' reading ability, whereas scores on a video test were unrelated to reading ability (Chan & Schmitt, 1997). Therefore, if reading is not required on the job, or if the test is not needed to measure reading ability, then a video-based test might be preferable. However, despite these advantages, there is a serious disadvantage. Video-based situational tests can be very expensive to produce, especially if professional actors are used. Weekley and Jones (1997) reported that the cost of developing the video test for their study was about $1,500 per finished minute.

**Developing a Situational Judgment Test**    The basic construction of a situational judgment test is done similarly for both written and video formats. In both cases, the process is lengthy, as it involves multiple steps (Motowidlo, Hanson, & Crafts, 1997). In the first stage of development, the test developer must identify situations that actually occur on the job. This is the distinctive feature of all job simulation methods. The situations selected should be ones that represent a challenge for the employee. Each one should be something that is important to handle appropriately and in which employees vary as to how successful they are. Response alternatives need to be developed at this same time. They should describe behaviors that vary in effectiveness—from the best to the worst thing an employee could do. Obviously, a job analysis is necessary in order to define and describe work situations and response alternatives. The critical incidents technique is particularly helpful because it identifies the critical aspects of work, which not all employees can perform. Recall from previous discussion of this job analysis method that each critical incident includes a description of the background situation, details on exactly what an employee did that was effective or ineffective, and an outline of the consequences. Thus, a critical incidents analysis provides the basic material for developing a job simulation.

As an example, Motowidlo and his associates (1997) outlined the steps they used to develop a situational test for a skilled electrician's job. First, they collected a large number of critical incidents and organized these according to their behavioral content. They grouped the incidents into three categories, including planning and organizing the work, troubleshooting, and supervising. These categories suggested the performance dimensions on which effective and ineffective electricians differed. Second, because the researchers needed more detailed information on the situations surrounding these performance dimensions, another group of SMEs—experienced electricians—was assembled. They were asked to develop full descriptions of a problem, which they had encountered and handled, that exemplified one of the performance dimensions. To accomplish this, the researchers instructed the SME to describe the problem in detail, state how it was resolved, and identify the relevant performance dimension. Third, they then sorted these problem descriptions according to the type of work activity addressed. This resulted in another set of performance categories. For example, some of the problems described dealt with blueprint reading, completing jobs on time, and working with overly demanding customers. Finally, a selection of the problems were drawn from each category to make up the items in the situational judgment test. Problems were selected so as to represent the important kinds of situations that occurred on the job. The proportion of items from each category depended on how important the category was to successful job performance.

As a last step in developing a situational judgment test, response alternatives for the individual items need to be created. Motowidlo et al. (1997) described their procedure for doing this. They presented test items, open-ended to a sample of relatively inexperienced job incumbents, and asked them to write a description of how they would handle each problem. The researchers then selected a set of five response alternatives from the incumbents' answers for each item. They recommended that the response alternatives selected should represent a range of strategies that applicants might use to handle a problem. Next, a panel of SMEs rated each response alternative as to its effectiveness for solving the problem. The researchers used these ratings to identify the best and worst alternative for each question and to develop a scoring key.

**Validity Studies**   Reviews of research conclude that written situational judgment tests that are well-developed and content-valid also have criterion-related validity. Various criterion measures have been used in the validity studies, including promotion rate, turnover, and supervisors' ratings of performance. For example, Rosen (1961) reviewed the evidence on the "How Supervise?" test (File, 1945), which is a standardized situational test used to evaluate supervisory and managerial job candidates. Although the validation studies reported a range of validity coefficients, Rosen concluded that the research evidence was strong enough to support the measure as valid for predicting supervisory performance. More recently, reviewers have evaluated validity evidence for various written situational judgment tests. In general, the scores correlate significantly with ratings of job performance, producing validity coefficients ranging from .20 to .50 (Motowidlo et al., 1997). For example, Motowidlo and his associates (1990) developed a situational judgment inventory for selecting junior-level managers for a consortium of companies in the telecommunications industry. Using a sample of relatively new managers to validate the instrument, the researchers found that the scores on the inventory correlated from .28 to .37 with supervisors' ratings of performance on the job. Criterion-related validity also has been shown for written situational tests of other types of abilities. Using performance ratings as criteria in validating her tests, Phillips (1992, 1993) reported significant validity coefficients of .18 and .24 for a test of sales skills and coefficients ranging from .41 to .45 for a test of negotiation skills.

Because video-based simulations are a more recent innovation, not much research has been published on their validity. Still, there have been some studies, and some of the results are positive. Jones and DeCotiis (1986) compared scores on a video-based situational test for hotel employees with supervisors' ratings and found a significant correlation of .38. Clearly, however, the criterion-related validity of video-based tests varies. Dalessio's (1994) cross-validation[2] study, using insurance agents, showed a significant but low correlation of .13 with a criterion measure of turnover. Smiderle et al. (1994) reported that they were unable to find criterion-related validity in their attempt to validate a video test of interpersonal skills required of transit operators. More recently, Weekley and Jones (1997) conducted validation studies on two video-based situational judgment tests, using samples of retail store employees and nursing home caregivers. Test scores of cross-validation samples were correlated with supervisory ratings of performance. Validity coefficients of .22 were obtained in the retail store study and .24 in the nursing home study. When corrected for probable unreliability in the criterion measure, the validities rose to the middle .30s. These results provide at least some indication that video-based situational tests can be valid for selecting employees.

## Work Sample Performance Tests

A work sample used as a performance test is considered to be a high-fidelity simulation.[3] The work sample test is a complex measure and constitutes a miniature replica of the job. As such, it is near a job tryout in terms of realism. Asher and Sciarrino (1974) reviewed research conducted between 1940 and 1970 on various types of work sample tests that were used for selection during that time. They found that the tests could be categorized into two groups, one involving physical manipulation or *motor* activities, and the other involving language- and people-oriented problems or *verbal* activities. For example, a test requiring an applicant to type a sample of material drawn from a secretary's

---

[2]Cross-validation is an empirical method for confirming a previously obtained validity coefficient. In a cross-validation study, a second sample is independently drawn from the same population as the original validation sample. The test is administered and criterion data are collected on the new sample. Analysis yields a new validity coefficient.

[3]Because of their high fidelity to the job, work sample tests are sometimes used as criterion measures—instead of supervisors' ratings of performance—to evaluate the validity of another predictor measure. Similarly, they can be used as criterion measures to assess the validity of training programs.

**EXAMPLES OF MOTOR AND VERBAL WORK SAMPLE TESTS**

| Test Category | Type of Performance | Examples of Tests |
|---|---|---|
| Motor | Physical object manipulation | Drill press and lathe operation tests for wood shop workers |
| | | Repair of a vehicle engine for mechanics |
| | | Stitching test for sewing machine operators |
| | | Typing test for office clerks |
| | | Complex circuit simulation test for electricians |
| | | Driving test for vehicle operators |
| Verbal | Communication or interpersonal interactions | Leaderless group discussion for supervisors |
| | | In-basket simulation for managers |
| | | Customer service role-playing test |
| | | Language translation for interpreters |
| | | Simulation of testimony-taking for government inspectors |
| | | Business letter–writing test for administrators |

Based on information from "Realistic Work Sample Tests: A Review," by J. J. Asher and J. A. Sciarrino, 1974, *Personnel Psychology, 27*, pp. 520–522.

work is a motor work sample test because of the use of the typewriter or computer keyboard. A telephone interaction with a customer, such as might occur in customer service work, is an example of a verbal work sample test. Table 12.1 lists other examples of work sample tests.

**Development**    Work sample tests are constructed from the job, using a detailed job analysis. The contents of the job are carefully analyzed to obtain a certain sample of required work activities. The best sample includes the most important job activities, but it omits those that are learned on the job. To the extent that work sample tests are developed this way, they are considered to be content-valid. Cascio and Phillips (1979) described the process of developing and content-validating work sample performance tests that were used to hire city government employees. The process began with a comprehensive job analysis, which formed the basis for constructing the tests. The job analysis was conducted using a task inventory analysis procedure. (Recall from the previous discussion of job analysis that this technique produces a full description of a job and its requirements, including the relative importance of tasks and KSAs.) From the task analysis, the developers selected tasks that would constitute the work sample tests. Also, performance standards were determined that described levels of acceptable performance on the tasks. These standards were used in developing instructions for test administrators on evaluating and scoring applicant performance. Finally, SMEs evaluated the work sample tests to establish that they were realistic and that they covered the essential job requirements. Through this process of thorough job analysis and use of SMEs to confirm that the tests constituted representative samples of the job, content validity was established.

**Validity Studies**   In addition to content validity, work sample tests often have been found to have criterion-related validity (cf. Robertson & Kandola, 1982). This is not surprising, considering the high realism in such tests. Compared to more abstract and less factual predictor measures, content-valid work sample tests might be expected to have high validity for predicting performance criteria. In a review of studies, Asher and Sciarrino (1974) argued that, in general, a point-to-point correspondence between test content and the contents of criterion measures would lead to the highest levels of validity. When they examined work sample test validities, they did find strong evidence of criterion-related validity. However, the level of validity depended on whether the work sample involved motor or verbal performance. It also depended on what criterion was being predicted. The reviewers found that two types of criteria had been evaluated in these studies: job proficiency and training success. When the criterion was job proficiency, a majority of the studies of motor work sample tests showed significant validity coefficients of .30 or better. In fact, almost half of the motor test validities reached at least .50. Verbal work sample measures were less effective than the motor tests in predicting job proficiency, although more than half of the studies did show significant validities of .30 or higher. The verbal tests actually were better at predicting training success. The reviewers found that a majority of the studies using verbal tests reported validities of at least .30 and that almost 40 percent had validities of .50 or higher. Motor work sample tests also were able to predict a training criterion measure, although not quite as well as the verbal tests. Overall, these values indicate that work sample performance tests, whether they are motor or verbal tests, show high criterion-related validity (Asher & Sciarrino, 1974).

Work sample tests have other advantages. They show little indication of adverse impact, and applicants react positively toward them (Robertson & Kandola, 1982; Schmidt, Greenthal, Hunter, Berner, & Seaton, 1977). Cascio and Phillips (1979) reported that the work sample tests they developed showed no signs of adverse impact against minorities or women. In addition, the tests were cost effective and resulted in decreased turnover rates. Turnover dropped from an average of 40 percent to less than 3 percent during the period following the introduction of work sample testing. The researchers surmised that this may have resulted because performance of the work sample actually behaved as a realistic job preview. That is, the work sample test allowed applicants to experience what the job was like before they accepted it.

## Conclusions

Job simulations—especially work sample tests—are versatile assessment methods. They may play either of two roles in assessment. Historically, job simulations have been used in selection, as predictors of job performance. However, when other selection instruments are being validated, job simulations are sometimes used as criterion measures. Their versatility demonstrates the close relationship between the concepts of predictor and criterion. To determine whether a measure is a predictor or a criterion, we must look at how it is being used. Some measures, such as applications and biodata instruments, are used *only* as predictor measures in validation studies. However, work samples and certain other measures, such as situational interviews, can be used as either predictor or criterion measures in validation studies. We are most likely to see that measures involving ratings play this role. Obviously, ratings are used as criterion measures; supervisors routinely rate the job performance of employees and, thus, provide the criterion measure for criterion-related validation. However, ratings also are collected with certain other measures, such as situational interviews and job simulation evaluations. These ratings can be used either to predict performance or as a criterion measure of performance.

A requirement of measures that are used as either predictors or criteria concerns the extent to which the measure replicates the job. A work sample or other job simulation does not have to be an exact replica of a job in order to be a valid predictor or selection measure. In previous chapters, I discussed selection methods that are quite abstract, such as cognitive ability tests, and yet that have been shown to have high validity. However, when used as a criterion measure, a job simulation does need to assess all critical tasks. Felker and Rose (1997) argued that work samples are effective, not only as predictor measures but also as criterion measures, precisely because they meet this requirement. Work sample performance tests that are well-constructed using a thorough job analysis are commonly recognized as having the highest fidelity to the job and as being the most valid indicators of actual job performance.

Predictor and criterion measures do not produce identical results. There are at least two important aspects of the measurement process that contribute to the differences. First, interviewers and observers of applicants on job simulations have a different focus than supervisors who observe and rate the performance of their employees. Observers of applicants focus on evaluating potential for job proficiency rather than actual proficiency. Second, an applicant behaves differently while being observed for selection purposes, than an employee who is performing the job (Sackett, Zedeck, & Fogli, 1988). An applicant probably exhibits his or her *maximum* performance, whereas an employee exhibits a lower, more *typi-*

*cal* performance. This difference occurs because the conditions vary. When applicants are evaluated for selection, they know they are being observed and they try to do their best during the observation period. The observation period is relatively short, so they are able to maintain their maximum performance level. Employees, however, are not always being observed, and they do not continually work at maximum capacity. These two differences in measurement imply that it is unlikely for any predictor measure and criterion measure to correlate exactly. The differences in the conditions under which applicants and employees are evaluated will limit the correlation. For such reasons, many researchers consider carefully how a validation study was done, when they evaluate the criterion-related validity of a selection measure.

# ASSESSMENT CENTERS

An assessment center is a complex selection method that incorporates multiple simulations, tests, exercises, and other measures which job candidates perform in a simulated work environment. Special assessors are trained, and they observe and evaluate job candidates' performance of the assessment activities. Because assessment centers are meant to simulate important aspects of a job, and because they may include work sample tests or other simulations, they are categorized as high-fidelity measures.

Assessment centers have an interesting history. They were first designed during World War II to meet the needs of the U.S. government's Office of Strategic Services (OSS). The OSS needed an effective way to select secret service agents. The work of an agent involved complex tasks, ambiguity, and high-stress situations. It was especially important that agents performed well under stress. At the time, a team of psychologists were working on a personality research project that seemed relevant to the government's need (Murray, 1938). The research involved a new procedure for assessing personality by having clinical psychologists observe volunteer research participants and evaluate them using various clinical methods. The OSS adopted a similar strategy to develop an assessment center for selecting new secret service agents (Murray & MacKinnon, 1946). OSS assessors observed job candidates and evaluated their performance in various individual and group activities. One of the activities was a leaderless group interaction. This exercise was used to obtain assessments of candidates' teamwork, initiative, and leadership behavior, which were behavioral dimensions required on the job. Because stress was an important part of secret service work, the OSS assessment center also was designed to present potentially stressful activities. Candidates had to meet tight deadlines, overcome obstacles, and deal with unpredictable events. For example, one assignment required the candidate to perform a task with the assistance of two "helpers" who actually were obstructive and generally uncooperative.

Since this beginning, the assessment center has become a commonly used method for making hiring and promotional decisions, especially on jobs that involve complex interpersonal behavior.[4] Many assessment centers have been designed for selecting managers and executives. In addition, professional, technical, and sales personnel have been evaluated in assessment centers. Research conducted at American Telephone and Telegraph (AT&T) is well known for its influence in initiating the managerial assessment center. Bray and his colleagues (Bray, 1982; Bray & Campbell, 1968; Bray, Campbell, & Grant, 1974) used assessment center methodology at AT&T to conduct longitudinal studies of career progress among managerial and sales personnel. They found that assessment center evaluations could be used to predict the career development patterns of individuals over long periods, sometimes as long as 20 years.

Currently, assessment centers are used widely by many different organizations and in various industries, such as manufacturing, service, banking, and government (Spychalski, Quiñones, Gaugler, & Pohley, 1997). Various public sector organizations, including the military and police and fire departments, have developed assessment centers for hiring and/or promoting employees. For example, a survey of federal, state, and local government agencies reported in 1982 that 44 percent were using assessment centers at that time (Fitzgerald & Quaintance, 1982). Another survey also documented that 44 percent of metropolitan fire departments were using assessment centers (Yeager, 1986). A later survey suggested that public sector use of assessment centers has increased considerably since these earlier studies were done. Data collected in 1992 showed that at least one assessment center was regularly being administered by 62 percent of the organizations in a sample of government employers (Lowry, 1996). Assessment centers also are being used outside of North America. Research papers indicate that they have been used in Singapore (Chan, 1996), Israel (Tziner, Ronen, & Hacohen, 1993), and Western Europe. Several studies have reported on their use in the United Kingdom (e.g., Robertson, Gratton, & Sharpley, 1987). For example, one use of assessment centers in the U.K. was to select candidates for naval officer training (cf. Jones, Herriot, Long, & Drakeley, 1991).

## STRUCTURING AN ASSESSMENT CENTER

As you can see in Figure 12.2, preparing an assessment center is a multiple-phase process. The developer must analyze the job and identify required behavioral dimensions. Dimensions often found to be required in managerial

---

[4]Assessment centers have uses other than selection. For example, they are used in employee training.

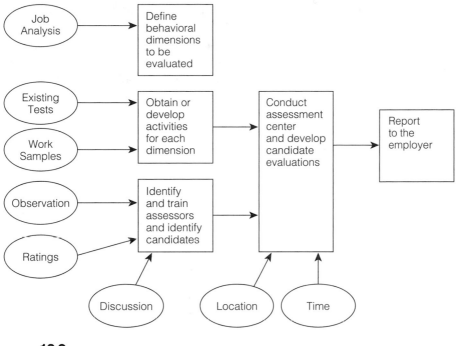

**FIGURE 12.2**

The process of developing and conducting an assessment center.

jobs include decision making, planning, leadership, oral communication, and stress tolerance. Once the required dimensions have been identified, activities for assessing them need to be obtained or developed. Some existing exercise forms are well known, such as the leaderless group discussion, and these can be adapted to suit the needs of a job. Other measures may have to be constructed outright. For example, simulations such as work sample tests sometimes have to be developed to assess certain dimensions.

Information and direction are readily available to those who plan to develop and use assessment centers. A document titled *Guidelines and Ethical Considerations for Assessment Center Operations* was published (Task Force on Assessment Center Standard, 1989) expressly for this purpose. In the *Guidelines,* the structural components of an assessment center are outlined, and variables are identified that the task force considered likely to affect the validity of the method. Steps for developing an assessment center are specified. First, a job analysis is necessary to determine the dimensions of job performance that are critical to success on the job. Assessment center activities must be designed to measure these dimensions. Multiple exercises will be needed for the assessment center, mainly because the jobs for which the assessment center is useful are likely to be quite complex. Second, multiple assessors must be retained to observe and evaluate candidates' performance in the activities. Assessors must be trained on what to observe and evaluate and how to prepare a written assessment of a candidate's performance. Also, a valid procedure is needed through which to integrate the multiple assessors' evaluations on each candidate. Third, assessment centers should be pretested, and ratings of candidates need to be evaluated for their reliability and validity in predicting a criterion measure.

## Assessment Center Activities

A wide variety of activities can be used in assessment centers. Written job knowledge tests and personality tests may be administered. Work sample performance tests and other job simulations routinely are included, as are situational and other structured interviews. Both individual and group exercises are used to simulate certain aspects of a job. Role-play exercises sometimes are included. For example, a role-play exercise may be conducted that simulates a meeting with a "difficult" employee. The candidate interacts with a trained role player, who acts as the employee. The purpose of the exercise is to determine how the candidate would supervise and handle employee problems.

**In-Basket Exercise**    One commonly used activity, which is appropriate for many managerial assessment centers, is the in-basket exercise. This activity functions as an individually administered work sample test. The contents of the work sample are a collection of materials such as might have accumulated in the message in-basket of a manager who has been away from the office. Typically, the in-basket materials are letters, memoranda, telephone messages, reports, records, and various other items. Some of these demand the manager's attention and need to be handled immediately and personally. Some cite deadlines and contain requests that are urgent, whereas others concern more routine matters.

A candidate is allowed a limited period of time to handle the in-basket items, and then assessors evaluate the candidate's performance in terms of specific behavioral dimensions. Two behavioral dimensions that are commonly assessed by in-baskets are the abilities to assign priorities and to appropriately delegate responsibilities. Depending on the particular abilities and skills that a job analysis indicates are necessary on the job, in-basket contents may be designed so as to elicit several different performance behaviors. For example, Brannick, Michaels, and Baker (1989) designed two in-basket forms and developed assessors' scoring keys for five behavioral dimensions on each. These dimensions were (1) organizing and planning, defined in terms of prioritizing and setting times for handling items; (2) perceiving relationships implied in the items; (3) delegating appropriately; (4) leadership, as in taking responsibility and supervising; and (5) decision making.

**Leaderless Group Discussion**    Another frequently used exercise is the leaderless group discussion. In this activity, candidates meet as a group and, without having any assigned roles, they discuss some issue of common concern. The discussion topic is defined for the group and usually focuses on a job-related problem that requires group interaction to solve. The nature of the problem depends on the behavioral dimensions that need to be assessed with the exercise, although there is usually some urgency and candidates often must deal with unanticipated events. For example, a group may be misinformed, or it may lose budgetary resources during the course of handling a problem.

The problem structure and the relationship between group members can be designed to create and encourage a certain interaction pattern in the leaderless group discussion. Depending on what the job analysis reveals about necessary interactions, the activity can be designed to promote either a cooperative group interaction or a win–lose competition. This can be accomplished by varying the instructions given the group about its purpose and the nature of individual and group tasks and goals. For example, Schneider and Schmitt (1992) designed two leaderless group discussion activities by varying how group members' goals and tasks were related. In a group designed to be cooperative, the group members' goals and tasks were highly interdependent. The overall goal of the group was to collectively manufacture a product for sale; thus, members' goals overlapped the group's goal. Tasks were interrelated, as well. Each group member was given a packet of instructions. However, these were incomplete, which meant that members had to pool their information in order to perform their tasks. In the group designed to be competitive, members' goals and tasks were *not* interdependent. Members worked separately to design individual projects, and their interactions involved competing for funding of their projects from a limited budget.

## Administrative Structure

The assessment center is a relatively "rich" selection method in terms of the amount of time and attention devoted to job candidates. Although most assessment work is done in groups—that is, groups of candidates and groups of assessors—considerable time is spent in the evaluation process. It is not unusual for as many as four to six assessors to be engaged for an assessment center to evaluate six to twelve candidates. Such a selection method often is considered to be worth the cost because of the importance of making the right decision in placing employees in high-paying managerial or professional positions or on jobs that have a sensitive nature, such as protective service or money-handling. In addition, the cost might be justified by the assessment center's related developmental purpose. Assessment center participants often are selected from among an organization's employees for development and promotion because they appear to have potential for high-level positions.

**Assessors**   Because assessors play an extremely important role, assessment center developers should consider carefully whom they ask to perform as assessor. Sometimes, clinically trained psychologists are retained for this purpose. Studies have shown that assessment centers using psychologists have higher validities than assessment centers using other assessors (Gaugler, Rosenthal, Thornton, & Bentson, 1987). However, a survey of organizational practice found that few psychologists (6 percent of the sample) actually perform this role (Spychalski et al., 1997). Usually, an organization engages its own employees to perform as assessors. Most are administrators or managers whose positions are somewhat higher in the organizational hierarchy than the job for which candidates are being considered. One possible reason for not using psychologists is the belief that managers are better able to assess candidates because of their working familiarity with the job and organization. Also, hiring psychologists or other consultants is costly relative to using the organization's own staff.

Assessors' responsibilities include conducting certain assessment procedures, such as situational interviews, and observing and evaluating candidates' performance in all assessment center activities. An important part of their work involves meeting as a group and, in what is known as an "integrative" discussion, coming to agreement in their evaluation and recommendation of each candidate. The assessors develop a written report for the employer that provides detailed information on assessment center performance and evaluates each candidate's potential for the job.

All assessors, regardless of their backgrounds, need to be trained. The Task Force's 1989 *Guidelines* on assessment centers emphasized the need for assessor training. Trainers should provide information and give specific instruction on (1) the nature of the job, (2) dimensions to be assessed and their relationship to performance on the job, (3) techniques for notetaking, (4) use of rating scales or other methods of assessment, (5) performance standards and behavior that might be observed, (6) the process of integrating assessors' evaluations, and (8) procedures for feedback to participants. Most organizations report that their assessor training covers these areas of content. Spychalski et al. (1997) found that assessor training programs usually included explanations of the assessment center method and the exercises to be used. Most of them included demonstrations of observing and evaluating, gave information about rating errors, and described the assessors' integrative discussion. However, the survey also showed that there were some weaknesses in these training programs. The *Guidelines* recommend that assessors be evaluated at the end of training to establish that they are qualified. Only 52 percent of the organizations surveyed said they did this. This is a serious weakness. If the training is not evaluated, it is unclear whether assessors learned what they need to know to perform well.

| TABLE 12.2 | A 3-Day Assessment Center, Including 2 Days of Candidate Participation in Exercises and 3 Days of Assessor Observation, Evaluation, and Report Development | |
|---|---|---|
| | **Candidate Activities** | **Assessor Activities** |
| **1st Day** | Structured interview | Conduct interview, observe, take notes |
| | In-basket | Evaluate interviews |
| | Leaderless group discussion (cooperative) | Observe, take notes |
| | (break) | Evaluate participants' group interactions |
| | Role-play (supervision) | Observe, take notes |
| | (end of day) | Evaluate role-play behavior<br>Evaluate in-baskets |
| **2nd Day** | Situational interview | Conduct interview, observe, take notes |
| | (break) | Evaluate interviews |
| | Leaderless group discussion (conflict) | Observe, take notes |
| | Written report<br>Prepare for oral report | Evaluate participants' group interactions |
| | Oral report | Observe, take notes |
| | (end of day) | Evaluate oral reports<br>Evaluate written reports |
| **3rd Day** | | Integrative discussion<br>Evaluate candidates' overall performance |
| | | Develop employer report on candidates |

**Time and Place Arrangements**    The length of time needed to conduct an assessment center can vary from 1 day to as long as a week. A sample of studies evaluated by Gaugler et al. (1987) indicated that most organizations require observations of candidates over a period of 2 or 3 days. Table 12.2 shows an example of a 3-day assessment center with 2 days of candidate observation.

Assessment centers may be conducted on-site, but away from the job, using the organization's own physical facilities. They also may be conducted off-site, such as in a hotel or other public facility that offers meeting rooms for rent. Off-site assessment centers can be advantageous in that they take assessors and candidates away from their daily work routine, which allows them to focus more completely on the assessment center. However, assessment centers generally are considered to be among the most expensive of selection methods. As I mentioned earlier, this is partly because of the expense of consultants who are retained to develop the center and/or act as assessors. Administration of the center also can be expensive. If an assessment center takes several days to run and is conducted off-site, it can be especially costly for a company.

# Conclusions

Assessment centers provide a simulation of the job in which candidates can be evaluated. In this sense, they are categorized as a job simulation selection method. Assessment centers are different in some ways from all other selection methods that I have discussed. What distinguishes them most is their "multiple assessment" nature. An assessment center involves multiple assessors and multiple activities. Unlike the individually oriented procedures described in previous chapters, in which job applicants are taken one at a time and evaluated with tests, interviews, and other such individual techniques, the assessment center uses the group as the unit of evaluation. In many of the activities, a group of candidates are immersed in interaction, and assessors base their evaluations on the candidates as performers in the group interaction. Another feature that distinguishes the assessment center is its aim of obtaining multiple measures of behavioral dimensions from multiple exercises.

## ASSESSMENT CENTER EFFECTIVENESS

Do assessment centers work? The answer depends on whom we ask and on what aspect of effectiveness we consider. Those who design and use them probably will defend their assessment centers as being effective. Also, there is evidence that supports the criterion-related validity of the assessment center method. However, as you will see, evidence of reliability and validity is not always strong, and it has been especially difficult to determine exactly what constructs are being measured. It is not clear why assessment centers are effective, even when the empirical evidence shows that they are.

One important question is whether assessment centers are designed and conducted according to accepted professional practice. This was the focus of a survey of assessment center developers and administrators (Spychalski et al., 1997). The survey showed that most assessment centers had been designed by consultants and, for the most part, the 1989 *Guidelines* had been followed. Almost all the organizations (93 percent) had used job analysis to develop the assessment center, and most (80 percent) reviewed the center periodically to maintain its job relevance. They made use of multiple exercises, and a little more than half of the sample said they pretested the exercises before using them. In certain ways, however, the organizations had failed to follow the professional guidelines. First, relatively few had evaluated the reliability and validity of their assessment centers. Only half of the sample (52 percent) had gathered reliability evidence. A somewhat greater number (69 percent) said they had evidence of validity. However, most of this number were claiming content validity based on the fact that they had used a job analysis to develop the center. Few had conducted criterion-related or other empirical validation studies. Second, candidates rarely were given adequate information. The 1989 *Guidelines* recommended that participants be thoroughly briefed. They should be told the purpose of the assessment center and how results would be used, how participants were selected, and the consequences of not participating. In fact, most participants knew little about what to expect. Some (35 percent) were given general information about assessment centers. However, a few (11 percent) received no information at all (Spychalski et al., 1997).

## Content Validity

Because the assessment center is a job simulation, it is reasonable to document the relationship between the contents of a job and assessment center exercises, and to claim content validity. This is certainly appropriate validity evidence when the exercises clearly constitute samples of important tasks performed on the job. However, when a job is complex and interactive, it can be difficult to establish that assessment center activities actually sample the job, and assuming content validity may be unwarranted.

For an assessment center to have content validity, it is not enough merely to note that a job analysis was done and to assert that the exercises are job-related. Content validity is more than the simple appearance of validity. A review of research on the in-basket exercise found that face validity and content validity often had been confused (Schippmann, Prien, & Katz, 1990). None of the content validation studies indicated that job-related tasks or KSAs had been systematically sampled in developing the exercise, as is required in developing and content-validating a test. The reviewers emphasized that "simply eyeballing test content with reference to the job analysis results and proclaiming the procedures to be content valid is unacceptable" (p. 851). To have content validity, a job analysis must identify the important dimensions of job content, and assessment center activities must clearly address this content. Also, the developer must document that the job has been adequately sampled and is well-represented by the activities.

To content-validate an assessment center, the developer must address validity issues in all aspects of the assessment center. Obviously, identifying important job dimensions and developing appropriate exercises are essential steps. In addition, both the administration and evaluation processes need to be standardized. Otherwise, inconsistencies can be introduced that lower reliability and validity. One issue that developers often neglect in content-validating an assessment center is the extent to which standardized instructions are given to participants. Research has found that assessment center participants often are told little other than to be as accurate as possible or to work as fast as possible. They are rarely informed about the kinds of behavior being evaluated in an exercise. Unless a dimension being measured is transparent enough that they can decipher it on their own, participants may not know what is being asked of them (Kleinmann, 1993). Another need is to extend the content-validation effort to the scoring process. Developers should consider carefully how exercises will be scored because evaluation procedures can affect how well a dimension is measured. For example, Sackett (1987) described three different ways that an in-basket could be scored. In two procedures, an assessor reads a candidate's responses and then either (1) rates several behavioral dimensions or (2) interviews the person about reasons for each response and then rates the dimensions. In the third procedure, an administrative clerk reads each response, finds the nearest match from a list of responses on a scoring key, and assigns the associated score points. These three ways of evaluating candidates' responses potentially can result in three different scores for essentially the same performance. The developer needs to purposely define how scoring will be done. Otherwise, the validity of the exercise might be compromised.

In summary, there are a number of requirements for establishing that an assessment center has content validity. One is that the behavioral dimensions represent what is required on the job. Another is that the exercises clearly reflect job content or work requirements. Also, developers must standardize the administration, observation, and scoring processes. All participants need to be adequately and similarly informed; and assessors must have standardized methods for observing and evaluating candidates. Assessment centers need to have a solid foundation in the job. As you will see, when there are problems in showing content validity, empirical validation also is affected.

## Criterion-Related Validity

Research on assessment centers has indicated a very wide range of criterion-related validities. A review of 107 validation studies showed validity coefficients ranging from a low of −.25 to a high of +.78. Using these studies, Gaugler et al. (1987) conducted a meta-analysis expressly to estimate true assessment center validity. They applied the statistical corrections permitted by the meta-analysis, including weighting the validity coefficients by sample size and correcting for range restriction and unreliability in the criterion measures. As a result, they were able to show strong supportive evidence of validity. The overall mean validity coefficient was .37. This value indicated that, on average, assessment centers are valid for predicting criterion measures.

Earlier studies of assessment centers had indicated that the level of criterion-related validity depended on the criterion measure being predicted. For example, assessment centers were found to be more valid for predicting ratings of potential, likelihood of promotion, and career progress than they were for predicting job performance criteria (Klimoski & Strickland, 1977). Gaugler et al. (1987) found the same result. Their meta-analysis showed average corrected validities of .53 for potential and .36 for job performance. There are various explanations as to why this might occur. One possibility is that assessors know more in general about what it takes to get promoted than they know about day-to-day performance on a particular job (Klimoski & Strickland, 1977). This suggests that assessors are not basing their evaluations on a candidate's performance in the assessment center. Instead, they seem to be guessing how promotable a candidate will appear to a supervisor or manager who makes the promotion decision. Another, more troubling possibility is that the criterion used in these predictive validity studies is contaminated. This might happen because data gathered in the assessment center while it was being validated were considered in making the very promotional decisions that were to be used as the criterion measure (Klimoski & Brickner, 1987). Employers must not do this. It can inflate the true association between the assessment center and promotions. Remember, as I discussed previously, a validation study cannot accurately assess whether or not an instrument is a valid predictor if the instrument's scores are used to make personnel decisions while the validation study is ongoing.

## Construct Validity Studies

We can conclude from the criterion-related validity evidence that, in general, assessment centers are valid for predicting criterion measures. Still, many researchers have questions about what assessment centers actually measure that validly predicts a criterion, especially given the difference in the assessment center's ability to predict candidate potential rather than performance.

Construct validation is a way to study the dimensions assessed and find out why assessment centers are valid. Recall, from the discussion in Chapter 7, that both convergent and discriminant validity are required in order for a measure to have construct validity. Convergent validity of assessment center dimensions is shown when different measures of the same dimension are highly correlated. Discriminant validity is shown when the measures of one dimension are not highly correlated with the measures of other dimensions. For instance, suppose oral communication is included among the dimensions a center is meant to assess. In order for this dimension to have convergent validity, the measures of oral communication taken in different exercises need to be highly correlated. In addition, for the dimension to have discriminant validity, the measures of oral communication should *not* be strongly correlated with measures of other dimensions in the exercises, such as planning or leadership.

**Dimension Validity Versus the Exercise Effect**   During the 1970s and 1980s, many studies were conducted that attempted to determine the construct validity of assessment centers (e.g., Sackett & Dreher, 1982; Silverman, Dalessio, Woods, & Johnson, 1986; Turnage & Muchinsky, 1982). None of

TABLE

**12.3**  RESULTS OF FACTOR ANALYSIS SHOWING THE EXERCISE EFFECT

| Dimensions | Exercises | Factors I | II | III |
|---|---|---|---|---|
| Problem analysis | Staffer role-play | | | .79 |
| Problem solution | Staffer role-play | | | .80 |
| Leadership | Staffer role-play | | | .85 |
| People sensitivity | Staffer role-play | | | .48 |
| Sense of urgency | Staffer role-play | | | .77 |
| Communication | Staffer role-play | | | .67 |
| Problem analysis | Customer role-play | | .79 | |
| Problem solution | Customer role-play | | .84 | |
| Leadership | Customer role-play | | .86 | |
| People sensitivity | Customer role-play | | .64 | |
| Sense of urgency | Customer role-play | | .82 | |
| Communication | Customer role-play | | .78 | |
| Problem analysis | In-basket | .85 | | |
| Problem solution | In-basket | .91 | | |
| Leadership | In-basket | .86 | | |
| People sensitivity | In-basket | .61 | | |
| Sense of urgency | In-basket | .83 | | |
| Communication | In-basket | .83 | | |

*Notes:* (1) Rotated factor loading matrix of assessment ratings. Ratings made at the end of each exercise, as per the within-exercise method of instructing assessors. (2) Only factor loadings greater than or equal to .35 are presented.

From "Influence of Assessment Center Methods on Assessors' Ratings," by W. H. Silverman, A. Dalessio, S. B. Woods, and R. L. Johnson, Jr., 1986, *Personnel Psychology, 39*(3), table 3, p. 574. Copyright 1986 by Personnel Psychology, Inc., Bowling Green, Ohio. Reprinted by permission.

these studies, nor others conducted during or after this time, were able to establish that assessment center dimensions have construct validity. Although they usually found evidence of convergent validity, researchers were unable to establish that the dimensions had discriminant validity. In fact, what they found was contrary to what they expected. Different dimensions within a single exercise actually were correlated more strongly than the same dimensions in different exercises. In other words, the "constructs" being measured in assessment centers were not the specified dimensions but, rather, appeared to be the exercises. This result has been observed in study after study, and it has come to be known as the "exercise effect." Although this effect can be identified by using various statistical techniques, factor analysis is particularly capable of illustrating the exercise effect. See Table 12.3 for an example.

**Explanation: Evaluation Method**    Researchers have offered a number of possible explanations for the persistent exercise effect and to account for the difficulty in showing construct validity. Sackett and Dreher (1982) suggested that the problem occurs because of variations in the way candidate performance is evaluated in assessment centers. One method of evaluation, called the AT&T model,[5] requires that all exercises be completed and, before candidates are evaluated, assessors meet and discuss their observations. Only then do the assessors individually rate candidates, and they rate them on all dimensions. A second method, which is more commonly used, requires assessors to evaluate a candidate on all dimensions immediately after each exercise is completed. These two methods of evaluation might differentially influence assessors' cognitive organization and processing of information and, in turn, affect the ratings they give candidates. That is, using the AT&T method, assessors might engage in cognitively chunking or summarizing their observations of a candidate over *all* exercises as they rate each dimension. However, the typical method essentially instructs the assessors to focus on how well a candidate performed in the single exercise and to rate dimensions on this basis.

Other researchers agreed that such differences could be a source of the difficulty. Silverman and his associates (1986) conducted an experimental study, using two assessor groups instructed differently, in order to evaluate the effects of varying how and when performance dimensions were rated. One group of assessors, who received across-exercise instructions, used the AT&T method of evaluation. They observed all exercises and then shared their observations before they rated candidates on all dimensions across exercises. The other group of assessors received within-exercise instructions. They used the typical method of evaluation and rated candidates on all dimensions immediately after each exercise. The researchers hypothesized that this manipulation would influence how assessors processed assessment center information and that the manner of information processing would affect construct validity. They thought the exercise effect occurred whenever assessors operate under within-exercise evaluation instructions, as most assessment centers provide. Thus, they expected to find better evidence of validity when assessors were given across-exercise instructions.

Results of this study showed that construct validity could be improved somewhat by making such procedural changes. Analysis of the ratings confirmed that the dimensions had convergent validity and, as expected, it was stronger in the ratings given by the group who followed across-exercise instructions. The researchers applied multiple methods of analysis in an effort to determine whether there was any evidence of discriminant validity. In one

---

[5]This is called the AT&T model because it was the method used in the early assessment center studies conducted at American Telephone & Telegraph (cf. Bray & Campbell, 1968).

statistical analysis, there was an indication of discriminant validity. Average dimension correlations were somewhat higher than average exercise correlations, especially in the group using across-exercise instructions. In addition, a factor analysis revealed that this group's ratings were more complex than the ratings given by the group receiving within-exercise instructions. Some dimensions loaded on more than one factor, which would be expected if dimensions—rather than exercises—were being rated. The researchers interpreted this as meaning that the assessors who were instructed to rate dimensions across exercises had found it necessary to think broadly in terms of behavioral similarities. In contrast, the factor structure in the ratings given by the within-exercise group was different. The factor analysis results for this group are those shown in Table 12.3. As you can see, the ratings fell into three very clear factors that corresponded exactly to the three exercises, demonstrating the exercise effect. As Silverman et al. (1986) had proposed, the effect was shown most clearly by the group of assessors who rated the dimensions immediately after each exercise.

**Explanation: Rating Error**    Another explanation for the usual failure to show construct validity considers the difficulty that assessors might have in rating performance on complex tasks. It is possible that the exercise effect is due partly to rater errors, especially to one known as *halo* error.[6] Although halo error usually is considered a problem of employee performance appraisal, it can occur whenever an evaluator rates an individual's traits or behavior for other purposes. Apparently, the error occurs when an evaluator lacks information on a behavioral dimension and, in the absence of the specific information, uses his or her general impression of the individual to rate the dimension. Thus, a person is likely to be rated high (or low) on a performance dimension depending on how well, overall, he or she has performed. The key condition is that the rater has limited information on the dimension. Researchers have pointed out that assessment center exercises vary as to the opportunities they provide for participants to demonstrate performance dimensions (Sackett & Dreher, 1982). In certain exercises, a candidate may have little or no chance to do anything that would provide information to assessors on a particular dimension. For this reason, it seems likely that assessment center evaluations do contain halo error. Assessors probably use their general impression or overall assessment of a candidate's performance in an exercise to rate the dimensions on which they have limited information. If the different ratings within an exercise are based on the assessor's impression of overall performance, then we could expect that they would be correlated. Thus, the exercise effect could result from halo error in the ratings.

---

[6]I discuss halo and other performance rating errors in more detail in Chapter 14.

**Explanation: Assessor Workload**    The difficulty of rating performance dimensions might be due to the heavy workload of information processing that is required of assessors. Consider the cognitive demands on someone who must observe two or three candidates in three to six exercises and rate each candidate's performance on each exercise along multiple dimensions. Consider, also, that these dimensions may be neither independent of one another nor clearly defined in operational terms, which increase the demands for decision making. That is, an assessor must decide if, and to what extent, an exhibited behavior demonstrates a dimension. Reilly, Henry, and Smither (1990) were able to devise a procedure for lightening the assessor's heavy cognitive workload, which also improved the construct validity of the assessment center ratings. They developed a behavioral checklist containing examples of dimension-relevant behavior that assessors used at the end of an exercise to record their observations. Compared to the ordinary ratings given by the assessors, the checklist scores showed greater construct validity. Correlation of checklist scores on the same dimension across exercises (convergent validity) increased from .24 to .44, and correlation within an exercise (discriminant validity) *decreased* appropriately from .47 to .38. Therefore, the checklist yielded more construct-valid evaluations than did the assessors' ratings.

**Explanation: A True Exercise Effect**    A final explanation for the difficulty in showing construct validity considers the nature of the exercises themselves. Schneider and Schmitt (1992) questioned whether exercise design features might be responsible for the continued showing of the exercise effect. They reasoned that the *form* of an exercise can change the situation that participants encounter and can influence the kinds of behavior they are able to demonstrate. For example, a group discussion would not present the same opportunities for demonstrating oral communication ability that making a speech would. In addition, candidates are likely to vary individually in their abilities to communicate in these different situations. Such exercise-form characteristics, if they are unique to an exercise, could be expected to increase the correlation of different dimensions within the exercise and to produce an exercise effect. In their study, Schneider and Schmitt (1992) experimentally manipulated the form and contents of assessment center exercises in order to evaluate the effects on ratings. Two group discussion and two role-play activities, involving either cooperative or competitive interactions, were designed. Three behavioral dimensions—problem solving, interpersonal skill, and initiative—were assessed in each exercise. By controlling exercise design, the researchers expected that assessors would have more opportunity to observe dimension-relevant behaviors, and that their ratings would show discriminant validity. However, the data analysis exposed a dominant exercise effect. There were high correlations among the different dimensions within an exercise and no significant evidence of discriminant validity.

Considering the difficulty researchers have had in dispelling the exercise effect as an error, we might ask whether there is a true exercise effect. Neidig and Neidig (1984) suggested that there is. They proposed that job candidates actually perform dimensions differently in various exercises and that this occurs because people are more adept in certain activities than they are in others. Schneider and Schmitt (1992) also discussed this as a possible explanation for the exercise-form effect they found. They thought certain assessees might have been better able to perform in one-on-one role-play situations than in the group discussions.

If a true exercise effect does account for some of the variation in participant behavior, then studies that address the participant's experience might be helpful. Some research has suggested that giving in-depth instruction to participants might increase construct validity. In one study, researchers attempted to make exercise dimensions highly transparent to participants (Kleinmann, Kuptsch, & Köller, 1996). As a result, both convergent and discriminant validity were improved. However, there also was an exercise effect. The researchers discussed this exercise effect as possibly having occurred because the amount of dimension-relevant behavior varies among exercises as a product of exercise content. That is, whereas some exercises elicit behavior information on multiple dimensions, others may yield information essentially on one dimension only.

## Conclusions

Criterion-related validity studies have shown that assessment centers vary in their ability to predict job success. However, across these studies, the average level of criterion-related validity is substantial and indicates that assessment centers can be valid. Other studies, meaning to identify the constructs being measured in the dimension ratings, have not been so successful. Construct validity usually is not demonstrated. Even the best-controlled studies generally fail to show discriminant validity. In the construct validity research, it appears that if there is anything consistent about the ratings collected, it is that they reflect the exercises themselves, rather than the dimensions that are supposedly being measured. Study after study has reported a strong exercise effect. So, what is the meaning of this? Possibly, the exercise effect is an unusually difficult error to control. Many researchers have considered it to be an error, because it seems to interfere with showing discriminant validity. Some found that experimental interventions designed to "correct" the error did improve the evidence of discriminant validity, although an exercise effect usually remained.

I conclude, as others have, that the effort to determine what assessment centers measure needs to be reconceptualized. I am convinced by all of the four explanations discussed above. I think they each have merit in finding the answer to the question of what assessment centers measure. Whereas any one of them alone might not be able to explain the difficulty in showing construct validity, each can contribute a piece of the puzzle. For example, when assessors are instructed to evaluate candidates after each exercise, this seems to be an invitation for them to evaluate the candidates on the exercise, rather than on the dimensions. In the process, the stage is set for halo error to occur. Further, we should keep in mind that part of the difficulty in showing discriminant validity might be because the supposedly "different" dimensions are not all that different. If they are similar in meaning, then a positive correlation between them would not be a sign of error. Rather, it would be a reflection of a real association. (In performance appraisal ratings, this is known as *true* halo.[7]) We should also recognize that assessors are asked to do difficult work. Observing and rating performance are not easy tasks. Some of the difficulty in establishing construct validity might be related to the assessors' heavy information-processing workload. Interventions that help assessors organize their observations might make it easier for them to produce reliable dimension ratings. Finally, because the exercise effect has been found repeatedly, even in studies designed to control extraneous variables, perhaps it is not entirely due to error. A true exercise effect might occur because of several reasons. One possibility is that the defined dimensions are not equally reflected in the different exercises. Perhaps, they are no more so in assessment centers than they are in interviews, tests, and other selection methods. With such a complex method as the assessment center is, we might do well to consider all of these possibilities.

## SUMMING UP

Job simulations are the most realistic of all selection methods, and they can have high levels of measurement quality. In this chapter, the purpose has been to examine the various ways of simulating a job and using the simulation for selection purposes. We can sum up the discussion with the following points:

- Because they use samples of job content and performance dimensions, simulation methods must be grounded in job analysis.
- In situational judgment tests, items refer to hypothetical work situations.
- A work sample performance test, to the extent that it is a miniature replica of the job, is a content-valid measure.
- There is evidence that situational judgment tests and work sample tests have criterion-related validity.

---

[7]The concept of true halo is discussed in Chapter 14.

- An assessment center is a complex job simulation, which includes tests, interviews, and exercises conducted in a simulated work environment.
- Managerial assessment centers evaluate candidates on dimensions such as decision making, planning, and oral communication.
- Dyadic and group exercises are useful if a job involves interpersonal behavior.
- The in-basket, leaderless group discussion, and role-play activity are commonly used exercises.
- On average, criterion-related validity of assessment centers is strong.
- Construct validity of assessment center dimensions has not been established. Instead, an exercise effect usually appears.

## InfoTrac College Edition

Want to learn more about the issues discussed here? Use your subscription to InfoTrac College Edition to access an online library of research journals and other periodicals. Go to http://www.infotrac-college.com/wadsworth and enter a search term. Any of the following terms can be used in a keyword search to find articles about some topics reviewed in this chapter. (Note: Adding an asterisk at the end of a word allows a search for other forms of the word, such as the plural of a singular term.)

Assessment center*              Work sample test*
Person–job fit                  Design and (job or organizational)

# THE NATURE OF PERFORMANCE

What is the real measure of a successful employee—that is, one whom the employer should make an effort to keep or one who deserves a raise? Is this person one who knows the job and how to do it? Is he or she one who works hard on doing it right, putting in overtime if necessary? Is this the person who goes beyond the minimum requirements of the job, helps coworkers, and makes an extra effort to help customers? Which quality might be most important? These are practical questions, and people in organizations have various ways of defining what a successful employee is and does. For example, a business manager recently discussed an employee's work performance. The employee had been working long and hard –13 hours a day for the past year— and he was known throughout the company as one whose work was flawless. Apparently, he believed that long hours and high-quality work were the way to get a pay raise, and he expected a big one. In the manager's view, however, a pay raise was not warranted because the employee's job performance had not proportionately increased the productivity of the company. The extra effort the employee had made simply had not been worth it. The employee had not adequately distinguished between what is important to do well and what is not. For example, there is no point in spending hours polishing something that does not matter to anyone. In the manager's opinion, certain tasks do need to have an individual's very best effort. However, not all things at work need to be treated as if they were highly important because, in fact, they are not. Sometimes, the manager pointed out, it is better to do a task quickly, and less than perfectly, and move on to more important activities (McCormack, 1999).

In Chapters 8 through 12, I discussed the use of performance criteria in the course of developing and validating measures used for selection purposes. In those chapters, the focus was directly on selection. In this and the next two chapters, the focus is on employee performance and the methods of evaluating performance. In the present chapter, I discuss the nature of performance and its relationship to selection decision making. Job performance is an important criterion that selection methods are meant to predict. In the first section of this

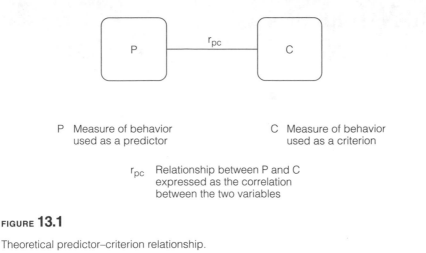

FIGURE **13.1**

Theoretical predictor–criterion relationship.

chapter, I describe the predictor–criterion relationship and discuss the performance criterion as an integral part of the validation process. In the second section, I discuss various dimensions of performance and describe theoretical models relating to both job-specific and general work performance.

## PREDICTORS AND CRITERIA

The emphasis of this text is on selection and on methods that employers can use to predict employee behavior. Throughout, an effective selection method has been considered to be one that can assess whether an applicant would be a valuable employee. In previous chapters, I discussed the development, evaluation, and use of measures that aid an employer in making the best selection decisions. Evaluation of a selection measure was couched in terms of the measure's validity for predicting one or more criterion measures of employee effectiveness. Generally, discussions of selection measures follow the classical measurement model, which relates one predictor to one criterion. According to this model, the ability of a test or other selection measure to predict a performance criterion measure can be shown by the extent to which the two measures are correlated. Figure 13.1 is a simple depiction of the theoretical relationship between a predictor measure and a criterion measure.

Most of the research literature on the predictor–criterion relationship has focused on predictors. Relatively speaking, criteria have been ignored, especially in the past. Although researchers recognized the need for understanding performance criteria, most were interested only in developing tests and other selection measures. For example, in 1946, Jenkins reviewed the research and practice that had taken place during the 1920s and 1930s. He reported that much work had been done on selection measurement. However, almost no attention had been given to the performance criteria that the selection measures were supposed to predict. Field researchers apparently made little effort to purposely choose criteria or to develop criterion measures. Instead, the criteria used in studies were whatever was found just "lying around." One possible reason for the widespread lack of interest was that performance criteria were viewed as being important primarily to those doing scientific studies in the research lab, whereas selection specialists working in organizations had to find ways to make the personnel decisions that were needed almost daily.

There still is relatively less attention given to performance criteria than to selection measures. However, there is more interest now than there was in the past. What is responsible for the change? You might wonder whether the increased interest in performance has come from the field setting. Employers often have strong opinions about what effective performance is. As the example at the start of the chapter suggests, many believe that an organization's success is an important element of individual employee performance and that it should be considered in HR decision making. Organizations need to accomplish their missions, and their employees, to a great extent, do make this possible. Therefore, employers must be able to recognize the kinds of employee behavior that might help an organization succeed. They especially need effective tools for evaluating performance—for example, in order to identify successful employees and to make reasoned decisions about promotions and raises. Despite these needs, however, the increased interest in performance seems not to have come from the business setting. Rather, the improvement appears to have resulted from the work of researchers studying the construct validity of selection measures. Currently, researchers are interested in discovering what constructs are actually being measured by tests and other such instruments. As a result, there is greater recognition that both predictors and criteria draw from the same basic domains of performance behavior. The increased understanding of performance has come, after all, from those working on selection problems in the research lab.

## Validation of Predictors and Criteria

Predictors and criteria are inextricably linked. Let me briefly review some issues relating to validity that were discussed previously, in order to demonstrate what I mean. First, the terms "predictor" and "criterion" refer to roles played by behavioral variables in selection research, rather than to the variables themselves. The variables playing the predictor and criterion roles in one validation study do not necessarily play the same roles in another study. Second, although many of the selection measures discussed in previous chapters—tests, biodata, and interview assessments, for example—usually perform as predictor measures, not all such measures have this single purpose. Depending on how it is used, a test might play the role of predictor in a criterion-related validity study or the role of criterion in a construct validity study. Third, some measures function only as criterion measures, such as the objective procedures for assessing absenteeism and turnover. However, others can play either role. Work samples, which usually fill the role of predictor, can be used as a criterion measure in the validation of another instrument. Supervisors' ratings of performance frequently are used as the criterion measure in a test validation study and as the predictor measure in selection decisions involving promotions. Finally, a criterion measure does not always refer directly to performance of a job's tasks. Data on promotions, salary history, absenteeism, and turnover—in addition to measures of performance—frequently are used in criterion-related studies to assess the predictive validity of a selection instrument. Thus, it is the use of a measure—not specifically the measure's own inherent qualities—that defines it as a predictor or a criterion.

**The Criterion Problem**   A validity study may be conducted with criterion-related, content, or construct validation strategies. For any of these validation strategies to be successful, it is critically important that a clear connection be established between the predictor measure and the performance criterion. Sometimes, in criterion-related validity studies, establishing this connection is difficult. The reason for the difficulty is not always obvious. Did the validity study fail because the predictor measure was not valid? Or did it fail because the criterion measure was not an adequate representation of the performance construct? It might be either. Sometimes, a validation study fails because the criterion measure itself has not been established as being a valid indicator of job performance. The difficulty occurs frequently and is called the *criterion problem*. It is particularly difficult to resolve when the criterion measure used in a study is not an adequate representation of job performance, but when no better criterion measure is available.

So, what is the big deal? Why not first validate the measure or use something else to assess the performance criterion? Partly, the difficulty is due to the lingering tendency to view criteria as being whatever is at hand. That is, nothing more valid may appear to be "lying around" at the workplace. However, it is possible to validate the measure to be used as a criterion. Because validity refers to the role a measure plays, we would approach such a validation effort by hypothesizing that the "criterion" measure actually does predict the performance criterion, and proceed by testing this hypothesis. Conceivably, such a study could be done using the criterion-related validation strategy. Researchers studying performance appraisal methods have used this strategy to evaluate the validity of supervisors' ratings. However, they have found that empirical, criterion-related validation of a performance rating measure is difficult to accomplish. Mainly, the problem is one of finding another criterion measure with which to correlate supervisors' ratings in such a study. Usually, researchers wish for a "true score" of performance to use in the correlational study. Hypothetically, true scores of performance exist. However, they are difficult to locate in reality. Even the so-called objective measures of performance, such as production and personnel data, may not be what is desired in a true score. Production measures (i.e., counts of whatever is produced) can be deficient by not including important behaviors other than production outcomes. Personnel data relating to performance, such as promotions and salary increases, are not fully objective because such decisions are based on someone having previously made a judgment or rating of employee behavior. You can see that the problem becomes one of circular reasoning, when criterion-related validity is sought.

Criterion-related validation is not the only validation strategy available, of course. A thorough job analysis, especially one conducted with the critical incidents technique, can provide the necessary data for developing and content-validating an instrument to be used as a performance criterion measure. This, as you will see in Chapter 14, has been the most effective strategy for handling the problems of inaccuracy and irrelevance that often are found in supervisors' ratings of employee performance. In addition, content validation has the potential of resolving the "criterion problem."

## Relationships Between Constructs and Measures

Using the reasoning of construct validation, Binning and Barrett (1989) developed a theoretical framework for identifying the relationships between the multiple hypothetical constructs and measures that make up the selection process. Their discussion begins with some important definitions. The term "construct" is a label for a cluster of behaviors that covary. That is, when one behavior changes, the others change also. A construct is hypothetical. It functions as a hypothesis about the behaviors that might be expected to relate in such-and-such a way. The construct validation process involves developing measures that can be hypothesized to show certain relationships to a construct and to each other. Binning and Barrett (1989) used Nunnally's (1978) reasoning to describe four inferences, referring to relationships or links between constructs and measures. These four inferences constitute the basic construct validation process. They are defined in the following statements:

1. Measures X and Y are related in a certain way (measure–measure link).
2. X is a measure of construct A (construct–measure link).
3. Construct A and construct B are causally related in a certain way (construct–construct link).
4. Y is a measure of construct B (construct–measure link).

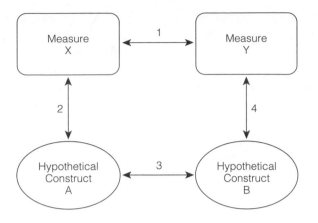

Note: The double-headed arrows indicate that the relationship between the two connected elements is bi-directional.

FIGURE **13.2**

Inferential links between measures and constructs in the construct validation process.

Adapted from "Validity of Personnel Decisions: A Conceptual Analysis of the Inferential and Evidential Bases," by J. F. Binning and G. V. Barrett, 1989, *Journal of Applied Psychology, 74*, p. 479. Copyright 1989 by American Psychological Association, Washington, DC. Adapted by permission.

The inferences are presented graphically in Figure 13.2. In the complete validation process, each of the inferential links connecting elements of the framework needs to be justified or provided with evidence that indicates the extent to which the relationship is valid. Direct, empirical evidence can be provided, through criterion-related validity studies, only for the link described in inference 1. Because inferences 2, 3, and 4 each involve a hypothetical construct (A or B), only indirect, rational evidence can be obtained for these inferences. This evidence is obtained through content validation studies using job analytic data.

Undoubtedly, you will recognize the terms and at least some of the above four inferences from previous discussion of construct validity studies of selection measures. Generally, selection specialists have been most concerned with construct-validating the link between a predictor measure and its underlying psychological construct (inferences 2 and 4). For example, an employer might have developed a new instrument, X, and now needs to confirm that it is a valid measure of a certain psychological construct, A. The basic logic of this construct validation process is useful for establishing the validity of any of the links depicted. For example, we might want to examine the relationship between two constructs (inference 3), such as intelligence and personality. Suppose we have two tests: a general mental ability test and a personality test.

Suppose, also, that existing evidence allows us to accept each of these tests as a valid measure of its individual construct—intelligence or personality. We now can conduct a correlational study, using scores from each of the tests, to determine the extent that the tests are related. Then, on the basis of the resulting correlation coefficient, *plus* the preexisting evidence of the tests' own construct validity, we can conclude that the two underlying constructs themselves are related (inference 3). In other words, we use existing evidence of two predictor measures' construct validity (links 2 and 4), along with new evidence of the relationship between the two measures (link 1), to *infer* the hypothesized relationship between the two constructs (link 3). Obviously, this validation process involves multiple studies; it cannot be done with one study. The researcher may use either empirical or rational evidence to justify the inference in question. In any single study, two of the inferential links are assumed (based on existing evidence or reasoning). New evidence is gathered on another link, and the researcher uses it to infer the validity of the remaining link (Binning & Barrett, 1989).

**The Performance Domain as a Construct**    Is it reasonable to consider job performance as a construct? If so, can we validate a performance measure using the kind of reasoning and evidence gathered in validating predictor measures of constructs? The answer to both questions is yes. Binning and Barrett (1989) pointed out that the performance domain fits the definition of a construct equally well as psychological constructs underlying predictors. It is an intact cluster of related, covarying behaviors. Like a psychological construct, job performance represents a behavioral domain. The differences between the two types of constructs stem mainly from the fact that the behavioral clusters are identified in different ways. Specifically, psychological constructs have been defined by measurement specialists, who use formal methods of correlation and experimentation and describe constructs in terms of personal attributes. Performance domains are defined by organizational designers, who use informal and rational methods to translate organizational goals into employee behavior and goal-related outcomes. This method defines the performance domain at a different, more concrete level of abstraction than the psychological construct. As a result, it presents the possibility that the performance construct is subsumed into the more basic psychological construct.

**Predictors Related to the Performance Construct**    Binning and Barrett (1989) use the inferential links defined in the construct validation process to describe the relationship between the job performance construct and measures used as predictors. Figure 13.3 shows their theoretical framework, which identifies the relevant inferences that need to be confirmed as valid. Observe that inferences 5, 6, 7, and 8 are comparable to inferences 1, 2, 3, and 4 listed above and shown in Figure 13.2.[1] Other elements and inferential links are new. Notice that job performance is identified in the framework as a construct and that it is made up of two "internal" constructs: performance behavior and outcomes. The performance construct is linked in four ways to other elements of the structure. Inferential link 10 connects the construct to the actual job. Link 8 expresses the extent to which a performance criterion measure is representative of the performance construct. Link 7 indicates the relationship of the performance construct to the psychological construct. Notice also that inference 9 has been *added* to the basic construct validation process. This is a unique construct–measure link that has particular meaning for employee selection. This link is inferred to exist between the predictor measure being used and the performance construct. Practically speaking, it is the most important inference in workplace studies of validity. Selection specialists are primarily interested in getting evidence for inference 9. That is, they want to justify the conclusion that a given selection measure can predict the performance domain.

Binning and Barrett (1989) described three ways to justify concluding that inference 9 is valid. First, we can attempt to support a *direct* link between the predictor measure and the performance construct. Using a content validation procedure, it may be possible to demonstrate that the predictor is *interchangeable* with the performance construct. This strategy yields rational evidence, based on job analytic data, which shows that the predictor measure is a representative sample of performance behavior required on the job. With such evidence, inference 9 is justified, and scores on the predictor measure can be accepted as valid for predicting performance.

A second approach provides an *indirect* justification of inference 9. Using the reasoning and methods of construct validation, it may be possible to show that the predictor measure is linked to the psychological construct (inference 6 in Figure 13.3) and, in turn, that the psychological construct is linked to the performance construct (inference 7). Thus, the predictor measure would be indirectly linked to the performance construct. To show this, we would begin by establishing that the predictor instrument is a measure of a certain psychological construct. This is done with the usual procedures for determining convergent and discriminant validity of a selection instrument, as I discussed in previous chapters. Next, the psychological construct underlying the predictor measure would need to be linked to the performance construct. To demonstrate that the two constructs are linked, we would use a job analysis method that can identify the necessary KSAs for a job. This indirect justification of inference 9 allows the predictor measure to be accepted as valid for predicting performance.

The third approach provides a different, indirect justification for inference 9. The *criterion* measure is considered linked to the performance construct (in-

---

[1]Inferences 1 and 5 are measure–measure links; 2 and 4 are the same construct–measure links as 6 and 8; and inferences 3 and 7 are both construct–construct links.

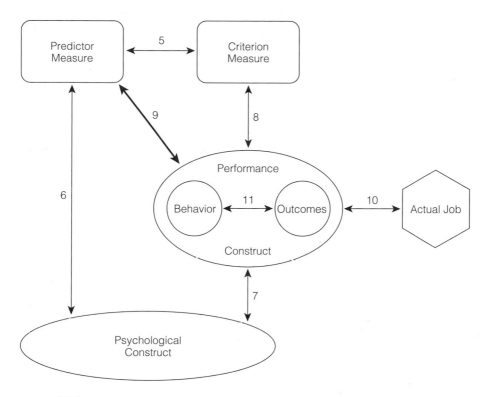

FIGURE **13.3**

A conceptual framework showing measures, constructs, and inferential links.

Adapted from "Validity of Personnel Decisions: A Conceptual Analysis of the Inferential and Evidential Bases," by J. F. Binning and G. V. Barrett, 1989, *Journal of Applied Psychology, 74*, p. 485. Copyright 1989 by American Psychological Association, Washington, DC. Adapted by permission.

ference 8), with the predictor measure being linked to the criterion measure (inference 5). Evidence supporting these inferences would allow us to conclude that the predictor measure also is indirectly linked to the performance construct. To gain supporting evidence, we would first establish that the criterion measure is a valid assessment of the performance construct. For this, the criterion measure must be validated. As detailed in the section below, validation of the criterion may involve correlational studies or job analyses. To establish that the predictor measure can validly predict the criterion measure, we would conduct an empirical validity study, correlating scores on the predictor and criterion measures. Evidence supporting the two inferences provides the justification for inference 9. However, it is absolutely necessary that the relationship between the criterion measure and the performance construct be established. Otherwise, we cannot infer that a predictor measure, which can predict the criterion measure, also is valid for predicting the performance construct.

**Validating the Performance Criterion**   The same basic procedures are used to validate criterion measures and to obtain evidence for the inferential links involving a criterion measure and the performance construct, as shown in Figure 13.3 (Binning & Barrett, 1989). First, we might seek empirical evidence for a *direct* link between the performance criterion measure and the performance construct (inference 8). An empirical, criterion-related validity study might be done to show this direct link, if "true scores" of performance are available. Most likely, no such scores are available, however, and we will need another approach.

The second method of validating the criterion measure presumes both that the criterion measure is linked to the performance construct (inference 8) and that the performance construct is linked to the actual job (inference 10). Content validation based on job analysis is used to support both inferences. However, the job analysis must be well-designed and carefully conducted. It must show that the criterion measure adequately represents the important behaviors and outcomes that define the performance construct. It also must demonstrate that the performance construct is representative of the job itself. This means that the job analysis must identify actual job demands and demonstrate that these demands are expressed in the behaviors constituting the performance construct. The critical incidents method of job analysis is an effective way to gather this type of information. As you recall from previous discussion, the critical incidents method produces detailed information on what employees actually do on the job that has important outcomes. In Chapter 14, you will see that this method of job analysis is used to develop some of the most effective rating scales for performance appraisal purposes.

## Conclusions

The performance criterion is an integral part of developing and validating selection measures. To devise effective measures, one must have a good reason to assume that the performance criterion represents the actual job that employees must perform and that this meaning is carried forward into the criterion measure. Although it is possible to empirically validate a performance criterion measure, generally this is difficult because no other measures are available for the required correlational study. More likely, a content validation study, using job analysis, will be conducted to obtain evidence for inferring validity.

The quality of the job analysis is the key point in substantiating the links between a performance criterion measure and the actual job. Used for this purpose, job analysis yields a basis for inferring validity. Yet, job analysis is itself an inferential process, specifically in identifying KSAs required for a job. If you refer back to Chapter 3, you will see that job analysis methods vary in terms of how KSAs are determined. For example, in the task inventory analysis, job analysts first identify clusters of related tasks in the job, and the needed KSAs are inferred from these task clusters. In the job element analysis, the basic data are KSA elements, which SME-groups of job incumbents and/or supervisors have inferred to be required on the job.

In job analysis, even at its best, the inferential link between the job and KSAs represents a weak point. For job analyses that are not well done, the weakness can be devastating. Binning and Barrett (1989) discussed the difficulties inherent in relying on the typical job analysis done in many organizations. Although job analysis does have the capacity to justify the multiple inferences involved in validating criteria, the justification is weak if it is based on nothing more than someone's opinion that actual job demands have been identified (inference 10), behavior–outcome links have been established (inference 11), all necessary KSAs have been identified (inference 7). and all critical job behaviors are represented in the criterion measure (inference 8). These inferences are too important to be based on opinion. At least, there must be documentation in the job analysis on how the judgments were made.

# PERFORMANCE BEHAVIOR

As I have described performance so far, it appears to be an abstract behavioral construct that is enmeshed in a complex theoretical structure of relationships and roles. Let us now begin to address the issue in more concrete terms. What is job performance? We can answer this question in different ways. One way is to consider whether performance is a unity or a multiplicity. Some researchers and practitioners treat performance as if it were a unit or a single thing and as if a single measure could assess it. For example, a researcher may be interested in developing an instrument to predict performance as a whole. Similarly, an employer may view employee performance simply as being an effect on company profits. The more widely accepted view among I/O psychologists is that performance is multifaceted in form and involves multiple behaviors. This generally means recognizing the need for multiple measures. However, for some purposes, the measures may best be combined into a single composite measure. For example, when an employer needs to evaluate performance for making personnel decisions, such as promotion or termination, then he or she can use a composite measure to assess the overall value of the employee's performance. For other purposes, such as assessing predictor–criterion links in validation studies, independent measures of the multiple aspects of performance are more useful (Borman, 1991).

Another way to answer the question is to consider what makes up the performance construct. It is possible to describe performance in terms of a hierarchy of levels. At a high point in the hierarchy, employee performance might be described as the extent to which organizational goals are met. However, broad organizational goals are influenced by a variety of factors, not simply an employee's behavior. Therefore, at lower levels in the hierarchy, these goals must be translated into individual performance behaviors, which can be analyzed further in even more specific terms. At the level of the person, performance is behavior. It can be openly observable behavior, such as physical actions, and it can be internal or cognitive processes, such as problem solving (Campbell, 1990a).

In a related fashion, performance behaviors can be described in terms of their stability over time. Ghiselli (1956) proposed that job performance changes systematically as an employee learns and becomes adept on a job and that this enters into the definition of performance requirements. For example, for a new salesperson, the most important performance may be to establish contacts. For a seasoned sales employee, it may be better to work on developing effective client relationships (Bass, 1962; Ghiselli & Haire, 1960). The question, of course, is whether such variations are important enough to change the performance requirements of a job. In an attempt to answer this question, Barrett, Caldwell, and Alexander (1985) reviewed data from previous studies on the hypothesized dynamic nature of performance. They concluded that there was little need for concern about such systematic changes, because they did not find strong support for the view that performance requirements fluctuate to any great degree. Still, not all researchers are convinced, and they argue in favor of defining performance dynamically (e.g., Austin, Humphreys, & Hulin, 1989).

# A THEORETICAL MODEL OF PERFORMANCE

Campbell and his associates (Campbell, 1990a; Campbell, Dunnette, Lawler, & Weick, 1970) defined performance in terms of employee behavior. In their view, performance is what people do in the context of their jobs, relative to the organization's goals. Campbell (1990a) also described what performance is *not*. He noted that although performance behavior may need to be inferred from its outcomes, it is not synonymous with the outcomes. Rather, performance is the action itself. In addition, performance is not the same as effectiveness. The latter is an evaluation of the organizational outcomes of performance, and these outcomes are influenced by factors of a larger scale, such as the state of the economy and the extent of consumer product demand. Performance is even less directly related to productivity. Productivity is the relationship between the level of organizational effectiveness and the organization's costs of achieving that level (Mahoney, 1988).

**Determinants of Performance**   Campbell (1990a) distinguished between the determinants and the components of performance. The determinants constitute the underlying psychological construct of the behaviors that make up the performance construct. He proposed that any specific performance component can be considered to be "a function of three, and only three, major determinants—declarative knowledge, procedural knowledge and skill, and motivation" (p. 705).

The three determinants of performance are defined as follows: *Declarative* knowledge is knowledge of information. This concept refers to understanding the requirements of a task, such as knowing task-relevant facts, rules, and goals. It also includes self-understanding. *Procedural* knowledge and skill is a matter of knowing both what to do in order to perform a task and how to go about doing it. As you can see from the definition, this determinant of performance depends on declarative knowledge, and it is gained after declarative knowledge has been attained. It includes a range of skills, from cognitive and perceptual to physical and interpersonal. Individuals are likely to differ on both of these factors. Campbell pointed out that individual differences in work and educational experience and in stable characteristics, such as abilities and personality, will affect levels of declarative knowledge and procedural knowledge and skill. In other words, our backgrounds and personal characteristics determine what we know and can do. *Motivation* is a direct determinant of performance. It is defined as the combined effect of three behavioral "choices," as follows: An individual chooses to make an effort on a task, decides how much effort to make, and chooses to persist on the task. For performance to occur at all, Campbell proposed that motivation would need to be at some level greater than zero. In addition, a performer would need at least a threshold level of procedural knowledge and skill, which depends on the development of some basic declarative knowledge. Poor performance, therefore, might be due to a person not making the necessary effort, or not knowing what to do or how to do it, or both.

The basis for these propositions on how performance is determined was empirical research done by Campbell and his colleagues in a large-scale study of major importance, called *Project A*. The researchers studied various aspects of the performance of soldiers who had been assigned to entry-level jobs in the U.S. Army (cf. Campbell, 1990b). For example, McCloy, Campbell, and Cudeck (1994) evaluated Campbell's (1990a) model of performance determinants, using data on eight jobs studied in the course of conducting Project A, and found that it could be used effectively to explain behavior on these jobs.

**Components of Performance**   Campbell (1990a) was interested in identifying the structure of the performance construct. To do this, he developed a taxonomy of behavioral variables, which he proposed constitute the performance construct. Eight factors were identified to describe the most general dimensions of performance. These are listed in Table 13.1. Although not all of the factors are expected to be relevant to all jobs, Campbell stated that the eight fac-

<table>
TABLE
13.1    COMPONENTS OF WORK PERFORMANCE
</table>

| Factor Label | Relationship to Work |
|---|---|
| Job-specific task proficiency | Major component of any job<br>Job-related behavior<br>Specific to the job |
| Non-job-specific task proficiency | May be component of some jobs<br>Job-related behavior<br>Not specific to a job |
| Written and oral communication | May be component of some jobs<br>Job-related behavior<br>Not specific to a job |
| Demonstrating effort | Major component of any job<br>Work-context-related behavior |
| Maintaining personal discipline | Major component of any job<br>Work-context-related behavior<br>Avoidance of negative behavior |
| Facilitating peer/team performance | May be non-job-specific component of a job<br>Job-related behavior in team positions |
| Supervision | Component of only some jobs<br>Job-related behavior in supervisory jobs |
| Management/administration | Component of only some jobs<br>Job-related behavior in managerial jobs |

Based on information from "Modeling the Performance Prediction Problem in Industrial and Organizational Psychology," by J. P. Campbell, 1990a, in M. D. Dunnette and L. M. Hough (Eds.), *Handbook of Industrial and Organizational Psychology* (2nd ed., vol. 1), pp. 708–710.

tors, or a subset of the eight, could be used to describe performance on any job in any occupation. He considered three of the factors—job-specific task proficiency, demonstrating effort, and maintaining personal discipline—to be major components of every job. Other factors, however, pertain only to certain jobs. The eight factors are as follows:

1. *Job-specific task proficiency.* This factor refers to performance of technical tasks or the basic substance of a job. Examples include sorting mail, doing word processing, conducting a store inventory, drawing architectural plans, running medical laboratory tests, and developing lectures for a college course. (Notice that supervision and other interpersonal tasks are not indicated. These are included in other factors.)
2. *Non-job-specific task proficiency.* This dimension reflects performance behaviors that are not specific to any particular job but, rather, may be required of any employee in an organization. For example, any employee might be expected to help meet the needs of clients, respond appropriately in case of an emergency, or serve on a committee as a representative of a work group.

3. *Written and oral communication.* For many jobs, the basic ability to write and/or to speak in front of an audience is required, regardless of the technical aspects of the job.
4. *Demonstrating effort.* This factor reflects the consistency of an employee's motivation to perform. It indicates the degree to which an employee shows commitment, even when working conditions are adverse or when putting in extra time is necessary.
5. *Maintaining personal discipline.* This element of performance refers to aspects of general work behavior, particularly the avoidance of actions that have negative effects, such as excessive absenteeism or drug use.
6. *Facilitating peer and team performance.* For jobs involving coworking relationships, this factor is important. It refers to being supportive and helpful, showing commitment to one's work group, and helping the group to function well through informal leadership.
7. *Supervision.* This factor includes all aspects of interpersonal behavior that are intended to influence the behavior of subordinates. It is distinct from factor 6 because of the difference between formal supervisory leadership and the informal leadership of peers.
8. *Management/administration.* Included here are the major aspects of managerial work that are independent of supervision, such as planning, identifying organizational goals, and solving problems or dealing with crises.

Campbell's theoretical model of performance provides a valuable framework for understanding the nature of performance. How well the propositions describe reality, of course, depends ultimately on whether research that attempts to test the theory will be able to show support for it. However, as I mentioned above, the model was developed empirically, from the results of the Project A studies conducted by Campbell and his associates (cf. Campbell, 1990b), which had been done in order to improve selection and classification of U.S. Army recruits in entry-level jobs. Among the studies conducted in Project A was research on performance criterion variables. For example, in one such study, Campbell, McHenry, and Wise (1990) collected data from a sample of soldiers working on 19 different entry-level jobs. The researchers hypothesized that two general types of performance would be exhibited in these jobs. One was job-specific, reflecting technical competence. The other was non-job-specific, reflecting performance components that were required in all the jobs. This was the beginning of the working theoretical model. At this point, the researchers viewed performance as multifaceted within these two general categories. The results of the study indicated that five dimensions of behavior could be used to describe performance on these jobs. These dimensions included several that are similar to those which Campbell incorporated into his eight-factor model: technical task proficiency, non-job-specific proficiency, personal discipline, and effort and peer leadership.

## Performance Related to Tasks and Work Context

Task- and job-related behaviors contribute directly to the organization's product or service. Such performance behaviors, and the KSAs required for them, are identified through job analysis, and they are considered in selection procedures. The potential for task- and job-related performance is the reason people are hired. Campbell (1990a) considered valuable job performance to include job-specific and non-job-specific *task* performance, as well as other job-related behaviors that are prescribed by the work roles of certain jobs, such as written and oral communication, supervision, and leadership. Motowidlo and Van Scotter (1994) drew a further distinction between various job-related performance behaviors. They defined one category of task behavior as consisting of production performance activities, in which raw materials are transformed into goods and services and delivered to customers and clients. Another category is made up of task behavior that plays a supportive role. This type of performance supports the production work of an organization and includes such activities as product distribution, organizational planning, and supervision of production and service employees. This treatment of task performance corresponds to the traditional distinction between line and staff employees.[2]

## Contextual Performance Behavior

Another group of work behaviors, including certain of Campbell's (1990a) concepts, such as demonstrating effort and maintaining personal discipline, are not directly task related. They have more to do with the context of work than with the tasks of a job. This category focuses specifically on the types of performance that often are referred to as pro-social organizational behavior and organizational citizenship.

Pro-social organizational behavior is oriented toward helping or promoting the welfare of someone with whom the employee interacts on the job. The employee exhibits such behavior during the course of performing his or her job, although the person's actions may extend beyond the work role. That is, depending on the nature of the job, pro-social organizational behavior may be either role-prescribed or extrarole behavior. Helping coworkers on job-related activities and taking extra steps to help and show courtesy to clients and customers are examples of this type of behavior (Brief & Motowidlo, 1986). Pro-social behavior is thought to have a basis in the individual's affective or emotional state. Researchers have investigated the relationship of pro-social behaviors to other constructs that have emotional components, such as job

---

[2]Line employees are those whose jobs clearly reflect the profit-making purpose of an organization. They perform work resulting in production of goods and services. Staff employees provide various kinds of administrative support for the production line.

satisfaction and feelings of being treated fairly (cf. Organ & Konovsky, 1989). Being in a good mood at work, which is an emotional state, also has been studied. George (1991) found that employees whose mood was positive were significantly more likely to engage in both role-prescribed and extrarole pro-social behavior.

Organizational citizenship is similar to pro-social organizational behavior in some respects. Being a good organizational citizen can mean that one is voluntarily helpful and supportive of one's coworkers. Other behaviors of the good citizen relate to nonsocial aspects of organizational life, such as making suggestions for company improvements and showing a positive attitude (Organ, 1988). Smith, Organ, and Near (1983) found evidence of two general dimensions within the construct of organizational citizenship. One, which they labeled altruism, included spontaneous pro-social organizational behavior. The other dimension was strongly related to the personality factor of conscientiousness. Individuals showing this form of organizational citizenship are likely to comply with the employer's expectations, such as for being on time for work and refraining from using company time for personal needs.

Borman and Motowidlo (1993) summarized organizational citizenship and pro-social behaviors as being forms of contextual performance. For example, they labeled the following as contextual performance behaviors: (1) volunteering to do work that is not part of one's own job, (2) persisting with extra effort on one's own tasks, (3) being cooperative and helpful to others, (4) following rules and using proper procedures even when it is inconvenient, and (5) endorsing and showing support for the organization. Although contextual behavior can contribute to task performance, this is not its main feature, and it is distinguished from task-oriented behavior in several ways. Contextual performance is extrarole behavior, and it has a direct effect on the organization. The social environment of work is improved by contextual performance. In contrast, task performance is role-directed behavior, and its direct effect is on the job. Contextual performance generally is discretionary behavior. It is an expression of initiative, extra effort, or enthusiasm in performing one's tasks, and it usually is not an employee's explicit responsibility. Contextual performance is more general in nature and common to all jobs. Volunteering, exhibiting motivation, helping others, following rules, and supporting the organization are valuable behaviors of employees in any job. These are different from task activities, which vary widely according to the job. Contextual performance also appears to be determined differently than task performance. Contextual performance behavior is believed to spring from a person's motivation and personality (Borman & Motowidlo, 1993), whereas task performance depends most strongly on the level of an individual's knowledge, skills, and abilities for the tasks.

Clearly, extrarole performance behaviors are valuable to the employing organization. However, to the extent that they are discretionary and not part of the minimum requirements for a job, it is inappropriate to demand them as a condition of hiring someone. You might ask, however, whether an employer has any way to encourage employees to behave in this manner. There is some indication that employers actually consider extrarole behavior in employee performance evaluation and in decisions about pay increases. There also appears to be a positive relationship between task performance and contextual performance that may affect the decision to reward employees (Kiker & Motowidlo, 1999).

## A Taxonomy of Generic Work Performance

Hunt (1996) introduced the term "generic work behavior" to describe and summarize a variety of non-job-specific components of performance. He defined the term as referring to both task-role-prescribed and extrarole activities, including organizational citizenship and other forms of pro-social organizational behavior. The concept of generic work behavior encompasses both productive behaviors that contribute to the organization and counterproductive actions that detract from organizational effectiveness. Negative behaviors, such as excessive absenteeism, theft, drug use, and other forms of employee misconduct, are components of generic work behavior. Thus, the construct represents a somewhat larger set of contextual performance behaviors than I have discussed so far.

Hunt (1996) developed the construct and proposed a taxonomy of generic work behaviors, based mainly on the analysis of performance data collected from a large sample of hourly-paid, entry-level employees in retail stores. He reasoned that because hourly, entry-level jobs require relatively little in the way of specific KSAs, performance on these jobs is highly dependent on general rather than job-specific work behavior. Although general work capacities and behaviors can be considered necessary for all employees, regardless of the job, they are especially important for employees performing hourly, entry-level jobs. Therefore, studying the performance of such jobs can expose the nature of generic work performance.

As shown in Figure 13.4, the taxonomy includes eight dimensions of generic work behavior. Hunt organized the eight dimensions under two higher-order categories: organizational citizenship and minimum performance behavior. Organizational citizenship subsumes three factors referring to productive behavior. One, *schedule flexibility*, refers to the individual's willingness to change his or her work schedule to accommodate the employer, to work overtime, and to come in when the employer needs extra help. The other two factors—industriousness and thoroughness—are closely related and appear to reflect a work ethic. *Industriousness* means focusing on the work and making a constant effort to get it done. This is similar to other motivational and personality constructs, such as effort, willingness, enthusiasm, and conscientiousness.

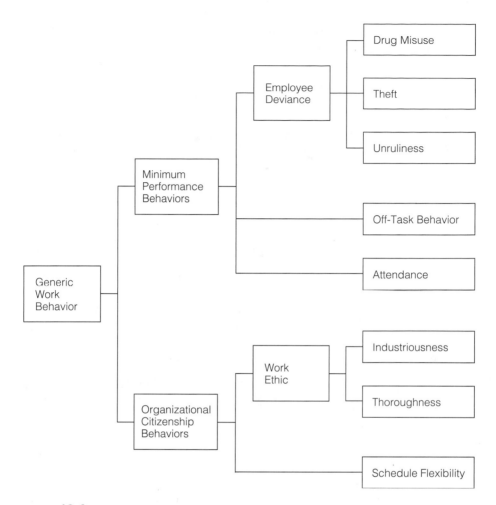

FIGURE **13.4**

Theoretical framework showing relationships between generic work behavior dimensions.

From "Generic Work Behavior: An Investigation into the Dimensions of Entry-Level, Hourly Job Performance," by S. T. Hunt, 1996, *Personnel Psychology, 49*, p. 75. Copyright 1996 by Personnel Psychology, Inc., Bowling Green, Ohio. Reprinted by permission.

*Thoroughness* reflects work quality, as when an employee takes responsibility and does more than the job requires. Minimum performance behavior encompasses five factors, including both productive and counterproductive dimensions. *Attendance,* a productive behavior, means coming to work, being punctual, and staying for the full shift. It contrasts with absenteeism and other forms of counterproductive time use, such as taking long breaks. *Off-task behavior,* which is counterproductive behavior, means using work time to engage in nonwork activities, such as making personal phone calls. Three dimensions of counterproductive behavior were described as forms of employee deviance.

*Unruliness* refers to abrasive and inflammatory actions. *Theft* includes stealing or helping others steal money or merchandise from the organization. *Drug misuse* refers to using alcohol as well as illegal drugs at work.

**Generic Work Behavior and Employee Selection**    Should an employer expect non-job-specific behavior? Should such behaviors be considered in the screening of applicants? As I mentioned above, employees sometimes are recognized for their organizational citizenship and other contextual performance behaviors, and certain personnel decisions, such as raises and promotions, take this performance into account. However, such behaviors are not listed among a job's duties and responsibilities and are not evaluated in the selection process because they are beyond the minimum requirements for the job. In contrast, some non-job-specific behaviors are unspoken requirements for employment that are understood as being necessary for any job. The generic work behaviors listed in Hunt's (1996) category of minimum performance behaviors are examples. Attendance is a widely recognized requirement of employment. Being at one's work station—regardless of where it is located—and staying for the full work period is understood to be necessary for retaining one's job, and employers expect this behavior. In addition, employers can expect employees to refrain from counterproductive behavior, including off-task activities, unruliness, drug or alcohol use, and theft. These behaviors are not specifically job-related and will not appear in a job analysis. However, they are understood to be generally necessary work performance behaviors, and an employer can use information about them to make selection decisions.

## Conclusions

This section has explored the nature of performance. Theorists and researchers have identified various components of work performance. Generally, these fall into one of two categories of behavior needed by employers—task-role-prescribed and extrarole performance. Most importantly, employers must obtain effective task performance from employees. In all jobs, performance consists of proficiency in the core substance or technical tasks of the job for which the employee was hired. Task performance is required behavior, and it forms the bulk of an employer's selection procedures. Other performance behaviors are considered highly valuable because they benefit the organization or improve the context of the job. However, such behaviors usually are not considered to be job requirements.

There appear to be jobs that require performance behaviors that fall between the categories of task-role-prescribed and extrarole performance. Jobs that involve teamwork provide examples of how requirements for interpersonal activities can be blended with required technical tasks and result in jobs in which certain pro-social organizational behaviors become role-prescribed activities. Campbell's (1990a) model of performance included a component—facilitating peer and team performance—which reflects helping and other organizational citizenship behaviors. Hunt (1996) also considered teamwork as a potential component of generic work behavior because interacting with coworkers is required on most jobs and is an explicit part of the work required in team-based jobs. This means that employers can expect and consider such behaviors in their selection procedures when hiring employees for teamwork.

It is important to recognize that certain performance behaviors, while being largely contextual for most employees, in fact, should be considered as job-specific for employees who work closely in pairs or in teams. This implies that employers can consider job-specific pro-social behaviors, along with technical task behaviors, as requirements for such jobs. Teams do perform technical tasks. However, team activities also involve interpersonal interaction and require knowledge that often is not necessary for individually performing technical tasks. Team members must have communication skills, knowledge of the effects of interpersonal processes on team performance, an understanding of group decision making, and conflict management skills. Team members need to exhibit helping behavior and other explicitly pro-social behavior, such as cooperating. In addition, they must refrain from counterproductive behaviors that are related to teamwork. For example, one potentially serious counterproductive behavior that has been observed in work teams is called "social loafing" (Latané, Williams, & Harkins, 1979). Team members who exhibit this behavior do less work as a member of the group than they do when working alone. It is counterproductive because their fellow team members must make up the difference.

## SUMMING UP

The purpose of this chapter is to consider the criterion behavior that selection procedures are meant to predict and to explore the behavioral nature of work performance. Summing up, we can make the following conclusions:

- In the past, researchers often neglected performance criteria and correlated scores on selection measures with whatever was available.
- The "criterion problem" occurs when no "true scores" can be found with which to validate a criterion measure. A solution is to content-validate it.
- A theoretical framework shows how constructs and measures are linked and identifies inferences that must be confirmed in validation.
- Job performance is a hypothetical construct. Underlying it is a psycho-

logical construct of personal capacities.
- A theoretical model identified eight components of performance. Three are major factors on any job: job-specific task proficiency, effort, and personal discipline.
- Pro-social organizational behavior and organizational citizenship are usually extrarole, but highly valuable, performance behaviors.
- Generic work behaviors are non-job-specific but include behaviors that are widely recognized requirements for employment which, like job-specific behaviors, can be considered in selection.

## InfoTrac College Edition

To learn more about the issues discussed here and about related topics in research and practice, use your subscription to InfoTrac College Edition to access articles from research journals and other publications. Go to http://www.infotrac-college.com/wadsworth to start your search of this online library. You can enter search terms of your own choosing, or you can use the following keywords to find articles relevant to this chapter.

Job performance predictor*        Organizational citizenship
Employee absenteeism              Employee work ethic
Organizational commitment

# PERFORMANCE APPRAISAL METHODS

Almost everyone complains about performance appraisal. Supervisors complain because they have to take time out to do them—and to do the frequently unpleasant task of discussing them with employees. Employees complain because getting an appraisal is a nerve-racking process, and it may or may not lead to anything good happening. Others—observers of business practices, mostly—complain that performance appraisal is pointless. They charge that it does not improve performance or motivation and that it is not a reasonable basis for making important decisions, such as giving raises and promotions. Sometimes, the results are absurd. Inflated performance ratings can cause even the terms to lose meaning. For example, one observer noted that according to a "nearly useless performance appraisal system," federal government employees are not only all "above average," but almost all are "outstanding" (Light, 1999).

Is performance appraisal really such a useless exercise? Could employers simply discard it without any harm? I think not. For one thing, some of the complaints actually are about errors and inadequacies in the procedure used, not the concept of performance appraisal itself. It is not necessary to discard the system in order to deal with the problems. In addition, many complaints refer to the administrative uses of performance appraisal—granting raises, promoting, terminating, and the like. These are important. However, as you know, performance information also is important in validating selection measures. This use is not so well known to the public, but it is as important as the administrative uses of performance appraisal.

In this chapter, the emphasis is on methods of performance appraisal. I begin by considering the various approaches to performance measurement, including both objective and subjective methods, as well as the sources of performance information. Next, I discuss the quality of performance appraisals and pay close attention to rater errors and biases. The remainder of the chapter covers the different types of procedures and instruments that are used to conduct performance appraisals. You will see that many of these methods resulted directly from researchers' efforts to correct rater errors and to help raters more effectively evaluate employee performance.

## APPROACHES TO MEASURING PERFORMANCE

In this chapter, I use the term "rater" to refer to any person who conducts an evaluation of another's performance. This is usually the supervisor, but not always. Sometimes other sources of performance appraisal are tapped, as I discuss later. Also, I use the term "rating" to refer to any performance appraisal measure or method. In fact, although these terms are commonly used this way, the usage is not exact. Not all performance measures involve subjective judgments or ratings; therefore, not all sources literally are raters. However, the general use of the terms is convenient because many performance appraisals do involve a subjective process of judging someone's behavior and producing some type of rating.

### *Objective Measures of Performance*

We might expect objective measures to be especially valuable because they appear to provide an unbiased, bottom-line assessment, rather than being based on someone's personal opinion. However, objective measures have both advantages and disadvantages. Two types of objective performance measures can be obtained: production measures and personnel-related measures.

Production measurement refers to whatever is produced on the job. For example, the number of items constructed or assembled, or the dollar amount of sales, can be used. Similarly, production data can include the number of mistakes, the amount of material wasted, and the extent of customer complaints. Production data are appropriate to collect when a job involves observable and countable results or products. However, these measures can be *deficient* in assessing performance on certain jobs, because it may not be possible to count the important outcomes of performance. The important results of a manager's job or of a college professor's job usually cannot be counted in any meaningful way. It is hard to guess what outcomes or products could be counted in assessing a professor's teaching performance, for example. Production measures also can be *contaminated* by factors that are not under the employee's control. For example, performance on a sales job might be contaminated by changes in consumer demand for the product sold. A manager's performance can be influenced by the work of others, as can the performance of employees who work on team projects. Because of the potential for deficiency and contamination, therefore, production measures do not always provide the best appraisal of performance.

Personnel data can include information on various work behaviors, such as unsafe behavior, unruliness, theft, and other forms of misconduct. However, the personnel data that are most commonly used in performance appraisal are measures of attendance. Incidents of tardiness and absenteeism are recorded, as are rates of turnover. In Chapter 13, I discussed performance behaviors that are general requirements of all employees, although not job-specific. Attendance is one such behavior. It is essential to an organization's success that all employees come to work, come on time, and keep their jobs. Both turnover and attendance problems can be dysfunctional. When valuable employees leave or when employees do not do their work because they are late or absent, there are costs to the organization. Therefore, it is reasonable to include measures of attendance in performance appraisal. However, attendance measures are deficient—because they do not address job-specific performance. They should be used as only one part of a performance assessment. Also, attendance measures can be contaminated. If they are used in performance appraisal, the type of absence should be determined. Involuntary, legitimate absences (such as taking time off from work because of illness) need to be distinguished from voluntary, illegitimate absences (such as taking time off for leisure activities). Only voluntary, illegitimate absences should be counted. These absences are thought to reflect employees' motivation or willingness to work (Borman, 1991). However, it is not always easy to distinguish voluntary from involuntary absences. Harrison and Hulin (1989) studied variables that might predict voluntary absenteeism. They reported two interesting results. One, voluntary absences occurred during certain time periods. Employees were more likely to be absent on a Friday than other workdays and during certain months such as December. Two, an individual's propensity to be voluntarily absent changed over time, depending on how many absences had already been taken. Those who were voluntarily absent tended to spread their absences out over the year. Therefore, a year's total of absences for each employee might be more useful in performance appraisal than data collected over a shorter or longer period.

## Subjective Measures of Performance

Subjective measures are based on human judgments, and they are the performance ratings most commonly used in performance appraisal. Subjective measures can be obtained when production measures cannot be, such as on jobs in which there is little of anything relevant to be counted. Even on jobs in which objective measures can be taken, performance ratings also can be obtained. However, at least to some extent, subjectivity probably runs through most types of measures that are touched by human hands. Certainly, subjectivity is apparent in performance ratings. Even production and personnel data are thought likely to contain a certain amount of subjectivity due to the individuals who provide or collect these data. In actuality, we have no measures that we can be sure are unaffected by people. The best we can do in deciding what measure to use is to begin by defining what is needed in performance appraisal, discovering the strengths and weaknesses of available measures, and taking these into account when making the decision. In some cases, production and personnel data are the most appropriate. In other cases, performance ratings are the best choice.

Performance ratings do have problems that must be controlled, even when they are the most appropriate measure to use. In rating someone's performance, a rater uses his or her own understanding of the person's behavior to make a value judgment concerning the performance. This subjective process leaves the rater open to making various types of observational, judgment, and rating errors. These errors have been studied extensively, and there are strategies for dealing with them. I will have more to say about rater errors in later sections.

Because of their ready availability, most employers and researchers have come to rely on subjective measures to provide for all performance appraisal needs. However, we must not be misled by this widespread acceptance. Ratings do not satisfy all performance appraisal needs, and they should not be substituted for objective measures when these are available. A meta-analysis of performance measures found an overall mean correlation of .39 between objective and subjective measures (Bommer, Johnson, Rich, Podsakoff, & MacKenzie (1995). This value, though substantial, indicates that performance ratings are not interchangeable with objective measures,. The authors concluded that if employers are most interested in their employees' objective performance levels, such as productivity, then objective measures, rather than performance ratings, must be used.

## Sources of Performance Appraisal

Who should be the raters? Because of the importance of performance appraisal and the difficulty of using some measures, particularly those requiring hard judgments, performing the rating task requires someone with special knowledge and ability, and someone who can observe the performance of the ratee. Usually, performance appraisals are conducted by employees' supervisors. Sometimes, however, such as when an employee does not work under close supervision, others will be asked to rate the person's performance. Any of several such sources might be available, including customers and clients. Most likely, however, ratings will be collected from coworkers or peers and the employees themselves. Table 14.1 provides a brief summary of appraisal sources.

**Supervisor Appraisals**   Generally, an employee's immediate supervisor is considered to be the best source of high-quality appraisals. A supervisor's job

TABLE

14.1
**TABLE 14.1   COMMON SOURCES OF PERFORMANCE APPRAISAL**

| System | Source | Comments |
|---|---|---|
| Single source | Supervisor | Ratings tend to be reliable |
| | | Acceptable to ratees |
| | Peer | Correlate with supervisor ratings |
| | Self | Often inflated |
| | | Do not correlate with other ratings |
| | Customer/client | Useful when work closely with outsiders |
| Multisource | Combination of single sources | Multiple perspectives on performance |
| | | Useful for coworking employees |
| Upward | Subordinate | Managerial appraisal |
| | | Upward feedback for development |
| 360-degree | Combination of upward, downward, lateral, and self | Managerial appraisal |
| | | Multiple perspectives on performance |
| | | Feedback used for development |

routinely requires overseeing and evaluating employees' work activities. Anyone holding a supervisor's position is expected to have the basic knowledge and ability to conduct performance appraisal on his or her own subordinates. In addition, it is widely accepted that reliable and accurate evaluation depends on a rater having had sufficient opportunity to observe. The supervisor is considered to be in the best position for this. Research has shown that performance appraisals are more reliable when they are based on a longer period of observation, especially when performance on the job is relatively complex and the supervisor must evaluate many different tasks (Rothstein, 1990). Employees accept the supervisor as being the most appropriate to evaluate their job performance, and they consider feedback from the supervisor to be more relevant and useful than feedback from others (Becker & Klimoski, 1989; Herold, Liden, & Leatherwood, 1987).

**Peer Appraisals**   Coworkers or peers can be good sources of performance information. Employees who work together, either in a coworking relationship or as members of a team, are in a position to observe and often are aware of how well their coworkers perform on the job. Peer appraisals are preferred to supervisor appraisals when the supervisor does not have much direct contact with an employee and cannot observe the individual's work. When employees work in teams, peer ratings are desirable, either in addition to or instead of supervisor ratings. Increasingly, employers are including peer raters along with others, in multisource appraisal systems.

Peer appraisal seems to be acceptable to ratees, especially those who previously received positive ratings and who perceived the peer rating as being unbiased and fair (McEvoy & Buller, 1987). We might reasonably question whether peer ratings are as accurate as those given by supervisors. Employees are less likely to have experience in conducting performance appraisals; therefore, they might not have the same capability that supervisors have. Another reason to expect differences in their ratings is that peers and supervisors probably are exposed to different aspects of employee performance, and these different exposures might influence the ratings they produce. A study of military personnel indicated that peers and supervisors did vary somewhat with respect to the type of information they used in making their ratings. Specifically, supervisors put more emphasis on a ratee's ability and technical proficiency than peer raters did (Borman, White, & Dorsey, 1995). However, early reviews of research concluded that peer appraisal is a reasonably reliable technique (Kane & Lawler, 1978; Reilly & Chao, 1982) and, later, a meta-analysis found that agreement between peer and supervisor ratings was actually quite strong, with an average correlation of .62 (Harris & Schaubroeck, 1988).

**Self-Appraisals**   It can be useful to collect self-appraisals from employees, especially when an employee works alone or is relatively independent of others, such as managers, sales personnel who travel extensively, and those who work at home.

Apparently, employees have quite a different view of their performance than others who rate them, and this is expressed in self-ratings that do not correlate very strongly with ratings from other sources (Thornton, 1980). In a meta-analysis of the three main sources of performance appraisal, the relationship between self-ratings and both peer and supervisor ratings was found to be quite weak (Harris & Schaubroeck, 1988). Why self-ratings are not highly correlated with ratings from others is not entirely clear. Explanations often point to the self-rater's personal bias. You might think that given the opportunity, people are likely to overrate their performance. Although not everyone does do this, it appears that many employees' self-ratings are more positive than the ratings they receive from others. Some have suggested that the tendency to inflate self-ratings varies across cultures and that non-Western employees might be more modest in rating themselves. A study conducted in Taiwan found that employees' self-ratings were less favorable than their supervisors' ratings (Farh, Dobbins, & Cheng, 1991). A study of mainland Chinese workers, however, failed to show the expected modesty effect. Employees' self-ratings were more favorable than their supervisors' ratings, as they generally are in the United States (Yu & Murphy, 1993).

Low agreement between self-ratings and ratings from peers and supervisors might be due to the raters' having different perspectives. First, differences in perspective could result from the work relationship between the rater and the ratee. For example, Saavedra and Kwun (1993) wanted to know whether a peer rater's own job performance might affect the ratings he or she gives others. In studies using students working on team projects, the researchers found that outstanding team performers were the most capable of distinguishing between levels of performance in rating their peers. Second, the nature of the job being performed also appears to affect the level of rater agreement. In their 1988 meta-analysis, Harris and Schaubroeck found better agreement between self-ratings and supervisor ratings on blue-collar and service jobs than on managerial and professional jobs. Possibly, supervisors of managerial and professional employees were less able to observe than the supervisors of blue-collar and service employees. Third, low agreement with supervisors' ratings might occur if individuals' self-ratings are based on somewhat different standards. When Schrader and Steiner (1996) investigated this, they found that raters evaluated performance differently depending on the standards they used. Also, giving supervisors and employees the same explicit and objective comparison standards resulted in high agreement between self- and supervisor ratings.

**360-Degree Appraisals**   The current fashion in managerial performance appraisal is the 360-degree system. This is a multisource performance appraisal system in which managers do self-ratings and are rated by relevant others in all directions—downward by superiors, laterally by peers, and upward by subordinates.

A decade or two ago, *upward appraisal* made its first appearance. This was an early version of the 360-degree system. Since then, these programs have been implemented in a great number of organizations. In 1986, Bernardin reported that less than 10 percent of the companies surveyed were using upward appraisal. By 1989, use had gone up to about 20 percent of companies. Adoption of these programs continued to increase over the next few years (Tornow, 1993). In 1993, an entire issue of the practitioner journal *Human Resource Management* was devoted to 360-degree appraisal programs, and in 1997, a special issue of *Group & Organization Management* also focused on these programs. During this brief history, 360-degree appraisals have changed from an innovation used by a few companies to evaluate senior managers, to a performance appraisal method used in many organizations for all managerial levels. However, it may be that the widespread use of these programs is premature. Antonioni (1996) stated that some companies rush into implementing a 360-degree appraisal system before fully considering what they need or even what is possible to accomplish with such a system.

Many employers believe 360-degree appraisals can be especially useful for developing managerial talent. The interest in using these appraisals for this purpose appears to be based on the belief that behavioral change occurs through increasing self-awareness, which results when a person compares his or her self-ratings with ratings from others. While managerial development seems to be the most obvious use of 360-degree appraisals, they also are used for other purposes, including administrative decision making and actions affecting managers, such as promotions (Church & Bracken, 1997).

In using a 360-degree system, rater accountability and the confidentiality of ratings are highly important. When an organization plans to implement any appraisal program using subordinate ratings, these issues must be considered carefully. Bernardin (1986) identified a number of reasons why both managers and subordinates might not be favorable toward upward appraisals. For example, managers might be concerned that some subordinates will rate them negatively because the manager has disciplined the employee in the past. Also, subordinates are likely to fear reprisals if they give negative ratings. One response to these concerns is to allow subordinates to provide anonymous ratings and for the manager to keep the ratings confidential.

The dilemma of accountability is that no one wants it for themselves, but everyone wants others to have it. London, Smither, and Adsit (1997) report that subordinate raters usually prefer not to identify themselves. Managers generally prefer that they be able to identify the rater and that they be allowed to keep the rating confidential. Antonioni (1994) conducted a field study on rater anonymity. Managers were more favorable toward upward appraisals when subordinate raters were identifiable and could be held accountable for the information. However, subordinates were more favorable when they could rate their supervisors anonymously. When subordinates were required to identify themselves, they produced ratings that were significantly more positive than when they rated anonymously. Therefore, even though managers prefer that subordinates be held accountable, the effect of this is inflated ratings, which are unlikely to be helpful in the manager's developmental process. Antonioni recommended that organizations allow subordinate ratings to be given anonymously. Because of the manager's powerful position relative to the subordinate's, reprisals could be costly to the employee, and the fear of this is likely to make identified subordinate appraisals useless. However, London et al. (1997) recommended that both the subordinate and the supervisor be held accountable. Information from ratings can easily be ignored, especially if the ratings are anonymous. Further, a 360-degree appraisal program will have little impact if the employer does not hold managers accountable for using the information. The manager may make no improvements—and may have no intention of improving—if there is no consequence for failure to use the information. Walker and Smither (1999) reported evidence supporting this view. They found that managers who held group meetings with their subordinates—specifically to discuss the upward feedback they had received—improved more than other managers.

## Conclusions

Organizations can approach performance appraisal in several ways, using different types of measures and collecting information from different sources. Irrespective of these variations, performance appraisal depends on observation. Supervisors usually have ample opportunity for observation. However, additional appraisal sources may be sought, such as peers and subordinates. The general assumption is that different raters observe a ratee from different vantage points and that this is an advantage because it implies that a ratee's performance has been more fully observed and assessed. However, research has found that ratings from various sources are not always in agreement. Self-ratings, especially, may not agree with supervisor and peer ratings. We might expect this lack of interrater agreement, given the different perspectives of the raters. However, questions arise about whether one rater's perspective is more appropriate than another and whether one rating is more accurate than another. We might have cause for concern if the difference in perspective refers to the job's tasks or the importance of certain tasks that are being performed. There also might be cause for concern if the disagreement is between the self-rater and the supervisor. An employee may feel unfairly treated if the supervisor's rating departs from the person's own conception of effective performance on the job, and he or she may react negatively. This is a time for sensitive communication with the employee, especially if the organization uses the appraisal for administrative decisions and personnel action, such as raises and promotions (Cheung, 1999).

## PERFORMANCE MEASUREMENT QUALITY

No doubt, you will not be surprised to learn that the quality of performance measurement depends on the instrument, the rater's ability, and how the employer uses the information. Some critics, such as those mentioned at the start of this chapter, do not consider such differences in quality, but, rather, view performance appraisal as a simply bureaucratic routine that has outlived its usefulness. Some performance appraisal forms and procedures probably are so completely worthless that the employer should discard them. However, they will have to be replaced. Performance appraisal is a necessity, not an option.

Measurement quality needs to be assessed in any performance appraisal system. Ratings should be examined for their reliability and to determine whether biases or common errors are present. If problems are discovered, something should be done to address them. Unfortunately, in some companies, such an assessment may never be done, which may be the reason performance appraisal is disparaged.

## Reliability

The first requirement of high-quality measurement is reliability. As I discussed in Chapter 7, measurements must be consistent. Only if an instrument is reliable and consistent can it be a valid measure. This requirement applies to all instruments, whether they are used as predictors for employee selection purposes or as criterion measures of job performance.

Reliability can be assessed in various ways, depending on the nature of the instrument and the use of the reliability information. However, because of the extensive use of judgments or ratings to measure performance, an assessment of ratings reliability usually is required. A frequently used index of reliability is interrater reliability. The standard procedure for studying interrater reliability involves the use of one rating instrument by two or more raters, to evaluate two or more performers, on multiple dimensions of behavior. This procedure yields an assessment of agreement between raters, and it shows the extent of consistency in the distributions of rating scores, per dimension and per ratee.

What is desirable to find, in a reliability study, is that different raters produce similar ratings of all performance dimensions in a sample of ratees. Such a finding would mean that the raters at least are paying attention to the same kinds of ratee behavior. This is especially reasonable to expect if the raters are at the same organizational level. If there is inconsistency in the ratings produced by a homogeneous sample, such as all supervisors, then the ratings must be considered unreliable and the inconsistency due to error. Some amount of inconsistency might not be surprising if a mixed sample of supervisor, peer, and self-ratings is collected. As I discussed above, the inconsistency might be related to differences in the raters' organizational roles and perspectives on the employee's performance. However, accuracy should not be assumed. The ratings simply may be unreliable and the inconsistency due to differences—including organizational roles—that function as error variables.

Supervisor ratings appear to be the most reliable. Through a meta-analysis, Viswesvaran, Ones, and Schmidt (1996) found an average interrater reliability coefficient of .52 for supervisors, as compared to .42 for peer raters. These values were consistent with reliability estimates ranging from .43 to .48, which were obtained earlier from mixed samples (Schmidt, Hunter, Pearlman, & Hirsh, 1985). Rothstein (1990) found average interrater reliability coefficients of .48 and .52 in samples of supervisors, and she was able to suggest a reason for supervisors' high levels of reliability. Specifically, she found a strong association between the length of a rater's exposure to ratees and the reliability of the ratings produced. That is, reliability was greater when raters had

PERFORMANCE APPRAISAL METHODS **375**

TABLE

**14.2** SUMMARY OF RATER ERRORS

| Category | Error | Description | Appearance in Rating |
|---|---|---|---|
| Observational error | Knowledge | Ratings based on general impression | Not apparent |
| | Recency | Ratings based only on recent observations | Not apparent |
| Distributional error faulty standards, restricted range, inadequate ratee differentiation | Leniency | Low performance standards; ratings higher than deserved | Ratings concentrated at high end of scale |
| | Central tendency | All rated average | Ratings concentrated at middle of scale |
| | Severity | High performance standards; ratings lower than deserved | Ratings concentrated at low end of scale |
| Rating scale error high correlations, inadequate differentiation of dimensions | Halo | Items assumed related rated the same | Correlation between similar items |
| | Proximity | Items grouped together rated the same | Correlation between adjacent items |
| | Logical | Semantically similar items rated the same | Correlation between similar-sounding items |

longer experience on a job that required evaluating others—such as a supervisory job requires. Rothstein also found there was a limit to the effect of this exposure. As a rater continued on the job, especially during the first year, the rate of increase in the reliability of ratings was rapid. After that point, the effect of increasing months of exposure to ratees gradually leveled off, and a ceiling or upper limit on the reliability coefficient appeared at roughly .60. As this reliability level was approached, the effect of additional time on the job was relatively minor, and there was little further improvement in reliability even for raters with 10 or more years in the supervisory position.

## Rating Errors

It has long been recognized that ratings are not always accurate, and many studies were done in the past to determine the kinds of errors raters make. The point was, if errors could be identified, corrections could be made, and more reliable and accurate performance appraisals might result. The research did reveal certain errors that raters tended to make. In general, these errors can be differentiated as being related to (1) inadequate observations, (2) faulty standards or expectations about performance, and (3) difficulties in using a rating scale. These errors are summarized in Table 14.2 and discussed in this section.

**Observational Errors**   Observation is necessary for accurate performance appraisal. A rater who has had little direct contact with a ratee cannot be expected to make accurate judgments about performance. At best, a rating that is based on inadequate observation of an employee will reflect the rater's general impression of the individual. Sometimes, however, a rater has observed, but not throughout the entire appraisal period. A busy supervisor may neglect to pay much attention to an employee until just shortly before the performance appraisal is due. As a result, the appraisal will show *recency* error. Because the rating is based on observations of recent behavior only, it is likely not to fully represent the ratee's performance. In other situations, the problem may not be a lack of observation. A rater may have had enough contact with an employee, but has neglected to make any record of observations. The rater probably expects to remember enough detail from the observations to accurately rate the employee when the time comes. Some raters may be able to remember well enough, especially if only an overall evaluation is required. However, there is a good chance that this is not what actually happens. During the time between the observation and the appraisal, cognitive demands from the rater's other tasks can interfere with and reduce his or her memory of the observation. Consequently, if ratings of performance dimensions are based on memory only, they are likely to be inaccurate because the memory of observations has degraded.

**Distributional Errors**   Some errors reflect differences in raters' standards and expectations of employees in general. We can detect these errors by examining the distributions of rating scores that are produced by different raters. The errors are expressed in features of the score distribution, specifically, the mean score, the amount of variance, and the general shape of the distribution. Leniency, severity, and central tendency errors are distributional errors, and they result from use of faulty standards for judging performance.

   *Leniency* is shown when a rater has low performance standards and rates employees more positively than their performance actually deserves. The mean rating score is high, variance among scores is low, and scores are concentrated at the high end of the distribution. This error has long been recognized as a stable response tendency of raters (Guilford, 1954). The anecdote presented at the start of this chapter, in which all employees had been judged to be above average and most were outstanding, is a demonstration of leniency. Although this is a laughable example and the author meant to poke fun at government bureaucrats, lenient ratings are not uncommon in any organization. A study of ratings collected in three different field settings found that rater leniency was a stable response tendency, irrespective of whether the raters were evaluating nurses, police officers, or social workers (Kane, Bernardin, Villanova, & Peyrefitte, 1995).

   You might ask, Is it not possible that what appears to be rater leniency actually is the accurate evaluation of a group of high-quality performers? This a reasonable question. However, because raters vary in their tendency to give high ratings, it is commonly accepted that this rating effect has less to do with the employee's performance than it does with the rater's characteristics. Bernardin, Cooke, and Villanova (2000) reported a study showing that certain personality variables—conscientiousness and agreeableness—affected the tendency of raters to give high ratings. In an experimental lab study of peer appraisals, the researchers found that those who scored low on conscientiousness and high on agreeableness gave the highest ratings and that their ratings were most likely to contain leniency error.

Leniency can be a serious problem for an organization. Bretz, Milkovich, and Read (1992) reported that a large majority of business firms considered leniency to threaten the validity of their appraisal systems. Excessively lenient evaluations are not meaningful to employees. For example, a raise is not a reward for quality performance if raises are given to everyone. Also, when ratings are inflated, their value in making personnel decisions is reduced. Although giving high ratings allows a rater to avoid having to confront employees who have performance problems, this also can create a situation in which it is difficult for an employer to legally terminate an ineffective employee.

Two other distributional errors are sometimes observed, although less frequently than leniency. *Central tendency error* is shown when a rater evaluates almost no one as either superior or inferior. Everyone is considered about average, and ratings are concentrated in the middle of the score distribution. *Severity* is the reverse of leniency. The severe rater appears to have excessively high standards and rates employees' performance lower than they deserve. As a result, the mean score is low, variance is low, and the distribution of scores is skewed toward the low end of the rating scale. This is probably an infrequent error in reality. Most supervisors will find it difficult to justify giving low ratings to all or most of their subordinates. Also, if the organization's employee selection methods are effective at all, one would expect that few truly unsatisfactory employees would have been hired in the first place.

Restriction of range is a problem with all of these distributional errors. The mean scores will differ depending on which error is present, as I state above. However, the range of scores in each distribution is narrow. That is, ratings are restricted to one section of the rating scale. Despite any actual performance differences that might exist, raters showing these error tendencies fail to differentiate among ratees. All are given highly similar ratings. This is a problem in at least two ways. First, sets of ratings collected from raters showing the different errors cannot be combined or compared directly. Employees rated by one rater may appear to be superior to those rated by another rater. Yet, the apparent difference in their performance quality may not be real but, rather, due to the leniency or severity of the rater. Second, the use of ratings as a performance criterion measure in validation studies can be severely limited when the range of scores is restricted. As mentioned previously, a criterion measure of performance is inadequate if it does not distinguish among individuals who actually do perform at different levels. For this reason, a set of ratings that are restricted in their range are not useful as criterion data in validating a predictor measure, because both low and high predictor scores must be correlated with the same narrow band of rating scores.

Efforts to correct distributional errors involve applying statistical controls, revising the rating scale, and training raters, as I discuss in later sections. For example, statistical corrections can be used to salvage ratings and make them comparable across raters. A commonly used strategy for this is to convert the different sets of ratings to standard scores or $z$-scores. As discussed in Chapter 7, scores on two different distributions can be converted to a single distribution of standard scores. For example, we can use ratings from a lenient and a severe rater if we calculate $z$-scores for all ratings given by both raters. This places the ratings on a single distribution and allows us to compare the performance of individuals in the different groups. This also makes it possible to determine whether an employee in one group is actually superior, equal, or inferior to employees in a different group.

**Halo and Other Rating Scale Errors**   Some rating errors appear to be the result of using a rating scale. *Proximity error* appears to be due to the particular ordering of performance dimensions on a rating scale. In this, dimensions that are located next to each other are rated similarly. *Logical error* occurs when two performance dimensions are rated the same, not because the rater actually knows the ratee's performance is the same, but because the dimensions appear to refer to logically related or semantically similar categories. That is, the terms suggest that the dimensions ought to go together. It is difficult to distinguish this error from halo error. Some researchers have regarded semantic similarity in dimensions as a type or a source of halo error (cf. Balzer & Sulsky, 1992; Cooper, 1981; Kozlowski, Kirsch, & Chao, 1986).

*Halo error* is thought to be present when there is a high correlation between two or more rated dimensions in a rating. Halo was described by early researchers as being due to a rater's tendency to think of the ratee as being either a good or a poor employee, and to allow this general impression to color his or her thinking about different aspects of the employee's performance (Thorndike, 1920). Consequently, when the rater evaluates the employee high (or low) on a performance dimension, it is not because the rater has *observed* the ratee's performance on the dimension, but because of the influence of the general impression on the rater's information processing ability. Other researchers—although recognizing that general impressions can have this effect—believe that halo might also occur because of the semantic relationships between dimensions. That is, a rater might form an impression of one dimension and then use this impression to decide the rating of another dimension. This might happen because the dimensions appear to be related or because the rater simply cannot distinguish between them (cf. Balzer & Sulsky, 1992; Cooper, 1981; Kozlowski et al., 1986). A study designed to test these perspectives using experimental manipulations found that the better explanation of halo error was that the rater was using a general impression of the ratee (Lance, LaPointe, & Stewart, 1994).

Of all the errors raters make in evaluating performance, halo error has been the most interesting to researchers. Many studies have attempted to cast light on the nature of halo error and predict when it might occur. Cooper (1981) reviewed the early research and concluded that halo was present everywhere—in most ratings, in most settings. However, he noted that not all of what was being called halo error actually was error. The halo effect contained both true halo and illusory halo. The concept of true halo refers to a naturally occurring relationship between dimensions. The dimensions actually are related, and that is why it seems appropriate to rate them alike. Illusory halo is just that. The apparent relationship between dimensions is not real, and rating the dimensions the same is incorrect. The research indicated that it is illusory halo which occurs when a rater is unfamiliar with a performance dimension. Thus, the high intercorrelation of dimension ratings that frequently had been observed appeared to be a combination of accuracy and error.

In another review, Murphy, Jako, and Anhalt (1993) stated that researchers had made too much of halo error. In the past, halo had appeared to be commonplace. The presence of high correlations between performance dimensions was assumed to reflect halo error and to mean that raters were unable to distinguish between dimensions. Because halo appeared to seriously affect the quality of ratings, certain interventions, such as training, were suggested as corrections. However, later studies reported that dimension intercorrelations were not excessively high (e.g., Fisicaro, 1988; Lance, Fisicaro, & LaPointe, 1990). From their review of this more recent research, Murphy et al. (1993) concluded that halo error is not commonplace and actually is not much of a problem. Signs of halo in ratings do not always indicate inaccuracy. In fact, attempts to suppress the effect have been known to create greater inaccuracy. For example, after being trained to avoid the error, raters sometimes reduce the intercorrelation of dimensional ratings to a level lower than would be expected given the existence of true halo between the dimensions (Murphy & Reynolds,1988).

**Rater Training**    One way to deal with rater errors is to train raters to avoid making them. Raters can be told about the kinds of errors they might make, and they can be taught strategies to use to avoid these errors. Rater-error training was expected to be a good solution. However, it did not always seem to have much effect. Probably, it depended on how the training was done. One rater-error training program that is often cited as an effective method is the workshop developed by Latham, Wexley, and Pursell (1975). Latham and Wexley (1981) described some of the differences between the workshop and other rater-error training programs. One of the most important differences was the amount of time devoted to training. They pointed out that some rater instruction had taken less than 1 hour. Not surprisingly, such rater training had not brought about lasting change. In the Latham et al. (1975) workshop, 6 to 8 hours were required for trainees to learn about and work on just four rating errors. This amount of time was thought necessary because rating-error tendencies are ingrained habits and are difficult to change. Raters in training need enough time to observe how other raters make such errors, to learn about their own rating tendencies, and to practice effective strategies for reducing errors.

Rater-error training had an unexpected effect. Although raters could learn to avoid the classic errors, the ratings they produced were not always more accurate. This seemed completely contradictory. How could reduction of error decrease accuracy? The explanation offered most often was that in their effort to avoid making one error, raters were making some other error. With respect to halo, perhaps they were trying too hard to avoid the error and were responding to truly related dimensions as if they were not related at all.

Frame-of-reference (FOR) training is a method that was meant to increase rating accuracy. The intention was to help raters develop better standards or frames of reference. Clearly, some raters were using their own idiosyncratic interpretations of the different dimensions of job performance, and these were not congruent with the organization's standards. The purpose of FOR training was to establish a common frame of reference among rater trainees and to guide raters in observing employee behavior and producing more reliable appraisals (Bernardin & Beatty, 1984; Bernardin & Buckley, 1981). In essence, FOR training involves teaching raters a more effective model or way of looking at performance. Performance dimensions and standards are defined. Raters learn how to categorize ratee behavior into dimensions and how to evaluate the performance level of the behaviors they observe.

Is accuracy training more effective than error training? Actually, these types of training accomplish different objectives. Each can be effective in its own way. When raters receive well-designed error training, they commit fewer specific errors. Those who receive FOR training learn how to produce ratings that are more accurate overall (Woehr & Huffcutt, 1994). Studies suggest that FOR training can be durable over time and that it helps raters develop better conceptions of effective performance (Sulsky & Day, 1992, 1994).

## Personal Biases in Ratings

Some effects on ratings are due to the rater's response to the ratee's personal characteristics or to the relationship the rater has with the ratee. For example, a biasing effect was observed and labeled in early studies as the "similar-to-me" error. Raters make this error because of their tendency to judge someone more favorably if they perceive the person to be similar to themselves, even though the similarity might be entirely irrelevant to performance on the job (Latham &

Wexley, 1981). Many studies have been conducted in an attempt to determine what personal characteristics might influence ratings. Race, gender, age, disability, and experience have been considered. Also, the rater's cognition, motivation, and emotion have been studied. The most frequently studied influences are race and gender and the rater's cognitive processes in conducting an appraisal.

**Race and Gender Effects**    Early research, examining racial differences in the performance appraisals of Black and White employees, sometimes found effects due to race and sometimes did not (Landy & Farr, 1980). Gradually, the reasons for this inconsistency became more apparent. Research showed that Black employees received slightly lower ratings than White employees, but this depended on who was giving the rating. Raters of either race gave more positive ratings to members of their own race (Ford, Kraiger, & Schechtman, 1986; Kraiger & Ford, 1985). The view that "Black raters rate Blacks higher and White raters rate Whites higher" was accepted. Soon, however, research began to question this conclusion (e.g., Pulakos, White, Oppler, & Borman, 1989). Sackett and DuBois (1991) found that Black raters and White raters differed very little in their evaluations of White employees. Most of the difference between them was shown in how they evaluated Black employees. Blacks were rated lower by both raters, although Black raters evaluated these employees somewhat higher than White raters did. A later study further clarified the race effect. Mount, Sytsma, Hazucha, and Holt (1997) collected performance data from subordinates, peers, and supervisors of a sample of managers. The data showed the same-race effect for all black raters. From all perspectives— whether supervisor, peer, or subordinate—Black raters gave better ratings to the Black managers than they gave to the White managers. Ratings given by White raters depended on the rater's relationship to the manager. White supervisors showed the same-race effect. They gave better ratings to the White managers than to the Black managers. To some extent, White peer raters did the same. However, in the ratings given by White subordinates, there was no difference due to the race of the manager. So, do raters give better ratings to employees of their same race? Yes, to a great extent, they do.

Gender effects in performance appraisal likewise appear to involve complex relationships between the rater and the ratee. Sex bias is not simply a matter of raters giving better ratings to those of their same sex. A review of the early research suggested that we also need to give serious thought to the sex stereotype of the job being performed (Landy & Farr, 1980). Specifically, male employees could be predicted to get more positive ratings than females in traditionally masculine jobs or "men's work," and females to get better ratings than males in feminine jobs or "women's work." Actually, there has been very little support for either of these predictions. In their sample of military personnel, Pulakos et al. (1989) did see evidence of such a job type/ratee sex interaction, but the overall effect on ratings was trivial. If there is such a gender effect in ratings, it must be more complex than this.

One possibility is that ratings are affected by the extent to which an employee's sex-typed personal characteristics are congruent with the job's sex stereotype. That is, independent of being a man or a woman, an employee who shows masculine or feminine characteristics might be rated higher or lower depending on whether their characteristics match the type of job being performed. When both men and women work on a masculine-type job (such as management or many military jobs), we could expect that their ratings would reflect the extent to which they each show masculine behavior (e.g., aggressiveness). Maurer and Taylor (1994) found evidence of this in their study of college teaching—which is regarded as being a fairly masculine type of work. Perceptions of masculinity in the instructor's behavior contributed to the favorability of ratings given to both men and women. However, the rater's attitude about the appropriate sex-typed characteristics of someone performing this work influenced the ratings given the male instructors only. Specifically, when the rater held negative attitudes toward women as instructors, male instructors who showed more masculine characteristics received better ratings. When the rater held positive attitudes toward women instructors, it was not necessarily an advantage for male instructors to be more masculine. Obviously, more study is needed to clarify the nature of such gender effects in ratings.

**Rater Cognitive Processes**   To understand and predict performance appraisal accuracy, a good approach might be to study the rater's thought processes. In the late 1970s, many researchers were influenced by developments in cognitive psychology. A catalyst for the increasing interest in rater cognition was the research being reported on cognitive complexity.[1] For example, Schneier (1977) found a strong effect in performance ratings that was due to rater differences on this variable. Raters who exhibited high cognitive complexity produced performance appraisals that contained few signs of rater error. Other researchers were not always able to replicate this particular result, possibly because of the inherent difficulty in defining and measuring the construct (Bernardin & Beatty, 1984). Still, interest in rater cognition endured. Theoretical models were offered (e.g., DeNisi, Cafferty, & Meglino, 1984) that focused on how a rater collected, processed, and interpreted information about the person being evaluated. A key construct in rater cognition is the cognitive categorization of information. Theoretically, in the process of receiving information (such as by observing someone's work behavior), perceptions are compared to cognitive schemas and prototypes of the type of behavior[2] and are categorized accordingly. For example, observations of an employee's work activities would be compared with the observer's conception of how an effective or ineffective

---

[1] "Cognitive complexity" refers to the ability to think in multidimensional terms.

[2] A "schema" is a term for a cognitive category and includes a prototype or model that is used in making comparisons. The sex-stereotype of a job is a schema, and sets of behaviors shown by certain job performers would be prototypes.

employee would behave. Relevant to this, a study of subordinate ratings of managers revealed that ratings were more accurate when a manager acted as the rater expected; that is, when the manager's behavior was congruent with the rater's prototype of managerial behavior (Mount & Thompson, 1987).

Many laboratory studies were conducted during the 1980s using students to perform rating tasks that more or less resembled those performed by raters at work. Questioning the relevance of these studies, DeNisi and Peters (1996) conducted a set of field experiments to determine whether the results of the studies could be used to understand performance appraisal in real organizations. Building on laboratory reports that cognitive organization in memory is important to rating accuracy, the researchers tried out two interventions— structured diary-keeping and structured recall—to help raters organize and remember information on employee performance. The results of their experiments showed that knowledge of rater cognitive processes is useful in the workplace. Raters who kept structured diaries of their observations and who used the structured recall method were better able to remember performance information than those who did not. They produced ratings that showed less leniency and that differentiated more effectively between ratees. Also, the trained raters reacted more positively toward the appraisal process than those who had not used these methods.

## Conclusions

Throughout this section, I have discussed how raters influence the quality of performance appraisal. Rater effects often appear to be the result of the rater's own personal ways of thinking and behaving. Sometimes, in an effort to control these effects, interventions are designed to bring about changes in a rater's cognitive processes and abilities. For example, consider the following:

1.  Individuals differ in their ability to handle a cognitive workload of difficult information processing and decision making, such as performance appraisal requires. Compared to other raters, however, supervisors produce the most reliable ratings, especially when they have been performing the rating task for some time. Perhaps this is because they, more than those in other jobs, have learned effective cognitive strategies for handling the difficult workload of performance appraisal tasks.
2.  Raters have standards or frames of reference concerning what they believe is effective or ineffective performance, and these can enter into the ratings they produce. If a rater's conception of performance is well-founded, it contributes to the rater's ability in providing an accurate assessment of employee performance. Raters' standards can

be faulty, however, and they can cause rating errors and biases. Certain interventions can help raters cognitively restructure their frames of reference to reflect more appropriate organizational standards.

3. Novice raters make rating errors. Typically, they do not systematically observe or record their observations. At the time of rating, they cannot remember what they have observed because, in the interim, there have been demands made on their attention, information processing, and memory. Because they cannot remember specifics about the performer, they use a general impression of the ratee as a basis for rating dimensions. This results in ratings with very little differentiation among dimensions or among ratees. Through rater training, raters can learn new cognitive skills that are helpful in rating, such as active observation, use of memory aids, and the avoidance of common errors in categorizing performance information.

In these examples, notice that the rater's unique cognitive processes are implicated. You can see how difficult it is to understand rater errors and biases without delving into the rater's thought processes. Much of what we know about the errors and biases of performance appraisal is based on an increased understanding of the cognitive processes that are relevant to the rating task.

## Appraisal Techniques and Instruments

The techniques and instruments that have been used in performance appraisal can be distinguished in several ways. One, they are not all ratings per se, because some do not involve the use of a rating scale. Two, they vary in terms of how easily developed they are. Some instruments require almost no time to develop. A procedure for ranking or a simple rating scale can be drawn up in a matter of minutes. Other instruments require a special job analysis and complex procedures for developing and scaling items. Three, appraisal instruments differ in the amount and kind of information they yield. They range from a simple description of an employee's overall acceptability on the job to a full evaluation of multiple attributes of performance. Four, appraisal techniques and instruments vary as to their use. Some appear to have no purpose except for the company to have something in place. Other techniques have been designed specifically to address an employer's need for more valid and error-free performance information. As such, they can be used to provide the basis of personnel decisions and employee development or to provide criterion data for validation of other measures. In the following sections, I discuss appraisal techniques and instruments in terms of these distinctions. In addition, I have more to say about their uses in the next chapter.

## Checklists and Employee Comparisons

Although most performance appraisal is conducted by means of a graphic rating scale, some appraisal methods use other instruments or procedures. Two types are checklists and employee comparisons.

**Weighted and Forced-Choice Checklists**    Performance appraisal can be conducted by using checklists with items describing various behaviors that employees might exhibit which have been scaled as being more or less valuable in performance. The two most commonly used are weighted checklists and forced-choice checklists.

Developing a weighted checklist can be a time-consuming process because it requires several labor-intensive steps. An SME-group of supervisors usually is established to generate a pool of behavioral statements and to evaluate these statements in terms of their importance to the job. Traditionally, Thurstone's (1928) method of equal-appearing intervals has been used to do this. First, SMEs evaluate each statement and assign a score from a scale of values, such as on a scale of 1 to 9 with 9 high. Second, the SME-group's mean score and standard deviation for each statement are calculated. The standard deviation is used to identify items on which SMEs do not agree in their evaluations. These items are considered to be unclear and, therefore, are discarded. Only those on which SMEs agree are retained. To construct the checklist, the item mean scores are used to select specific items. An item representing each scale value needs to be included. The selected item's mean score is used as the item's scale value or weight in scoring a checklist, although item weights are not shown on the checklist.

Weighted checklists are easy to use and because of this they generally are acceptable to raters. The rater simply checks the statements that describe either the employee's highest performance or typical performance. Ordinarily, a rater can check as many or as few of the items as apply. Then someone other than the rater, such as an HR analyst, calculates an overall performance score. A scoring key showing the item weights is used, and the scorer sums the scale values of the items that have been checked. Because item weights are not shown on the checklist itself, rater errors, such as leniency, should not be much of a problem, especially if the items are not transparent as to their desirability.

The forced-choice checklist is another method of rating by checking statements on a checklist, although it differs from the weighted checklist in certain respects. To develop a forced-choice checklist, scores on a pool of behavioral statements are obtained on a sample of employees. Next, these scores are correlated with the employees' performance scores on other measures. Then, on the basis of the correlational data, statements are selected to go on the forced-choice checklist according to the extent that they are found to discriminate between good and poor performance. Sets of two to four behavioral statements

**Instructions**

From each set of four items, first indicate the statement that most describes the ratee by writing "M" in the blank and, second, indicate the statement that least describes the ratee by writing "L" in the blank.

1.

    _____   Takes initiative in starting new projects
    _____   Provides helpful information for planning work on new projects
    _____   Is dependable and will get the work done on time
    _____   Works cooperatively with others on the team

2.

    _____   Shows resistance to changes in procedures
    _____   Spends too much time on details
    _____   Waits until the last minute to get reports done
    _____   Often is in a bad mood

FIGURE **14.1**

Example items for a forced-choice checklist.

---

each are listed on the checklist. The sets of items are established by grouping items together that appear to be equally desirable, but that are different in level of good or poor performance. The reason for this is to prevent a rater from producing an overly lenient rating or from rating an employee on the basis of the apparent social desirability of the item.

In use, the forced-choice checklist places imitations on the rater's freedom in checking statements. It requires that the rater respond to each of the sets of behavioral statements. Often, a rater must select one item from each set of two as the most descriptive of a ratee's behavior. When sets of four statements are used, the rater may be asked to select the one that is most descriptive and the one that is least descriptive of the employee, such as shown in Figure 14.1. Raters may not respond well to the forced-choice checklist, particularly when they have to select items from sets in which none seem right. Like the weighted checklist, the forced-choice method does not show the item values on the checklist itself. As a result, rater leniency should be controlled as it is on the weighted checklist. However, a rater using either of these procedures will have little feedback information to use.

**Comparison and Ranking Methods**    Performance appraisal is based on the premise that employees vary in how well they perform. Some perform extremely well, while others hardly perform at all. An effective method of appraisal will show the actual variation among performers. Whenever performance appraisals show restricted range of differences because of rater tendencies, such as leniency, levels of employee performance are not distinguished, and the appraisals are not very useful. Methods that make specific comparisons among employees, however, can be especially effective in differentiating levels of performance. All employee comparison methods produce a ranked list of the ratees and, in this way, distinguish among employees. Another advantage of employee comparison and ranking methods is that no form or instrument is needed. Thus, these procedures are quick and easy to develop. The main problem with these methods is that they, like checklist methods, yield little information that employers can use for employee feedback.

The rank order comparison technique is easy to use. The rater simply thinks of the entire group of ratees at once and then ranks them from the highest to the lowest. The rater usually ranks overall performance quality only, although separate rankings can be done for different performance dimensions. Because it often is difficult to distinguish between *average* performers, a variant of this procedure can be used. In this ranking process, the rater writes the name of each employee on a separate card. Next, the names of the best employee and the poorest employee are selected out and placed at the boundaries of the ranking. Then, from the remaining cards, the rater again selects the best and the poorest and places their cards in the ranking layout. The rater continues—each time removing the best and the poorest from the remaining cards—until all employees have been ranked. Although the rank order procedure yields information about differences in employee performance—by virtue of the ranks—the method does not show the distance between employees' ranks. The assumption of rank ordering is that the difference between individuals is equal, which probably is not true. Yet, there is no way for a rater to indicate that one employee is much better or only a little better than another or that two employees are equally good.

The paired comparison technique is a solution to this problem. A ranking is produced that does show the extent of differences between ratees. Also, the process of paired comparisons is easier than that of the rank order method because it focuses on comparing just two individuals at a time. Using a list of the employees to be evaluated, the rater takes each name on the list and pairs it once with every other name. Then, the rater randomly selects one of the pairs, decides which of the two is the better performer, records this decision, and continues with a second pair. An individual's score is equal to the number of times he or she was considered to be the better performer of a pair. The ranking that results from scoring in this way shows the difference between the performers, including the possibility of tied scores. (See Figure 14.2 for an example.)

The disadvantage of the paired comparison method is that the rating task can be laborious if the number of comparisons is large. The number of pairs that the rater must compare depends on the number of evaluations needed and the number of ratees. Although it is possible to evaluate specific performance dimensions, usually only a single overall evaluation is obtained, especially if many employees must be evaluated. To obtain an overall rating for each employee, the number of comparisons needed will equal $n(n - 1)/2$. If a supervisor has only four subordinates, then the number of pairs is 4(3)/2, or 6.

Step 1   List all employees to be evaluated

A - Anna      E - Ellen
F - Frank     J - Jason
L - Linda     M - Mark

Step 2   Pair each name with each other name for $n(n-1)/2$ pairs.

AE
AF      EF
AJ      EJ      FJ
AL      EL      FL      JL
AM      EM      FM      JM      LM

Step 3   Conduct comparisons.

J:L = J         E:M = M         A:E = A
E:F = E         A:F = A         A:L = L
A:J = J         E:J = J         F:J = J
F:M = M         E:L = L         A:M = A
J:M = J         L:M = M         F:L = L

Step 4   Count number times each employee was evaluated as the better performer and list scores in rank order.

Scores                    Ranks
  Anna      3       Highest  5  Jason
  Ellen     1                4
  Frank     0                        ⎡ Anna
  Jason     5                3 ⟵⟶ ⎢ Linda   Tied ranks
  Linda     3                        ⎣ Mark
  Mark      3                2
                             1  Ellen
                   Lowest    0  Frank

**FIGURE 14.2**

Steps in paired comparisons.

This is an easy enough task if only an overall evaluation is needed, and it might be manageable if three performance dimension ratings are needed instead, in which case the comparisons would equal three times that number, or 18.

The forced distribution[3] is another employee comparison that yields information about how performance differs among employees. It is especially useful when many employees have to be evaluated and when a single overall evaluation will suffice. You will see that the forced distribution does not make fine distinctions between ratees. To use this method, the rater compares the work behavior of a group of employees and makes a judgment of the perfor-

---

[3]Some methods used for performance appraisal are used in other contexts. You might recognize the forced distribution as being the "curve" or distribution of scores your instructor uses to assign grades.

mance level of each. Based on these judgments, the rater assigns each ratee to an appropriate performance level at some point on a distribution. The shape of the distribution can vary, but often the normal, bell-shaped curve is used to define the levels. Typically, the following categories of performers are defined: the highest, or best, 10 percent; the next best 20 percent; the middle 40 percent, or average performers; the next lower 20 percent; and the lowest 10 percent, or poorest performers. Suppose, for example, there are 30 people who have to be evaluated. Using this distribution, the rater could select out the best three (top 10 percent) and the poorest three (bottom 10 percent) and record these decisions. Then, of the remaining ratees, the rater would identify the next best six (upper 20 percent) and the next to lowest six (lower 20 percent) and record their names at these levels of the distribution. Then, the remaining 12 employees would be listed at the 40 percent or average level of performance. Obviously, with a group of employees no larger than this, the time and work involved would not be burdensome.

## Graphic Rating Scales

The most common way for a rater to express his or her judgment of a ratee's job performance is with a graphic rating scale. Such scales provide for rating along a continuum from low to high performance levels. Basically, graphic rating scales vary in terms of the type and orientation of the response continuum, and the number and anchoring of scale points. Rating scales can be horizontal, as you see in Figures 14.3, 14.4, and 14.5. However, the same scales could be presented vertically. Points on a rating scale are weighted by anchors that are placed at mid- and/or endpoints on the scale. Anchors can be verbal and/or numerical. They can contain single numbers, words, phrases, or some combination of these. When a line is used to represent the continuum, the rater can respond by checking a scale point or between points, as shown in Figure 14.3. If between-point responses are not acceptable, the continuum line must be replaced by some other response continuum that encourages discrete responding, such as shown in Figures 14.4 and 14.5. These scales require the rater to fit the response to the nearest appropriate scale point. Rating scales vary in terms of the numerical value of the high versus low endpoints on the continuum. In business firms, some like to think of the best performer as "#1" and find this easy to carry over to a rating scale. Personnel analysts and researchers usually prefer to assign larger numerical values to the best performers because it is conceptually easier to interpret analyses of scores. Rating scales also vary in the number of scale points. Five-point scales, such as in part b of Figure 14.3, are commonly used. Scales with fewer than this will probably be "converted" to five-point scales by raters who respond between the points, as you see in part a of the figure. Seven-point scales are not unusual. Scales with more than nine points are rare, mainly

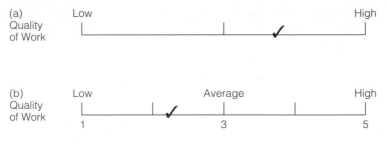

FIGURE **14.3**

Graphic rating scales, allowing on- and between-point responses. (a) 3-point scale, verbal endpoint anchors only. (b) 5-point scale, verbal and numerical end- and midpoint anchors.

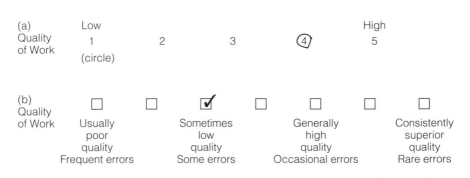

FIGURE **14.4**

Graphic rating scales, allowing on-point responses only. (a) 5-point scale, verbal and numerical endpoint anchors. (b) 7-point scale; verbal phrases; end- and midpoint anchors.

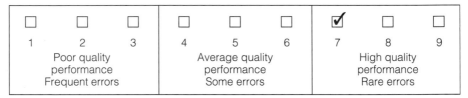

FIGURE **14.5**

Graphic rating scale, allowing on-point responses only; 9-point scale, numerical and verbal, end- and midpoint anchors.

because they are difficult to use. If such scales are used, they are likely to contain a "grouping" device in which the points are organized into related categories, such as is shown in Figure 14.5.

Graphic rating scales are versatile. They are used to obtain evaluations of overall performance and specific performance dimensions. Dimensions that are commonly rated in many appraisals include quality of work, which is relevant to many jobs, as well as dependability and responsibility, which are more job specific. However, the dimensions to be rated must be relevant to the job. Appropriate dimensions are identified through job analysis of the jobs that employees are performing. A rating scale that includes dimensions which are irrelevant to performance on a particular job will contribute error to the performance appraisal. This means that if an employer has several different jobs being performed, a *general* graphic rating scale should not be adopted for company-wide use. Rather, the employer should develop a new scale or customize an existing scale to apply to specific jobs.

What is critical about effective rating scale design is the amount of meaning that the response options provide about the rating dimension. For example, although some of the verbal anchors shown in the figures are wordier than others, they probably do not provide much more meaning for the rating scale continuum. Although all the scales shown in the figures ask for evaluations of the quality of work, relatively little information is available to define different performance levels on that dimension. Even the scale in Figure 14.5, which is more detailed than the others, is inadequate in defining the performance dimension. Improvements in performance measurement need to go beyond the largely cosmetic variations seen in most graphic rating scales and increase the amount of information they provide to the rater about the performance dimensions.

## Specialized Appraisal Instruments

The first major step that researchers took to improve the performance appraisal process was to create methods which would provide more information for raters. Their hope was that the new methods would make the rater's judgmental task easier and result in more reliable and accurate appraisals. In the following sections, I describe four appraisal methods that yield far more than just another rating scale. These are the Behaviorally Anchored Rating Scale, the Behavior Summary Scale, the Behavioral Observation Scale, and the Mixed Standard Scale.

**Behaviorally Anchored Rating Scale (BARS)**   As I have discussed, raters often find it difficult to evaluate performance because of the long period of time since the last evaluation and because they have neither observed systematically nor recorded the observations, which means they have to do the rating from memory. Making it still more difficult is that they might be asked to use a graphic rating scale on which dimensions are undefined traits. In such a case, raters will have to apply their own interpretations of dimensions and do their

| | TABLE 14.3 | STEPS IN DEVELOPING BARS ITEMS |
|---|---|---|

| Step | Group | Activity |
|---|---|---|
| 1 | SME group 1 | Identify dimensions and write critical incidents |
| 2 | SME group 2 | Sort shuffled incidents into dimensions |
| | | Write behavioral statements for high to low performance levels |
| 3 | SME group 3 | Sort shuffled statements |
| | | Retranslate into dimensions |
| 4 | SME group 4 | Independently evaluate and assign rating values to behavioral statements |
| 5 | Analysts | Calculate means and standard deviations |
| | | Use to select behavioral statements to anchor dimension scales |

best to relate these to their memories of how a ratee behaved. The likely result is an inaccurate rating.

Smith and Kendall (1963), the originators of the Behaviorally Anchored Rating Scale, or BARS, proposed a rating method that would handle such difficulties, making the rater's task easier and the rating more accurate. The BARS method requires observation and use of the observation to infer the nature and level of a ratee's performance. Smith and Kendall proposed an extensive developmental process that results in a separate rating scale for each performance dimension. Each scale is anchored with uniquely relevant behavioral statements. These anchors describe the kinds of behavior that a rater would have observed and would have used to infer what could be *expected* from an employee.[4] For each dimension, the rater should be able to identify one of the scale anchors as being "the kind of thing I've learned to expect from this employee." Thus, the rater's judgmental task should be easier when using the scale, because there is no need to guess at the meaning of the dimensions (Bernardin & Smith, 1981).

As outlined in Table 14.3, a BARS is customed-developed for a single job or job family, using a multiphase procedure based on Flanagan's (1954) critical incidents method of job analysis. First, an SME-group, such as supervisors, is convened. In a group session, they identify the performance dimensions that need to be rated. They also describe as many real incidents as possible in

[4]Originally, because expected behavior was inferred from observed behavior, Smith and Kendall's instrument was called the Behavioral Expectation Scale, or BES. Occasionally, I still see the term used.

which an employee has been observed to be effective or ineffective on the job. Second, the critical incidents are given to a different SME-group, who identify the performance dimension described in each incident. They sort these into dimension categories. Then, using the sorted incidents, they write behavioral statements, attempting to describe behavior at high, average, and low performance levels on each dimension. Third, the behavioral statements are shuffled together and given to another group who "retranslates" them into what appear to be the dimensions being addressed. This ensures that there is agreement among job experts on the meaning of the dimensions and the behaviors describing performance levels. That is, we must be sure that we are still talking about the same thing and that nothing is lost in "translation." If the SMEs do not agree in the retranslation of a behavioral statement, then it is discarded. Fourth, the dimensions and behavioral descriptions on which there was agreement in the retranslation group are given to another group. These SMEs work independently. They evaluate the behavioral statements, assigning a numerical scale value to each. Finally, the group's data are combined, and an analyst calculates means and standard deviations for each statement. Those statements on which the SMEs did not agree in their assignment of scale values (i.e., those with a large standard deviation) are discarded. Of the remaining behavioral statements on each dimension, those that have a mean value at the top, middle, and bottom levels of the scale are accepted as representing levels of performance on the dimension. These statements are entered as anchors on a vertical scale. Numerical values are added to mark the scale points, and a brief definition of the dimension is included. An example of a BARS is shown in Figure 14.6.

Use of the BARS begins with observation. A rater is given BARS blanks showing the anchored scale for each performance dimension. These are used as observation worksheets. The rater is instructed to use them to record behavior as it happens. Each observation is recorded on the appropriate dimension scale. The date, details of the behavior, and estimated scale level of the performance are written on the blank. The rater continues this process throughout the performance observation period. Any number of observations might be described and rated on each dimension. At the end of the observational period, the performance appraisal is done by taking the mean value of the recorded behaviors on each dimension. The ratings are justified by examples taken from the observation worksheets. When viewed in this way, it is clear that a BARS is much more than a rating scale. By encouraging and guiding the observational process, it is a rating system that can make the final rating task easier and less subjective.

BARS development clearly is time consuming, and proper use of the system means that raters must observe and record ratings throughout the appraisal period. However, if more reliable and valid observations and performance appraisals result, it could be worth the time and effort. The question is,

**Teamwork** Participation and contribution to team projects.
Making an effort; initiating team projects; contributing to discussion; helping others.

**Ratee can be expected to . . .**

9 ——— Make an extra effort and put in extra time to help team finish a project

7 ——— Initiate team discussion on how to solve problems

——— Participate in problem solving by sharing good ideas

5 ——— Be friendly and cooperative while working with others

3

——— Be argumentative in group problem sessions

——— Socialize while other team members are working

1

**FIGURE 14.6**

Example of a BARS type rating scale.

Does this technique result in better performance appraisal? Actually, it is difficult to answer this question because many who have created "BARS" instruments have not followed the BARS developmental procedure or used the scales for observation. Rather, they have subverted the developmental process by an intention to quickly create a rating form. A scale is produced that is a BARS in appearance only. The behavioral anchors may look like BARS anchors, but not have come from a BARS study, as it is easy enough to fabricate such items. Also, the rating form is used, not to register and evaluate observations, but only to produce a final performance rating. When the performance appraisal is due, the rater is expected to use the BARS-like form as he or she would use any other graphic rating scale. Scale points are checked according to what seems to describe the person's behavior.

These spinoffs of the BARS that mainly produce graphic rating scales have been evaluated in research. Reviewers have reported that the reliability, validity, and error control of the various BARS-like forms are no better than any other graphic rating scale. Thus, the reviewers conclude, because one is no better than another, the user can follow his or her own personal preferences about what rating format to use (Jacobs, Kafry, & Zedeck, 1980; Landy & Farr, 1980). Unfortunately, it appears that the distinctions between the typical BARS-like instrument and the Smith and Kendall BARS system often have been ignored in the research evaluating these instruments.

There has not been much research assessing the value of the complete BARS developmental procedure or use of the scales in observation. Still, there is much to recommend Smith and Kendall's (1963) BARS technique, and we should not abandon the method, especially if there is nothing better (e.g., Guion, 1998b; Murphy & Cleveland, 1991). Although development of BARS admittedly is time-consuming, the thorough job-analysis-based process is a source of several strengths. One, because raters (as SMEs) are involved in BARS development from the start, they are likely to have gained an increased understanding of the job and to be more accepting of the rating system. Two, when used as an observational aid—as it is meant to be—the BARS produces ample material that can be used for employee feedback. Three, because the BARS is drawn from the job itself, we can expect it to have content validity. When Bernardin and Beatty (1984) considered the available research and their own experience in using the BARS, they concluded that error control and reliability also are relatively good and that the approach is useful in developing criterion measures for selection research.

**Behavior Summary Scale (BSS)**    Despite its apparent advantages, raters sometimes have had difficulty using the BARS (Borman, 1979). They may find it hard to identify the performance dimension of an observed behavior or to match the behavior with a behavioral anchor on the scale. As I describe above, BARS anchors tend to be brief statements that individually have been shown to reflect only certain critical behaviors, and they are placed at some but not all scale points. Therefore, if an observed behavior is not exactly the same as one of the anchor statements, it can be difficult for a rater to judge how to evaluate it. Responding to this difficulty, Borman (1979) conceived of a variant of the BARS that anchors scale points with more general behavioral descriptions. With the Behavior Summary Scale (BSS), Borman meant to create a scale that raters could use more easily to identify the relevant performance dimension of an observed behavior and to match the behavior to an anchor statement on the dimension's rating scale.

Because the BSS is an adaptation of Smith and Kendall's (1963) method, it retains certain features of the BARS. For one, development of a BSS requires a critical incidents job analysis. The critical incidents are used to produce behavioral anchors for performance dimension scales. Thus, the BSS is drawn from the job itself, a strategy that yields content validity. The process of development, however, is shorter and involves fewer participants than BARS development. Only a few steps are required. First, the SME-group examines the contents of all critical incidents and categorizes them according to the performance dimensions to which they refer. Next, taking each category one at a time, the SME-group evaluates the incidents on a numerical scale (e.g., from 1 to 9, with 9 high) as to the level of performance. Then, they write general statements that summarize the meaning of the incidents rated as reflecting a

| Critical Incident | BSS Anchor Statement |
|---|---|
| A prospective recruit said he wanted the nuclear power program or he would not enlist. When he did not qualify for this, the recruiter did not give up. Instead, he persuaded the young man to go into electronics by emphasizing the technical training he would receive. | Often mentions specific benefits that are likely to persuade a prospective recruit to enlist in the navy; describes navy life well; can counter commonly heard objections about navy service. |

Performance Dimension
Salesmanship as a navy
recruiter

Performance Effectiveness Level
Effective; Rating Scale Points 6, 7,
or 8

FIGURE **14.7**

Example of a BSS rating scale anchor statement showing an example critical incident used as one of several sources.

Based on information from "Format and Training Effects on Rating Accuracy and Rater Errors," by W. C. Borman, 1992, *Journal of Applied Psychology, 64,* pp. 412–413.

certain performance level. BSS statements are constructed to describe a wider range of behavior than is shown by a single incident and, in fact, a statement can reflect the meaning common to multiple incidents rated at about the same scale point. This means that when a rater uses the scale, there is a good chance that one of the scale anchors will match an observed behavior. (See Figure 14.7 for an example of a critical incident and the type of summary statement that might be written to cover this and related critical incidents.)

Borman (1986) summarized the conceptual advantages of the BSS as making the meaning of behavioral dimensions more evident and increasing the ease of use, relative to the BARS. However, there has been little direct study of these advantages. In Borman's own (1979) research, even though the BSS performed as well as the BARS and other rating methods in producing accurate ratings, he was not able to show that it was any better. However, while the BSS might not be a superior measure, users have found value in it. Raters are reported to react more positively to the BSS than to the BARS, apparently because—as Borman hoped—it is easier for them to see the relevance of the summary statements anchoring the scales (Pulakos, 1997).

**Behavioral Observation Scale (BOS)**   The Behavioral Observation Scale (BOS) is another procedure that was based on Smith and Kendall's (1963) BARS rationale for reducing subjectivity and error in performance appraisal (Latham & Wexley, 1977, 1981). The BOS was designed to emphasize assess-

Knows the prices of competitive products.

| 1 | 2 | 3 | 4 | 5 |
|---|---|---|---|---|
| Never | | Sometimes | | Always |

FIGURE **14.8**

Example BOS item for rating sales personnel.

Based on information from "Behavioral Observation Scales for Performance Appraisal Purposes," by G. P. Latham and K. N. Wexley, 1977, *Personnel Psychology, 30,* p. 257.

ment of observed performance behaviors. In use, the BOS allows the rater simply to report how often a ratee has been observed to exhibit a described behavior.

Like the BARS, the BOS is developed specifically for a job. A job analysis is required, using the critical incidents technique. From the critical incidents, SMEs identify job dimensions and develop behavioral statements. The BOS statements describe specific behaviors that might be observed on the job, and these should be useful for a rater in reporting observed behavior. The BOS differs from the BARS in certain ways. Most importantly, it uses a different rating format. BOS statements describing observable behaviors are listed as items, in survey-like fashion, and a rater responds to each item using a simple graphic rating scale. The anchors used on the rating scale are frequency terms. For example, as shown in Figure 14.8, the anchors may combine numerical values with verbal anchors, such as "always" and "never," or may indicate time frequencies, such as "less than 20%, 20–39%, 40–59%," and so on. The rater responds to each item by marking the appropriate scale point to estimate how often he or she has observed the ratee to show the behavior. The ratings given to related items are summed to obtain dimension scores.

There are advantages in using the BOS. To the extent that its items are developed from a representative sample of critical behavior on the job, the BOS can be accepted as content-valid.[5] The frequency scale is a reasonable way to maintain an emphasis on actual job performance. If job-relevant behavior is observed, then reporting these observations should provide a valid performance appraisal. On the other hand, the BOS does have certain weaknesses. The phrasing of BOS statements tends to be transparent as to how positive or important the behaviors are. Considering this transparency, it would be easy enough for a rater to respond simply by using his or her overall evaluation of the ratee. Although the BOS is meant to encourage reports of observation,

[5]To claim content validity for any of the specialized instruments discussed in this section, keep in mind that content validity depends on how well the job analysis has been done. If a thorough job analysis is not already available, then one will have to be done. Shortcuts must not be taken in the job analysis or in developing items.

some raters will not respond to the scale in this way, but will simply use it to give an employee a certain rating. Therefore, transparency in the scale values might mean that subjectivity and rating errors are not resolved with the BOS, any more than they are with simpler graphic rating scales. Research on the cognitive processes of rating with the BOS suggests this interpretation (Murphy, Martin, & Garcia, 1982). It might be especially likely for the problems to remain when there are many items to rate. In complex jobs, a very large number of items—sometimes as many as 80—are included on the BOS (Latham & Wexley, 1977). Obviously, such a large number might be needed to provide an adequate sample of behavior on the job. It also means that completing the rating can be time consuming, and a rater might be inclined to take a shortcut and simply rate the employee according to an overall impression, rather than report observed behavior.

**Mixed Standard Scale (MSS)**    A third, highly specialized appraisal technique is the Mixed Standard Scale (MSS) (Blanz & Ghiselli, 1972). The creators of this scale wanted to provide a way to deal with subjectivity and rating errors, particularly halo and leniency.

Like the scales discussed above, the MSS begins with a thorough job analysis. SME-groups generate critical incidents that distinguish between different levels of performance. The SMEs use these incidents to identify performance dimensions and to develop behavioral statements representing various levels on each dimension. To construct the MSS, three descriptions per dimension are selected to represent three levels—good, average, and poor performance. These behavioral descriptions are the "standards" against which a ratee's performance is to be compared. Blanz and Ghiselli (1972) pointed out that many rating methods present the rater with descriptions of performance at different levels and require the rater to mark the one that best describes the ratee. In using the MSS, however, the rater does much more than this. The rater must respond to every statement. As you can see in Figure 14.9, the rater responds to an item by entering a plus (+) sign if the person's performance is *better* than that described, a zero (0) if the performance *fits* that description, or a minus (−) sign if the person's performance is *worse* than that described. A score on the dimension can range from a low of 1 in which all three statements are given minuses, to a high of 7 in which all three are given pluses.

To assemble the MSS, the items for all dimensions are shuffled together and drawn up as a single list. This produces an instrument in which it is not easy for a rater to form a clear picture of the dimension and performance level being assessed. As a result, the rater must respond separately to each item. However, like other performance appraisal procedures that purposely disguise performance dimensions and levels, the MSS leaves the rater not only without any clear sense of how good a rating has been given, but also with very little information that he or she can use for feedback to the ratee.

---

**Instructions** Rate each item by selecting and entering one of the following responses in the space provided:

+   ratee's performance is better than this
0   ratee's performance fits this description
−   ratee's performance is worse than this

---

_____   Participates very little in meetings and conferences, and as a result does not have much influence on the decisions made. (I,p)

_____   Plays an active part in most meetings and conferences, and sometimes influences the outcomes of the discussion. (I,a)

_____   Rarely has original ideas, and almost always deals with problems in the routine fashion. (II,p)

_____   Fully appreciates the value of proven ways of dealing with problems, but also thinks creatively and has many new ideas. (II,g)

_____   Contributes in many ways in any meeting or conference; plays an active part in discussion and has very real influence on the outcomes and decisions made. (I,g)

_____   Does have some ideas, but usually is content with the customary and familiar solutions. (II,a)

---

Notes: The codes in parenthesis at the end of each item refer to the dimension and the performance level. Dimension I is "participation in meetings" and dimension II is "originality of ideas." The performance levels are good (g), average (a), and poor (p). The codes are not included on the actual instrument.

---

FIGURE **14.9**

MSS item examples from two performance dimensions.

Adapted from "The Mixed Standard Scale: A New Rating System," by F. Blanz and E. E. Ghiselli, 1972, *Personnel Psychology, 25*, table 2, pp. 191–192. Copyright 1972 by Personnel Psychology, Inc., Bowling Green, Ohio. Adapted by permission.

---

The purpose of the cloaked arrangement is to ensure that the rater does not simply use an overall impression of the ratee and produce a rating that contains errors, such as leniency and halo. How well does the MSS do in controlling rater errors? Although not a lot of research has evaluated it, the MSS does not appear to have fully realized its goal of error control (Finley, Osburn, Dubin, & Jeanneret, 1977; Saal & Landy, 1977). Even so, rater error is a problem for all subjective rating procedures, and the MSS is probably as good as many other techniques. Also, the originators pointed out how the MSS can detect logical errors and carelessness. For example, if a person is rated *better* than the statement representing good performance and *worse* than the statement representing poor performance, the scorer knows this is nonsense and may infer that the rater was not paying attention.

## Conclusions

Historically, it has been difficult to obtain accurate performance information. Researchers and practitioners looking for reliable and valid performance appraisal methods have been plagued by the problems of subjectivity and rater error. From the 1960s to the 1980s, many studies focused on new rating scales designed specifically to address these problems. Each new scale proposed to provide better performance information and more effective error controls than the one before. For a while, it looked as if these new instruments would solve the problems. They did improve things. For example, by including supervisors in the construction of job-specific rating scales, such as the BARS, improvements were made. A rater's knowledge of performance dimensions often was increased, and raters became more accepting of the rating process. However, the new rating scales did not solve all the problems. Research attempting to show that one rating format was better than another largely was unable to do so. Landy and Farr (1980) reviewed this research, found that rating scale format accounted for very little of the variance in ratings, and concluded that it hardly mattered what type of rating scale was used. Many researchers lost interest in studying rating scales. If the specialized, difficult-to-develop rating systems did not do any better than a simple graphic rating scale, then these methods were not worth the trouble it took to develop them. Still, not everyone found performance appraisal methodology to be in such poor shape. Although rating scale format might not matter much, job-based rating systems constitute much more than format, and both Borman (1991) and Guion (1998b) reflected on the potential value of putting such a system in place. Developed carefully, rating systems can guide a rater's actions. They help the rater know what to look for in observing performance and how to translate observations into rating scale values.

In the 1980s and 1990s, studies of the rater's cognitive processes began to highlight the difficulty of performance appraisal, noting that raters have to observe, remember, and translate performance information into rating dimensions. Also, because performance probably varies over the appraisal period, a rater has to take this into account, as well. Of course, if a rater has observed throughout the period and has used some systematic method for this, such as a BARS system, the cognitive workload at the time the rating is due should not be too heavy. However, if a rater has not used any such observational system, it will be difficult to remember and subjectively average performance levels over the appraisal period. Once again, it became obvious to researchers that raters needed help in doing performance appraisal and, once again, it appeared that a new rating system might do the trick.

Some researchers were interested in a system that could track performance over time and minimize the amount of subjective "averaging" that was necessary. Kane's (1986) Performance Distribution Assessment (PDA) model was meant to do this. In his model, performance is conceptualized as a set of distributions showing the levels of work quality achieved over repeated performances of a task or duty within a specified time period. Development of this rating system requires a lengthy process of defining dimensions and identifying expected levels of performance. To use the rating system, the rater must estimate the percentage of time a ratee has achieved each level of performance on each dimension, at various points throughout the appraisal period. These multiple ratings over time yield distributions of performance on different dimensions. When the performance appraisal is due, the "average" performance levels are assessed, not subjectively, but statistically from the distributions.

When Kane's PDA was introduced in the 1980s, it drew little attention, possibly because the system is complex and not easy to develop or analyze. More recently, a few studies have evaluated distributional ratings. In one study, actual performance variability was controlled in a laboratory setting, and both distributional ratings and BOS ratings were collected from observers of videotaped performers (Steiner, Rain, & Smalley, 1993). In a field study, distributional ratings were compared to an objective measure of productivity and to ratings on an ordinary graphic rating scale (Deadrick & Gardner, 1997). In both studies, distributional ratings were found to reflect the actual variability in performance. However, in neither of the studies did these ratings perform any better than the nondistributional rating scales in providing a measure of average performance. If nothing more than the level of average performance is needed, then distributional ratings might not be worth the effort.

## SUMMING UP

The purpose of this chapter is to describe the methodology of performance appraisal and to discuss the attendant problems and issues. Summing up, we can make the following conclusions:

- Two types of performance measures are used—objective and subjective.
- Employees' supervisors are considered the best source of appraisal.
- For employees who work in teams, self and peer ratings are possible.
- Many employers use 360-degree systems for managerial assessment.
- Performance appraisals must be checked for reliability and accuracy.
- Raters may make errors because they do not adequately observe and because they are lenient.

- Accurate performance rating is a cognitively difficult task made easier by learning strategies for observing, remembering, and drawing inferences.
- Some appraisal methods use checklists and ranking procedures.
- The most frequently used appraisal method is a graphic rating scale.
- Several specialized rating scales have been created, expressly to improve the rating process, including the BARS, BSS, BOS, and MSS.

## INFOTRAC COLLEGE EDITION

Want to learn more about the issues discussed here? Use your subscription to InfoTrac College Edition to access an online library of research journals and other periodicals. Go to http://www.infotrac-college.com/wadsworth and enter a search term. Any of the following terms can be used in a keyword search to find articles about some topics reviewed in this chapter. (Note: Adding an asterisk to a keyword allows a search for other forms of the word, such as the plural of a singular term.)

Employee performance and (appraisal or evaluation)
360-degree appraisal*

Criterion measures
Performance rating technique*

# USES OF PERFORMANCE APPRAISAL

Does every organization have a formal performance appraisal system? Only a few surveys have been done to determine how widespread formal appraisal is. However, it appears that most companies do conduct performance appraisals. Surveys reported in the 1970s and 1980s indicated that between 74 percent and 96 percent of U.S. organizations, and a comparable proportion of British firms, had a formal performance appraisal system in place. Large, complex organizations—more than small firms—were especially likely to conduct formal appraisals (Cleveland, Murphy, & Williams, 1989; Murphy & Cleveland, 1991). It may appear that where you work, there is no appraisal system. If you are unaware of ever having had your performance assessed in any formal manner, it may be that you work for one of the companies that has no such system. If you have had a performance appraisal, you probably are aware of at least one of the organization's purposes in conducting appraisals. You may have been given feedback on how you could improve, or the appraisal may have been the basis for a raise or promotion. These are common organizational uses of performance appraisal.

## USING PERFORMANCE APPRAISAL FOR EMPLOYEE SELECTION PURPOSES

For what purpose is performance appraisal needed? Mainly, there are three important uses. All—either directly or indirectly—relate to employee selection. First, performance is the criterion behavior being predicted by selection measures. Therefore, performance appraisal is needed to establish the validity of the selection instrument. Second, because performance appraisal is used as justification for making administrative decisions, we can consider it to have a "selection" use. That is, on the basis of their performance appraisals, employees are "selected" to be retained or terminated, or to be granted a raise, promotion, or transfer. Third, administrative decisions made on the basis of performance appraisal can affect the need for recruiting and hiring new employees. For example, when positions are vacated by transferring or promoting employees or by terminating poor performers, the positions must be filled again. Ultimately, this brings us back to the beginning of the selection process, at which point we need to hire employees for the position openings. When the impact of using performance appraisal for administrative purposes results in open positions, a company can handle this need for additional selection in two ways: (1) by further use of performance appraisal to fill the positions from within, through promoting or transferring current employees, or (2) by recruiting and hiring new employees from outside the organization.

All of these uses are possible. The question is whether employers actually use performance appraisal in these ways. A survey of industry practices showed that they do. Most importantly, in the organizations contacted, performance appraisal was used to make individual employee assessments and identify employees' strengths and weaknesses in order to provide feedback. These organizations also used performance appraisal to make between-employee comparisons, for the purpose of recognizing individual employees, and to identify poor performers. Some organizations used performance appraisal to provide for research and documentation, especially for documenting personnel decisions and meeting legal requirements (Cleveland, Murphy, & Williams, 1989).

In this chapter, I discuss these important relationships between performance appraisal and employee selection.

## VALIDATION OF SELECTION MEASURES

Performance appraisal is used in validation studies of selection measures. As such, the appraisal functions as the criterion measure in criterion-related validity studies. Such studies often are conducted in research laboratories. They can similarly be conducted in field studies, when an organization develops and validates its own selection measures. Recall from previous discussion that criterion-related validation involves administering a selection instrument to a sample, collecting their scores, and correlating these with the sample's scores on a performance criterion measure. To ensure that the selection measure is valid, it must be documented that the measure can predict the performance criterion. The correlation can show the extent to which this can be assumed. However, the fault for a low correlation may lie with either the selection measure or the performance criterion measure.

Use of performance appraisal as the criterion measure requires evidence that the appraisal is an accurate assessment of job performance. That is, to determine whether the selection instrument is valid, we must first establish that the performance appraisal instrument is itself a reliable and valid measure. It is difficult to empirically validate a performance criterion measure, usually because nothing is available with which to correlate performance ratings. However, if the performance appraisal has been developed through job analysis, as some appraisals are, then content validity can be argued. I discussed several of these methods in Chapter 14.

A reliability estimate will give some information about the validity of a performance criterion measure. Briefly, if the measure is highly reliable, it *may* be valid; if it is not reliable, it also is not valid. What we need in pursuing evidence of criterion validity is to obtain a measure of interrater reliability. This is commonly used to show the stability of the measure across raters. In contrast, intrarater reliability refers to the consistency of single raters in using the different rating items or dimensions, and it is expressed as the rating's internal consistency. Because of the differences in how they are conceptualized and assessed, these two indices of reliability are not equivalent, and they should not be treated as such (Viswesvaran, Ones, & Schmidt, 1996). The difference is a matter of how to interpret the raters' personal influences on ratings. In interrater reliability, a rater's individual ways of perceiving and understanding employee performance are considered to be sources of error in ratings, rather than true differences among ratees. In intrarater reliability assessments, however, the influences of raters cannot be distinguished from real variation in ratee performance. Viswesvaran et al. (1996) found that estimates of reliability yielded by the two techniques were not equal. The average interrater reliability coefficient was .52, whereas the average intrarater or internal consistency estimate was .86. Certainly, it can be helpful to obtain the two reliability estimates, such as in designing rating procedures. However, only the more conservative, interrater reliability estimate is appropriate for use in validity studies because it is less likely to overestimate validity.

Some researchers have speculated that using performance appraisals collected routinely for administrative uses is not a good way to validate selection measures. One reason is that rater leniency can be a serious problem. Excessively lenient ratings cannot provide a useful criterion measure for validation studies because they do not give information about low performance. This information is essential if the selection measure is to be accurate in identifying and rejecting applicants who are likely to be low performers. Lenient ratings might be more likely when raters must conduct appraisals for multiple, rather than single, uses. For example, industry practice suggests that when multiple uses are planned, raters will first assess the potential consequences of each use of the performance appraisal, and then conduct the appraisal according to what they believe is its most important purpose (Longenecker, Sims, & Gioia, 1987). If the main purpose is to determine pay increases for employees in a unit, then we might expect ratings to be more lenient than if the purpose is to identify individuals' strengths and weaknesses. Ratings conducted for administrative purposes might not be useful for validation research, not only because of leniency, but also because they might consider personal variables, such as seniority, which are irrelevant and a source of error in research-oriented appraisals. A field study was conducted which demonstrated that administrative-based ratings were more lenient than research-based ratings. They also reflected the employee's level of seniority, whereas the research ratings did not. Most importantly, only the research ratings were correlated with a predictor measure, indicating that the ratings done for administrative purposes were not useful as a criterion measure for a selection validation study (Harris, Smith, & Champagne, 1995).

## EMPLOYEE DEVELOPMENT

The organization has two other, closely related purposes for performance appraisal—employee development and administrative decisions on employee status. In both, the retention or termination of employees is affected. For example, if employees are satisfactory performers, the employer will want to retain them—for two reasons. One, continued employment of these individuals is economical because they perform effectively on what they were hired to do. Two, by retaining satisfactory performers, the company saves the expense of replacing them with new employees whose performance may or may not be satisfactory.

What does employee development entail, from the standpoint of the employer? Most importantly, employee development requires feedback from performance appraisal. All employees need to receive information about the extent to which their performance is satisfactory. Feedback from an accurate performance appraisal can inform an employee about strengths and weaknesses, and it can identify actions he or she can take to improve on the job or to increase qualifications for advancement. For a borderline satisfactory performer, employee development can include sending the person to training or making changes in work assignments or transfers, in order to increase the person's chances for retention. For high-performing employees, performance feedback can provide rewards and motivation, such as when the quality of their performance warrants a pay increase. Development of these employees can involve identifying ways to become qualified for promotion to higher positions in the organization, and it may include training.

### Performance Improvement

One of the most important uses of performance appraisal is to increase the potential for performance improvement. Most employees can improve in some way. Even those who are effective performers usually have certain weaknesses, and they can benefit from having these identified, especially if the employee

seems interested in his or her own career development. It is essential that the employer provide feedback to employees who are at or below the minimum satisfactory levels of performance. For these employees, the purpose of the feedback is corrective. Even though it may not be pleasant to have one's errors pointed out, receiving such information can serve as a warning, and hearing the supervisor's suggestions for what to do instead can help the person improve. Feedback is considered necessary when someone is in training to learn a new skill or area of knowledge. Likewise, when an employee is new to a job, feedback is necessary.

How does feedback about previous work performance improve performance in a later period? One possibility is that feedback—especially if it is negative—can motivate change. When employees receive only positive feedback from a review, the message is that they are performing satisfactorily and that no changes need to be made. When employees receive some amount of negative feedback, however, a different message is received. It means that in some way performance is not effective and improvements should be made. This implies that we can expect to see greater change in the behavior of those who receive negative feedback than in the behavior of those who receive only positive feedback. There is evidence of this effect, although it depends on whether the feedback is believable. The more credible the feedback information, the stronger the effect of negative feedback on later performance (Podsakoff & Farh, 1989).

When is feedback more acceptable to an employee? One possibility is that it is more acceptable when it is consistent with one's own self-assessment. Korsgaard (1996) reported evidence of this from a study using self-appraisals along with appraisals from others. Feedback that was consistent with the person's self-appraisal was accepted. However, there was greater performance improvement when the feedback was more positive than the self-appraisal. This result suggests that personal variables might affect the acceptability and use of performance feedback. Nease, Mudgett, and Quiñones (1999) pointed out that when employees must learn new skills on the job, it is not uncommon that they receive repeated negative evaluations. The researchers reasoned that the employee might not react the same to later negative evaluations as to the initial evaluation and that this might be determined in part by the employee's personal characteristics. In their study, they found that some employees did not react the same and that the individual's sense of self-efficacy had an important impact in determining the reaction. Specifically, those with high self-efficacy were less accepting of repeated negative feedback than they were of the initial evaluation. For those with low self-efficacy, there was no difference in their reactions to the initial and later evaluations. The researchers interpreted these results as meaning that employees with high self-efficacy become frustrated with the apparent ineffectiveness of their efforts to improve and begin to doubt the authenticity of the negative feedback. Those with low self-efficacy seemed more willing to accept that their efforts to improve had not been successful.

**Giving Feedback**    Employers can get expert advice on how to conduct both the appraisal process and the feedback interview, either directly from the research literature or from consultants who have knowledge of this literature. However, some experts think employers either are not interested or, for some other reason, are not listening. For example, in an article addressed to managers in government organizations, Kikoski (1999) repeated several points of advice on handling performance appraisals that had been made in a much earlier article (Kikoski & Litterer, 1983). In the first article, because they had noted that public agency managers appeared to resist giving performance feedback, the authors hoped to advise managers on how to conduct the appraisal interview and communicate more effectively. In the later article, Kikoski reported that the problem of inadequate feedback interviews appeared to be worse than before. The problem at both times was ineffective interpersonal communication that left the employee out of the process. Providing employees with feedback about their performance can help them in several ways. Feedback can provide positive reinforcement for good performers. It can be directive for both good and poor performers. It can identify specific areas in which an employee can improve. It can identify appropriate paths for an employee to take to enhance career development. Why, then, do supervisors resist giving feedback?

Research (e.g., Larson, 1986) has documented the tendency for supervisors to avoid giving feedback to poor performers or to distort the information to make it seem less negative. There appear to be a number of reasons for this. Sometimes, a supervisor simply wants to give an employee a break or wishes to avoid confronting an employee. However, the failure to provide accurate feedback can signal a deliberate misuse of the performance appraisal system. Positive appraisals may be given to a poor performer in order to justify promoting the employee and moving him or her up and out of the department (Longenecker, Sims, & Gioia, 1987). Some research has been done in an effort to determine what brings managers to avoid or subvert their responsibility to such an extent. Larson (1984) suggested that the perception of an employee's responsibility for performance outcomes might affect whether the supervisor gives feedback. Specifically, the extent of a person's responsibility for an outcome can explain his or her actions and, in this way, can affect the supervisor's willingness to provide feedback. In a laboratory study, Moss and Martinko (1998) evaluated the effect of effort and ability attributions in determining a supervisor's feedback behavior toward a poor performer, under conditions in which the supervisor's own rewards depended on the subordinate's performance. They found that the combined effects of these variables could explain the type of feedback given. When the supervisor's rewards were dependent on the subordinate, more punitive feedback was given to poor performers who were seen as not making an effort. In contrast, more corrective feedback was given to poor performers who were seen as having low ability. These results indicate that the relationship between the supervisor and the employee can determine the nature and extent of the feedback given.

## Absenteeism

Although job-specific feedback obviously is useful for employee development, information about more general employee behavior can be discussed in feedback interviews. As you know, attendance is a general work requirement, and data on absenteeism can be collected as an objective measure of performance. Nonlegitimate absences represent a problem to be handled, and employees need to understand the employer's policy on absenteeism.

Absenteeism can be understood in terms of its relationship to job performance. In their review of theory and research, Harrison and Martocchio (1998) found several studies reporting evidence that absenteeism is negatively correlated with job performance (e.g., Bycio, 1992). That is, employees who are excessively absent are less likely to be high performers. Performance is seen to decline following absences, possibly because the employee has lost opportunities to keep up with what is going on at work. To the extent that pay is performance-contingent, the absences and the associated decline of performance can lead to lost pay and fewer promotions. Although absenteeism often is described as a simple form of withdrawal from work, currently, it is being treated as a productivity problem. Harrison and Martocchio (1998) found several studies placing absenteeism in the same category as other nonproductive and counterproductive behaviors, such as idling, off-task behavior, unruliness, and drug use. These behaviors involve deliberate reductions of attention and effort and disrupt productivity.

Absenteeism has long been considered to be dysfunctional to the organization. It is costly, for a number of reasons. For some nonlegitimate absences, paid sick leave is taken. In addition, bringing in replacements to do the absent employee's work may be necessary. Both coworkers and supervisors have reactions to an employee's absence. Coworkers may have to pick up the slack.

Supervisors usually have to decide what to do about nonlegitimate absences. Absenteeism also may be an antecedent of voluntary turnover. Mitra, Jenkins, and Gupta (1992) reported a correlation of .33 between absence-taking and turnover. The progression from absenteeism to turnover might be a rather short-term process, with increased absenteeism a few weeks before the person quits (Harrison & Martocchio, 1998).

What can be done about nonlegitimate absences? Information about inappropriate and excessive absenteeism can be collected as part of performance appraisal and discussed with the employee in the feedback interview. Some organizations have a formal policy, which treats unexcused absences as a violation of acceptable employee behavior and provides for disciplining absence-takers. If a formal absence control policy is in place, it is easier for supervisors to determine what to do about an absence problem. A supervisor can feel justified in disciplining employees for excessive absences if he or she has the backing of the organization through such a policy.

Research suggests there might be several factors that influence the decision to apply discipline for unexcused absences. For example, these factors might include the employee's employment status, history of absences, level of job performance, and how critically needed the employee is. Martocchio and Judge (1995) asked supervisors and subordinates what should be done about absenteeism. Respondents were in strong agreement that disciplinary action should be taken in response to unauthorized absence. Although there were some differences, in general, supervisors and subordinates agreed that more severe disciplinary decisions were appropriate when the employee had a history of absenteeism, performed at a below-average level on the job, or when the person was a new employee.

## Conclusions

Is performance appraisal helpful to employees in maintaining a high level of job performance and effective work behavior? We can conclude that it is. Conducting a performance review tells employees that performance matters to the employer and that someone is paying attention to how employees behave at work, including the extent of their absenteeism. What is most helpful is direct and honest feedback from the performance appraisal. Feedback that addresses relevant and important aspects of job-specific performance and general work behavior especially can be helpful to an employee who needs to make adjustments. Of course, these benefits depend on whether and how feedback is delivered. Sometimes, the actual usefulness of feedback depends on how the employer conveys it, because communication can determine whether the employee accepts the information.

# Administrative Decision Making and Action

Performance appraisal is the basis for administrative decision making and action, such as salary administration, promotions, and terminations. This use of performance appraisal clearly is connected to employee development. However, it can be distinguished from employee development by the frame of reference that must be adopted by the rater. Let me explain. To assess an employee's strengths and weaknesses for employee development purposes, the rater adopts a within-individual frame of reference. Focusing on the single employee, the rater evaluates the person's performance on each dimension, relative to his or her performance on other dimensions. When the purpose of performance appraisal is to have a basis for making administrative decisions that affect all employees, a between-individuals frame of reference is necessary. In this, each employee's performance is compared to the performance of other employees.

The need to shift from one frame of reference to another brings up the question of whether multiple uses of the same performance appraisal are reasonable. Within-individual and between-individuals comparisons result in two different kinds of performance information. This means that these uses of performance appraisal may be in conflict, just as they are when appraisals are done for administrative versus research uses. Raters probably will be able to provide only one type of information in conducting any single performance appraisal. Appraisals that have been prepared for one organizational use are likely to be inadequate for a different use. For example, for employee development, specific information about an employee's performance over time is needed, and the performance appraisal focuses on that single individual. For administrative decision making, performance appraisal must provide information about how one employee's performance compares to the performance of other employees. If a rating satisfies one of these conditions, it probably does not satisfy the other. It would be best to conduct more than one set of performance appraisals whenever the uses are in conflict. In practice, however, organizations usually conduct only one appraisal per employee, and the appraisals are forced to satisfy at least two purposes even though the purposes may conflict (Cleveland et al.,1989).

## *Retention and Voluntary Turnover*

Employers value and want to retain employees who perform well on the job and who contribute to the operation and success of the organization. Therefore, they are likely to provide monetary rewards, such as raises and bonuses, and developmental opportunities, such as training and promotions, in order to retain high performers and prevent their voluntary turnover. Employers also want to retain average performers and are likely to provide rewards to encourage these employees to stay. They may invest in the retention of borderline performers, such as by providing remedial training, if it appears that the employee can improve and raise the level of performance. When employees do not improve to an acceptable level, it is sometimes possible to retain them by transferring or demoting them to jobs they can perform. Otherwise, termination is a better solution. Although there are costs in terminating an employee, the costs can be greater when a poorly performing employee is retained.

For some years now, researchers have been studying the nature and possible effects of voluntary turnover. In particular, they have been interested in determining who is likely to quit their jobs and whether there is any reason for employers to worry about the possibility that their most valued employees might quit. Under certain conditions, it appears that voluntary turnover is not always dysfunctional but, rather, can actually benefit the employer. For example, when poor rather than good performers quit, when the costs of replacing a quitter are low, and when the *replacement* is likely to be a high performer, then turnover is considered to be functional for the organization.

The interest in this question was piqued some years ago, when researchers—who assumed turnover to be dysfunctional because of good performers leaving—actually found that poor performers were somewhat more likely to leave than good performers (e.g., McEvoy & Cascio, 1987). Later studies confirmed the finding that poor performers are likely to quit. However, the result was found to be stronger in organizations using performance-contingent reward systems. That is, low-performing employees were more likely to leave when earnings were contingent on the level of performance (Williams & Livingstone, 1994). When the compensation system provided relatively little base pay, with a large proportion of earnings coming from commissions, the relationship between low performance and turnover was pronounced. The effect was strongest among sales employees who worked under a commission-only system, which is a maximally contingent reward system with pay based entirely on performance (Harrison, Virick, & William, 1996). These studies suggest that an employer who chooses to reward only good performance can encourage good performers to stay on the job and poor performers to leave.

The remaining question is whether the relationship between performance and turnover is as linear as these studies seem to imply. That is, because low performers are more likely to quit, does this mean that average performers are moderately likely to quit and high performers are least likely to quit? This is a linear interpretation, and it might be a good assumption, although not necessarily so. Another interpretation suggests that the relationship might be curvilinear. That is, both low and high performers might be more likely to leave their jobs than average performers (Jackofsky, 1984). For example, low performers might leave, even though their prospects for another job might not be

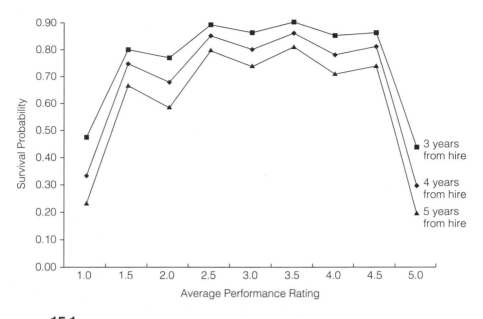

good, because they feel threatened by the possibility that they might be fired. High performers might leave because they have good prospects for other jobs, especially if they have had promotions and other career development opportunities while with the company. However, average performers are not likely to quit. They do not have the alternatives for other jobs that high performers have. Also, their performance is good enough that they are not threatened by the possibility of being fired.

Trevor, Gerhart, and Boudreau (1997) examined the curvilinearity hypothesis in a study using salaried employees. The results showed the hypothesized relationship with turnover being substantially greater for both the lowest and highest performers, than for the average performers. Figure 15.1 shows the inversion of this relationship. Each curve indicates the probability of survival or retention on the job, at different levels of performance. The three curves show the proportion of employees who remained on the job for 3, 4, or 5 years. Notice that for each tenure level, the probability of staying was low at the lowest levels of performance, increased as performance improved, leveled off at higher performance levels, and then sharply declined at the highest performance level. This means that many low and high performers had quit their jobs. The

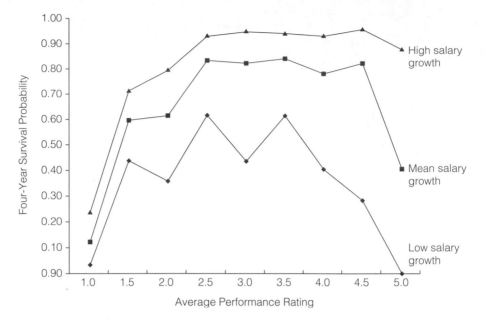

FIGURE **15.2**

Probability of four-year survival or retention of employees by performance level and rate of salary growth. The graph demonstrates a curvilinear relationship between performance and retention, moderated by salary growth.

Adapted from "Voluntary Turnover and Job Performance: Curvilinearity and the Moderating Influences of Salary Growth and Promotions," by C. O. Trevor, B. Gerhart, and J. W. Boudreau, 1997, *Journal of Applied Psychology, 82*, (1), figure 3, p. 57. Copyright 1997 by American Psychological Association, Washington, DC. Used by permission.

researchers further explored whether salary growth might moderate the relationship between performance and turnover. They looked at the rate of increase in pay at different performance levels. They found that pay increased at a more rapid rate for employees performing at the *lower* levels than for those performing at *higher* levels. The most severe effect of low salary growth was at the highest performance levels. Among top performers, low salary growth predicted extremely high turnover. You can see this in Figure 15.2. The implication is clear: If employers fail to pay top performers commensurate with their high performance levels, they are likely to lose their very best employees.

## *Termination*

Much of the movement out of organizations is through voluntary turnover. This type of turnover serves the departing employees' needs. However, some turnover is involuntary from the employee's standpoint and serves the organization's needs. Two forms of involuntary turnover—firing and laying off—are meant to be functional for the organization.

For what reasons do employers terminate employees? When an employee is fired, research indicates that the most common reason is poor performance. For example, in a study of terminations in different organizations, the strongest determinant was the level of performance. Performance of terminated employees was significantly lower than the performance of retained employees and of employees who had quit their jobs (Wanous, Stumpf, & Bedrosian, 1979).

Are layoffs conducted on the same basis, or do employers have other reasons for letting employees go? Employers must lay off a percentage of the workforce when their organization is undergoing a downsizing effort. They often start by laying off poor performers. Other employees are likely to leave in exchange for a beneficial termination package, such as early retirement benefits. These two categories of workforce reduction may not fill the need for downsizing, however, and other employees probably will have to be laid off. To be as functional as possible, the layoff should not include the company's high performers. However, it is likely that the company will have to lay off some employees whose performance is at least somewhat satisfactory and who, under ordinary conditions, would be allowed to remain on their jobs. Barrick, Mount, and Strauss (1994) were interested in discovering the basis for decisions to lay off average performers, and they studied the decision-making process of an active reduction-in-force. They found that the strongest predictor of a layoff decision was job performance, as measured by supervisory ratings and an objective production measure. Because of the strong effects of performance levels on layoff decisions, the researchers reasoned that other variables which relate to performance might also have an effect on the layoff decision, and the results of their study confirmed this. They found that general mental ability and conscientiousness affected layoff decisions. Specifically, high ability and conscientious employees performed at higher levels and in turn were less likely to be laid off during a downsizing. The study also showed that the employee's tenure was an important contributor to the layoff decision, although not in the direction you might think. The organization did not follow the "last hired, first fired" convention. Newer employees were not more likely to be laid off. The strategy of laying off more senior employees—who also were more highly paid—was seen as a cost savings, which was consistent with the purpose of downsizing.

From these studies showing that the level of performance is the primary basis for termination, we can conclude that performance appraisal has an important and direct role to play in the decision to fire or lay off an employee. Because emotions usually run high at time of termination, employers need to establish that they are using effective appraisal techniques and to conduct the termination interview with sensitivity. Karl and Hancock (1999) contacted employers about the extent to which they had followed the advice of experts in conducting termination interviews. The employers appeared to be following expert advice about who should be present. Conventional wisdom is that termination interviews should be conducted by at least two individuals, such as the immediate supervisor and the HR manager. However, those who had followed this advice had not had the expected experience. Instead, they reported higher hostility from the terminated employee than when the supervisor alone conducted the interview. The researchers found that most employers were not following expert advice about the best location and time for such interviews (e.g., during the week instead of Friday afternoon). However, their experiences were more positive than when they had followed expert advice. It is questionable, therefore, whether the current expert advice is "expert" after all. Perhaps, better study is needed to determine what actually works, before employers are advised about this.

## Legal Issues

**Fair Employment**    Performance appraisals can be central to legal actions taken against an employer. As I discussed in Chapter 6, several fair employment laws have been enacted over the past decades. Title VII of the 1964 Civil Rights Act prohibits employer practices that result in adverse impact on employment opportunity. Clearly, as it is interpreted by the EEOC's *Uniform Guidelines* (1978), the law addresses selection procedures used for the initial hiring of employees. However, selection is interpreted broadly to include other decisions that can affect employment opportunity, including those that result in salary increases, promotions, and terminations. By this interpretation, performance appraisal is used to "select" those who will be given a raise, promoted, or terminated. This means that performance appraisals are subject to legal scrutiny, and it suggests also that performance appraisal methods might need to be evaluated for their reliability and validity as "selection" measures.

Establishing the validity of a performance appraisal instrument is not easy to do, as I have discussed. However, it appears that the courts which hear employee termination cases often do not seek empirical evidence of validity in considering the use of performance information for termination decisions. Instead, organizations have successfully defended their performance appraisal systems by showing that they were based on job analysis and a rational or content-oriented developmental procedure (Feild & Holley, 1982). Werner and Bolino (1997) found that the U.S. circuit courts were actually more concerned about fairness and the due process of law than validation of the performance appraisal instrument. The reviewers found that case outcomes more often were determined by whether (1) the performance appraisal was based on a job analysis, (2) written instructions were given to raters, and (3) the appraisal was reviewed with the employee. In addition, the courts seemed interested in whether there was interrater agreement when multiple raters were used. Although there was not a great deal of emphasis on validity studies, validation was not entirely unimportant in these cases. Out of 295 cases, the researchers identified only 9 in which the court actively considered validation. In these 9 cases, however, the issue was highly important, and the decision was determined by the validation evidence. When a high-quality validity study could be submitted for review, the court decision favored the organization.

**Employment-At-Will**     Traditionally, U.S. employers have had the right to terminate an employee with no legal requirement to justify the action. This right is part of what are commonly known as "employment-at-will" rights. Employers still hold these rights, although they have been limited somewhat by fair employment laws that prohibit terminations based on discriminatory practices, for example. However, through certain of their actions, employers can effectively reduce their own at-will rights. Sometimes, employers make promises, offer bonuses, or even draw up official contracts to get applicants to accept employment offers or to discourage current employees from leaving. These actions can restrict the employer's right to terminate the employee, especially during the term of such agreement. Employers also can limit their employment-at-will rights in other ways, such as by what is implied in interactions with an employee. For example, an employee may be misled by representatives of the employer into believing that he or she has high job security or even permanent employment. It may further be implied that the company will not terminate the person except for extreme misbehavior or seriously deficient job performance. The employee might understand this as an "implied contract" and believe it to be substantiated when satisfactory performance evaluations are received over a long period. Termination, then, can look like a violation of the implied contract. For example, in one situation, an employee was fired after having been with the company for 32 years. Over the years, the individual had been promoted from an unskilled job up through the ranks to a high-level managerial position. The employee claimed that an "implied contract" had existed affirming that he would not be terminated without cause, and he based the claim on his years of satisfactory performance reviews (*Pugh v. See's Candies*, 1981).

Wrongful discharge lawsuits may be considered with respect to the legal principle of "implied covenant of good faith and fair dealing," which refers to the behavior of parties who have established a contract. According to the legal principle, neither party may deprive the other of the benefits of the contract. In a wrongful discharge lawsuit, the employee tries first to convince the court that there was reason to believe that a contract had been implied, and second to show that the termination was made without cause, such as by presenting evidence of satisfactory performance. In response, the employer tries to show either that there was no implied contract—and employment-at-will-rights had been retained—or that the termination was made with cause, such as by presenting evidence that performance or general work behavior was substandard. It also can be helpful for the employer to show that the employee was informed of the problem and given an opportunity to improve. Obviously, because of the potential problems and costs of making such agreements, employers are advised to think carefully about drawing up formal contracts and strictly to avoid any implication that a contract exists when in fact it does not. For this reason, some employers protect their rights by including "at-will" termination language in employee handbooks and by doing their best to conduct performance appraisals accurately.

## *Conclusions*

Organizations need to be in control of employee retention and turnover. The use of reliable and valid performance appraisal methods and a rational salary administration plan can make this possible. Performance appraisal can identify employees who should be retained, and a pay-for-performance compensation plan can be applied appropriately to reward and encourage high and average performers to remain with the company.

Employee turnover is not always dysfunctional. Either voluntary or involuntary turnover of poorly performing employees can be functional for the organization, especially if the replacement personnel are at least satisfactory. Voluntary turnover can be dysfunctional, however, when it involves a company's best performers. In preventing this type of turnover, the employer needs to compare the costs of paying for the high performance with the costs of losing such valuable employees and having to replace them with other individuals whose performance levels may be more or less known to the company.

## SUMMING UP

The purpose of this chapter is to complete the discussion of performance appraisal by addressing the organizational uses of appraisal. Briefly summing up, we can make the following conclusions:

- Performance appraisal is the basis for decisions such as promotion or termination of an employee.
- Job-specific and general work performance is discussed with employees in feedback interviews.
- Employee retention is an important action involving both performance appraisal and salary administration.
- Turnover and termination of poor performers can be functional for an organization.

- Voluntary turnover follows a curvilinear pattern, with both low and high performers more likely to quit their jobs.
- Some legal actions taken against employers involve terminations.

## InfoTrac College Edition

Would you like to learn more about the issues reviewed in this chapter? If you purchased a new copy of this book, you received a complimentary subscription to InfoTrac College Edition with your purchase. Use it to access full-text articles from research journals and practice-oriented publications. Go to http://www.infotrac-college.com/wadsworth to start your search. You might open current issues of a journal that you know is likely to have relevant articles, such as *Personnel Psychology*. You probably will want to do a keyword search. The following keywords can be used to find articles related to the topics of this chapter.

Employee performance
  evaluation feedback
Employee discipline
Employee turnover

Wrongful discharge
Salary increases
Employee and (termination or layoff)

# EMPLOYEE TRAINING

At one point or another, I ask the students in my class what they think will have a big impact on employment in the future. Invariably, one of the first answers I get is "Computers!" When I hear this, I ask them what could happen as a result of advances in computer technology. Some say this technology will drastically change the work we do. We will be able to get our work done more quickly and with less effort. We will not have to do boring, repetitive work. Perhaps, we will have time for more interesting and satisfying things. Whatever unlikely outcomes some students might suggest, the class usually agrees that the workplace of the future will be computerized and that computing skills will be required for almost all jobs. Next, I ask the students to think about what could be an obstacle for employers in this new world of computerized work. Eventually, a student will respond tentatively, "What if not everyone has computer skills?" This, of course, is an issue of great importance. It is important to employers who already have computerized the work they do and to those who are planning to do so. Employers must have capable and skilled employees. Currently, an obstacle facing employers is that not enough people are available who already have computer skills.

How do people develop the skills required for new areas of work or for using new equipment? Some might have developed these in school or college. However, this means they will have had to be in school at a time when the subject was taught and to have taken advantage of the opportunity to learn it. Many older workers were educated at a time when typewriters were used for "processing words" and computers were mainly what scientists used to analyze their data. Younger employees also may not have learned computer skills in school. Some have had few years of education and/or little access to instruction in using computers. Others have had access, but no interest. Where else, if not in school or college, does one learn these skills?

Sometimes, government-sponsored training programs are provided for those who are not equipped to work because they lack knowledge and skill. Gattiker (1995) described a program sponsored by the Canadian government for semiskilled workers. Computer training was provided for employed clerical workers who had less than 12 years of schooling and no vocational training. The training included general instruction in computer and software use provided by an outside agency, and business-specific practice and training provided by the trainee's employer. Such sponsored programs are rather unusual, however. Many job-relevant training programs are provided by employers. Organizations budget specifically for employee training. Often, the investment is quite large. In one business firm, over a 4-year period, $240 million was spent on training (Morrow, Jarrett, & Rupinski, 1997).

In this chapter, we concentrate on employee training. In the first sections, I describe how to assess the needs for training, how to design a program, and how to evaluate training success. In addition, I include an overview of the methods of training and describe some topics featured in workshops. The final section of the chapter covers research on basic learning processes that are relevant to training, including practice, feedback, and individual differences in ability and motivation.

## TRAINING NEEDS ASSESSMENT

Employees are likely to need training under certain conditions. A training needs assessment is a process for exploring these conditions and determining exactly what training is needed. The basic needs assessment is conducted from three different perspectives or levels of analysis. These are organizational analysis, task analysis, and person analysis (McGehee & Thayer, 1961).

### Organizational Analysis

Traditionally, organizational analysis was meant to determine *where* in the organization training might be needed (McGehee & Thayer, 1961). For example, organization-wide records of productivity, absenteeism, and turnover can spotlight departments in which there are needs for some type of intervention, possibly training. Currently, organizational analysis takes a broader and more future-oriented perspective, and its purpose is to provide general direction for employee training. Consulting high-level managers is a way to get information about organizational structure and goals that will be useful in this analysis. Plans and strategies being developed by the organization can create needs for training in several ways. First, if a company changes its line of business, or if equipment is introduced that employees have never used, training will be needed. Second, if new jobs are developed or if existing jobs are redesigned to include new responsibilities, at least some training will be necessary. Third, if groups of new employees are hired who are not fully qualified, they will need training to increase their knowledge and skills.

## Task Analysis

Although organizational analysis provides for overall direction, it is too general for the kinds of details needed for training program design. Task analysis is necessary for this purpose. Task analysis is specific to the job. It defines *what* needs to be trained and specifies the objectives of the training.

In Chapter 3, I discussed task inventory analysis (also called task analysis) as a method for studying jobs. This same technique is used for training needs assessment. If a task analysis has already been done, such as for job design or selection purposes, it can be used also to determine training needs. Recall that the primary aim of task inventory analysis is to identify the essential tasks that must be performed. A complete inventory of a job's tasks is developed, consisting of written task statements that say exactly what an employee does on the job. The task inventory itself is useful for some purposes, such as job design. However, for other purposes, including training, the task analysis must be taken a step further. The KSAs that are required for effective performance must be determined. Recall that these are inferred from the task statements. Task analysts and other SMEs make judgments about what an employee needs to know in order to accomplish each task. Then they consolidate the KSAs into groups showing the knowledge and skill requirements for the entire job. These requirements are used to guide training design.

## Person Analysis

A person analysis identifies individual needs for training: who needs to be trained, what training they need, and how much training they need. When continuing employees' jobs have changed, or when employees are newly hired into positions for which they may not be fully prepared, their individual needs for training must be determined.

There are several sources of information about individual training needs. Information about the needs of new employees can be obtained from selection records. A person's KSAs at the time of hire can be compared to the required KSAs, as identified by the task analysis. Information about transferring or continuing employees who have been on the job for some time can come from performance appraisals. Supervisors are in a position to observe employees' work behavior and can provide information about their training needs. Performance appraisals can be useful in two ways. Borderline performers can be given remedial training to improve their performance. Superior performers can be given advanced training to develop them for higher-level jobs. Self-assessment is a third source of information for personal analysis. Employees often can identify aspects of their work with which they have difficulty, and they may be able to identify areas of knowledge they need in order to progress in their careers. Self-assessment is commonly used to identify the training needs of managerial employees.

While we might assume that self-assessment provides accurate information about training needs, Ford and Noe (1987) found that individuals' personal opinions about available training affected their self-assessed needs. Those who viewed training as being useful were more likely to report high needs for training. The researchers concluded that even when high-quality training is being offered, such as that needed for managers to stay current in their fields, those who have negative attitudes toward training may perceive it to be of no use and report that they have no need for it. Guthrie and Schwoerer (1994) also found that those who were positive toward training had higher self-assessed training needs. Delving into what might predict a positive attitude toward training, the researchers found that those who were more positive were also more likely to feel high self-efficacy or confidence in their ability to benefit from training and to perceive their superiors as being supportive of them.

## Conclusions

Because training needs assessment requires all three levels of analysis, it is helpful to think of these analyses as distinct perspectives. Actually, however, they overlap and it is often difficult to discuss one analysis without discussing the others. For example, when an organizational analysis identifies a department in which productivity and attendance records indicate there is a problem, further analysis is necessary. A person analysis should help to determine whether training is needed to solve the problem. Sometimes, the reason for a problem is that employees lack knowledge, and this indicates a training need. At other times, however, the problem is complicated because it reflects needs other than training. As discussed in other chapters, the study of work performance shows two basic determinants of performance: (1) knowledge and skill and (2) motivation. As you can see in Figure 16.1, performance requires making an effort, and effort depends on both knowledge and motivation. If a problem of work performance has motivational components, the appropriate intervention is one that includes some type of incentive. Motivational incentives often are needed in connection with training programs. For example, an employee's effort to use what has been learned in training can be enhanced—or blocked—by the level of encouragement and support received from a supervisor.

If a company is making plans that will change the organization, these plans must be identified in organizational analysis because they determine training needs and represent motivational opportunities and obstacles. Supervisors need to be aware of the organization's plans, since they play a critical role in determining whether training will be effective. Unless supervisors support newly trained employees and provide opportunities for them to apply what they have learned, the training will be a waste of time and money (Goldstein, 1991, 1993).

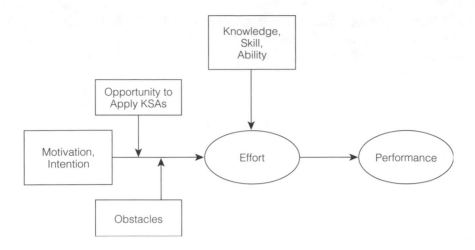

FIGURE **16.1**

The relationship of KSAs and motivation to effort and performance. Opportunities and obstacles are considered as moderators of the effect of motivation on effort.

## TRAINING PROGRAM DESIGN

Much of the training provided by organizations today is conducted away from the job in formal training workshops and programs. Employees are given time off to attend training sessions that take place either in training classrooms at the worksite or at some off-site location. The design of this formal training is a deliberate process of thinking through, defining, and structuring the learning experience. A first requirement in design is that the results of the training needs assessment provide the basis of program development. I want to emphasize that it is absolutely necessary for a training program to reflect the training needs that have been identified. Unfortunately, it is easy to lose sight of this requirement if an employer "goes shopping" for a ready-made training program. Although many such programs are attractive and may be useful for their stated purpose, an employer must be very careful about accepting one "straight off the shelf." Rather, training programs must be custom-designed to fit the needs revealed in the training needs assessment.

Educational design theory can be helpful in developing training because it offers a framework for structuring a program on the basis of actual needs (Bauman, 1977). The first step in design is to identify the nature and extent of the training needs, using information from the organizational, task, and person analyses. For example, suppose an organization plans a massive expansion that will result in the eventual recruitment and hiring of a much larger workforce. To conduct the recruitment, the company has hired new HR assistants, but

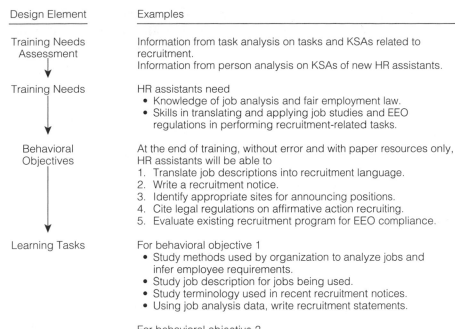

| Design Element | Examples |
| --- | --- |
| Training Needs Assessment ↓ | Information from task analysis on tasks and KSAs related to recruitment.<br>Information from person analysis on KSAs of new HR assistants. |
| Training Needs ↓ | HR assistants need<br>• Knowledge of job analysis and fair employment law.<br>• Skills in translating and applying job studies and EEO regulations in performing recruitment-related tasks. |
| Behavioral Objectives ↓ | At the end of training, without error and with paper resources only, HR assistants will be able to<br>1. Translate job descriptions into recruitment language.<br>2. Write a recruitment notice.<br>3. Identify appropriate sites for announcing positions.<br>4. Cite legal regulations on affirmative action recruiting.<br>5. Evaluate existing recruitment program for EEO compliance. |
| Learning Tasks | For behavioral objective 1<br>• Study methods used by organization to analyze jobs and infer employee requirements.<br>• Study job description for jobs being used.<br>• Study terminology used in recent recruitment notices.<br>• Using job analysis data, write recruitment statements.<br><br>For behavioral objective 2<br>• Study recruitment terminology used by organization.<br>• Study job analysis data and other descriptive material.<br>• Write a recruitment notice.<br><br>For behavioral objective 3<br>• Study local labor statistics to determine location of applicant populations.<br>• Study community media and directories indicating public posting sites.<br>• Study procedures for posting used by organization. |

FIGURE **16.2**

Training design from need assessment to learning tasks performed in training.

Adapted from *Psychology at Work: An Introduction to Industrial and Organizational Psychology,* 2nd ed., by L. M. Berry, 1997, figure 6.2, p. 160, and table 6.2, p. 161. Copyright 1997 by The McGraw-Hill Companies, Inc. Adapted by permission.

these individuals have little knowledge of recruitment, job analysis, or fair employment law. This training need would be revealed in the needs assessment, specifically by the organizational analysis.

The second step in training design is to derive behavioral objectives. Information for this purpose also is drawn from the needs assessment, specifically from the task and person analyses. As you see in Figure 16.2, behavioral objectives are explicit statements which specify the knowledge and skills that should be developed in training. Behavioral objectives guide the instruction because they comprise end-of-training or "terminal" behaviors that show the extent to which learning has occurred. Terminal training behaviors represent the kind of performance that is needed on the job and that training is meant to produce.

They are observable actions, elicited at the end of training, that demonstrate whether trainees have acquired the KSAs necessary for performance. Well-defined behavioral objectives specify the conditions or necessary aids to performance, such as equipment or materials, and the standards of performance quality. Standards are used in evaluating trainees' acquisition of the expected KSA levels. Therefore, they define exactly what constitutes successful performance on the tasks being trained. To set standards, the training designer must decide whether anything less than perfect performance can be allowed in training. I have defined very high standards (i.e., zero errors) in the example in Figure 16.2, although this is not always necessary. Often, some errors can be tolerated, especially on tasks in which errors do not create costly or dangerous situations.

The third step in training design constitutes a bridge to the instructional phase. At this point, learning tasks are defined for each behavioral objective. These are the learning experiences through which knowledge and skill are to be developed, and they provide directions for the trainer who conducts the instruction. Usually, multiple learning tasks can be extracted from each behavioral objective, especially from complex objectives. In developing learning tasks, the training designer determines what trainees must do in order to learn the material or actions described in behavioral objectives. For example, to develop a skill, trainees may need to study written materials and then practice performing some procedure. In Figure 16.2, to reach the first two objectives, trainees study source materials covering job analysis methods, existing job descriptions, and common recruitment terminology. Then, using samples of job analysis data, trainees practice writing recruitment notices. When learning tasks have been identified for all behavioral objectives, the training designer organizes these in some coherent structure. This organization provides a basic framework for training sessions (Berry, 1997).

The final step in training design is to select appropriate training techniques and to plan how training sessions will cover the learning content within a specified time period. Developing a formal structure and schedule—or lesson plan—for each training session is a way of making sure that each element of the training content gets the appropriate attention. This plan is helpful to a trainer because it outlines exactly what learning content will be covered in a session and by what methods. In developing the structure for training, a number of issues and decision points will have to be addressed, including the following:

1. Is there a necessary order among the learning tasks, such that certain content must be learned before other content?
2. How much time is required for each learning task and/or to use a training method?
3. Are "double-duty" training methods needed by which the trainer can address more than one learning task at a time?

4. Are there important knowledge or motivational differences among trainees that need to be taken into account?
5. Will all learning tasks be accomplished in the classroom or will some be done elsewhere, such as in homework assignments or on the job?

Decisions on these points will be reflected in the training design. For example, the first session of a training program might be structured around learning tasks that develop basic knowledge, which is necessary for later sessions. This decision addresses a requirement for order in covering learning tasks. It also takes into account that more advanced trainees might omit this session and join the class later, when the training is more appropriate for their level of ability. When learning tasks do not have to be covered in order, there is greater freedom in planning activities to fit the available time. For example, a training session might be structured to focus mostly on one complex learning task and to use a time-consuming method. However, a less complex learning task, which requires less attention and uses a different method, might be squeezed into the time available, for a refreshing change of pace. Another way to use training time effectively is to incorporate outside assignments, such as readings or individual projects. This allows learning experiences for which there might not be enough class time, and it extends the training beyond the classroom.

## TRAINING METHODS AND TECHNIQUES

There are two categories of training methodology. In one category are the methods used for formal training workshops and programs that take place away from the job in a separate on-site or off-site location. In another category are the methods used for training on the job. In the following pages, I will describe several examples of each category.

### Methods for Training Workshops and Programs

In planning a training session, training techniques must be chosen carefully. Certain techniques are effective for developing knowledge of facts and information. These are general and multipurpose methods that can be used for a variety of subject matter, and they tend to be economical in terms of time and material costs. Other methods are more appropriate for developing procedural knowledge or skills in technical areas. Some related techniques have been developed for use in training interpersonal skills, such as communication. Some of the skills training techniques are highly specialized, as they have been developed for a single type of training, and they can require special equipment and/or extensive training time. The training designer needs to be aware of the variety of available training techniques and to understand their strengths, as well as the constraints they impose. Some techniques are easy to use; others are complicated, and a trainer must be trained expressly to use them.

**Techniques for Training Knowledge and Skill**    An important distinction between training techniques is the extent to which a technique involves active trainee behavior and practice in the training session. In the following list of training techniques, notice that the first few techniques allow trainees to be rather passive listeners while the trainer is highly active. In the middle of the list are techniques requiring that trainees play a more active part. The trainer gives up some responsibility for the instruction to the trainees themselves, who become more responsible for their own learning. The last technique in the list involves only the trainee.

1. *Lectures.* Lectures are used more often than any other single training technique. A well-prepared lecture is a relatively quick and economical technique for conveying large amounts of information—facts, ideas, and opinions. A lecture can be used not only to inform trainees, but also to motivate and inspire them. It can be used to give procedural instructions; however, because trainees are passive, a trainer should not rely on the lecture as the sole method for developing skills. Often, a lecture is combined with other methods in a training session.
2. *Moderated panel discussions.* Although it is less formal, a panel discussion is similar to the lecture in being useful for conveying information, ideas, and points of view. The panel of experts discuss and explore a topic while the trainer, acting as moderator, keeps the discussion on track. The advantage is that a panel can provide a breadth of information because of the experts' differing perspectives on the topic. In addition, when added to a series of lectures, the method can provide change of pace.
3. *Listening teams.* Depending on their knowledge of a topic, trainees sometimes are selected to form a listening team. A listening team responds to a lecturer, such as by asking for elaboration or clarification of points that are relevant to the class. This can be a useful technique—especially when a guest lecturer is not fully aware of what the trainees need to learn—and also an interesting experience for trainees.
4. *Question–answer periods.* Trainees usually are encouraged to ask questions, and sometimes specific periods of time are scheduled for this purpose. Question–answer periods often are used as a follow-up to a formal guest lecture or panel discussion. This can be a valuable technique if trainees are alerted to the importance of their participation and are encouraged to write down questions for the speaker's response.
5. *Demonstrations.* Demonstration of a work procedure is well known as an effective technique for skills training. A demonstration can be introduced by a lecture in which procedural information is presented. Performance

of the procedure is then demonstrated, step by step, allowing trainees to observe the action. A demonstration can be done by the trainer personally or by using audiovisual materials. An effective follow-up of a demonstration is trainee practice of the procedure.

6. *Discussion groups*. Trainees play a more active role in their learning when there is a discussion group. To use this informal method, the trainer moderates a discussion among a small group of trainees. Trainees can raise questions, identify points and controversies, and present their own experiences and views. A carefully moderated discussion group can add to the breadth of learning and create high interest among trainees.

7. *Case studies*. A case study is an organizational "story" that gives a somewhat detailed description of a work problem that is relevant to the content of the train-ing session. Individuals or teams of trainees analyze the case and develop a plan of action for handling the problem. Case studies are helpful for developing analytical and problem-solving skills and for giving trainees practice in applying what they have learned in previous training sessions.

8. *Simulation*. Through imitation of an actual work situation, a simulation provides for realistic practice and feedback for skill-building. Trainees must already have received training for basic knowledge and skill and must be ready to be highly active participants. The nature of simulation training varies widely, as it is used to train both technical and interpersonal skills. A simulation may use work samples or case studies. Some managerial training includes "business games" that simulate aspects of a manager's work. In other simulation training, sophisticated equipment is required for a computer-generated simulation. For example, pilot-training simulators present visual, auditory, and kinesthetic sensory information, which gives realistic feedback in response to a trainee's actions in "flying" the simulator.

9. *Programmed instruction*. In programmed instruction, materials are provided for a trainee to use in self-instruction. Trainees individually study and are examined on information presented in workbooks or computer programs. Programmed instruction is best used for learning work-related information, although work procedures can be described and pictured graphically. If ready-made programmed instruction for a topic is available, the method is convenient and can be effective, especially if employees must be trained singly. If the instruction is not available, it can be produced. However, production is extremely time consuming when training content is complex, and it may not be worth the cost.

**Interpersonal Skills Training**    Interpersonal skills are required for most employees and especially for those who work in teams. However, nowhere are interpersonal skills more important than they are in managerial work. Managers spend their workdays in communication and interaction with others, in dyads and groups, both inside and outside the organization.

Interpersonal skills training uses some of the same techniques that are used for developing more technical knowledge and skill. For example, it can be helpful for trainees to receive information from the research on communication and interaction processes. This information can be presented through lectures, and interaction problems can be explored through case studies. In addition to these training methods, other techniques have been developed specifically for use in interpersonal skills training. Like other skills training techniques, they require high trainee activity. The following are some examples:

1. *Role-play*. By using role-play, trainers can help trainees become more aware of the social roles they play and the effects of these roles in their interactions. A role-play activity can be conducted using a small group of trainees as performers, while the remaining trainees serve as observers. The trainer provides information about a situation the role players are facing. This can be real or hypothetical, but it must involve an interactional problem. The trainer also assigns a role to each trainee. For example, depending on the interactional problem, trainees may be given roles that are in conflict. No scripts are provided; trainees play their roles as themselves. After a period of interaction, the trainer stops the role-play and leads the class in discussion of the interactional processes that took place.

2. *Behavior modeling*. In behavior modeling activities, trainees observe, perform, and practice complex interpersonal behavior. For example, supervisory problems, such as disciplining an employee, can be addressed in behavior modeling sessions. First, an actor—either live or on videotape—models the desired behavior in front of the trainees. (Sometimes the actor also demonstrates ineffective behavior to show what *not* to do.) The trainer may point out important aspects of the model's behavior, during or after the performance. Then trainees practice the desired behavior in front of the class, and the trainer provides corrective feedback.

3. *Structured experiences*. People learn through experience. In training, experiences can be created especially for displaying the nature of interpersonal dynamics that trainees need to learn. Structured experiences are "barely" structured. Typically, they allow a group to generate and use its own interactions. For example, a listening exercise may be structured simply by assigning the roles of speaker and listener, setting time limits, and disallowing interruptions. The trainer encourages trainees to pay attention to the interpersonal processes that play out in a group's interaction, and discusses these with the trainees.

## On-the-Job Methods of Training

Years ago, two major distinctions were considered to exist between schooling and work training: (1) how general or specific the learning was and (2) whether the learning took place on the job or at some other location. Education, provided by schools, was viewed as being general in nature and concerned with preparing students for many aspects of life. Employee training, conducted on the job, was narrowly focused on preparing employees to perform their work. Today, it is not so clear that these distinctions hold. Although businesses do invest heavily in employee training that is specifically job oriented, some of this training addresses more general topics. For example, many employers are interested in their employees' having had a broad and general education—especially their high-level managers—and often they are willing to help pay for this education (Saari, Johnson, McLaughlin, & Simmerle, 1988). Also, although it is no longer true that work training is conducted only at work, some training does take place on the job while the employee is working.

**On-the-Job Training (OJT)**    Training that is usually referred to as on-the-job training, or OJT, is carried out in the midst of ongoing work activity, usually at the new employee's workstation. The training is brief and informal, and the "trainer" is the supervisor or an experienced coworker. Typically, the training includes a demonstration of procedures to be followed. Sometimes, an explanation of the reasons for the procedure is given, and sources of further information are identified for the trainee. Essentially, the new employee watches the other person perform some part of the job and later tries to imitate the performer's actions. The trainer may observe and guide the new employee's performance. Often, however, the trainer returns to his or her own job, and the new employee begins work. The trainer may have no further involvement except as a contact, in case the trainee has questions. (Many of us have had this type of "training.")

The main advantage of OJT is that it can be highly relevant to performance on the job. The work sample used in training can be a close simulation of the entire job. To employers, OJT may appear to have other advantages. It does not require a special trainer, and an employee can go to work right away. However, the extent to which these are real advantages depends on the purpose of the training. In practice, OJT is used in three ways: (1) to introduce new employees who were hired to do jobs that require little knowledge or skill, (2) to introduce new employees who already have the necessary skills for the job they were hired to do, and (3) to provide training for new employees who do not have the required KSAs for the job. In the first two uses, the need is largely for orientation to the workplace. For this purpose, OJT can provide an adequate learning experience. For the third use, in which the purpose is to provide job training, OJT may not be effective. It can be too brief or superficial, and the employee can be left having to figure out what to do. Such a problem is compounded when the "trainer" has limited knowledge of the job and/or weak training skills or is an experienced employee who resents having this responsibility thrust upon him or her. Therefore, for training important areas of knowledge and skill, OJT can be costly. Inadequately trained, a new employee may be unproductive, waste materials as a result of making mistakes, or interact poorly with customers or clients.

**Apprentices and Interns**    As a training method, apprenticeship occupies a place on the boundary between formal education and informal OJT. The training combines off-site education at a vocational school or college with a job placement in which the apprentice receives OJT and gains experience. In off-site education, the apprentice learns the basic subject matter and methods. The job placement offers opportunities for applying the basic learning, gives training in job-specific procedures, and provides for practice. Apprenticeship has a long history of use in preparing people for the skilled trades, such as carpentry and electrical work. A trades apprentice typically is assigned to work with a skilled and experienced worker—called a journeyman—who demonstrates procedures and guides the apprentice's work practice. At the end of a successful apprenticeship (which can last for a year or more), the apprentice becomes a journeyman in his or her own right.

A similar form of training is an internship that is incorporated into the career preparation of professionals, such as physicians, psychologists, and school teachers. In preparing for the profession, the person begins with a general college education. Formal education is continued in an advanced university program that focuses on the professional specialty. Professional training culminates with a specialized internship or job placement at a worksite in the professional field. In the job placement, the intern works as an assistant to a professional practitioner. Like the trades journeyman, the practitioner demonstrates work procedures and applications of academic knowledge, and guides the intern's practice.

**Job Rotation**    Job rotation is a form of training on the job that often is offered to employees who are being prepared for managerial positions. In job rotation, the employee spends a period—sometimes several months—moving from one position to another in related jobs. This gives the trainee exposure to various tasks and responsibilities, and it offers learning opportunities for developing new knowledge and skill. A job rotation has the potential for making an employee more promotable and can contribute to the person's career development in general. As a result of going through a job rotation, the individual becomes a more versatile employee. When the organization has the need, this employee can more easily step into vacated positions and begin working right away.

**Mentoring**   In discussing their careers, managers and professionals often credit their mentor as having had a notable influence on their development. The learning they gain from the tutorial relationship with a mentor can be highly beneficial to their performance and career success. Studies have shown that careers can be advanced, with higher earnings and promotions resulting from having a mentor (e.g., Dreher & Ash, 1990).

A mentor is an experienced and high-ranking individual in an organization who supports and enhances the development of a more junior employee. There are several ways that a mentor can benefit the protégé. The mentor can share information about the inner workings of the organization and can be a work-role model. Because of the mentor's influence in the organization, he or she may be able to sponsor and create opportunities for the protégé. In addition, mentors offer friendship and informal counseling that can strengthen the protégé's psychosocial development (Kram, 1985).

The relationship between mentor and protégé usually develops informally and spontaneously. However, it is possible to encourage the process by formalizing it through an organizational structure. Companies that want to encourage such relationships sometimes develop a formal process. In some mentoring programs, an individual is *assigned* to a mentor. The mentor is expected to participate in the socialization and development of the junior employee. In other formalized programs, the arrangement is made with a softer touch and is meant to facilitate the development of relationships. For example, in one organization, newly hired employees were given information about senior managers who were willing to be mentors, and they were encouraged to initiate an assignment to one (Seibert, 1999). Very little is known about the effects of formalized mentoring. The few studies that have been done indicate that it does not yield the same benefits as informally established relationships. Although protégés in formalized mentorships receive psychosocial benefits, the extent of career-related benefits appears quite limited (Chao, Walz, & Gardner, 1992; Noe, 1988; Seibert, 1999).

Much has been written on the success of mentoring. A few researchers have also considered the possibility that not all mentoring has positive outcomes. Although it is relatively rare, dysfunctional mentoring does occur. In one study, interviews with mentors and protégés revealed that even though they began productively, some relationships became dissatisfying and destructive, and one or both parties felt angered and frustrated (Kram, 1985). Protégés sometimes terminate a mentorship, for any of a number of reasons. Some terminations are positive; the mentorship has served its purpose and the protégé is moving on. Other terminations are due to the relationship having become dysfunctional. For example, some protégés end a relationship because they feel dependent or suffocated or because they believe the mentor is jealous and has withdrawn support (Ragins & Scandura, 1997). Scandura (1998) suggested that termination is the best outcome when a mentorship is dysfunctional. If such a relationship continues, it can result in negative outcomes for both parties. The protégé may experience damaged self-esteem and dissatisfaction with work. Mentors may undergo stress. Neither may be willing to mentor others in the future. Because of such possibilities, it might be best for an organization to forgo formalizing mentorships and to let them develop spontaneously, as they will.

## Conclusions

Training can take any of several different approaches and may or may not require a trained trainer. It can be oriented toward the long-term development of single individuals, as in job rotation, and in some cases can engender close working relationships, as in apprentice training and mentoring. On the other hand, many employees are trained in groups, using methods that are effective for workshops and relatively short-term programs. Some techniques, such as lecture and demonstration, are highly versatile. They can be used in different contexts, on or off the job, to instruct trainees on various subjects. Other methods are content-specific, having been developed expressly for training particular skills. Some are used to train technical skills; others are for developing interpersonal skills. Simulation and behavior modeling are examples. Most of the methods used in workshop training require a knowledgeable and skilled trainer. For some, the trainer must have extensive training in handling the learning experience.

## TRANSFER OF TRAINING

Transfer of training refers to the generalization and use of learning in performance on the job. This is the main reason for employee training. There is little point in paying the cost of training unless trainees learn and then transfer what they have learned to perform their work.

Researchers have concluded that processes of stimulus-response generalization and discrimination underlie the transfer of training (cf. Houston, 1986). That is, when learning involves stimuli in one situation (such as a training classroom), similar situations (such as a trainee's job) will tend to elicit the response that was learned. Therefore, designing training so as to reflect the job should enhance the likelihood that actions learned under training conditions will generalize to the work setting. Training conditions do not have to be exactly the same as on the job and, in some cases, may not be very similar. According to Goldstein (1993), learning the underlying principles of an issue in training can be sufficient for the trainee to generalize the learning and use it in solving problems on the job. A concept similar to generalization is stimulus-response discrimination, in which complex distinctions between stimuli are learned and transferred. Notice that in learning complex skills, what you learn often is a response contingency. The contingency tells you to make response X in one situation and response Y in a different situation. What you have to learn and transfer to work activities is the distinction between the two situations. The distinction can be subtle. For example, suppose you must park a car along a crowded street, and you find an empty space between two vehicles. You must determine whether this is a situation in which you can do X (park the car) or a situation in which you must do Y (drive on and find a larger space). To be able to make such a distinction requires you to have learned how much space you need in order to park and how to estimate the size of empty spaces. Transferring this learning means you make the appropriate response.

Training programs need to be designed to maximize the likelihood that learning will be transferred and used on the job. Training developers need to be concerned, not only about the immediate transfer of newly trained KSAs, but also about their maintenance over time. Baldwin and Ford (1988) noted that even when learning is transferred from training to job performance, the use of trained skills and knowledge often declines over time. They suggested that the decline may occur when rarely used skills become "rusty" or when motivational obstacles in the work setting interfere with the employee's use of new skills. The researchers identified five problems relating to the transfer of training. These are described by the curves in Figure 16.3. The curve for type A shows transfer, but it is not maintained long. The skills are gradually lost, possibly indicating that they are not often needed on the job. In type B, learning fails to transfer; no effort is made to use the skills. In C there is transfer, and it is maintained for a while, but then it declines rapidly to the pretraining level. This probably reflects an obstacle, such as lack of supervisory support for use of the learned skills. The curves for D and E show that not much was learned and so there is little to transfer. In type D, what transfer there was, is not maintained. The curve for E, however, shows a very different picture. The transferred skill—although minimal at the start—is maintained and then increases rapidly to a high level. This may reflect supervisory support for making use of the learning. It also may describe a trainee who learned general principles in training and then developed these through practice on the job.

What can be done when transfer is not maintained? One possibility is to offer refresher training. This can help to enhance low-level learning or to restore previously learned material that was lost. Another possibility is to identify obstacles that might prevent a trained employee from applying the learning on the job. A trainer can attempt to discover whether there is organizational support for employees to use what they learn. If the immediate supervisor does not encourage using the learning, but insists that work be done as usual, then transfer is unlikely to be maintained (Baldwin & Ford, 1988). The nature of the organizational environment can affect transfer of training. In some

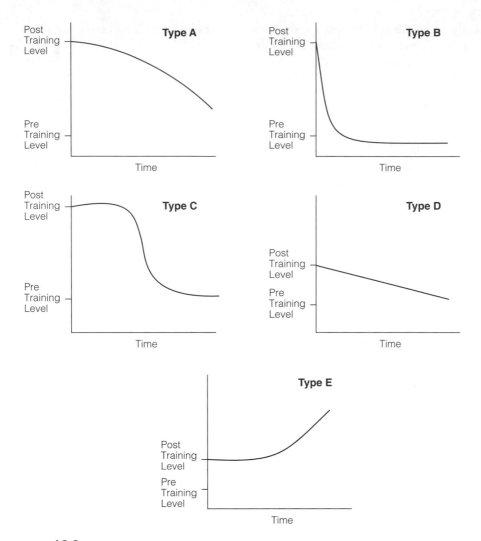

FIGURE **16.3**

Patterns of transfer of training and maintenance. (A) strong learning; transferred; failed to maintain; gradual loss. (B) strong learning; failed to transfer. (C) strong learning; transferred; maintained briefly then sudden loss. (D) weak learning; transferred; failed to maintain. (E) weak learning; transferred; maintained and learning increased.

From "Transfer of Training: A Review and Directions for Future Research," by T. T. Baldwin and J. K. Ford, 1988, *Personnel Psychology, 41,* figure 2, p. 97. Copyright 1988 by Personnel Psychology, Inc., Bowling Green, Ohio. Reprinted by permission.

organizations, a climate exists in which training is valued and transfer is encouraged. Also, some organizations reflect what is known as a continuous-learning culture, in which knowledge and skill are valued. The results of a field study demonstrated that these organizational characteristics can have positive effects on the transfer of training (Tracey, Tannenbaum, & Kavanagh, 1995).

# SPECIAL TOPICS IN TRAINING

Training workshops are offered by many organizations. Some workshops provide orientation training for all new employees. Others focus on topics of common interest to different employee groups. For example, some workshops are meant to draw supervisory and managerial employees from various departments and to prepare them for responsibilities they have in common, such as employee motivation, performance appraisal,[1] and leadership. Training workshops also may be developed covering issues that are currently important to the organization and for which policies and procedures may have been developed, such as employee termination, sexual harassment, diversity, and international business. These workshops usually are offered mainly to managerial employees.

## *Orientation*

One purpose of orientation training is to introduce the organization. New employees learn about organizational policies and procedures that affect them, how they fit into the organizational structure, and what behavior is expected of them. Such training often recognizes that starting a new job can be stressful. Therefore, a second purpose is to enhance the new employee's ability to adjust.

Orientation training is widely available. Whether it is actually effective is not clear. Probably, the effects of orientation training depend on the purpose emphasized and the kinds of information provided. Waung (1995) was interested in discovering whether routine orientation training is adequate for helping employees handle stress. She reasoned that it might be more beneficial to provide training—using stress inoculation techniques—through which employees could learn to anticipate stressful situations and to manage their emotional responses to these. Waung tested this idea in a field experiment, expecting to find that individuals prepared by stress inoculation training would manage their job stress better and show lower levels of turnover than those given the usual orientation. In fact, there was a significant effect. However, it was opposite to that predicted. Employees given stress inoculation training showed higher turnover, with 37 percent of the group quitting within the first 4 weeks on the job. Only 10 percent of the others did so. To explain this surprising result, Waung suggested that the stress inoculation itself had created anxiety in these new employees. A previous study on realistic job previews had found similar effects.[2] Meglino, DeNisi, Youngblood, and Williams (1988)

---

[1]See Chapter 14 for a discussion of rater training workshops.

[2]Information provided in orientation training is similar to that provided in realistic job previews given to job applicants (see Chapter 5). The difference is that orientation training is given after the person is hired.

evaluated turnover of military trainees who were given information about potentially stressful military life and suggestions on how to cope. The trainees showed higher turnover than those given an ordinary preview. In discussing the effect, the researchers surmised that the suggested coping strategies "may have actually increased apprehension in the same way that providing shark repellent could increase a swimmer's apprehension about shark attacks" (p. 265). Waung (1995) concluded that she, too, may have inadvertently included a "shark repellent" in the stress inoculation training she provided.

## MANAGERIAL AND SUPERVISORY TRAINING TOPICS

**Organizational Leadership**    Having an effective leader can mean the difference between success and failure for a business. Over the past several decades, theorists and researchers have studied leadership and, as a result, there are some answers to questions about how to obtain better organizational leadership. Reflecting on what has been learned over years of study, Fiedler (1996) pointed out two important inferences of the research. First, how well a leader performs is a result of a highly complex interaction between the individual's behavior and elements of the situation in which he or she operates. A leader's knowledge, abilities, and behavioral style are important in this interaction, as is the extent to which the leader is able to influence the work situation. Second, the necessary KSAs for leadership are learned, and training can be devised to develop these.

Most large organizations provide training for their managerial employees, and much of it addresses one or more aspects of leadership (Burke & Day, 1986; Saari, Johnson, McLaughlin, & Zimmerle, 1988). A manager's work can include multiple leadership roles and responsibilities. Depending on a manager's organizational level, any of the following leadership activities might be part of the individual's work and an area in which the manager needs training: (1) motivating employees to reach their goals, (2) stimulating and guiding teamwork, (3) solving problems and handling conflicts, (4) representing and making decisions for the organization, and (5) planning for the organization's future.

Training workshops have been developed that focus specifically on leadership style, as viewed by theorists. The Leader Match training program, which is based on Fiedler's leadership contingency theory, was one of the earliest of these (Fiedler, Chemers, & Mahar, 1976). It is meant to help managers assess and understand their personal styles of interacting with employees and learn how to use or change the work situation to match their styles. Leader Match has been shown to be a valid and cost-effective technique for training managers in leadership (cf. Burke & Day, 1986). Training based on transformational leadership theory also has been conducted. Briefly, transformational leadership theory incorporates three concepts: (1) charisma, in which a leader communicates a passionately held vision; (2) intellectual stimulation, by which a leader changes followers' views; and (3) individualized consideration, through which a leader encourages and supports subordinates or team members (Bass, 1985). Barling, Weber, and Kelloway (1996) designed a program for training managers in transformational leadership. Their evidence showed the training to be effective. The trained managers' subordinates perceived them as having more charisma, being more intellectually stimulating, and expressing more individual consideration in their interactions.

**Cross-Cultural Interaction**    International organizations often send technically skilled domestic employees to work in a foreign branch. Almost certainly, managers will be sent to oversee foreign operations. Undoubtedly, the personal and family lives of both technical and managerial employees will change in the new culture, and the employer needs to provide at least some general training for those sent abroad. Managerial employees have especially great needs for training because of the nature of the work they do. Managerial work is largely interactional and depends heavily on the cultural context. For this reason, cross-cultural training is essential. Training should be based on a needs assessment that considers differences between a manager's domestic job and the job in the new location. It should cover differences between the two cultures and give close attention to interpersonal interactions that are likely to require special knowledge of the host culture. If the host culture is very different from the home culture, then managers will have special needs for training to prepare for these interactions. Without training, there is a good chance of failure on the assignment, and the manager may return home early. Such premature returns are expensive for the company. Not only are there payroll costs, but also an entire household may need to be moved, sometimes after only a short time abroad.

In the past, employees often were sent on foreign assignments without training. Tung reported in 1981 that 70 percent of companies with foreign operations provided no training at all for employees sent on these assignments. Apparently, in those days, it was expected that on-the-job experience in the foreign country would provide the necessary learning. Even when it could have been expected that there would be major cultural differences and misunderstandings, expatriates often were given little training to prepare for these. A survey of American multinational companies indicated that during the early 1980s, one of the two most frequent work assignments was in the Far East. Yet, almost one-fourth of the companies gave their expatriate employees no training (Inman, 1985). Have things changed? Unfortunately, it seems that change in this area is slow. Recently, Kim (1999) discussed the growing need for government officials to learn how to interact across cultures. (In attracting foreign investments, they must interact with representatives of foreign corporations.) Kim was interested in developing cross-cultural training for public sector managers and hoped to follow the corporate example of preparing managers for foreign assignments. However, he found little help in the private sector. Many business organizations were depending on the foreign assignment itself to develop cross-cultural ability. That is, expatriate managers were still having to learn on their own.

I do not mean to suggest that nothing is done to prepare expatriates. Many HR directors are keenly aware of the need to train managers for foreign work. About one-third of those surveyed by Saari et al. (1988) reported that managers in their organizations needed training with more emphasis on international issues. Also, workshops have been developed and used for cross-cultural training. Black and Mendenhall (1990) reviewed 29 studies evaluating cross-cultural training and found moderately strong evidence that the training was effective. There are a number of reasons why such training is not *more* effective. For one thing, it may be too brief. Because the culturally relevant behaviors that managers need to learn are likely to be complex and difficult, the usual 1- or 2-day workshop is probably not enough. Further, these programs vary widely in their contents. Some simply convey general information—facts and figures on various topics such as climate, food, and customs. This type of training is not very helpful. Hesketh and Bochner (1994) stated that such programs "convey a mostly superficial, incoherent, and misleading view of a society, fail to deal with its more fundamental aspects, and give the false impression that a culture can be learned instantly" (p. 213).

Cross-cultural training is likely to be more effective if it actively engages trainees. Hesketh and Bochner (1994) described one such example—the Contrast-American exercise, which incorporates role-play. The exercise is meant to help trainees understand the cultural basis of behavior. Trainees interact with a trained actor who behaves in ways that contrast sharply with the behavior of the (American) trainees. Another cross-cultural training method, called the *cultural assimilator*, uses programmed materials for self-instruction (Fiedler, Mitchell, & Triandis, 1971). The purpose is to help trainees understand the people of another culture by learning to use the same explanations for behavior that those individuals themselves would use. The materials consist of written descriptions of problematic interactions that occur between people of different cultures, and alternative explanations of the problem, which are to test oneself.

**Diversity Management**   In an earlier chapter, I discussed steps some organizations are taking to move away from affirmative action hiring and toward hiring a fully heterogeneous workforce. Ideally, a diverse workforce is varied in many respects, certainly in race, gender, and age, but also in other ways, such as cultural background and linguistic ability. Top management in many organizations recognizes the value of having a diverse workforce and, by developing a diversity policy, the organization formally endorses this value. A training program can provide a means for implementing and creating support for the policy.

In such training, the trainer presents and discusses the policy and the procedures for implementing it. Managers need to know what actions to take in managing the initiative and how to turn diversity policy into reality. Garcia (1995) outlined a training process both to address implementation and to train interpersonal skills for interacting with diverse groups. Where there is high diversity, individuals must learn to interact with others whose backgrounds may be quite different from their own. Some may never have worked with or supervised anyone from a different ethnic or cultural group, for example.

A 1994 survey found that many organizations had endorsed the value of diversity and that managers expected that workforces would become more diverse. However, not many managers were prepared for what this would mean for their organizations. Less than one-third of the companies sampled had diversity training programs (Hopkins, Sterkel-Powell, & Hopkins, 1994). Whether diversity training is offered appears to depend on certain organizational factors. Rynes and Rosen (1995) found that diversity training was more likely to be available in large organizations, especially where a diversity manager had been appointed to oversee the initiative. Training was also more likely to be available if top management considered diversity to have high strategic value and visibly supported it. However, the researchers found that diversity training had not been entirely successful. Although the immediate reactions to the training had been positive, in the majority of organizations, the effects had not been long-lasting. Apparently, the problem had been a failure to maintain the transfer of training, due to declining support from top management. Specifically, lower-level managers were not being rewarded for increasing diversity in their departments.

## Conclusions

This sampling of special-topic training shows that there are good reasons for offering such programs. Orientation can be beneficial for all employees, although trainers should be careful about what is included. Special-topic workshops clearly are useful to those performing supervisory and managerial work. For example, leadership skills can be improved by training, and many organizations provide this, with good results. However, some managerial training needs are not being satisfied. Managers need to learn cross-cultural interaction skills before departing for foreign work assignments. Yet, effective cross-cultural training may not be available. This is one instance of a shortcoming in training that organizations need to correct. Another is the failure to maintain diversity policy implementation. Diversity training often yields good short-term results, but long-term results may not be supported. In both instances—that is, in failing to train expatriates, and in failing to support diversity implementation—organizations do not fully capitalize on the initial investments they make.

# TRAINING PROGRAM EVALUATION

Training is expensive, and an organization cannot be expected to support a training program that does not accomplish its purpose. When training developers construct a program of learning experiences based on a thorough needs assessment, they expect the training to be successful—that trainees will learn and the learning will transfer. Training evaluation is done in order to determine whether these expectations are met and to identify problems that can be corrected. To conduct a training evaluation, the researcher needs to know about criterion measures and procedures for assessing the validity of training and to be able to use applied research methods to carry out the study.

## Evaluation of Training Validity

The aim of training evaluation is to assess the validity of training for accomplishing its objectives. We can think of training validity in much the same way that we think of test validity. In either case, we need to know whether an intervention actually does what it is supposed to do. Training usually is designed to accomplish several goals, as identified by a needs assessment. The goals may include trainee learning, improved job performance, and organizational gains. An evaluation study is designed to test hypotheses about validity—that is, about the extent to which one or more of these goals are attained. Hypotheses about internal validity predict that trainee learning will occur, and they address the training itself. Collecting measures of learning and testing hypotheses about internal validity is the first step in training evaluation. Only if learning has occurred is it reasonable to test additional hypotheses about training effects on job performance and organizational outcomes. Hypotheses about external validity (also called transfer validity) predict that the learning produced in training was transferred and had effects on job performance and organizational success.

**Criterion Measures** Most training evaluation researchers refer to Kirkpatrick's (1967) discussion of training criterion measures in deciding what measures are appropriate to use for assessing training validity. Internal criterion measures include reaction and learning measures, which focus on what took place during the training. A *reaction* measure is obtained with a questionnaire handed out at the end of a training program. Usually, the questionnaire asks whether trainees enjoyed the training or felt that they learned something. This is the most frequently used criterion measure, but also the weakest. An experience can be enjoyable and yet not teach us anything—or at least not anything that is useful on the job. Trainees may enjoy off-site training because it gets them away from the daily routine or because it takes place in a vacation spot.

Also, trainees may not know whether what they learned will be useful until they are back at work and have an opportunity to use it. *Learning* measures provide a more direct and useful assessment of what was learned in training. These measures are appropriate to use in evaluation studies that test hypotheses about the internal validity of training. Learning can be measured in different ways. Written tests can be used to assess knowledge gained from material covered in training. Performance tests can be used if the training is for skill development (cf. Kraiger, Ford, & Salas, 1993).

External measures of training criteria address the longer-term outcomes that occur after the training. *Behavior* measures indicate whether trainees' job performance actually changes once they are back at work. These measures play an important role in establishing external or transfer validity. Performance appraisals can be used as behavior measures for training evaluation. However, it is essential that the appraisal include the specific aspects of performance that training was meant to improve. *Results* measures of training criteria provide a broader assessment of external validity by indicating whether organizational goals are reached more effectively as a result of employee training.

## Designing Studies of Training Validity

Any of several different research designs can be used to evaluate hypotheses about internal or external validity of training.[3] However, be aware that some are better than others for testing hypotheses and for controlling error variables that can contaminate validity evidence.

**Threats to Training Validity**  To establish training validity, it is necessary to show not only that there was a change, but also that the change resulted from the training and not from some other influence. Goldstein (1993) discussed various ways in which extraneous, irrelevant factors can affect training outcomes. Many things happen both during and after training that are not part of the training, but nevertheless affect trainees' learning experience. The problem for the evaluation study is that these events and influences might as easily account for training outcomes as the training itself. For this reason, they are referred to as *validity threats*. In evaluation designs that incorporate experimental research procedures, many of these validity threats can be prevented or their effects identified and taken into account. In some other studies, there may be no way to control the operation of validity threats.

---

[3]If you want to learn more about evaluation research methodology, consult Cook and Campbell (1979) or Cook, Campbell, and Peracchio (1990). (Full citations are in the References section.) These sources give explanations and examples showing how various evaluation research designs are used in field studies.

Several different validity threats have been identified. Many of these affect internal validity and make it difficult to determine whether or not a training program has been effective in producing learning. First, certain events and processes can influence trainee behavior, and the effects can easily be confused with the results of training. *History* threats refer to events that occur while the training is being evaluated. Suppose, for example, that during the evaluation of a training program on safety, a serious accident occurs at the workplace. The training about safety precautions might become more meaningful because of the event, and trainees' learning could be affected. Unless recognized, such an effect could make the training appear to be more valid than it actually is. *Maturation* threats similarly occur during training. However, maturation threats are personal processes that develop over time rather than events that occur. For example, trainees may become fatigued, lose interest, or learn from other experiences. These individual changes also are not due to the training, and they need to be taken into account in the evaluation.

Second, some threats to internal validity have to do with a study's design or participants' reactions. For example, in some studies, volunteers are assigned to the group being trained, and other employees are used as an untrained control group. This procedure can result in a *biased assignment* of participants to groups, and it constitutes a validity threat. A second threat of this type refers to personal reactions to the experience of being in a study. Evaluation studies are conducted with participants' awareness and consent, of course, and individuals' *reactions to research* can operate as a threat to training validity. For example, members of a control group may resent not being trained. Those receiving training may feel pressured to do well and may try harder than if they were in a program not being evaluated. A final example of this type of threat is *pretesting sensitization*. Here, the practice of pretesting participants prior to training—which is a common strategy—can itself influence learning. The contents of a pretest can give a participant advance notice of what he or she should learn in training. This might be no great problem, except that it creates a different kind of training for the evaluation study than for that offered later in ordinary employee training without pretests.

**One-Group Designs**    Some evaluation studies use only one training group, as described in Figure 16.4. The simplest, but also the weakest, is the one-group design with a single posttest. This evaluation is not much better than doing nothing. The training may have had no effect. However, there is no way to tell because there is nothing with which to compare the measure. The trainees may have learned, but the study does not establish that the learning was due to the training. The design provides no way to assess validity threats. A second one-group design is somewhat better, but not much. The improvement is that a measure is taken both before and after training. These pre- and posttest

| Time | 1 | 2 | 3 | 4 | 5 | |
|------|---|---|---|---|---|---|
| | T | M | | | | (a)  One-Group Design |
| | M | T | M | | | (b)  One Group Pre- and Posttest Design |
| | M | M | T | M | M | (c)  Simple Interrupted Time Series Design |

Legend: T = Train, M = Measure

FIGURE **16.4**

One-group designs using nonrandom assignment of participants.
(a) posttest measure only. (b) pre- and posttest measures. (c) multiple pre- and posttest measures.

scores can be compared to see whether any change occurred. However, if there is a change, there is no way to confirm that it resulted from training rather than from history or maturation threats. A third design using one group is better because it involves more extensive pre- and posttesting. As outlined in part c of Figure 16.4, multiple measures are taken before and after training. This is called a simple interrupted time series design. (That is, the series of measures is "interrupted" by training.) Although this design does not assess the effects of all validity threats, it does give some information. The multiple measures make it possible to detect maturation threats. For example, if the pretest scores do not change, then maturation processes probably are not affecting the data. If there are changes, however, then maturation effects are a possibility. If pretest scores are showing a trend of improvement before the training is given, and the same trend continues in the posttest scores, then maturation effects are indicated. Something other than training is causing the scores to improve. Such an impact would not be apparent in a study that uses only a single pre- and posttest measurement, and the change would mistakenly be attributed to training. This is the real advantage of the interrupted time series design (Cook, Campbell, & Peracchio, 1990).

**Experimental Designs**   Experimental designs, which incorporate one or more control groups, are the most powerful methods to use in training evaluation studies. The key feature of experimental design is the random assignment of participants to groups. As you know, researchers conducting laboratory experiments randomly assign subjects to experimental and control groups.

| Time | 1 | 2 | 3 | |
|------|---|---|---|---|
| **Group** | | | | |
| E | T | M | | |
| C | | M | | (a)  Basic Experimental Design |
| | | | | |
| E | M | T | M | |
| C | M | | M | (b)  Pretesting Experimental Design |
| | | | | |
| $E_1$ | M | T | M | |
| $C_1$ | M | | M | |
| $E_2$ | | T | M | |
| $C_2$ | | | M | (c)  Solomon Four-Group Design |

Legend: T = Train, M = Measure; E = Experimental, C = Control

**FIGURE 16.5**

Experimental designs with randomized group assignments. (a) basic experimental design with one control group and posttest measure. (b) experimental design with pre- and posttesting measures. (c) Solomon four-group design with control for pretesting effects.

Likewise, to use an experimental design for an evaluation study, they randomly assign participants to groups. This controls the threat of biased group assignments. If randomization is not possible, as I discuss below, a quasi-experimental design is a good alternative (Cook et al., 1990).

Figure 16.5 outlines three experimental designs that evaluation researchers can use to evaluate training. In the basic experiment, the experimental group is given training, whereas the control group is left untrained. A test on the training material is then administered to both groups, and the test scores of the groups are compared. Because participants are randomly assigned, the groups can be assumed not to have differed at the outset of the study. For example, prior knowledge of the training content can be assumed to have been roughly the same in both groups. Therefore, any difference between the groups' test scores can be attributed to the training. History and maturation threats are controlled because—being drawn from the same employee population—the groups are equally subject to such effects. In a slightly different experiment, a pretest is administered to the two groups, as shown in part b of Figure 16.5. In all other respects, this design is the same as the first. Also, except for the possibility of pretesting sensitization—which is not controlled in this design—the same protection against validity threats is offered. The third experiment, called the Solomon four-group design, is more extensive (Solomon, 1949). In this, the above two designs are combined, as you can see in part c of Figure 16.5. The Solomon four retains the power of the basic experiment for assessing training and controlling validity threats. It has an advantage over the pretesting design because it can account for pretesting sensitization. This threat is evaluated by comparing posttest scores of *pretested* participants (groups 1 and 2 in the figure) with posttest scores of those *not* pretested (groups 3 and 4). If the posttest scores are the same, then pretesting sensitization has not had an effect. If they are different, then this threat cannot be ruled out.

**Quasi-Experimental Designs**   When studies are conducted in the workplace, there often is resistance to the use of experimental design. For example, people may be unhappy about having to delay the training of some employees while a program is being evaluated. The need for random assignment to groups may not be understood or accepted. Participants assigned to control groups may complain. Also, there may be too few employees available at any one time to make up an adequately large sample for a study.

Field researchers often use quasi-experimental procedures to accommodate such constraints. One quasi-experimental design is the simple interrupted time series, using one group, as discussed above. A second, more complex design uses multiple groups and incorporates control elements in the manner of experimental methods. At least one pre- and posttest measurement is taken from trainees in each of several groups. As shown in Figure 16.6, by controlling the timing of testing and training, the procedure creates groupings that can be used as if they were experimental and control groups. Notice that each group can function as an untrained "control" group at one time, and later as a trained "experimental" group. For example, in the figure, look at the relationship of group 2 to groups 1 and 3. First, in playing the role of control group, pretests from group 2 are used for comparison with the posttests of group 1, which has finished its training. Second, as an experimental group, group 2 is trained and is given a posttest. The posttests are then compared with what are actually the pretests of group 3, which is next in line for training. This quasi-experimental design provides controls for certain validity threats. For example, although random assignment may not be possible, the groups' pretests can be compared to determine whether there are systematic differences between the groups, which would indicate biased assignments. Maturation effects can be assessed by varying the design slightly and collecting multiple pre- and posttests. For example, multiple tests are shown for groups 4 and 5 in the figure. Comparison of multiple tests is used to detect maturation trends, in the manner I described for the simple interrupted time series design.

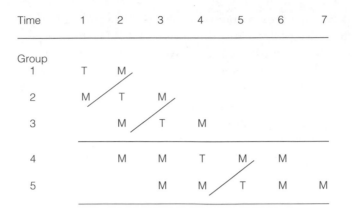

FIGURE **16.6**

Complex time series using nonrandom assignment. In this quasi-experimental design each group performs as both "experimental" and "control" groups. Multiple pre- and posttesting is used to assess maturation effects.

## Conclusions

Once internal validity has been established, evaluation can be directed toward assessing external validity, using the same research methods. Studies to evaluate external validity use behavioral and/or results measures, and their purpose is to determine whether learning was transferred and used on the job and, if so, whether it resulted in organizational gains. For example, in an evaluation of a leadership training program for bank managers, Barling, Weber, and Kelloway (1996) obtained behavior measures of the managers' performance from their subordinates. These measures showed that the training had transferred. The researchers also took two results measures: the number of credit card sales and personal loans, which indicated that the training had enhanced the bank's financial performance.

Organizational results of training also can be assessed in dollar-value terms using utility analysis.[4] This method can be used to assess the results and value of single training programs and also to assess training in organizations that run multiple training programs. Morrow, Jarrett, and Rupinski (1997) reported an example of the latter. They conducted the study in response to an opportunity provided by the company president, who rejected an anecdotal report on the value of training and asked instead for a

[4]Utility analysis is discussed in Chapter 7 as a way to put a dollar value on employee selection. Utility analysis can be applied similarly to many organizational interventions, including training.

scientific study to evaluate the worth of the company's investment. The researchers used quasi-experimental procedures to study the internal validity of a sample of 18 different programs used for training managerial, sales, and technical personnel in the organization. Using the evidence of internal validity, the researchers then conducted a utility analysis to show the monetary value of training. The utility analysis demonstrated that the training was worth its cost, especially the training being provided for sales and technical employees.

## LEARNING PROCESSES IN TRAINING

In these final pages, you will see that training has a strong basis in the research on human learning. Over the long period of time that psychologists have been studying the processes of learning, an enormous body of research literature has accumulated. This literature is relevant to many fields, including industrial and organizational psychology. Weiss (1990) discussed the relevance of learning theory and research to various organizational issues, ranging from the socialization of organizational members, to the diagnosis of organizational behavior management problems. On none of these has the study of learning had a greater impact than on training.

Until now, I have used the term "learning" with its ordinary, everyday meaning. Now, to discuss the nature of learning, I need to define the term. In its scientific sense, learning is a relatively permanent change in behavior that occurs through practice or experience (Houston, 1986). Let us examine this definition in detail and differentiate learning from related aspects of behavior. First, not all changes in behavior are due to learning. Some relatively permanent changes in behavior result from the physiological processes of maturation that all of us experience in our development. Similarly, certain temporary changes, such as those that result from illness or fatigue, are not learned. Second, some aspects of behavior are closely related to learning. Training provides the experience and practice required for learning to occur. Memory refers to the storage and retention of what has been learned. Learning itself is a hypothetical construct. Like other constructs, it cannot be observed directly but must be inferred from some form of performance behavior, such as answering test questions or performing a task. It is sometimes difficult to determine whether someone has learned because learning can occur without the acquired knowledge being expressed. The reason has to do with motivation. As I discussed earlier in this chapter, both ability and motivation are necessary for performance, but neither alone is sufficient. A person can learn something but—through lack of motivation—make no effort to use the knowledge in taking action. Likewise, a person can be motivated but not perform because he or she has not learned what is necessary to know and has no idea what to do.

## *The Importance of Practice*

For learning to occur, and especially for learned material to be retained in memory, some amount of practice is required. Research has made it clear that simple exposure to training material is not enough (Houston, 1986). Mainly, practice involves repetition. It can be physical repetition, such as when an action sequence is repeated. For example, a child learns to stay upright on a bicycle by repeating a certain sequence of actions, day after day. Practice also can be cognitive repetition. What we call "studying" is largely cognitive repetition. To study for an exam, you probably read through your textbook assignments and lecture notes, think about what you are reading, make notes on your thoughts, highlight or underline passages, and then review and rethink the material.

**Mental Practice**    The repetition required in practice can involve visualization or mental imagery. Mental practice is guided mental rehearsal of an action series without any physical movement (Richardson, 1967). Mental practice is not the same as the cognitive repetition I describe above; for one thing, that example contains several physical elements. Neither is it the same as mental preparation, in which positive imagery is used to reduce fears. Rather, mental practice is a special training technique by which the procedure for performing some task or action is rehearsed with mental processes only (Driskell, Copper, & Moran, 1994). Trainees are instructed in how to use mental imagery to practice an action sequence. The task to be learned is identified, and the actions for performing it are described. To practice, a trainee sits quietly, without moving, and visualizes performing each action.

Does this really help a person learn? Mental practice might reasonably help in learning things that are symbolic or cognitive, such as composing an article or a report. However, is there any reason to believe that it can help a person learn physical or motor skills, such as swimming? A meta-analytic review by Driskell et al. (1994) indicated that mental practice does improve performance, especially on tasks that contain more cognitive elements. The researchers also found that certain conditions moderated the effectiveness of the method, including the learner's existing knowledge of the task. Inexperienced trainees benefited more from mental practice when a cognitive task was being learned. With experienced trainees, however, mental practice was helpful regardless of whether the task was cognitive or physical. The timing and scheduling of practice sessions further influenced the usefulness of mental practice. Beyond about 20 minutes, the longer the period of practice, the *less* beneficial it was. The best scheduling was immediately before the actual performance.

Trainees in certain job training programs might benefit from mental practice sessions. For example, if opportunities for trial runs are limited, or if such performance is dangerous, then mental practice might be the only way to practice. Mental practice also can be used to supplement ordinary training sessions. It was recently used this way to follow a communications training workshop conducted for supervisors (Morin & Latham, 2000). The purpose was to give the supervisors a way to practice the communication skills they had learned in training and to increase their confidence in their ability to communicate effectively. Trainees were instructed on how to visualize themselves engaging in an interpersonal interaction and using the communication skills. Results of the study indicated that mental practice was helpful. The supervisors' communications improved, and they reported feeling more confident of their abilities. However, the effectiveness of the practice depended on how capable the supervisor was in visualizing. This means that if a trainer plans to introduce mental practice, trainees must be instructed and given time to learn the technique.

**Feedback in Practice**   When a trainee practices a task he or she receives at least some information from the sheer act of performing it. This is internal or task feedback. Task feedback gives the learner information about how accurate or successful the performance was and about errors that were made. In addition to task feedback, a learner may get information from an external source. For example, a supervisor or a training instructor may observe a trainee's practice, identify mistakes, and tell the trainee how to correct them.

How much feedback is optimal for learning? Research has found that a high level of task feedback is highly beneficial to trainee performance in practice sessions (e.g., Earley, Wojnaroski, & Prest, 1987). Apparently, as a result of task feedback, the learner engages in processing task information, envisions what might be more effective strategies for performing the task, and then tries out these strategies in further practice. External feedback can improve performance, but it does not affect learning to the extent or in the same way that task feedback does. Although it would seem likely that more feedback is better than less, this is not necessarily so. Learning can occur even though the trainee receives no external feedback. Goodman (1998) reviewed research indicating that the amount of feedback needed depends on the source (task versus external) and on the stage of learning in which the feedback is received (early versus late). Although frequent external feedback can improve task performance during practice, when the retention of learned skill is measured, the measure shows that this feedback can have a detrimental effect. Providing external feedback only infrequently during practice, and then eliminating it altogether toward the end, has a better overall effect. Performance during practice may be decreased, but posttraining skill retention is greater (cf. Salmoni, Schmidt, & Walter, 1984; R. A. Schmidt, 1991). As you might guess, an explanation for this lies in the coincidental effects on task feedback. Although external feedback is functional for directing a learner to correct performance errors made during practice, it also can reduce the learner's need to engage in active information processing, such as paying attention to the task and noticing the effects of certain actions. Essentially, external feedback can interfere with or deny the learner the beneficial effects of making errors and discovering how to correct them.

Goodman (1998) designed an experiment by which to vary the availability of task and external feedback and to evaluate the effects on both practice performance and long-term learned performance. The study confirmed that task feedback during practice is beneficial, although its greater effect was on the retention of learning. The study also showed that external feedback improved performance during practice. However, the improvement did not carry over to the later evaluation of learned performance, unless task feedback also had been available. When task feedback was *not* available, having external feedback contributed to neither learning nor retention. This finding confirmed the earlier research showing that external feedback could be detrimental.

These studies suggest that training designers may want to think carefully about the availability of feedback in practice sessions, and attempt to arrange for the most favorable combination of external and task feedback. Because acquisition and long-term retention are the most important outcomes of training, sometimes the best overall strategy is to give only infrequent external feedback and allow trainees to learn through a trial-and-error process using task feedback.

## Designing Practice Sessions

To schedule practice sessions, the trainer must consider two related issues: massed versus distributed practice and part versus whole learning. The important distinction between massed and distributed practice is the existence of a time interval between practice periods. When there is no break, it is massed practice. When practice is interspersed with training activities or rest breaks, it is distributed practice. For example, an educational course that alternates lecture sessions with laboratory work in which you perform tasks based on lecture material is a distributed practice design.

Which form of practice is better will depend on what is being practiced. A meta-analysis of research found that trainees in distributed practice usually performed better than those in massed practice, but this depended on the complexity of the task being learned (Donovan & Radosevich, 1999). The learning of relatively simple psychomotor tasks with high physical requirements, such as typing, was reported to benefit from distributed practice. However, the practice of such tasks was actually more beneficial when the interspersed time interval was very brief—less than 1 minute, which essentially is massed practice. For more complex tasks that involve high-level information processing and judgment as well as machine control, such as vehicle operation, distributed practice with longer intervals is essential for learning.

The issue of part versus whole learning concerns the amount and nature of the material to be practiced. In whole learning, practice is designed so that a learner practices the entire task at once. In part learning, the task is broken into components that the learner practices separately. Discussions of the research literature suggest that the nature of the task will determine whether it is better to practice it whole or practice the parts separately (cf. Houston, 1986). If a task is simple and its components are interrelated (such as typing), it should be practiced as a whole. If a task is complex and its components are not highly interrelated, practicing the parts is more effective. In some complex tasks, the sequence in which components are performed is critical. Practice for such tasks is focused first on learning the parts. Once these are learned, the whole is practiced, with all components in proper order. For example, in learning to operate a motor vehicle, a learner benefits from having distributed practice of some components of driving, such as starting the engine, operating the gear shift, backing up, and so on. Still, it is the sequence in which the actions are performed that is most important in driving. Therefore, after the basic elements are learned, the tasks in sequence are practiced as a whole. Many work tasks have such requirements, ranging from machine operation to food production to analysis of medical tests.

## Individual Differences Among Trainees

Trainees' personal characteristics are important to consider. A training designer should think about trainees' existing knowledge and ability in deciding what material to cover and in how much depth. Also, trainers should have some idea of whether trainees are interested and motivated to learn.

**Differences in Knowledge and Ability**    Differences in individuals' levels of general mental ability and job knowledge have long been recognized as influences on work performance. For example, in Chapter 10, I discussed research on the Schmidt-Hunter theoretical model showing that general mental ability had an important, indirect impact on performance, through its effect on job knowledge (Schmidt, Hunter, & Outerbridge, 1986). Ree, Carretta, and Teachout (1995) thought training might be affected similarly. They proposed that trainees' general mental ability and prior knowledge of the tasks being trained would influence new learning. In an Air Force pilot training program, the researchers took measures of trainees' general mental ability, prior knowledge of flying, knowledge acquired in training, and work sample performance. The results of the study were consistent with the Schmidt-Hunter model. General mental ability had a strong indirect influence on work sample performance through its effects on trainee knowledge. The level of general mental ability predicted both prior knowledge of flying and knowledge acquired in training. In turn, these sources of knowledge had direct effects on work sample performance.

For certain complex tasks, the impact of general mental ability is more direct. According to Ackerman's (1988, 1992) theoretical model, as depicted in

Ability Structure                           Skill Acquisition

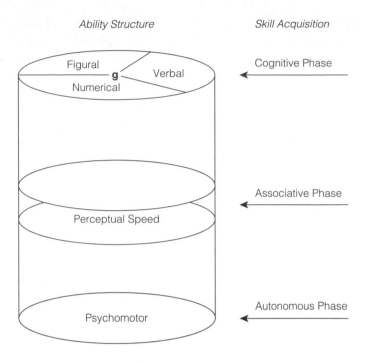

Legend:  **g** = general mental ability

FIGURE **16.7**

Ability requirements at different stages of skill acquisition, according to Ackerman's theoretical model.

From "Predicting Individual Differences in Complex Skill Acquisition: Dynamics of Ability Determinants," by P. L. Ackerman, 1992, *Journal of Applied Psychology, 77*, figure 1, as adapted from Ackerman (1988), p. 599. Copyright 1992 by American Psychological Association, Inc. Reprinted by permission.

Figure 16.7, different abilities are associated with different stages of learning. Cognitive abilities, including general mental ability, are important in the first phase of skill acquisition. Perceptual speed is important in the second phase, in which performance procedures are being developed. Psychomotor abilities are important in the final phase, in which performance is being polished and automatized. Ackerman proposed that certain task attributes can either advance or impede skill development, beyond the cognitively controlled first stage of learning. One such attribute is the consistency of information processing required by a task. In many tasks, information-processing requirements are consistent. That is, stimuli and correct responses are stipulated so as to allow performance with complete accuracy, once the relationships are learned. No limits are imposed, and learning can reach the autonomous phase. The trainee learns the appropriate response to each task stimulus with such certainty that the response becomes automatic. At this point, performance requires little attention or cognition. Driving is like this. Once a person has learned, he or she can drive without thinking about it. On other tasks, learning does not proceed beyond the first stage because information processing is inconsistent. Such tasks do not become easier with practice, and they never become automatic. Each performance must be cognitively controlled. Examples are tasks that involve monitoring, signal detection, and making decisions under time pressure—such as in air traffic control. Few actions in such work can be performed accurately without paying attention. Even well-trained and experienced performers must continually engage in information processing. Ackerman (1992) proposed that a person's level of cognitive ability would have direct benefits for the performance of such tasks and would also be related to success in the training of them. He found evidence of this in an extensive training program using an air traffic control simulation. The results showed that performance was directly controlled by cognitive abilities throughout the entire training period and that the level of general mental ability could be used to predict successful performance.

An important implication of these studies is that an effective way to select individuals for training on highly complex tasks is to accept trainees on the basis of their scores on general mental ability tests (Ree et al., 1995). In organizations that use general mental ability tests for employee selection purposes, the information is already available and should be identified by the person analysis in training needs assessment. Depending on the type of tasks being trained, other tests and assessments are possible. A job knowledge test might be helpful for determining whether a trainee's preparation is adequate given the level of the training. Another option is to administer a trainability test. In this, brief instruction is given showing how to perform a work sample, followed by a performance test on the tasks demonstrated. A trainability test can assess both the aptitude for learning and the existence of previously developed skills (Robertson & Downs, 1989).

**Motivation**    In the past, many theorists and researchers studied the effects of motivation on job performance, but they gave little attention to motivation in training. Because learning theory addressed motivation only in terms of reinforcing behavior, learning researchers likewise showed little interest in the motivation to learn. Now, that has changed. Currently, there is a large body of theory and research on motivational effects in training, and interest in this issue is growing. In this section, I will overview two theories that are relevant to motivation in training and discuss some of the research.

Reinforcement theory originated as learning theory, and it was meant to guide the scientific study of how behavior develops and changes (Skinner, 1954). The basic idea of reinforcement theory is that any action is strengthened or weakened by its consequences. That is, in the process of learning, people form associations between their actions and whatever happens as a result. These action–outcome associations are stored in memory and are used to guide subsequent behavior. In forming an association, the individual is generally assumed to have an emotional response to the consequence of the action. This response is critical in the development of behavior. If the out-come of a person's action feels pleasant or satisfying, then the action is rein-forced by this feeling, and the person will take the same action when the next opportunity arises. In contrast, if the outcome is unpleasant or not satisfying, then he or she will tend not to repeat the action. In reinforcement theory, what makes an outcome reinforcing is largely an individual matter. No action outcome operates universally as a reinforcer, although money comes fairly close. A reinforcer can be anything the individual values, including tangible goods or social rewards, such as praise and recognition. Reinforcement also can be intrinsic to the task being learned, such as when a task is interesting or when performance yields a feeling of accomplishment. Intrinsic reinforce-ment may have particular relevance to employee training. For example, the high value of task feedback in practice sessions may be due to both its infor-mational and motivational contributions.

Goal-setting theory originated as a work motivation theory meant to ex-plain the effects of intentions or goals on job performance (Locke & Latham, 1990). The central feature of motivation in goal-setting theory is the goal. As a motivational concept, goals are assumed to determine choice of work activity and to direct and sustain behavior. Goals are defined in terms of how specific or general and how difficult or easy they are. Research has found that these goal attributes have important effects on an individual's motivation. Many stud-ies have demonstrated that specific and challenging goals have strong effects on work performance (cf. Mento, Steele, & Karren, 1987). The basic motiva-tional process includes setting a goal and developing strategies for attaining it. Certain personal factors are assumed to determine commitment to the goal and the level of performance. These include knowledge and ability for goal-re-lated work, and the individual's sense of self-efficacy.[5] The source of the goal is another important factor, also affecting goal commitment and performance. Goals can be self-set, or they can be assigned by someone else, such as a super-visor or a trainer. Acceptance of an assigned goal and commitment to attaining it can occur because the individual accepts the influence of the goal source or even because monetary rewards are expected. However, goal acceptance is more likely when the person is consulted in the goal-setting process. This al-lows the goal to be at least partly self-set (Locke, Latham, & Erez, 1988).

In their review, Colquitt, LePine, and Noe (2000) observed that the recent interest in training motivation has generated a considerable body of literature. Generally, this work has proceeded along one of two lines: (1) study of specific individual differences and situational variables that might be related to the motivation to learn, and (2) development of theoretical models showing how these factors influence learning motivation. The result of this, according to Colquitt et al. (2000), has been an "extensive nomological network for training

---

[5]Self-efficacy refers to a person's beliefs about his or her capacity to successfully perform a task (Bandura, 1991). This motivational concept has been studied in the context of training.

motivation, but at the cost of convergence and clarity regarding which specific factors can be leveraged to improve it" (p. 678). In other words, there is presently a lot of information available, but as a whole it is fragmented and disordered, and we are not sure how to make use of it.

Colquitt et al. (2000) attempted to clarify the meaning of this accumulated literature. First, they conducted a meta-analysis of the research data. This showed that several personal and situational variables predicted the motivation to learn. These included personality characteristics, such as locus of control, conscientiousness, and anxiety, as well as other personal factors, such as self-efficacy and outcome valence.[6] Next, they conducted a path analysis to determine how these variables are related to motivation and learning. They considered theoretical models that differed in their prediction of these relationships. Mainly, the difference between the models is whether such variables are considered to have direct effects or indirect, mediated effects on learning. In the path analysis, the researchers found that a model which could accommodate both direct and indirect effects on motivation and learning was a better fit for the research data. First, concerning the influence on motivation, the analysis showed that personal variables, both directly and indirectly, determined motivational levels. Personality characteristics—specifically, locus of control, conscientiousness, and anxiety—influenced self-efficacy and outcome valence and, through these mediators, indirectly affected the level of motivation. Also, locus of control and anxiety had direct effects on motivation. Second, concerning the influence on learning, the analysis confirmed that cognitive ability was the greatest overall determinant. However, motivation did have a significant effect on knowledge and skill acquisition, beyond that due to cognitive ability. Further, personality traits had direct and independent effects on learning. Together, these three sources—cognitive ability, motivation, and personality—were able to account for almost all the variation in levels of knowledge and skill acquisition.

## Conclusions

In the past, the emphasis in training development was on methods and the setting in which training was to take place. Neither researchers nor training developers gave much thought to the person being trained. Gradually, however, it became apparent that even within the same program, using the same methods for all participants, some trainees were learning more than others. At this point, researchers began to take notice. Their review of experimental research on basic learning processes suggested certain changes in training design. For example, studies of learning had demonstrated that

---

[6]Valence refers to how desirable or attractive a performance outcome is. It is a motivational concept, similar to reinforcement, used in some work motivation theories.

trainees need practice and at least some reinforcing feedback. However, it was often difficult to discern the practical messages of this largely academic research on learning. More recently, industrial and organizational psychologists have begun to study individual differences in trainees and to provide the needed practical emphasis. They have been particularly interested in trainee characteristics, such as cognitive ability and motivation, that might explain the differential results of training programs. Their research has demonstrated that what trainees already can do and want to learn are extremely important to consider in training.

Currently, training research is exploring differences in trainees' personalities that might either facilitate or obstruct the training process. For example, Martocchio and Judge (1997) studied the behavior of highly conscientious trainees. They proposed that individuals who are highly conscientious in personality have two other traits that affect their learning as well as their later use of the learning. One is high self-efficacy. Highly conscientious trainees believe in their ability to succeed. As a result, they are likely to learn more and perform better than trainees with low self-efficacy. The other trait is self-deception. Self-deceiving individuals hold a positive but biased view of themselves. Self-deception can have positive effects. Self-deceivers ignore minor criticisms and do not dwell on past failures. However, self-deception can interfere with learning. Because self-deception can prevent a person from confronting performance errors, a self-deceiver might not learn much from making mistakes in training. Results of Martocchio and Judge's (1997) study showed that highly conscientious trainees did not perform as well in training as others did, which supported the predictions. It was troubling, however, that this result seemed to contradict other studies showing that conscientious employees are strong performers (e.g., Barrick & Mount, 1991). To explain, the researchers pointed out that while conscientious trainees may learn less in training, they may be much better at using what they do learn because of the self-discipline and organization that is characteristic of conscientiousness. Later evidence supported this interpretation. Colquitt et al. (2000) found conscientiousness to be negatively associated with performance in training, but there was a strong positive association between conscientiousness and the transfer of training to the job. More of what the training offered was being used by these individuals.

## SUMMING UP

Employee training is offered by many organizations to prepare new employees and to further develop continuing employees. The purpose of this chapter has been to examine the nature of training from multiple perspectives. We can sum up as follows:

- Training needs assessment is the basis for effective employee training.
- Effective design requires learning experiences that accomplish training objectives and that fit within time and place constraints.
- Training techniques can be used in on- or off-site programs to develop technical and/or interpersonal knowledge and skill.
- Traditional training is conducted on the job by a trainee's supervisor or coworker.
- Apprenticeship, job rotation, and mentoring are on-the-job methods.
- Transfer of training to use on the job is the main reason for training.
- Employers offer workshops on various topics of common interest, including diversity training.
- To assess the success of training, a controlled evaluation study is required.
- Practice and performance feedback are essential for effective learning and transfer. Task feedback is especially important.
- The level of a trainee's general mental ability predicts the extent to which the individual will benefit from training.
- Trainee motivation and personality can impact learning, beyond the effects of cognitive ability.

## INFOTRAC COLLEGE EDITION

Want to learn more about the issues discussed here? Use your subscription to InfoTrac College Edition to access an online library of research journals and other periodicals. Go to http://www.infotrac-college.com/wadsworth and enter a search term. Any of the following terms can be used in a keyword search to find articles about some topics reviewed in this chapter.

Interpersonal skills training       Internships
Mentoring                           Employee orientation
Diversity training                  Instructional design
Organizational leadership
    training

# References

Aamodt, M. G., Bryan, D. A., & Whitcomb, A. J. (1993). Predicting performance with letters of recommendation. *Public Personnel Management, 22,* 81–90.

Ackerman, P. L. (1988). Determinants of individual differences during skill acquisition: Cognitive abilities and information processing. *Journal of Experimental Psychology: General, 117,* 288–318.

Ackerman, P. L. (1992). Predicting individual differences in complex skill acquisition: Dynamics of ability determinants. *Journal of Applied Psychology, 77,* 598–614.

Adams, J. S. (1965). Inequity in social exchange. In L. Berkowitz (Ed.), *Advances in experimental social psychology* (Vol. 2, pp. 267–299). New York: Academic Press.

*Adarand Constructors v. Peña, U.S. Secretary of Transportation* (1995). 115 Sup. Ct. 2097.

Adler, R. S., & Peirce, E. R. (1996). Encouraging employers to abandon their "no comment" policies regarding job references: A reform proposal. *Washington & Lee Law Review, 53,* 1381.

Adventures in interviewing, or college grads say and do the darndest things. (1998). *Office Systems, 15*(8), 9.

Age Discrimination in Employment Act (1967). 29 U.S.C. 621.

Albert, S., & Whetten, D. A. (1985). Organizational identity. In L. L. Cummings & B. M. Staw (Eds.), *Research in organizational behavior* (Vol. 7, pp. 263–295). Greenwich, CT: JAI Press.

*Alexander v. Gardner-Denver Company* (1974). 415 U.S. 36.

Alfredsson, L., Akerstedt, T., Mattsson, M., & Wilborg, B. (1991). Self-reported health and well-being amongst night security guards: A comparison with the working population. *Ergonomics, 34,* 525–530.

Alkhadher, O., Clarke, D. D., & Anderson, N. (1998). Equivalence and predictive validity of paper-and-pencil and computerized adaptive formats of the Differential Aptitude Tests. *Journal of Occupational & Organizational Psychology, 71,* 205–217.

Allport, G. W., & Odbert, H. S. (1933). Trait-names: A psycho-lexical study. *Psychological Monographs, 47,* 171–220.

Alvares, K. M. (1997). The business of human resources. *Human Resource Management, 36*(1), 9–15.

Americans with Disabilities Act (1990). 42 U.S.C. 12101.

Anastasi, A. (1982). *Psychological testing* (5th ed.). New York: Macmillan.

Anderson, P., & Pulich, M. (2000). Recruiting good employees in tough times. *Health Care Manager, 18*(3), 32–40.

Andersson, L. M., & Pearson, C. M. (1999). Tit for tat? The spiraling effect of incivility in the workplace. *Academy of Management Review, 24,* 452–471.

Angoff, W. H. (1971). Scales, norms, and equivalent scores. In R. L. Thorndike (Ed.), *Educational measurement* (pp. 508–600). Washington, DC: American Council on Education.

Antonioni, D. (1994). The effects of feedback accountability on upward appraisal ratings. *Personnel Psychology, 47,* 349–356.

**460**

Antonioni, D. (1996). Designing an effective 360-degree appraisal feedback process. *Organizational Dynamics, 25,* 24–38.

Argyris, C. (1957). *Personality and Organization.* New York: Harper & Row.

Armstrong, M., & Brown, D. (1998). Relating competencies to pay: The UK experience. *Compensation and Benefits Review, 30*(3), 28–39.

Arthur, W., Jr., & Doverspike, D. (1997). Employment-related drug testing: Idiosyncratic characteristics and issues. *Public Personnel Management, 26,* 77–87.

Arvey, R. D., & Begalla, M. E. (1975). Analyzing the homemaker job using the Position Analysis Questionnaire (PAQ). *Journal of Applied Psychology, 60,* 513–517.

Arvey, R. D., & Campion, J. E. (1982). The employment interview: A summary and review of recent research. *Personnel Psychology, 35,* 281–322.

Ash, P. (1991). Law and regulation of preemployment inquiries. *Journal of Business and Psychology, 5,* 291–308.

Ash, R. A., & Levine, E. L. (1985). Job applicant training and work experience evaluation: An empirical comparison of four methods. *Journal of Applied Psychology, 70,* 572–576.

Asher, J. J., & Sciarrino, J. A. (1974). Realistic work sample tests: A review. *Personnel Psychology, 27,* 519–533.

Ashforth, B. E., & Kreiner, G. E. (1999). "How can you do it?": Dirty work and the challenge of constructing a positive identity. *Academy of Management Review, 24*(3), 413–434.

Austin, J. T., Humphreys, L. G., & Hulin, C. L. (1989). Another view of dynamic criteria: A critical reanalysis of Barrett, Caldwell, & Alexander. *Personnel Psychology, 42,* 583–596.

Avoiding "truth or dare" in reference checks. (2000). *HR Focus, 77,* 5–6.

Baldwin, T. T., & Ford, J. K. (1988). Transfer of training: A review and directions for future research. *Personnel Psychology, 41,* 63–105.

Baltes, B. B., Briggs, T. E., Huff, J. W., Wright, J. A., & Neuman, G. A. (1999). Flexible and compressed workweek schedules: A meta-analysis of their effects on work-related criteria. *Journal of Applied Psychology, 84,* 496–513.

Balzer, W. K., & Sulsky, L. M. (1992). Halo and performance appraisal research: A critical examination. *Journal of Applied Psychology, 77,* 975–985.

Bandura, A. (1991). Social cognitive theory of self-regulation. *Organizational Behavior & Human Decision Processes, 50,* 248–287.

Barber, A. E., Daly, C. L., Giannantonio, C. M., & Phillips, J. M. (1994). Job search activities: An examination of changes over time. *Personnel Psychology, 47,* 739–765.

Barber, A. E., Hollenbeck, J. R., Tower, S. L., & Phillips, J. M. (1994). The effects of interview focus on recruitment effectiveness: A field experiment. *Journal of Applied Psychology, 79,* 886–896.

Barling, J., Weber, T., & Kelloway, E. K. (1996). Effects of transformational leadership training on attitudinal and financial outcomes: A field experiment. *Journal of Applied Psychology, 81,* 827–832.

Barrett, G. V., Caldwell, M. S., & Alexander, R. A. (1985). The concept of dynamic criteria: A critical reanalysis. *Personnel Psychology, 38,* 41–56.

Barrett, G. V., Phillips, J. S., & Alexander, R. A. (1981). Concurrent and predictive validity designs: A critical reanalysis. *Journal of Applied Psychology, 66,* 1–6.

Barrick, M. R., & Mount, M. K. (1991). The Big Five personality dimensions and job performance: A meta-analysis. *Personnel Psychology, 44,* 1–26.

Barrick, M. R., Mount, M. K., & Strauss, J. P. (1994). Antecedents of involuntary turnover due to a reduction in force. *Personnel Psychology, 47,* 515–535.

Barry, B., & Bateman, T. S. (1996). A social trap analysis of the management of diversity. *Academy of Management Review, 21*(3), 757–790.

Bartlett, C. J., Bobko, P., Mosier, S. B., & Hannan, R. (1978). Testing for fairness with a moderated multiple regression strategy: An alternative to differential analysis. *Personnel Psychology, 31,* 233–241.

Barton, J. (1994). Choosing to work at night: A moderating influence on individual tolerance to shift work. *Journal of Applied Psychology, 79,* 449–454.

Barton, J., & Folkard, S. (1991). The response of day and night nurses to their work schedules. *Journal of Occupational Psychology, 64,* 207–218.

Bass, B. M. (1962). Further evidence on the dynamic character of criteria. *Personnel Psychology, 15,* 93–97.

Bass, B. M. (1985). *Leadership and performance beyond expectations.* New York: Free Press.

Bauer, T. N., Maertz, C. P., Jr., Dolen, M. R., & Campion, M. A. (1998). Longitudinal assessment of applicant reactions to employment testing and test outcome feedback. *Journal of Applied Psychology, 83,* 892–903.

Bauman, A. R. (1977). *Training of trainers: Resource manual.* Washington, DC: U.S. Government Printing Office.

Baxter, J. C., Brock, B., Hill, P. C., & Rozelle, R. M. (1981). Letters of recommendation: A question of value. *Journal of Applied Psychology, 66,* 296–301.

Becker, B. E., & Huselid, M. A. (1992). Direct estimates of SDy and the implications for utility analysis. *Journal of Applied Psychology, 77,* 227–233.

Becker, T. E., & Colquitt, A. L. (1992). Potential versus actual faking of a biodata form: An analysis along several dimensions of item type. *Personnel Psychology, 45,* 389–406.

Becker, T. E., & Klimoski, R. J. (1989). A field study of the relationship between the organizational feedback environment and performance. *Personnel Psychology, 42,* 343–358.

Berkowitz, L., Fraser, C., Treasure, F. P., & Cochran, S. (1987). Pay, equity, job gratifications, and comparisons in pay satisfaction. *Journal of Applied Psychology, 72,* 544–551.

Bernardin, H. J (1986). Subordinate appraisal: A valuable source of information about managers. *Human Resource Management Journal, 25,* 421–439.

Bernardin, H. J., & Beatty, R. W. (1984). *Performance appraisal: Assessing human behavior at work.* Boston: Kent.

Bernardin, H. J., & Buckley, M. R. (1981). A consideration of strategies in rater training. *Academy of Management Review, 6,* 205–212.

Bernardin, H. J., Cooke, D. K., & Villanova, P. (2000). Conscientiousness and agreeableness as predictors of rating leniency. *Journal of Applied Psychology, 85,* 232–234.

Bernardin, H. J., & Smith, P. C. (1981). A clarification of some issues regarding the development and use of Behaviorally Anchored Rating Scales (BARS). *Journal of Applied Psychology, 66,* 458–463.

Bernstein, A. (1987, October 19). Dispelling the myths about a higher minimum wage. *Business Week,* p. 146.

Berry, L. M. (1997). *Psychology at work: An introduction to industrial and organizational psychology* (2nd ed.). Boston: McGraw-Hill.

Binet, A., & Simon, T. (1916). *The development of intelligence in children.* (E. S. Kite, Trans.) Baltimore: Williams & Wilkins.

Binning, J. F., & Barrett, G. V. (1989). Validity of personnel decisions: A conceptual analysis of the inferential and evidential bases. *Journal of Applied Psychology, 74,* 478–494.

Binning, J. F., Goldstein, M. A., Garcia, M. F., & Scattaregia, J. H. (1988). Effects of preinterview impressions on questioning strategies in same- and opposite-sex employment interviews. *Journal of Applied Psychology, 73,* 30–37.

Black, J. S. (1988). Work role transitions: A study of American expatriate managers in Japan. *Journal of International Business Studies, 19,* 277–294.

Black, J. S., Gregersen, H. B., & Mendenhall, M. E. (1992). *Global assignments.* San Francisco: Jossey-Bass.

Black, J. S., & Mendenhall, M. (1990). Cross-cultural training effectiveness: A review and a theoretical framework for future research. *Academy of Management Review, 15,* 113–136.

Black, J. S., Mendenhall, M., & Oddou, G. (1991). Toward a comprehensive model of international adjustment: An integration of multiple theoretical perspectives. *Academy of Management Review, 16,* 291–317.

Black, J. S., & Porter, L. W. (1991). Managerial behaviors and job performance: A successful manager in Los Angeles may not succeed in Hong Kong. *Journal of International Business Studies, 22,* 99–113.

Black, J. S., & Stephens, G. K. (1989). The influence of the spouse on American expatriate adjustment and intent to stay in Pacific Rim overseas assignments. *Journal of Management, 15,* 529–544.

Blanz, F., & Ghiselli, E. E. (1972). The mixed standard scale: A new rating system. *Personnel Psychology, 25,* 185–199.

Boehm, V. R. (1977). Differential prediction: A methodological artifact? *Journal of Applied Psychology, 62,* 146–154.

Bohle, P., & Tilley, A. J. (1998). Early experience of shiftwork: Influences on attitudes. *Journal of Occupational & Organizational Psychology, 71,* 61–79.

Bolton, B. (1992). Review of the California Psychological Inventory, Revised Edition. In J. J. Kramer & J. C. Conoley (Eds.), *Eleventh mental measurements yearbook* (pp. 138–139). Lincoln: University of Nebraska Press.

Bommer, W. H., Johnson, J. L., Rich, G. A., Podsakoff, P. M., & MacKenzie, S. B. (1995). On the interchangeability of objective and subjective measures of employee performance: A meta-analysis. *Personnel Psychology, 48,* 587–605.

Bordens, K. S., & Abbott, B. B. (1996). *Research design and methods: A process approach* (3rd ed.). Mountain View, CA: Mayfield.

Borgatta, E. F. (1964). The structure of personality characteristics. *Behavioral Science, 9,* 8–17.

Borman, W. C. (1974). The rating of individuals in organizations: An alternate approach. *Organizational Behavior & Human Performance, 12,* 105–124.

Borman, W. C. (1979). Format and training effects on rating accuracy and rater errors. *Journal of Applied Psychology, 64,* 410–421.

Borman, W. C. (1986). Behavior-based rating scales. In R. A. Berk (Ed.), *Performance Assessment: Method and applications.* Baltimore, MD: Johns Hopkins University Press.

Borman, W. C. (1991). Job behavior, performance, and effectiveness. In M. D. Dunnette & L. M. Hough (Eds.), *Handbook of industrial and organizational psychology* (2nd ed, vol. 2, pp. 271–326). Palo Alto, CA: Consulting Psychologists Press.

Borman, W. C., Dorsey, D., & Ackerman, L. (1992). Time-spent responses as time allocation strategies: Relations with sales performance in a stockbroker sample. *Personnel Psychology, 45,* 763–777.

Borman, W. C., & Motowidlo, S. J. (1993). Expanding the criterion domain to include elements of contextual performance. In N. Schmitt & W. Borman (Eds.), *Personnel selection in organizations* (pp. 71–98). San Francisco: Jossey-Bass.

Borman, W. C., White, L. A., & Dorsey, D. W. (1995). Effects of ratee task performance and interpersonal factors on supervisor and peer performance ratings. *Journal of Applied Psychology, 80,* 168–177.

Botkin, M. D. (1995). Review of the Revised NEO Personality Inventory. In J. C. Conoley & J. C. Impara (Eds.), *Twelfth mental measurements yearbook* (pp. 862–863). Lincoln: University of Nebraska Press.

Bouchard, T. J. (1972). *A manual for job analysis.* Minneapolis: Minnesota Civil Service Department.

Boudreau, J. W. (1991). Utility analysis for decisions in human resource management. In M. D. Dunnette & L. M. Hough (Eds.), *Handbook of industrial and organizational psychology* (2nd ed., Vol. 2, pp. 621–745). Palo Alto, CA: Consulting Psychologists Press.

Brannick, M. T., Michaels, C. E., & Baker, D. P. (1989). Construct validity of in-basket scores. *Journal of Applied Psychology, 74,* 957–963.

Bray, D. W. (1982). The assessment center and the study of lives. *American Psychologist, 37,* 180–189.

Bray, D. W., & Campbell, R. J. (1968). Selection of salesmen by means of an assessment center. *Journal of Applied Psychology, 52,* 36–41.

Bray, D. W., Campbell, R. J., & Grant, D. L. (1974). *Formative years in business: A long-term AT&T study of managerial lives.* New York: Wiley.

Bretz, R. D., Jr., Boudreau, J. W., & Judge, T. A. (1994). Job search behavior of employed managers. *Personnel Psychology, 47,* 275–302.

Bretz, R. D., & Judge, T. A. (1994). The role of human resource systems in job applicant decision processes. *Journal of Management, 20,* 531–551.

Bretz, R. D., Jr., & Judge, T. A. (1998). Realistic job previews: A test of the adverse self-selection hypothesis. *Journal of Applied Psychology, 83,* 330–337.

Bretz, R. D., Milkovich, G. T., & Read, W. (1992). The current state of performance appraisal research and practice: Concerns, directions, and implications. *Journal of Management, 18,* 321–352.

Brief, A. P., & Motowidlo, S. J. (1986). Prosocial organizational behaviors. *Academy of Management Review, 11,* 710–725.

Brogden, H. E., & Taylor, E. K. (1950). The dollar criterion—applying the cost accounting concept to criterion construction. *Personnel Psychology, 3,* 133–154.

Brown, C. (1990). Firms' choice of method of pay. *Industrial and Labor Relations Review, 40,* 165–182.

Brownas, D. A., & Bernardin, H. J. (1988). Critical incident technique. In S. Gael (Ed.), *The job analysis handbook for business, industry, and government* (Vol. 2, part 9.8, pp. 1120–1140). New York: Wiley.

Burke, M. J., & Day, R. R. (1986). A cumulative study of the effectiveness of managerial training. *Journal of Applied Psychology, 71,* 232–245.

Burnett, J. R., Fan, C., Motowidlo, S. J., & Degroot, T. (1998). Interview notes and validity. *Personnel Psychology, 51,* 375–396.

Burns, J. A., Jr. (1997). Employment references: Is there a better way? *Employee Relations Law Journal, 23,* 157–168.

Burrington, D. D. (1982). A review of state government employment application forms for suspect inquiries. *Public Personnel Management, 11,* 55–60.

Bycio, P. (1992). Job performance and absenteeism: A review and meta-analysis. *Human Relations, 45,* 193–220.

Cable, D. M., & Judge, T. A. (1994). Pay preference and job search decisions: A person–organization fit perspective. *Personnel Psychology, 47,* 317–348.

Caggiano, C. (1999). The truth about internet recruiting. *Inc, 21*(18), 156.

Campbell, D. T. (1960). Recommendations for APA test standards regarding construct, trait, and discriminant validity. *American Psychologist, 15,* 546–553.

Campbell, J. P. (1990a). Modeling the performance prediction problem in industrial and organizational psychology. In M. D. Dunnette & L. M. Hough (Eds.), *Handbook of industrial and organizational psychology* (2nd ed., Vol. 1, pp. 687–732). Palo Alto, CA: Consulting Psychologists Press.

Campbell, J. P. (1990b). An overview of the Army selection and classification project (Project A). *Personnel Psychology, 43,* 231–239.

Campbell, J. P., Dunnette, M. D., Lawler, E. E., & Weick, K. E. (1970). *Managerial behavior, performance, and effectiveness.* New York: McGraw-Hill.

Campbell, J. P., McHenry, J. J., & Wise, L. L. (1990). Modeling performance in a population of jobs. *Personnel Psychology, 43,* 313–333.

Campion, M. A., Campion, J. E., & Hudson, J. P., Jr. (1994). Structured interviewing: A note on incremental validity and alternative question types. *Journal of Applied Psychology, 79,* 998–1002.

Campion, M. A., Cheraskin, L., & Stevens, M. J. (1994). Career-related antecedents and outcomes of job rotation. *Academy of Management Journal, 37,* 1518–1542.

Campion, M. A., Palmer, D. K., & Campion, J. E. (1997). A review of structure in the selection interview. *Personnel Psychology, 50,* 655–702.

Campion, M. A., Pursell, E. D., & Brown, B. K. (1988). Structured interviewing: Raising the psychometric properties of the employment interview. *Personnel Psychology, 41,* 25–42.

*Canada NewsWire.* (2000, March 24). Details on pay equity payments.

Cannon-Bowers, J. A., Oser, R., & Flanagan, D. L. (1992). Work teams in industry: A selected review and proposed framework. In R. W. Swezey & E. Salas (Eds.), *Teams: Their training and performance.* Norwood, NJ: Ablex.

Cappelli, P., & Crocker-Hefter, A. (1996). Distinctive human resources are firms' core competencies. *Organizational Dynamics, 24* (3), 7–22.

Carlson, K. D., Scullen, S. E., Schmidt, F. L., Rothstein, H., & Erwin, F. (1999). Generalizable biographical data validity can be achieved without multi-organizational development and keying. *Personnel Psychology, 52,* 731–755.

Carroll, J. B. (1993). *Human cognitive abilities: A survey of factor-analytic studies.* New York: Cambridge University Press.

Cascio, W. F. (1991). *Applied psychology in personnel management.* Englewood Cliffs, NJ: Prentice Hall.

Cascio, W. F., Alexander, R. A., & Barrett, G. V. (1988). Setting cutoff scores: Legal, psychometric, and professional issues and guidelines. *Personnel Psychology, 41,* 1–24.

Cascio, W. F., Outtz, J., Zedeck, S., & Goldstein, I. L. (1995). Statistical implications of six methods of test score use in personnel selection. *Human Performance, 4,* 233–264.

Cascio, W. F., & Phillips, N. F. (1979). Performance testing: A rose among thorns? *Personnel Psychology, 32,* 751–766.

Cascio, W. F., & Ramos, R. A. (1986). Development and application of a new method for assessing job performance in behavioral/economic terms. *Journal of Applied Psychology, 71,* 20–28.

Casperson, D. M. (2001). Mastering the business meal. *Training & Development, 55,* 68–69.

Cattell, R. B. (1947). Confirmation and clarification of primary personality factors. *Psychometrika, 12,* 197–220.

Chan, D. (1996). Criterion and construct validation of an assessment centre. *Journal of Occupational & Organizational Psychology, 69,* 167–181.

Chan, D., & Schmitt, N. (1997). Video-based versus paper-and-pencil method of assessment in situational judgment tests: Subgroup differences in test performance and face validity perceptions. *Journal of Applied Psychology, 82,* 143–159.

Chan, D., Schmitt, N., DeShon, R. P., Clause, C. S., & Delbridge, K. (1997). Reactions to cognitive ability tests: The relationships between race, test performance, face validity perceptions, and test-taking motivation. *Journal of Applied Psychology, 82,* 300–310.

Chaney, F. B., & Owens, W. A. (1964). Life history antecedents of sales, research, and general engineering interest. *Journal of Applied Psychology, 48,* 101–105.

Chao, G., Walz, P., & Gardner, P. (1992). Formal and informal mentorships: A comparison of mentoring functions and contrast with nonmentored counterparts. *Personnel Psychology, 45,* 619–636.

Cheung, G. W. (1999). Multifaceted conceptions of self–other ratings disagreement. *Personnel Psychology, 52,* 1–36.

Church, A. H., & Bracken, D.W. (1997). Advancing the state of the art of 360-degree feedback: Guest editors' comments on the research and practice of multirater assessment methods. *Group & Organization Management, 22,* 149–161.

*City of Richmond v. Croson* (1989). 488 U.S. 469, 109 Sup.Ct. 706.

Civil Rights Act (1964). 42 U.S.C. 2000.

Civil Rights Act (1991). 42 U.S.C. 2000.

Clause, C. S., Mullins, M. E., Nee, M. T., Pulakos, E., & Schmitt, N. (1998). Parallel test form development: A procedure for alternate predictors and an example. *Personnel Psychology, 51,* 193–208.

Cleary, A. (1999). C. V. analysis: The new rock 'n' roll. *Insurance Brokers' Monthly and Insurance Adviser, 49,* 17, 22.

Cleary, T. A. (1968). Test bias: Prediction of grades for Negro and White students in integrated colleges. *Journal of Educational Measurement, 5,* 115–124.

*Cleveland Board of Education v. LaFleur* (1974). 414 U.S. 632.

Cleveland, J. N., Murphy, K. R., & Williams, R. E. (1989). Multiple uses of performance appraisal: Prevalence and correlates. *Journal of Applied Psychology, 74,* 130–135.

Clifford, J. P. (1996). Manage work better to better manage human resources: A comparative study of two approaches to job analysis. *Public Personnel Management, 25,* 89–102.

Cohen, S. G., & Ledford, G. E., Jr. (1994). The effectiveness of self-managing teams: A quasi-experiment. *Human Relations, 47,* 13–43.

Colquitt, J. A., LePine, J. A., & Noe, R. A. (2000). Toward an integrative theory of training motivation: A meta-analytic path analysis of 20 years of research. *Journal of Applied Psychology, 85,* 678–707.

Conley, P. R., & Sackett, P. R. (1987). Effects of using high- versus low-performing job incumbents as sources of job-analysis information. *Journal of Applied Psychology, 72,* 434–437.

Conlin, M., Mandel, M., Arndt, M., & Zellner, W. (2001, April 16). Suddenly, it's the Big Freeze: As the economy cools, the hiring door slams shut on job seekers. *Business Week,* 38–39.

Conoley, J. C., & Impara, J. C. (Eds.). (1995). *Twelfth mental measurements yearbook.* Lincoln: University of Nebraska Press.

Conway, J. M., Jako, R. A., & Goodman, D. F. (1995). A meta-analysis of interrater and internal consistency reliability of selection interviews. *Journal of Applied Psychology, 80,* 565–579.

Cook, T. D., & Campbell, D. T. (1979). *Quasi-experimentation: Design and analysis issues for field settings.* Chicago: Rand McNally.

Cook, T. D., Campbell, D.T., & Peracchio, L. (1990). Quasi experimentation. In M. D. Dunnette & L. M. Hough (Eds.), *Handbook of industrial and organizational psychology* (2nd ed., Vol. 1, pp. 491–576). Palo Alto, CA: Consulting Psychologists Press.

Cooper, W. H. (1981). Ubiquitous halo. *Psychological Bulletin, 90,* 218–244.

Cordery, J. L., Mueller, W. S., & Smith, L. M. (1991). Attitudinal and behavioral effects of autonomous group working: A longitudinal field study. *Academy of Management Journal, 34,* 464–476.

Cornelius, E. T., III. (1988). Analyzing job analysis data. In S. Gael (Ed.), *The job analysis handbook for business, industry, and government* (Vol. 1, part 3.1, pp. 193–204). New York: Wiley.

Costa, P. T., Jr. (1996). Work and personality: Use of the NEO-PI-R in industrial/organisational psychology. *Applied Psychology: An International Review, 45,* 225–241.

Costa, P. T., Jr., & McCrae, R. R. (1995). Domains and facets: Hierarchical personality assessment using the Revised NEO Personality Inventory. *Journal of Personality Assessment, 64,* 21–50.

Cowan, T. R. (1987). Drugs and the workplace: To drug test or not to test? *Public Personnel Management, 16,* 313–322.

Craig, A., & Condon, R. (1984). Operational efficiency and time of day. *Human Factors, 26,* 197–205.

Cronbach, L. J. (1970). *Essentials of psychological testing* (3rd ed.). New York: Harper & Row.

Cronbach, L. J., & Gleser, G. C. (1965). *Psychological tests and personnel decisions* (2nd ed.) Urbana: University of Illinois Press.

Cronshaw, S. F. (1997). Lo! The stimulus speaks: The insider's view on Whyte and Latham's "The futility of utility analysis." *Personnel Psychology, 50,* 611–615.

Cudeck, R. (1985). A structural comparison of conventional and adaptive versions of the ASVAB. *Multivariate Behavioral Research, 20,* 305–322.

Cunningham, M. R., & Ash, P. (1988). The structure of honesty: Factor analyses of the Reid Report. *Journal of Business and Psychology, 3,* 54–66.

Cunningham, M. R., Wong, D. T., & Barbee, A. P. (1994). Self-presentation dynamics on overt integrity tests: Experimental studies of the Reid Report. *Journal of Applied Psychology, 79,* 643–658.

Cureton, E. E. (1965). Reliability and validity: Basic assumptions and experimental designs. *Educational and Psychological Measurement, 24,* 327–346.

Dalessio, A. T. (1994). Predicting insurance agent turnover using a video-based situational judgment test. *Journal of Business Psychology, 9,* 23–32.

Dawis, R. V. (1991). Vocational interests, values, and preferences. In M. D. Dunnette & L. M. Hough (Eds.), *Handbook of industrial and organizational psychology* (2nd ed., Vol. 2, pp. 833–871). Palo Alto, CA: Consulting Psychologists Press.

Day, J. (2000). Online job ads with a human touch. *HRMagazine, 45*(3), 140–142.

Deadrick, D. L., & Gardner, D. G. (1997). Distributional ratings of performance levels and variability. *Group & Organization Management, 22,* 317–342.

Deci, E. L. (1972). The effects of contingent and noncontingent rewards and controls on intrinsic motivation. *Organizational Behavior and Human Performance, 8,* 217–229.

Delaney, J. T., & Huselid, M. A. (1996). The impact of human resource management practices on perceptions of organizational performance. *Academy of Management Journal, 39,* 949–969.

DeNisi, A. S., Cafferty, T. P., & Meglino, B. M. (1984). A cognitive model of the performance appraisal process. *Organizational Behavior & Human Decision Processes, 33,* 360–396.

DeNisi, A. S., & Peters, L. H. (1996). Organization of information in memory and the performance appraisal process: Evidence from the field. *Journal of Applied Psychology, 81,* 717–737.

Devine, D. J., Clayton, L. D., Philips, J. L., Dunford, B. B., & Melner, S. B. (1999). Teams in organizations: Prevalence, characteristics, and effectiveness. *Small Group Research, 30,* 678–711.

*Dictionary of occupational titles* (4th ed., Rev.). (1991). U.S. Employment Service. Washington, DC: U.S. Government Printing Office.

Digman, J. M. (1990). Personality structure: Emergence of the five-factor model. *Annual Review of Psychology, 41,* 417–440.

Donovan, J. J., & Radosevich, D. J. (1999). A meta-analytic review of the distribution of practice effect: Now you see it, now you don't. *Journal of Applied Psychology, 84,* 795-805.

Dougherty, T. W., Ebert, R. J., & Callender, J. C. (1986). Policy capturing in the employment interview. *Journal of Applied Psychology, 71,* 9–15.

Dougherty, T. W., Turban, D. B., & Callender, J. C. (1994). Confirming first impressions in the employment interview: A field study of interviewer behavior. *Journal of Applied Psychology, 79,* 659–665.

Drasgow, F., & Hulin, C. L. (1990). Item response theory. In M. D. Dunnette & L. M. Hough (Eds.), *Handbook of industrial and organizational psychology* (2nd ed., Vol. 1, pp. 577–636). Palo Alto, CA: Consulting Psychologists Press.

Dreher, G. F., & Ash, R. A. (1990). A comparative study of mentoring among men and women in managerial, professional, and technical positions. *Journal of Applied Psychology, 75,* 539–546.

Driskell, J. E., Copper, C., & Moran, A. (1994). Does mental practice enhance performance? *Journal of Applied Psychology, 79,* 481–492.

Drug-Free Workplace Act (1988). 41 USC 701 et seq.

*Duffield v. Robertson Stephens & Company* (1998). WL 467389.

Dunnette, M. D. (1962). Personnel management. *Annual Review of Psychology, 13,* 285–314.

Dunnette, M. D. (1999). Introduction. In N. G. Peterson, M. D. Mumford, W. C. Borman, P. R. Jeanneret, & E. A. Fleishman (Eds.), *An occupational information system for the 21st century: The development of O\*NET* (pp. 3–7). Washington, DC: American Psychological Association.

Dye, D., & Silver, M. (1999). The origins of O\*NET. In N. G. Peterson, M. D. Mumford, W. C. Borman, P. R. Jeanneret, & E. A. Fleishman (Eds.), *An occupational information system for the 21st century: The development of O\*NET* (pp. 9–19). Washington, DC: American Psychological Association.

Earley, P. C., Wojnaroski, P., & Prest, W. (1987). Task planning and energy expended: Exploration of how goals influence performance. *Journal of Applied Psychology, 72,* 107–114.

Ebel, R. L. (1972). *Essentials of educational measurement.* Englewood Cliffs, NJ: Prentice Hall.

Employee Polygraph Protection Act (1988). CFR 29 Chap V, Part 801.

England, G. W. (1971). *Development and use of weighted application blanks.* (Rev. ed., Bulletin 55). Minneapolis: University of Minnesota, Industrial Relations Center.

Equal Pay Act (1963). 29 U.S.C. 206.

Erbe, B., & Shiner, J. (1999, October 24). Gender gaps in the paycheck. *Washington Times.*

Farh, J., Dobbins, G. H., & Cheng, B. (1991). Cultural relativity in action: A comparison of self-ratings made by Chinese and U.S. workers. *Personnel Psychology, 44,* 129–147.

Feild, H. S., & Holley, W. H. (1982). The relationship of performance appraisal system characteristics to verdicts in selected employment discrimination cases. *Academy of Management Journal, 25,* 392–406.

Felker, D. B., & Rose, A. M. (1997). Tests of job performance. In D. L. Whetzel & G. R. Wheaton (Eds.), *Applied measurement methods in industrial psychology* (pp. 319–351). Palo Alto, CA: Davies Black.

Felson, L. (2001). Undergrad marketers must get jump on networking skills. *Marketing News, 35* (8), 14–15.

Ferris, G. R., Hochwarter, W. A., Buckley, M. R., Harrell-Cook, G., & Frink, D. D. (1999). Human resources management: Some new directions. *Journal of Management, 25,* 385–415.

Fiedler, F. E. (1996). Research on leadership selection and training: One view of the future. *Administrative Science Quarterly, 41,* 241–250.

Fiedler, F. E., Chemers, M. M., & Mahar, L. (1976). *Improving leadership effectiveness: The Leader Match concept.* New York: Wiley.

Fiedler, F. E., Mitchell, T., & Triandis, H. C., (1971). The culture assimilator: An approach to cross-cultural training. *Journal of Applied Psychology, 55,* 95–102.

File, Q. W. (1945). The measurement of supervisory quality in industry. *Journal of Applied Psychology, 29,* 323–337.

Fine, S. A., & Wiley, W. W. (1971). *An introduction to functional job analysis.* Kalamazoo, MI: W. E. Upjohn Institute for Employment Research.

Finley, D. M., Osburn, H. G., Dubin, J. A., & Jeanneret, P. R. (1977). Behaviorally based rating scales: Effects of specific anchors and disguised scale continua. *Personnel Psychology, 30,* 659–669.

Fisicaro, S. A. (1988). A reexamination of the relation between halo error and accuracy. *Journal of Applied Psychology, 73,* 239–244.

Fiske, D. W. (1949). Consistency of the factorial structures of personality ratings from different sources. *Journal of Abnormal and Social Psychology, 44,* 329–344.

Fitz, A. (1999). The debate over mandatory arbitration in employment disputes. *Dispute Resolution Journal, 54*(1), 34–41.

Fitzgerald, L. F., & Quaintance, M. K. (1982). Survey of assessment center use in state and local government. *Journal of Assessment Center Technology, 5,* 9–21.

Flanagan, J. C. (1954). The critical incident technique. *Psychological Bulletin, 51,* 327–358.

Fleishman, E. A. (1992). *Fleishman-Job Analysis Survey (F-JAS).* Bethesda, MD: Management Research Institute.

Flynn, G. (1999a). High-profile age discrimination suit moves forward. *Workforce, 78*(10), 126–128.

Flynn, G. (1999b). Who's left in the labor pool? *Workforce, 78*(10), 34–40.

Fogli, L., & Whitney, K. (1998). Assessing and changing managers for new organizational roles. In R. Jeanneret & R. Silzer (Eds.), *Individual psychological assessment: predicting behavior in organizational settings* (pp. 319–351). San Francisco: Jossey-Bass.

Ford, J. K., Kraiger, K., & Schechtman, S. L. (1986). Study of race effects in objective indices and subjective evaluations of performance: A meta-analysis of performance criteria. *Psychological Bulletin, 99,* 330–337.

Ford, J. K., & Noe, R. A. (1987). Self-assessed training needs: The effects of attitudes toward training, managerial level, and function. *Personnel Psychology, 40,* 39–53.

Freda, L. J., & Senkewicz, J. J. (1988). Work diaries. In S. Gael (Ed.). *The job analysis handbook for business, industry, and government* (Vol. 1, part 5.5, pp. 446–452). New York: Wiley.

Frey, T. L. (2001). Help abundant when marketing job seekers tap into networks. *Marketing News, 35*(8), 16–17.

Freyd, M. (1923). Measurement in vocational selection: An outline of research procedure. *Journal of Personnel Research, 2,* 215–249, 268–284, 377–385.

Friedman, C. E. (1997). Fair and equitable treatment: A progress report on minority employment in the federal government. *Review of Public Personnel Administration, 17*(4), 9–21.

Friedman, L. (1990). Degree of redundancy between time, importance, and frequency task ratings. *Journal of Applied Psychology, 75,* 748–752.

*Frontiero v. Richardson* (1973). 411 U.S. 677.

Gael, S. (1988). Interviews, questionnaires, and checklists. In S. Gael (Ed.). *The job analysis handbook for business, industry, and government* (Vol. 1, part 5.1, pp. 391–414). New York: Wiley.

Garcia, M. H. (1995). An anthropological approach to multicultural diversity training. *Journal of Applied Behavioral Science, 31,* 490–504.

Gardner, S. E., & Daniel, C. (1998). Implementing comparable worth/pay equity: Experiences of cutting-edge states. *Public Personnel Management, 27,* 475–489.

Gattiker, U. E. (1995). Firm and taxpayer returns from training of semiskilled employees. *Academy of Management Journal, 38,* 1152–1173.

Gaugler, B. B., Rosenthal, D. B., Thornton, G. C., III, & Bentson, C. (1987). Meta-analysis of assessment center validity (Monograph). *Journal of Applied Psychology, 72,* 493–511.

Gavin, A. T. (1977). *Guide to the development of written tests for selection and promotion: The content validity model* (Technical memorandum 77-6). Washington, DC: U.S. Civil Service Commission, Personnel Research & Development Center.

Geidt, T. E. (Ed.). (1991–92). Landmark federal civil rights act is signed into law. *SKOB Update, 10*(1), 2. San Francisco: Schachter, Kristoff, Orenstein, & Berkowitz.

Geidt, T. E., & Cobey, C. E. (Eds.). (1998). Ninth circuit prohibits mandatory arbitration of discrimination claims. *SKOB Update, 16*(2), 4, 7. San Francisco: Schachter, Kristoff, Orenstein, & Berkowitz.

George, J. M. (1991). State or trait: Effects of positive mood on prosocial behaviors at work. *Journal of Applied Psychology, 76,* 299–307.

Gerhart, B. (1990). Voluntary turnover and alternative job opportunities. *Journal of Applied Psychology, 75,* 467–476.

Gerhart, B., & Milkovich, G. T. (1992). Employee compensation: Research and practice. In M. D. Dunnette & L. M. Hough (Eds.), *Handbook of industrial and organizational psychology* (2nd ed., Vol. 3, pp. 481–569). Palo Alto, CA: Consulting Psychologists Press.

Ghiselli, E. E. (1956). Dimensional problems of criteria. *Journal of Applied Psychology, 40,* 1–4.

Ghiselli, E. E. (1966). *The validity of occupational aptitude tests.* New York: Wiley.

Ghiselli, E. E., & Barthol, R. P. (1953). The validity of personality inventories in the selection of employees. *Journal of Applied Psychology, 37,* 18–20.

Ghiselli, E. E., & Haire, M. (1960). The validation of selection tests in the light of the dynamic character of criteria. *Personnel Psychology, 13,* 225–231.

Gibson, C. B. (1999). Do they do what they believe they can? Group efficacy and group effectiveness across tasks and cultures. *Academy of Management Journal, 42,* 138–152.

*Gilmer v. Interstate/Johnson Lane Corporation* (1991). 500 U.S. 20.

Goldberg, L. R., Grenier, J. R., Guion, R. M., Sechrest, L. B., & Wing, H. (1991). *Questionnaires used in the prediction of trustworthiness in pre-employment selection decisions: An APA Task Force report.* Washington, DC: American Psychological Association.

Goldsmith, D. B. (1922). The use of the personal history blank as a salesmanship test. *Journal of Applied Psychology, 6,* 149–155.

Goldstein, I. L. (1974). The application blank: How honest are the responses? *Journal of Applied Psychology, 64,* 491–494.

Goldstein, I. L. (1991). Training in work organizations. In M. D. Dunnette & L. M. Hough (Eds.), *Handbook of industrial and organizational psychology* (2nd ed., Vol. 2, pp. 507–619). Palo Alto, CA: Consulting Psychologists Press.

Goldstein, I. L. (1993). *Training in organizations: Needs assessment, development, and evaluation* (3rd ed.). Pacific Grove, CA: Brooks/Cole.

Gomez-Mejia, L. R., & Balkin, D. B. (1984). Faculty satisfaction with pay and other job dimensions under union and nonunion conditions. *Academy of Management Journal, 27,* 591–602.

Goodman, J. S. (1998). The interactive effects of task and external feedback on practice performance and learning. *Organizational Behavior & Human Decision Processes, 76,* 223–252.

Gottfredson, G. D., & Daiger, D. C. (1977). Using a classification of occupations to describe age, sex, and time differences in employment patterns. *Journal of Vocational Behavior, 10,* 121–138.

Gottfredson, L. S. (1988). Reconsidering fairness: A matter of social and ethical priorities. *Journal of Vocational Behavior, 33,* 293–319.

Gough, H. G. (1971). The assessment of wayward impulse by means of the Personnel Reaction Blank. *Personnel Psychology, 24,* 669–677.

Gough, H. G. (1987). *California Psychological Inventory: Administrator's guide.* Palo Alto, CA: Consulting Psychologists Press.

Graves, L. M., & Karren, R. J. (1992). Interviewer decision processes and effectiveness: An experimental policy-capturing investigation. *Personnel Psychology, 45,* 313–340.

Greaud, V. A., & Green, B. F. (1986). Equivalence of conventional and computer presentation of speed tests. *Applied Psychological Measurement, 10,* 23–34.

Green, R. M., & Reibstein, R. J. (1988). *Negligent hiring, fraud, defamation, and other emerging areas of employer liability.* Washington, DC: Bureau of National Affairs.

Greer, C. R., Youngblood, S. A., & Gray, D. A. (1999). Human resources management outsourcing: The make or buy decision. *Academy of Management Executive, 13*(3), 85–96.

*Griggs v. Duke Power Company* (1971). 401 U.S. 424.

Grossman, R. J. (2000). Is diversity working? *HRMagazine, 45*(3), 46–50.

Guilford, J. P. (1954). *Psychometric methods.* New York: McGraw-Hill.

Guilford, J. P., & Lacey, J. I. (Eds.). (1947). Printed classification tests. *AAF aviation psychology research program reports,* No. 5. Washington, DC: Government Publications Office.

Guion, R. M. (1976). Recruiting, selection, and job placement. In M. D. Dunnette (Ed.), *Handbook of Industrial and organizational psychology* (pp. 777–828). Chicago: Rand McNally.

Guion, R. M. (1991). Personnel assessment, selection, and placement. In M. D. Dunnette & L. M. Hough (Eds.), *Handbook of industrial and organizational psychology* (2nd ed., Vol. 2, pp. 327–397). Palo Alto, CA: Consulting Psychologists Press.

Guion, R. M. (1995). Review of the Employee Reliability Inventory. In J. C. Conoley & J. C. Impara (Eds.), *Twelfth mental measurements yearbook* (pp. 348–350). Lincoln: University of Nebraska Press.

Guion, R. M. (1998a). Review of the Gordon Personal Profile—Inventory (Revised). In J. C. Impara & B. S. Plake (Eds.), *Thirteenth mental measurements yearbook* (pp. 466–468). Lincoln: University of Nebraska Press.

Guion, R. M. (1998b). *Assessment, measurement, and prediction for personnel decisions.* Mahwah, NJ: Erlbaum.

Guion, R. M., & Gottier, R. F. (1965). Validity of personality measures in personnel selection. *Personnel Psychology, 18,* 135–164.

Gullett, C. R. (2000). Reverse discrimination and remedial affirmative action in employment: Dealing with the paradox of nondiscrimination. *Public Personnel Management, 29,* 107–118.

*Gunther v. County of Washington* (1981). 456 U.S. 161.

Guthrie, J. P., & Schwoerer, C. E. (1994). Individual and contextual influences on self-assessed training needs. *Journal of Organizational Behavior, 15,* 405–422.

Guzzo, R. A., & Dickson, M. W. (1996). Teams in organizations: Recent research on performance and effectiveness. *Annual Review of Psychology, 47,* 307–338.

Guzzo, R. A., & Shea, G. P., (1992). Group performance and intergroup relations in organizations. In M. D. Dunnette & L. M. Hough (Eds.), *Handbook of industrial and organizational psychology* (2nd ed., Vol. 3, pp. 269–313). Palo Alto, CA: Consulting Psychologists Press.

Hamner, W. C., & Smith, F. J. (1978). Work attitudes as predictors of unionization activity. *Journal of Applied Psychology, 63,* 415–421.

Harris, M. M. (1989). Reconsidering the employment interview: A review of recent literature and suggestions for future research. *Personnel Psychology, 42,* 691–726.

Harris, M. M., & Schaubroeck, J. (1988). A meta-analysis of self-supervisor, self-peer, and peer-supervisor ratings. *Personnel Psychology, 41,* 43–62.

Harris, M. M., Smith, D. E., & Champagne, D. (1995). A field study of performance appraisal purpose: Research versus administrative-based ratings. *Personnel Psychology, 48,* 151–160.

Harrison, D. A., & Hulin, C. L. (1989). Investigations of absenteeism: Using event history models to study the absence-taking process. *Journal of Applied Psychology, 74,* 300–316.

Harrison, D. A., & Martocchio, J. J. (1998). Time for absenteeism: A 20-year review of origins, offshoots, and outcomes. *Journal of Management, 24,* 305–350.

Harrison, D. A., Virick, M., & William, S. (1996). Working without a net: Time, performance, and turnover under maximally contingent rewards. *Journal of Applied Psychology, 81,* 331–345.

Hartigan, J. A., & Wigdor, A. K. (Eds.). (1989). *Fairness in employment testing: Validity generalization, minority issues, and the General Aptitude Test Battery.* Washington, DC: National Academy Press.

Hartwell, T. D., Steele, P. D., & Rodman, N. F. (1998). Workplace alcohol-testing programs: Prevalence and trends. *Monthly Labor Review, 121,* 27–34.

Harvey, R. J. (1991). Job analysis. In M. D. Dunnette & L. M. Hough (Eds.), *Handbook of industrial and organizational psychology* (2nd ed., Vol. 2, 71–163). Palo Alto, CA: Consulting Psychologists Press.

Harvey, R. J., & Lozada-Larsen, S. R. (1988). Influence of amount of job descriptive information on job analysis rating accuracy. *Journal of Applied Psychology, 73,* 457–461.

Hatcher, L., & Ross, T. L. (1991). From individual incentives to an organization-wide gain-sharing plan: Effects on teamwork and product quality. *Journal of Organizational Behavior, 12,* 169–183.

Hattrup, K. (1995). Review of the Differential Aptitude Tests, Fifth Edition. In J. C. Conoley & J. C. Impara (Eds.), *Twelfth mental measurements yearbook* (pp. 302–304). Lincoln: University of Nebraska Press.

Hattrup, K., Rock, J., & Scalia, C. (1997). The effects of varying conceptualizations of job performance on adverse impact, minority hiring, and predicted performance. *Journal of Applied Psychology, 82,* 656–664.

Hazer, J. T., & Highhouse, S. (1997). Factors influencing managers' reactions to utility analysis: Effects of SDy method, information frame, and focal intervention. *Journal of Applied Psychology, 82,* 104–112.

Heilman, M. E. (1983). Sex bias in work settings: The lack of fit model. *Research in organizational behavior, 5,* 269–298.

Heilman, M. E., & Saruwatari, L. R. (1979). When beauty is beastly: The effects of appearance and sex on evaluations of job applicants for managerial and nonmanagerial jobs. *Organizational Behavior & Human Performance, 23,* 360–372.

Henderson, R. I. (1988). Job evaluation, classification, and pay. In S. Gael (Ed.), *The job analysis handbook for business, industry, and government* (Vol.1, part 2.2, pp. 90–118). New York: Wiley.

Heneman, H. G., III, & Schwab, D. P. (1985). Pay satisfaction: Its multidimensional nature and measurement. *International Journal of Psychology, 20,* 129–141.

Heneman, R. L. (1990). Merit pay research. *Research in Personnel and Human Resource Management, 8,* 203–263.

Henly, S. J., Klebe, K. J., McBride, J. R., & Cudeck, R. (1989). Adaptive and conventional versions of the DAT: The first complete test battery comparison. *Applied Psychological Measurement, 13,* 363–371.

Herold, D. M., Liden, R. C., & Leatherwood, M. L. (1987). Using multiple attributes to assess sources of performance feedback. *Academy of Management Journal, 30,* 826–835.

Hersey, R. B. (1936). Psychology of workers. *Personnel Journal, 14,* 291–296.

Herzberg, F. (1966). *Work and the nature of man.* Cleveland: World Publishing.

Hesketh, B., & Bochner, S. (1994). Technological change in a multicultural context: Implications for training and career planning. In M. D. Dunnette & L. M. Hough (Eds.), *Handbook of industrial and organizational psychology* (2nd ed., Vol. 4, pp. 191–240). Palo Alto, CA: Consulting Psychologists Press.

Hickens, M. (1999). Labor-strapped companies turn to college. *HR Focus, 76*(9), 1, 10.

Highhouse, S., Stierwalt, S. L., Bachiochi, P., Elder, A. E., & Fisher, G. (1999). Effects of advertised human resource management practices on attraction of African American applicants. *Personnel Psychology, 52*, 425–442.

Hill, E. J., Miller, B. C., Weiner, S. P., & Colihan, J. (1998). Influences of the virtual office on aspects of work and work/life balance. *Personnel Psychology, 51*, 667–683.

Hofstede, G. (1980). *Culture's consequences: International differences in work-related values.* Beverly Hills, CA: Sage.

Hogan, J. C. (1991). Physical abilities. In M. D. Dunnette & L. M. Hough (Eds.), *Handbook of industrial and organizational psychology* (2nd ed., Vol. 2, pp. 753–831). Palo Alto, CA: Consulting Psychologists Press.

Hogan, J., & Brinkmeyer, K. (1997). Bridging the gap between overt and personality-based integrity tests. *Personnel Psychology, 50*, 587–599.

Hogan, R. (1971). Personality characteristic of highly rated policemen. *Personnel Psychology, 24*, 679–686.

Hogan, R. T. (1991). Personality and personality measurement. In M. D. Dunnette & L. M. Hough (Eds.), *Handbook of industrial and organizational psychology* (2nd ed., Vol. 2, pp. 873–919). Palo Alto, CA: Consulting Psychologists Press.

Hogan, R., Carpenter, B. N., Briggs, S. R., & Hansson, R. O. (1985). Personality assessment and personnel selection. In H. J. Bernardin & D. A. Brownas (Eds.), *Personality assessment in organizations* (pp. 21–52). New York: Praeger.

Hollenbeck, J. R., & Whitener, E. M. (1988). Criterion-related validation for small sample contexts: An integrated approach to synthetic validity. *Journal of Applied Psychology, 73*, 536–544.

Holzer, H. J. (1990). Wages, employer costs, and employee performance in the firm. *Industrial & Labor Relations Review, 43*(3), 147–164.

Hopkins, W. E., Sterkel-Powell, K., & Hopkins, S. A. (1994). Training priorities for a diverse work force. *Public Personnel Management, 23*, 429–435.

Hough, L., Eaton, N., Dunnette, M., Kamp, J., & McCloy, R. (1990). Criterion-related validities of personality constructs and the effect of response distortion of those validities. *Journal of Applied Psychology, 75*, 581–595.

Houston, J. P. (1986). *Fundamentals of learning and memory* (3rd ed.). New York: Academic Press.

Hudson, J. P., Jr., & Campion, J. E. (1994). Hindsight bias in an application of the Angoff method for setting cutoff scores. *Journal of Applied Psychology, 79*, 860–865.

Huffcutt, A. I., & Arthur, W., Jr. (1994). Hunter and Hunter (1984) revisited: Interview validity for entry-level jobs. *Journal of Applied Psychology, 79*, 184–190.

Huffcutt, A. I., & Roth, P. L. (1998). Racial group differences in employment interview evaluations. *Journal of Applied Psychology, 83*, 179–189.

Hull, C. (1928). *Aptitude testing.* Great Britain: World Book.

Hunt, S. T. (1996). Generic work behavior: An investigation into the dimensions of entry-level, hourly job performance. *Personnel Psychology, 49*, 51–83.

Hunter, J. E. (1983). A causal analysis of cognitive ability, job knowledge, job performance, and supervisory ratings. In F. Landy, S. Zedeck, & J. Cleveland (Eds.), *Performance measurement and theory.* Hillsdale, NJ: Erlbaum.

Hunter, J. E. (1986). Cognitive ability, cognitive aptitudes, job knowledge, and job performance. *Journal of Vocational Behavior, 29*, 340–362.

Hunter, J. E., & Hunter, R. F. (1984). Validity and utility of alternative predictors of job performance. *Psychological Bulletin, 96*, 72–98.

Hunter, J. E., & Schmidt, F. L. (1982). Fitting people to jobs: The impact of personnel selection on national productivity. In M. D. Dunnette & E. A. Fleishman (Eds.), *Human performance and productivity: Human capability assessment* (pp. 233–284). Hillsdale, NJ: Erlbaum.

Hunter, J. E., & Schmidt, F. L. (1990). *Methods of meta-analysis: Correcting error and bias in research findings.* Newbury Park, CA: Sage.

Hunter, J. E., Schmidt, F. L., & Hunter, R. (1979). Differential validity of employment tests by race: A comprehensive review and analysis. *Psychological Bulletin, 86,* 721–735.

Hunter, J. E., Schmidt, F. L., & Jackson, G. B. (1982). *Meta-analysis: Culminating research findings across studies.* Newbury Park, CA: Sage.

Iaffaldano, M. T., & Muchinsky, P. M. (1985). Job satisfaction and job performance: A meta-analysis. *Psychological Bulletin, 97,* 251–273.

Immigration Reform and Control Act (1986). Pub. L. 99-603.

Inman, M. (1985). Language and cross-cultural training in American multinational corporations. *Modern Language Journal, 69,* 247–255.

International Personnel Management Association. (1999a, October). IPMA/NASPE HR benchmarking project: Best practices for attracting and retaining IT professionals. *IPMA News: Newsletter of the International Personnel Management Association.*

International Personnel Management Association. (1999b, October). HR insider: Rumors about print's demise greatly exaggerated. *IPMA News: Newsletter of the International Personnel Management Association.*

Ivancevich, J. M., & Gilbert, J. A. (2000). Diversity management: Time for a new approach. *Public Personnel Management, 29,* 75–92.

Jackofsky, E. F. (1984). Turnover and job performance: An integrated process model. *Academy of Management Review, 9,* 74–83.

Jacobs, R., Kafry, D., & Zedeck, S. (1980). Expectations of behaviorally anchored rating scales. *Personnel Psychology, 33,* 595–640.

Jacoby, S. M. (1999). Are career jobs headed for extinction? *California Management Review, 42*(1), 123–145.

Jamal, M., & Baba, V. V. (1992). Shiftwork and department-type related to job stress, work attitudes and behavioral intentions: A study of nurses. *Journal of Organizational Behavior, 13,* 449–464.

Jenkins, J. G. (1946). Validity for what? *Journal of Consulting Psychology, 10,* 93–98.

Jenner, L. (1994). Family-friendly backlash. *Management Review, 7,* 83.

Jensen, A. R. (1984). Test validity: g versus the specificity doctrine. *Journal of Social and Biographical Structures, 7,* 93–118.

*Job analysis handbook for business, industry, and government* (Vol. 1). (1988). New York: Wiley.

Johnson, L. B. (1965). Executive Order 11246. *Federal Register, 30,* 12319.

Johnson, M. (2000). Virtual recruitment. *Corporate Report Wisconsin, 15*(6), 16–19.

*Johnson v. Transportation Agency, Santa Clara County* (1987). 480 U.S. 616, 107 Sup. Ct. 1442.

Johnston, W. B. (1987). *Workforce 2000: Work and workers for the 21st century.* Indianapolis: Hudson Institute.

Jones, A., Herriot, P., Long, B., & Drakeley, R. (1991). Attempting to improve the validity of a well-established assessment centre. *Journal of Occupational Psychology, 64,* 1–22.

Jones, C., & DeCotiis, T. (1986, August). Video-assisted selection of hospitality employees. *Cornell Hotel and Restaurant Administration Quarterly,* 67–73.

Jones, J. E., Jr. (1985). The genesis and present status of affirmative action in employment: Economic, legal, and political realities. *Iowa Law Review, 70,* 901–944.

Joyce, A. (1999, December 7). Coaxing staffers to aim hire: At Freddie Mac, big rewards for referring new employees. *Washington Post,* Final ed., pp. E1–E2.

Judge, T. A., & Higgins, C. A. (1998). Affective disposition and the letter of reference. *Organizational Behavior & Human Decision Processes, 75,* 207–221.

Juni, S. (1995). Review of the Revised NEO Personality Inventory. In J. C. Conoley & J. C. Impara (Eds.), *Twelfth mental measurements yearbook* (pp. 863–868). Lincoln: University of Nebraska Press.

Kane, J. S. (1986). Performance distribution assessment. In R. A. Berk (Ed.), *Performance assessment* (pp. 237–273). Baltimore: Johns Hopkins University Press.

Kane, J. S., Bernardin, H. J., Villanova, P., & Peyrefitte, J. (1995). Stability of rater leniency: Three studies. *Academy of Management Journal, 38,* 1036–1051.

Kane, J. S., & Lawler, E. E., III. (1978). Methods of peer assessment. *Psychological Bulletin, 85,* 555–586.

Karl, K. A., & Hancock, B. W. (1999). Expert advice on employment termination practices: How expert is it? *Public Personnel Management, 28,* 51–62.

Kay, A. S. (2000, March 20). Recruiters embrace the internet. *Informationweek,* 72–80.

Kellough, J. E., Selden, S. C., & Legge, J. S., Jr., (1997). Affirmative action under fire: The current controversy and the potential for state policy retrenchment. *Review of Public Personnel Administration, 17*(4), 52–74.

Kiess, H. O. (1989). *Statistical concepts for the behavioral sciences.* Boston: Allyn & Bacon.

Kiker, D. S., & Motowidlo, S. J. (1999). Main and interaction effects of task and contextual performance on supervisory reward decisions. *Journal of Applied Psychology, 84,* 602–609.

Kikoski, J. F. (1999). Effective communication in the performance appraisal interview: Face-to-face communication for public managers in the culturally diverse workplace. *Public Personnel Management, 28,* 301–322.

Kikoski, J. F., & Litterer, J. A. (1983). Effective communication in the performance appraisal interview. *Public Personnel Management, 22,* 33–42.

Kim, A. Y. (1998). Arbitrating statutory rights in the union setting: Breaking the collective interest problem without damaging labor relations. *The University of Chicago Law Review, 65*(1), 225–254.

Kim, P. S. (1999). Globalization of human resource management: A cross-cultural perspective for the public sector. *Public Personnel Management, 28,* 227–243.

Kirkman, B. L., & Shapiro, D. L. (1997). The impact of cultural values on employee resistance to teams: Toward a model of globalized self-managing work team effectiveness. *Academy of Management Review, 22,* 730–757.

Kirkpatrick, D. L. (1967). Evaluation of training. In R. L. Craig & L. R. Bittel (Eds.), *Training and development handbook.* New York: McGraw-Hill.

Kitzman, B. C., & Stanard, S. J. (1999) The job of police chief in the state of Illinois. *Public Personnel Management, 28,* 473–499.

Kleinmann, M. (1993). Are rating dimensions in assessment centers transparent for participants? Consequences for criterion and construct validity. *Journal of Applied Psychology, 78,* 988–993.

Kleinmann, M., Kuptsch, C., & Köller, O. (1996). Transparency: A necessary requirement for the construct validity of assessment centres. *Applied Psychology: An International Review, 45,* 67–84.

Klimoski, R., & Brickner, M. (1987). Why do assessment centers work? The puzzle of assessment center validity. *Personnel Psychology, 40,* 243–260.

Klimoski, R. J., & Strickland, W. J. (1977). Assessment centers—valid or merely prescient? *Personnel Psychology, 30,* 389–401.

Kluger, A. N., & Colella, A. (1993). Beyond the mean bias: The effect of warning against faking on biodata item variances. *Personnel Psychology, 46,* 763–780.

Korsgaard, M. A. (1996). The impact of self-appraisals on reactions to feedback from others: The role of self-enhancement and self-consistency concerns. *Journal of Organizational Behavior, 17,* 301–311.

Kossek, E. E., & Nichol, V. (1992). The effects of on-site child care on employee attitudes and performance. *Personnel Psychology, 45,* 485–509.

Koubek, R. J., Salvendy, G., & Noland, S. (1994). The use of protocol analysis for determining ability requirements for personnel selection on a computer-based task. *Ergonomics, 37,* 1787–1800.

Kozlowski, S. W. J., Kirsch, M. P., & Chao, G. T. (1986). Job knowledge, ratee familiarity, conceptual similarity and halo error: An exploration. *Journal of Applied Psychology, 71,* 45–49.

Kraiger, K., & Ford, J. K. (1985). A meta-analysis of ratee race effects in performance ratings. *Journal of Applied Psychology, 70,* 56–65.

Kraiger, K., Ford, J. K., & Salas, E. (1993). Application of cognitive, skill-based, and affective theories of learning outcomes to new methods of training evaluation. *Journal of Applied Psychology, 78,* 311–328.

Kram, K. E. (1985). *Mentoring at work.* Boston: Scott, Foresman.

Krueger, A. B. (1988). The determinants of queues for federal jobs. *Industrial & Labor Relations Review, 41*(4), 567–581.

Kurutz, J. G., Johnson, D. L., & Sugden, B. W. (1996). The United States Postal Service employee assistance program: A multifaceted approach to workplace violence prevention. In G. R. VandenBos & E. Q. Bulatao (Eds.), *Violence on the job: Identifying risks and developing solutions* (pp. 343–352). Washington, DC: American Psychological Association.

Lance, C. E., Fisicaro, S. A., & LaPointe, J. A. (1990). An examination of negative halo error in ratings. *Educational & Psychological Measurement, 50,* 545–554.

Lance, C. E., LaPointe, J. A., & Stewart, A. M. (1994). A test of the context dependency of three causal models of halo rater error. *Journal of Applied Psychology, 79,* 332–340.

Landy, F. J., & Farr, J. L. (1980). Performance rating. *Psychological Bulletin, 87,* 72–107.

Larson, J. R. (1984). The performance feedback process: A preliminary model. *Organizational Behavior & Human Performance, 33,* 42–76.

Larson, J. R. (1986). Supervisors' performance feedback to subordinates: The impact of subordinate performance valence and outcome dependence. *Organizational Behavior & Human Decision Processes, 37,* 391–408.

Latané, B., Williams, K. D., & Harkins, S. (1979). Many hands make light the work: The causes and consequences of social loafing. *Journal of Personality & Social Psychology, 44,* 78–94.

Latham, G. P., Saari, L. M., Pursell, E. D., & Campion, M. A. (1980). The situational interview. *Journal of Applied Psychology, 65,* 422–427.

Latham, G. P., & Wexley, K. N. (1977). Behavioral observation scales for performance appraisal purposes. *Personnel Psychology, 30,* 255–268.

Latham, G. P., & Wexley, K. N. (1981). *Increasing productivity through performance appraisal.* Reading, MA: Addison-Wesley.

Latham, G. P., Wexley, K. N., & Pursell, E. D. (1975). Training managers to minimize rating errors in the observation of behavior. *Journal of Applied Psychology, 60,* 550–555.

Latham, G. P., & Whyte, G. (1994). The futility of utility analysis. *Personnel Psychology, 47,* 31–46.

Lawler, E. E. (1969). Job design and employee motivation. *Personnel Psychology, 22,* 426–435.

Lawler, E. E., III. (1989). Pay for performance: A strategic analysis. In L. R. Gomez-Mejia (Ed.), *Compensation and benefits* (Vol. 3, pp. 136–181). Washington, DC: Bureau of National Affairs.

Lee, R. A. (1999). The evolution of affirmative action. *Public Personnel Management, 28,* 393–408.

Leonard, J. S. (1988). Wage structure and dynamics in the electronics industry. *Industrial Relations, 28,* 251–275.

Leong, F. T. L. (1992). Review of the Miner Sentence Completion Scale. In J. J. Kramer & J. C. Conoley (Eds.), *Eleventh mental measurements yearbook* (pp. 536–537). Lincoln: University of Nebraska Press.

Leventhal, G.S. (1976). The distribution of rewards and resources in groups and organizations. In L. Berkowitz & E. Walster (Eds.), *Advances in experimental social psychology* (Vol. 9, pp. 92–131). New York: Academic Press.

Levin, L., Oler, J., & Whiteside, J. R. (1985). Injury incidence rates in a paint company on rotating production shifts. *Accident Analysis and Prevention, 17,* 67–73.

Levine, D. I. (1993). What do wages buy? *Administrative Science Quarterly, 38,* 462–483.

Levine, E. L., Ash, R. A., & Bennett, N. (1980). Exploratory comparative study of four job analysis methods. *Journal of Applied Psychology, 65,* 524–535.

Levine, E. L., Bennett, N., & Ash, R. A. (1979). Evaluation and use of four job analysis methods for personnel selection. *Public Personnel Management, 8,* 146–151.

Levine, E. L., & Flory, A., III. (1975). Evaluation of job applicants: A conceptual framework. *Public Personnel Management, 4,* 378–385.

Light, P. C. (1999). Behold Lake Wobegon East. *Government Executive, 31*(10), 12.

Likert, R. (1967). *The human organization.* New York: McGraw-Hill.

Lin, T., Dobbins, G. H., & Farh, J. (1992). A field study of race and age similarity effects on interview ratings in conventional and situational interviews. *Journal of Applied Psychology, 77,* 363–371.

Lindell, M. K., Clause, C. S., Brandt, C. J., & Landis, R. S. (1998). Relationship between organizational context and job analysis task ratings. *Journal of Applied Psychology, 83,* 769–776.

Lipman, M., & McGraw, W. R. (1988). Employee theft: A $40 billion industry. *Annals of American Academy of Political and Social Sciences, 498,* 51–59.

Locke, E. A. (1976). The nature and causes of job satisfaction. In M. D. Dunnette (Ed.), *Handbook of industrial and organizational psychology* (pp. 1297–1349).Chicago: Rand McNally.

Locke, E. A., & Latham, G. P. (1990). *A theory of goal setting and task performance.* Englewood Cliffs, NJ: Prentice Hall.

Locke, E. A., Latham, G. P., & Erez, M. (1988). The determinants of goal commitment. *Academy of Management Review, 13,* 23–39.

London, M., Smither, J. W., & Adsit, D. J. (1997). Accountability: The Achilles' heel of multisource feedback. *Group & Organization Management, 22,* 162–184.

Longenecker, C. O., Sims, H. P., & Gioia, D. A. (1987). Behind the mask: The politics of employee appraisal. *Academy of Management Executive, 1,* 183–193.

Lord, F. M., & Novick, M. R. (1968). *Statistical theories of mental test scores.* Reading, MA: Addison-Wesley.

Lovelace, H. W. (2001). Would you interview you? *Informationweek, 836,* 163–164.

Lowry, P. E. (1996). A survey of the assessment center process in the public sector. *Public Personnel Management, 25,* 307–321.

Lubinski, D., & Dawis, R. V. (1992). Aptitudes, skills, and proficiencies. In M. D. Dunnette & L. M. Hough (Eds.), *Handbook of industrial and organizational psychology* (2nd ed., Vol. 3, pp. 1–59). Palo Alto, CA: Consulting Psychologists Press.

Luthans, F., Welsh, D. H. B., & Rosenkrantz, S. A. (1993). What do Russian managers really do? An observational study with comparisons to U.S. managers. *Journal of International Business Studies, 24,* 741–761.

Macan, T. H., & Dipboye, R. L. (1988). The effects of interviewers' initial impressions on information gathering. *Organizational Behavior & Human Decision Processes, 42,* 364–387.

Macan, T. H., & Dipboye, R. L. (1994). The effects of the application on processing of information from the employment interview. *Journal of Applied Social Psychology, 24,* 1291–1314.

Macan, T. H., & Highhouse, S. H. (1994). Communicating the utility of human resource activities: A survey of I/O and HR professionals. *Journal of Business and Psychology, 8,* 425–436.

Mahoney, T. A. (1988). Productivity defined: The relativity of efficiency, effectiveness, and change. In J. P. Campbell & R. J. Campbell (Eds.), *Productivity in organizations.* San Francisco: Jossey-Bass.

Mahoney, T. A., Jerdee, T. H., & Carroll, S. J. (1965). The jobs of management. *Industrial Relations, 4*(2), 97–110.

Manz, C. C. (1992). Self-leading work teams: Moving beyond self-management myths. *Human Relations, 45,* 1119–1140.

*Marks v. Loral Corporation* (1997). Ca. Ct. Appeal.

Marlowe, C. M., Schneider, S. L., & Nelson, C. E. (1996). Gender and attractiveness biases in hiring decisions: Are more experienced managers less biased? *Journal of Applied Psychology, 81,* 11–21.

Maroney, T. (2000). Web recruiting is fine, but we like a job fair. *Fortune, 141*(6), 236–238.

Martinez, M. N. (1998). To have and to hold. *HRMagazine, 43*(10), 130–139.

Martinko, M. J. (1988). Observing the work. In S. Gael (Ed.), *The job analysis handbook for business, industry, and government* (Vol. 1, part 5.3, pp. 419–431). New York: Wiley.

Martocchio, J. J., & Judge, T. A. (1995). When we don't see eye to eye: Discrepancies between supervisors and subordinates in absence disciplinary decisions. *Journal of Management, 21,* 251–278.

Martocchio, J. J., & Judge, T. A. (1997). Relationship between conscientiousness and learning in employee training: Mediating influences of self-deception and self-efficacy. *Journal of Applied Psychology, 82,* 764–773.

Maslow, A. H. (1943). A theory of human motivation. *Psychological Review, 50,* 370–396.

Maurer, T. J., & Taylor, M. A. (1994). Is sex by itself enough? An exploration of gender bias issues in performance appraisal. *Organizational Behavior & Human Decision Processes, 60,* 231–251.

Mayfield, E. C. (1964). The selection interview: A re-evaluation of published research. *Personnel Psychology, 17,* 239–260.

McCabe, B. C., & Stream, C. (2000). Diversity by the numbers: Changes in state and local government workforces 1980–1995. *Public Personnel Management, 29,* 93–106.

McCann, B. A. (1996). Attitudes about and experiences of workplace violence: Results of a survey of construction and other workers. In G. R. VandenBos & E. Q. Bulatao (Eds.), *Violence on the job: Identifying risks and developing solutions* (pp. 251–259). Washington, DC: American Psychological Association.

McCloy, R. A., Campbell, J. P., & Cudeck, R. (1994). A confirmatory test of a model of performance determinants. *Journal of Applied Psychology, 79,* 493–505.

McCormack, M. H. (1999, November 16). Only work hard on things that need hard work. *Plain Dealer,* p. 4C.

McCormick, E. J. (1976). Job and task analysis. In M. D. Dunnette (Ed.), *Handbook of industrial and organizational psychology* (pp. 651–696). Chicago: Rand McNally.

McCormick, E. J. (1979). *Job analysis: Methods and applications.* New York: Amacom.

McCormick, E. J., Jeanneret, P. R., & Mecham, R. C. (1972). A study of job characteristics and job dimensions as based on the Position Analysis Questionnaire (PAQ). *Journal of Applied Psychology, 56,* 347–368.

McDaniel, M. A., & Schmidt, F. L. (1985). *A meta-analysis of the validity of training and experience ratings in personnel selection.* Washington, DC: U.S. Office of Personnel Management, Office of Staffing Policy.

McDaniel, M. A., Schmidt, F. L., & Hunter, J. E. (1988). Job experience correlates of job performance. *Journal of Applied Psychology, 73,* 327–330.

McDaniel, M. A., Whetzel, D. L., Schmidt, F. L., & Maurer, S. D. (1994). The validity of employment interviews: A comprehensive review and meta-analysis. *Journal of Applied Psychology, 79,* 599–616.

McEvoy, G. M., & Buller, P. F. (1987). User acceptance of peer appraisals in an industrial setting. *Personnel Psychology, 40,* 785–797.

McEvoy, G. M., & Cascio, W. F. (1985). Strategies for reducing employee turnover: A meta-analysis. *Journal of Applied Psychology, 70,* 342–353.

McEvoy, G. M., & Cascio, W. F. (1987). Do good or poor performers leave? A meta-analysis of the relationship between performance and turnover. *Academy of Management Journal, 30,* 744–762.

McGarity, L. J. (2000). Disabling corrections and correctable disabilities: Why side effects might be the saving grace of *Sutton. Yale Law Journal, 109,* 1161–1197.

McGehee, W., & Thayer, P. W. (1961). *Training in business and industry.* New York: Wiley.

Mead, A. L., & Drasgow, F. (1993). Equivalence of computerized and paper-and-pencil cognitive ability tests: A meta-analysis. *Psychological Bulletin, 114,* 449–458.

Meglino, B. M., DeNisi, A. S., Youngblood, S. A., & Williams, K. J. (1988). Effects of realistic job previews: A comparison using an enhancement and a reduction preview. *Journal of Applied Psychology, 73,* 259–266.

Mento, A. J., Steele, R. P., & Karren, R. J. (1987). A meta-analytic study of the effects of goal setting on task performance: 1966–1984. *Organizational Behavior & Human Decision Processes, 39,* 52–83.

Messick, S. (1995). Validity of psychological assessment: Validation of inferences from persons' responses and performance as scientific inquiry into score meaning. *American Psychologist, 50,* 741–749.

Milkovich, G. T., & Newman, J. M. (1987). *Compensation* (2nd ed.). Plano, TX: Business Publications, Inc.

Mills, C. J., & Bohannon, W. E. (1980). Personality characteristics of effective state police officers. *Journal of Applied Psychology, 65,* 680-684.

Miner, J. B. (1985). Sentence completion measures in personnel research: The development and validation of the Miner Sentence Completion Scales. In H. J. Bernardin & D. A. Bownas (Eds.), *Personality assessment in organizations* (pp. 145–176). New York: Praeger.

Mintzberg, H. (1980). *The nature of managerial work.* Englewood Cliffs, NJ: Prentice-Hall.

Mirvis, P. H. (1997). Human resource management: Leaders, laggards, and followers. *Academy of Management Executive, 11*(2), 43–56.

Mitchell, O. S. (1983). Fringe benefits and the cost of changing jobs. *Industrial and Labor Relations Review, 37,* 70–78.

Mitchell, T. R., & Mickel, A. E. (1999). The meaning of money: An individual-difference perspective. *Academy of Management Review, 24,* 568–578.

Mitra, A., Jenkins, G. D., Jr., & Gupta, N. (1992). A meta-analytic review of the relationship between absence and turnover. *Journal of Applied Psychology, 77,* 879–889.

Morgeson, F. P., & Campion, M. A. (1997). Social and cognitive sources of potential inaccuracy in job analysis. *Journal of Applied Psychology, 82,* 627–655.

Morin, L., & Latham, G. P. (2000). The effect of mental practice and goal setting as a transfer of training intervention on supervisors, self-efficacy and communication skills: An exploratory study. *Applied Psychology: An International Review, 49,* 566–578.

Morrow, C. C., Jarrett, M. Q., & Rupinski, M. T. (1997). An investigation of the effect and economic utility of corporate-wide training. *Personnel Psychology, 50,* 91–119.

Moss, S. E., & Martinko, M. J. (1998). The effects of performance attributions and outcome dependence on leader feedback behavior following poor subordinate performance. *Journal of Organizational Behavior, 19,* 259–274.

Motowidlo, S. J. (1983). Predicting sales turnover from pay satisfaction and expectation. *Journal of Applied Psychology, 68,* 484–489.

Motowidlo, S. J., Dunnette, M. D., & Carter, G. W. (1990). An alternative selection procedure: The low-fidelity simulation. *Journal of Applied Psychology, 75,* 640–647.

Motowidlo, S. J., Hanson, M. A., & Crafts, J. L. (1997). Low-fidelity simulations. In D. L. Whetzel & G. R. Wheaton (Eds.), *Applied measurement methods in industrial psychology.* Palo Alto, CA: Davies Black.

Motowidlo, S. J., & Van Scotter, J. R. (1994). Evidence that task performance should be distinguished from contextual performance. *Journal of Applied Psychology, 79,* 475–480.

Mount, M. K., Sytsma, M. R., Hazucha, J. F., & Holt, K. E. (1997). Rater–ratee race effects in developmental performance ratings of managers. *Personnel Psychology, 50,* 51–69.

Mount, M. K., & Thompson, D. E. (1987). Cognitive categorization and quality of performance ratings. *Journal of Applied Psychology, 72,* 240–246.

Mount, M. K., Witt, L. W., & Barrick, M. R. (2000). Incremental validity of empirically keyed biodata scales over GMA and the five factor personality constructs. *Personnel Psychology, 53,* 299–323.

Mroczkowski, T., & Hanaoka, M. (1997). Effective rightsizing strategies in Japan and America: Is there a convergence of employment practices? *Academy of Management Executive, 11*(2), 57–67.

Muchinsky, P. M. (1979). The use of reference reports in personnel selection: A review and evaluation. *Journal of Occupational Psychology, 52,* 287–297.

Mullins, W. C., & Kimbrough, W. W. (1988). Group composition as a determinant of job analysis outcomes. *Journal of Applied Psychology, 73,* 657–664.

Mumford, M. D., Costanza, D. P., Connelly, M. S., & Johnson, J. F. (1996). Item generation procedures and background data scales: Implications for construct and criterion-related validity. *Personnel Psychology, 49,* 361–398.

Mumford, M. D., & Peterson, N. G. (1999). The O°NET content model: Structural considerations in describing jobs. In N. G. Peterson, M. D. Mumford, W. C. Borman, P. R. Jeanneret, & E. A. Fleishman (Eds.), *An occupational information system for the 21st century: The development of O°NET* (pp. 21–30). Washington, DC: American Psychological Association.

Mumford, M. D., & Stokes, G. S. (1992). Developmental determinants of individual action: Theory and practice in applying background measures. In M. D. Dunnette & L. M. Hough (Eds.), *Handbook of industrial and organizational psychology* (2nd ed., Vol. 3, pp. 61–138). Palo Alto, CA: Consulting Psychologists Press.

Murphy, K. R. (1994). Potential effects of banding as a function of test reliability. *Personnel Psychology, 47,* 477–496.

Murphy, K. R. (1995). Review of the Reid Report. In J. C. Conoley & J. C. Impara (Eds.), *Twelfth mental measurements yearbook* (pp. 848–849). Lincoln: University of Nebraska Press.

Murphy, K. R., & Cleveland, J. N. (1991). *Performance appraisal: An organizational perspective.* Boston: Allyn & Bacon.

Murphy, K. R., Jako, R. A., & Anhalt, R. L. (1993). Nature and consequences of halo error: A critical analysis. *Journal of Applied Psychology, 78,* 218–225.

Murphy, K. R., Martin, C., & Garcia, M. (1982). Do behavioral observation scales measure observation? *Journal of Applied Psychology, 67,* 562–567.

Murphy, K. R., Osten, K., & Myors, B. (1995). Modeling the effects of banding in personnel selection. *Personnel Psychology, 48,* 61–84.

Murphy, K. R., & Reynolds, D. H. (1988). Does true halo affect observed halo? *Journal of Applied Psychology, 73,* 235–238.

Murphy, K. R., Thornton, G. C., III, & Reynolds, D. H. (1990). College students' attitudes toward employee drug testing programs. *Personnel Psychology, 43,* 615–631.

*Murphy v. United Parcel Service* (1999). 119 Sup. Ct. 2133.

Murray, H. A. (1938). *Explorations in personality.* New York: Oxford University Press.

Murray, H. A., & MacKinnon, D. W. (1946). Assessment of OSS Personnel. *Journal of Consulting Psychology, 10,* 76–80.

Nease, A. A., Mudgett, B. O., & Quiñones, M. A. (1999). Relationships among feedback sign, self-efficacy, and acceptance of performance feedback. *Journal of Applied Psychology, 84,* 806–814.

Neidig, R. D., & Neidig, P. J. (1984). Multiple assessment center exercises and job relatedness. *Journal of Applied Psychology, 69,* 182–186.

Neuman, G. A., & Wright, J. (1999). Team effectiveness: Beyond skills and cognitive ability. *Journal of Applied Psychology, 84,* 376–389.

Noe, R. A. (1988). An investigation of the determinants of successful assigned mentoring relationships. *Personnel Psychology, 41,* 457–479.

Norman, W. T. (1963). Toward an adequate taxonomy of personality attributes: Replicated factor structure in peer nomination personality ratings. *Journal of Abnormal and Social Psychology, 66,* 574–583.

Normand, J., Lempert, R. O., & O'Brien, C. P. (Eds.). (1994). *Under the influence: Drugs and the American workforce.* Washington, DC: National Academy Press.

Normand, J., Salyards, S. D., & Mahoney, J. J. (1990). An evaluation of preemployment drug testing. *Journal of Applied Psychology, 75,* 629–639.

Northwestern National Life Insurance Company. (1993). Fear and violence in the workplace: A survey documenting the experience of American workers. Minneapolis: Author. Main report reprinted in G. R. VandenBos & E. Q. Bulatao (Eds.), *Violence on the job: Identifying risks and developing solutions* (pp. 385–398). Washington, DC: American Psychological Association.

Nunnally, J. C. (1978). *Psychometric theory.* New York: McGraw-Hill.

Office of Technology Assessment. (1990). *The use of integrity tests for pre-employment screening.* Washington, DC: Congress of the United States, Office of Technology Assessment.

Older Workers Benefit Protection Act (1991). 29 U.S.C. 623.

Olea, M. M., & Ree, M. J. (1994). Predicting pilot and navigator criteria: Not much more than g. *Journal of Applied Psychology, 79,* 845–851.

Ones, D. S., Viswesvaran, C., & Reiss, A. (1996). Role of social desirability in personality testing for personnel selection: The red herring. *Journal of Applied Psychology, 81,* 660–679.

Ones, D. S., Viswesvaran, C., & Schmidt, F. L. (1993). Comprehensive meta-analysis of integrity test validities: Findings and implications for personnel selection and theories of job performance. *Journal of Applied Psychology, 78,* 679–703.

*O°NET.* (2001). http://www.onetcenter.org/.

Organ, D. W. (1988). *Organizational citizenship behavior: The good soldier syndrome.* Lexington, MA: Lexington Books.

Organ, D. W., & Konovsky, M. A. (1989). Cognitive versus affective determinants of organizational citizenship behavior. *Journal of Applied Psychology, 74,* 157–164.

Orpen, C. (1971). The fakability of the Edwards Personal Preference Schedule in personnel selection. *Personnel Psychology, 24,* 1–4.

Osterman, P. (1995). Work/family programs and the employment relationship. *Administrative Science Quarterly, 40,* 681–700.

*Oubre v. Entergy Operations, Inc.* (1998, January 26). 96 Sup. Ct. 1291.

Overton, R. C., Harms, H. J., Taylor, L. R., & Zickar, M. J. (1997). Adapting to adaptive testing. *Personnel Psychology, 50,* 171–185.

Owens, W. A. (1976). Background data. In M. D. Dunnette (Ed.), *Handbook of industrial and organizational psychology* (pp. 609–644). Chicago: Rand McNally.

Page, K. C., & Gomez, L. R. (1979). *The development and application of job evaluation systems using the Position Description Questionnaire* (Personnel Research Report No. 162-79). Control Data Corporation.

Paley, M. J., & Tepas, D. I. (1994). Fatigue and the shiftworker: Firefighters working on a rotating shift schedule. *Human Factors, 36,* 269–284.

Pape, E. S. (1988). Work sampling. In S. Gael (Ed.). *The job analysis handbook for business, industry, and government* (Vol. 1, part 6.3, pp. 518–535). New York: Wiley.

Parsons, C. K., & Liden, R. C. (1984). Interviewer perceptions of applicant qualifications: A multivariate field study of demographic characteristics and nonverbal cues. *Journal of Applied Psychology, 69,* 557–568.

Patton, K. R., & Daley, D. M. (1998). Gainsharing in Zebulon: What do workers want? *Public Personnel Management, 27,* 117–131.

Paulhus, D. L. (1986). Self-deception and impression management in test responses. In A. Angleitner & J. S. Wiggins (Eds.), *Personality assessment via questionnaires.* Berlin: Springer-Verlag.

Peres, S. H., & Garcia, J. R. (1962). Validity and dimensions of descriptive adjectives used in reference letters for engineering applicants. *Personnel Psychology, 15,* 279–296.

Peterson, N. G., Mumford, M. D., Borman, W. C., Jeanneret, P. R., & Fleishman, E. A. (1999). *An occupational information system for the 21st century: The development of O°NET.* Washington, DC: American Psychological Association.

Pfeffer, J. (1995). Producing sustainable competitive advantage through the effective management of people. *Academy of Management Executive, 11*(1), 55–72.

Phillips, J. F. (1992). Predicting sales skills. *Journal of Business & Psychology, 7,* 151–160.

Phillips, J. F. (1993). Predicting negotiation skills. *Journal of Business & Psychology, 8,* 403–411.

Phillips, J. M. (1998). Effects of realistic job previews on multiple organizational outcomes: A meta-analysis. *Academy of Management Journal, 41,* 673–690.

Phillips, J. S., & Freedman, S. M. (1985). Contingent pay and intrinsic task interest: Moderating effects of work values. *Journal of Applied Psychology, 70,* 306–313.

Pingitore, R., Dugoni, B. L., Tindale, R. S., & Spring, B. (1994). Bias against overweight job applicants in a simulated employment interview. *Journal of Applied Psychology, 79,* 909–917.

Podsakoff, P. M., & Farh, J. (1989). Effects of feedback sign and credibility on goal setting and task performance. *Organizational Behavior & Human Decision Processes, 44,* 45–67.

Powell, G. N., & Goulet, L. R. (1996). Recruiters' and applicants' reactions to campus interviews and employment decisions. *Academy of Management Journal, 39,* 1619–1640.

Pregnancy Discrimination Act (1978). 92 Stat. 2076.

Premack, S. L., & Wanous, J. P. (1985). A meta-analysis of realistic job preview experiments. *Journal of Applied Psychology, 70,* 706–719.

Primoff, E. S. (1975). *How to prepare and conduct job-element examinations* (U.S. Civil Service Commission, Technical study 75-1). Washington, DC: U.S. Government Printing Office.

Primoff, E. S., & Eyde, L. D. (1988). Job element analysis. In S. Gael (Ed.), *The job analysis handbook for business, industry, and government* (Vol. 2, part 8.1, pp. 807–824). New York: Wiley.

Primoff, E. S., & Fine, S. A. (1988). A history of job analysis. In S. Gael (Ed.). *The job analysis handbook for business, industry, and government* (Vol. 1, part 1.2, pp. 14–29). New York: Wiley.

*Pugh v. See's Candies* (1981). Cal. App. 3d.

Pulakos, E. D. (1997). Ratings of job performance. In D. L. Whetzel & G. R. Wheaton (Eds.), *Applied measurement methods in industrial psychology* (pp. 291–317). Palo Alto, CA: Davies-Black.

Pulakos, E. D., & Schmitt, N. (1995). Experience-based and situational interview questions: Studies of validity. *Personnel Psychology, 48,* 289–308.

Pulakos, E. D., Schmitt, N., Whitney, D., & Smith, M. (1996). Individual differences in interviewer ratings: The impact of standardization, consensus discussion, and sampling error on the validity of a structured interview. *Personnel Psychology, 49,* 85–102.

Pulakos, E. D., White, L. A., Oppler, S. H., & Borman, W. C. (1989). Examination of race and sex effects on performance ratings. *Journal of Applied Psychology, 74,* 770–780.

Quiñones, M. A., Ford, J. K., & Teachout, M. S. (1995). The relationship between work experience and job performance: A conceptual and meta-analytic review. *Personnel Psychology, 48,* 887–910.

Ragins, B. R., & Scandura, T. A. (1997). The way we were: Gender and the termination of mentoring relationships. *Journal of Applied Psychology, 82,* 945–953.

Ramsay, S., Gallois, C., & Callan, V. J. (1997). Social rules and attributions in the personnel selection interview. *Journal of Occupational & Organizational Psychology, 70,* 189–203.

Raza, S. M., & Carpenter, B. N. (1987). A model of hiring decisions in real employment interviews. *Journal of Applied Psychology, 72,* 596–603.

Ree, M. J., Carretta, T. R., & Teachout, M. S. (1995). Role of ability and prior job knowledge in complex training performance. *Journal of Applied Psychology, 80,* 721–730.

Ree, M. J., & Earles, J. A. (1991). Predicting training success: Not much more than *g. Personnel Psychology, 44,* 321–332.

Ree, M. J., Earles, J. A., & Teachout, M. S. (1994). Predicting job performance: Not much more than *g. Journal of Applied Psychology, 79,* 518–524.

*Regents of the University of California v. Bakke* (1978). 438 U.S. 265.

Rehabilitation Act (1973). 29 U.S.C.706.

Reilly, R. R., Brown, B., Blood, M. R., & Malatesta, C. Z. (1981). The effects of realistic previews: A study and discussion of the literature. *Personnel Psychology, 34,* 823–834.

Reilly, R. R., & Chao, G. T. (1982). Validity and fairness of some alternative employee procedures. *Personnel Psychology, 35,* 1–62.

Reilly, R. R., Henry, S., & Smither, J. W. (1990). An examination of the effects of using behavioral checklists on the construct validity of assessment center dimensions. *Personnel Psychology, 43,* 71–84.

Reiter-Palmon, R., & Connelly, M. S. (2000). Item selection counts: A comparison of empirical key and rational scale validities in theory-based and non-theory-based item pools. *Journal of Applied Psychology, 85,* 143–151.

Riccucci, N. M. (1997). The legal status of affirmative action: Past developments, future prospects. *Review of Public Personnel Administration, 17*(4), 22–37.

Richardson, A. (1967). Mental practice: A review and discussion, Part I. *Research Quarterly, 38,* 95–107.

Richman, W. L., & Quiñones, M. A. (1996). Task frequency rating accuracy: The effect of task engagement and experience. *Journal of Applied Psychology, 81,* 512–524.

Robertson, I. T., & Downs, S. (1989). Work-sample tests of trainability: A meta-analysis. *Journal of Applied Psychology, 74,* 402–410.

Robertson, I. T., Gratton, L., & Rout, U. (1990). The validity of situational interviews for administrative jobs. *Journal of Organizational Behavior, 11,* 69–76.

Robertson, I., Gratton, L., & Sharpley, D. (1987). The psychometric properties and design of managerial assessment centres: Dimensions into exercises won't go. *Journal of Occupational Psychology, 60,* 187–196.

Robertson, I. T., & Kandola, R. S. (1982). Work sample tests: Validity, adverse impact and applicant reaction. *Journal of Occupational Psychology, 55,* 171–183.

Robinson, S. L., & Bennett, R. J. (1995). A typology of deviant workplace behaviors: A multidimensional scaling study. *Academy of Management Journal, 38,* 555–572.

Robinson, S. L., & Rousseau, D. M. (1994). Violating the psychological contract: Not the exception but the norm. *Journal of Organizational Behavior, 15,* 245–259.

Romano, C. (1994). Workplace violence takes a deadly turn. *Management Review, 83*(7), 5.

Rose, A. M., Hesse, B. W., Silver, P. A., & Dumas, J. S. (1999). Database design and development: Designing an electronic infrastructure. In N. G. Peterson, M. D. Mumford, W. C. Borman, P. R. Jeanneret, & E. A. Fleishman (Eds.), *An occupational information system for the 21st century: The development of O\*NET* (pp. 273–287). Washington, DC: American Psychological Association.

Rosen, N. A. (1961). How Supervise?—1943–1960. *Personnel Psychology, 14,* 87–99.

Rosen, T. H. (1987). Identification of substance abusers in the workplace. *Public Personnel Management, 16,* 197–207.

Rosse, J. G., Stecher, M. D., Miller, J. L., & Levin, R. A. (1998). The impact of response distortion on preemployment personality testing and hiring decisions. *Journal of Applied Psychology, 83,* 634–644.

Rothausen, T. J., Gonzalez, J. A., Clarke, N. E., & O'Dell, L. L. (1998). Family-friendly backlash—fact or fiction? The case of organizations' on-site childcare centers. *Personnel Psychology, 51,* 685–706.

Rothstein, H. R. (1990). Interrater reliability of job performance ratings: Growth to asymptote level with increasing opportunity to observe. *Journal of Applied Psychology, 75,* 322–327.

Rotundo, M., & Sackett, P. R. (1999). Effect of rater race on conclusions regarding differential prediction in cognitive ability tests. *Journal of Applied Psychology, 84,* 815–822.

Russell, T. L., & Peterson, N. G. (1997). The test plan. In D. L. Whetzel & G. R. Wheaton (Eds.), *Applied measurement methods in industrial psychology* (pp. 115–139). Palo Alto, CA: Davies-Black.

Ryan, A. M., & Lasek, M. (1991). Negligent hiring and defamation: Areas of liability related to pre-employment inquiries. *Personnel Psychology, 44,* 293–319.

Ryan, A. M., Ployhart, R. E., & Friedel, L. A. (1998). Using personality testing to reduce adverse impact: A cautionary note. *Journal of Applied Psychology, 83,* 298–307.

Rynes, S. L. (1987). Compensation strategies for recruiting. *Topics in Total Compensation, 2,* 185–196.

Rynes, S. L. (1991). Recruitment, job choice, and post-hire consequences: A call for new research directions. In M. D. Dunnette & L. M. Hough (Eds.), *Handbook of Industrial and Organizational Psychology* (2nd ed., Vol. 2, 399–444.). Palo Alto, CA: Consulting Psychologists Press.

Rynes, S. L., Orlitzky, M. O., & Bretz, R. D., Jr. (1997). Experienced hiring versus college recruiting: Practices and emerging trends. *Personnel Psychology, 50,* 309–339.

Rynes, S. L., Schwab, D. P., & Heneman, H. G., III. (1983). The role of pay and market variability in job application decisions. *Organizational Behavior and Human Performance, 31,* 353–364.

Rynes, S., & Rosen, B. (1995). A field survey of factors affecting the adoption and perceived success of diversity training. *Personnel Psychology, 48,* 247–270.

Saal, F. E., & Landy, F. J. (1977). The mixed standard rating scale: An evaluation. *Organizational Behavior & Human Performance, 18,* 19–35.

Saari, L. M., Johnson, T. R., McLaughlin, S. D., & Zimmerle, D. M. (1988). A survey of management training and education practices in U.S. companies. *Personnel Psychology, 41,* 731–743.

Saavedra, R. & Kwun, S. K. (1993). Peer evaluation in self-managing work groups. *Journal of Applied Psychology, 78,* 450–462.

Sackett, P. R. (1987). Assessment centers and content validity: Some neglected issues. *Personnel Psychology, 40,* 13–25.

Sackett, P. R., Burris, L. R., & Callahan, C. (1989). Integrity testing for personnel selection: An update. *Personnel Psychology, 42,* 491–529.

Sackett, P. R., & Dreher, G. F. (1982). Constructs and assessment center dimensions: Some troubling empirical findings. *Journal of Applied Psychology, 67,* 401–410.

Sackett, P. R., & DuBois, C. L. Z. (1991). Rater–ratee race effects on performance evaluation: Challenging meta-analytic conclusions. *Journal of Applied Psychology, 76,* 873–877.

Sackett, P. R., & Ellingson, J. E. (1997). The effects of forming multi-predictor composites on group differences and adverse impact. *Personnel Psychology, 50,* 707–721.

Sackett, P. R., & Harris, M. M. (1984). Honesty testing for personnel selection: A review and critique. *Personnel Psychology, 37,* 221–245.

Sackett, P. R., & Ostgaard, D. J. (1994). Job-specific and national norms for cognitive ability tests: Implications for range restriction corrections in validation research. *Journal of Applied Psychology, 79,* 680–684.

Sackett, P. R., & Roth, L. (1996). Multi-stage selection strategies: A Monte Carlo investigation of effects on performance and minority hiring. *Personnel Psychology, 49,* 549–572.

Sackett, P. R., & Wanek, J. E. (1996). New developments in the use of measures of honesty, integrity, conscientiousness, dependability, trustworthiness, and reliability for personnel selection. *Personnel Psychology, 49,* 787–829.

Sackett, P. R., & Wilk, S. L. (1994). Within-group norming and other forms of score adjustment in preemployment testing. *American Psychologist, 49,* 929–954.

Sackett, P. R., Zedeck, S., & Fogli, L. (1988). Relations between measures of typical and maximum job performance. *Journal of Applied Psychology, 73,* 482–486.

Saks, A. M. (1994). A psychological process investigation for the effects of recruitment source and organization information on job survival. *Journal of Organizational Behavior, 15,* 225–244.

Salgado, J. F. (1998). Sample size in validity studies of personnel selection. *Journal of Occupational & Organizational Psychology, 71,* 161–164.

Salmoni, A. W., Schmidt, R. A., & Walter, C. B. (1984). Knowledge of results and motor learning: A review and critical reappraisal. *Psychological Bulletin, 95,* 355–386.

Sanchez, J. I., & Fraser, S. L. (1992). On the choice of scales for task analysis. *Journal of Applied Psychology, 77,* 545–553.

Scandura, T. A. (1998). Dysfunctional mentoring relationships and outcomes. *Journal of Management, 24,* 449–467.

Scandura, T. A., & Lankau, M. J. (1997). Relationships of gender, family responsibility and flexible work hours to organizational commitment and job satisfaction. *Journal of Organizational Behavior, 18,* 377–391.

Schiller, B. R., & Weiss, R. D. (1979). The impact of private pensions on firm attachment. *Review of Economics and Statistics, 61,* 369–380.

Schippmann, J. S., Prien, E. P., & Katz, J. A. (1990). Reliability and validity of in-basket performance measures. *Personnel Psychology, 43,* 837–859.

Schmidt, F. L. (1985). Review of Wonderlic Personnel Test. In J. V. Mitchell, Jr. (Ed.), *Ninth mental measurements yearbook* (pp. 1755–1757). Lincoln: University of Nebraska Press.

Schmidt, F. L. (1991). Why all banding procedures in personnel selection are logically flawed. *Human Performance, 4,* 265–277.

Schmidt, F. L., Caplan, J. R., Bemis, S. E., Decuir, R., Dunn, L., & Antone, L. (1979). *The behavioral consistency method of unassembled examining* (Technical memorandum 79-21). Washington, DC: U.S. Office of Personnel Management.

Schmidt, F. L., Greenthal, A. C., Hunter, J. E., Berner, J. G., & Seaton, F. W. (1977). Job sample vs. paper and pencil trades and technical tests—adverse impact and examinee attitudes. *Personnel Psychology, 30,* 187–197.

Schmidt, F. L., & Hunter, J. E. (1981a). Two pitfalls in assessing fairness of selection tests using the regression model. *Personnel Psychology, 35,* 601–607.

Schmidt, F. L., & Hunter, J. E. (1981b). Employment testing: Old theories and new research findings. *American Psychologist, 36,* 1128–1137.

Schmidt, F. L., & Hunter, J. E. (1995). The fatal internal contradiction in banding: Its statistical rationale is logically inconsistent with its operational procedures. *Human Performance, 8,* 203–214.

Schmidt, F. L., Hunter, J. E., McKenzie, R. C., & Muldrow, T. W. (1979). Impact of valid selection procedures on work-force productivity. *Journal of Applied Psychology, 64,* 609–626.

Schmidt, F. L., Hunter, J. E., & Outerbridge, A. N. (1986). Impact of job experience and ability on job knowledge, work sample performance, and supervisory ratings of job performance. *Journal of Applied Psychology, 71,* 432–439.

Schmidt, F. L., Hunter, J. E., & Pearlman, K. (1981). Task differences as moderators of aptitude test validity in selection: A red herring. *Journal of Applied Psychology, 66,* 166–185.

Schmidt, F. L., Hunter, J. E., Pearlman, K., & Hirsh, H. R. (1985). Forty questions about validity generalization and meta-analysis. *Personnel Psychology, 38,* 697–798.

Schmidt, F. L., Hunter, J. E., & Urry, V. W. (1976). Statistical power in criterion-related validation studies. *Journal of Applied Psychology, 61,* 473–485.

Schmidt, F. L., Pearlman, K., & Hunter, J. E. (1980). The validity and fairness of employment and educational tests for Hispanic Americans: A review and analysis. *Personnel Psychology, 33,* 705–724.

Schmidt, R. A. (1991). Frequent augmented feedback can degrade learning: Evidence and interpretations. In J. Requin & G. E. Steimach (Eds.), *Tutorials in motor neuroscience* (pp. 59–75). London: Kluwer.

Schmitt, N. (1976). Social and situational determinants of interview decisions: Implications for the employment interview. *Personnel Psychology, 29,* 79–101.

Schmitt, N., Rogers, W., Chan, D., Sheppard, L., & Jennings, D. (1997). Adverse impact and predictive efficiency of various predictor combinations. *Journal of Applied Psychology, 82,* 719–730.

Schneider, B. (1996). Whither goest personality at work? Overview of the special issue on "work and personality." *Applied Psychology: An International Review, 45,* 289–296.

Schneider, B., & Konz, A. M. (1989). Strategic job analysis. *Human Resource Management, 28,* 51–63.

Schneider, J. R., & Schmitt, N. (1992). An exercise design approach to understanding assessment center dimension and exercise constructs. *Journal of Applied Psychology, 77,* 32–41.

Schneier, C. E. (1977). Operational utility and psychometric characteristics of behavioral expectation scales: A cognitive reinterpretation. *Journal of Applied Psychology, 62,* 541–548.

Schrader, B. W., & Steiner, D. D. (1996). Common comparison standards: An approach to improving agreement between self and supervisory performance ratings. *Journal of Applied Psychology, 81,* 813–820.

Schriesheim, C. A. (1978). Job satisfaction, attitudes toward unions, and voting in a union representation election. *Journal of Applied Psychology, 63,* 548–552.

Scott, K. D., Markham, S. E., & Vest, M. J. (1996). The influence of a merit pay guide chart on employee attitudes toward pay at a transit authority. *Public Personnel Management, 25,* 103–117.

Seberhagen, L. W., McCollum, M. D., & Churchill, C. D. (1972). *Legal aspects of personnel selection in the public service.* Chicago: International Personnel Management Association.

Seibert, S. (1999). The effectiveness of facilitated mentoring: A longitudinal quasi-experiment. *Journal of Vocational Behavior, 54,* 483–502.

Shaffer, G. S., Saunders, V., & Owens, W. A. (1986). Additional evidence for the accuracy of biographical information: Long-term retest and observer ratings. *Personnel Psychology, 39,* 791–809.

Shareef, R. (1998). A midterm case study assessment of skill-based pay in the Virginia Department of Transportation. *Review of Public Personnel Administration, 18,* 5–22.

Shavelson, R. J. (1996). *Statistical reasoning for the behavioral sciences* (3rd ed.). Boston: Allyn & Bacon.

Silverman, W. H., Dalessio, A., Woods, S. B., & Johnson, R. L., Jr. (1986). Influence of assessment center methods on assessors' ratings. *Personnel Psychology, 39,* 565–578.

Skinner, B. F. (1954). *The behavior of organisms.* New York: Appleton-Century-Crofts.

Slack, J. D. (1997). From affirmative action to full spectrum diversity in the American workplace: Shifting the organizational paradigm. *Review of Public Personnel Administration, 17*(4), 75–87.

Smiderle, D., Perry, B. A., & Cronshaw, S. F. (1994). Evaluation of video-based assessment in transit operator selection. *Journal of Business Psychology, 9,* 3–22.

Smith, C. A., Organ, D. W., & Near, J. P. (1983). Organizational citizenship behavior: Its nature and antecedents. *Journal of Applied Psychology, 68,* 453–463.

Smith, P. B., Peterson, M. F., & Misumi, J. (1994). Event management and work team effectiveness in Japan, Britain and the USA. *Journal of Occupational & Organizational Psychology, 67,* 33–43.

Smith, P. C., & Kendall, L. M. (1963). Retranslation of expectations: An approach to the construction of unambiguous anchors for rating scales. *Journal of Applied Psychology, 47,* 149–155.

Smith, P. C., Kendall, L. M., & Hulin, C. L. (1969). *Measurement of satisfaction in work and retirement.* Chicago: Rand McNally.

Smither, J. W., Reilly, R. R., Millsap, R. E., Pearlman, K., & Stoffey, R. W. (1993). Applicant reactions to selection procedures. *Personnel Psychology, 46,* 49–76.

Society for Industrial and Organizational Psychology, Inc. (1987). *Principles for the validation and use of personnel selection procedures* (3rd ed.). College Park, MD: Author.

Solomon, R. L. (1949). An extension of control group design. *Psychological Bulletin, 46,* 137–150.

Spearman, C. (1904). "General Intelligence, " objectively determined and measured. *American Journal of Psychology, 15,* 201–293.

Spearman, C. E. (1927). *The abilities of man.* New York: Macmillan.

Spence, M. A. (1973). Job market signalling. *Quarterly Journal of Economics, 87,* 355–374.

Spencer, D. G., & Steers, R. M. (1981). Performance as a moderator of the job-satisfaction-turnover relationship. *Journal of Applied Psychology, 66,* 511–514.

Spriegel, W. R., & James, V. A. (1958). Trends in recruitment and selection practices. *Personnel, 35,* 42–48.

Spychalski, A. C., Quiñones, M. A., Gaugler, B. B., & Pohley, K. (1997). A survey of assessment center practices in organizations in the United States. *Personnel Psychology, 50,* 71–90.

Steiner, D. D., Rain, J. S., & Smalley, M. M. (1993). Distributional ratings of performance: Further examination of a new rating format. *Journal of Applied Psychology, 78,* 438–442.

Sternberg, R. J., & Kaufman, J. C. (1998). Human abilities. In J. T. Spence, J. M. Darley, & D. J. Foss (Eds.), *Annual review of psychology* (Vol. 49). Palo Alto, CA: Annual Reviews.

Stevens, C. K. (1998). Antecedents of interview interactions, interviewers' ratings, and applicants' reactions. *Personnel Psychology, 51,* 55–85.

Stokes, G. S., Hogan, J. B., & Snell, A. F. (1993). Comparability of incumbent and applicant samples for the development of biodata keys: The influence of social desirability. *Personnel Psychology, 46,* 739–762.

Stone, J. E. (1980, March). Age Discrimination in Employment Act: A review of recent changes. *Monthly Labor Review,* 31–37.

Sulsky, L. M., & Day, D. V. (1992). Frame-of-reference training and cognitive categorization: An empirical investigation of rater memory issues. *Journal of Applied Psychology, 77,* 501–510.

Sulsky, L. M., & Day, D. V. (1994). Effects of frame-of-reference training on rater accuracy under alternative time delays. *Journal of Applied Psychology, 79,* 535–543.

Sundre, D. L. (1998). Review of the Personnel Reaction Blank. In J. C. Impara & B. S. Plake (Eds.), *Thirteenth mental measurements yearbook* (pp. 758–760). Lincoln: University of Nebraska Press.

*Sutton v. United Airlines* (1999). 119 Sup. Ct. 2139.

Tajfel, H., & Turner, J. C. (1986). The social identity theory of intergroup behavior. In S. Worchel & W. G. Austin (Eds.), *Psychology of intergroup relations* (2nd ed.). Chicago: Nelson-Hall.

Task Force on Assessment Center Standards (1989). Guidelines and ethical considerations for assessment center operations. *Public Personnel Management, 18,* 457–471.

Taylor, F. W. (1916, December). The principles of scientific management. Originally published in Bulletin of the Taylor Society. Reprinted in D. Mankin, R. E. Ames, Jr., & M. A. Grodsky (Eds.). (1980). *Classics of industrial and organizational psychology.* Oak Park, IL: Moore.

Taylor, H. C., & Russell, J. T. (1939). The relationship of validity coefficients to the practical effectiveness of tests in selection: Discussion and tables. *Journal of Applied Psychology, 23,* 565–578.

Tepper, B. J. (1994). Investigation of general and program-specific attitudes toward corporate drug-testing policies. *Journal of Applied Psychology, 79,* 392–401.

Terpstra, D. E., & Rozell, E. J. (1997). Sources of human resource information and the link to organizational profitability. *Journal of Applied Behavioral Science, 33,* 66–83.

Tett, R. P., Jackson, D. N., & Rothstein, M. (1991). Personality measures as predictors of job performance: A meta-analytic review. *Personnel Psychology, 44,* 703–742.

Thayer, P. W. (1985). Review of Revised Minnesota Paper Form Board Test. In J. V. Mitchell, Jr. (Ed.), *Ninth mental measurements yearbook* (pp. 1279–1280). Lincoln: University of Nebraska Press.

Thomas, R. G. (1985). Review of Minnesota Clerical Test. In J. V. Mitchell, Jr. (Ed.), *Ninth mental measurements yearbook* (pp. 993–994). Lincoln: University of Nebraska Press.

Thorndike, E. L. (1920). A constant error in psychological ratings. *Journal of Applied Psychology, 4,* 25–29.

Thornton, G. C., III (1980). Psychometric properties of self-appraisals of job performance. *Personnel Psychology, 33,* 263–271.

Thurow, L. (1975). *Generating inequality.* New York: Basic Books.

Thurstone, L. L. (1928). Attitudes can be measured. *American Journal of Sociology, 33,* 529–554.

Thurstone, L. L. (1938). *Primary mental abilities.* Psychometric Monographs, No. 1.

Thurstone, L. L. (1947). *Multiple factor analysis.* Chicago: University of Chicago Press.

Tornow, W. W. (1993). Editor's note: Introduction to special issue on 360-degree feedback. *Human Resource Management, 32,* 221–229.

Totterdell, P., Spelten, E., Smith, L., Barton, J., & Folkard, S. (1995). Recovery from work shifts: How long does it take? *Journal of Applied Psychology, 80,* 43–57.

Tracey, J. B., Tannenbaum, S. I., & Kavanagh, M. J. (1995). Applying trained skills on the job: The importance of the work environment. *Journal of Applied Psychology, 80,* 239–252.

Treiman, D. J. (1977). *Occupational prestige in comparative perspective.* New York: Academic Press.

Treiman, D. J., & Hartmann, H. I. (Eds.). (1981). *Women, work, and wages: Equal pay for jobs of equal value.* Washington, DC: National Academy Press.

Trevor, C. O., Gerhart, B., & Boudreau, J. W. (1997). Voluntary turnover and job performance:

Curvilinearity and the moderating influences of salary growth and promotions. *Journal of Applied Psychology, 82*, 44–61.

Triandis, H. C. (1989). The self and social behavior in different cultural contexts. *Psychological Review, 96*, 506–520.

Truxillo, D. M., & Bauer, T. N. (1999). Applicant reactions to test score banding in entry-level and promotional contexts. *Journal of Applied Psychology, 84*, 322–339.

Tse, D. K., Francis, J., & Walls, J. (1994). Cultural differences in conducting intra- and inter-cultural negotiations: A Sino-Canadian comparison. *Journal of International Business Studies, 25*, 537–556.

Tung, R. L. (1981). Selection and training of personnel for overseas assignments. *Columbia Journal of World Business, 16*, 68–78.

Tung, R. L. (1988). *The new expatriates: Managing human resources abroad.* Cambridge, MA: Ballinger.

Turban, D. B., Campion, J. E., & Eyring, A. R. (1995). Factors related to job acceptance decisions of college recruits. *Journal of Vocational Behavior, 47*, 193–213.

Turban, D. B., Forret, M. L., & Hendrickson, C. L. (1998). Applicant attraction to firms: Influences of organization reputation, job and organizational attributes, and recruiter behaviors. *Journal of Vocational Behavior, 52*, 24–44.

Turnage, J. J., & Muchinsky, P. M. (1982). Transsituational variability in human performance within assessment centers. *Organizational Behavior and Human Performance, 30*, 174–200.

*Tuttle v. Missouri Department of Agriculture* (1999). No. 98-1686, 8th Cir.

Tziner, A., Ronen, S., & Hacohen, D. (1993). A four-year validation study of an assessment center in a financial corporation. *Journal of Organizational Behavior, 14*, 225–237.

Ulrich, L., & Trumbo, D. (1965). The selection interview since 1949. *Psychological Bulletin, 63*, 100–116.

Uniform guidelines on employee selection procedures. (1978). *Federal Register, 43*(166), 38290–38309; also in 29 CFR 1600 et seq.

U.S. Department of Labor. (1972). *Handbook for analyzing jobs.* Washington, DC: U.S. Government Printing Office.

U.S. Department of Labor. (1978). *The earnings gap between women and men.* Washington, DC: U.S. Government Printing Office.

U.S. Department of Labor. (1991). *Dictionary of occupational titles* (4th ed., Rev.). Washington, DC: U.S. Government Printing Office.

U.S. Department of Labor. (1993). *The new DOT: A database of occupational titles for the twenty-first century.* Washington, DC: U.S. Government Printing Office.

U.S. Department of Labor. (1994). *Working women count! A report to the nation.* Washington, DC: USDOL, Women's Bureau.

U.S. Department of Labor. (2000a). *Women's earnings as percent of men's.* Washington, DC: USDOL, Women's Bureau.

U.S. Department of Labor. (2000b). *Local area unemployment statistics: Regional and state employment and unemployment summary.* http://stats.bls.gov:80/news.release/laus. nr0.htm; downloaded April 21, 2000.

U.S. Department of Labor. (2000c). *Futurework: Trends and challenges for work in the 21st century: 1— the workforce.* http://www.dol.gov/dol/asp/public/futurework/report/chapter1/main.htm; downloaded April 21, 2000.

U.S. Department of Labor. (2000d). *Futurework: Trends and challenges for work in the 21st century: 1— the workforce* (continued). http://www.dol.gov/dol/asp/public/futurework/report/chapter1/main2.htm; downloaded April 21, 2000.

U.S. Equal Employment Opportunity Commission. (1978). Uniform guidelines on employee selection procedures. *Federal Register, 43*(166), 38290–39313; also in 29 CFR 1600 et seq.

U.S. Equal Employment Opportunity Commission. (1979). Adoption of questions and answers to clarify and provide a common interpretation of the *Uniform Guidelines on Employee Selection Procedures* (1978). *Federal Register, 44J*(43), 11996–12009.

U.S. Equal Employment Opportunity Commission. (1982). *Guidelines on discrimination because of sex.* 29 CFR 1604 et seq.

U.S. Equal Employment Opportunity Commission. (1990). *Policy guidance on current issues of sexual harassment.* http:www.eeoc.gov/docs/currentissues.html

U.S. Equal Employment Opportunity Commission. (1999). *Affirmative action appropriate under Title VII of the Civil Rights Act of 1964, as amended.* 29 CFR 1608

U.S. Equal Employment Opportunity Commission. (2000a). *About the Commission: EEOC enforcement activities.* http:www.eeoc.gov/enforce.html

U.S. Equal Employment Opportunity Commission. (2000b, January 7). *Press releases: $1.3 million settlement in EEOC racial and sexual harassment suit against Foster Wheeler Constructors.* http:www.eeoc.gov/pr.html

U.S. Equal Employment Opportunity Commission. (2000c). *Compliance manual section 902.* http:www.eeoc.gov/docs/902cm.html

U.S. Office of Personnel Management. (1979). *Equal employment opportunity court cases* (152-46). Washington, DC: Office of Intergovernmental Personnel Programs.

U.S. Office of Personnel Management, Workforce Relations (1998). *A review of federal family-friendly workplace arrangements: A report to Congress by the U.S. Office of Personnel Management.* Washington, DC: Author.

*United Steelworkers of America v. Weber* (1979). 443 U.S. 193; 99 Sup. Ct. 2721.

Van de Vijver, F., & Harsveld, M. (1994). The incomplete equivalence of the paper-and-pencil and computerized versions of the General Aptitude Test Battery. *Journal of Applied Psychology, 79,* 852–859.

Van De Voort, D. M., & Stalder, B. K. (1988). Organizing for job analysis. In S. Gael (Ed.), *The job analysis handbook for business, industry, and government* (Vol. 1, part 4.1, pp. 315–328). New York: Wiley.

VandenBos, G. R., & Bulatao, E. Q. (1996). Workplace violence: Its scope and the issues. In G. R. VandenBos & E. Q. Bulatao (Eds.), *Violence on the job: Identifying risks and developing solutions* (pp. 1–23). Washington, DC: American Psychological Association.

Varca, P. E., & Pattison, P. (1993). Evidentiary standards in employment discrimination: A view toward the future. *Personnel Psychology, 46,* 239–258.

Viswesvaran, C., Ones, D. S., & Schmidt, F. L. (1996). Comparative analysis of the reliability of job performance ratings. *Journal of Applied Psychology, 81,* 557–574.

Viteles, M. (1932). *Industrial psychology.* New York: W. W. Norton.

Vodanovich, S. J., & Lowe, R. H. (1992). They ought to know better: The incidence and correlates of inappropriate application blank inquiries. *Public Personnel Management, 21,* 363–370.

Wagner, J. A., III, Rubin, P., & Callahan, T. J. (1988). Incentive payment and nonmanagerial productivity: An interrupted time series analysis of magnitude and trend. *Organizational Behavior & Human Decision Processes, 42,* 47–74.

Wagner, R. (1949). The employment interview: A critical summary. *Personnel Psychology, 2,* 17–46.

Walker, A. A., & Smither, J. W. (1999). A five-year study of upward feedback: What managers do with their results matters. *Personnel Psychology, 52,* 393–423.

Wallace, S. R., Jr., & Weitz, J. (1955). Industrial psychology. *Annual Review of Psychology, 6,* 217–250.

Wanous, J. P., Stumpf, S. A., & Bedrosian, H. (1979). Job survival of new employees. *Personnel Psychology, 32,* 651–662.

*Wards Cove Packing Company v. Atonio* (1989). 490 U.S. 642.

Waung, M. (1995). The effects of self-regulatory coping orientation on newcomer adjustment and job survival. *Personnel Psychology, 48,* 633–650.

Weekley, J. A., & Jones, C. (1997). Video-based situational testing. *Personnel Psychology, 50,* 25–49.

Weiner, N. (1980). Determinants and behavioral consequences of pay satisfaction: A comparison of two models. *Personnel Psychology, 33,* 741–757.

Weiss, D. J. (1976). Multivariate procedures. In M. D. Dunnette (Ed.), *Handbook of Industrial and organizational psychology* (pp. 327–362). Chicago: Rand McNally.

Weiss, D. J., & Vale, C. D. (1987). Adaptive testing. *Applied Psychology: An International Review, 36,* 249–262.

Weiss, H. M. (1990). Learning theory and industrial and organizational psychology. In M. D. Dunnette & L. M. Hough (Eds.), *Handbook of industrial and organizational psychology* (2nd ed., Vol. 1, pp. 171–221). Palo Alto, CA: Consulting Psychologists Press.

Welbourne, T. M., & Cable, D. M. (1995). Group incentives and pay satisfaction: Understanding the relationship through an identity theory perspective. *Human Relations, 48,* 711–726.

Weldon, E., & Weingart, L. R. (1993). Group goals and group performance. *British Journal of Social Psychology, 32,* 307–334.

Werner, J. M., & Bolino, M. C. (1997). Explaining U.S. courts of appeals decisions involving performance appraisal: Accuracy, fairness, and validation. *Personnel Psychology, 50,* 1–24.

Wernimont, P. F. (1988). Recruitment, selection, and placement. In S. Gael (Ed.), *The job analysis handbook for business, industry, and government* (Vol. 1, part 3.1, pp. 193–204). New York: Wiley.

Wernimont, P. F., & Campbell, J. (1968). Signs, samples, and criteria. *Journal of Applied Psychology, 52,* 372–376.

West, M. A., & Anderson, N. R. (1996). Innovation in top management teams. *Journal of Applied Psychology, 81,* 680–693.

Whyte, G., & Latham, G. (1997). The futility of utility analysis revisited: When even an expert fails. *Personnel Psychology, 50,* 601–610.

*Wichman v. Board of Trustees of Southern Illinois University* (1999). No. 97-2902, 7th Cir.

Wilk, S. L., Desmarais, L. B., & Sackett, P. R. (1995). Gravitation to jobs commensurate with ability: Longitudinal and cross-sectional tests. *Journal of Applied Psychology, 80,* 79–85.

Wilkinson, R. T. (1992). How fast should the night shift rotate? *Ergonomics, 35,* 1425–1446.

Williams, C. R., & Livingstone, L. P. (1994). Another look at the relationship between performance and voluntary turnover. *Academy of Management Journal, 37,* 269–298.

Williamson, L. G., Campion, J. E., Malos, S. B., Roehling, M. V., & Campion, M. A. (1997). Employment interview on trial: Linking interview structure with litigation outcomes. *Journal of Applied Psychology, 82,* 900–912.

Wise, S. L. (1995). Review of Differential Aptitude Tests—Computerized Adaptive Edition. In J. C. Conoley & J. C. Impara (Eds.), *Twelfth mental measurements yearbook* (pp. 300–301). Lincoln: University of Nebraska Press.

Woehr, D. J., & Huffcutt, A. I. (1994). Rater training for performance appraisal: A quantitative review. *Journal of Occupational & Organizational Psychology, 67,* 189–205.

Yeager, S. J. (1986). Use of assessment centers by metropolitan fire departments in North America. *Public Personnel Management, 15,* 51–64.

Yu, J., & Murphy, K. R., (1993). Modesty bias in self-ratings of performance: a test of the cultural relativity hypothesis. *Personnel Psychology, 46,* 357–363.

Yuce, P., & Highhouse, S. (1998). Effects of attribute set size and pay ambiguity on reactions to "Help wanted" advertisements. *Journal of Organizational Behavior, 19,* 337–352.

Yukl, G. (1989). Managerial leadership: A review of theory and research. *Journal of Management, 15,* 251–289.

Zedeck, S., & Cascio, W. F. (1984). Psychological issues in personnel decisions. *Annual Review of Psychology, 35,* 461–518.

Zedeck, S., Tziner, A., & Middlestadt, S. E. (1983). Interviewer validity and reliability: An individual analysis approach. *Personnel Psychology, 36,* 355–370.

# Author Index

**490**

# Subject Index

## TO THE OWNER OF THIS BOOK:

I hope that you have found *Employee Selection* useful. So that this book can be improved in a future edition, would you take the time to complete this sheet and return it? Thank you.

School and address: _____

_____

Department: _____

Instructor's name: _____

1. What I like most about this book is: _____

_____

_____

2. What I like least about this book is: _____

_____

_____

3. My general reaction to this book is: _____

_____

_____

4. The name of the course in which I used this book is: _____

_____

5. Were all of the chapters of the book assigned for you to read? _____

   If not, which ones weren't? _____

6. In the space below, or on a separate sheet of paper, please write specific suggestions for improving this book and anything else you'd care to share about your experience in using this book.

_____

_____

_____

_____

_____

OPTIONAL:

Your name: _____ Date: _____

May Wadsworth quote you, either in promotion for *Employee Selection* or in future publishing ventures?

Yes: _____ No: _____

Sincerely yours,

*Lilly M. Berry*